nation-building
discourse
post-colonialism ($)
capitalism
feminism imperialism colonialism ($)
Marx
militarism
Durkheim
tical thinking

AN INTRODUCTION TO
CRITICAL SOCIOLOGY

From modernity to postmodernity

AMIR MIRFAKHRAIE
CHARLES QUIST-ADADE

Kendall Hunt
publishing company

Cover image © Shutterstock, Inc.

Kendall Hunt
publishing company

www.kendallhunt.com
Send all inquiries to:
4050 Westmark Drive
Dubuque, IA 52004-1840

Copyright © 2013 by Amir Mirfakhraie and Charles Quist-Adade

ISBN 978-1-4652-9989-5

Printed in the United States of America
10 9 8 7 6 5 4 3 2 1

Contents

Preface

We are caught in an inescapable network of mutuality, tied in a single garment of destiny. Whatever affects one directly, affects all indirectly. I can never be what I ought to be until you are what you ought to be. This is the interrelated structure of reality.

Martin Luther King, Jr. (A Letter from Birmingham Jail, 1963)

"The first wisdom of sociology is … that things are not what they seem", observed Peter Berger (1965). This book will, among other things, uncover those layers of meaning and the invisible processes involved in the **construction of social reality**. The book will introduce you to the **critical sociological perspective** and shed light on the place of the individual in society by critically examining how people relate to, shape, and are shaped by society. Our primary purpose is to explore the relationships between individuals and the larger societal structures to which they belong.

We approach sociology from a critical, transhistorical, global, and transnational perspective. We also approach sociology as public discourse. From this discursive perspective, how we think about, talk about, and see social reality is determined by historical forces, power dynamics, and sociocultural factors. We trace and examine the multiple factors and forces that have shaped our societies from the premodern to the postmodern world. We explore the most significant ideas, theories, and theorists that have formed our understandings of the social world, locally and globally. Thus, ideas from the Renaissance, the Enlightenment, the Modern, and the Postmodern epochs are explored.

While we adopt a multi-perspectival and intersectional approach in investigating social issues and phenomena, we place a premium on the critical perspectives with a focus on the intersections of local, regional, and global factors and relations. In other words, while we introduce students to different sociological perspectives, we privilege the critical constructivist, global, and transnational perspective. We introduce students to those approaches that view social reality as contested, contextual, ever-changing, and value-laden, while at the same time universal and global.

A central theme in sociology is how subgroup affiliations and mechanisms for empowerment influence one's vision of oneself, one's country, and the world. Exploring sociocultural differences, such as "race," ethnicity, gender, and class, provides insight into ongoing constraints and opportunities that shape the life chances of individuals and groups. A sociological approach to any of these differences begins with the assumption that **social structures**, the enduring systematic patterns of social interaction that order and constrain social life, and **social institutions** are human creations or **social constructs.** This means that subgroups or **collectives**, such as the family, are neither natural phenomena nor divinely created entities. They are human-made and tied to, and vary, significantly across time and place. It also means that these phenomena ultimately rest on supra-individual processes of group boundary formation, segregation, and the creation of inter-group (i.e., racial) hierarchies.

In this book, we engage in a sustained critique of concepts, such as "race", ethnicity, class, power, globalization, and sexual orientation from critical theoretical standpoints. The basic 2objective of the book is to understand:

1. the social, cultural, political, and historical conditions under which structural hierarchies and conflicts, such as racism, classism, and heterosexism emerged;

2. the **institutions** (i.e., structures and mechanism of social order) through which structural boundaries and hierarchies are produced and reproduced in Canada and in other cultural settings. We also look at human agency, the activities of individuals and collectives, in effecting change in this country and globally;

3. the intersection of "race", class, gender, and sexual orientation;

4. the connections between personal experiences, actions, and inactions (between biographies and the larger society).

In short, we will explore these issues and other social phenomena through **macro** and **micro** lenses or approaches. We will examine the categories of "race", gender, class, and sex not as isolated, independent entities, but as intersecting and interlocking, fluid, and contingent realities. By this, we mean that none of these social categories exists in isolation. For example, one's "race" affects and is affected by one's social class and gender. In other words, there is no "race" without sex and no sex without class (Rothenberg, 2011, p. 2).

This book will offer you a lucid lesson in the global sociological imagination. The global sociological imagination points to the fact that our individual biographies are not written or created by us, as individuals, alone, but are also the collective products of many other people, who may live in far-flung corners of our global landscape, and whose paths may never cross ours in our lifetime. Having the global sociological imagination will enable you to develop a keen awareness of the fact that our actions, seemingly inconsequential, do have ramifications for others, rippling far beyond our immediate environments and our shores.

It is our hope that this book will ignite your own global sociological imagination.

We are indebted to Margaret Bru (Acquisitions Editor) and Sara McGovern (Project Coordinator) at Kendall Hunt Publishing Company for their attention to details, professionalism, and all the help they have provided us for the last one year during the process of writing and revising this book. We could not have finished this book without their immense support and assistance.

Amir Mirfakhraie's wife, Sabrina, has also played a significant role in providing him unconditional support over the years. Her enthusiasm, attention to details, and critical thinking skills have been central in Amir's approach to teaching and learning sociology. He dedicates this book to her.

Charles Quist-Adade dedicates this book to his family, Geralda, Maayaa, Christopher, and Malaika. Their patient encouragement and inspiration provided me the much-needed boost to complete this book.

Amir Mifakharie, PhD

Charles Quist-Adade, PhD.

Kwantlen Polytechnic University

CHAPTER ONE

· ·

Introducing the Book and Critical Sociology

Introduction

· ·

Amir Mirfakhraie took interest in sociology after taking an introduction to Anthropology course that explored the effects of racism around the world. He wanted to find out why he viewed himself as a "White" person when others categorized him as a "person of colour" in North America. He has been doing research in the fields of identity construction, education, immigration, and textbook studies. Charles Quist-Adade became a sociologist when he realized that his education in Journalism did not prepare him for a comprehensive understanding of the effects of social, economic, and political factors on the lives of the people about whom he was writing. He has been involved in multidisciplinary approaches to sociological and media studies. This book is a reflection of our journeys as students of sociology with keen interests in teaching social justice in hopes of igniting in our students a passion and a willingness to help transform the world by addressing many issues of equality and inequality.

In this book, we offer a historical and analytical overview of the context in which sociology was developed. We explore the social, cultural, political, and economic factors and relations that have been instrumental in the rise of sociology as a "social science". Sociology explores and analyzes what people do in their day-to-day interactions and how they live their lives, not simply as individuals, but also as members of collectivities and social categories (Turner, 2003, p. 1). A **social category** refers to a group of individuals who are identified by references to some specific cultural, economic, political, or racial characteristic. These characteristics have positive/negative effects on one's social position within society. From a sociological point of view, human actions, belief systems, and likes or dislikes are considered to be the end result of their memberships in groups and their participations in the wider social structures and institutions that they often have no control over but nevertheless influence them. In studying the **personal problems** of individuals and the issues that they face in their daily activities, sociologists pay specific attention to political, cultural, economic, and social dimensions of interactions within social structures, such as the family and education system. For example, in order to study the life experiences of Aboriginal peoples as a social category in Canada, it is important to account for the consequences of colonial and imperialistic policies, relations, and structures on them.

In this chapter, we offer an overview of our approach to sociology and briefly introduce the reader to some of the concepts that are explored in more detail throughout this book. We view sociology as a critical discourse of analyzing human relations and structures of society. Several important terms and ideas are explored and discussed in detail in this chapter: **discourse, perspective, seeing the general in the particular, seeing the strange in the familiar, commonsense knowledge, ideology, hegemony, the sociological imagination, public discourse, personal troubles, social issues, quality of mind, false-consciousness, intersectional analysis, transnationalism,** and **dialectics.** This chapter is divided into two parts. In Part One, we introduce the reader to some of the general concepts in sociology. In Part Two, we explore our approach to sociology as **public discourse.**

Part One
....
A Brief Overview of Sociology

Sociology is defined as the "scientific" study of human relationships and behavior. "Science" refers to a process of developing theories that are tested and then rejected, modified, or retained until a more comprehensive theory is developed (Turner, 2003, p. 2). Sociologists test these theories against empirical cases to determine if and the extent to which they are plausible and applicable (Perry, 2001, p. 374). **Sociological theories** or **paradigms** are ways of understanding the effects of social forces on individuals as members of groups and social categories (Lemert, 2005, p. 10). We put the term "science" in quotation marks to highlight the fact that "science" is not "**value-free**" (i.e., it is informed by the theoretical and methodological biases of the researcher), and is affected by the **ideology** and interests of the researcher, a point that will be elaborated later in the next few chapters. Hiller (2006, p. 126) maintained that the lenses social actors employ to interpret the world around them and make sense of their social relations with others is referred to as ideology. It is composed of a series of values, assumptions, and beliefs that assist social actors to understand complex social phenomena they observe and face in their day-to-day interactions (Hiller, 2006, p. 126). Ideology enables us to judge other people and evaluate their actions and intentions in the context of social relations and structures. Depending on one's ideology, social actors view and evaluate the world around them in different lights.

As a "science", sociology develops theories that explain the social world (Turner, 2003, p. 2). The **aim of sociology** is to offer "**objective**" and "**value-neutral**" accounts of the social world through unambiguous terms and concepts (Turner, 2003). Sociological knowledge is both **objective** and **subjective.** It studies society as an entity that is external to individuals and stands above them (objective, i.e., in terms of rates of suicide, divorce, and school drop-outs) and as a "thing" that is produced through actions of individuals (subjective). Sociologists use various methods of collecting data, such as observation, experiment, and surveys by ensuring the highest level of "objectivity" and standards of ethics and conduct that are set by their respective professional associations.

Sociology studies those factors and structures as well as historical periods that have resulted in its inception and progress as a "social science" discipline and its institutionalization as an academic subject. Sociological ideas and theories have also been shaped by the same social, political, and economic processes that initially led to its emergence during the nineteenth century as a discipline and its development since then (Turner, 2003, p. 2). Sociology has been influenced by major structural, ideological, and historical changes, such as **industrialization, urbanization, scientific revolution, political revolutions, capitalism, nationalism, colonialism, postindustrialism, feminism, the gay movement, student movement, the Civil Rights movement,** and **postcolonialism.** These processes and changes have greatly affected:

1. how sociologists have conceptualized, theorized, and analyzed the world;

2. how social actors have interacted with the world; and

3. how individuals and groups have viewed themselves in the world.

In general, sociology is concerned with **social processes** and **structures**:

1. how people interact with one another in the context of social institutions (i.e., the family) and organizations (i.e., the government);

2. how individuals are affected by social structures (i.e., the economy); and

3. how they also affect social structures and change the structures of society.

Sociology consists of broad and diverse subjects "and any simple generalizations about it as a whole are questionable" (Giddens, 1990, p. 10). Sociology is a controversial field and sociologists have studied and examined contentious relations and complex issues. There are many disagreements among sociologists of different theoretical traditions about, for example, how society is organized and how society affects the lives of individuals. Some sociologists have adopted "scientific" lenses to explicate the fundamental forces that have shaped human societies in the past, present, and future by looking at social, economic, political, and social processes (Turner, 2003, p. 227). Others have looked at specific time periods and aimed at interpreting social events. They all, nevertheless, have developed analytical frameworks to understand the world and human interaction as well as behaviour (Turner, 2003, p. 227). Sociological ideas are not fixed. They change and theoretical perspectives are always revised in light of new data and ideas. At the same time, ideas that were rejected and criticized at one time are resurrected in new lights and under new socioeconomic conditions. This is called **paradigm shift.**

We can conceptualize the changes that have shaped sociological theories and concepts into **traditional, modern,** and **postmodern** factors and historical epochs. Turner (2003, p. 227) asserted that sociology is a self-conscious discipline that was created to explore the transformations of society from **agrarian societies** to **industrial capitalism,** or what has been referred to as **modernity.**

In more recent years (since the 1960s), sociologists have theorized about how the changes in modern societies have altered the structures of the economic institutions, cultural norms, and social relations in the era of **postmodernity**. For now, suffice to say that modernity was a period during which it was believed that "science" could solve all human ills and social problems; postmodernity refers to a period during which modernity's goals are questioned based on a **critique** of "science" and the belief that "science" is not "value-free" and is not capable of resolving humanity's problems. We explore these ideas in more detail in the following chapters. **Critical/Critique** in popular usage is understood as negatively evaluating something. In the sense it is being used here, the term means careful analysis. Critiquing is thus an attempt at objective understanding so as to determine the merits, faults, and other attributes of analysis. It means studying the nature of something in order to determine its essential features and the relations between them. In critique, we try to separate "facts" in order to make decisions or judgments.

In narrating the history of sociology, we will introduce the reader to a number of these modern and postmodern perspectives, theories, and their basic assumptions. Our knowledge about the history of sociology is also influenced by and is a product of modern and postmodern societies. It is reflective of the priorities, attitudes, perspectives, theories, and research techniques popularized by both modern and postmodern scholars and social thinkers (Brown, 1996, p. 101). Our narration of sociology and sociological knowledge is influenced by ways of thinking that were not the concerns of classical sociologists. It is in this light that we feel it is important to briefly highlight our theoretical approaches to sociological issues and concerns for the reader.

We approach sociology from **critical** and **transnational** (global) **perspectives**. We adopt a multi-perspectival and intersectional approach in investigating social issues and phenomena. Our approach is critical of the Eurocentric history of sociology. **Eurocentrism** refers to an interlocking system of values and beliefs that promotes the supremacy of Euro-Western cultural values, ideas, and peoples over other peoples' values and norms. According to this **discourse**, European culture is viewed as the main "vehicle" through which progress towards liberalism and democracy is possible. In this light, Eurocentrism is not critical of the role of Europeans and Westerners in promoting and reproducing the oppressive systems of colonialism and racism, locally and globally (Henry & Tator, 2010, p. 381, Glossary). According to this worldview, Western Europe and Western European cultures, conceptualized as the centre of the universe, define humanity and its characteristics.

As a Western-centric "science", sociology, nevertheless, is practiced and influenced by non-Western intellectuals from across the globe, including non-European and non-White researchers residing in the West. It is influenced by a number of traditions and theoretical perspectives that stem from the experiences of marginalized people in both Western and non-Western countries. It has also been a tool in promoting emancipatory politics in many non-Western parts of the world.

We place a premium on critical sociological perspectives with a focus on the intersections of local, regional, and global events and relations. Critical sociological knowledge and theories provide social actors with **macro-** and **micro-perspectives** that are drawn from various disciplines. Critical and intersectional sociology enables social actors to have a holistic and comprehensive understanding of how economic, social, historical, and cultural structures and relations influence them and others as members of different social categories, both similarly and differently, due to the intersections of factors such as "race", social class, gender, sex, sexuality, political ideology, ethnicity, ability, and age. Critical sociology enables individuals to understand how global relations affect them (**macro**), and how their actions and everyday practices reproduce or bring about changes in their immediate localities and other parts of the world (**micro**).

While we attempt to introduce students to different sociological perspectives, we privilege those theories that view social reality as contested, contextual, ever-changing, and value-laden. We believe the aim of sociology should be to liberate humans from being oppressed and from oppressing others. We hope sociological analyses will enable social actors to account for their own life experiences, both as those who promote and benefit from inequality and those whose lives are affected negatively by social, economic, and political inequities. One of the aims of critical sociology is to empower social actors to become active members of their communities in promoting social justice *for* and *with* marginalized groups. We maintain that social actors are both oppressors and oppressed due to their diverse locations and **positionalities,** which are influenced by factors, such as "race", gender, class, and ethnicity, to name a few, in the context of various social institutions, such as the family, economy, and education system.

In this book, our approach to sociology focuses on how inequalities are formed and "evolved" and affect various groups of individuals in different parts of the world. Critical sociologists focus on a number of interrelated and intersectional "isms", such as:

- **heterosexism**, referring to those sets of belief and practice that are used to classify individuals and groups based on their perceived sexual orientations. It legitimizes and privileges heterosexuals, and it negatively constructs and targets lesbians, gay men, and bisexuals in such ways that they are disadvantaged in society (Schniedewind & Davidson, 1998, p. 16). Heterosexism is considered as the norm in modern societies and as a powerful discourse of control that defines how men and women should behave and construct their identities.

- **racism**, referring to those beliefs, ideas, and social practices (behaviours) that assume individuals and groups have distinctive characteristics and that one racial group is more advanced and superior to other groups and, as a result, entitled to more power and resources. Racism has been the foundation of colonial and imperialist interventions in various parts of the world that justified the exploitation of non-Western people by Western societies. The consequences of racism have resulted in the creation of unequal relations between, for example, Blacks and Whites in North America and between dominant and subordinate groups in other parts of the world.

- **sexism**, referring to a set of complex ideas, social practices, and beliefs that consider males to be more superior to females. It assumes that men are endowed with distinctive characteristics that entitle them to more access to positions of power and economic and political resources (Schniedewind & Davidson, 1998, p. 8). Sexist values justify institutional and individual domination of women by men in structural and personal relations. Sexism is a prevalent form of discrimination that affects the lives of women. It has resulted in unequal wage-earnings between men and women and occupational segregation.

- **ableism**, an important form of oppression that disadvantages people with learning, emotional, and physical disabilities and provides unearned advantages and privileges to those considered as abled bodies (Schniedewind & Davidson, 1998, p. 20). People with disabilities have been organizing themselves in the United States, Canada, and other countries to promote their civil rights. They have been pushing for legislation that ensure their members have the same access to services that others already have.

- **linguicism**, referring to those ideologies and structures that legitimize and reproduce unequal divisions of power and distribution of resources between groups on the basis of language. Language oppression often intersects other forms of inequalities and discrimination based on factors, such as "race", ethnicity, gender, age, sexuality, and class (Schniedewind & Davidson, 1998, p. 18). It can be stated that all countries around the world are multilingual and their citizens speak a number of languages. In general, Indigenous languages are facing extinctions in various parts of the world. In addition, people whose mother tongue is different from the national language face disadvantages in schools due, for example, to their unfamiliarity with the language of instruction.

- **ageism**, referring to those attitudes, behaviours, and institutional structures that subordinate a person or a group because of age, "or any assignment of roles in society on the basis of age" (Schniedewind & Davidson, 1998, p. 15). In recent years, youth culture has come under attack and demonized in the United States (Giroux, 2012). Youth are problematized. Youth problems and issues are increasingly dealt with in the court system and in the context of the criminal code. Discrimination against seniors also falls under this category.

- **classism**, or the unequal and differential treatments of groups and individuals due to their class backgrounds and economic positions in society and the reinforcement of those inequalities and differences through, for example, the dominant cultural values in the media and practices prevalent in other social institutions, such as schools. Class refers to a person's location in society based on factors, such as income, money, education, occupation, power, and access to resources (Schniedewind & Davidson, 1998, p. 12). In North America, many working class students are **streamed** toward technical subjects that limit their rates of success in universities since they are not prepared for university education.

Sociology and Discourse

We conceptualize sociology and sociological knowledge as a collection of **discourses**. These discourses are constituted by a series of sub-discourses on topics such as the economy, politics, culture, and society, which are drawn upon to analyze human relations and human societies (Brown, 1996, p. 101). These discourses are contradictory and view society and human relations through conflicting lenses (We discuss these discourses in Chapter Ten: **structural functionalism**, **conflict theory**, **feminism**, and **symbolic interactionism**). In commonsense language, **discourse** refers to "a coherent or rational body of speech" (Hall, 1996b, p. 201). In academic writings, discourse refers to particular ways of representing a "thing" and its relations to other "things" (i.e., "social facts") (Hall,

1996b, p. 201). Discourse consists of a group of statements that allow us to conceptualize a "topic" or to depict a "social group" in relation to other "social groups". It enables us to formulate knowledge about the "topic" under consideration (i.e., White people, crime, or environmental issues). **Discourse is how we think about, imagine, and talk about social reality**.

Discourses are those frameworks that shape how we come to think about "social issues" and the types of concepts and language we use to speak about them. Discourses are values, norms, and ideas that are found in various cultural texts, such as popular magazines to scientific journals, that are used to construct and relate one set of "issues" and "social things" to another (Baumann, 2006, p. 47). We use various discourses to talk about immigration, poverty, unemployment, terrorism, youth culture, political affairs, and other countries.

Discourse, then, refers to how **knowledge is produced through language and social practices** (Henry & Tator, 2010; Hall, 1996b, p. 201). Knowledge is not "objective" but is produced from a specific vantage point (Hall, 1996b, p. 201). That is, we produce specific meanings about a "topic" or a "thing" through a discourse that reflects our ideologies, values, and political, economic, and cultural norms. Discourse structures how we think about "issues" by predisposing us "towards specific assumptions and specific forms of inquiry" (Brown, 1996, p. 101).

Discourse also entails actions that reproduce certain meanings about a "thing" or a "group". Discourse does not simply refer to ideas and values, but also to how we act upon those ideas and values that shape our worldview about a specific "topic" in the social world. These meanings about a "group" or a "thing" are produced through **social practices**. This is referred to as **discursive practices** (Hall, 1996b, p. 201). Discursive practices refer to those social actions and practices through which meaning is produced (Hall, 1996b, p. 201). Discursive practices are rules by which discourses are formed. Discursive practices, or "preexisting conceptual elements" (Omi & Winant, 2001, p. 9), determine what can be said about a "group" or a "thing", what cannot be said and by whom (that is, who has the authority to speak about a "group", a "concept", or a "political event") (McLaren, 1998, p. 184). These rules govern how we conceptualize a "thing", what we say about a "topic", a "group", or a "thing", and what we do not say about a "group" or a "thing". In other words, they dictate what can be mentioned about a "topic" and what must remain unsaid about "an issue" or "a thing". Discursive practices determine who has the power to speak about "a topic" from the position of authority, whose views are the truth about "a thing", and who must listen to those with authority to speak about specific "topics" or "groups" (McLaren, 1998, p. 184).

Discursive practices are embodied in institutions, such as the family, education, legal, and economic systems, and shape how we behave. This entails that knowledge is power and it is produced by those people who control the means of producing information, laws, and data (i.e., the media, the education system, and publishing firms). That is, although a discourse entails a specific way of viewing the world, it does not necessarily reflect the "real world" out there. Discourse reflects social, economic, and cultural power differences in society. It is reflective of "a particular position" about the world within a specific historical time frame (Fleras & Elliot, 2002, p. 267). Discourse highlights that the production of meaning is a power issue (i.e., certain "meanings" are considered as more legitimate than others). For example, we can talk about immigration and citizenship policies and laws as discourses that allow us to imagine who is an insider or who is an outsider; who should be considered as a Canadian and who should not be admitted into the country.

A **racist discourse** attempts to view humans based on a set of assumptions that link cultural and biological differences with differences in intelligence and mental abilities in a hierarchy in which one group is assumed to be superior to another group (Henry & Tator, 2010, p. 383, Glossary). A **racist discourse refers to how society gives voice to racism**. It consists of a series of narratives, images, representations, explanations, and social practices that result in establishing, maintaining, reproducing, and reinforcing relations of power that privilege one group over others and are oppressive (Henry & Tator, 2010, p. 383, Glossary). The Canadian immigration laws prior to the 1960s reform were based on the assumption that only White people should be admitted into Canada as immigrants. That is, the national identity of Canadians was based on the **discourse of Whiteness**. There were laws enacted that prohibited, for example, the immigration of the Chinese and other "unwanted" groups into Canada. A racist discourse does not allow space for the inclusion of non-White cultures and points of views as legitimate frameworks in, for example, constructing national identity and in determining the characteristics of the nation-building process.

On the other hand, an **antiracist discourse** is a critical discourse that points to the extent to which Eurocentric views have informed our views and knowledge about difference and diversity. Antiracism analyzes the effects of raced thinking and racism on individuals and groups (Dei, 1996). Antiracist discourse attempts to **decentre White hegemony** and to account for the voices of other groups in the margins of the dominant society in developing different types of political and economic systems that are democratic and inclusive. Antiracism is an action-oriented discourse that requires social actors to question how they are implicated in reproducing inequality individually, systemically, and institutionally, locally and globally. This implies that victims of racism and marginalized people and those who are critical of racism must become involved in actions that aim at eliminating various forms of discrimination.

When we view the world from a racist discourse, we may think that the problems that Blacks face are cultural and the solution to poverty or inequality that they face should be sought through the adaptation of dominant cultural values by Black people. It is often assumed that they can escape poverty by becoming culturally assimilated into the dominant society. That is, poverty and their subordinate socioeconomic and political positions are explained by their lack of individual initiatives. Solutions to economic inequalities are sought through cultural means (i.e., by changing one's attitudes, it is possible to become successful). From an antiracist point of view, on the other hand, solutions to poverty are sought through politicized actions and knowledge that aim at eliminating oppression and injustices structurally (McLaren, 1998, p. 185). That is, the socio-political-economic position of "minorities" in society is understood by analyzing how goods and services are unequally distributed at both local and global levels. In order to eliminate poverty, this discourse argues that we need to think of ways in which the economic and political structures of society should be altered to make the system more equal.

Orientalism is another dominant discourse that informs our knowledge and the ways in which we come to think about, imagine, and talk about how Western countries are related to non-Western societies, for example, in the Middle East (Said, 1978). Said (1978, p. 3) maintained that Orientalism is a "Western style for dominating, restructuring, and having the authority over the Orient, [or the Middle Eastern countries and societies]". In this discourse, Western countries, conceptualized as the "**us**" category, are often constructed as modern, democratic, open, developed, and affluent. In contrast, non-Western Middle Eastern societies, constructed as the "**them**" category, are often depicted as non-modern, traditional, despotic, nondemocratic, underdeveloped, and poor.

Using Orientalism as an example, we can state that discourse consists of a group of statements that allow us to formulate knowledge about "a topic", for example, the Middle East or Middle Eastern societies in the West (Hall, 1996b, p. 201). As mentioned, as "a family of concepts", discourse reflects power relations (McLaren, 1998, p. 184). As such, only the views of the most powerful groups in Western societies are considered valid and the "truth" about Middle Eastern people and their societies. Westerners are the ones who have the authority to produce knowledge about other peoples.

In constructing the Middle East, different discourses (statements) are drawn upon to depict it as something "tangible" and "objective". Each discourse draws on other discourses, which may not seem to be connected or have the same meanings (Hall, 1996b, p. 202). However, these statements work together and are informed by the same set of rules; each statement implying relations to all other statements. For example, consider the following ways that the West talks about the Middle East. Westerners construct the Middle East as economically "**underdeveloped**". They depict the Middle East as a mystical, patriarchal, and **traditional** set of societies. They talk about the fundamentalist Moslem governments of the Middle East as examples of **authoritarian** and **undemocratically-based regimes**. And, Westerners argue that women in the Middle East are **second class citizens** and face severe forms of discrimination and **sexism**. They also assume that the Middle East is an unsafe place due to religious and ethnic conflicts. These depictions find expressions in classic writings, travellers' accounts, and scientific journals. These are all different types of statements produced in different sites (i.e., artistic fields, movies, and books) that allow social actors to imagine the Middle East. Yet, they all say the same thing. Middle Easterners are not like Westerners: modern, democratic, peaceful, and nonsexist.

Much in the same way, sociology also consists of a series of discourses that allow us to think about society and social groups from various perspectives. They are frameworks or paradigms that are used as methodological tools that give structure to analyses of society. These discourses, such as **feminism, structural functionalism, symbolic interactionism**, and **conflict theory**, are discussed in more detail in Chapters Two and Ten.

Sociology as a Discourse of "Seeing the General in the Particular" and "the Strange in the Familiar"

Peter Berger (1963, p. 4) maintained that sociology is "not a practice like [social work] but an attempt to understand" social relations and a desire to see how general patterns affect the lives of particular individuals. He argued that sociology enables us to see **the general in the particular**. Sociology examines how the categories to which we belong (the **general**) determine and affect our relations with other people and influence our life-chances and experiences (the **particular**) in society. For example, in our individualistic society, social actors often assume that marriage is a personal decision that reflects their own individual choices and likes and dislikes regarding their partners. However, viewed from this sociological perspective, the choice of marriage partner in society is affected and influenced by a range of intersecting factors, such as gender, sexuality, "race", ability, social class, religious affiliation, political ideology, ethnicity, period of immigration, etc. For example, Jewish Iranians in the United States may decide to marry other Jewish Iranians or non-Iranian Jewish persons rather than marry Moslem Iranians. In this case, marriage is influenced by religious membership of individuals. On the other hand, a gay Jewish Iranian may decide to marry a gay Catholic Irish person. In this case, sexuality and prevalent homophobic views influence the choice of marriage partner rather than nationality/ethnicity or religion.

Sociology also helps us to see **the strange in the familiar**. Berger (1963, p. 21) asserted that sociology is a fascinating field of study because of the fact that sociological perspectives enable social actors to view and understand the very world in which they have lived from new lenses. Sociology helps social actors to transform familiar social situations and practices into their strange connotations and meanings (Berger, 1963, p. 21). Sociological knowledge and research can assist us to question the understandings, and the values, norms, and beliefs that inform those understandings we once assumed to be true, and explain the familiar scenes we have been encountering in our day-to-day lives (Berger, 1963, p. 22).

Sociological knowledge points out things are often not what they seem to be. For example, we may think we live a **multicultural society** that is open to diversity and celebrates ethnic and religious pluralism. But, upon a closer examination, we may conclude that **multiculturalism is in fact a discourse of power and an ideological tool in the hands of the elite to construct Canada as a symbol of liberalism and a democratic society**, without seriously dealing with structural factors that restrict opportunities available to marginalized ethnic and racialized groups. As an ideology, it assumes that some perspectives, norms, and values are more important than others. They are privileged over others as natural, normal, and superior (Fleras & Elliott, 2002, p. 35). That is, multiculturalism determines and forms what we should consider as the "truth" about the world, how we should think about diversity in the world around us, what kinds of and whose cultural practices we should practice and experience, and how we should relate to other individuals, groups, and the world at large (i.e., from specific and predetermined vantage points) (Fleras & Elliott, 2002, p. 35). As a dominant ideology, it privileges certain cultural perspectives, norms, and values (i.e., those promoting the interest of the ruling classes) through its ability to influence debates over what are acceptable, natural, or normal social practices and behaviours (Fleras & Elliott, 2002, p. 36). For example, those cultural norms and values that undermine Christian, White, and Anglo cultural norms and values are shunned and denied legitimacy in Canada (i.e., the anti-veiling policies of the Canadian government in the last few decades; rejection of Sharia Islamic Laws, and criminalization of female circumcision practices). By problematizing the dominant discourse of multiculturalism as something **familiar**, sociology highlights the hegemonic aspects of multiculturalism as **strange**.

Sociological lenses or discourses allow us to see how society shapes our decisions and interactions with other peoples and influences our membership in groups. We live in an individualistic society in which we have the notion that we are the authors of our lives. For instance, we may think that we and our partners decide how many children we should have or adopt. We may consider this as a private decision. However, when viewed from the sociological perspective, we can discern certain trends in modern societies that suggest that many individuals living in **postindustrial societies** (i.e., societies in which services rather than manufacturing dominate the economy) will have fewer children due to the constraints of social life and changes in attitudes about the role of women, the availability of resources and opportunities for women, and the need for dual income earners in order to satisfy the needs of family members in terms of survival requirements, such as shelter, food, and services.

Sociology also assists us to see and understand individual actions in light of the broader history of humanity and societal pressures and structures. For example, we can analyze immigration as a "social fact" by focusing on the out-migration of Iranians from Iran since the late 1970s. One of the reasons why many Iranian single males left Iran during the 1980–1998 period was due to the effects of the Iran-Iraq War (1980–1998). They did not want to be drafted into the armed forces and many of them left or escaped Iran and applied for refugee status in various parts of the world, including Canada. In fact, 33% of all Iranian immigrants arriving in Canada between 1980 and 1998 were accepted as refugees (Mirfakhraie, 1999). Here, we see how political events in one part of the world have consequences for other countries. The movement of Iranians to Canada has resulted in the formations of large Iranian communities in cities, such as Vancouver and Toronto, adding to the complexity of ethnic and racialized relations in Canada.

Sociology as a Discourse of Debunking Our Commonsense Knowledge: questioning hegemonic ideologies

Before we can change the world, we need to become critical of our taken-for-granted ideas and assumptions. The first step in this direction is to interrogate one's own views, knowledge, conceptions, and values. We should account for our own biases and their effects on how we approach other peoples from culturally, economically, and socially diverse groups. Critical knowledge, as the basis for making and changing history, first needs to be adopted by social actors and be internalized and filtered through the self-understandings of social agents (Giddens, 1990, p. 15). Sociological perspectives pave the road for you to achieve this goal.

One of the aims of sociology is to debunk our knowledge about the social word. Sociology interrogates what is often referred to as **commonsense knowledge**. Most people have a commonsense notion of how human society operates. However, this commonsensical notion is often based on the façade or surface realities of society. Social actors often confuse the tip of the iceberg with the iceberg itself. It is in this vein that Peter Berger urged us to go beyond the façade, because like an onion, social reality has many layers of meaning, and the discovery of each new layer results in how we perceive the whole onion (Berger, 1965, p. 23).

Sociology impels us to question our preconceived ideas about society and political, economic, cultural, and social relations and structures. Sociology asks us to debunk our biases about how society works and why people behave the way they do. **Sociological knowledge assists us to become critical and radical thinkers.** Émile Durkheim's study of suicide is a classic example of debunking. Many of us may think people who commit suicide are affected by mental illness. Sociological knowledge makes us question our commonsense knowledge. He repudiated the conventional wisdom of his days that viewed suicide as an individual act and the result of psychological factors by showing that suicide is a social act and is affected by societal factors and structures. Durkheim demonstrated that the less one is integrated into his or her community the more likely that person would take his or her own life in times of economic, political, and social crisis. This is not to say that our commonsense is wrong, or it is not something that we should rely on in interpreting the world around us. Rather, the aim of sociology is to incorporate critical thinking and "scientific" knowledge as part of the commonsense.

Sociological approaches to social issues require us to start questioning our taken-for-granted assumptions about how the world works. A central theme in sociology is how subgroup affiliations and mechanisms for empowerment influence one's vision of oneself, one's country, and the world. Exploring sociocultural differences, such as "race," ethnicity, gender, and class, provides insight into ongoing constraints and opportunities that shape one's identity. For example, many of us may believe that the reason why some people are poor is due to their lack of hard work. Sociology looks at the structural causes of poverty, and enables us to see that many people do work hard, but due to the effects of sexism, racism, and/or ethnocentrism, certain groups of people, such as women, racialized people, people with disabilities, and nondominant ethnic groups as well as working classes, face inequality more than dominant members of society.

Sociological knowledge enables us to subvert dominant views that serve the interests of the elite groups within society. Karl Marx defined dominant views (**ideology**) "as a system of ideas, attitudes, and beliefs that stem from the social relations within a particular system of production" (Pampel, 2007, p. 31). According to Karl Marx, the capitalist class controls the noneconomic and economic institutions of society. That is, the capitalist class not only controls the **means of production** (i.e., factories, land, and machines), but also the means through which dominant ideas are produced in society (i.e., the media) (Pampel, 2007, p. 31). He asserted that ideology justifies and reproduces the material interests and position of the dominant capitalist class (Pampel, 2007, p. 31). The ideology of the dominant society influences the structures of life and other institutions in modern society, such as the legal and political institutions. Karl Marx maintained that the state (i.e., the government) functions to reproduce unequal social relations (Pampel, 2007, p. 32). For example, the state in various parts of the world has used the legal system and the police to eliminate and crush workers' rebellions, demonstrations, and strikes since the 1800s. Governments also pass laws that reinforce the ideals of the dominant society. **Dominant ideology** refers to those sets of complex ideas that aim at explaining, justifying, legitimating, and perpetuating the social, economic, and political conditions that are faced by a group or community (Henry & Tator, 2006, p. 16). Ideology, then, refers to those views and ideas that rationalize and promote the vested interests of elite groups, which often distort social reality (Berger, 1963, p. 41). For example, American physicians who have maintained that if the fee-for-service method of payment is abolished, this policy would result in the lowering of medical and health standards is an ideological argument. This argument attempts to promote their interests by keeping such services private and resisting attempts to socialize the cost of the health care system (Berger, 1963, p. 41).

Liberalism is also a form of dominant ideology. It is an important aspect of capitalism and capitalist societies that assumes society is a collection of free individuals. Liberals maintain that it is the duty of the state to protect the rights and freedoms of individuals. According to liberalism, the most important human rights are considered the freedom of an individual to hold private property and to freely participate in economic activities. As such, the role of the state is to make sure that individuals have access to opportunities in order to achieve their personal goals and objectives (Hiller, 2006, p. 127). A critical analysis of the distribution of opportunities in society, however, reveals that many people do not have equal access to these opportunities and the state impedes their access to such opportunities through laws and regulations.

Dominant ideology, then, informs how members of a society should behave and make sense of the world. It imparts "meaning to life, instilling a common bond among group members, and explaining situation" that reflect a specific group's history, language, and class, political, and cultural interests (Henry & Tator, 2010, p. 382, Glossary). As such, ideology is a framework that justifies and maintains relations of power in society (Henry & Tator, 2006, p. 16). It provides concepts and a framework of systems of dominance that excludes a large portion of society (Henry & Tator, 2006, p. 16). Ideology is related to **discourse** in a sense that it informs cultural, educational, political, and legal institutions and policies as well as group identities, norms, and practices, and how history is understood and interpreted. To illustrate this, let us consider the following arguments.

Is the belief in individualism, hard work, and **deferred gratification** an aspect of the dominant ideology? Have they become an integral part of our consciousness, influencing how we approach and understand life and think about class relations in modern societies? A popular modern myth in capitalist and liberal societies is the belief in **individualism**. Individualism assumes that we all have the same level of free will and choices in life and that the level of our success in society depends on the extent to which we use our free will and make appropriate choices in life. The ideology of individualism rests on the assumption that social actors are autonomous and independent individuals apart from those social groups and institutions to which they belong (Bulman, 2004, p. 24). We believe that as individuals we have the power to effect change and if we try hard enough, we can alter our economic fortunes. Bulman (2004, pp. 26–38) argued that individualism is an important aspect of the middle class value system in the United States that assumes hard work, deferred gratification, and frugality are the most important characteristics for success in America. In this discourse, America is conceptualized as the land of opportunities, and it is up to individuals to take advantage of all the resources available to them. If one is not successful and is experiencing poverty, one's condition has nothing to do with the effects of racism or sexism, but it is due to lack of hard work. Many of us do not critically think about how we came to view society through such a lens.

Can we really change our fortunes simply due to our will power? Or is it that individualism is an aspect of the dominant ideology that informs our socialization in schools and through the media? Commonsense knowledge asserts that the poor or the homeless face poverty because they are lazy. In this way, it explains poverty by reference to the lack of proper individual aptitudes and characteristics. This commonsense understanding functions in an ideological way, which blames the victims for the conditions they face. It does not account for how government policies and economic factors and trends that are outside individuals' control affect them and "cause" hardships and/or poverty or homelessness. As such, this commonsense knowledge ends up reproducing dominant ideology that highlights individual responsibility and middle class value system. Sociologists, for instance, have argued that youth homelessness has been rising due to other factors, such as abuse at home and reduction in social services available to youth older than sixteen. Moreover, gay and lesbian youth may leave home due to the consequences of parental violence at home or the fact that they have to hide their identities from homophobic parents. They move out of their households and find themselves in urban centres without any skills, help, or assistance. They are homeless not due to laziness, but due to the effects of social, cultural, and ideological factors.

Individualism is an important defining characteristic of modern Western societies. As such, it is important to begin to question the commonsense knowledge about the power of individuals and the idea of individualism. Such ideas are so central to the dominant society that they are also reflected in the popular culture and the movies that we watch about high school life. In most of these movies, students are portrayed in light of **utilitarian** and **expressive** forms of **individualism**. The former is used to depict working class high school students and the latter informs how middle class high school students are portrayed.

Bulman (2004, p. 19) maintained that the main theme in the films about urban schools is **utilitarian individualism**. Utilitarian individualism assumes that ideals, such as hard work, materialism, and individual self-sufficiency, are important characteristics of individuals. In movies about urban schools, the hero, who is depicted as a middle-class teacher, encourages his or her impoverished and marginalized students to adopt the qualities of utilitarian individualism (i.e., they should study hard in school, have high goals for themselves, and take personal responsibility and attempt to escape the culture of poverty (Bulman, 2004, p. 19). An example of such genre of films is *Dangerous Minds*. Since the majority of inner-urban school students are "minorities", such as African Americans, Latinos, recent immigrants, and poor or working class students; for these students, it is assumed that all they need to do in order to succeed in America is to adapt to the values of the dominant society. In other words, they need to change their attitudes. The solution to poverty is sought in light of individual solutions rather than changing the structure of schools and society that reproduce inequality.

Expressive individualism, on the other hand, refers to the idea that nonconformity to the rules is an important aspect of insuring that individuals truly follow their interests and do not simply accept the norms and the values of society about what it means to be successful. They should reject the conventional measures of success and resist the prevailing social pressures (Bulman, 2004, p. 28). This form of individualism does not consider and value material achievements as the end goal. It celebrates the discovery of one's unique identity, and highlights the importance of freedom of individuals and self-expressions (Bulman, 2004, p. 20). Good examples of this genre of movies are *Risky Business* and *Ferris Bueller's Day Off*. The context of these movies is the middle class suburban United Sates. In these movies, middle class students are told to discover themselves. Teachers are not considered as the saviour of students. Students are told not to follow the established norms. Rather, they should emphasize exploring their individualities by going against the established norms that are set by incompetent school officials.

As the above arguments and examples point out, it can be argued that individualism and liberalism are **hegemonic ideologies** and **discourses**. Hegemonic ideologies and discourses are those dominant views and ideas that have become acceptable explanations of reality. They are presumed to promote the interest of all people. They are considered as normalized aspects of the everyday culture. Through **hegemony**, the most powerful classes in society win the approval of those classes that are oppressed (McLaren, 1998, p. 177). Hegemony refers to a process through which the oppressed classes unknowingly participate in their own domination (McLaren, 1998, p. 178). It is a form of moral and intellectual domination that is achieved not through coercion or force but through "the general winning of consent of the subordinated class to the authority of the ruling class" (McLaren, 1998, p. 178). It is not a form of active coercion and domination. It is a process of structuring the culture, norms, values, and experiences of the subordinated groups and manufacturing their dreams and values in such a way that the dominant values and norms become aspects of the culture of the subordinated groups (McLaren, 1998, p. 178). According to Gramsci (as cited in Turner, 2003, p. 204), the ruling party (social class) is hegemonic since they determine and control not only the means of production and the political structure but also reproduction of ideology. Culture is propagated through the dominant classes' control over the media and other institutions that promote the ideas of the ruling class. In other words, hegemony is "cultural leadership exercised by the ruling class" (Ritzer, 2000, p. 275).

Sociology assists us to become aware of hegemonic ideologies and to debunk them. For example, a working class student may blame his/her school failure and the fact that he/she dropped out of school and did not graduate from high school on his/her lack of hard work and the fact that he/she did not listen to the advice of his/her teachers. His/her **personal trouble** is explained by reference to individual characteristics. However, Marxist and conflict theorists argue that schools are based on the culture of the dominant society and if one wants to succeed, he/she better belong to that culture. In other words, they argue that schools are based on the **cultural capital** of middle class people. Schools promote middle class values, norms, behaviour, language codes, knowledge, and understanding of history. Working class students' socializations in their families do not prepare them for success in schools because they are often unfamiliar with what is expected of them in schools. Their histories and social, cultural, economic, and political issues that they face daily are not taught in schools and do not find expressions in school textbooks. As a result, they become **alienated** from school activities, and for some, the solution is to drop out. Working class and other marginalized students, on the other hand, are also **streamed** into vocational type education that does not prepare them for university education. In this sense, the *personal trouble* of dropping out of school becomes a **social issue** and something that also affects others in the same way. When we offer an explanation of personal failure and the fact that one did not do well in school because of his/her own lack of initiatives and hard work, we in an ironic way promote the ideology of the dominant society, mainly the culture of individualism and personal responsibility as well as the **discourse of equal opportunity** (i.e., liberalism). We assume that schools in the working class areas have the same facilities and standards as middle class schools, and it is up to "minorities" to take advantage of these institutions. The effects of poverty, violence, and unemployment, to name a few factors, are not considered as part of the exploration why people experience schooling so unequally and differently.

Sociology as a Discourse of Public Philosophy

We approach sociology as a **discourse of public philosophy** (Seidman, 1994a, p. 286). Public philosophy is "an alternative to the standard view of scientific sociology" (Seidman, 1994a, p. 286). As a public form of philosophy, sociology is refashioned into a more public- or people-centered and interdisciplinary inquiry that combines empirical social analysis and moral advocacy to promote shared understandings based on the diversity of values and views in society (Bellah, as cited in Seidman, 1994a, p. 286). In this light, sociology is conceptualized as a tool and medium that promotes social and cultural harmony, criticism, and hope, reflecting social values, ideologies, and aspirations of various social actors from different backgrounds (Seidman, 1994a, p. 288). For Bellah, the aim of sociology is to offer newly formulated and synthetic ways of looking at the world that are critical and are based on integrated or holistic views of society (Seidman, 1994a, pp. 286–287). Sociology's main objective should be to provide spaces for all members of society for dialogues or conversations with others about social, economic, cultural, and moral issues, such as what it means to be free, social justice, moral order, conceptions of community, or the role of supranational organizations and the state in designing and implementing social policy (Seidman, 1994a, p. 288).

The central audience of sociology as public philosophy shifts from academics to the critically conscious public (Seidman, 1994a, p. 287). In fact, one of the criticisms against sociology has been that it has turned inwards and tends to only speak to sociologists as "experts". Sociological theories are not discussed by the everyday person, and have not become an aspect of the citizens' vernacular (language) of the everyday life or the *lifeworld* (Seidman, 1994a, p. 287). The results of sociological studies are exclusively published in professional journals. Sociology has become a technical and specialized discipline and has been influenced by **quantitative approaches** to social issues. A quantitative approach assumes there is an external reality that can be known **objectively** and empirically by applying positivistic methods to studies of society (See Chapter Two). This "scientific" sociological approach has ignored the "broad moral and political implications of social events" and how social actors make sense of their routines of daily lives (Bellah, as cited in Seidman, 1994a, p. 287).

Although sociologists have attempted to avoid moral values in order to legitimize their claim to producing objective knowledge, we agree with Bellah that sociology has inherently been value committed (Seidman, 1994a, p. 288). We need to highlight how each tradition promotes and envisions specific social and moral sentiments and to analyze and state their implications for our lives (i.e., the consequences and influences of certain ideas about self, freedom, and social justice) (Seidman,

CHAPTER ONE • Introducing the Book and Critical Sociology 17

1994a, p. 288). We believe that a moral commitment and ethics based on social justice values is central to promoting **sociological imagination**. In this sense, instead of trying to neutralize the value-laden characteristics of our ideas, we should recognize the moral foundations of our approaches to sociology and be explicit about our assumptions (Seidman, 1994, p. 288). Sociology as public philosophy explicitly emphasizes its moral meanings.

Our approach to sociology as public philosophy that is influenced by sociological imagination is based on a set of frameworks that allow us to speak from specific **standpoints** or traditions (i.e., paradigms). The following standpoints set our goals. **First**, it is important to become **reflexive**; that is to reflect critically upon ourselves and the world and use that information and critical outlook to reconsider how we think about the world and ourselves, and how we act and behave in society. **Second**, it is as important to elucidate the core beliefs, ideologies, and hopes underlying our political, economic, and legal institutions that control, guide, and inform our behaviours. **Third**, we also need to evaluate these social norms and ideals in light of a desire to advocate social change *with* and *for* marginalized groups, locally and globally (Seidman, 1994a, p. 288). These goals are based on a definition of sociology that highlights reformulating public-centred ethical values that account for the ideas of "minorities", women, and gay and lesbian peoples. In this way, they become multiple and inclusive of sameness (i.e., we are all Canadians), diversity, and difference (i.e., Indo-Canadians, Jewish-Canadians, and Chinese-Canadians). In this light, like C. W. Mills, we approach sociology as historically situated and "publicly engaged social discourses" of conversation between different people from diverse historical backgrounds and ideologies (Seidman, 1994a, p. 162).

Part Two

• •

The Sociological Imagination and Public Philosophy

We believe that one of the best ways to learn sociological theory is to practice them and to apply what we learn in our everyday activities and social relations. It is important that as social actors we become both producers of theory and its practitioners (Ritzer, 2000). We can practice sociology through the concept of **sociological imagination**. The sociological imagination combines theory and practice (Ritzer, 2000, p. 282). Through this concept, C. W. Mills merged macro- and micro-sociological analysis in his attempts to offer holistic approaches to understanding social issues that would lead to implementing social policy and changes in the organization and operation of social structures (Ritzer, 2000). Mills approached sociological theory "with an eye to the social consequences rather than exclusively focusing on their absolute truth", or objectivity (Seidman, 1994a, p. 162).

Mills distinguished between micro-level *personal troubles* of milieu and macro-level **public issues** of social structures in his attempt to analyze social, political, and economic issues (Ritzer, 2000, p. 498; Mills, 1959, p. 7). He argued that in order to understand the lives of social actors, we need to understand the history of a society (**macro**); and, in order to understand the history of a society, we also need to understand the lives of individuals that compose it (**micro**) (Mills, 1959,

p. 3). He maintained that people need to define the **troubles** they face in light of *public issues* and historical changes and structural contradictions (Mills, 1959, p. 3).

Personal troubles are those issues that have consequence for an individual and for those in face-to-face relations with him or her (Ritzer, 2000, p. 498). Mills asserted that troubles happen within the individual and within the array of his or her relations with others. They are related to his or her self and to those limited areas of everyday realities, which he or she is directly and personally aware (Mills, 1959, p. 8). Troubles happen in the contexts of those social settings that are directly experienced by a social actor and reflect his or her willful involvement (Mills, 1959, p. 8). In other words, troubles are private matters and are related to those values that are cherished by an individual and are considered to be threatened (Mills, 1959, p. 8). Divorce and unemployment are good examples of *personal troubles*. Divorce can have devastating consequences for men and women and children. As a result of a divorce, one may feel depressed and angry, act irrationally, and lose friends and family support. When one loses his/her job, the individual may not feel empowered anymore, as he/she may not consider him/herself a productive member of society, not being able to provide for him/herself or one's family. During economic bust, when corporations lay off workers, individuals face many *personal troubles*. They may lose their homes because they forfeit on their mortgages. As a result, they may become homeless. Unemployed men may turn to alcohol consumption as a way of dealing with pressures of being unemployed. They may also become violent and abuse their spouses.

Public issues refer to those macro-oriented factors that have consequences for a large number of people and society (Ritzer, 2000, p. 498). The effects of **deindustrialization** in Canada in terms of the loss of manufacturing and unionized jobs and the rise of unemployment in industrialized parts of the country are examples of *public issues* that affect many people. Changes to divorce laws are another example that made it easier for women and men to proceed with divorce. It is important to note that there is a dialectical relationship between the *personal troubles* and *public issues*: "wide spread *personal troubles* can become a public issue and a public issue can cause many people personal troubles" (Ritzer, 2000, p. 498).

The sociological imagination is a way of realizing that what we consider as *personal troubles* are in fact *public issues*. It is a reflection of social, economic, political, and cultural relations and structures (Lemert, 2005, p. 10). The sociological imagination leads us to understand the social causes of our *personal troubles*: *personal troubles* of people are actually problems that are the end result of the ways in which the social world is structured (Lemert, 2005, p. 15). In this light, sociology is not just for the professional sociologist. The value of sociology lies in its ability to enrich our lives since it enables us to comprehend how **social things** (i.e., unemployment, divorce, and suicide) that are external to us affect us. In other words, the sociological imagination is a systematic way of relating oneself to others in the context of historical, analytical, and systematic approaches to the relationship between **agency** and **social structure** (Lemert, 2005, p. 11). **Agency** refers to how we reproduce or alter society through our conscious activities. **Social structure** refers to those regularized patterns of social relations that inform and "dictate" how we should behave, act, and approach others in our day-to-day interactions.

'Discursive Sociological Knowledge' and Quality of Mind

The sociological imagination is one way of developing explanations of why and how different individuals belonging to different groups experience life differently (Lemert, 2005, p. 10). It enables us to draw upon **discursive sociological knowledge**. This term refers to the ability and willingness to talk about issues that focus on *public issues* (Lemert, 2005, p. 29). The important aspect of discursive knowledge is that as we begin to talk about structural factors in public not only do we learn more about the structures of society and ourselves, but we also begin to teach others how the world affects us; thus, we may become involved in actions that attempt to change those realities. In other words, the aim is not simply to discuss social issues for the sake of discussion, or understanding for the sake of understanding. Rather, the goal is to introduce change based on actions that derive from critical, analytical reflections that account for the voices and histories of nondominant societies, thus avoiding **ethnocentric views**.

Mills proposed that social actors must develop their sociological imagination. The sociological imagination enables people to understand how macrostructures in the external world affect them. As Mills stated, the sociological imagination also highlights the relationship between biography and history (Mills, 1959, p. 6). He asserted that social actors need to read their personal biographies in light of contemporary and historical events in order to make sense of how political, economic, social, and cultural surroundings/situations affect them.

Sociological imagination enables social actors to understand the consequences of historical relations and epochs in terms of their meanings for "the inner life and the external career of a variety of individuals" (Mills, 1959, p. 5). In other words, it enables us to develop an understanding of what may be happening within ourselves in the context of the social, economic, and political factors (Mills, 1959). The sociological imagination is the ability to understand the consequences of the relationships between various macro-elements of society on individual life chances. This requires social actors to locate themselves in the context of historical processes and to imagine themselves in relation to other people. As such, for example, the sociological imagination requires us to question our understandings of the discourse of individualism, which implies we are in control of our own lives, and account for the ways in which who we are is partly a reflection of events and cultural practices over which we may have no control. Through the application of sociological knowledge, then, social actors are able to better understand themselves and other people's behaviours.

To practice sociological imagination, Mills maintained, social actors need to develop what he called a **quality of mind**, which will assist people to use knowledge and "to develop reason in order to achieve lucid summations of what is going on in the world and what may be happening within themselves" (Mills, 1959, p. 5). By the *quality of mind*, Mills referred to an anthropological, historical, and systematic analysis of the relationship between the self and other people in the context of social structures, such as the state, education system, the economy, and families. *Quality of mind* is the capacity that brings to the foreground the impacts of the relationships between elements of society on the life chances of social actors.

The Sociological Imagination Framework

As already mentioned, sociological imagination is the ability to view and understand our lives in the context of relations of power in local, national, and global contexts and to relate them to our immediate life situations (Naiman, 2004, p. 22). The sociological imagination accounts for the relationship between social structures (i.e., the family, the education system, and the economy) and their effects on individuals. In order to develop sociological imagination, social actors need to ask several inter-related sets of questions. By answering these questions, we can situate ourselves in the context of the wider societal events from a historical perspective (Mills, 1959, pp. 6–7):

- What is the structure of my society like?

- What are its main components?

- How are these essential parts related to one another?

- How does the structure of my society differ from other varieties of social order in other parts of the world?

- What is the function of any aspect and part of my society for its reproduction and transformation? For example, what are the aims of the education system, and how does the education system satisfy the economic needs of my society? How are changes in the economic system reflected in changes in the education system?

- Where is my society located in the context of human history?

- What are the basic ways and characteristics in which my society is changing? In what ways?

- How does my society contribute to the general development of humanity and how is it related to the history of progress?

- How is my society affected by the historical events and period in which it exists? How does it affect the features of the historical period and events?

- How does the current period differ from previous periods? For example, what are the differences and similarities between traditional, modern, and postmodern epochs?

- What are the characteristics of the various groups of men and women that make up my society?

- How are individuals in my society repressed? How are they oppressed? How are they liberated?

- How are humans exploited? How do they fight and resist exploitation?

As Mills pointed out, the main lesson of sociological imagination is that we as individuals have the power to understand our own experiences and measure our own fate by locating ourselves within the historical period in which we live. Knowing oneself also requires that social actors become aware and cognizant of the circumstance of the lives of their fellow citizens and individuals who share his or her circumstances (Mills, 1959, p. 5). For example, as students you pay tuition in order to take college credit courses at institutions of higher learning. Many of you express your frustrations over the rising cost of textbooks and tuition. As the cost of higher education increases, many poor, underprivileged, and working class people may not be able to afford going to college, even if they have the grades and the necessary credentials. During the early 1990s, for example, the cost of nine credit courses at Langara College in Vancouver, British Columbia was less than 330 Canadian dollars. Today, at Kwantlen Polytechnic University, Canadian students pay more than 1,500 Canadian dollars for nine credit hours. How come, you may ask, in a span of a few decades the cost of education has increased so much? Not accounting for the effects of inflation, it can be argued that the rise in tuition fees is correlated with the rise of **neoliberal policies** in Canada. The implementation of neoliberal policies that aim at **privatizing social services**, such as higher education, has been responsible for the reduction in government investment in education. Neoliberals argue that governments need to be fiscally responsible and control their spending. They maintain that governments must cut social services as a way to achieve this goal. As governments cut the budgets of universities, these institutions need to somehow find money needed to cover the capital cost of running a university or college. One way to achieve this goal is to increase the tuition fees. So, as a result, students and their families become responsible to pick up the tab for their educational costs. In fact, another premise of neoliberalism is that individuals and families must become responsible for providing welfare measures for themselves. As this ideology informs government policies, it also affects people in various other areas of life. For example, neoliberal policies have had devastating consequences for women and children in British Columbia. Cuts to welfare programs, after school programs, child-care, and disability programs have made life more difficult for marginalized people, such as single parents.

As you can see, one's *personal troubles* when viewed in the context of history and societal structures turn into *public issues*. What affects you and a single mother, although differently with different consequences, is due to the effects of neoliberal policies that are now the dominant ideology of the capitalist ruling class in the West and other parts of the world. Universities across the world are experiencing the same phenomenon due to the implementation of similar policies. It is in this sense that the sociological imagination is a structural and historical approach to understating society at both local and global levels. The sociological imagination employs anthropological and critical perspectives in situating the self in the context of societal change and conflicts.

It is in this light that we conceptualize the sociological imagination in the context of the **discourse of transnationalism**. **Transnationalism** highlights local, national, and individual interactions in the context of global structures of power. It is a way to conceptualize how nations, individuals, and groups are hierarchically categorized and related to one another (Mirfakhraie, 2011). It explores how ethnic, religious, and (im)migrant groups connect nation-states through nongovernment organizations, such as religious institutions. **Transnational sociological imagination**, then, analyzes *personal troubles* and political issues in the context of national and global relations that have contradictory effects on one another.

The Sociological Imagination, Ethnocentrism, and False-Consciousness

One of the main premises of sociological imagination is to avoid **ethnocentric** views. **Ethnocentrism** refers to a propensity to view events and social relations from the perspective of one's own culture and its norms and values that tend to result in misunderstandings or diminishing the worth of other groups and constructing them as inferior (Henry & Tator, 2010, p. 381, Glossary). We should avoid assuming that our norms and cultural values are "superior" to others and they are the only ways of approaching and understanding society around us. By avoiding ethnocentric approaches to social issues, it is possible to see ourselves through the lenses of other cultural and social groupings. As such, we become open to the voices of other people, their histories, and their undertakings of the social world.

Sociology introduces us to various worldviews and information that are often not available to us in our daily face-to-face activities and relations. We can learn from others by viewing life through the lenses and life experiences of those who seem to be strange to us. If we choose to view life and society from the perspectives of transgendered, female, Black, or Aboriginal individuals, we may note how sexuality, gender, "race", and colonialism affect one's life, and how **racial ideology** or **racist discourses** influence the life chances of racialized individuals in comparison to the life chances of White, male, and heterosexual individuals. **Racist ideology** refers to interlocking concepts, ideas, images, and modern institutions that act as frameworks to interpret and give meaning to racialized values, practices, and behaviours in society. It produces and reproduces systems of domination that reify "race" in the context of various institutions of socialization and those social structures responsible for the transmission of culture, "such as the mass media, schools, and universities, religious doctrines, symbols and images, art, music, and literature" (Henry & Tator, 2010, p. 383, Glossary). For example, during both World War I and World War II many Black Canadians were refused admission into the Canadian armed forces because it was assumed that as Black people they could not be trusted (Fleras, 2010, p. 55). Black males are also often depicted as good athletes who are not academically oriented (Kelly, 1998). In addition, according to the Ontario Human Rights Commission report of 2005, racialized people experienced poverty more than their White counterparts; they were overrepresented in the prison system; and they were underrepresented in the types of position that were bestowed with prestige and power (as cited in Fleras, 2010, p. 56). Calliste (2001, p. 158) maintained that during harsh economic periods and downturns, the first group of nurses to be suspended, demoted, and summarily dismissed are Black nurses due to factors and reasons, such as "alleged incompetence or for not following standard nursing procedures, or for 'unacceptable behaviour'". As Fleras (2010, p. 149) also indicated, formal and personal testimonies and accounts by Aboriginal women show that they are one of the most severely disadvantaged groups in Canada. Furthermore, more women than men also face poverty in Canada and in the rest of the world (Duffy & Mandell, 2010, p. 256). **Feminization of poverty** is a term that refers to this fact. Related to the feminization of poverty is the poverty of children. In 2006, 760, 000 Canadian children grew up in low-income families (Duffy & Mandell, 2010, p. 259). In this sense, we can see the extent to which discrimination based on factors, such as "race", gender, age, and class, limit the possibility of achieving desired positions in society.

The sociological imagination is also based on the **discourse of hope**, allowing us to have the optimism that by realizing and comprehending what is going on in the world and in ourselves (through an analysis of how our personal biographies and histories intersect one another within the operation of the social world), we can change the world (Mills, 1959, p. 7). The sociological imagination is a way of coming to terms with how larger social forces limit and constrain individuals and using this knowledge to transform the world and promote social justice (Lemert, 2005, p. 14). It makes individuals become aware of the opportunities available to them. It is also a way to become aware of our **false-consciousness** (Mills, 1959, p. 7).

When we fail to recognize the effects of these larger social forces on us, we develop what has been referred to as **false-consciousness**, a Marxist terminology referring to the condition and characteristic of work in the capitalist societies in Western Europe during the nineteenth century (Lemert, 2005, p. 16). False-consciousness is the end result of people not using their sociological imagination. It is due to the inability of people to understand how the larger social forces cause their *personal troubles* (Lemert, 2005, p. 15). False-consciousness is the outcome of thinking about and approaching life through the lenses of the dominant society. As Marx would have argued, for example, the workers face oppression due to the fact they are taught to think like the dominant groups, whose control over the media and schools excludes the ideologies of the working classes as part of school knowledge, norms, and values (Lemert, 2005, p. 17). If we are taught to think that individuals are free acting agents and participate in the labour market on their own accords and that our freedom is a gift given to us by our societies and liberal governments, then we may tend to blame ourselves and not the society for our economic, cultural, social, and political problems (Lemert, 2005, p. 18). In this sense, people who face inequalities, violence, sexism, racism, and homophobia explicate their *personal troubles* by references to the lack of individual efforts and hard work rather than by accounting for the social forces that have caused them (Lemert, 2005, p. 16). False-consciousness stems from our inability to locate the real sources of our personal problems in the social structures, rules, regulations, and values that are imposed on us (Lemert, 2005, p. 16). In other words, we tend to misidentify the causes of our private troubles, blaming ourselves instead of social structures. As mentioned, many people who have lost their jobs since the 1970s, due to the changes in the economic structure of society from a shift from manufacturing and industrial occupations to service sector economy, may have felt alienated and became depressed due to the effects of unemployment. They may have felt worthless because they were not able to provide for themselves and their families. Although how they felt had psychological bases, "the reality of the causes and effects of their feeling is sociological" and due to the capitalist relations and economic changes (Lemert, 2005, p. 16).

High unemployment and the lack of high-paying jobs are reflections of the changes in and failures of the larger economic and political structures that cause impossible troubles for the citizens of many societies. This fact is not the focus of the media and politicians (Lemert, 2005, p. 16). Rather, many of our politicians in Canada, Europe, and the United Sates promote the discourse of blaming immigrants and illegal aliens for our social problems during harsh economic times. They maintain that these people are depleting our resources and stealing social services and educational opportunities from the rest of us; yet, such pessimistic analysis do not often mention that these unwanted "guests" have been needed by profit hungry capitalist classes who want to pay the lowest possible wages for their labour (Lemert, 2005, p. 18). As we incorporate the views of the dominant society to analyze our own conditions, we begin to offer solutions that promote the interests of the dominant society. For example, we blame ourselves for not seeking re-skilling or blame the most vulnerable people in the society for problems that are caused by the policies of the most powerful. It is in this light that the sociological imagination allows us to critically evaluate and understand how various societies control and shape their members. Thus, the sociological imagination makes us activists, arousing in us a keen desire to fight, to transform, and to uproot those structures that promote our varied and multiple oppressions.

The Sociological Imagination, Public Philosophy, and Dialectical Analysis

One of the most important aspects of our approach to the sociological imagination and sociology as public philosophy is the concept of **dialectics**. The term dialectics is defined as the struggle and unity of opposites (i.e., ideas). A dialectical approach looks at the totality of human societies and assumes that no part can be understood in isolation from the consideration of the whole (Ritzer, 2000, p. 282). Dialectical relationship does not promote "a simple, one-way, cause and effect relationship among the various parts of the social world" (Ritzer, 2000, p. 42). For example, in order to understand educational issues, it is important to also discuss political and economic factors that have been influential in the rise of educational institutions. In addition, it is also important to account for the experiences of teachers and students in schools if we are to really comprehend what takes shape in schools. Marxist researchers have argued that educational reforms in the United States and Canada reflect political and economic changes, both locally and globally. Beginning in the 1960s, Canada began to introduce more science and math courses as part of the school curriculum during the technological space-war and the arms race (Wotherspoon, 2009). The West viewed Soviet-style communism as a menace that must be contained in order to save the "free and democratic" world (i.e., capitalist countries). At the time, it was assumed that schools were failing students and Canada was losing ground in the global political economy. The fear of communism and the scientific achievements of the Soviet Union were underlying factors in the revision of the curriculum both in Canada and the United States.

Dialectical analysis has several key features:

1. A dialectical analysis of social relations accounts for the reciprocal relationships between social factors in the context of the totality of social life (Ritzer, 2000, p. 42). For example, one of the consequen.ces of the capitalist system of exploitation of workers may be the rise of alienation and dissatisfaction among workers. But, as workers become more militant and organize against the owners of capital, the capitalist class may in turn increase their exploitive measures.

2. A dialectical approach highlights that it is almost impossible to be "value-free" and to keep values and ideologies out of the analysis of social reality and the world. It also points out that a value-free approach to understanding human behaviour and social reality is undesirable since it results in the type of sociological approach to knowledge and information

production that is dispassionate and inhumane. This type of sociology would have nothing to offer to individuals who are in search of answers to some of the problems they confront. It is important to take into consideration that facts and values are intertwined aspects of sociological analysis. That is, studies of social phenomena, relations, and structures are value-laden (Ritzer, 2000, p. 43).

3. It is undesirable to see social phenomena as binary oppositions (i.e., in the form of "either/or" or "us/them" divisions/categories) and as fixed and static. Different aspects of the social world blend into one another. Many people may move between classes and/or exist in the interstices between the two classes, for example, of capitalist and working classes (Ritzer, 2000, p. 43). We can also apply the dialectic approach to understanding how factors, such as gender, class, "race", ethnicity, and sexuality, blend with one another, resulting in different consequences for different types of people. For example, a Black woman may face both racism and sexism. A middle-class White woman may only face sexism. A lesbian working-class White woman may experience classism, homophobia, and sexism. Sociologists refer to such phenomena as **multiple jeopardy**. According to this term, women face discrimination due to the intersections of the effects of "race", ethnicity, sexuality, class, and age. When women face discrimination due to the consequences and effects of gender and "race"/ethnicity, this phenomenon is referred to as **double jeopardy**.

In general, a dialectical approach is in tune with intersectional analyses of social factors.

An **intersectional analysis** does not treat "race", ethnicity, class, and gender as separate, fixed, and static phenomena/entities. It does not ignore diversity *between* and *within* each of these categories. An intersectional perspective highlights the extent to which different aspects of one's social identity relate to one another in the context of different systems of oppression (Fleras, 2010, p. 153). As Fleras (2010, p. 374) pointed out, as a theoretical approach that studies inequalities and analyzes their effects, intersectional analysis looks at the interplay of gender, social class, age, sexuality, "race", and ethnicity. Although gender is considered as the central aspect of analyzing, for example, women's issues, it is acknowledged that it intersects other factors, resulting in the creation of interlocking patterns of domination that deepen the exploitation of women as a "minority" group and a form of **otherness**.

According to Rothenberg (2010, p. 2), **intersectional approach** is to acknowledge that there is "no gender without race, no race without class, no class without gender". She pointed out that the intersectional approach provides holistic and multiple lenses to see and appreciate the dialectical relationship between self and society and between the individual and the collective. An intersectional approach explores the multiple layers of social inequality and allows us to see how the layers play off each other to complicate rather than simplify the process of identity construction (Rothenberg, 2010, p. 2).

Several assumptions undergird intersectionality. **First**, our individual life chances are affected and shaped either positively or negatively by our birth assignments, as men, women, blacks, browns, whites, heterosexuals or homosexuals, able-bodied or disabled bodies. **Second**, these intersecting and interacting categories are fluid, changing, and contextual. At any given time, place or circumstance, one or a combination of these categories, may work to our advantage or disadvantage, since they are not immutable or cast in stone. **Third**, each individual may be a beneficiary or a victim of a single or a combination of these categories. In other words, these categories come with multiple advantages and disadvantages, depending on the circumstance, time, and place (Quist-Adade, 2012).

In short, intersectional analyses account for multiple forms of oppression that affect the lives of marginal groups differently in both contemporary and historical contexts. This perspective allows social actors to become **self-reflective** and question their own roles as social actors in promoting oppression or in subverting it (Glesne, 2011, p. 11). The aim of self-reflection is to act upon critical knowledge and to become involved in the politics of everyday interactions, dismantling structures that lead to oppression. The final step in self-reflection is to become allies of the marginalized groups and to join them in struggles against poverty, violence, and injustices.

4. Those who apply a dialectical analysis take a relational view of the social world. They tend to focus on the relations *between*, *within*, and *among* various aspects of the social world. They look at multiple relations and multiple factors, even if they focus on one or two specific phenomena. That is, a person who practices dialects would not focus on one social unit in isolation from other social factors (Ritzer, 2000, p. 46). For example, Mirfakhraie (in press, 2014) in analyzing curricular reform in Iran also accounted for how theories of global education, developed by two Canadian educators, informed the revision of school textbooks in Iran.

5. A dialectician is concerned with a historical analysis of social phenomena that looks at the past in order to understand the present and use that knowledge to "predict" the future. They tend to focus on understanding the historical roots of social reality in a way that such analysis can be used in predicting and informing the future directions of society (Ritzer, 2000, p. 46). It is in this sense that a dialectical approach to sociology is also considered as a political act.

6. A dialectical approach is critical of deterministic understandings and explanations of the world. It posits that we cannot understand the social world through the application of a simple deterministic model (Ritzer, 2000, p. 46). That is, a dialectical thinker avoids dealing in grand abstractions. In other words, it is important to avoid thinking in terms of a grand-theory that attempts to explain everything in the social world. It is also important to avoid explaining the world in terms of a single cultural, social, and/or economic factor, structure, or relation. That is, it is essential to understand that any given social reality is influenced by multiple factors. A dialectical approach is multidisciplinary and multi-theoretical. For example, in understanding the effects of racism and sexism, it is critical to approach these issues by drawing upon, for example, anthropological and sociological theories and political science discipline and from the perspectives of feminist and antiracist discourses rather than by simply relying on economic explanations using a Marxist lens.

7. A dialectical approach emphasizes the effects of conflict and contradictions. It is concerned with the process of change that results from conflicts between various levels of social reality over, for example, control of the economic, cultural, social, and political resources and

structures in society (Ritzer, 2000, p. 47). It does not ignore how societies form cohesion, but it offers a critical understanding of shared norms in light of the concept of ideology. A dialectical thinker asks how shared norms and values promote the interests of a few over others.

8. A dialectical thinker is also interested in the relationship between actors and social structures. It does not assume that social actors are entirely powerless in the face of powerful social structures (i.e., the family, economy, religion). Social relationship is not a zero-sum game. People have agency, and they often do exercise it. That is, social structures do not simply determine who and what we are. A dialectical thinker also assumes that social actors either reproduce or change the nature of these structures through their actions. As Marx stated, "while men are changed by circumstances, circumstances are changed precisely by men" (as cited in Ebenstein 1960: 410).

In short, the dialectical approach to sociology is both a way of thinking as well as a construct of the world. As a construct, it emphasizes the importance of conflicts, contradictions, dynamics, and processes. It is critical of static ways of thinking about the social world. It is also a discourse, a way of talking about the world that is made of dynamic and contradictory structures and relations (Ritzer, 2000, p. 19). This dialectical approach forms the basis for the **critical paradigm**.

Critical Sociology Discourse

As mentioned, our approach to teaching sociology highlights the importance and interrelationship between **macro-** and **micro-sociological** analyses and understandings. It is also influenced by **critical pedagogy** and **sociology**, which analyze the effects of oppressions and inequalities on groups and individuals. This approach looks at how groups and individuals resist the effects of global and local forms of inequities. It also seeks to explicate how individuals and groups reproduce various forms of oppression through their interactions in social structures. **Critical pedagogy** refers to a set of theories and practices that aim at debunking dominant forms of teaching methods and curriculum. It emphasize that in teaching and learning about a topic one needs to account for the needs of students, their perspectives, and, at the same time, to introduce them to histories and social issues that marginalized groups face in their struggles towards achieving equality and ending oppression.

Critical theorists are not simply concerned with description (i.e., asking questions, such as "what is"), but are concerned with questions, such as "what could be" (Glesne, 2011, p. 9). We define **critical** as the process of debunking and unmasking those values, norms, beliefs, and social, political, and economic practices that limit and undermine human and group freedom, social justice, and democracy (Glesne, 2011, p. 9). Critical theorists offer critiques of society, social structures, and practices that go beyond a descriptive depiction of the status quo (Wotherspoon, 2009). They focus on analysis of structural inequalities that affect human interactions. They analyze how the systems of power promote the interests of the elite groups in society and work against the subordinate classes and their political, social, and economic interests. This theoretical perspective questions the status quo, and argues that social structures do not benefit all equally (Wotherspoon, 2009). They focus on the effects of social change. They also promote social change that results in the advancement of equality and equity. Critical sociology is inclusive of various interpretations of social reality (Glesne, 2011, p. 9). As such, it is multidimensional.

Critical theorists offer holistic analysis of social phenomena by looking at the economic, social, cultural, and political factors. Although they are critical of the economic determinism of classical Marxism and some neo-Marxists, "they do not argue that [these theorists] were wrong in focusing on the economic realm but that they should have been concerned with other aspects of social life as well", such as cultural factors (Ritzer, 2000, p. 276). They are critical of a simple focus on structures within society as explanatory factors that exclude the experiences of individuals within society as factors in understanding human relations (Ritzer, 2000, p. 277).

The aim of critical sociology is to question and to offer critiques of structural and historical conditions of oppression that many groups have, and continue to face. The other aim is to transform these conditions in order to put an end to various forms of oppression. The focus of critical sociology is to highlight and to bring to the centre of theory building the worldviews and standpoints of the oppressed groups and their experiences and perspectives in order to critically understand how cultural, social, political, and economic conditions serve and promote the interests of certain groups and not others (Glesne, 2011, pp. 9–10). They want to account for the interaction between individual and society (Ritzer, 2000, p. 277). That is, critical theory explores social, economic, political, and cultural issues by drawing upon **standpoint epistemologies**.

Epistemology refers to the study of knowledge and how knowledge comes to be created (Glesne, 2011, p. 5). It refers to the ways in which we perceive and know our social world. **An epistemological position, thus, states how we know what we know. Standpoint epistemologies** reflect and are based on the experiences, values, and interests of the oppressed or excluded groups (i.e., women, gay and lesbian groups, racialized populations, and colonized groups) (Glesne, 2011, p. 10). That is, the aim is to produce knowledge that is based on the understandings of marginalized people. By being inclusive of this knowledge base, we can achieve the main aim of critical sociology: subverting dominant discourses of power and deconstructing the dominant forms of narrations and exposing their racist, sexist, homophobic, ableist, and Eurocentric aspects (Glesne, 2011, p. 10). Such an approach requires an intersectional analysis of social relations. **Intersectional analyses** and **multicentric approaches** provide comprehensive frameworks that offer alternative approaches to reductionist explanations of Marxist class analysis, an overemphasis by antiracists on racism and "race" as explanations for inequalities faced by non-White populations, and the role feminists attach to gender as a central factor in explaining patterns of power inequalities and social and economic privileges, historically and across time and space (Fleras, 2010, p. 153). It is in this light that as critical sociologists we cannot ignore the individual and his/her experiences if we want "to say anything meaningful about political changes that could lead to a just and humane society" (Ritzer, 2000, p. 277).

Briefly, there are several characteristics of critical theorists that have already been identified:

1. They consider research to be a political act of questioning dominant forms of power. In their analysis and critique of those who have power, they account for the perspectives of nondominant and subordinated groups in society (Glesne, 2011, p. 10).

2. Critical theory and research focus upon language and the unspoken rules that determine and regulate what can and cannot be said about a "topic"; who has the authority and the right to

speak about a "topic"; who is considered as the subordinate; whose views are erroneous and unimportant; and who must accept the knowledge and social constructions of experts about a "topic" as the truth about the world (Kincheloe and McLaren, as cited in Glesne, 2011, p. 10). In other words, they look at how discourses are positioned from a historical perspective and how they perpetuate structures and unequal relations of power (Glesne, 2011, p. 10).

3. Critical theorists emphasize **praxis**. They argue that just talking about issues and changing peoples' views are not enough nor adequate efforts to bring about change. One also must act upon ideas to materialize them and put them into practice. That is, praxis refers to the dialectical relationship between thought and practice, theory and action (Glesne, 2011, p. 10). Sociology based on dialectical approach highlights praxis. By this we mean that theory is informed by practice and practice is shaped by theory (Ritzer, 2000, p. 282).

4. The aim of critical theory is to increase awareness among social actors about their conditions in terms of how they are dominated and subjugated. In other words, critical theorists want to raise social actors' class, racial, gender, sexual, and ethnic consciousness, to name a few.

Conclusion

In this book, we offer a general framework to narrate the development of sociology and sociological knowledge from a critical perspective. We examine the political, economic, social, and cultural changes that have been influential in the rise of sociology. We also explore the tremendous consequences that these factors have had on various groups across the globe (Ritzer, 2000, p. 6). Sociology looks at how human civilizations have been formed, changed, and reproduced; and how humans interact, behave, and organize themselves in face-to-face, institutional, local, national, and global contexts. Sociological knowledge and theories are not static and they change; they reflect the changes in society at local and global levels.

We approach sociology as a micro- and macro-multidimensional discourse that seeks to disrupt and challenge the existing social world and to make it far more open, equal, and diverse. The aim is to open up spaces for the voices of marginalized people as important sources of knowledge and perspectives about the world. The goal is to offer theories that reflect their interests and knowledge systems so that we can "change social structures [cultural norms], and the prospects for individuals" (Ritzer, 2000, p. 225).

Chapter Review Questions

1. Define sociology and explain the paradigm shifts that have influenced sociology.

2. Explain what sociologists mean by the term discourse. Discuss by providing examples.

3. What is meant by "sociology as a discourse"? Explain.

4. Why should we approach sociology as "public discourse"?

5. What are some of the characteristics of critical transnational perspective?

6. Is sociology Eurocentric? Explain.

7. Why is the concept of the sociological imagination an important term/idea in sociology?

8. Distinguish between agency and social structure.

9. What does Peter Berger mean by "seeing the general in the particular" and "seeing the strange in the familiar"?

10. What are some of the examples of discrimination? Define the different forms of "isms" that sociologists explore in their analysis of society.

11. Define ideology (dominant ideology) and provide examples to illustrate the basic characteristics of the term.

12. Distinguish between personal troubles and public (social) issues.

13. What is meant by the term quality of mind?

14. What is meant by the term intersectional analysis?

15. Define dialectics and explain the main assumptions of dialectical analyses.

16. What is mean by false-consciousness?

17. What is meant by the terms positionality and reflexive thinking?

18. Distinguish between expressive and utilitarian individualism.

19. Define and explore the significance of the term, feminization of poverty, in analysis social issues in today's world.

Critical Thinking Questions

1. How can sociology help you to become a critical thinker?

2. What are some of the commonsense knowledge that people adhere to that result in the perpetuation of dominant social structures and ideologies?

3. What do you need to do in order to become a dialectical thinker and practice your sociological imagination? Explain.

4. In what ways might you adhere to and practice racist or antiracist discourses and ideologies? Explain.

CHAPTER TWO

Sociology, Sociological Theories, Controversies, and Debates

Introduction

In this chapter, we explore the subject matter of sociology (i.e., what sociologists study). We briefly discuss the main theoretical perspectives in sociology and examine some of the main sociological controversies and debates within the field (Wotherspoon, 2009). We introduce the reader to concepts and ideas, such as **science, positivism, synchronic** and **diachronic approaches, agency, social structure, micro-** and **macro-analyses, objective** and **subjective knowledge, structuralist** and **constructivist approaches** to the social world, and **qualitative** and **quantitative methodologies**. We also examine the different ways sociologists explain related concepts, such as **socialization, gender, objectivity, subjectivity, value, norm, ontology, racialized identity,** *othering,* **gazing, suicide, discrimination, prejudice,** and **stereotype**.

This chapter is divided into two parts. In Part One, we define sociology as a multidisciplinary field and explore the elements of social structure. We also distinguish between sociology and other social science disciplines, and introduce the reader to the main perspectives in sociology. In Part Two, we distinguish between macro-objective-quantitative and micro-subjective-qualitative sociology. We end the chapter by arguing that the best way to approach social issues is by incorporating both macro- and micro-sociological analysis and theories.

Part One

Sociology as a "Scientific Discipline"

Sociology is a systematic study of social conditions and phenomena through observation, gathering of data, analysis of the data, and drawing of conclusion. This makes sociology a "scientific" discipline. The term "**science**" implies that there is an "objective" reality that can be comprehended rationally through the application of "scientific" methods of observation and experimentation (Perry, 2001, p. 374). "Science" is based on the assumption that the regularities in the social world that we observe in the past and present will be repeated in the future (Perry, 2001, p. 374). The "scientific" method is based on the premise that the natural world is guided by natural laws and the duty of the scientist is to discover these laws through observation and analysis of data. In the same view, sociologists embark on the study of society with the presumption that society is organized by societal laws and their task is to discover these laws, using the same methods of the natural/physical sciences. Sociologists call this approach **positivism**. As a "science", sociology proposes abstract theories and tests these theories against empirical cases to determine if they are credible (Turner, 2003, p.2). Sociologists generalize from research, analysis, and observation to better understand how societies operate.

Sociology is not simply concerned with developing theoretical, "scientific", and empirical approaches to understanding human societies and behaviour. It is also a "tool-kit" to critique society and to use this critical knowledge to act upon the world in order to bring about equality and equity in terms of attributes, such as "race", gender, sexuality, social class, religion, region, etc. Sociological knowledge makes more sense when it is practiced in our day-to-day interactions. That is, sociological knowledge needs to be **authenticated**. From a critical theory perspective, **authentication** happens when individuals and groups who have been the victims of distorted and hegemonic communication and information draw upon sociological research and knowledge and use it to free themselves and others from the systems of exploitation and hegemony (Ritzer, 2000, 282). In this sense, sociology acts as an **anti-hegemonic discourse** that questions and critiques commonsense and dominant forms of knowledge.

Sociology draws upon both **synchronic** and **diachronic approaches** to contemporary economic, social, cultural, and political issues. A **synchronic** view tends to be concerned with specific factors within a specific setting and historical period (Ritzer, 2000, p. 282). For example, looking at how men and women who experience divorce deal with their anxieties, dilemmas, and problems associated with separating from their partners. A **diachronic** approach is concerned with the historical roots of contemporary societies and with where they might be going in the future (Ritzer, 2000, p. 282). For example, sociologists may study the consequences of changes in technology for how work is organized and how people experience work. In short, while the synchronic view looks at "the then and the now", the diachronic approach focuses on the "yesterday, today, and tomorrow" of social phenomena.

Sociology seeks to understand how individuals live in society and how society is reflected in the actions, thoughts, and behaviours of individuals, both synchronically and diachronically. Sociology aims at understanding and providing explanations about how and why humans behave, think, and organize themselves the way they do (Turner, 2003, p. 1). Sociology studies how human behaviour is affected by the participation of individuals as members of social categories in groups, organizations, and institutions from both **macro** and **micro perspectives**. Sociology examines how changes in economic, cultural, social, and political spheres affect individuals in the context of **micro-level** (i.e., face-to-face interactions) or **macro-level** relations (i.e., social structures and global contexts). Sociology explores the consequences of social structures and institutions, such as schools, the workplace, and the legal system, on how individuals perform their duties and how they are socialized to think in certain ways and to act in particular manners (See Box 2.1 - Elements of Social Structures). Sociologists focus on the effects of social structures that influence the ways in which social actors experience life. At the same time, sociologists are also interested in determining how individuals through their actions and interactions with others affect change in the structure of social institutions. In other words, sociology studies how human behaviour is affected by their socialization and experiences in social structures, and how they reproduce or transform such institutions through active and passive participation in day-to-day relationships.

BOX 2.1 - Elements of Social Structures

Social structures refer to those well-established large scale and long-term patterns of organization. **Status, role, value, norm, social institution, group,** and **organization** are examples of social structures. These elements of social structure in addition to culture allow people whose experiences are different to act in predictable ways and to cooperate with one another despite their differences. Both culture and social structures influence human actors to behave in various ways in different social situations depending on factors, such as gender, "race", and ethnicity, to name a few. Accordingly, social actors adjust their behaviours according to the expectations that are placed on them by others in different social situations.

We can conceptualize social structures as a set of social positions or a set of **statuses** that relate to one another, such as the relationship and expectations imposed on people who are labelled as "doctor, nurse, and patient" or as "principal, teacher, parent, and student". Ralph Linton (1961, p. 202) argued that a status is "distinct from the individual who may occupy it. [It] is simply a collection of rights and duties". As individuals, we are assigned statuses that are interrelated. There are two main types of status: **ascribed** and **achieved**. **Ascribed statuses** are assigned to individuals and are not related to the innate characteristics of individuals (Linton, 1961, p. 203). Age, sex, and family relations are examples of ascribed status. We are assigned a sex at birth due to our biological characteristics. We are often trained for performing the status of a male or female from the moment of birth (Linton, 1961, p. 203). We learn how to behave, think, and act according to the statuses we occupy. In interactions with one's sister, one acts as a brother. In interaction with a teacher, one acts not as a brother but as a student.

In contrast, **achieved statuses** are not assigned at birth, but reflect the characteristics of individuals and their individual efforts (Linton, 1961, p. 203). For example, we are sociology instructors, because we registered for postsecondary education in sociology, received our Ph.D.'s in this discipline, and applied for a job at Kwantlen Polytechnic University to teach this subject. We achieved this status because we attained the necessary credentials, a Master of Arts and/or a Ph. D. in sociology, anthropology, and mass communication, and became knowledgeable in the theories and methods of sociology that are necessary to obtain such a job.

Status is related to the concept of **role**. When an individual acts upon the rights and duties that constitute a status, he or she is performing a role (Linton, 1961, p. 202). A role is a dynamic aspect of a status, and the two are inseparable from one another. Roles are evaluative forms that allow individuals to organize their lives, attitudes, and behaviours in such a way that they are meaningful to other members of society (Linton, 1961, p. 202). For example, as instructors in an institution of higher learning we cannot share students' information with their parents or other students. Strict institutional rules also govern the interactions between instructors and their students. For example, instructors should not accept gifts from students who are currently registered in their classes, as this may be perceived as biasing their assessment of students' evaluation in the class. Roles are not individual expectations but societal ones that determine how people occupying different statuses should behave and interact with one another and what to expect from one another in social interactions.

Robert Merton (1976, p. 245) distinguished between role and **role-set**. He maintained that a specific status can also be defined by a number of roles. For example, a medical student (a social position) is not simply defined in terms of its relation to his or her teachers/instructors. He or she is also involved in a series of role-relationships that diversely relate him/her to a collection of other statuses, such as physicians, nurses, medical technicians, other students, and social workers (Merton, 1976, p. 245). Here, Merton (1976, p. 246) is reminding us that even the ostensibly simple forms of social structure are very much complex and composed of many parts.

Statuses and roles make sense and become operative in the context of social institutions. A social institution is another element of social structure. **Social institution** refers to those patterns of beliefs and behaviour that are organized and designed to satisfy human needs and wants. It is defined as organized interactions of sets of roles, social expectations, and statuses that are related and complementary to one another (O'Brian, 2004, p. 149). Examples of social institutions are the family, the economy, and the education system. They provide us with roles, statuses, and rules that inform our social interactions. Our identities are formed in the context of our relationships with other people as members of various groupings in the context of these social institutions. From a **structural functionalist perspective**, the main **functions of the family** are to:

1. ensure that society has a stable source and supply of new members by regulating sexual reproduction and the socialization of children to learn the appropriate values, norms, and attitudes prevalent in society;

2. provide a source of economic support for its members; and

3. "provide emotional support for family members by providing intimacy, warmth, safety, and protection" (Mitchell, 2003, p. 32).

In contrast, the **conflict perspective** sees the family as the source of economic inequality. For example, if one is born into an affluent family, he/she is afforded more opportunities than a person who is born into a family living in poverty. According to this perspective, the class position of parents affects the type of socialization children receive. Working class parents emphasize conformity, neatness, and orderliness. In contrast, middle class parents socialize their children according to characteristics, such as self-reliance and critical thinking (i.e., problem solving). As such, their socialization in the family prepares them for the types of jobs and occupations that enable them to reproduce their class positions.

According to **symbolic interactionism**, the family is the outcome of the interactions of its members and is socially constructed. This implies that there are various types of families possible, which questions the structural functionalist view that family is a natural and standard structure (Mitchell, 2003, p. 37). In fact, **feminists**, such as Margaret Eichler, have pointed out that sociological analysis of the family in the past had been affected by what they call a **monolithic bias**, through which only one ideal type of family (the nuclear family) is celebrated as "normal" (Mitchell, 2003). Feminism also points out that the family is socially constructed and is not a "natural" institution. Families are diverse and not uniform. They maintain that it is in the context of the family that women and girls face violence. They problematize the role of men in perpetuating violence against women. They maintain that violence against females in the family is not a rare incident. In general, they highlight that women are discriminated in the family and other institutions and experience inequalities due to the effects of sexism and patriarchal values and belief systems that reinforce sexual violence against women in both public and private spaces (this is referred to as the **matrix of domination**).

It is in the context of social institutions that we learn about the **values** and **norms** in society. Values and norms are two other elements of social structure. **Value** refers to conceptions of right and wrong within society. They are factors/beliefs that are considered as desirable, proper, and good by most members of a given culture/social group. Values dictate how we should behave and judge other peoples' behaviours. **Norms** refer to those rules, regulations, and behaviours that are universally observed by the members of society and have moral significance and consequences for the operation of society. Laws (legal codes) are examples of norms that are formal and written down. Simply put, norms, as a prescription for proper behaviour, point to the "dos" and "don'ts" in a given culture.

Groups are organized people with shared norms and values. A group consists of two or more individuals who identify and interact with one another regularly. Group members share similar experiences and have common loyalties and interests. They also share similar values and adhere to shared norms. We share views and values as participants in group activities. Groups can be formed on long-term and short-term basis. They bring social actors who have a common interest together. Examples of groups are **peer groups**, **"minority" groups**, **ethnic groups**, or **primary groups**. Groups assist in transmitting culture from one generation to another.

A **peer group** consists of individuals who have similar interests, hobbies, and belong to the same age category. Peer groups play an important role in the socialization of adolescents. Wirth (1961, p. 309) defined a **"minority"** as a group of people who due to their cultural, religious, or physical characteristics are singled out from other groups, are affected by differential and unequal treatments, and consider themselves as being the object of discrimination. The fact that there are "**minority**" **groups** in society implies that there is also a "majority" group that enjoys power and higher social status and access to privileges that are closed to other members of society. In comparison to the **dominant group** in society, "minority" groups lack access to the positions of power and social, economic, and political opportunities in society (Wirth, 1961, p. 309). As Wirth (1961) asserted, by "minority" or "majority" groups we are not referring to the size of these groups. Rather, the reference is to the extent to which they have power in society. In South Africa, during the era of Apartheid, for example, Black people who outnumbered Whites in society were considered a "minority" group. In general, a "minority" group refers to people who belong to specific "racial", sexual, religious, or cultural groups that experience social disadvantages due to their "racial", sexual, religious, or cultural characteristics and membership or assumed membership in the group. Members of "minority" groups do not have control over their everyday relations in comparison to members of the dominant group whom have greater control over their lives.

An **ethnic group** refers to the actual lived communities that are composed of individuals who share similar cultural norms, religions, and rituals, and distinguish between themselves and others by keeping ethnic boundaries through, for example, marriage rules that may prohibit marrying someone from outside the group (they practice **endogamy**). An ethnic group shares a common heritage, culture, language, and religion that bond its members into a homogenous community who show loyalty and adhere to specific customs, beliefs, and value systems (Henry & Tator, 2010, p. 381; Glossary). In general, members of an ethnic group have a common language and culture and share similar norms and behaviours. We can also speak of **primary groups**. Charles Horton Cooley (1961, p. 315) defined a primary group as "those characterized by intimate face-to-face associations and cooperation", such as the family, playground, community group of elders, and neighbourhood. They are primary in a sense that they play an important role in "forming the social nature and ideals of the individual" (Cooley, 1961, p. 315).

Formal Organizations are large specialized secondary groups that are structured to achieve maximum efficiency and predetermined and specific goals. In formal organization, its members play roles that are stable with clearly defined boundaries and are easily recognized by others (Wosley, ed., 1976, p. 255). **Bureaucracies** are examples of formal organizations. They are structures that facilitate the operation and management of large-scale groups. Examples of such formal organizations are the national **post office**, **corporate fast-food restaurants**, and **universities** and **colleges**. They are designed in such a way as to perform specific tasks efficiently. They are hierarchical and operate according to preestablished written rules. They are characterized by a division of labour and hierarchy of authority. They are also impersonal, and employment in these organizations is based on technical qualifications (Weber, 1976, pp. 265–269).

Sociology as a Multi- and TransDisciplinary Field: what do sociologists do?

Sociology produces knowledge about society and generalizes from observation. Sociology is also a transdisciplinary field due to its emphasis on historical and comparative analysis and the fact that it draws upon knowledge produced by scholars from various parts of the world. Sociology adopts the **subjective approach** to understanding society and **objective methods** of investigating and exploring the social world.

Although sociology is distinguished from psychology, anthropology, political science, philosophy, history, and literary studies, to name a few disciplines, it draws upon all these fields of studies to offer comprehensive analyses of human relations and behaviours. In this sense, it is a **multidisciplinary field**. In the following paragraph, we offer a general understanding of these other disciplines to distinguish them from sociology.

Anthropology is concerned with studying all peoples of past and present, including nonindustrial and modern societies/cultures in systematic and comparative manners (Erickson, 1998, p. 13). It approaches studying societies from a holistic approach. It consists of several subfields: sociocultural (i.e., studying cultural elements such as kinship), linguistic (i.e., "concerned with the nature of language" and how language has been used and evolved), physical (i.e., analyzing human fossils), and archaeology (i.e., studying artifacts and their importance) (Erickson, 1998, p. 13). **Economics** studies how goods and services are produced, distributed, and consumed and the impact of government policies on these factors. It is subdivided into: macro- (i.e., national and international levels) and micro-subfields (i.e., individual level, firm level analysis). **Political Science** studies the political system. It explores how governments are formed/change and how states are formed and function. It is interested in developing theoretical propositions regarding power and government. It offers a comparative study of all levels of power structures and the decision-making processes at the social and political levels. **Psychology** is an analytical approach to understanding human behaviour. Psychologists study the mind, personality formation, and individual behaviours. They gather data and interpret those data in order to formulate theories. They often employ lab experiments to produce data about human behaviours. Psychology consists of many subfields, such as clinical, experimental, behavioural, and applied psychology. **History** is concerned with events and factors that have shaped societies through the ages. It is descriptive and has not developed theoretical approaches to studying societies in comparison to other fields. In contrast, sociology makes its theoretical approaches explicit because the aim is to test these theories. Nevertheless, historians study the human and social development in order to determine the extent to which these events were unique parts of the larger processes, thus pointing to their patterns and regularities. **Philosophy** also employs analytical approaches and aims at both refining and testing its theories. However, it is not empirical. That is, it does not gather data and information in order to test its theories. It is more concerned with the internal logic of its theories and arguments.

As it can be gathered from the above paragraph, sociology differs from other disciplines which study human society and behaviour. In comparison to psychologists, for example, sociologists study what happens between individuals and collectives/groups rather than focusing on what happens *within* (inside) individuals. Sociology emphasizes social patterns of human behaviour rather than episodic or random occurrences. In other words, sociologists tend to be more interested in recurrent or repeated and ritualistic behaviours and phenomena. For instance, a sociologist will be less inclined to investigate why a student arrived late to class a couple of times. Most people occasionally arrive late to events and appointments. However, if a student was half the semester late to class, then that is a pattern: something must be happening, which causes the lateness. Similarly, if a couple of students come to class occasionally late, this will not occasion a sociological investigation. However, if half the class was late most of the semester, then there must be something going on either in the class (i.e., boring lectures) or in the larger society that is preventing students to come to class on time (i.e., the students are working two jobs to make ends meet or do not have access to adequate means of transportation). Let's look at another example: If millions of Canadians are unemployed as it is the case in almost the entire span of Canadian history, then that indicates a clear pattern and it would certainly call for a sociological investigation to find out what is causing so many people to be unemployed.

Sociology is also composed of many subfields, each studying and analyzing specific issues and factors, such as educational, racialized, ethnic, religious, and political. Sociology studies social change, deviance, crime, social movements, nationalism and nation-building processes, economic and political structures, and population trends and their consequences for groups and individuals. Sociologists study how human interactions are affected by the media, family values, ethnicity, gender, sexuality, racial identity, and government policies. A Sociologist may ask why people commit suicide. Another may ask how Black students in Edmonton, Alberta, Canada construct their identities. Some sociologists focus on analyzing the effects of public policy on various regions in Canada and across the globe. They may explore the effects of public policy and the implementation of laws on the life chances of the members of specific groups. For example, sociologists may examine how environmental issues and factors affect the health of different individuals and groups similarly or differently. Sociology also examines the consequences of human interactions in diverse settings in terms of people's level of access to social, economic, and cultural opportunities, wealth, power, knowledge, goods, and services. For example, sociologists are concerned with how socioeconomic inequalities are reproduced and the extent to which power differences and income inequalities affect individuals and groups based on various factors, such as gender, "race", ethnicity, and social class. According to Murphy and Rosenbaum (as cited in Barak, Leighton, & Falvin, 2007, p. 197), "being black and poor places a person in closer geographical proximity to opportunities to buy and/or smoke cocaine and to become criminal subject of the administration of justice". In contrast, White and middle class individuals can "hide" their addictions in their middle class homes and neighbourhoods, thus making them invisible to the criminal justice system.

Sociologists have also been interested in urban and rural studies, sports, gender studies, and the effects of sexuality and ability on individuals and groups. Sociology of education, nationalism, families, work, knowledge, and religion are examples of other subfields within the discipline of sociology. Due to its multiple focuses in various interrelated topics and areas of inquiry, sociology, as a "scientific" approach to analyzing society and its many elements, provides us with a range of different and holistic approaches and understandings of issues and factors that have shaped human societies both locally and globally (See Box 2.2 - Sociology, Discrimination, and Prejudice).

BOX 2.2 - Sociology, Discrimination, and Prejudice

Many sociologists study the causes and effects of **discrimination** on groups based on multiple social categories, such as gender, "race", ethnicity, ability, social class, political ideologies, religious beliefs, and sexuality. Discrimination refers to the act of treating someone unequally due to perceived prejudiced views. That is, it is the differential and unfair treatment of individuals because of their membership in a group or in a category that lacks power in society. Discrimination is defined as "illegitimate forms of treatment" (Francis, as cited in Driedger, 2003, p. 246). Fleras (2010, p. 71) offered a useful definition of discrimination: it is any intentional or unintentional act that adversely affects others based on factors other than one's aptitudes, merits, or abilities. Allport (as cited in Driedger, 2003, p. 246) suggested that discrimination implies "action" by social actors and institutions. That is, discrimination is the end process of putting prejudgments about a group into practice (Fleras, 2010, p. 71). For example, people with disability continue to face discrimination in society that has made them vulnerable to the effects of poverty: the average income of individuals with disability in 2001 dollars was $22,200 in comparison to $30,800 for nondisabled people (Mitchell, 2009, p. 274). According to the Campaign 2000's Report Card on Poverty, Children of **visible minority** backgrounds (visible minority is defined as those people who are neither White nor Aboriginal) are "twice as likely to live in poverty as all children in Canada" (Mitchell, 2009, p. 85). According to one report, moreover, amongst the recent immigrants about 49 percent of children live in poverty (Mitchell, 2009, p. 85). A study by Head in 1981 (as cited in Driedger, 2003, p. 250) also suggested that 90 percent of Black and 72 percent of South Asian respondents in his research about discrimination in housing, employment, and community services reported "'some' or 'a great deal of' discrimination, in contrast to 35 percent of European respondents".

Sociologists distinguish between discrimination and **prejudice.** Fleras (2010, p. 71) pointed out that discrimination can exist without prejudice. This is the case in instances that institutionalized discrimination is well ingrained into the fabric of society. Prejudice is defined as irrational views that are generalizations about a group of people that are either depicted in negative or positive lights. Prejudice refers to those ideas that presume one group of people is more superior to another. **Prejudice** is a mental attitude that negatively and unfavourably prejudges members of a group by attributing to every individual in that group characteristics that are incorrectly attributed to the whole group (Henry & Tator, 2010, p. 383, Glossary). Prejudice refers to "illegitimate forms of categorization" or stereotyping (Francis, as cited in Driedger, 2003, p. 246). They arise in unequal contexts and reflect the attempts of some groups to control others in the competition for scarce resources (Fleras, 2010, p. 69). We have preconceived ideas about other people based on what we think of the group and the type of information and knowledge that we have about the members of that group. In these cases, individual characteristics/merits are ignored and denied, and we conceptualize individuals based on the information that we attribute to the whole group. In other words, individuals are viewed in light of perceived group characteristics. Prejudice, then, refers to **positive** and **negative attitudes** (Driedger, 2003, p. 246). In Canada, many people hold **positive prejudice** towards the **charter groups** (i.e., British-Canadians and French-Canadians) and **negative prejudice** towards Indigenous peoples, Black Canadians, Chinese-Canadians, and Indo-Canadians. Two good examples are how Moslems have been depicted as "terrorists" and "fundamentalist irrational religious" individuals since Sept. 11, 2001 in the media and the rise of **Islamophobia,** or the fear of Moslem immigrants and Islam in general in Western parts of the world. They are often constructed as "militants" who are willing to use violence to achieve their political goals in the dominant media. As such, they are viewed as *outsiders* who should be controlled and put under **surveillance**. Fleras (2010, p. 73) argued that Islamophobia reflects Western fears, anxieties, and distrusts of Moslem societies that are ingrained in Western imagination and have not been critically examined. In general, the actions and beliefs of a small number of individuals within the diverse Islamic world are portrayed by the media to represent the whole group.

It is also important to note that there is a difference between prejudice and ignorance: a prejudiced person holds on to his/her views despite being confronted with evidence that question and subvert his/her views (Fleras & Elliot, 2002, p. 232). Prejudice is closely related to the concept of **stereotype**. Stereotyping involves categorization. It refers to those generalizations about others that are unwarranted and unfounded and are not based on evidence (Fleras, 2010, p. 69). Stereotypes have two important functions (Taylor, as cited in Driedger, 2003, p. 244). First, when little is known about a group, social actors have the tendency to "'fill in missing information". In contrast, when social actors are faced with too much information, they tend to simplify it. However, the process of choosing which information to exclude or include is influenced by biases, prejudiced views, and misinformation. An example of stereotype is when social actors assume that "Jews are shrewd, industrious, grasping, intelligent and ambitious" (Driedger, 2003, p. 245). Another example is when the media portrays stereotypical images of adult children who continue to live at home with their parents. They are often depicted as slackers, moochers, or as mamma's boys. The parents are depicted as victims of their children who are constructed as greedy and lazy individuals (Mitchell, 2009, p. 209). The multicultural policy in Canada has also been criticized for resulting in the production of stereotypes. It is argued that a focus on cultural events and characteristics defines culture based on the lowest common denominator. Viewing cultures based on factors, such as food and dance, do not account for diversity and difference/inequalities *between* and *within* ethnic/cultural groups. For example, most youth in Canada when celebrating the multicultural day in their schools participate in events that often focus on dance, music, and food from different cultural backgrounds rather than on the histories and contributions of various cultural groups to the nation-building in Canada. The consequence of such a focus is that we often ignore the political and economic contributions of various cultural groups to the development of Canada as a nation. In this sense, multiculturalism emphasizes *what people are* rather than on *who they are*.

Prejudices and stereotypes are world-ordering schemes, helping us to understand a seemingly chaotic reality. In general, prejudice is a negative or positive belief or feeling about a particular group of individuals. Prejudices are often passed on from one generation to the next. Although it may serve as a cementing factor for in-group members, promoting solidarity and members' self-image, prejudice is considered largely destructive. Prejudice is believed to be pervasive because it serves many psychological, social, and economic functions:

1. prejudice allows people to avoid doubt and fear;

2. prejudice gives people scapegoats to blame in times of trouble;

3. prejudice can boost self-esteem;

4. prejudice allows people to bond with their own group by contrasting it with outsider groups; and

5. prejudice legitimizes discrimination because it apparently justifies one group's dominance over another.

Sociologists also analyze the causes and consequences of **institutional discrimination**. They distinguish between two forms of institutional discrimination: **systematic** (implying intent) and **systemic** (referring to their effects). Institutional discrimination refers to explicitly condoned sets of organizational policies and practices that negatively affect "minority" groups (Fleras, 2010, p. 76). **Systematic discrimination** is defined as those practices, ideas, and values that openly and deliberately deny and exclude "minorities" from equal participation in society, and is conveyed by those employees who act on behalf of the organization and implement organizational policies and their action is approved by the organization (Fleras, 2010, p. 76). In Canada and the United States, immigration laws have been used as ways to deny entrance to people and groups that were/are deemed unwanted and were/are not considered as ideal future citizens of these countries (i.e., Roma people, whose refugee statuses are denied in Canada). These laws exclude(d) people and groups based on factors, such as religion, gender, marital status, ability, and "race".

Systemic discrimination refers to the idea that when the rules and practices of an institution are evenly and equally applied to everyone, they may have negative consequences for some and not others. They are not intentionally set or practiced based on prior knowledge and awareness of their negative effects. Fleras (2010, p. 76) maintained that systemic discrimination points out that the rules and procedures of institutions can very well be discriminatory by design, in practice, or in terms of their outcomes, even if those working for the organization are not prejudiced and do not believe in discriminating against others. They are part of normal operation of institutions. Nevertheless, the groups that are often affected are "minorities" due to no fault of their members, but by virtue of their membership in "minority" and devalued groups. For example, height requirements for firefighters may exclude people who are short but are nevertheless very capable to do this kind of job. In fact, this requirement may discriminate against those ethnic/racial/national groups who are genetically shorter than European groups (notwithstanding height diversity within each group). Although the intention was never to exclude people based on their ethnicity, this rule actually may discriminate against those who were very much able to become good firefighters. As the old saying goes, *the road to hell is often paved with good intensions.*

One of the main topics of investigation for sociologists is the process of **socialization**, or the ways and means through which social actors learn to be human. **Socialization** refers to the processes through which we learn about norms and values that are prevalent in our society from infancy to old age. Mitchell (2009, p. 139) defined socialization as a complex process through which "behavioural patterns, attitudes, values, and knowledge" that play a central role in developing self-identity are passed from one generation to another. Socialization, in other words, refers to the process of learning the culture that is prevalent in a group or society from childhood to death (i.e., the life course). Sociologists consider the state, siblings, peer groups, schools, the media, and the family as important **agents of socialization**. Agents of socialization are those social institutions and social actors within them that play an important role in the development of our personalities and identities (Albanese, 2009, p. 27). Socialization processes in the family, school, workplace, and other organizations and social networks make us who we are or who we will become. We become familiarized with societal expectations and acceptable behaviour as we participate in these social institutions. Sociologists distinguish between **primary socialization** and **secondary socialization**. Primary socialization takes place during childhood, mainly in the context of the family. Secondary socialization happens outside of the family structure through which individuals are introduced to new roles and identities that reflect the changing expectations of society of individuals, as they move through the life course (i.e., as teenagers, friends, parents, workers, and retirees) (Albanese, 2009, p. 26).

Our socialization takes shape in micro, macro, and global levels. At the micro-level (i.e., in the context of the family), we learn about expectations that society places on individuals and how social actors are supposed to behave in various contexts with various types of people. Older siblings, for example, can be the source of information for the younger siblings and they can also be role models for younger brothers and sisters. At the same time, the opposite is also true: siblings can be become sources of conflict as they may compete for parents' attention and/or familial resources (Mitchell, 2009, p. 140). We also learn about gender roles in various agents of socialization: how to act as boys and girls. At the macro-level, cultural norms and values are transmitted from one generation to another, thus allowing society to reproduce itself based on a set of generalized and universal norms and values (i.e., in schools we learn about Canadian values, national identity, and history). Socialization is not an apolitical process (i.e., politically neutral process). For example, the values and norms that social actors are introduced to in schools often exclude the histories and experiences of "minority" groups in society; thus perpetuating the status quo (i.e., the dominant ideology). Through participation in religious functions, social actors are inculcated with proper parent-child relations specific to a religion that may undermine child-rearing practices in other religious groups (Mitchell, 2009, p. 141). However, it is important to note that due to the effects of globalization, socialization also takes shape in the context of cultural norms and values that are more than ever global in scope. For example, many of us watch American films and may be influenced by their depictions of the ideals of individualism that inform our self-conceptions and personalities. Many Indo-Canadians watch **Bollywood** movies that may inform their understanding of the Indian society and its cultural norms and practices (See Hirji, 2010). In the same way, many Nigerian-Canadians learn new norms or reinforce pre-learned ones by watching **Nollywood** films (the Nigerian equivalent for Hollywood and Bollywood).

The media also influences how social actors may conceptualize **gender relations**. **Gender** refers to those characteristics that are associated with being male or female in society. Johnson (2011, p. 202) maintained that in cartoons women's roles "lack cleverness and depth of their male counterparts". Women are often depicted as "helpless" and "ignorant" and as needing the help of men to rescue them. That is, they are constructed as not being able to defend or help themselves. Jackson Katz (as cited in Hofmann, 2011, p. 210) explained that through toys, video games, and Hollywood movies boys are socialized to be tough, "solitary, independent, and often violent". The main message through the popular media is that boys who show their emotions are conceived as "sissies". Most toys for boys are also solitary and do not offer avenues for verbal or social development (Hofmann, 2011, p. 210). As Dorman argued (as cited in Christensen, 2011, p. 191), mass produced images and culture do not simply entertain us but also provide us with a secret education: "we are not only taught certain styles of violence, the latest fashions, and sex roles by TV, movies, magazines and comic strips, we are also taught how to succeed, how to love, how to buy, how to conquer, how to forget the past and suppress the future". In other words, as Kilbourne maintained (as cited in Chavanu, 2011, p. 26), media images and advertisements "shape our values". They do not simply attempt to sell us products, but they also define our dreams, wants, and needs. Through media produced images corporations sell ideas about sex, love, romance, capitalism, success, beauty, and power that reflect and perpetuate their ideologies (Kilbourne, as cited in Chavanu, 2011, p. 28).

In general, through the socialization process, social actors learn how to construct their **identities** (self-images); **personalities** (or, one's usual patterns of attitudes, needs, and characteristics), and concepts of **self** (or, those peculiar characteristics that form social actors' identities and distinguish them from other individuals). By emphasizing on the processes of socialization, sociologists examine:

1. how social actors create society, and how social structures, as agents of socialization, influence who they are;

2. how social actors conceptualize categories, such as beauty, sex, consumption, war, violence, mother, women, father, men, gay/lesbian//transgendered people, and African-Americans, and how such conceptualizations affect the way they behave and interact with others; and

3. how social actors make sense of their social realities and interactions in various social institutions.

Sociology, Paradigms, and Theories

Sociology, as a "science" that attempts to understand the relationship between individual and society, is influenced by several controversies and debates. These debates and controversies raise several questions that define how sociologists study society and individuals within it (Wotherspoon, 2009, p. 6). Should sociologists use the individual or society as the unit of analysis? Is it society (and social structures) that produce individuals; or is society (and social structures) the product of individuals and their interactions? To what extent do social conflict or social stability and consensus define the social world? To what extent would sociologists attempt to provide observable facts and laws? Should sociologists focus on how individuals interpret their social surroundings (Wotherspoon, 2009, p. 6)? These questions determine the types of frameworks, guidelines, and orientations that sociologists draw upon to produce knowledge about society and individuals. For example, the **conflict** and **structural functionalist** paradigms highlight a very significant debate that has been influential in sociological theories and analysis: the contrast between **social order** and **conflict** (Sears, 2008, p. 30) (See Box 2.3 - Debates and Controversies in Sociology: order versus conflict and individual versus society).

BOX 2.3 - Debates and Controversies in Sociology: order versus conflict and individual versus society

One of the most important debates in sociology is characterized by the emphasis of some sociologists (mainly **structural functionalists**) on the importance of **social order** in social organization of life. These sociologists conceive of sociology as a "science" that produces "objective" knowledge about society. In this definition, society is conceived as an "objective material thing" with real effects on individuals. The assumption is that knowledge about society can be utilized in the maintenance of social order. By understanding the laws that govern society, we can apply them to society and its structures and make sure that we can control the effects of social change and promote consensus and order. According to this view, change and progress, if they must happen, must be gradual or evolutionary, not revolutionary. That is, rapid social change is viewed as an abnormal state of society. The emphasis is on a "stable social order" (Wotherspoon, 2009, p. 6).

One of the most important proponents of social order was **Émile Durkheim**, who defined sociology as the scientific study of "**social facts**". According to him, "social facts" are "things" that impact individuals' ways of thinking and acting. Durkheim assumed that society affects individuals and their life chances, actions, and behaviours. In this sense, society is assumed to have a real "objective" reality that can be studied by employing scientific methods. In his view, the aim of sociology was to find the "normal characteristics" of society, which could then be employed in the integration of individuals as valuable citizens who are well integrated into society and its many institutions (Wotherspoon, 2009, p. 16).

For Talcott Parsons (whose ideas are also essential to our understanding of the structural functionalism paradigm), for example, the main objective of sociology was to find solutions to the 'problem of order' (Giddens, 1990, p. 14). In this light, the emphasis on order requires sociologists to focus on **issues of integration,** or those factors and structures that hold the system together despite existing divisions of interests, which divide among the members of a society (Giddens, 1990, p. 14). In this sense, sociology provides us with knowledge about society that can be used to establish some sort of control over its institutions, much like the natural sciences that provide information to control nature (Giddens, 1990, p. 15). For example, Parsons and his colleague Bales maintained that the family performs its function in the most efficient way when men are socialized according to **instrumental traits** and women according to **expressive traits** (Mitchell, 2003, p. 32).

According to Parsons, differences in gender socialization are central to the normative social integration of individuals (Macionis, Benoit, & Janssen, 1999, p. 246). Gender roles provide complementary sets of expectation and norm that socialize men and women into the circle of family unit. The division of labour between men and women in the family is considered to be functional for the normal operation of society. That is, gender differentiation is considered to contribute to the stabilization of society: the division of labor at home and within the family is vital to the operation of society. In this perspective, women are conceptualized as sensitive to others, expressive, emotional, and responsible for the operation of the family and household activities (i.e., women are viewed as "household managers" responsible for the consumption of goods and services within the family). In contrast, men are conceptualized as practical, instrumental, rational, self-assured, competitive, and responsible for the maintenance of the relationship between the family and other social institutions (i.e., men work outside home). To ensure the orderly operation of society, then, boys should be socialized to be rational, self-assured, competitive, and instrumental. In this context, **instrumental** refers to emphasis on responsibilities, focus on more abstract and impersonal goals, and a focus on external relationships between one's nuclear family and other social institutions. In contrast, girls should be socialized to be expressive, emotional, and sensitive. In this light, **expressiveness** "denotes concern for maintenance of harmony and the internal emotional affairs of the family" (Macionis et al., 1999, p. 246).

Marriage is also defined as the union between a man and woman with aim of biological reproduction of society. This definition derives from a **heterosexist view** of society, which normalizes heterosexual roles and attributes while treating other forms of sexuality as "deviant". This stereotypical construction of an ideal type family is best depicted in the sitcom "Leave It to Beaver". In this TV program, the father performs his instrumental roles as the breadwinner of the family and is depicted as a hardworking and confident male. In contrast, the wife in this show is portrayed as a caring mother (one of her expressive roles), whose main responsibility is the management of the household (Mitchell, 2003, p. 32). When the tasks and needs of the family are met according to a division of labour based on sex, this insures the reproduction of family in an orderly manner. Both men and women are socialized based on an understanding of their roles and obligations, which are thought to be instrumental in the reproduction of society and achieving system prerequisites. In this sense, as Malinowski argued in the early decades of the last century, the main function of family is to provide a home, organize sexual reproduction, and provide nurturance and love to its members (Mitchell, 2003, p. 32). In short, the division of labour between men and women based on instrumental and expressive traits is central in achieving continuity, homeostasis, and equilibrium.

On the other hand, other sociologists such as the proponents of the **conflict theory** state that social change is the outcome of **struggles** based on social, economic, political, and cultural interests and factors, such as class differences. As groups attempt to have their demands met and to make sure that their interests are accounted for, societies go through social change. In this sense, the aim of sociology is to understand how class and other forms of inequality and conflict, such as gender, racial, ethnic, and sexual, are related to the social circumstances and institutional arrangements that are based on the dominant ideology and promote the interest of the elite groups in society. They argue that a simple focus on shared norms that lead to a normative reproduction of society does not account for the effects of sexism, classism, and racism, to name a few, on social categories and individuals. As Mitchell (2003, p. 35) pointed out, **feminists** have also been critical of structural functionalist approaches to family studies, in that it does not account for the effects of power and inequality and how family relations are structured by the intersections of factors, such as gender, "race", class, and disability. For example, parenting advice in parenting magazines is still written for mothers and instils stereotypical gender socialization based on traditional gender roles (Albanese, 2009, p. 66).

As we have been arguing, sociological knowledge assists individuals to better understand how they relate to others in the context of local and global power relations. Sociology attempts to explain how and why socioeconomic as well as cultural, religious, and political, events, relations, and structures happen and for what ends through developing theoretical frameworks and paradigms. A **paradigm** or **perspective** is a general way of understanding and seeing the world that organizes our reality and provides us with the tools and ground rules to analyze society and social issues (Babbie, 1986, p. 32). **Sociological paradigms** enable individuals to view the world through different theoretical perspectives and lenses, each lens offering a specific understanding of the world of human interactions and behaviours. Paradigms are akin to windows of a building. If you look through one window, you only see a partial view of the outside world. Hence, it is always important to use more than one perspective (i.e., multi-perspectives) when analyzing any given social issue. The multiple-perspective approach allows for a more holistic understanding of the social world.

The birth and rise of sociology and its development over the years have been characterized by **shifts in paradigms** that also coincide with shifts from **traditional** type societies, to **modern**, and in the most recent years to **postmodern** societies (We explore the history of sociology in more detail in Chapter Three). Shifts in paradigms bring with them shifts in how we understand the world.

As mentioned, paradigm is a collection of ideas, values, principles, and facts that are interconnected and offer a general overview of the natural and social world, and how to think about them (Hamilton, 1996, P. 22). It is a central model and a fundamental system for understanding social reality and structures (Babbie, 1986, p. 29). It functions as a discourse or framework with a specific philosophy of science, and puts forward certain assumptions about the structure and functions of society (i.e., it proposes the kinds of questions scientists should explore and the ways in which they should go about exploring and investigating them (Glesne, 2011, p. 5).

Each paradigm is based on a set of ontological assumptions. **Ontology** refers to those ideas and beliefs that are used in defining what we mean by *reality* and the kinds of things that structure the world, and explores whether the world exists, how it exists, and in what form (Glesne, 2011, p. 5). Ontology, then, is the study of being, or what *is* and what exists. Thus, taking a particular ontological position articulates your assumptions about the nature of social reality and what is 'knowable' to the social scientist. For example, some social scientists have adopted the ontological approach of the **positivistic method of research**. The term **positivism** was coined by French sociologist Auguste Comte, who insisted that social scientists must use the same methods employed by natural scientists (i.e., observation, collection of data, analysis of the data, drawing conclusions, etc.) to study human society. Just as the natural world is guided by natural laws, positivists contend that society is guided by societal laws and the duty of the social scientist is to discover these laws, in order to properly understand and control the workings of the social world.

As Wotherspoon (2009, p. 9) maintained, sociologists use guidelines that allow them to focus their observations and analyze what they study and explore. These guidelines are referred to as *sociological perspectives*: **symbolic interactionism, social systems** (or **structural functionalism**), **conflict theory**, and **feminism**. Each one offers us a specific view of society, human relations, and behaviours. They are systems of organizing our thoughts about society, through which we think about and attempt to analyze social relations and interactions.

The **symbolic interactionist paradigm** asserts that humans create shared social meanings through face-to-face interactions (Babbie, 1986, p. 30). The main question that they ask is how humans construct meaning and understand their social surroundings in the context of **social processes** rather than **social structures** (Wotherspoon, 2009, p. 11). They focus on day-to-day relations, face-to-face interpersonal, and micro-interactions and how individuals make sense of other people's behaviours. This perspective is also referred to as **micro-sociology** (Wotherspoon, 2009, p. 11). Micro-sociologists are concerned with how humans form their identities and a conception of self. They assert that the **definition of situation** that is based on our interpretations of the social situations we are involved in guide our actions (Wotherspoon, 2009, p. 31). According to this paradigm, social reality is a construction. This theory "grew from reactions to the macro-level focus of structural functional and conflict theories, which focused on structures and process of organizations" to the exclusion of small-scale, interpersonal interactions (Ballantine, 2001, p. 13). Two examples of symbolic interaction theories are **labelling** and **exchange theories. Labelling theorists,** such as Becker, maintained that, for example, when teachers label their students as "smart" or "slackers", these labels function as **self-fulfilling prophecies** that determine how students behave and act in the classrooms

(Wotherspoon, 2009, p. 32). These labels are often based on the assumptions and expectations of teachers that reflect their commonsense knowledge and the general background information they have of students that do not reflect the aptitudes and merits of students. In this light, a student who is labelled as a "slacker" will behave according to this conception of the teacher of him/her and will not perform as well as a student who is labelled as "smart". **Exchange theory**, on the other hand, asserts that our behaviours and actions are based on conscious evaluations of costs and rewards involved in our interactions with other members of society (Ballantine, 2001, p. 13).

The structural functionalist paradigm argues that society consists of different parts that are integrated and each element plays a part (or has a role and function) in the survival of the whole system (Babbie, 1986, p. 30). This theory asks how society is ordered. It focuses on factors that result in the perpetuation of social stability (Wotherspoon, 2009, p. 9). This perspective equates society to a social organism that is made of different parts (this is referred to as an **organic** or **organismic analogy**). Like the human body, which has different parts—limbs, lungs, liver, etc.—society is conceived of consisting of various interdependent structures and institutions, such as the family and education system. According to this perspective, an orchestra could be equated to a society or a social group, and each member of the orchestra, who plays a different musical instrument, can be imagined as a part in society, whose music and the sounds he/she makes plays a different function in the creation of musical play as a whole (Babbie, 1986, p. 30). The social order model informs the works of scholars, such as Hobbes, Comte, Durkheim, Parsons, and W. W. Rostow, and it forms the basis of structural functionalism, the dominant form of theory in the United States until the 1960s (Sears, 2008, p. 31). This model assumes that a society that is well-regulated aids the interests of all its members by protecting them against the threat of disorder and violence that exist within each member and throughout human civilizations (Sears, 2008, p. 31). Structural functionalists argue that a strong set of shared norms and values is central to maintaining social order (Sears, 2008, p. 32). In this sense, the education system transmits values and knowledge that brings the various elements of society together and teaches those aptitudes and roles that are necessary for individuals in their future statuses in society (Wotherspoon, 2009, p. 10). Structural functionalism is an abstract theory. Research based on this perspective tends to produce positivistic knowledge (Wotherspoon, 2009, p. 10). Structural functionalism does not take into consideration how humans make sense of their interactions with others. It is an example of **macro-sociology**. It also does not account for how inequalities are structurally reproduced. That is, it does not account for the consequences of conflicts and struggles that shape the social world.

In contrast to structural functionalism, others have focused on:

1. how **conflicts** over the distribution of resources and power in society have resulted in the creation of various forms of inequalities and

2. how political, social, cultural, and economic conflicts and inequalities shape the structures of society.

The **conflict paradigm** maintains that social life is characterized by inherent inequalities and conflicts over the distribution of resources and power between different classes of society in such a way that dominant groups have power over subordinate ones (Babbie, 1986, p. 30; Wotherspoon, 2009, p. 12). Those who subscribe to this paradigm envision society in the context of "haves" and "have-nots" and ask how inequalities are reproduced and what their effects are on marginalized groups. The conflict paradigm examines how society's institutions maintain the privileges of some groups and reproduce the subservient positions of other groups. Conflict is not considered as a destructive element. Rather, conflict is viewed as a normal and an expected aspect of any social organization that needs to be analyzed in order to promote social justice and equity within society. Conflict is considered as the force behind social change (Wotherspoon, 2009, p. 12). The existence of conflict points to problems that need solutions. As Max Weber argued, conflicts are not simply due to class differences alone and can arise due to value or status differences. Conflict can be found in any society or institution; it is not peculiar to capitalist societies. Conflicts and power differences exist in all societies as groups attempt to promote their interests. Gender inequality, racial discrimination, ethnic divisions, ageism, and ableism determine the extent to which individuals have access to positions of power in society. However, this paradigm overlooks how shared values generate unity within society and between members of society.

Feminism is another important perspective in sociology. One of the criticisms against classical theories of sociology has been their **androcentric characteristics** (Ritzer, 2000, p. 8). Prior to the 1960s, feminist theories and concepts were peripheral to the main sociological knowledge, and were only reflected in either the research of marginal male theorists or female theorists whose work was also increasingly marginalized within the sociological canon (Ritzer, 2000, p. 8). This is despite the fact that since the 1800s women have played an important role in the mobilization against slavery, promoting social reforms during the era of Progressivism in the United States, and in organizing the women's suffrage movements across the world (Ritzer, 2000, p. 8). Feminism as a multilayered paradigm has questioned the **malecentric** (or, **androcentric**) and **Eurocentric** basis of sociological knowledge and theories.

Androcentrism refers to the fact that knowledge about society is often produced by men about men. That is, androcentrism excludes women's perspectives and analyses of social institutions as part of the canon of sociological knowledge. As Abu-Laban and Gabriel (2002, p. 24), quoting Sandra Burt, asserted, **androcentricity** is "a view of the world from a male perspective". In this view, women are considered passive social actors and objects of observation, rather than acting subjects with historical roots (i.e., they are perceived as objects who are acted upon by society) (Abu-Laban & Gabriel, 2002, p. 24). It is in this light that feminists highlight the importance of incorporating knowledge about women based on their perspectives and experiences as the basis for theorizing about society and for revising sociological theories by offering analysis of gender as a social factor. In short, feminist theorists are both inclusive of female perspectives and revisionist of male-centred epistemologists and sociological canons. They ask how gender organizes social life.

Feminism is also critical of **patriarchal** relations, or those structures and relations that promote the interests of men over women. Feminists argue that sociological analysis and social policy in general lacks a **gender based analysis** (Abu-Laban & Gabriel, 2002, pp. 26–27). This form of analysis is based on the standpoint that policy issues cannot be understood outside an analysis of gender issues, and that gender issues are intrinsically linked to economic, cultural, racial, and sexual factors, relations, and structures. Such an approach questions the belief that there are natural differences between men and women. Rather, feminists view **gender** as socially constructed and account for how differences between men and women find cultural manifestations and economic consequences. They point out that it is important to understand how the actions of men and women are influenced by their gender and socially sanctioned behaviours, beliefs, and ideas about what it means to be a male or female in both dominant and nondominant groups.

Feminism also asserts that gender based studies need to account for the effects of other factors, such as race, ethnicity, social class, disability, age, and sexuality in better understanding the diverse and conflicting experiences of men and women in society. In general, feminists attempt to offer analysis of the social world that is attentive to the differences between men and women and among women. They highlight the web of power relations that reproduce gender inequality at both micro and macro structural and ideological levels. There are many different forms of feminism, including Marxists, socialists, standpoint, poststructuralists, liberal, and neo-Marxists, which will be discussed in more detail in chapter Ten.

The aforementioned theories are ways of organizing knowledge about society and the world. Depending on the theoretical perspective(s) of sociologists, they disagree with one another on how to analyze and view the social world. Conflict theorists and feminists maintain that structural functionalists promote the status quo. They argue that functionalists do not account for the fact that the shared norms and values they focus on reflect the ideology of the dominant groups in society (i.e., male, White, and Anglo-Saxon-Protestant) and serve their interests. Unlike functionalism, these paradigms tend to disrupt the existing social world in order to make it more open to diversity. Feminists and symbolic interactionists also share a concern over how social actors through their subjectivity give meaning to other people's actions and behaviours (i.e., how men and women construct gender identity).

Sociology is informed by multilayered theoretical perspectives that can offer social actors diverse and conflicting understandings of human behaviours, groups, and interactions by accounting for historical changes in cultural, political, social, and economic spheres of life. Despite the similarities and differences between different perspectives in sociology, it is important to learn about and become familiar with the basic arguments of these theories. We believe that having a good grasp of theory is an important component of becoming involved in movements and struggles that seek human rights and social justice (Sears, 2008, p. 27). In this light, theoretical thinking should not be confined to, and be a property of, a handful of "experts"; instead it needs to become part of the public discourse. A public discourse informed by theory enables us to analyze and conceptualize human behaviours and relations in many divergent ways.

One of our aims in this book is for you to analyze your experiences in the light of sociological knowledge and theories, and to apply them to your own situations to better situate yourself within local and global events. An understanding of theories in sociology leads us to find our voice and to express ourselves logically and systematically (Sears, 2008, p. 27). A strong theoretical basis is also central to becoming a good practicing sociologist. Sociological theories, as ways of seeing, viewing, and planning, enjoin us to relate a new situation to an old one, in such ways as to explicate patterns in social relations and structures and to decipher what may happen next (Sears, 2008, p. 16). As you read about different theories throughout this book, the challenge is for you to develop your own insight and analytical perspectives that will then serve as a framework to write and talk about social issues (Sears, 2008, p. 27).

Becoming a Theorist: why is theory important?

Why is theory important? What are the differences between commonsense and theoretical thinking? Theory has a number of functions. **First**, it provides researchers patterns and frameworks that are used in interpreting data. **Second**, it assists researchers to link one study to another. **Third**, it offers frameworks, concepts, and variables that have specific meanings and applications. **Fourth**, theory enables researchers to interpret the larger meanings of the findings of their specific research on specific topics for the society as a whole (i.e., for better understanding human behaviour and relations) (Hoover, 1988, p. 35). In other words, theory allows us to discern how and why economic, political, social, and cultural events, relations, and structures are related. Theory provides us with a framework to explain social problems/concerns, actions, and behaviours.

Although we are all unconsciously philosophers in our own ways (Antonio Gramsci, as cited in Sears, 2008, p. 27), one's commonsense understanding reflects our day-to-day philosophizing as opposed to a conscious effort to theorize about the world around us. Although your opinions, commonsense knowledge, and experiences are necessary to become sociologically engaged, on their own, they are not sufficient (Sears, 2008, p. 27). This is partly due to the fact that commonsense is exclusive and ideological: it often reflects the interests of the dominant society. As Gramsci asserted, it is necessary to critically and consciously configure our own conceptions of reality and the world "and thus, in connection with the labour of one's own brain, choose one's sphere of activity, take an active part in the creation of the history of the world, be one's own guide …" (as cited in Sears, 2008, p. 28). That is, if we want to create a better world that is inclusive of the voices and experiences of marginalized groups, such as women and racialized people, it becomes necessary to dispel our commonsense knowledge that we have obtained due to our socialization in various social institutions, such as schools, the media, and the economy, and start imagining and working towards a different kind of society that reflects our critical theoretical reflections *on the world* as the bases of acting *upon the world* (Sears, 2008, p. 27). It is through a critical understanding of approaches to sociological theories that we can develop such a framework and become conscious of our philosophizing powers and to draw upon them to bring about equality and social justice, locally and/or globally.

Social actors need to ask whose ideas and perspectives inform their views and for what purposes and ends. Who benefits from our way of thinking about the world and from the ways in which we act upon the world based on our commonsense knowledge? Who does not? One way of answering these and other similar questions is "to make the familiar strange" (Sears, 2008, p. 29). In other words, we need to de-familiarize ourselves from what we think we know about the world by looking at issues as if we are doing it for the first time (Sears, 2008, p. 29). A very useful way of achieving this goal is to view the world through the lenses and understanding of other peoples'. In this way, we start questioning our own **ethnocentric** views, or the ways in which we judge other peoples' behaviour and actions based on our own cultural values that do not include and reflect other peoples' understandings of the world. In other words, the first step is to become **self-reflective** and put our views, values, ideas, and assumptions under critical introspection. It is important to ask whose frameworks we use to make sense of peoples' actions, behaviours, and the world around us.

A good grip of social theory will enable you to critically reflect on your own experiences. By reflecting on sociological theory, you can become aware and critical of your own biases and commonsense knowledge that generally frame our vision of the world, and account for the extent to which such commonsense knowledge reflects the dominant ideology and reproduces the unequal political, economic, and cultural relations and structures, locally and globally (Sears, 2008, p. 28). For example, many of us may think that racism is not an important factor in determining people's interactions and life chances in the United States, especially since the election of an African-American person to the presidency of that country. However, educational and sociological analysis of existing data points to the fact that many Black and Latino students drop out of school partly due to the continuing effects of racism in schools and in the wider society (Nieto, 2000). Educational and sociological research indicates that "race" is an important factor in the process of **streaming** racialized students into nonacademic subjects in schools, which does not prepare them for university education, and, thus, excludes them from obtaining higher paying professional jobs that require university degrees. **Streaming** refers "to the placement of students into different programs based on their aptitude, ability, or special interests and needs" (Wotherspoon, 2009, p. 118). However, streaming students into various programs and fields of study reflects the existing patterns of economic, racial, ethnic, gender, and class inequalities prevalent in society. For example, according to Jane Gaskell (as cited in Wotherspoon, 2009, p. 119), in comparison to men, women tend to enrol in nursing, education, the fine arts, and most humanities disciplines. Although we cannot ignore the effects of individuals' preferences on their decision-making processes to choose one program over the other, it is important to also account for the effects of organizational features on how men and women are streamed into different fields. Henry and Tator, for example, pointed out that Black students are disproportionally streamed into low-level academic and vocational programs (Wotherspoon, 2009, p. 122). In contrast, "Asian" students are concentrated in mathematics, sciences, and computer programs, especially in postsecondary programs.

A theoretical understanding of world affairs allows you to name the world and to understand it from multiple perspectives (i.e., women's perspectives and working class worldviews). Theoretical perspectives enable you to better configure who you are, how you have been affected by the structures of society, the extent to which you actively or passively reproduce the existing social structures and relations, and/or whether or not you attempt to use your agency and power as critical social actors to effect change in society. Sociological theories, despite their varied and conflicting focuses, provide us with a set of tools and frameworks that assist social actors to have power over the world as they develop insights for understanding the way social structures and relations affect human beings and groups (Sears, 2008, p. 16).

Part Two

∙∙∙

Agency and Structure: social constructionism versus structuralism views

As mentioned, sociology studies the relationship between individuals and society. However, sociologists are not simply concerned with understanding individual behaviours and beliefs in isolation from other individuals. Sociology is concerned with the relationships between **agency** and **social structure**. They analyze human relations in the context of face-to-face interactions (directly) or the social structures (indirectly) (Wotherspoon, 2009, p. 6). Sociologists have been interested in examining the extent to which social actors have free choice and how this free choice affects their interactions with others in society (Wotherspoon, 2009, p. 7). The division between individual/agency and society/social structure remains one of the main debates in sociology (Wotherspoon, 2009). This debate revolves around two main trajectories: **social constructionism** and **structuralist perspectives** (these approaches have also been referred to as *individual-first* and *society-first theories*; See Lemert, 2005).

Agency refers to the ability of individuals to act consciously by becoming active in the processes of change through participation in decision making procedures and social practices (O'Brian, 2004, p. 149). The assumption is that through their agencies social actors are capable of influencing and altering social structures. The concept of agency implies that society is reproduced or recreated through people's actions and their relationships with other people. Human actors are viewed as active "agents whose behaviour and thoughts make society possible" (Wotherspoon, 2009, p. 6). In other words, individuals are said to be the architects of their own lives. In addition, they argue that human beings are like chameleons, changing their behaviours to match the situations in which they find themselves. For example, you may act, talk, and dress differently when in a lecture hall than when you are in a church or at a nightclub. This perspective is referred to as **social constructionist**. According to this view, society and social relations are socially constructed. **Social constructionism** is based on the assumption that there is nothing natural or normal about the world we inhabit. Rather, social reality is created by individuals to reflect certain interests in a world not necessarily of their making. Humans make meaning of messages they receive based on the reality of everyday existence. Thus, there are different realities of everyday existence. This perspective maintains that subgroups or **collectives,** such as the family and ethnic/"race" groups, are neither natural phenomena nor divinely created entities, but that they are (wo)man-made and tied to, and vary, significantly across time and place. It also means that these phenomena ultimately rest on supra-individual processes of group boundary formation, segregation, and the creation of intergroup (i.e., racial, gender, and class) hierarchies.

Social constructionism emphasizes how meanings that are produced by individuals are dependent on the context, historical period, one's position in social structures, and ideological constraints prevalent in society. For example, we can investigate the different and conflicting meanings that arise from messages transmitted by the mass media. On May 1, 2011 US President

Barack Obama in an address to the nation announced the killing of Osama Bin Laden by US Navy Seals. CNN and other news outlets carried the same message, which was received by millions of viewers around the world. From the social construction perspective, each one of the millions of viewers will read different meanings, or interpret the news about Bin Laden's death differently. So what do you think? What different meanings might this news take on? Let us consider the following scenarios:

- To a relative of a victim of the terrorist attacks on the World Trade Centre and the Pentagon on September 11, 2001, which is believed to have been masterminded by Osama Bin Laden,

- To a supporter of Osama Bin Laden and his Al Qaeda terrorist group,

- To a member of Al Qaeda,

- To relatives of Osama Bin Laden,

- To a peace activist, and

- To a human rights lawyer or activist.

The meanings that the millions of television viewers made of Bin Laden's death stemmed in large measure from the realities of their lived life experiences, ideological beliefs, or their lifeworlds. Berger and Luckmann (1996) pointed out that these realities are **intersubjective**, the notion that each individual's meanings (one's understanding of a situation) relate to, and to some extent depend on, the meanings of other individuals (other people's understandings of the same situation). What this means is that there is a dialectical relationship between a person's meaning and the meanings of others. In other words, in a conversation, what each interlocutor says depends largely not only on what she/he communicates, but also on who the listener is in terms of factors, such as gender, class, "race", ethnicity, age, and sexuality. Other factors, such as time, place, and even the mood of the interlocutors, play significant roles in determining the direction of the conversation. For example, when Afghanistan was invaded by the Soviet Union's forces, Osama Bin Laden was considered as an ally in fighting the Soviets by the United States government. He was supported and financed by the CIA.

Not everyone viewed the killing (or murder) of Osama Bin Laden in the same manner. Some described the Navy Seal action as a terrorist act and murder, while others saw it as assassination. Although large crowds of US citizens celebrated the death of "America's Enemy Number One", the reaction in the rest of the world was more muted and less celebratory. Supporters of Al Qaeda, of course, were furious, with pledges to avenge their leader's death at the hands of American troops. Despite the fact that the US described Osama Bin Laden as "Number One Enemy," his supporters and sympathizers hailed him as a hero and conceptualized his death in light of the discourse of "martyrdom".

As people with agency, we have also internalized the values deemed important in our societies and are constrained by the existing rules and norms prevalent in social institutions, such as the family, education system, and the economy (Wotherspoon, 2009, p. 6). This is referred to as the **structuralist** view. This perspective emphasizes that humans are the product of their societies. Our personalities and identities are shaped by **social structures**.

As mentioned, social structures are a "relatively enduring pattern of [social interaction] within society and social life" that order and constrain relationships between individuals (Wotherspoon, 2009, p. 7). Social actors are born into societies with specific social structural arrangements or social institutions such as the family, the economy, government, and the education system. Human behaviours and interactions are governed by specific rules and expectations within these institutions, and these rules and expectations put boundaries on their choices to achieve desired goals and ends. Structuralists argue that behaviour is socially and culturally determined, and it is possible to "predict" how social actors may behave by analyzing the social structures and cultural beliefs that are prevalent in various social settings. In short, structuralists maintain that social actors are not independent of the social forces and contexts that are governed by specific rules, norms, values, and expectations that determine how we should act, behave, and think, thus constraining our agencies. For example, the dominant view of Bin Laden in the Western world promoted in the media (a social structure) is one of a terrorist and a fundamentalist Moslem. This view reflects the dominant ideology in the West that justified killing and eliminating Bin Laden. Many Americans and Canadians, in fact, label Bin Laden and his organization as a terrorist group. In contrast, a small number of people in other parts of the world consider him and his organization as an anti-imperialist force. People in different parts of the world reacted differently after hearing about his death: many Americans, for example, celebrated his death, as if it is a national holiday or the Fourth of July.

In general, structuralists argue that social structures determine what is available to us and they place limitations on us based on factors, such as gender, social class, "race", etc. Structuralism asserts that social actors cannot escape the constraints of the structural components of their social and cultural environments. They play an active and important part in their lives. As Wilden (1987, p. 125) put it:

> Many of our apparently unique personal opinions are in fact derived from social conditioning by dominant codes of values transmitted by others, beginning in the cradle and including the media of family, school, and popular entertainment, rather than from personal and informed decisions that we actually made for ourselves.

In contrast, social constructionists argue that society is created through people's interactions as active subjects.

Macro- and Micro-Sociology

Another debate in sociology revolves around how best to explain human relations and examine social structures and their effects. Should sociologists focus on face-to-face interactions? Or, should they mainly put their emphasis on what happens to individuals due to the effects of the institutions in which they are socialized? Sociology focuses on both micro and macro issues and contexts and/or large-scale and small-scale theories (Ritzer, 2000, p. 494). **Macro-sociology** (macro-sociological theory) tends to look at the big picture and the consequences of large-scale social structures, such as the family, economy, education, and religion on groups and individuals (Kennedy, Zusman, Schachrt, & Knox, 2011, p. 62). Macro-sociology focuses on the world systems, societies, and organizations, and studies large scale social categories (Ritzer, 2000, p. 636, Figure A.1). Macro-sociologists focus on complex social patterns that have been formed over time.

Structural functionalism, conflict, and neo-Marxist paradigms are examples of macro-sociological theories (Ritzer, 2000, p. 494). The unit of analysis of these theories is the social network and not the individual. Karl Marx, for example, applied the political economy approach to examine the consequences of capitalism in England and other parts of Europe. A study of the causes and consequences of Italian immigration to Canada from 1945 to 2008 based on statistical analysis of available data in terms of factors, such as income, educational level, and occupational categories, is another example of macro-sociology. From a critical perspective, macro-sociological analyses can also assist us in better understanding how the education system, for example, benefits some groups of people, and how it perpetuates the reproduction of class inequalities by analyzing education as a system of power and by looking at the statistical analysis of, for example, graduation rates for women, members of ethnic minority, racialized groups, and people with disabilities; or by comparing the availability of resources in middle class schools versus working class schools.

A classic example of macro-sociological study is Émile Durkheim's analysis of suicide rates in Europe. Durkheim wanted to study suicide not as a personal and individualized act that has psychological roots, but as a "thing" that is influenced by society and its organization. He was not interested to learn about the individual reasons for attempting or committing suicide. In fact, individual intentions are left out of his analysis (Berger, 1963, p. 40). Durkheim compared the rates of suicide to determine the effects of social control on individual behaviour. In his study, he showed that "social facts" are "things" that are external to individuals and influence their behaviours, that is, they are coercive of individuals (Ritzer, 2000, p. 84).

In fact, Durkheim defined sociology as the science of "**social things**" (Lemert, 2005, p. 7). "Social things" are defined as "**social facts**", or realities that are the products of social structures. Durkheim argued that "a social fact is distinct from its individual manifestation" (Durkheim, 1938, p. 7). For him, a "social fact" referred to a "group condition repeated in the individual because [it is] imposed on him [sic]. It is to be found in each part because it exists in the whole, rather than in the whole because it exists in parts" (Durkheim, 1938, p. 9).

Durkheim maintained that "a social fact is to be recognized by the power of external coercion which it exercises or is capable of exercising over individuals, and the presence of this power may be recognized in its turn either by the existence of some specific sanction or by the resistance offered against any individual effort that tends to violate it" (Durkheim, 1938, p. 10). "Social things" or "social facts" refer to those structures and social statuses or roles that define how individuals ought to behave and interact with one another. That is, **"social things"** "exist in their own right, apart from the individuals they affect" (Lemert, 2005, p. 26). "Social things" have immense power over us: they can control us, which at times we do not even recognize, as we may have internalized the values and norms of society as the truth about the world (Lemert, 2005, p. 27).

In short, Durkheim maintained that society "exists outside the individual consciousness" and has an objective manifestation, independent of individuals within it (Durkheim, 1938, pp. 1–2). In other words, Durkheim argued that society and social norms are external to the individual, outlive the individual, and can be studied as "social facts". Babbie defined **objective** as "that which is external to mind" (Babbie, 1986, p. 23). The source of "social fact" is not the individual. Durkheim argued that "most of our ideas and our tendencies are not developed by ourselves but come to us from without" (Durkheim, 1938, p. 4).

As Wotherspoon (2009, p. 6) also pointed out, "social facts" refer to those elements of society, such as rates of suicide, dropout rates, and social institutions of religion, law, and economy, that exist separately from the individual and influence a social actor's thoughts and actions. By analyzing these rates, we are not studying individual characteristics or circumstances; we are analyzing these as the aggregate of individual actions that have social causes (Durkheim, 1938, p. 8). Suicide, thus, is a group condition that finds individual manifestations. Through his analysis of suicide, Durkheim was able to legitimize sociology as a science (Seidman, 1994a, p. 64). His aim was to determine the causes of suicide as a social phenomenon. He maintained that studying suicide was one way of analysing "social facts" in order to determine how the decline in social bonds between individuals in modern societies and the weakening of the moral fabric of society was affecting social actors (Pampel, 2007, p. 69). He found that "race" was not a factor in determining the level of suicide within a group as the rates of suicide varied widely within a racial group (Ritzer, 2000, p. 85). For example, Durkheim discovered that although Jews had higher insanity rates, they committed less suicide than White Protestants, making him to conclude that stronger social bonds and group solidarity among persecuted Jewish communities in Europe explained the lower suicide rates instead of their assumed racial characteristics (See Box 2.4 - Durkheim's Study of Suicide: an example of macro and positivist sociology).

BOX 2.4 - Durkheim's Study of Suicide: an example of macro and positivist sociology

As mentioned above, Durkheim was not interested in explanations that focused on exploring individuals' reasons for suicide. Durkheim compared the rates of suicide to determine the effects of social control on individual behaviour. He saw society as a reality *sui generis*, which cannot be reduced to, for example, psychological factors (Berger, 1963, p. 39). That is, he argued we are creations of society. As Goffman maintained, as social actors and performers of various statuses, we act in such ways that do not undermine accepted social rules and norms and conform to them (Lemert, 2005, p. 26). We reflect the moral values of society that are imposed upon us from without due to our socialization and participation in social structures and relations (Lemert, 2005, pp. 25–26). In this light, sociology, as the study of "things" that have influences over us, moves away from explanations that blame the individual for experiencing, for example, violence and inequality.

Integration and Regulation

Durkheim identified four types of suicide, which relate to the "different social condition of **integration** and **regulation**" (Seidman, 1994a, p. 64). **Integration** refers to the extent to which values, norms (or, collective sentiments) are shared among the members of a group (Ritzer, 2000, p. 86). Integration is a characteristic of groups. It highlights the degree of social cohesion and how strong the values and norms are shared within society among individuals (Pampel, 2007, p. 70). **Regulation** refers to the extent to which we are constrained and controlled by external forces (Ritzer, 2000, p. 86).

Egoistic Suicide

Durkheim concluded that in societies where individuals are not well integrated we find **egoistic suicide**. These societies are characterized by low integration, which results in a state of meaninglessness among individuals. They are also characterized by overt or excessive individualism, which may lead to individual dissatisfaction and to suicide since not all of one's needs could be satisfied. In contrast, those societies that offer their members a strong sense of **collective consciousness** provide them "with a sense of broader meaning of their lives" (Ritzer, 2000, p. 86). That is, when a person finds social meaning in his/her life, due to, for example, strong bonds between family members, their bonds reduce the rate of egoistic suicide (Pampel, 2007, p. 70).

By analyzing statistical data in Western European countries, Durkheim showed that Catholics had a lower level of suicide than Protestants (Seidman, 1994a, p. 65). One of the reasons for this difference was the individualistic aspect of the Protestant faith. They are not socially well-integrated into their groups and communities (Seidman, 1994a, p. 65). This is due to the fact Protestantism allows more personal leeway in interpreting the Bible, and, as result, it undermines the social control of the congregation on individuals since it focuses on the individual relationship of a practitioner to his/her God (Pampel, 2007, p. 70). The Catholic system, on the other hand, which is organized around a centralized bureaucracy, imposes on its members a unified/bureaucratic faith (Seidman, 1994a, p. 65). Catholics are more likely to be well integrated into their community since it stresses and promotes social responsibility of the individual to the religious community (Pampel, 2007, p. 70). Durkheim concluded that as social integration decreases, suicide increases. In this light, in societies that lack a well-defined social structure and framework, individualism becomes a social menace (Seidman, 1994a, p. 65).

Altruistic Suicide

Durkheim also argued that too much social integration has consequences for individuals in society. **Altruistic suicide** is the flipside of egoistic suicide (i.e., altruism versus egoism).

Altruistic suicide is the end result of the condition where there is high integration (Ritzer, 2000, p. 87). The mass suicide of members of a cult is a good example of this type of suicide. In such communities, the values and norms of the group limit the expression of individuality of its members and "extinguish separate individual existence" (Seidman, 1994a, p. 65). The important message here is that too much group control is not healthy (Seidman, 1994a, p. 65). Suicide is justified because the members of, for example, a cult feel it is their duty to die for a cause (Ritzer, 2000, p. 87).

Anomic Suicide

Anomic suicide is another form of suicide that Durkheim refered to, which occurs in those communities and societies where their regulative powers are disrupted (Ritzer, 2000, p. 88). In these types of society, there is little control over individual wants and needs, which cannot be satisfied as they become involved in a greedy race to gratify their needs (Ritzer, 2000, p. 88). Anomic suicide occurs in times when there are structural changes in society, such as during economic recession or booms, which result in a decrease in the power of collectivity to influence the actions of individuals.

Social control is low in such societies, which results in what Durkheim refered to as **anomie**, or "moods of restlessness and normlessness" (Ritzer, 2000, p. 88). For example, when a factory closes down, the factory worker is cut off from the structure of work that provides him/her with meaningful ways of interacting and giving meaning to his/her life. In such cases, there is limited external control and constraint and as such people become slaves to their passion and as a result commit destructive acts (Ritzer, 2000, p. 88). That is, the individual does not have access to sufficient social direction (Seidman, 1994a, p. 66).

Durkheim pointed out that the unregulated desires, wants, and needs of individuals are produced by the society. Due to lack of social organization in times of chaos (i.e., structural changes), individuals become incapable of managing themselves and organizing their lives in manners that are orderly and coherent (Seidman, 1994a, p. 66). As such, economic decline results in a lack of moral order, which is the main cause of anomic suicide.

In general, the cause of anomic suicide is due to a lack of external social control since the family or the community no longer have authority over the individual (Pampel, 2007, p. 71). The important point in this discussion of suicide is the message that order and stability based on shared norms, values, and moral standards are the requirements for the growth and socialization of individuals, providing them with a framework to behave and act with purpose. So, accordingly, any solution to deal with suicide must be a social one. The workplace and professional association, according to Durkheim, would provide individuals in modernity with moral and social centres to participate in social relations with intent and direction (Seidman, 1994a, pp. 66–67).

Fatalistic Suicide

The last form of suicide is **fatalistic suicide**. It occurs in societies and communities where there is high regulation. That is, the individual's every action is controlled by the "oppressive discipline of everyday action" (Durkheim, as cited in Ritzer, 2000, p. 88). Slaves who take their own lives are good examples of this type of suicide.

What do we learn from this analysis of suicide?

As a solution to anomie and unchecked individualism, Durkheim maintained that the aim should be to integrate individuals into the complex and differentiating world of modern society. Group identity can enforce social regulation that would encourage a sense of duty and obligation as well as discipline on individuals as a way to check their unregulated desires (Pampel, 2007, p. 71). In other words, the aim should be to curb and sacrifice selfish pleasure for the good of the group and society (Pampel, 2007, p. 72). As such, there is a need to develop new group memberships that are based on specialization: for example by forming economic groups and building communities and by participating in such organizations (i.e., Association of Sociologists). Durkheim also argued that the dignity of the individual provided a value that would transcend membership in a specialized group (Pampel, 2007, p. 72). Individualism, here, means a shared value that brings people together (Pampel, 2007, p. 72). At the same time, in his analysis of suicide, as Seidman (1994a, p. 66) argued, Durkheim pointed out that freeing individuals from repressive social control, as espoused by liberals and socialists at the time, would result in suicide as a form of escape "from the tyranny of freedom".

As the above discussions point out, Durkheim's study of suicide was also an attempt to prove that society was not reducible to the actions and psychology of individuals (Seidman, 1994a, p. 64). He maintained that society was not the end result of the actions of an aggregate of individuals, a view that was popular at the time. Individual psychology of individuals could not be used as an explanatory factor to analyze social issues (Seidman, 1994a, p. 64). This is not to say that psychological and personal factors do not explain individual acts of suicide. His main point was that "social conditions produce [the] suicidal disposition" (Seidman, 1994a, p. 64).

In general, Durkheim laid the foundation for a **positivistic approach** to sociology, which is reflected in his argument that "social facts" be treated as "things" (Bocock, 1996, p. 155). **Positivism** is a belief in science. It implies that a single scientific method is applicable to all fields of study (Ritzer, 2000, p. 277). Positivists assert that knowledge gained through scientific procedures is inherently neutral (Ritzer, 2000, p. 277). The main argument of positivists is that it is possible to keep "science" "value-free". They distinguish between facts and values (Hamilton, 1996, 41). That is, positivists posit that social scientists should keep their human values and ideologies out of their work. In this light, it is assumed that science should not be advocating any particular form of social action (Ritzer, 2000, p. 277). It is not the duty of the social scientists to change society, positivists contend. Their task is to merely study and analyze society and leave social change or improvement to those whose duty it is to effect change, i.e., social workers and politicians.

The critical school of sociology is opposed to positivism (Ritzer, 2000, p. 277). It argues that positivists reify the social world as an object and view it in light of the standards of natural/physical sciences (Ritzer, 2000, p. 277). Positivists assume that the methods and assumptions of physical sciences should form the standards for all disciplines. Positivists tend to downplay the role of actors and their subjective understanding of the world. They relegate social actors as passive individuals who are simply influenced by social forces (Ritzer, 2000, p. 277). Ritzer (2000, p. 277) concludes that "positivism is assailed for being content to judge the adequacy of means toward given ends and for not making a similar judgment about ends". Critical theorists argue that it is also important to focus on human activities and how these activities influence the larger social structures (Ritzer, 2000, p. 277). They fault positivism for its conservative "nature" and for its lack of challenging the existing systems of power (Ritzer, 2000, p. 277).

Micro-sociology, on the other hand, explores the relationship between human beings in face-to-face relations in the context of specific social structures, such as the family or the education system. It tends to study individual thought and action by emphasizing interaction and examining human groups (Ritzer, 200, p. 636, Figure A.1). Micro-sociology is sometimes called **interpretative sociology** since it views individuals as social actors in relation to other individuals, not as isolated units but as active producers of social meanings (Wotherspoon, 2009, p. 11). Symbolic interactionism and exchange and rational choice theory are examples of micro-sociological paradigms (Ritzer, 2000, p. 494).

Micro-sociology, also called **social psychology**, focuses on explicating how human identities are formed in interactions with other human beings not as passive but active social actors (Wotherspoon, 2009). It focuses on how meanings are produced and shared through social interaction. It is a descriptive approach to understanding human relations with no emphasis on explaining these relations in terms of power relations (Wotherspoon, 2009). That is, it tends not to ask and account for whose views inform our understanding of the world. On its emphasis on here and now (i.e., how social actors are creating and interpreting social reality), micro-sociology adopts an ahistorical approach to analysis of social relations and interactions (See Box 2.5 - Constructing Black Identities in Canada: a micro-sociological and subjective approach).

Since micro-sociology is more concerned with how individuals in the context of localized social structures make sense of their everyday interactions (Kennedy et al., 2011, p. 62), it highlights the role of subjectivity in understanding human relations. **Subjectivity**, Babbie (1986, p. 22) maintained, refers to "the quality or condition of viewing things exclusively through the medium of one's own mind or individuality". It is also defined as "the characteristics of existing in the mind only" (Babbie, 1986, p. 22). This approach is similar to how Max Weber defined sociology as the interpretative study of social action.

Weber was critical of the view that sociology should be modeled after the physical and biological sciences with an emphasis on positivism and objectivity. Weber (1947, p. 88) asserted that "sociology is a science which [should] attempt the interpretative understanding of social action in order thereby to arrive at a causal explanation of its causes and effects". As Ritzer (2000, p. 9) argued, Weber "thought that distinctive characteristics of social life made wholesale adoption of a scientific model difficult and unwise". Such positivistic approach could not analyze and delve into how people make sense of their realities. This requires a subjective approach to understating human action. By "**action**", Weber (1947, p. 88) referred to "all human behaviour when and in so far as the acting individual attaches a subjective meaning to it". An acting individual takes account of the behaviour of others (See intersubjectivity).

Weber used the term *Verstehen* (i.e., emphatic understanding) to highlight his approach to sociological action. Talcott Parsons (1947, p. 87, Footnote # 2) asserted that the primary reference of this term in Weber's work is "to the observation and theoretical interpretation of the subjective 'state of mind' of actors". For him, sociological analysis must account for how social actors make sense of their social surroundings in the contexts of the constraints and opportunities that social structures provide (or do not provide) them. Weber (1947, p. 103) concluded that in the social sciences we can achieve an important goal that is not attainable in the natural sciences, "namely the subjective understanding of the actions of the component individuals".

Although we can divide sociology into macro and micro perspectives, it is important to note that, as Ritzer (2000, p. 494) argued, Karl Marx, Max Weber, Émile Durkheim, and George Simmel, who influenced sociological thinking and theorizing during its early years (1800–1920s), "were generally concerned with the micro-macro linkages". Marx, for example, looked at the consequences of capitalist society and its coercive and alienating structures on individual workers and capitalists (Ritzer, 2000, p. 494). Weber, on the other hand, was interested in "the plight of the individual within the iron cage of a formally rational society", and Simmel was interested in the interplay between objective (macro) and subjective (micro) cultures (Ritzer, 2000, p. 494). In fact, Ritzer (2000, p. 494) pointed out that Émile Durkheim was also interested in the effects of macro-level factors ("social facts") on the behaviours of individuals.

A satisfactory framework for analyzing the social world, then, must include both elements of macro- and micro-sociology. This framework "must be able to move from the level of the person to that of large-scale social structure and back again" (Stryker, as cited in Ritzer, 2000, p. 375). Social structures, as elements that define and limit what people should and can do are not static. Although social structures exist above and beyond individuals, it is only through human interactions that these structures are reproduced, or altered, changed, and replaced with new forms that will in turn influence how people think, behave, and act. Knowledge about society is more useful and meaningful when these two approaches are integrated and combined (Ritzer, 2000, p. 495).

Quantitative and Qualitative Sociology

Durkheim's and Kelly's research discussed above also highlight the distinction between **quantitative** and **qualitative sociology**. In fact, another debate in sociology is how to approach researching society and how best to gather data and analyze them. Should we draw upon quantitative or qualitative methods of analysis to produce knowledge about social relations and human behaviour?

BOX 2.5 - Constructing Black Identities in Canada: a micro-sociological and subjective approach

A good example of micro-sociology that attempts to understand actors' meanings and understandings is Jennifer Kelly's research that explores how Black students in Edmonton, Alberta, Canada constructed their identities as Blacks in a White dominated society (Kelly, 1998, p. 6). Her aim was to show "how **racialization** ([or] giving raced meanings to social situations) takes place in the lives of young Black students" (Kelly, 1998, p. 6). She defined **identity** as "an individual's sense of uniqueness, knowing who one is, and who one is not" (Kelly, 1998, p. 6).

Kelly's research was guided by several interrelated questions (Kelly, 1998, p. 7). How do Black students construct their identities? How do they relate to their peers? What are the significances they assign to being 'Black' in a White dominated society? How do they interpret and internalize Western popular forms of media? How do they interact with and relate to their teachers and school? She interviewed twenty-six females and twenty-three males in grades ten, eleven, and twelve (Kelly, 1998, p. 14). She interpreted students' narratives of their lives and experiences in light of an understanding of identity as something that is learned; that is, identity formation is conceptualized as the outcome of social interactions with others. Who we are partly depends on how others construct us (i.e., how Black people are constructed by White people and White institutions, such as schools and the media).

Kelly stressed that identity is "a subjective sense of coherence, consistency, and continuity of self, rooted in both personal and group history" (Henry & Tator, 2010, p. 382, Glossary). In this sense, identity is understood in light of how the individual views him/herself; how the individual views him/herself in relation to others; and "how these social constructions of identities reflect or do not reflect what people do in their day-to-day interactions (Dei, as cited in Kelly, 1998, p. 10).

Putting it differently, **identity** is formulated based on what we are not; that is, in relation to the "other" (Castagna & Dei, 2001, p. 28). Identity construction and formation is the outcome of the dialectical relationship between the "self" and the "other" (Castagna & Dei, 2001, p. 28). Identity is based on a sense of uniqueness (selfhood), sameness, and difference (relations with/to others that bring people together at the same time as distinguish between people) (Castagna & Dei, 2001, p. 28). For example, when Brazilians immigrate to Canada, they may form community organizations based on their national origin (i.e., sameness). At the same time, due to differences in terms of "racial" characteristics and/or ethnic backgrounds they may distinguish amongst themselves and create organizations that reflect these characteristics (i.e., White Portuguese-Brazilian associations or Black-Brazilian organizations).

In order to better understand how Black students construct their identities, Kelly pointed to an important distinction between **racial identity,** which refers to "[having] a **given** racial identity" (Castagna & Dei, 2001, p. 29), and **racialized identity**, which is conceptualized as "the act of becoming or assuming an identity" (Castagna & Dei, 2001, p. 29). The term "**racialized**" refers to "processes by which meanings are attributed to particular objects, features and processes, in such a way that the latter are given significance and carry or are embodied with a set of additional meanings" (Henry & Tator, 2010, p. xxvi). For example, in Iran, Iranians are constructed as White and Aryans in their school textbooks. In the United Sates, in popular culture, Iranians are depicted as brown or non-White; however, according to the US Census, Iranians are categorized as Whites. In Canada, according to Census Canada, Iranians are identified as visible minorities, or as non-Aboriginal and non-White. In this light, Amir Mirfakhraie was given a racial identity in Iran as a White/Aryan person. After immigrating to the United States and Canada, and as a result of how the dominant society views him, he has formed a racialized identity as a "non-White person".

As Kelly argued, Amir in Canada, like Black students, is affected by the process of *othering*; that is, "of being put outside of the dominant group" due to how his skin colour is interpreted (Kelly, 1998, p. 7). She maintained that her research points out how the process of *othering* affects the way Black youths socialize and interact with their peers and how they talk about the popular culture they face and experience at school (Kelly, 1998, p. 7). Kelly concluded that although many of the students whom she interviewed were born in Canada, they expressed that the dominant society often constructed them "as not belonging", as not "really Canadian". In other words, the definition of the ideal Canadian is based on the discourse of **Whiteness**.

The **discourse of Whiteness** assumes that White people define the norms, and anything else is considered as the *other*, or constructed as not belonging and as **abnormal**. In Canada, Black students are not considered as part of the norm. In this sense, they are marked by virtue of their skin colour and their skin colour categorizes them as the *other*. The common experience of Black students is their reaction of being marked as Blacks in a White-dominated society. According to **Thomas Theorem**, social situations that are defined as real by social actors become real in their consequences and manifestation. Kelly argued that since one's **definition of the situation** shapes one's social reality, it is significant to account for the extent to which students' definitions of social definition and their "racialized frame of reference—which shapes that definition—informs their social actions and thereby their social reality" (Kelly, 1998, p. 11).

The meaning of social reality is established through interactions; and reality is socially constructed and is reflective of power differences between groups. The lack of inclusion of Black histories in the curriculum and school culture and the fact that they are Black and live in a society that is constructed as White results in Black students' *othering*. Since Black students are visible due to their colour of skin, they are under constant supervision/surveillance or the gaze of the dominant society that has the power to enforce its rules and regulations and categorize certain groups as the *other*. As such, the ways in which Black students use social space is monitored and questioned by those authorities who view them and categorize them as outsiders.

Gazing *otherness* is a powerful tool of social control that gives the ability to certain groups to regulate "the social spaces and social interactions of all [*other*] groups" (Kelly, 1998, p. 19).

As Black students are gazed at by the dominant culture and society, the end result is making Black students both visible and invisible. They become visible as "troublemakers" and "school skippers". As they are made visible, Black students may wish to become invisible. That is, as Black students are made visible by the dominant society in negative lights, they begin to police and "restrain" themselves. As such, Black students become involved in their own social control. They come to identify themselves as Blacks as a result of the extent to which they come to see themselves as the *other* and consider altering or not altering their behaviour and identities (Keely, 1998, p. 17). She also asserted that Black identity is not an essentialist identity; that is, it is not a homogenous and a fixed identity. Her research pointed to the importance of accounting for "multiple Black identities and varied Black experiences" (Kelly, 1998, p. 10).

Quantitative sociology takes a positivistic approach to understanding the social world. It emphasizes the analysis of numerical data. Quantitative research promotes **objectivity**, which is defined as an attempt to neutralize personal biases. **Qualitative sociology** is an interpretative approach to analyzing human relations and structures. It examines how humans make sense of their surroundings and construct their social realities. Qualitative sociology offers **subjective** analysis of social relations. That is, it is based on subjective interpretations.

Quantitative sociology is based on the ideas of **logical positivism**. **Positivism** is a term that was developed by Comte in the nineteenth century as an approach to social sciences based on methods of natural sciences in order to produce knowledge that is reliable and concrete as the basis for our actions to change the social world for the better (Glesne, 2011, p. 6). As Glesne maintained, many social scientists from various disciplines drew upon positivist methods and concepts, such as validity and reliability in their research and studies. The ontological belief of positivist researchers asserts that a fixed reality external to people exists, and this reality can be measured and understood accurately (Glesne, 2011, pp. 6–7).

This paradigm argues that "knowledge [is] limited to what could be logically deduced from theory, operationally measured, and empirically validated" (Glesne, 2011, p. 5). According to Hamilton (1996, p. 37), **empiricism** refers to knowledge and information that proceeds out of experience. Empiricism was the dominant research method during the Age of Enlightenment. The Enlightenment was developed and flourished out of the Renaissance (1450–1600), as a way of questioning the power of religion and religious beliefs as the main explanations of natural and physical events in the world (Glesne, 2011, p. 6). The **empiricists** argue that they "could explain the world and find truth through observation and experimentation" (Glesne, 2011, p. 6). Levine (1995) maintained that empiricists ask questions which their answers depend upon sensory observation, as a precondition of objectivity. In other words, knowledge about the social world should be based on empirical facts: things that people can understand and apprehend through their senses (Hamilton, 1996, p. 23). Empirical data, then, are observable and objective facts through seeing, smelling, touching, and hearing. **Objectivity** implies that findings of research are "subject to independent corroborations by other investigators" (Levine, 1995, p. 20).

As a positivist, your aim is to come up with a generalization about various social phenomena, to offer explanations about the causes of social phenomena, and to develop predictions regarding those phenomena (Glesne, 2011, p. 7). This knowledge about the social world is obtained through "objective observations, measurements, and carefully designed experiments" (Glesne, 2011, p. 7). In this approach to research, you begin with a theory about the phenomena that you are analyzing and investigating. You use the theory to propose certain hypotheses. You test them through methods that are considered to be objective, for example, to make sure that you do not influence the observations and responses of the participants in your research (Glesne, 2011, pp. 7–8). After you collect your data, the data is "reduced to numerical indices or quantifiable bits of information and analyzed statistically" (Glesne, 2011, p. 8). These procedures are called quantitative methods. In general, as a positivist, you use **deductive methods** in your research. A deductive method proceeds from the general to the particular. In a sense, positivist views are similar to the **realist** conception of the social world that asserts the world exists outside the individual and is independent of the knower (Glesne, 2011, p. 8).

By the 1930s and 1940s, however, the ontology which **logical positivism** was built upon, that a fixed reality existed that could be measured and known, was criticized by the **idealists. Idealists** argued that the world "cannot exist independently of the mind or the ideas"; they maintained that it is through the mind that the world is interpreted (Glesne, 2011, p. 8). **Idealism** downplays the importation of the material world and emphasizes the centrality of ideas and mental products (Ritzer, 2000, pp. 19, 20). They insist that the social definitions of the physical and material world matter most, and not "these worlds themselves" (Ritzer, 2000, p. 19). According to the idealists, the social world is not an objective entity that exists independently of individual consciousness (Perry, 2001, p. 373). It is through the individuals as knowing subjects and through his/her consciousness that the world and its forms are determined (Perry, 2001, p. 373). As Ritzer (2000, p. 19) maintained, in its extreme form, idealism argues that only the mind and psychological constructs exist. The aim of social scientists according to this view, then, is to access "others' interpretations of some phenomenon and of interpreting, themselves, other's actions, and intentions" (Glesne, 2011, p. 8). The focus of such analysis is to develop an understanding of ideas, actions, and interactions in specific social, cultural, or economic contexts and/or in terms of the wider social world and culture (Glesne, 2011, p. 8).

Idealism informs the basic assumptions of the interpretivist tradition. Their ontological assumptions assume that reality is socially constructed, and it is complex and ever changing (Glesne, 2011, p. 8). The most important information to obtain, according to this view, is how people make sense of the objects, events, actions, and perceptions around them and how they interpret the social world in which they function. As Glesne (2011, p. 8) reminded us, such constructed realities are considered as existing not only in the minds of social actors, but also as social constructions that are the outcomes of individualistic interpretations in the context of linguistic rules and the existing knowledge bases available in the wider society.

The main research method employed by these researchers is interaction with people in their social settings and "talking with them about their perceptions" (Glesne, 2011, p. 8). As an interpretive researcher who uses qualitative research methods, you are often involved in the types of research that are based on in-depth, long-term interactions "with relevant people in one or several sites"

(Glesne, 2011, p. 8). In this type of research, you may begin with site-specific hypothesis, but, most likely, you approach your research with an "exploratory, open mindset to the variety of perspectives and issues that might arise" (Glesne, 2011, p. 8). These methods are called qualitative. They are based on **inductive philosophy**. That is, you start with a specific context; study the context; gather data; analyze your data; and based on your data, you develop a theory to explain the data. Thus, such methods proceed from the particular to the general.

Going Beyond Agency versus Social Structure, Objective versus Subjective, and Macro- versus Micro-Sociology Debates

As Ritzer (2000, p. 496) stated, all social analyses involve "micro and macro social phenomena [that] are also either objective or subjective". We can divide social analysis into four categories of macro-objective, macro-subjective, micro-objective, and micro-subjective (Ritzer, 2000, p. 498).

- **Macro-objective analysis** looks at material realities that are large-scale, such as society and bureaucracy.

- **Macro-subjective** analysis analyzes large-scale nonmaterial social facts, such as norms and values.

- **Micro-objective analysis** focuses on patterns of interaction and action in small-scale objective settings.

- **Micro-subjective analysis** emphasizes the small-scale mental processes through which individuals make sense of their day-to-day interactions with others.

In this book, we are concerned with the dialectical relationships between these four levels of social analysis (Ritzer, 2000, p. 219). A number of sociologists have tried to bridge the gap between macro- and micro-sociology. In European sociology, this has taken the form of looking at the relationship between agency and social structure (Ritzer, 2000, p. 211). It is important to note that agents can be both people (micro) and unions (macro), and "while structures are usually macro-level phenomena, we also find structures at the micro-level" (Ritzer, 2000, p. 220). Antony Giddens' **theory of structuration** is an example of agency-structure integration. His main point was that we cannot separate between the two. They are implicated in one another. That is, agency is involved in structure and structure influences agency (Ritzer, 2000, p. 220). In other words, social structures are not simply constraining (Durkheim's view), but they are also enabling (Ritzer, 2000, p. 220). For example, the structure of grass-roots organizations as forms of new social movements have enabled Indigenous people in the Americas to oppose the implementation of economic policies that aim at privatizing their lands and resources (See Prashad & Ballvé, 2006).

Another scholar who has also been concerned about the divide between agency and structure is Pierre Bourdieu. He looked at the relationship between **habitus** and **field**. **Habitus** refers to those mental structures that are internalized by social actors and are also employed by individuals to deal with the social world (Ritzer, 2000, p. 220). He argued that the ways in which social rules and practical actions are related has a lot to do with the habits of humans that inform their practices (Lemert,

2005, p. 33). Rather than view individuals as separate from the social groups to which they belong, Bourdieu examined the relationship between the two from a dialectical perspective (Lemert, 2005, p. 33). He maintained that as human beings involved in everyday interactions we produce the habitus. At the same time, habitus has the power of producing us, the social actors (Ritzer, 2000, p. 220). Habitus enables us to go beyond the assumption that habits function differently in individuals than they do in social groups and collectivities (Lemert, 2005, p. 33). Bourdieu argued that "most habitual practices are simultaneously a result of the forces of social rules and of their own individual flourishes" (Lemert, 2005, p. 38). Habitus brings to the foreground the need to account for the practices of social things and not just in the ways social actors think about social things (Lemert, 2005, p. 39). Thus, habitus explains how our practical actions that seem to be in compliance with the rules of society are at the same time potential ways for individuals to either obey the values of society or to resist them (Lemert, 2005, pp. 38–39). According to Bourdieu, "the practice of social life is not ever so simple a matter as an individual spontaneously proposing and organizing a social coming together, nor is it simply a mechanical thing mass-produced by society's expectation that individuals execute a [normalized] practice" (Lemert, 2005, p. 40). Habitus, then, is a set of or a system of "durable [and] transposable disposition" (Lemert, 2005, p. 41).

According to Bourdieu, the **field** refers to a set of a network of relations between individuals who occupy specific and objective social positions (Ritzer, 2000, p. 220). The function of the field is to constrain the activities of individuals, both as social actors and as collectivities. The field informs the habitus, and the habitus constitutes the field. The two are involved in dialectical relationships with one another (Ritzer, 2000, p. 220).

Jurgen Habermass also dealt with the divide between agency and structure through his term, "**the colonization of the life-world**" (Ritzer, 2000, p. 220). People who communicate with one another are involved in face-to-face relations in the micro-world of the **life-world**. The roots of society lie in the life-world, but it also develops structures with its own characteristics. These structures grow in power and become independent of the micro social-worlds of individuals, and exert greater control over their lives. In this sense, the system has come to control the life-world and to colonize it (Ritzer, 2000, p. 220). Also, the interdependence of the individual and society, the dialectical relationship between human agency (free will) and social structures is illuminated by Peter Beger and Thomas Luckman's theory of the duality of structure and agency (1996). The central premise of this theory is that while individuals act on things, their actions take place within the context of social structures. But those same structures can be changed by human action, as they (i.e., social structures) were created by human beings in the first place.

Conclusions

In this chapter, we discussed the main debates in sociology and briefly explored the basic arguments of the four sociological perspectives. In developing a holistic and complex understanding of sociology, it is important to become engaged with how the field of sociology and sociological knowledge has been shaped and affected by the various controversies and theoretical perspectives through a historical lens. In the next chapters, we offer a historical overview of sociology and explore some of the issues introduced in Chapters One and Two in more detail.

Chapter Review Questions

1. What is meant by authentication?

2. Distinguish between synchronic and diachronic approaches.

3. Distinguish between sociology and other disciplines.

4. Distinguish between micro- and macro-sociology. Provide examples.

5. Distinguish between systematic and systemic discrimination.

6. What do sociologists mean by prejudice and discrimination? Explain by references to appropriate examples.

7. Distinguish between idealism and realism.

8. What do sociologists mean by positivism?

9. Explore the main arguments of the different sociological perspectives.

10. Distinguish between quantitative and qualitative sociology.

11. Why is Durkheim's study of suicide important?

12. Distinguish between different forms of suicide and discuss the implications of his arguments for studies of "social facts".

13. Define androcentricity and patriarchy.

14. Distinguish between racial and racialized identities.

15. What does Bourdieu mean by the terms field and habitus? Explain.

Critical Thinking Questions

1. Develop your own micro- macro-approach to sociological issues.

2. Why should you as a sociologist be concerned about the consequences of prejudice and discrimination in society?

3. How does critical knowledge about society assist us in promoting social justice?

4. Could sociological knowledge promote and justify the interests of elite groups in society?

5. Why is having a solid theoretical understanding of social, economic, cultural, and political events, structures, and relations important? Explain.

CHAPTER THREE

From Premodernity to Modernity

Introduction

In this and the next five chapters, we offer the reader a general overview of the history of sociology and the factors and relations that have been influential in the development of the **field** since the sixth century. We examine and explore the history of Europe and other parts of the world in order to better understand how and why sociology evolved as a "social science". In narrating the history of sociology, we also provide several frameworks for analyzing and sketching these changes in light of various sociological theories. We explore the history of sociology by looking at three concepts that have come to capture the imagination of sociologists for the past three centuries: **modernity**, **postmodernity**, and **globalization**. These terms point to social changes across long periods of time. Although these periods may seem to be disjointed, distinctive, and isolated eras in human development, it is always difficult to demarcate the boundaries between them and to pinpoint the exact origin of each. **The late fifteenth century is nevertheless signaled as the early modern period** (Hall, 1996a, p. 16). This period signals a break with past and old systems of power, structures, and relations. In general, sociology matured and developed as a tool for a better understanding of the changes in modern European societies.

In this chapter, we introduce you to several factors and events that resulted in the transformation of premodern to modern societies. We focus on the history of European history to explore how sociology was influenced due to the consequences of intense periods of change in Europe. We examine this history in the context of conceptualizing sociology as a **multidisciplinary field**. The controversies and debates that have been central to sociology find their roots in the intellectual, political, social, and economic changes, starting in the fifteenth century.

The rise of sociology is linked to the history of **modernity, liberalism** as a political ideology, and the rise of **capitalism** as the dominant form of economic system. As you read these narratives and arguments, it is important to note that sociology also studies and explores the effects of **political revolutions, colonialism, industrialization, scientific revolution,** and **urbanization** on individuals, groups, and societies from historical, theoretical, and comparative perspectives. That is, there is a dialectical relationship between sociology and these important events and changes. In studying the history of sociology, we also want to emphasize the extent to which sociology has been influenced by diverse groups of people and social thinkers who viewed social change from different theoretical perspectives. This requires us to have broad global understandings of how our societies have been changing since the fifteenth century and what the consequences of these changes have been for various groups in different parts of the world. In other words, we want to highlight the global and multi-disciplinary aspects of sociological knowledge.

This chapter is divided into two parts. In Part One, we reexamine what we mean by sociology as a field of inquiry and the controversies and debates that have been central to sociological theories and analysis. We also narrate the rise of **modernity** in light of the economic, cultural, and social changes that are considered as significant in the development of sociology. As it has been argued, sociology must be understood "in the context of history driven by the diffusion of science, knowledge, and technological applications and innovations" (Hebron & Stack, 2009, p. x).

In Part Two, we offer two main sociological frameworks for understanding the changes from pre-modernity to modernity, those postulated by Ferdinand Tönnies (1855–1936) and Émile Durkheim (1858–1917).

Part One

Sociology as a Field: contextualizing the emerging sociological debates and controversies

As we pointed out in Chapter Two, we define sociology as a **field**. However, sociology in many textbooks is presented as a **discipline**. As Kubow and Fossum (2007, p. 7) maintained, the term discipline implies adherence to certain specific methods of investigation and examination of issues and variables. This indicates that each discipline follows a set of rules and standards in investigating social, cultural, political, psychological, and environmental issues. Each discipline may also reject methods and techniques used in other disciplines. However, an overemphasis on sociology as a discipline with specific discipline-specific modes of inquiry, we believe, can limit our understandings of social, political, cultural issues, structures, and relations. For this reason, in line with Kubow and Fossum's approach to comparative education, we emphasize that sociology is also a **field** that is constantly changing (2007, p. 7).

By **field**, we imply that sociology draws upon knowledge produced in various other disciplines in order to better understand the complexity of specific issues that are of concern to sociologists. In fact, many sociologists bring with them multidisciplinary approaches to understanding society and human behaviours. Charles Quist-Adade, for example, was trained as a journalist before receiving his Ph.D. in sociology. Amir Mirfakhraie received his B.A. in sociology and anthropology; his M.A. in anthropology, and his Ph.D. in educational studies, Faculty of Education, specializing in anthropology and sociology of education, with a focus on Iranian studies. George Herbert Mead, an influential micro-sociologist, was influenced by a set of diverse ideas and theories, such as **evolutionism**, **pragmatism**, **utilitarianism**, **behaviourism**, and the influential ideas of Charles Horton Cooley (also a symbolic interactionist) (Turner, Beeghley, & Powers et al., 2002, p. 434).

Sociology as a field has been and continues to be influenced by several themes and debates. These debates have had tremendous consequences for the production of sociological knowledge and how sociologists approach the study and understanding of society and human behaviours. As discussed in Chapter Two, Terry Wotherspoon (2009) identified several debates and controversies that have shaped and continue to influence sociological approaches to:

1. understanding human behaviours and group relationships and

2. applications of sociological perspectives to analysis of society.

    Sociologists have been asking several conflicting, contradictory, and interrelated questions, such as:

    a) Should we begin our analysis with society or the individual?;

    b) Are individuals the producers of society or are they the products of social structures?;

    c) Does social stability or social conflict characterize social life?; and

    d) Should we aim to establish laws of society or should we attempt and search for human interpretations of the social world (Wotherspoon, 2009, p. 6)?

These questions arise from the various interests and approaches adapted by different social thinkers in seeking to analyze and explicate the structures and processes that affect our societies.

For example, the **human agency approach** claims that our world is socially constructed and we make and remake our cultural norms, values, and institutions through human actions and activities (Wotherspoon, 2009, p. 7). That is, society becomes real through our actions. It is through our interactions and ways of thinking that we produce, reproduce, and change society. In this light, **social agency** is understood as the abilities of individuals who act as conscious beings whom are wilfully involved in the processes of change, social practices, and decision-makings (O'Brian, 2004, p. 149).

Structural determinists, on the other hand, argue that we are the products of our society. Our identities, who we are, our class positions, and our personalities are affected by social structures (i.e., by roles, statuses, groups, formal organizations, social institutions, and values prevalent in any given society). **Social structure** is defined as those patterns of social behaviour that are considered as relatively stable over time. Structural determinists claim that what we can do is limited and circumscribed by our memberships in social groups based on factors, such as gender, social class, ethnicity, wealth, sexuality, "race", and ability. They also maintain that social expectations within society are constraining factors that affect our chances in life, positively and negatively. As Karl Marx pointed out, we do make our own history but in the context of historical factors that are not the result of our actions but the actions and attitudes of other individuals who lived before us (as cited in Wotherspoon, 2009, p. 7).

Still other sociologists attempt to discover the laws that govern society. They rely on an approach that is known as **positivism**. Their assumption is that the structures of society can be objectively measured, classified, and observed in such a way that leads to an objective knowledge about the world around us (Wotherspoon, 2009). On the other hand, some sociologists claim that no one **theory** or **meta-narrative** can explain and describe society in an objective way. As discussed, a **perspective** or **paradigm** is a general way of seeing the world that allows researchers to ask specific questions and to come up with answers and ways of interpreting the data. In general, theory "provides patterns for the interpretation of data; it links one study with another; it suppl[ies] frameworks within which concepts and variables acquire special significance; and it allows us to interpret the larger meaning of our finding for ourselves and others" (Hoover, 1988, p. 35).

At the same time, it is important to note that the process of knowledge production is affected by the biases of researchers and their respective perspectives and worldviews. Each perspective assumes that certain factors or relations are more important than others. They are based on certain assumptions about society and human relations, and each studies human relations and social structures in different ways (i.e., by emphasizing how social order is achieved [i.e., **structural functionalism**] or how inequalities are reproduced [i.e., **conflict theory**]). In contrast, according to **symbolic interactionism**, one must understand social phenomena in their contexts and attempt to determine how meaning is constructed and attached (affixed) to a given social phenomenon by social actors, not as passive producers of social reality, but as proactive agents (Wotherspoon, 2009).

These debates and controversies are based on dichotomies and divisions that construct an **either/or** understanding of the world. In other words, they are based on dualistic ways of thinking that lead into a bifurcate (divisive) conceptualization of the social world. The eighteenth-century **Enlightenment culture** was based on such a dualist way of thinking about the social world (Seidman, 1994b, p. 13). Their ideas not only described the world but were also ways of conceptualizing the world and understanding it (Seidman, 1994b, p. 3).

In fact, sociology emerged with the rise of the **Enlightenment**. The Enlightenment was a movement led by eighteenth-century European intellectuals known as the *philosophes* who challenged the conventional and taken-for-granted assumptions of their era, such as the divine right of kings, absolutism, and religious explanations of social reality. The **Enlighteners**, as they are also called, placed a premium on reason and rationality as the basis of knowledge. They argued that social problems were created by human beings and the solutions to those problems should be sought here on earth, not in the high heavens or in the bosom of Kings and Popes.

One of the characteristics of the Enlightenment was its optimism towards the apparent success of "science" and technology in explaining various natural phenomena in rational and mechanical terms and in utilizing Nature for the improvement of life for "Man" (sic). This modern Enlightenment approach retained, for the most part, elements of a Christian world view, which assumed a separation of "Man" and "Nature" and mind and body, and thus the possibility of understanding human experience as distinct from natural events (Hall, 1996a). In general, the **Enlightenment thinkers** assumed that the truth about the world is produced through "scientific" approaches and this knowledge was preferred and considered more superior to religious, folkloric, and metaphysical knowledge. These other forms of knowledge were labelled as "opinions" and "ideologies" based on "faith" and political considerations (Seidman, 1994b, p. 3). Many of these thinkers separated between the mind and the world, and assumed that through mind and language it was possible to represent the world in an objective and neutral way (Seidman, 1994b, p. 3). In other words, knowledge was organized by invoking a series of oppositions, such as science/politics, science/literature, science/narrative (Seidman, 1994b, p. 13). "Science" was considered true knowledge that was drawn based on facts and reason. Narrative, literature, and politics were considered as belonging to the category of feelings and values (Seidman, 1994b, p. 13). The above oppositions were also related to a series of other binary oppositions, such as theory/narrative, reason/affect (emotion); masculine/feminine (Seidman, 1994b, p. 13). In these constructions, the first term is considered as more important and central than the second term. That is, "science" is presumed to be "true, rational, and useful; nonscience is fiction, figurative, [and] subjective" (Seidman, 1994b, p. 13). This aspect of the Enlightenment culture, referred to as **Cartesian dualism,** has been critiqued by a number of contemporary social thinkers. Cartesian dualism was a theory by Rene Descartes, the seventeenth Century French philosopher and mathematician, which posited that the mind and soul are separate, but work together.

Feminist scholars, for example, have been critical of the Cartesian and sociological conceptions of the subject (i.e., identity construction and images of the **self**), and have played an important role in *decentring* (unsettling and questioning) our understandings of the subject and self in modernity (i.e., who and what we are). **Feminism** was also influential in questioning the division between "inside" and "outside" and "private" and "public" in sociological thought. Feminism points out that "the personal is political" (Hall, 1996b, p. 611). That is, concepts, such as childrearing, domestic division of labour, and the family are "opened up to political contestation" from the perspectives of women (Hall, 1996b, p. 611).

Donna Harraway, a well-known contemporary feminist, argued that the Enlightenment culture functioned to oppress women despite its basic emancipatory politics (Seidman, 1994b, p. 7). Harraway argued that sociological "science" and the Enlightenment pundits ignored the different experiences of women as sources of knowledge in producing theories about society. In other words, the ways in which women come to see and relate the world have been ignored in the formation of "science" in Western traditions (Seidman, 1994b, p. 7). Feminists point out that men and women differ in the ways they understand and act in the world. Harraway agreed that identity construction is a gendered process, but she is critical of "a universal gender dichotomy" (Seidman, 1994b, p. 7). Not all women experience life in the same way. Black women experience racism, where as White women benefit from racism against Black women. Working class women deal with the consequences of class inequalities and lack of access to positions of power in contrast to middle class women who benefit from their underprivileged economic positions. Harraway pointed out that we need to account for the *de-centred* characteristic of the self: identities are multiple, not unitary. (i.e., one can be working class, Arab, Christian, homosexual, and ideologically conservative). This is what she refered to as *fractured* **nature of identity**.

In this light, feminism questions uncritical constructions of societal relations based on the Cartesian dichotomies and binary oppositions that are limiting in their application and ignore the existence of various ways of life. In fact, feminism has played an important role in interrogating **binary oppositions,** such as male and female, especially as they are applied to the construction of identities and subjectivities. Let us consider the words "man" and "woman". What is a "man"? When we define what we mean by a "man", we suggest that a "man" is not a "woman": we refer to those characteristics that do not define a "man". (i.e., what a "man" is not). "Men" do not cry; "men" control their emotions; and "men" are not "sissies". That is, the characteristics we associate with "men" exclude those characteristics we associate with "women". We may consider men as rational, endowed with leadership skills, more predisposed to be involved in public affairs, and more concerned with control and authority (Seidman, 1994b, pp. 18–19). Such **Cartesian dichotomies (dualities)** associate women's activities and roles with "private" affairs in the family (i.e., as mothers and daughters) and men's roles with "public" affairs (i.e., as politicians, wage-earners, and businesspeople). Moreover, such a binary opposition does not account for the existence of hermaphrodites and bisexual individuals. Accordingly, we conceptualize the world in light of feminine and masculine characteristics that are associated with females and males, respectively. That is, we gloss over the extent to which such characteristics are general cultural and social features rather than specific attributes defining either males or females.

In this book, we argue that although we need to account for these dualist ways of conceptualizing sociology and the social worlds, we also need to move away from bifurcate approaches to doing and learning sociology. As sociology students, our approaches must account for and incorporate all these controversies as part of our frameworks for analyzing and understanding social, economic, political, and cultural relations and structures. For example, rather than emphasizing the constructivist or structural deterministic approaches and views, as Anthony Giddens pointed out, we should seek to explain how individuals are both involved in the creation/reproduction of society (i.e., agency) and are influenced by the societal forces (i.e., social structures), a process that he called **double involvement** (as cited in Wotherspoon, 2009, p. 7). That is, society is more than a collection of humans and their actions. It creates us as much as we create it (Wotherspoon, 2009).

History and Sociology: an overview

In order to better understand the origin of sociological debates, it is important to develop a general framework of the historical events and factors that changed the face of Europe and its societies. Although the establishment of sociology was due to political, social, economic, and cultural changes in Europe, these changes were also partly influenced by events and structures of power in other non-European "countries". The transformation of European societies also had consequences for other parts of the world. As David Held (1996, p. 57) maintained, "European expansion and development has had a decisive role in shaping the political map of the modern world". As such, it is of paramount importance for sociology students to approach sociology from a historical perspective, situating its rise and development by references to political, cultural, social, and economic changes in Europe and other parts of the world. In this light, sociology, as the study of social, political, economic, and cultural changes in European societies in the contexts of their interactions with non-Western parts of the world since the 1400s, enables us to both develop an appreciation of how non-European "others" influenced sociology and how sociology became a "science" of society due to changes from premodernity to modernity in Europe. By exploring this history, **our goal is to demonstrate that the**

dichotomy of "civilized" West and "barbarous" East (another binary opposition) is a hegemonic construct that must be questioned and reformulated. Such a reconstruction will allow the reader to consider how events and policies in other parts of the world enter into an interconnected web of relations with local and global consequences for others (Held, 1996). In the following chapters, we offer general and eclectic accounts of these historical events and factors.

Several events, processes, and changes are considered as the precursors to the rise of sociology as a "science" during the eighteenth and nineteenth centuries. Sociology emerged out of the **Renaissance** (a term that means rebirth and refers to a period in European history from 1300 to 1600). Renaissance came about after centuries of political, economic, and cultural stagnation in Europe from the time of the fall of the Roman Empire in the sixth century to about the 1300s (Turner, 2003, p. 1). Another important process that also was influential in the rise of modernity was the **Reformation** that put an end to the medieval religious unity of Europe by dividing it into two camps of Protestantism and Catholicism (See Box 3.1 - The Reformation).

BOX 3.1 - The Reformation

Reformation was an important social movement that had tremendous influences in Europe. It began with the ideas of **Martin Luther** (1483–1546) that sparked a rebellion against the Catholic Church and put an end to the unity of Christendom. **Lutheranism** emphasized personal faith rather than the acceptance of the practices of the Catholic Church for salvation (Perry, 2001). Luther was critical of the practice of the Church to sell indulgences, which were designed to release individuals from some of the time they were thought to spend in purgatory (which refers to a period of penance for individuals who "have sinned excessively … but who have had the good fortune to repent before death") (Perry, 2001, p. 229). Indulgences were given to individuals because of their prayers, attending Mass, or giving charity. In contrast, Luther claimed that salvation is an individual journey and is achieved "through inner religious beliefs" and "a trust in God's mercy" (Perry, 2001, p. 229). He translated the New Testament into German and its followers became known as **Protestants**. John Calvin (1509–1564) also played an important role in spreading **Protestantism**. He maintained that salvation is a form of uncertain predestination (that is, God already knows who is destined to Heaven and who is condemned to Hell). Some of Calvin's followers argued that some activities were signs that God had chosen them for salvation. **Calvinist assumed that "hard work, diligence, dutifulness, efficiency, frugality, and a disdain for pleasurable pursuits" were signs that they were chosen for salvation** (Perry, 2001, p. 241). It is important to note that these characteristics are now central to business procedures and success in **capitalist societies**. In fact, Max Weber argued that Protestantism provided a religious framework for acceptance of moneymaking and businesspeople's way of life (Perry, 2001, 241). Moreover, Protestantism resulted in the formation of a strong sense of **individualism**, based on virtues, such as self-discipline and inner strength, which were also considered as necessary characteristics for middle classes striving for business success during the eighteenth and nineteenth centuries (Perry, 2001, p. 241).

Sociology was also influenced by the rise of the **Scientific Revolution** in the sixteenth and seventeenth centuries, during which scholars critiqued the medieval understanding of the universe based on **scientific research methods**, such as "rigours and systematic observation and experimentation" (Perry, 2002, p. 278). During this period, **the natural and physical world was viewed as a system that is governed by laws that could be represented and studied mathematically** (Perry, 2001, p. 278). The **Enlightenment** movement during the eighteenth century, which was influenced by the emphasis of the Scientific Revolution on reason, played another important role in the rise of sociology as a "science" of society due to the intellectual contributions of the *philosophes* in France and other parts of Europe (Turner, 2003, p. 2). In fact, sociology was the outcome of the intellectual debates generated by the French *philosophes*. One of the most important contributions of the Enlightenment thinking was that not only **progress** was possible, but it was also inevitable (Turner, 2003, p. 2). These *philosophes* also influenced future social thinkers who experienced the effects of the **French Revolution** (1789–1799) and the **Industrial Revolution**. Sociological knowledge, for example, was influenced by the intellectual contributions of August Comte. He was critical of the moral advocacy and detached scientific observation that was being promoted by the **Enlightenment thinkers** in France (Turner, et al., 2002, p. 4). He and other social thinkers became critical of the assumptions and arguments of the *philosophes*. In fact, the basic arguments of sociology were developed as a result of the **conservative reactions** to the ideas of Enlightenment and the rejection of several of its main principles. As Ritzer (2000, p. 11) claimed, sociology is the end result of the bumpy mixture of ideas promoted by the Enlighteners and counter-Enlighteners. As such, we can stipulate that one of the conditions that had a very important and everlasting consequence on the development of sociology was the **French Revolution** and its negative outcomes. Many scholars at the time of the French Revolution were concerned with the ensuing chaos and disorder that followed it. Although some thinkers proposed a return to past and traditional forms of organization, many attempted to envision new ways of achieving order in societies that had been affected by political revolutions during the eighteenth and nineteenth centuries (Ritzer, 2000, p. 6). Since then, one of the main concerns of some sociologists (i.e., **structural functionalists**), has been a preoccupation with the ideal of **social order**: how to achieve it in light of the changes in society that result in chaos and undermine the orderly reproduction of society (Ritzer, 2000, p. 6).

The rise of **capitalism**, the **Industrial Revolution**, and the processes of **urbanization and colonial expansions** into other parts of the world, the establishments of the **nation-state** (as the dominant form of political establishment in modernity), and the **American Revolution** were also the other significant historical changes and factors that explain the rise of sociology as a "scientific" endeavour to understand human societies and the consequences of social change. In the following chapters, we explore these main changes and events that have had tremendous consequences and effects on sociology and its development in more detail. In the following section, we offer two general frameworks to analyze and conceptualize the vagaries we have so far discussed. These two frameworks allow us to think systematically about the changes from traditional societies and forms of organization to modern ones.

Part Two

• •

From Premodernity to Modernity

How did the early sociologists distinguish between premodern and modern societies? How did they theorize about the changes from premodern to modern societies? An important and logical question to start the conversation about **modernity** is what existed before the modern era? What are the characteristics of premodern societies? **Premodern societies** were conceptualized as "primitive" societies, but they are now variously described as traditional, preindustrial, pretechnological, or "simple". Conley (2010, p. 726) described premodern society as "any society that has not industrialized or urbanized". These societies are characterized by sparse populations, "rudimentary" division of labour, "simple" technology, and "low degree" of literacy, where individuals live in small groups, such as villages (Conley, 2010, p. 726). Conley (2010) identified other characteristics of the premodern society. In these societies:

1. gods are the source of knowledge and spiritual leaders (shamans) are believed to be sole repositories and transmitters of this knowledge to the people;

2. tradition plays a pivotal role in organizing, protecting, and directing everyday life with customs serving as the basis of socialization and transmission of collective wisdom, as well as myths from generation to generation; and

3. myths or stories are used to explain the natural and social world.

   Although it is assumed that any society that has not industrialized or urbanized is premodern in its mode of organization, in today's global and interconnected world, it is difficult to categorize an entire society as premodern; however, "some tribal cultures deep in the rain forest of South America or located in other remote rural areas still socially distant from the rest of the world might fit the bill" (Conley, 2010, p. 726).

The idea of modernity became the main subject of social analysis during the nineteenth century as a result of the effects of the **Industrial Revolution** and the accompanying globalization of economy and the Westernization of the world (Hall, 1996a, p. 17). **Modernity** highlights a shift from and a break with traditional type societies. It is often viewed as an opposition to tradition (Kivisto, 2011, p. 132). The most important characteristic of modernity is that everything will eventually be transformed, reshaped, displaced, dissolved, and sped up (Hall, 1996a, p. 17). In modernity, society goes through industrialization, urbanization, and other social changes that completely alter the lives of individuals (Young, 2012). Modernity is also characterized as an era of rationality, bureaucratization, and objectivity. As Seidman (1994b, p. 1) maintained, the most important aspect of the modern West is the culture of the Enlightenment and their assumptions regarding the unity of humanity, the individual as the creator of history, the centrality of "science" as the truth about the world, and the emphasis on social progress.

Modernity is characterized by certain key signs: an industrial-based economy; the importance of unions, political parties, and interest groups (i.e., civil society); the centrality of a market economy;

"institutional differentiation and role specialization and professionalism within institutions (i.e., how Kwantlen Polytechnic University is composed of many departments, each with its own specialized and highly qualified staff); and a conceptualization of knowledge that is differentiated into various disciplines, each professing its contributions to the progress of humanity (Seidman, 1994b, p. 1).

Max Weber, an important sociologist who influenced structural functionalism, conflict theory, and symbolic interactionism, wrote extensively about modernity and its characteristics. Weber argued that there are differences between how people in premodern societies thought in contrast to people in modern societies (Lemert, 2005, p. 64). The focus of people in traditional societies was how to organize daily life so that they could protect time honored rituals that had persisted before them. They were not futuristic. He conceived traditional societies as the worlds of the "eternal yesterday[s]" (Lemert, 2005, p. 64). Life in traditional type and rural societies was very much ordered by the natural rhythm of events (Lemert, 2005, p. 64). In modern societies a new attitude becomes supreme: **rationality**. For Weber, rationality was "an attitude of future orientated calculations" (Lemert, 2005, p. 65). It was also an **ethic**, or a pervasive "shared social value that motivates practical behavior" (Lemert, 2005, p. 65). In this sense, modern societies are future oriented. The dominant culture in modernity is a rationalizing one in which people constantly calculate "the most efficient means to get to some future goal" (Lemert, 2005, p. 67). Weber viewed modern societies as being characterized by "the increasing *rationalization* of social life" (Longhofer & Winchester, 2012, p. 202). **Rationalization**, for Weber, meant the ways in which human action was becoming organized and driven by an emphasis on efficiency and calculation (Longhofer & Winchester, 2012, p. 202). He labelled it **instrumental rationality** and considered it as becoming omnipresent and affecting human lives in every aspect. Weber argued that this rationalization of the world would result in better control of our lives, but it would also result in the loss of meaning in our lives (Longhofer & Winchester, 2012, p. 202).

In the remaining part of this section, we discuss two main frameworks for conceptualizing traditional societies and modernity. First, we discuss how Ferdinand Tönnies (1855–1936) perceived the differences between the two eras. Second, we explore the ideas of Émile Durkheim (1858–1917) and how he made sense of a shift from traditional type societies to modern societies. We approach these conceptualizations as **ideal types** or as constructs that assist us in comparing and contrasting the changes that were influential in the transition from premodern to modernity. These are generalized constructs that are not necessarily found in the real world.

Ferdinand Tönnies, like other Europeans during the late nineteenth century, was fascinated with the consequences of modernity and wanted to better understand the dangerous effects of modernity through an analysis of social relations (McAreavey, 2012). As McAreavey (2012) argued, Tönnies' *gemeinschaft* and *gesellschaft* are conceptual terms that provide a framework for understanding relations within communities and societies. Tönnies described the premodern society as *gemeinschaft*, or a society which is maintained by traditional rules and a universal sense of solidarity (Levine, 1995, p. 203). In other words, traditional society is used to denote *community*. These types of societies have the following characteristics:

a) there is minimum division of labour;

b) relations take shape in the context of face-to-face interactions;

c) members share common values and experiences; and

d) there is very little acceptance and tolerance for diversity and deviance.

That is, in these societies, **ascribed statuses** are the dominant forms: there is very limited social change; and individuals' social, cultural, and economic obligations and roles are not divorced and separated from their personal and face-to-face relationships and interactions with other members of the community. In short, *gemeinschaft* is a term that allows us to conceptualize life in rural settings. In *gemeinschaft* types of society, social, cultural, and economic organizations are based on qualities, such as kinship, territory, language, and religion that are commonly shared by all the members of the community. In these societies, human will is perceived to be unreflective and characterized by spontaneous 'reactions' to natural predispositions (Levine, 1995, p. 203).

In contrast, Tönnies labeled modern societies that are organized based on contracts and characterized by shared constitutions *gesellschaft* (Levine, 1995, p. 203). That is, modernity highlights social relations in terms of **association** (Levine, 1995). Social interactions and relations are determined by social actors' occupations and roles that are attached to these occupations. In *gesellschaft* societies, social relations are based on impersonal interactions. They are based on social contracts. For example, the relationship between a mechanic and a customer often is based on impersonal relations, so are the interactions between someone who wants to buy a parking permit and a municipal official at the City of White Rock, British Columbia, Canada. In *gesellschaft* types of organization, human will is considered to be based on reflective, deliberate, and calculating approaches that highlight human voluntarism and free will. People are characterized as individuals who pursue their self-interests. Social relations are based on rational principles, which highlight business and economic principles. That is, the emphasis is on one's own needs rather than the needs and wants of other people. In such societies, social change is widespread and rampant. Although there is more tolerance for diversity in modern societies than in nonindustrial type societies and **achieved statuses** are considered as more important, these types of societies are, it is assumed, plagued with "loss of social solidarity". In general, Tönnies problematized the chasm between premodern and modern societies in terms of social organization and how individuals were perceived within them.

As mentioned in Chapter Two, Émile Durkheim believed that sociology should provide us with a plan to deal with the consequences of rapid and intensive social change. Durkheim was concerned with the effects of the division of labour on people's behaviour. He examined the emergence of modern society in light of an analysis of the loss of social integration and its relationship to the rise in suicide. He theorized that greater specialization leads to greater **anomie**, which is defined as a loss of direction that a society experiences when social control of individual behaviour becomes ineffective (Bocock, 1996, p. 177). Durkheim believed that in modernity, societies characterized by industrialization, lacked mechanisms for integration and solidarity that are central to ward off *anomie* (Longhofer & Winchester, 2012, p. 4).

Durkheim did not argue that modern societies are characterized by disintegration and conflict. Rather, he pointed out that as we move from traditional type of societies to modern ones, one form of social solidarity is replaced with other sets (Longhofer & Winchester, 2012, p. 4). As people began moving into urban centres, many young people and families found themselves without the support of their family members and close-knit communities. They were no longer under the scrutiny of their community members and did not have to abide to the social conventions prevalent in their societies that curbed and constrained their desires and wants. This lack of social control led them to explore their desires and needs, which in their own communities might have been labelled as problematic and unconventional since they were considered to undermine social norms and the fabric of the community. *Anomie*, then, refers to the "inability of social ties and norms to regulate … insatiable passions and aspirations of individuals left to their own devices" (Longhofer & Winchester, 2012, p. 4).

In traditional societies, the young men and women were expected to conform to the norms that were highly prized in their communities. If a person did not conform to these social expectations, they were ostracized and accordingly punished. In the city, such constraints were no longer present. As such, young men and women were able to experiment with those behaviours that they were denied before due to social control and pressures. The elite groups in the urban centres viewed these experimentations stemming from unconditional individualism as a menace and a sign of social disorder. Men were labelled as "rowdies" and women were called "immoral" or "loose" (Robbins, 2008, p. 60). Women who worked in the factories of New York City during the nineteenth and early twentieth centuries used their wages and their freedom from their families to date, shop, or dance. The behaviours of these women were seen as "immoral" and undermining the orderly reproduction of society by social reformers who wanted to protect these women from temptations of modernity (Robbins, 2008, p. 60). One of their solutions was the creation of Young Women's Christian Association (YWCA) to curb the "immorality" of these women and to reestablish order in society.

Almost a century later, female rural migrant workers in major urban centres of Malaysia are also experiencing similar trends. The media, politicians, and religious leaders are calling to control working women's leisure time. Female factory workers are depicted as pleasure seekers: "women are beginning to cross social boundaries, having 'illicit' relationships and marrying men of other ethnic groups (e.g., Chinese), something traditional family and [religious] authorities would never have allowed" (Robbins, 2008, p. 61). The dominant society has attempted to impose new forms of discipline on these factory wage-labourers due to the fact that the capitalist class needs and requires a disciplined and reliable workforce (Robbins, 2008, p. 61). As a tactic, factory owners and managers are drawing upon and appealing to the traditional practice that requires children and especially women to take care of their parents in old age so that these workers use part of their wages to "pay back what they owe their parents", thus having less to spend on "immoral" activities (Robbins, 2008, p. 61). Factory owners and managers have also attempted to establish links with women's home communities in order to enlist their assistance in monitoring and controlling these workers. For example, they have devised plans that allow parents to view and monitor the timesheets of the workers in order to determine how long they work and the time they spend on other activities.

Such views about the loss of social control were also echoed by German **neoconservatives** during the first five decades of the last century. According to these thinkers, modernity results in a loss of continuity between present and past that provided people a moral framework to behave and act in their societies (Giddens, 1994, p. 31). Durkheim was critical of these views that assumed social order was weakening and degenerating (Longhofer & Winchester, 2012, p. 4). Rather, he maintained that in the conditions of *anomie* people tend to have no sense of purpose or direction, especially during times of extreme change or upheaval, such as high unemployment and economic recession. But, as societies develop other forms of social control, new norms and values are instituted to give meaning to peoples' interactions and social relations.

For Durkheim, in premodern societies, individuals were endowed with a single status, which determined most of their activities (Giddens, 1994, p. 31). Status was always connected with specific conceptions of duties and rights towards the members of the community. Aspects of life in one social space (locality) were not easily transferrable to another locality. This is one of the reasons why there was not a lot of cultural diversity in premodern societies despite the fact that many diverse groups lived in close proximity to one another (Giddens, 1994, p. 31). In contrast, modern societies and institutions result in eradicating the particularities of **place** and have homogenizing consequences (Giddens, 1994, p. 31): structures and relations in one part of the world can be incorporated and adapted in other parts of the world.

Durkheim argued that premodern societies were governed by **mechanical solidarity,** which facilitates the social integration of members of a society who share common values and beliefs (Ritzer, 2000, p. 77). These common values and beliefs constitute a **collective conscience** that works internally in individual members to cause them to cooperate with one another. He defined collective conscience as "the totality of beliefs and sentiments common to average citizens of a society" (as cited in Wallace & Wolf, 2006, p. 20). In this type of society, the social structure is not significantly differentiated in terms of roles and statuses. That is, there is little or no division of labour. Durkheim emphasized on the division of labour as an example of a material *"social fact"* in order to gauge the extent to which societal tasks and responsibilities were becoming specialized and differentiated (Ritzer, 2000, p. 77). In societies characterized by *mechanical solidarity*, individuals within them can often perform a number of tasks that are essential for their survival. The characteristic of such societies is *sameness*. In other words, the members of such societies are all involved in performing similar tasks and have comparable responsibilities. For example, in a hunting and gathering society, the nutritional needs of the family are provided by fathers and mothers who hunt and gather food.

Modern societies are characterized by **organic solidarity.** Modern societies, unlike traditional societies, are characterized by *difference*. Solidarity in modern societies, is due to the fact that people have different responsibilities and roles (Ritzer, 2000, p. 78). In these types of society, solidarity is preserved through people's reliance on others to perform their varied tasks and jobs in society rather than on "shared labour, interests, and values" (Longhofer & Winchester, 2012, p. 4). In modern societies such as industrialized societies, the family relies on other groups to provide the basic needs of the family members. For example, bread is bought from the baker, meat from the butcher, and fruit and vegetables from the local market (Ritzer, 2000, p. 78). These individuals need the services provided by others in order to satisfy their needs. For example, they need the police to provide safety, lawyers for legal matters, and so on. It is important to note that since people are more *similar* in traditional type societies, there is higher likelihood that they will be in competition with one another over the natural resources. In contrast, in the case of *organic solidarity*, people, due to *differentiation* in society, are more likely to cooperate with one another and to be supported "by the same resource base" (Ritzer, 2000, p. 78). In this sense, Durkheim argued that societies that are characterized by *organic solidarity* lead to more solidarity and more individuality than it is possible in societies characterized by *mechanical solidarity* (Ritzer, 2000, p. 78). In these types of society, there is a rise in individualism.

As it can be deduced, these two models point to the complexity of modern societies. They are based on evolutionary ways of thinking that assume premodern societies were "simple". They highlight the process of progress in human societies by focusing on European societies. At the same time, they are concerned with a range of social issues that arose in modernity that did not exist in previous societies to the same extent. One of these issues is a concern with order and conflict and how modern societies reproduce themselves in an orderly manner, despite the breakdown of traditional forms of social relations and structures.

Conclusion

The change from traditional to modern societies is due to various factors and events. No single explanation can adequately explain the development of modern societies. It is in the nexus of political revolutions, scientific discoveries, technological innovations, and population movement that one can begin to develop a framework for understanding modernity as a historical epoch. In the next few chapters, we explore what is meant by modernity and describe its main characteristics from various theoretical perspectives. The history of sociology is ultimately linked to how sociologists and other social thinkers have theorized about these socioeconomic, cultural, and political changes that form the bedrock of sociology as a field of "scientific" inquiry.

The theories we discussed in this chapter are based on binary oppositions that have come to influence how we think about ourselves, society, the economy, culture, and politics. As it will be discussed in Chapter Nine, postmodernists have criticized modern conceptions of society, culture, politics, and other spheres of life by pointing to the fragmented aspects of the current structures of societies in local and global contexts.

Chapter Review Questions

1. What are some of the historical factors that influenced the rise of sociology?
2. Why are some contemporary scholars critical of Cartesian dualism? Explain.
3. Explore the impacts of the Reformation and the Enlightenment on European societies.
4. What are the differences between modern and traditional societies?
5. What is meant by the term "social fact"?
6. Define anomie.

7. How did Ferdinand Tönnies theorize the change from traditionalism to modernity? How do his ideas differ from Durkheim's theory of social change from premodern to modern societies? Explain.

8. Distinguish between human agency and structural determinist approaches.

9. What is meant by the term double involvement? Explain.

10. What does Donna Harraway mean by the fractured nature of identity?

Critical Thinking Questions

1. In what ways are there continuities between traditional and modern societies? Explain.

2. Are the ideas of Durkheim and Tönnies about social change Eurocentric? Why? Why not? Explain.

3. In what ways are dualist ways of thinking useful in promoting social order and harmony?

4. In what ways do you approach the world from a Cartesian dualist perspective? Offer a critique of your understanding of human relations based on such conceptions.

5. In what ways does your identity construction resemble what Donna Harraway refers to as the "fractured nature of identity" in modernity? Explain.

CHAPTER FOUR

Modernity and the Birth of Sociology

Introduction

In this chapter, we continue our exploration of the history of sociology by examining some of the general characteristics of modernity and those relations and factors that distinguish it from previous periods. We focus on the ideas of Anthony Giddens, who offered an exhaustive and illuminating account of the conditions and factors that gave birth to modernity. You are introduced to ideas and terms, such as **evolutionism, industrialism, Scientific Revolution**, the main **features of modernity**, the **Enlightenment, nation-states, disembedding, emptying of space** and **time, token symbols**, and **expert systems**. We also distinguish between **modernity,** as a historical epoch, and **modernism,** as the ideas and cultural values in modernity. In addition, we introduce you to the ideas of **Paulo Freire, liberation theory**, and **critical pedagogy**.

This chapter is divided into two parts. In Part One, we define modernity and explore its characteristics as a globalizing phenomenon. We examine what Giddens meant by time and space separation (distanciation) as the main features of the chasm between modern and premodern eras. In Part Two, we focus on the two mechanisms of disembedding and distinguish between modernity and modernism.

Part One

Modernity: a globalized and "runaway" world

As mentioned in the preceding chapter, modernity implies a shift away from traditional types of societies and their social, economic, and political worldviews. According to Giddens (1990, p. 1) **modernity** refers to those modes of organization and social life that emerged in Europe since the seventeenth century and became worldwide in their consequences and influences. Kivisto (2011) has noted that modernity is often associated with progress, advancement, development, liberation, growth, and betterment. It is also often "depicted as an expansive, and thus global, phenomenon" (Kivisto, 2011, p. 133). Giddens (1991, p. 16) has pointed out that modernity is a dynamic epoch in the history of human societies and is characterized by **discontinuities** that distinguish it from previous periods. He maintained that these discontinuities had not been fully appreciated due to the influences of evolutionist thoughts (1990, p. 5). **Evolutionism** assumes that human history is governed by several general dynamic principles and has an overall direction (Giddens, 1990, p. 5). This theory imposes an orderly picture on the history of human societies. "Human" history is told as a unified "story line" with specific characteristics. According to this theory, human history starts with small hunting-gathering communities, followed by crop-growing, agriculturalist settlements and pastoral nomad societies, and from there to the creation of agrarian states, ending in the rise of modern societies in the west (Giddens, 1990, p. 5). A critical look at evolutionism reveals that history should not be viewed as a unified entity with universal principles of organization and transformation (Giddens, 1990, pp. 5–6). Yet, such a critique does not imply that we cannot come up with certain characteristics of change that define the modern world. Giddens attempted to highlight these characteristics of modernity in his book, *The Consequences of Modernity*.

Giddens (1990) observed that modernity has a globalizing characteristic. In modernity, local relations and events are affected by political decisions, economic policies, and technological advancements in other parts of the world. What affects the local (where face-to-face relations and interactions take place) is decided and influenced by what occurs in other areas of the world. For example, economic recession in China will have consequences for economic growth and activities in the United States and Canada. Or, when the US housing market is in decline, there is less demand for lumber products used in construction projects in the United States; and, as a result, mills in British Columbia, Canada that supply lumber to the United States may close down or slow production, which often has devastating effects on the residents of towns and cities that rely on employment opportunities provided by these mills.

The modern world is a dynamic and "runaway world" (Giddens, 1991, p. 16). In the modern period, human population increased drastically, "and so did urban centers" (Brown, 1990, p. 93). Modern societies are societies that are affected by "constant, rapid, and permanent change" (Hall, 1996c, p. 598). One way of visualizing this aspect of modernity is to look at contemporary and historical pictures of the cities in which you reside and compare the images of specific intersections in your cities over time. As these pictures may attest, in a span of a few decades, specific geographical locations have gone through intense changes. For example, the area near East Hastings and Main Street in Vancouver, Canada used to be the centre of shopping and social activities for middle class individuals during the 1940s and 1950s. However, in 2013, it is considered to be one of the poorest communities/neighbourhoods in Canada. In contrast, Robson Street, which used to be a neighborhood where many German immigrants resided, is now home to high-end shopping and is the hub of social, commercial, and tourist activities.

In modernity, the increase in the commercial basis of social relations resulted in the new standards of consumption for many groups of people that were not conceivable previously (Brown, 1990, p. 93). Due to the improved standards in communication and production and movement of goods and services, people were able to travel more easily. Fashion trends and changes in consumer tastes in one part of Europe also more easily influenced trends of consumptions in other parts of Europe due to the ease of communication. In fact, the eighteenth century is considered as the time period during which a **consumer society** emerged. During this time period, entertainment, music, and the theatre were also beginning to become commercialized. They were now available to a larger portion of the population who could afford to buy tickets to attend such events. At the same time, we also notice an increase in the number of pubs, amusement parks, and coffeehouses during this period.

The modern world is a global world. Many of our daily activities are influenced by events and trends in other parts of the world. The fact that Canadians rush to buy the latest electronic gadgets, such as the iPhone developed by the Apple Inc. in the United States, is a reflection of how our actions and behaviours are influenced by technological development and consumer trends in other parts of the world. As consumers of goods, moreover, we seek cheaper products and bargains. We may choose to shop at Wal-Mart for its competitive prices. When we choose to shop at Wal-Mart, we become involved in the exploitation of labour, both locally and globally. This is not because we actually intend to exploit others, but it is due to Wal-Mart's labour policies and practices. In this sense, when we shop at this or similar stores that their products are made using cheap labour in unsafe working conditions in non-Western parts of the world, we are not simply acting locally as consumers satisfying our immediate needs. We become involved in a web of local and global relations that are often beyond our controls. Through our actions, we are also indirectly affecting and reproducing unequal social, economic, and political relations in other parts of the world. For example, consider the fact that many of the consumer items that we use and purchase are designed and conceived in the West, but they are produced and manufactured in non-Western parts of the world. It is in this sense that the modern world is a globalizing epoch and ever changing.

Modernity is also characterized by a belief in the power of "science" and technological development as tools in controlling nature and promoting continual human progress. Kivisto (2011) observed that modern culture is imbued with optimism about human abilities to resolve and find solutions for social problems and human suffering in order to improve social life (Yet, that optimism has been questioned by **postmodernist** thinkers that will be discussed in Chapter Nine in more detail). The history of such a belief is found during the intense periods of change starting in the sixteenth century. Due to the effects of the **Scientific Revolution**, for example, "scientific" knowledge gained prominence throughout society and competed with religion as the primary method of knowing, culminating in the eighteenth century **Enlightenment**. These thinkers, called the *Enlighteners* or *philosophes* proposed that **rationality** and **reason** were important bases or sources of knowledge, not faith, which formed the bedrock of the premodern era. They adopted **positivism,** or the application of "science", to the study of society. They rejected the idea that God was the source of knowledge.

Declaring their faith in **individual reason**, the Enlightenment scholars launched a barrage of attacks against three pillars of society of the day:

a) political authority,

b) religious revelation, and

c) existing social inequalities (these ideas will be explored in more detail in the next chapter).

The Enlightenment movement opposed **absolutism**, a system of political governance in which all power is vested in one ruler or authority figure. They were critical of the dominant views of the time that assumed kings derive their right to rule directly from God. During premodernity (i.e., the Middle Ages), the kings, popes, and bishops were viewed as God's representatives on earth. Disobeying them was considered disobedience of God, an act that would result in punishment in the form of death or other personal calamities, such as poverty, illness, and misery. In criticizing such views, the Enlightenment scholars argued that social problems were created by human beings themselves. They maintained that humans were capable of solving them here on earth, and not in the High Heavens. Human beings, they reasoned, were capable of creating good and evil. Thus, the issues of sin and salvation are human creations, not the result of some divine grand scheme. With their persistent critiques, it was not long before the old order began to crumble under the weight of the new ideas that were being proposed (See Hall, 1996c). Riding the crest wave of the Enlightenment ideas of individual agency, reason and rationality, "new political structures developed, with the rise of the modern nation-state and the process of urbanization" (Conley, p. 727). During this time, technological inventions and innovations also radically transformed agricultural production and forms of mass communication. In addition, increased **industrialization** and the specialization of labour revolutionized economic production. These general changes separated modern societies from previous generations. In the following section, we discuss the main features of modernity and explore the new institutional foundations of modernity in more detail.

Three Features of Modernity and New Modern Institutions

As mentioned, there are discontinuities between modern and traditional societies. Such breaks or chasms can be identified by references to three main features of modernity:

1. the **pace of change is faster** (the speed of change is great and extreme);

2. the **scope of change and how it affects social practices and behavioural modes** (the whole world is transformed); and

3. **the specific characteristics of modern social institutions** (Giddens, 1990, p. 6; 1991, p. 16).

Since the eighteenth century, changes in consumption habits, production, artistic expressions, behaviours, and cultural norms were swift and unpredictable. These changes were introduced as a result of structural vicissitudes in society. The speed of change in modernity is extreme. Technological innovations, such as the steam engine, that were introduced affected people's relations in various unpredictable ways (i.e., how work was organized in factories). As a result of the introduction of new machinery and management policies in factories during the late nineteenth and early twentieth centuries, for example, workers became deskilled and every aspect of their activities was under the control and surveillance of the managers and owners of capital. As a result of the introduction of agricultural technology and machinery and the implementation of "land-reforms", many rural people and peasants in Western European societies became landless-unemployed workers who had to move to cities in search of work in factories. This process was also accelerated by the improvement of communication means, such as roads.

Some of the institutions of modernity also did not exist in traditional type societies. For example, the political system of the **nation-state**; the general dependence of production on machines and nonanimal sources of power, and the commodification of the goods we purchase and human labour in the form of wage-labour are intrinsic to modern societies (Giddens, 1990, p. 6). In essence, modernity is characterized by a series of structural changes in the cultural, social, political, and economic spheres, which had trickle down effects on how individuals and groups lived their lives.

Let us consider the consequences of the rise of nation-states in Europe in more detail. **Nation-States** are political units that have definite and distinguishable political and geographical boundaries. The nation-state imposes a **national identity** on its citizens, which determine how they (citizens) define themselves through the invocation of national symbols, such as a common language, religion, ethnicity, and flag. In modern societies, the citizens of a nation show loyalty to the state, not to their clans, ethnic groups, occupational organizations, or religious denominations. As a result of the rise of nation-states, many people in Western Europe, despite their ethnic identities and national origins, had to be resocialized in order to learn how to act and behave as citizens of these newly established nation-states. For instance, many people in France did not speak French. In Germany, many people considered themselves as Polish. The aim of nation-building was to impose a uniform national identity on all the inhabitants of a nation-state. During the Middle Ages, in contrast, although national states were being formed by some kings, these kings had to reconcile political power with other influential segments of society, such as feudal lords, the clerics, free cities, and representative assemblies (Perry, 2001, pp. 244–245). There were a number of competing forms of power and authority that dictated the everyday interactions of people. People often viewed themselves as members of an estate, as aristocrats, as clergies, or as commoners, rather than as subjects and citizens of a nation-state (Perry, 2001, p. 245).

Furthermore, during most of the Middle Ages, the Church viewed the kings as deriving their power from God, and their rule was affirmed in accordance with the interpretations of God's commands by the clergy (Perry, 2001, p. 245). Starting in the sixteenth and seventeenth centuries, however, kings were able to dominate these other forces within society and subjected lords and the clergy to royal control (Perry, 2001, p. 245). This led to the gradual evolution of national states based on specific territorial boundaries. Kings established strong central states (i.e., governments) that used centralized bureaucracies, military force, and new technology to enforce their control over vast territories, home to different ethnic and linguistic groups. In these new forms of governance, the state was conceived as an autonomous political structure to which the subjects owed loyalty and towards which they had obligations and duties (Perry, 2001, p. 245). The states were now being conceived as sovereign entities.

As nation-states became a central feature of modern societies, elite groups within these nation-states were able to control all aspects of life within their borders. The main function of the state was to develop a sense of belonging amongst the people and to mold their attitudes in such a way that the people would serve the goals of the state (Perry, 2001, p. 245). In fact, by the nineteenth century, the European states, many of which were made of diverse ethnic, racial, and linguistic groups, formed universal and fixed national identities that reflected the culture of the dominant society and required their citizens to show devotion to, and express their pride in the nation by, for example, their willingness to die for it.

In the following sections, we offer a framework that was developed by Giddens to explore the changes from premodern to modern societies by examining three elements that characterize the dynamism of modernity. Giddens maintained that the dynamism of modernity derives from:

1. **separation of time** and **space**;

2. **disembedding of social institutions**; and

3. **reflexivity that is influenced by the constant input of knowledge "affecting human action and groups"** (See Ritzer, 2000, p. 558).

Before we explore the first two characteristics in more detail, it is important to note that modernity is characterized by an emphasis on constantly examining and reforming social practices in the light of incoming new information about these social practices that ultimately results in altering their characters (Giddens, as cited in Hall, 1996c, p. 598; Ritzer, 2000, p. 560). All aspects of life are affected by the process of *reflexivity*, which results in constant change, reformation, and an inescapable sense of uncertainty (Ritzer, 2000, p. 560). This is an important point to consider: the notion of *reflexivity* explains the nature of change and the differences between modern and traditional type societies in terms of discontinuities between the two periods. For example, in modernity, the **self**, or the ability to view and consider oneself as an object, is both an object and a subject (Ritzer, 2000, p. 351). We (as subjects) reflect on ourselves (as objects): how we present ourselves in social interactions depends on how we imagine other people see us. For instance, we view ourselves as good students because our teachers construct and label us as studious students. Their images of us as good students become parts of our self-images. If they view us as "bad" or mediocre students, we may perceive ourselves as nonacademic type students. The ways in which the self develops is due to its *reflexive* characteristics: the ability to position ourselves in places of others and to act as they might do by way of incoming information (Ritzer, 2000, p. 351). We discuss the construction of self and its reflexive character in more detail in Chapter Five.

In the following sections, we focus on the first two factors that shape the dynamism of modernity: the *separation of time* and *space* and *disembedding of social institutions*. In modernity, our conceptions of *time* and *space* began to change: social actors were no longer bounded by local events and natural conceptions of *time* that linked individuals to specific localities.

Time and Space Separation (Distanciation): the chasm between modern and premodern eras

Have you ever thought about how *time* and *space* are related? Two people in southern and northern British Columbia are simultaneously asked what *time* it is. They do not look at the location of the sun or other natural makers to tell the *time*. They look at either their watches or cell-phones to tell the *time* of the day. Their answer will be the same: it is 5:30 p.m. In traditional type societies, as Giddens (1990) pointed out, however, *time* and *space* were connected and not separate phenomena. One could not have meaning without the other. In fact, *time* was a local phenomenon and was not universalized. "Time of the day" meant different things to people living in various parts of Europe during the fourteenth century. The times to pray or harvest were localized events. Social, economic, and cultural activities were conceptualized in the context of local conceptions of *time* and within the confinement of local traditions.

In modernity, *time* and *space* are distinguished from one another. The day, for example, is divided into precise units of *time* that is measured using a mechanical device. The clock divides the day into 24 hours. This division of the day that is standardized all over the world allows for a management of activities and ordering of economic, social, and cultural activities across various geographical *places*. It allows the owners of factories to determine precisely how long a worker should work, how long their breaks should be, and when their lunch breaks will be. It allows for managing workers' activities in an efficient way. Regardless of the location of the factory in different time zones (*spaces*), all workers must follow the same time management rules. As such, work becomes regimented. One, for example, may have to arrive at 5:00 a.m. for work and take one's breaks at specific times, depending on how long one works in a day (i.e., if one works less than three hours, he/she is not entitled to a fifteen minute break).

In modernity, *time* is determined by the ways we measure it, using clocks, watches, and other devices (Robbins, 2008, p. 50). In the early stages of modernity, the workers in factories had to be disciplined to accept this new conception of *time* and its management by mechanical devices. In premodern societies, the *space* and *time* were always connected. In determining *time* (i.e., when), people often associated it with a specific *place* and/or natural occurring event (i.e., where). That is, telling *time* was conditional upon references to specific sociocultural markers in specific *localities* (Giddens, 1990, p. 17). In these societies, *time* was connected to specific tasks (that is, *time* was task oriented) and was directed by natural events and activities. In premodern Malaysia, one of the main markers of *time* was (is) the cycle of daily Islamic prayer, which differed depending on the region (time zone) one lived in. In contrast, in modern Malaysia, female labourers work for eight successive hours with only two fifteen-minute breaks and a half-hour lunch break (Robbins, 2008, p. 62). In Madagascar, *time* was measured by the *time* it took to cook rice (about half an hour). In seventeenth-century Chile, the *time* to cook an egg equaled the *time* to say an Ave Maria. In Burma, monks woke up when they could see their veins in the early daylight. In the Oceanside communities, *time* was related and depended on the movement of tides (Robbins, 2008, p. 50). E. E. Evans-Pritchard, an anthropologist who studied the Neur people in Africa, maintained that the Neur people did not seem to fight against *time* in the same way Europeans did in the 1930s and 1940s. The main points of reference in these societies were the social, economic, and religious activities that were mainly of leisurely nature. Events and activities were based on a logical order, but they were not determined by "man-made" mechanical devices and abstract systems of time; human activities did not have to precisely conform to preestablished time frame (as cited in Robbins, 2008, p. 50). The linking of *time* with *space* was not precise or constant in traditional societies.

As Giddens (1991, p. 16) pointed out, in premodern contexts *time* and *space* were linked because of the situatedness of *place*. The clock made possible the existence of *empty* (abstract) *time* that is not connected to a specific *space* or activity. As Giddens (1990, pp. 17–18) maintained, *time* and *space* (and *place*) were still connected until it was possible to uniformly measure *time* through the application of mechanical clocks, a process that was also accompanied with establishing uniform ways of socially organizing *time*. As mentioned, after the invention of the clock in the late eighteenth century, it was possible to divide the day into precise and predetermined universal zones for specific activities, such as the working day.

Modernity is characterized by the **separation of *time* from *space*** and the creations of precise *time-space* zoning of social life (Giddens, 1990, p. 17). Giddens defined separation of *time* and *space* as the bases for the "articulation of social relations across wide spans of time-space, up to and including global system" (Giddens, 1991, p. 20, Figure 1: the Dynamism of Modernity). For example, in Iran, the education system is nationally organized. All students at all levels of schools in this country use the same textbooks and instructional materials in the classroom. Regardless of where students live, teachers in primary schools must follow the prescribed weekly program that is set for them by the officials of the Ministry of Education and textbook experts (*Education in Islamic Republic of Iran, 2003*, p. 66). School activities are organized according to predetermined universal *time* periods for teaching and learning specific topics in grades One through Five in different geographical locations in Iran. This is the extent to which **bureaucracies** control our daily activities in modern societies, a point that Max Weber explored through his term, **rationalization**. In this context, the hours of instructions that should be allocated to each subject is predetermined and fixed, which also universalizes all school activities across Iran. That is, for example, all children in Grade One must be taught one hour of Qur'an, eleven hours of Persian Reading, two hours of art and eight hours of math and sciences during the week. This timetable regiments teachers' activities and determines what they teach.

Different social, ethical, and moral meanings were also being associated with the new concept of *time* in modernity. For example, at about the same time in the nineteenth century when our present sense of *time* became well established, the view that idleness was not an acceptable social practice became popular and dominant (Robbins, 2008, p. 50). *Time* began to be conceptualized as something that should not be wasted: *time* was now money (Robbins, 2008, p. 50). *Time* became a commodity that could not be undervalued. As such, leisure *time* was considered as something that should be avoided, since seeking amusement was considered to be sinful. In fact, any activity that did not contribute to producing goods and services was discouraged (Robbins, 2008, p. 50).

The second aspect of change that resulted in the separation of *time* from *space* was the standardization of *time* across regions; yet it is important to note that even in the late nineteenth century different regions within a nation-state followed different *times* and the situation was even worst between national borders (Giddens, 1990, p. 18). This process is referred to as ***emptying of time***, which is the prerequisite for the ***emptying of space*** (Giddens, 1990, p. 18). For example, consider the fact that people living on the West coast of the United States and Canada reside in the same time zone. If you call someone in California at 9:00 p.m. in British Columbia, Canada, it is also 9:00 p.m. in California. If you call someone in Ontario, Canada, one knows that they are three hours ahead: the time there will be 11:00 p.m. So, if you need to contact a government office located in Ontario from British Columbia, you know when you are supposed to call them during the working week (Monday-Friday) in order to reach a person or an office.

Emptying of time was also the end result of the standardization of world calendars: we follow the same dating system in organizing our activities and social, economic, and political relations (Giddens, 1990, p. 18). Although there are a number of "New Years" that are practiced in the world, the Christian calendar has become a universal way of organizing events, social relations, and movements of goods and services. This brings worldwide uniformity that enables firms, corporations, individuals, and governments to organize and coordinate events and social, cultural, and economic transactions irrespective of where one lives. If you need to discuss an important business matter with your investors who reside in California and Ontario, you can coordinate a "time" for a telecommunication with them despite the fact that all of you live in different geographical *places*. In coordinating a meeting between people living in China, Pakistan, Ghana, and Brazil, furthermore, we use the Christian calendar system to determine what day and what *time* the individuals could participate in a conference-call. This is an important characteristic of modern organizations that requires coordinating the actions of individuals who are not physically present at the moment (in other words, they are "absent from one another") since they reside in different *places* (Giddens, 1991, p. 17).

According to Giddens, in modernity, the control of *space* first required the coordination across *time* (Giddens, 1990, p. 18). By ***emptying space***, Giddens meant "**the separation of space from place**" (our emphasis) (1990, p. 18). Giddens defined **place** by reference to **locale**, or "the physical settings of social activity as situated geographically" (1990, p. 18). In premodern societies, *place* and *space* meant the same thing and referred to the same phenomenon (i.e., geographical position). This is due to the fact that human activities were localized. One acted locally and the consequences of one's actions had consequences within the immediate locality that were experienced by other local inhabitants in face-to-face relationships. In premodern societies, the social actors were present "at the same time and in the same place" (Ritzer, 2000, p. 525). In modernity, however, social system spread over *time* and *space* due to the consequences of new forms of communication and transportation (Ritzer, 2000, pp. 525–526).

The *development of empty space* also allowed for the representation of *space* without reference to a privileged *locale*, making it possible to substitute different spatial units for one another (Giddens, 1990, p. 19). Better transportation means resulted in the "discoveries" of various parts of the world and the exploitation of people, wealth, and the natural resources of non-Western nations during the era of **colonialism (the domination of non-Western parts of the world by Western European societies)**. Colonialism had devastating consequences for many peoples around the world. It, for example, resulted in altering the structure of family relations amongst some Aboriginal societies. European patriarchal relations and structures that reinforced men's power in society replaced matrilineal relations and structures prevalent in many Aboriginal societies, resulting in the diminution of women's power in these societies and modifying their egalitarian gender relations. The so-called "discovery" of previously uncharted parts of the world by European colonialists, travellers, and explorers was the necessary basis for *emptying of space* (Giddens, 1990, p. 19). Let us consider the implication of colonialism in terms of *emptying of space*. If we think of British Empire, we are no longer referring to England and its geographical location in Europe. The British Empire referred to various locations in various parts of the world in Asia, Africa, and the Americas. In this sense, *space* (British Empire) is torn away from *local* (England or London, as the centre of power). We could, for example, talk about "British India" without references to the cultural and economic structures prevalent in England. In modernity, *space* like *time* becomes an abstract phenomenon.

As the above example illustrates, the charting of the world and the publication of global maps also resulted in establishing "space as 'independent' of any particular place or region" (Giddens, 1990, p. 19). To determine where China is located, we do not use a specific *local* or *place*, such as Shanghai, London, Lisbon, or Tehran, as a reference point. We use coordinates on maps to locate where China is positioned. In contrast, as mentioned above, in traditional societies *space* and *place* meant the same thing and referred to the same geographical locations. One often did not travel far from one's birth place, and one's immediate needs were provided within one's localities. In modernity, one's immediate needs and wants are satisfied by purchasing products and goods that are manufactured in other regions and parts of the world: in *spaces* that are different than and separate from *places/locals* in which we reside. For example, with the establishment of British and French colonial posts in North America, lumber and fur were imported to European cities. Spices and silk were imported from China and other parts of Asia to Europe, and cotton that was grown in plantations in the United States using African slaves were used in mills and factories in England to manufacture fabrics in cities like Manchester. Industrial goods produced in England were then exported to other parts of the world, including to the colonies in North America, India, and China.

Let us consider another example to illustrate what Giddens meant by the *development of empty space*. In today's technologically advanced societies with the proliferation of the Internet, people in various parts of the world often communicate with others in different parts of the globe who live in different time zones. Youth playing Disney's Penguin on the web can communicate and play with other youth of different racial, sexuality, class, ethnic, and national backgrounds who live in different *locals* and time zones. *Space* in this context is a *cyber-space* that brings various *localities* under one umbrella.

In general, in modernity, the separation (or **distanciation**) of *time* from *space* resulted in multiple and variant combinations. Ritzer (2000, p. 559) argued that "time and space distanciation is important for several reasons". **First**, it is the prerequisite for the growth of rationalized organization (bureaucracies) and the rise of nation-states that connect local and global spheres. That is, it is one of the prerequisites for the **rationalization** of modern organizations of life (Giddens, 1990, p. 20). Modern institutions are based on bureaucratic standards that rely on *time* and *space* separation and, as such, they are able to affect the lives of many people by connecting *local* and global in ways that were not possible in premodern societies (Giddens, 1990, p. 20). Consider a Greyhound bus time-table, which highlights the schedule of the time when a bus arrives in different cities (Giddens, 1990, p. 20). This is not just a *time-based* sequential table. Rather, it is a *time-space* organizational tool that determines when and where busses arrive and leave specific *places/locations*. It allows for determining how to move people and goods from one part of the world (Canada or the United Sates) to another in a very systematic and efficient way. For example, a bus that is scheduled to leave Seattle, Washington at 9:00 am and is supposed to arrive in Chicago at 1:00 pm the next day enables the movement of people and goods across time zones and geographical "tracts of time-space" that connect Seattle and Chicago to many other cities and towns in the United States (Giddens, 1990, p. 20). **Second**, *distanciation* is also an important step leading to the second aspect of the dynamism of modernity: **disembedding**. The **disembedding process** requires the *separation of time and space*. In coordinating international air travel, for example, we use a Christian and Western dating system rather than Iranian or Moslem dating systems (i.e., *Hegirah*), which points to the extent to which modernity is also inherently a Westernizing and **Eurocentric** process. Nevertheless, the universalization of a dating system also provides a platform to view the past in unitary forms and ways, which is the **third** reason why *time* and *space distanciation* is an important analytical tool (Latouche, 1996, p. 22; Giddens, 1990, p. 20; Ritzer, 2000, p. 559). However, it is important to note that it was not until 1564 that January 1st became the fixed beginning of the legal year in France and other countries (Latouche, 1996, p. 23). Russia and England adopted this practice in 1725 and 1752, respectively. During the Middle Ages, in contrast, the first of the year in countries, such as Spain and Portugal, was on Christmas Day. In Venice, it was March 1st and in England March 25th. In Rome, it was either January 25th or March 25th. As Latouche (1996, p. 23) maintained, in France, "the legal year began on Easter Day, which was a movable feast: thus 'French-style' year varied between 330 and 400 days". Russia did not change its system of calendar from Julian to Georgian calendar until the formation of the Soviet Union; and, in Greece, this occurred in 1923. The Greenwich Mean Time (GMT) marks the victory of a Newtonian concept of *time* over the more traditional conceptualization of *time* that linked it to seasonal changes and the position of the stars (Latouche, 1996, p. 23).

Disembedding of Social Systems: the second source of dynamism in modernity

As mentioned above, related to the *time* and *space* separation is the process of **disembedding of social systems**, which Giddens identified as another aspect of the dynamism of modernity. The *disembedding of social systems* refers to the "lifting out" or disentangling of social relations from their local contexts and reformulating them across unlimited zones of *time-space* (Giddens, 1991, p. 18). *Disembedding*, then, refers to the idea of highlighting how local and global *spaces* become entangled into a web of relations that have dialectical and contradictory consequences for one another. In this sense, in order to understand what takes shape in a *locality*, we must contextualize it in light of global factors that affect it.

In the condition of modernity, *space* becomes increasingly torn away from *place* mainly because of the effects of the relationships between **absent others** who live in various parts of the world and regions of the country and who are not necessarily involved in face-to-face interactions (Giddens, 1990, p. 18). In other words, what happens in *localities* (i.e., *locales*) is affected by events and relations that are quite distant from them (Giddens, 1990, p. 19). That is, the events that structure *locales* are not "present on the scene", but are invisible distant activities that are far from the *locale* (Giddens, 1990, p. 19). For example, when American politicians passed the **Monroe Doctrine** in the nineteenth century, they devised a policy through which they were able to justify their military interventions in various parts of the world, which resulted in mass murder and loss of wealth and property in non-Western parts of world.

The *Monroe Doctrine* was passed in 1823 at the time when many Latin American countries were becoming independent and severing their relations with Spain. This imperialist and colonialist policy impelled and justified the United States' imposition of its power over regions freeing themselves from European control. According to one American politician, Albert J. Beveridge, US Senator from Indiana, American capitalists were producing more than the population of US could consume. As a result, America needed foreign markets for the extra manufactured industrial goods. The *Monroe Doctrine* was an ideological tool based on the belief that, "The trade of the world must and shall be [under the control of American capitalists]" (Zinn, 2008, p. 29). According to this doctrine and **The Open Door Policy** that was conceived later during the nineteenth century, the United Sates has inherent rights to economic development and resources in the Caribbean, Latin America, Pacific Islands, and Asian markets (Zinn, 2008, p. 28). Military force, invasions, and wars were deemed as appropriate tools and ways of achieving the goal of accessing and exploiting these resources in order to protect the economic interests of American capitalists. As a result, in 1853, 1855, and 1860 the United State intervened militarily in the political affairs of Nicaragua and Argentina, Uruguay, and Portuguese Angola, respectively (Zinn, 2008, p. 28). This example also highlights the fact that **violence** and **militarism** are important defining characteristics of modernity, which points to the connection between modern industrial innovations and the organization of military that dates back to the early days of industrialization (Giddens, 1990, p. 9).

As the above example points out, political documents and ideologies in one part of the world (i.e., the United Sates) had consequences for people in other parts of the world. These other people did not have any say in devising these documents, nor did they reflect their political, social, or economic interests. The *Monroe Declaration* and the *Open Door Policy* were based on the capitalist interests of White Anglo-American male industrialists, who assumed that the world is their oyster. They used racist arguments to assert their inherent rights to exploit labour and resources around the world. These racist arguments derived from and inspired by the ideas of "**American exceptionalism and Manifest Destiny**," which conferred on the US the **"God-given duty to introduce democracy and liberty to other parts of the world in line with the congruent view** that Americans are God's chosen people responsible for civilizing the rest of the world (the discourse of **Manifest Destiny**).

In general, this is an important point to consider in understanding the difference between modern and traditional societies. In modernity, who we are, how we view ourselves, what we consume, the ways in which we organize our lives are influenced by political, economic, and cultural realities, and events in other parts of the world (i.e., by technological trends and innovations and economic changes in other parts of the world). It is in this sense that modernity is considered as having a globalizing effect: it is more likely that we become involved in interactions and relations with individuals who are not physically present (they are absent) and live in other parts of the world (Ritzer, 2000, p. 559). In the above example, *time* and *space* are reformulated and reconstituted, forming a world-historical framework for performing and understanding human action and experience (Giddens, 1990, p. 21).

Part Two

Two Mechanisms of Disembedding: symbolic tokens and expert systems:

As we mentioned earlier in this chapter, **disembedding** refers to "lifting out" or *dislocating* social relations form their *local* contexts of interaction and reformulating them across infinite possibilities of *time-space* (Giddens, 1990, p. 21). *Disembedding* occurs through two main mechanisms of:

1. **symbolic tokens** (i.e., money) and

2. **expert systems**.

Money, as Karl Marx pointed out, is "the universal whore" (sic), which allows individuals to exchange any item for any other, regardless of whether or not they have anything in common (Giddens, 1990, p. 22). For example, a farmer can sell his/her farm products in the market for a fixed price and use the money earned to purchase farm equipment from a dealer of agricultural equipment and products, who then uses that money to order more farm equipment from various parts of the world or to purchase food and other goods for his/her family. These goods and services that are purchased are not equal in value, but money as a *symbolic token* allows for the exchange of such goods in local and global contexts. As Ritzer (2000, p. 559) highlighted, money makes possible the distanciation of *time* and *space* since it allows us to become involved in economic transactions with others who are separated from us by both *space* and *time*.

Expert systems refer to those systems of technical knowledge and professional expertise that are used to organize most aspects of lives in modernity (Giddens, 1990, p. 27). We tend to consult professionals about our taxes, family counseling, preparing a will, and buying or selling stock (Giddens, 1990, p. 27). We live in a system that has incorporated and integrated the knowledge of experts into the structures of life. Both the *expert systems* and *symbolic tokens* are *disembedding* because social relations are removed from the proximities of their contexts (Giddens, 1990, p. 27). For example, consider the reforms that are introduced in schools based on social policies that are decided by experts who are often not aware of the contexts in which teachers teach in different *localities*. These experts base their policy recommendations on quantifiable results of test scores that in themselves are not reflective of the problems and issues that different students in different *localities* face. For example, in a school with a high number of English learner students, students may not do as well on standardized English tests. This does not mean that they are not smart, or teachers are not doing their jobs of teaching them how to read and write. In fact, a qualitative analysis based on classroom observation may reveal that students might have improved greatly in learning grammar and syntax since the beginning of the school year. A universal change to teaching methods recommended by experts based on the result of standardized tests may in fact make the learning environment for the English learners more difficult and have negative consequences in terms of passing standardized English tests, because these studies and recommendations do not account for the context in which teachers teach. In general, although many of these experts have not taught in specific *localities*, their policy recommendation will affect how teachers teach and interact with their students in various *localities* (See Giddens, 1990, p. 28). This is a problem associated with **instrumentalism** (Kubow & Fossum, 2007. P. 14). In this sense, instrumentalism refers to using quantifiable means to evaluate teaching practices by experts who are not directly involved in local educational practices. Instrumentalism has several characteristics, which influence how teaching is evaluated and conceptualized:

a) it promotes predictability and replicability in teaching (one way of teaching suits all students);

b) how to teach is the outcome of scientific studies performed by outsiders with specialized expertise that exclude solutions by local practitioners (experts know better than teachers); and

c) effectiveness of a teacher or program is already decided in advance, with no reference to the contexts in which teaching and learning is shaped; thus, the failure of the teacher is viewed to be due to the fact that he/she did not follow the prescribed ways of teaching promoted by the experts.

Because of the influences of instrumentalism in the education systems across the world, "holistic appraisals that might rely on [teachers] input[s] … are devalued" (Kubow & Fossum, 2007. P. 14).

Another way to understand the effects of *expert systems* is to consider how knowledge about how to teach and what to teach produced in universities in various parts of the world are incorporated into educational policies and teacher education programs in Asia, the Americas, Europe, or Africa. For example, progressive educators who influenced the education system in the United States during the 1920s and 1970s also influenced how educators conceptualized an ideal education system based on student-centred pedagogy (i.e., theory of teaching based on the interests of students that reflect their strengths) in Iran, Russia, Vietnam, Canada, and China (Spring, 2006). Also, educational theories of Paulo Freire conceived in Brazil as a result of working with peasant societies have now become an important aspect of **critical pedagogy** (See Box 4.1-What is critical pedagogy?), as a theoretical and practical approach to educational issues in Canada and the United States and many other parts of the world. Paulo Freire in his books, *Pedagogy of Hope* and *Pedagogy of the Oppressed*, argued that education must be perceived as a process that involves a move towards permanent liberation (See also, Oakes & Lipton, 2003, pp. 34–35). He argued that the hope for better social conditions needs to be understood as an active struggle aimed at attaining better social conditions for all people. **Hope** needs to be seen as a theory of action and *praxis* (i.e., action and reflection). Hope is the central

BOX 4.1 - What is Critical Pedagogy?

Freire's ideas have also influenced **critical pedagogy**. Critical pedagogy is both a school of thought and a form of critique (Barakett & Cleghorn, 2000, p. 34). They criticize the overemphasis of Marxism on historical materialism. They shift the attention from an emphasis on class analysis to an emphasis on how we experience life as social actors and the extent to which the everyday life and culture "represent a new terrain of domination" (Barakett & Cleghorn, 2000, p. 34). They are concerned with the relationship between knowledge and power (Barakett & Cleghorn, 2000, p. 76). Knowledge is socially constructed and reflects the relations of power prevalent in any given society. They ask whose knowledge is considered as the legitimate knowledge and why. Why is it that only certain ways of constructing knowledge are considered as the truth by the dominant groups and other types of knowledge are ignored?

Their aim is to bridge the gap between theory and practice and to change the system. As a result of our education, we come to see the world through the lenses of the dominant society. This is hegemonic in a sense that the ruling elites control how we perceive the world and our place within the societal structures and relations. **Hegemony** refers to cultural and ideological control of the masses without force or coercion. In this sense, the views of the elite become an aspect of the everyday knowledge about the world around us. Putting it differently, the capitalist class, for example, cannot secure control through economic means alone but through ideological control over the civil society (Thompson, 1996, p. 410). Ideological domination (hegemony) coincides with and informs the everyday experiences of the working classes and other subordinated groups (their commonsense). The ways in which we come to understand our environment and social relations is based on terms of reference supplied by the dominant society (McLaren, 1998, p. 178–179). In hegemony, the less powerful are "unknowingly" involved in their own exploitation (McLaren, 1998, p. 178). In general, hegemony refers to domination through consensual forms at various levels: state, church, education, and mass media. For example, as schools promote the idea of individualism (which is central to our understanding of our identities in capitalist nations) they become hegemonic institutions. Individualism is a core aspect of our value system. Our success in school, the job market, and society at large is often viewed in the context of our own individual initiatives, aptitudes, and intelligence and other attributes associated with individual qualities, "while those elements and factors that result in our failure are viewed in the context of psychological ailments that can be remedied through changes in individual attitudes" (Wotherspoon, 2009, p. 113).

The solution is for the less powerful classes in society, such as the working classes, First Nations, and colonized peoples in Asia, Latin America, and Africa, to develop their own alternative counter-hegemonies, which is the goal that liberation theory and critical pedagogy attempt to achieve. Critical pedagogy uses a language of protest that analyzes how schooling and social structures contribute "to poverty, dehumanization, and hopelessness". This language of protest is endowed "with the promise of hope and prospects for meaningful change" (Wotherspoon, 2009, p. 49). It emphasizes that liberation should not be understood in the context of class relations (i.e., economic factors) alone, but also account for other spheres of life and factors, such as culture, religion, gender, "race", sexuality, and law (Barakett & Cleghorn, 2000, p. 35). It also emphasizes the idea that human behaviour is not only a reaction to and a direct result of economic relations and structures within society (Barakett & Cleghorn, 2000, p. 35). We also need to account for the needs, modes of thought, and the motivations of social actors that are shaped by their gender, sexuality, "race", ethnicity, religions, and age in the context of their interactions with others in various institutions, such as the family, media, and legal system. This requires us to be dialectical in our analysis and account for the relationship between social actors and social structures (Barakett & Cleghorn, 2000, p. 35).

According to this perspective, knowledge production is considered to be a political act (Nieto, 2000, p. 313). In other words, knowledge is power; and those who control knowledge production have power over others. School policies at all levels reflect the "political ideology and worldview of the decision maker[s]" (Nieto, 2000, p. 314). Critical pedagogy questions the everyday assumptions of individuals (their commonsense) and points to the contradictions of the myths we believe in (i.e., the discourse of individualism). It places emphasis on people's lived experiences within the context of power dynamics. Such an analysis can develop principles for social transformation, arming and empowering teachers and students to participate in the processes of decision making regarding curriculum construction and school policies (Wotherspoon, 2009). In this sense, it assumes that the best education is the one that starts with learners (Nieto, 2000, p. 318). Theory, they argue, must enable teachers to link their lifeworlds to the struggle for liberation. Critical pedagogy engenders in educators a keen sense of reflexivity, impelling them to remain critical of their own practices and conscious of the social contexts in which they teach and interact: how the context shapes what is possible and what is not.

aspect of sustaining the struggle for a better world: in other words, we must move away from arguments, such as: "there has always been inequality in the world and we will not be able to achieve equality". He maintained that the act of participation in struggles for equality is itself a process that will lead to "improvement" of social conditions. He asserted that without struggle, hope turns into alienation.

Freire's ideas were influential in the formation of **liberation theory**. Liberation theory points out that elite groups in the South (i.e., "underdeveloped" countries) control the system of power and use it to reproduce inequalities that benefit them, but have devastating consequences on the poor and underprivileged classes (Kubow & Fussom, 2007, p. 55). This theory asserts that in order to change the conditions of poverty, all efforts must become focused on bettering the conditions of life for the oppressed groups in the South (Kubow & Fussom, 2007, p. 55). This requires social actors to transform existing power and economic structures. The goals of this theory are to mobilize and awaken exploited and subjugated "minority" groups. An important goal of liberation theory is to provide space and opportunity to those who participate in educational services and programs to affect change. Education from a liberation theory perspective is a process in which the teacher is a facilitator, who instead of lecturing, focuses on problem solving strategies (Kubow & Fussom, 2007, p. 55).

In his book, *Pedagogy of the Oppressed*, Freire proposed that through critical education individuals become aware of their oppression and can act upon that knowledge in order to transform the structures of society that produce oppressive relations. He believed in human liberation through the application of **critical consciousness** and *dialogical methods* of conversation and interaction between individuals. He was critical of **banking approaches** to teaching that construct students as empty vessels who are passive learners. In a banking approach to education and teaching the goal of teachers is to "deposit" useful and official knowledge in the minds of students. In other words, "the teacher teaches and the students learn" (Freire, 2001, p. 89). That is, "the teacher talks and the students listen" (Freire, 2001, p. 89). In this sense, the producer of knowledge is the teacher and students are passive learners. Students do not choose the content of the curriculum (See Box 4.2-What is curriculum?). It is the teacher who determines the content of the program, and students who are not consulted simply adapt to the knowledge that teachers deem important (Freire, 2001, p. 89).

BOX 4.2 - What is curriculum?

Curriculum is defined in number of ways. In general, it can be understood as "what happens to students in school" and refers to all those school experiences that students are exposed to through planned or unplanned activities (Kubow & Fussom, 2007, p. 75). Sonia Nieto defined it as "the organized environment for learning what is thought to be important knowledge" (Nieto, 2000, p. 96). It also refers to a decision-making process that is affected by political, social, and cultural factors, structures, and relations. Curriculum can also be construed as the means through which the goals and objectives of schools are achieved (Henson, 2001, p. 7). For example, in Iran the aim of the education system is to educate students about Islamic tradition and norms. As a result, Iranian students are introduced to many hours of instruction in Islamic studies as part of their curriculum that excludes information about other religious minority groups. Curriculum, then, consists of: a) expressed-written goals, objectives, lesson plans, and units; and b) hidden elements (unintended positive and negative messages) (Nieto, 2000, p. 383). It is also defined as the "planned action for instruction" (Henson, 2001, p. 8). Curriculum, as "planned experiences", moreover, refers to "all the experiences that students have under the guidance of a teacher" (as cited in Henson, 2001, p. 9). School curriculum organizes students' experiences in the context of what is considered as desirable and accepted knowledge and values and norms by the dominant society (McLaren, 1998, p. 167). It reflects the interests of those who produce it (McLaren, 1998, p. 167). It promotes a particular vision of the past and specific values that are deemed important for the reproduction of society in such a way that it privileges the economic, social, and political position of elite groups. For example, Mexican-American students learn about the Westward expansion of the United States into Texas, but they do not learn about the long history and contributions of "Mexicans" to the development of California and Texas: Texas and California were part of Mexico before their annexation by the United States. In this sense, Mexican-American students do not learn about themselves and their roles in the development of North and Central American societies.

That is, the task of the teacher is to narrate facts: The capital of Iran is Tehran. There is no emphasis on a critical discussion of how social, economic, cultural, and political factors affected the establishment of this city as the capital beginning in the 1920s. In such a system, educators regulate how and whose knowledge is communicated and transmitted to students. The curriculum writers and teachers determine how the world is presented to students (Freire, 2001, p. 91).

In a *Banking system (approach)* to education, students are "considered in the world, not with the world or with others" (Freire, 2001, p. 90). That is, they are viewed as objects rather than subjects who are capable of abstract thinking and active participants in, and co-constructors of, their own learning. Students in the banking system are perceived as "spectator[s], not re-creator[s]" of knowledge (Freire, 2001, p. 90). Putting it differently, students are viewed not as conscious and active social actors capable of participating in the education process. They are only "possessor of a consciousness" without being able to use it. Freire argued that in order to achieve liberty and free the oppressed from the control of their oppressors, we need to change our approach to education. Freire maintained that "the interest of the oppressors lies in 'changing the consciousness of the oppressed, not the situation which oppresses them'; for the more the oppressed can be led to adapt to that situation, the more easily they can be dominated" (Freire, 2001, 89). That is, the main task of the elite groups and the dominant society is to control how the oppressed and nondominant classes think about themselves and their societies. If they approach their conditions in a noncritical way, they will not be able to see their conditions as oppressive that lead to their domination.

Freire proposed that students should not be manipulated and controlled in schools. Students must become involved in the process of dialogue with their teachers. The task of educators is to promote those practices that allow pupils to plan and act on the conditions of their lives both in and beyond schools. **Dialogue** plays an important role in a critical approach to education. The role of dialogue is to "validate the voices and subjective experiences of the oppressed [and also] to expose both the subjective and objective nature of ideology" (Barakett & Cleghorn, 2000, p. 73). In this light, education is viewed as *the practice of freedom*. **Dialogic pedagogy** (theory of teaching based on dialogue and analysis as well as action) allows students to narrate who they are, what they do, and why they do it and to act upon this information. For example, Freire attempted to help Brazilian farmworkers to become aware of their exploitation by developing a literacy program that used their experiences as teaching materials to educate them about why and how they are oppressed.

His literacy instructions focused on the social, cultural, political, and economic conditions of farmworkers' lives. He focused on exposing the oppressive structures and relations that resulted in their further marginalization. That is, he was a firm believer in the idea of *praxis*: how knowledge about oppression can be utilized to free individuals when this information forms the basis of human actions. He emphasized both analysis and action. He argued that when we see how power relations function, we then can and need to act upon the information and become effective social actors. In this sense, the act of knowing is considered as a political act. This approach to learning and teaching is in contrast to the ways in which the official knowledge is taught in schools that turns individuals to spectators since such knowledge removes their ideological bases from public debate and critical scrutiny.

As mentioned, Freire promoted the idea of **conscientization** (in Portuguese, *conscientização*) or *critical consciousness*, which refers to the process of awakening students. The aim of this type of education is to empower students to change the world based on their critical understandings of how they are exploited in the world as working class, gay, lesbian, ethnic minorities, peasants, and/or racialized peoples (Kubow & Fussom, 2007, p. 56). In this sense, his arguments are similar to Karl Marx's ideas that pointed to the "numbing effects of domination and alienation in which alienated people become unaware of their condition[s] and their potential[s] to change it" (Kubow & Fussom, 2007, p. 56). In this process, it is acknowledged that we cannot separate ourselves from our own personal worlds. So the best way to learn is to relate the material to the lived experiences of students. That is, school knowledge needs to account for the types of experiences and knowledge that students bring with them to classrooms. For example, when teaching in rural areas of the world, one should not use examples and illustrations of modern malls or elevators to discuss a topic to students who have never seen an elevator. To teach the topic more effectively, it is more logical to use examples from local settings that students can relate to and have experienced.

The practice of *conscientization* asserts that as social actors, we must become aware of how we are affected by structural and ideological factors and socioeconomic relations. In other words, in order to know ourselves and to change the world, the external world first needs to be known. This requires us to problematize the role of dominating structures and groups and their consequences on our and other peoples' lives. **Critical literacy** plays an important role in this process. Freire was able to teach illiterate peasants to become literate in 40 days through his literacy program, which resulted in the Brazilian government to cancel the program and exile him to Chile in 1964 (Kubow & Fussom, 2007, p. 56). The objective of this program was to empower poor Brazilians by making them aware of their conditions and using education as a means to give them the needed tools to confront and deal away with the conditions that resulted in their subordinate positions (Kubow & Fussom, 2007, p. 137). Freire criticized the **dependency theory**, a Marxist and conflict theory, as lacking an action plan to end economic dependency in South America. Dependency theory, which is explored in more detail in Chapter Eight, explains why and how Western countries, due to their exploitation of non-Western countries, became developed and non-Western countries have experienced inequality and became "underdeveloped" due to colonial and postcolonial relations (Kubow & Fussom, 2007, p. 51).

As the above example points out, how we teach is no longer a local process or based on local approaches *per se*, but is influenced by approaches that were (are) conceived in other parts of the world and in different social, economic, and cultural contexts. The same can also be said about the wholesale adaptation of child-rearing practices and ideas that were promoted by American psychologists during the period between 1920s and 1970s by non-Western elites. These ideas were translated into various languages and made accessible to middle class populations in Asia, Africa, and Latin America. This knowledge was used by parents in various parts of the world to socialize their teens based on scientific knowledge that was produced based on research on White, American, middle-class, Christian youth in the United States. In addition, Western knowledge about family relations and adolescence socialization was also incorporated into society and informed the approaches of local experts on family issues. In Iran, for example, experts informed rich and upper-class families that the movement of their children must be controlled and confined. It was suggested that "after sunset, the children should not leave the perimeters of the house for cruising, partying, or games" (as cited in Rejali, 1994, p. 90). These experts also asserted that parents should know the whereabouts of their children, and as such, children should constantly report to their parents, even if their sons are in their twenties (Rejali, 1994, p. 90). Many Iranian experts, furthermore, were given space in weekly radio shows to drive home the need for mental hygiene amongst the youth (Rejali, 1994, p. 86).

As the above discussions point to, modernity refers to the socio-political-cultural-economic changes introduced since the Industrial Revolution, which transformed traditional societies. Central to the characteristics of modernity is its dynamism. Modernity's dynamism is due to the *separation of time and space* and its reconfiguration at the global level and the effects of *disembedding processes*. Modernity is influenced by the rise of bureaucracies as central features of life that affect our everyday interactions. Now that we have a general understating of modernity, it is important to distinguish between **modernity** and **modernism**. In general, modernity refers to the political, philosophical and ethical contexts that "provide[s] the basis for the aesthetic aspects of modernism". In the next section, we briefly discuss modernism.

Modernism

Modernity refers to the historical period and its structural forms and characteristics that highlight the change from traditional societies to modern types. **Modernism** refers to the ideas that were prevalent in modern times. That is, modernism refers "to the philosophy or culture of modern period as a whole" (Cahoon, 1996, p. 13). Thus, modernism represents the aesthetic form of modernity. As alluded to above, modernity's culture is influenced by the "Cartesian binary and dualistic thinking[s] and rational and structural explanation[s] of reality" (Slattery, 1995, p. 16). The world is perceived as constituting realities of stark, irreconcilable opposites: male and female, developed and under-developed, rational and irrational, mind and body. As discussed above, the first term is assumed to be more superior to the second term. The second term defines what the first term is. What is a man? A man is not a female. In other words, a man is not "emotional", rather, he is "rational".

As discussed in Chapter Three, this dualist way of thinking promotes an *either/or* way of conceptualizing the world and ignores or glosses over the many possibilities that exist within the two categories of *difference*. For example, the dichotomy, heterosexual and homosexual, fails to account for the fact that many people are transgendered, bisexual, or asexual. It assumes that heterosexuality is *normal* and homosexuality *abnormal*. This dichotomy also assumes that male and female characteristics are fixed and **essential**. Femininity is defined by reference to the attribute of "caring", assuming that men are always "rational". As such, gay men are considered as "emotional", who act like females. Rather than thinking of these attributes as human qualities, they are conceived along the category of gender. An **essentialist argument** simplifies the multifaceted identities of a particular group and represents them by references to a set of streamlined characteristics, thus denying the individual qualities of its members (Henry & Tator, 2010, p. 381, Glossary). **Essentialism** is the naive and crude reduction of something, such as an idea or process, to a set of biological and/or cultural characteristics that are thought to define all the group members (Henry & Tator, 2010, p. 381, Glossary).

In modernity, the self is also considered as a fixed subject that can be objectively known and represented through "science". National Identity, for example, is assumed to be based on coherent and static entities, represented by references to specific characteristics and based on the norms and value system of the elite groups in society. In modernity, it is also assumed that "science" provides "us" with verifiable knowledge about the world. This knowledge is considered to be the "truth" about the world, which objectively represents and explains it (See Turner, 2003, p. 228). "Science" is viewed as an authoritative voice about the nature of society and natural and physical worlds. "Science" is considered to be *logocentric*. That is, "science" is viewed as a type of language that "reveal[s] truth, moral rightness and beauty" (Seidman, 1994a, p. 202). In modernity, philosophical languages aim at developing universal discourses, defining what is considered real, "true", right, and beautiful (Seidman, 1994a, p. 202). "Science" is considered as the product of unbiased rational approaches to the social, economic, and natural worlds. In the language of "science", reason is considered to be central in determining what is right, what is not acceptable, and what the "truth" is.

Modernity also signals the emergence of a period during which a number of new *avant-garde* movements in various fields, such as literature, "science", and philosophy became popular (Hall, 1996a, p. 16). Modernity requires new ways of reinterpreting the past (Brown, 1996, p. 92). These intellectual and artistic movements and ways of analyzing the past are referred to as **modernism**. Modernism refers to those cultural styles and movements that characterized the first half of the twentieth century (Thompson, 1996, p. 569). Modernism questioned and subverted the nineteenth century forms of **realism** by emphasizing impressionism and subjectivity in writing (Baldwin, Longhurst, McCeacken, Ogborn, & Smith, 2004, p. 400; Perry, Marvin, Peden, & Von Laue, 1995). Modernism focused on the role of the artist and political nature of art (Baldwin, et al., 2004, p. 400). As the domain form of literature and art, **realism** was based on the idea of "rigorous observation of reality" and depicting the world as it actually is: it attempted "to show things as they really are" (Lovell, as cited in Baldwin, et al., 2004, p. 61). In realist novels, the authors used real names for the characters of their novels and the storyline referred to places that were recognizable by the readers (Baldwin, et al., 2004, p. 61). For example, authors such as Émile Zola represented ordinary people, such as the poor, in their day-to-day activities (Perry et al., 1995, pp. 153–155). Charles Dickens also wrote novels about the harsh conditions of the working classes in England (Perry et al., 1995, p. 156). In general, unlike the **romantics** who focused on the inner life and feelings and intuitions, realists assumed that there is a need to shift away from an emphasis on individual human feelings to a focus on the external world (Perry et al., 1995, p. 153).

Modernism, Perry (Perry, 2001, 487) explained, is the continuation of **romanticism**. Modernism questioned the traditional unity and continuity of Western culture by liberating the imagination from those restrictions of realist movements and enabling the readers and viewers to become involved in the process of creation of art and literature (Perry, 2001, p. 488). They questioned the assumption that since the external world is orderly and based on mathematical order and logic, art should attempt to mirror this external and orderly world.

Modernist writers and artists explored *how seeing takes shape rather than what is being perceived and understood differently through different human senses*. Modernists questioned and critiqued essential and fixed narrative points of view and clear-cut moral positions. Rather than emphasizing *sameness*, they highlighted *fragmentation* and *difference* or "collage of different materials". They did not use harmonic chords to create music, or laws of perspective and proportion to create art (Perry, 2001, p. 488). They subverted any notion of objective reality of motion and time. Things do not have the same meanings to everyone, they claimed. They maintained that reality is perceived differently by different people. They posited that the world is created and recreated through human imagination and consciousness.

Modernism was less "concerned with the object itself than with how the artist experienced it" (Perry, 2001, 488). Modernists questioned the aim of the realist to produce an objective picture of reality (Perry, 2001, 488). They were more concerned with the formless, irrational, and mysterious aspects of life. Although modernism represents a fragmented view of subjectivity, it nevertheless considers this aspect of subjectivity as a tragic loss. They pointed out that despite such fragmentations, art can still depict unity, coherence, and meaning that were lost in modern life through promoting **avant-garde** representational and experimental techniques. An example of modernism is the paintings of Picasso (1881–1973) and his style of **cubism**. The cubists attempt to depict a *thing* from multiple perspectives. They do not represent a *thing* from a single point of reference in *space*. They achieve this by deliberately deforming objects in their paintings (Perry, 2001, p. 491). They also emphasized self-reflexivity and rejected the distinction between "high" and "low" as well as popular culture. Postmodernism argues that this style became institutionalized and functioned as the dominant international style. In other words, modernism became a *metanarrative* (i.e., skyscrapers in every modern city or housing projects that were built in major urban centres for the poor).

Conclusion

Modern societies are more complex than previous ones. Social, economic, political, and cultural relations in modern societies are globalized. *Localities* are more than ever directly or indirectly affected by relations and structures that are distant from them. Globalization is an important characteristic of modernity. The pace of change and its scope are accelerated in modern societies. These changes take the form of material, structural, and aesthetic. Modernity is filled with contradictions. It is based on the belief in "science" in promoting peace and prosperity for everyone. It is also a period during which European nations ideologically justified their domination over other groups and racialized nations, resulting in economic inequalities between Euro-Western nation-states and other countries around the world. While the Enlightenment provided a framework to rethink the role of powerful traditional power structures in Europe, the European nations became hegemonic and exploitive by way of their colonialist and imperialist interventions in the tri-continents of Africa, Asia, and Latin America. The separation of *time* and *space*, central to the formation of modern societies, served as a prelude to the globalization of the world. Our lives are more than ever determined by knowledge produced by experts who do not live in our nations, countries, or regions and who may have little or no understanding of and familiarity with our ethnic, racial, and cultural backgrounds in specific *localities*.

Chapter Review Questions

1. What is meant by the following statement: the modern world is a dynamic and "runaway world"?

2. In what ways is modernity characterized by a belief in the power of "science" and technological development as tools in controlling nature and promoting continual human progress?

3. Explore and explain the three main features of modernity.

4. Explain what Giddens meant when he stated that the dynamism of modernity derives from:
    1. separation of time and space;
    2. disembedding of social institutions; and
    3. reflexivity.

5. What did Giddens mean by the separation of time from space?

6. Explore the significance of Giddens' arguments regarding emptying of time and the emptying of space.

7. Distinguish between place and locale. What are the consequences of such a separation in modernity?

8. What are the consequences of the separation of space from place for modern social relations?

9. What were some of the consequences of colonialism?

10. What did Giddens mean by the disembedding process?

11. Explain consequences of the Monroe Doctrine and the Open Door Policy.

12. What are the consequences of symbolic tokens and expert systems in modernity?

13. Explore the main arguments of critical pedagogy.

14. Define and explain the term hegemony.

15. What are the main arguments of the liberation theory?

16. What is meant by critical consciousness?

17. Do you agree with banking approaches to education? Explain.

18. Define curriculum.

19. What does the term dialogic pedagogy imply? Explain.

20. What did Freire mean by the concept of *conscientization*?

21. Distinguish between modernity and modernism.

22. Critique the essentialist arguments.

23. What is meant by the term logocentrism?

24. Distinguish between realism and romanticism.

Critical Thinking Questions

1. In what ways is your life affected by the globalization of the economy and society?

2. Critically evaluate your K-12 educational experiences. Explain your points by providing examples.

3. In what ways do you use essentialist arguments to view and make sense of the world? Explain.

4. Do you think policies/ideologies, such as The Open Door Policy and Monroe Doctrine, still inform US policies around the world? Explain.

CHAPTER FIVE

Modernity, Historical Epochs, Nation-States, and Construction of Identity

Introduction

As mentioned in previous chapters, modernity refers to the historical epoch that accompanied intensive social changes and upheavals in Europe and the rest of the world. In this chapter, we explore the answers to several interrelated questions. What are the sources of these social, economic, cultural, and intellectual changes? What are their characteristics and consequences? How are individuals perceived in modernity? What are the relationships between society and the individual in the modern era?

This chapter is divided into two parts. In Part One, we explore some of the historical epochs that define and shape modernity and briefly explain how Karl Marx, Max Weber, Émile Durkheim, and George Simmel viewed modernity. We focus on the Renaissance and the Enlightenment periods and their consequences for the rise of sociology. We also provide the reader with a working definition of society that highlights the importance and rise of **nation-states** in modernity. We explore how various sociologists viewed society.

In Part Two, we distinguish between the *Enlightenment subject*, the *sociological subject*, and the *postmodern subject*. We examine the main arguments of symbolic interactionism. We also explore in detail how symbolic interactionists, such as **George Herbert Mead**, theorized about identity construction and the formation of **self** in modernity. We discuss the ways in which **utilitarianism, evolutionism, pragmatism, behaviourism**, and **Cooley's** conception of the *looking-glass self* influenced Mead's conception of the self, the *me* and the *I*.

Part One

· ·

Modernity and Historical Epochs

Modernity, for Karl Marx, was characterized by the rise of the capitalist economy (Ritzer, 2000, p. 556). For Max Weber, the modern world was characterized by the rise of formal rationality in the form of bureaucracies at the expense of other forms of rationality, resulting in the advent and rise of the iron cage of formal organizations with their grips on limiting and determining human actions (Ritzer, 2000, p. 556). For Émile Durkheim, modernity was distinguished by the rise of *organic solidarity* and the fading and waning of the *collective consciousness* (Ritzer, 2000, p. 556). George Simmel, for his part, explored the rise of modernity in the context of an analysis of city and money economy that were influential in diffusing modernity (Ritzer, 2000, p. 556). For Simmel, modernity takes shape in the city, which highlights the importance of **urbanism** (the movement of population from rural and agricultural settings to cities and towns as the centres of social, political, economic spheres). These are different approaches to understanding modernity. Together, these views offer us a somewhat holistic ways of looking at the changes that highlight modern societies. In general, modernity, it is suggested, unleashed certain human potentials that were repressed in traditional type societies.

We can conceptualize modernity by reference to the following **historical epochs** (Hall, 1996a, p. 16):

1. the Renaissance and the Reformation;
2. the Enlightenment;
3. the nineteenth century (the age of revolutions and social movements); and
4. the twentieth century.

These historical periods assist us to distinguish between modernity and premodernity by highlighting the discontinuities between modern and traditional societies. In this chapter, we focus on two of these epochs: the Renaissance (Rebirth) and the Enlightenment. The rise of sociology is inextricable from the influences of the Renaissance and the Enlightenment period and the ideas that became popular as a result of the structural changes that were introduced during these two eras in the history of (Western) European societies.

The Renaissance

The Renaissance gave birth to modernity, which began in Italy and eventually spread to other parts of Europe, such as Germany, France, and England (Perry, 2001, p. 213; Kagan et al., 1991, p. 349). During the period of Renaissance, from about the fifteenth century to the rise of the Enlightenment in the eighteenth century, the institutions of the Middle Ages were replaced with modern institutions and ways of thinking about the social, physical, and natural worlds. Europeans began to rethink their relations to the natural and physical world by reinterpreting Greek and Roman knowledge and learning (Perry, 2001, p. 212). Renaissance Europe was a society with a "growing national consciousness and political centralization; an urban economy based on organized commerce and capitalism; and ever greater lay and secular control over thought and culture, including religion" (Kagan et al., 1991, p. 349). Renaissance thinkers viewed the period between the fall of Rome to the 1300s as the Dark Ages and attempted to evoke the secular characteristics and spirit of antiquity (Perry, 2001, p. 212). During this period and by the late fifteenth century, European societies saw an increase in their populations that was decimated by widespread diseases during the Middle Ages. They also experienced a new political order of the nation-state that was being imposed by powerful monarchs and other rulers (Kagan et al., 1991, p. 343). After 1450, we witness the fall of the feudal order and the establishment of integrated and centralized national monarchies (Kagan et al., 1991, p. 344). At this time, the feudal nobility and the clergy were losing their grip on the power structure. In Italy, the city-states, which were developed urban centres, played an important role in changing the nature of feudal society since it was in these cities that people were able to accumulate wealth and relish in the fruits of worldly life (Perry, 2001, p. 213). In these cities, the feudal nobility had less power and were not involved in the political affairs of the city. The new-rich classes in Florence, composed of rising merchant classes, capitalists, and bankers, began to challenge the power of the old rich. By the twelfth century, many of these cities had developed independent political and republican self-government, "built around the office of a chief magistrate" (Perry, 2001, p. 213). These new economic classes with economic and political power used their wealth and had the freedom to promote arts and scholastic endeavours. The elite members of towns that were now playing important economic roles joined the kings and became involved in the administration of the government and the monarchy as advisors and staff (Kagan et al., 1991, p. 344). These monarchies also established standing armies. Professional soldiers and officers who were paid to fight were viewed as more efficient and useful than feudal lords and peasants who battled simply for honor's sake (Kagan et al., 1991, p. 354).

The Renaissance also resulted in the political thought that emphasized and highlighted the importance of **individualism**, which has since become a fundamental aspect of modernity (Perry, 2001, p. 213). This can be seen in the rival of Platonic thought by the Florence Academy. According to Kagan (et al., 1991, p. 349), platonism made a distinction between an eternal world of being and the perishable sphere in which humans actually lived and interacted with one another. It posited that human reason was an element of the eternal world and had preexisted in this pristine world and has continued "to commune with it, as the present knowledge of mathematical and moral truth bore witness". In this light, man (sic) was depicted as a creature who had the freedom, power, and will to be who he or she chooses, "able at will to rise to the height of angels or to descend to the level of pigs" (Kagan et al., 1991, p. 349).

By the fifteenth century, many of these republican forms of government were replaced by either despotic rulers or, in the case of Florence, they were controlled by powerful merchant families, such as the Medici. In these cities, merchants played an important role in political and artistic affairs. As commerce and industries expanded in the city-states, the ideals of individualism and ambition replaced the feudal emphasis on hereditary, social hierarchy, and military aptitudes (Perry, 2001, p. 214). Civic pride and patriotism was the focus of art. At the same time, Renaissance resulted in the rise of secularism and less emphasis on salvation (Perry, 2001, p. 216). Human nature was no longer viewed in light of Christian theology, which identified it as weak and sinful. Rather, the emphasis was on the human capacity, which came to be seen as boundless and infinite.

During this period, **humanism**, or the study of classical Geek and Roman literature, was also considered as central to becoming an educated person and a framework and guide to achieve a good life (Perry, 2001, p. 217). Although humanists did not challenge the Christian belief and the truth of the Bible, they analyzed moral problems from a secular perspective. Humanist scholars played an important role in inventing the idea of the **Middle Ages** in order to separate and distinguish between the ancient world and their own (Perry, 2001, p. 219). This is an example of what Giddens meant when he argued that universalized dating system provided a framework to view the past in unitary forms and ways (Giddens, 1990, p. 20). The humanist Lorenzo Valla (1406–1457), who was a Catholic, became a hero to later Protestants because of his defence of predestination against the advocates of free will. In fact, many early humanists became the supporters of Martin Luther (Kagan et al., 1991, p. 355). Italian humanists also promoted the usefulness of applied knowledge. They argued that education should emphasize individual moral excellence with a focus on public service (Kagan et al., 1991, p. 355). Renaissance art also emphasized and glorified "the secular world, secular learning, and purely human pursuits as ends in themselves" (Kagan et al., 1991, p. 357). It attempted to observe the natural world and highlight human emotions. Because of the new techniques of painting that were now available, they were able to rationalize space by painting a more natural world that was symmetrical and linear (they altered the size of figures and objects in order to provide the viewer a sense of continuity with the painting) (Kagan et al., 1991, p. 357). These artists started to depict more natural and real images of the world around them. The Northern Renaissance thinkers were more concerned with religious reforms and communicated their ideas with lay people, making use of the new printing press to popularize their views (Kagan et al., 1991, p. 367).

The Renaissance also resulted in the formation of new political ideas due to its emphasis on secular thought and rejection of Christian values and norms. **Niccolò Machiavelli** (1469–1527), for example, theorized about how rulers could increase the power of the state as a secular institution (Perry, 2001, p. 219). He maintained that the survival of the state is its main goal that goes above any moral or religious consideration. The ruler should use any means to make sure that the state survives even if that means that the ruler should not honour contracts with others and use violence to achieve this goal (Perry, 2001, p. 219). The main contribution of Machiavelli was that he decoupled political power from Christian and religious values and norms. He studied the state from the perspective of a scientist and from a secularized and rationalized political philosophy (Perry, 2001, p. 219).

Another important change during the era of Renaissance was the rise of vernacular languages and the decline of Latin as the language of communication amongst the elite. With the invention of new printing techniques, books could be written and distributed in the local languages, replacing Latin as the language of power.

The Enlightenment

The Enlightenment emerged in France beginning in the first quarter of the eighteenth century and by the last quarter of the eighteenth century the Enlightenment ideas had become a dominant intellectual canon and convention among the cultured European elites (Hamilton, 1996, p. 27). The Enlightenment paradigm consists of a number of key ideas, values, and principles that were used to understand society and human behaviour. These ideas were quite opposite to the dominant forms of religious ideology prevalent at the time. In general, the *philosophes* agreed on the following principles and ideas: **reason**, **empiricism**, **science**, **universalism**, **progress**, **individualism**, **toleration**, **freedom**, **uniformity**, and **secularism** (See Box 5.1 – The Key Principles of the Enlightenment).

BOX 5.1 - The Key Principles of the Enlightenment

The philosophes emphasized the importance of **reason** and **rationality** as means and methods of organizing information and knowledge based on experience and experiment (Hamilton, 1996, p. 23). They wanted to replace the existing and established forms of knowledge that were based on religious authority and Christian discourses of how the world was created (Hamilton, 1996, p. 30). Reason was viewed in opposition to authority, or those individuals or institutions that had legitimate control over the beliefs and actions of others, and revelation, or the religious ways in which knowledge was said to be communicated to the masses by the Church (Hadden, 1997, p. 16). Yet, as Giddens (1990, p. 48) pointed out, their emphasis on reason coincided with the rise of Europe as a dominant colonizer of the rest of the world. Nevertheless, the philosophes opposed all forms of authority in knowledge (Hadden, 1997, p. 15). They focused on criticizing conceptions of knowledge rather than taking up arms and attempting to dismantle existing social orders (Hadden, 1997, p. 16).

At the time, individuals' place within society, their obligations, and roles were viewed from the perspective of the Christian churches. The dominant view held that there was a Great Chain of Being and that all things in the world were hierarchically arranged with God occupying the highest position. In the middle of this hierarchal positioning of objects, humans, and things, society was separated into estates that were conceptualized in light of a hierarchy of positions (with nobility and clergy forming the highest category and serfs and peasants forming the lowest category). Each of these categories were viewed as either superior or inferior to others (Hadden, 1997, p. 17). This is an example of a **closed class system**, in which there was little to no social mobility between different "classes" in society. One's social position was based on birth and not on individual achievements and characteristics. This is an example of **ascribed status**. It is important to note that between the fourteenth and seventeenth centuries, feudalism, or estate system in the countryside, was being replaced as cities were growing in numbers, commerce developed immensely, and nation-states were substituting the local principalities in many parts of Europe, especially in Western European regions (Hadden, 1997, p. 18). As feudalism was falling, it was very difficult to justify the existing rationale for the hierarchical arrangement of society (Hadden, 1997, p. 18). Instead, the *Enlighteners* wanted to establish a knowledge base that emphasized reason as the progression of rational thought, based upon clear, intrinsic ideas that could be tested and their validity proved and demonstrated by any thinking person (Hamilton, 1996, p. 23).

The *philosophes'* idea of rationality as central in a **scientific** pursuit of knowledge production was allied with an emphasis on **empiricism**. They promoted a scientific approach that was based on experimental methods and observation as keys to developing and expanding all human knowledge (Hamilton, 1996, pp. 23, 28). In this sense, they argued that individuals can realize their potentials through the use of their mind (Hamilton, 1996, p. 28). That is, they believed that humans are capable to use their reason and act upon this understanding in their social, political, economic, and cultural endeavours (Hadden, 1997, p. 17). In other words, they assumed that knowledge was achievable by all and it could be the basis for self-reflection (Hadden, 1997, p. 18). Their conception of **individualism** was based on the notion of a human individual who is capable of reasoning freely as a self-determining and self-directed person (Hadden, 1997, p. 20). However, they did not view "science" as problematic or ideological. They assumed that "science" will produce "verifiable truths" about the social world. They believed that the application of scientific methods would lead to the creation of a new modern individual who through "his" (sic) "scientific" knowledge could master nature (Hamilton, 1996, p. 28).

They maintained that "scientific" knowledge was **universal**, and could be applied to any and every event and the principles of "science" were uniform and the same in all situations (Hamilton, 1996, p. 23). That is, they assumed the general laws of "science" govern the whole of universe without any exceptions.

The *philosophes* were also staunch believers in the idea of **progress**, which translated into the belief in the power of "science" to improve the natural and social conditions of humans. Through the application of "science" and reason, they argued that humanity can increase the level of happiness and well-being of all (Hamilton, 1996, p. 23).

The philosophes also asserted that one cannot subject individual reason to higher authorities. They viewed society as the sum or product of the actions and thoughts of a large number of individuals. That is, individuals were considered as the starting point of action and all knowledge (Hamilton, 1996, p. 23). Like John Locke (1632-1704), they asserted that the human mind at birth is similar to a sheet of paper on which nothing has been written (Hamilton, 1996, p. 37). As mentioned, knowledge was considered to be the product and property of individuals (Hadden, 1997, p. 19). Individuals were seen as having the ability to reason and gain knowledge by using their abstract thinking skills and acting in the world based on that knowledge. The concept of liberal individualism who is a free and independent person able to reason and produce knowledge was a central aspect of the Enlightenment. During this period, individuals involved in economic activities were acting as free and autonomous persons involved in contracts and making deals, which set the basic conditions for the *Philosophes* to theorize about individualism (Hadden, 1997, p. 21). It is the contract (agreement) between humans that governs their actions and relations that many *Philosophes* assumed to be the sources of society and the state (Hadden, 1997, p. 21). The emphasis on **individualism** was criticized by the founders of sociology. In fact, Comte argued that society is a "social fact", and it exists independent of human actions. In general, the individual was viewed as the central component of a liberated society, the source of knowledge, who could through application of reason solve human problems (Hadden, 1997, p. 22).

The Enlighteners also assumed that knowledge of humans and their emotions are the products of their experiences (Hamilton, 1996, p. 37). In other words, they were **empiricists**: they believed that knowledge proceeds from and is the outcome of human experience (Hamilton, 1996, p. 37).

They also maintained all human beings regardless of their differences in terms of religion or morality were practically the same. This is an important point since it was also argued that there is need to **tolerate** other people's culture, as non-European and Christian civilizations and cultural norms are not inherently inferior to that of Europeans (Hamilton, 1996, p. 23). Related to this element of their belief was the faith in **uniformity of human nature** and the idea that human nature was the same everywhere (Hamilton, 1996, p. 23). They assumed that "human nature possesses an essential uniformity" despite its varied empirical manifestations across the globe (Hamilton, 1996, p. 36). In fact, the *philosophes* viewed themselves as cosmopolitan intellectuals and citizens of the world who had the interest of humanity in mind, rather than a specific nation or clan; however, this emphasis was based on European cultural norms and as such was very Eurocentric (Hamilton, 1996, p. 26).

They also emphasized on the importance of **freedom**. They were very critical of the feudal and traditional norms that constrained people's freedom to communicate and determined how they lived their lives. They maintained that traditional norms inhibited the formation of new views, ideas, economic transaction, trade, communication, social interaction, sexuality, and ownership of property. Yet, for the *philosophes*, the extension of freedom, liberty, and democratic rights to women and the lower classes as subjects was problematic and viewed unfavourably (Hamilton, 1996, p. 23).

The *philosophes* were anti-clericalism and emphasized the idea of **secularism**. They pushed for secular knowledge that was free from religious orthodoxies (Hamilton, 1996, p. 23). In this sense, they challenged the traditional worldviews, which were dominated by Christianity (Hamilton, 1996, p. 24).

The era of the Enlightenment was influenced by the **Scientific Revolution** of the previous centuries and the political, social, and economic changes that were prevalent during the eighteenth century (Turner, et al., 2002, p. 2). The Enlightenment was not simply an intellectual revolution; its growth and importance was a response to economic and political changes in the organization of society (Turner, et al., 2002, p. 4). Ritzer (2000, p. 10) maintained that the Enlightenment thinkers were influenced by two currents of seventeenth-century philosophy and "science". Since the Renaissance, the dominance of the Catholic Church was being questioned by the rise of new religious ideas in Europe (i.e., the Reformation). At the same time, due to the effects of war and conquest, many people and groups were experimenting with new ideas that led to the formation and emergence of new political organizations (Turner, et al., 2002, p. 1). New ways of viewing the world through "scientific" lenses were being introduced to society (See Box 5.2 – The Rise of Scientific Methods). Sir Francis Bacon (1561–1626), for example, argued for the systematic approaches to understanding the nature of

BOX 5.2 - The Rise of Scientific Methods

An important change that was significant in bringing about social and cultural transformations since the sixteenth century was the rise in "science" that aimed at analyzing the physical world, nature, and society rather than simply philosophizing about the ideal world and society. In regards to society, the aim was no longer to determine how society ought to look like and be organized; rather the emphasis was on how society is actually organized and how people make sense of their day-to-day activities and relations. By the sixteenth century, the view that the earth was the centre of the universe was shattered, which also put into doubt the Christian belief that the universe has been created for humans by God and the aim of life was to achieve salvation (Perry et al., 1995, p. 31). In 1543, Copernicus (1473–1543) pointed out that the earth revolved around the sun. And the sun was the centre of the universe. His ideas were criticized by the religious order of the time who attacked him by arguing that his ideas went against the scripture that states the Sun is stationary and the earth revolves around it (Perry et al., 1995, p. 33). Galileo Galilei (1564–1642) also argued that knowledge about the physical and natural world must be sought through observation and based on mathematics (Perry et al., 1995, p. 31–32). He argued that nature is uniform everywhere and that one could not make any distinctions between heavenly and earthly bodies (Perry et al., 1995, p. 37). Johannes Kepler (1571–1630) found that planets moved not in a circle but in an ellipse. Sir Isaac Newton (1646–1723) also argued that the mechanical laws of motion and attraction governed and directed celestial (heavenly) and terrestrial (earthly) objects (Perry et al., 1995, p. 31–32). He argued that the same forces that cause an apple to fall from a tree also hold celestial bodies in their orbits (Perry et al., 1995, p. 50). Rene Descartes (1596–1650) also maintained that humans are capable of understanding the world through their mental capacities that follow logical principles and are based on inherent mathematical and causes and effects principles (Perry et al., 1995, p. 46). With these developments also came an emphasis on "scientific" methods based on **inductive** (i.e., empirical, based on experience and experimentation) and **deductive** (i.e., rational) approaches to understanding the universe. In general, as Hamilton (1996, p. 30) observed, Kepler's and Copernicus' astronomic discoveries during the sixteenth and seventeenth centuries that explored the nature of the universe, the explanations and observations of Galileo regarding the movements of the planets, the contributions of the emerging empirical "sciences", and the proliferation of accounts of and stories about distant and exotic societies that were becoming available in the form of traveller's tales, collectively provided an effective framework and base to challenge traditional cosmologies ("a **cosmology** is an intellectual picture or model of the universe") that were based on Christian belief system. "This Christian cosmology placed the earth at the centre of the universe, and Christendom at the centre of the world. This was fertile ground for the Philosophes [to oppose] traditional religious authority" (Hamilton, 1996, p. 30).

the universe. He maintained that such understandings should be verified and tested against facts that are observable (Turner, et al., 2002, p. 1). This view, which was a radical idea at the time, questioned the legitimacy of the Catholic Church's control over knowledge production. The basic assumption, here, is that individuals are capable to produce verifiable information based on experimentation and observation, not only based on religious dogmas. Bacon's argument was the precursor to the great achievements of the sixteenth and seventeenth centuries in astronomy, which culminated in Sir Isaac Newton's famous law of gravity (Turner, et al., 2002, p. 1). During the same period, thinking about the nature of the universe also became more abstract. That is, intellectuals began to articulate basic and fundamental relationships on highly general terms, and, as a result, looked into whether or not tangible and material events in the empirical world followed and conformed to the same general statements (Turner, et al., 2002, p. 2). This is the basic essence of "science".

During the seventeenth century scholars, such as Rene Descartes (1596–1650), Thomas Hobbes (1588–1679), and John Locke (1632–1704), attempted to produce abstract and general systems of ideas that were rational (Ritzer, 2000, p. 10). The Enlightenment thinkers adopted this way of approaching and understanding the social world and attempted to base and develop their ideas on, and from, the real world and to examine and test them in the real world (Ritzer, 2000, p. 10). Their aim was to amalgamate reason with empirical research. As Ritzer (2000, p. 11) asserted, for the Enlightenment thinkers, people were capable of understanding and controlling their social conditions and the world through application of reason and empirical research. The assumption was that the world is verifiable and objective and is governed by certain discoverable laws. These laws could be exposed by social thinkers through the application of reason and empirical research (Ritzer, 2000, p. 11). The ultimate goal was to use this knowledge to create a better and more rational world (Ritzer, 2000, p. 11).

The Enlightenment thinkers' emphasis on reason and empirical research resulted in questioning the importance of religious explanations of the world and the power of traditional authority (Ritzer, 2000, p. 11). The *philosophes* maintained that the world was an orderly and complex entity and it was possible to understand this complexity through reason and systematic accumulation of facts, just like in the physical sciences (Turner, et al., 2002, p. 2). Physics became the model upon which society should be studied and understood (Turner, et al., 2002, p. 3). One of the main concerns of the *philosophes* (or, the Enlighteners) was the freeing of thought about humans from an emphasis on religious speculation. Instead, they analyzed speculations from a "scientific" perspective that highlighted the importance of reason, which reflected their passionate search for "scientific" laws (Turner, et al., 2002, p. 3). The philosophes were critical of the old regimes of political power, and were supportive of the newly formed bourgeoisie, who were involved in and promoted "free trade, free commerce, free industry, free labour, and free opinion" (Turner, et al., 2002, p. 3). It is important to note that the ideas of the *philosophes* were not so much adopted by the poor and disfranchised as they were embraced by the emerging classes of the **bourgeoisie**. Their efforts were financed by the bourgeoisie, who were also the main readers of the *philosophes'* writings. The *Philosophes* argued that humans have certain 'natural rights' and these rights were fundamentally undermined by the existing structures of power. They maintained that the system of power needed to be changed and the new system of order must be compatible with the essence and basic needs of humankind (Turner, et al., 2002, p. 3). They wanted to change society through peaceful measures, such as legislative means. Nevertheless, their ideas indirectly influenced those participating in the French Revolution, which had violent consequences (Turner, et al., 2002, p. 3).

They also emphasized the importance of **progress** in human societies. They assumed that society was governed by the law of progress, much the same way as the law of gravitation was central to the physical world (Turner, et al., 2002, p. 3). The idea was that laws, such as the law of progress, can be used as tools to form a better society. The *philosophes* asserted that the principles of rational thought, "science", and personal freedom would replace religious myths and eliminate the power of the aristocracy and would create better societies and more content individuals (Pampel, 2007, p. 7). Unlike the traditional societies in which human nature, which was thought of as naturally good, had become corrupted, the new rational institutions of modern society would result in the improvement of social life (Pampel, 2007, p. 7).

It is important to note that the ideas of the *philosophes* were influenced by the changes in other aspects of society, such as technological innovations in agriculture, manufacturing, and new ways of warfare (Hamilton, 1996, p. 24). In England and Scotland, the Enlightenment was dominated by social thinkers whose vision of society both reflected and justified the **Industrial Capitalism** that was emerging in England in the nineteenth century (Turner, et al., 2002, p. 2). One of the most well-known of these thinkers was **Adam Smith** (1732–1790), who argued that the path to a better society was through individual freedom; that there should be no constraints placed on individuals in their creative activities. He maintained that when individuals are allowed to compete with one another freely, this would result in the creation of a better society (Turner, et al., 2002, p. 2). The freedom to pursue one's interests would result in economic expansion that would also have wider societal benefits. He also criticized the role of the state in economic affairs. He argued that the state's role should be limited to promoting law and order, defend the country, and administer justice (Perry, 2001, p. 304). Smith is known for his term, *laissez faire*: governments should not intervene in the market and the market should be left to its own devices and internal logic. This idea was in contrast to the **mercantilist theory** that argued governments should introduce laws and regulations to protect national industries by promoting exports and refraining imports (Perry, 2011, p. 304). It is important to note that these changes in the economic system were also accompanied with changes in the realm of ideas: that is, for example, there is a dialectical relationship between new ideas about the national self and the economic bases of society.

In general, the Enlightenment's ideas can be summarized as being characterized by four principles: **anti-clericalism**, which translated into opposing religious persecution; a belief in **empirical knowledge**; an enthusiasm for technological and medical **progress**, which was thought to cure all social ills; and a desire for **reform** in the form of constitutional changes as the *philosophes* questioned French absolutist regime in favour of British style constitution (Hamilton, 1996, p. 36).

Reactions to the Enlightenment

The p*hilosophes'* ideas were also viewed by the ruling classes as dangerous and revolutionary, despite the fact that the *philosophes* themselves did not consider themselves as rebels and revolutionaries.

They assumed that social change could result from the spread of their ideas among men of influence; that is they were **idealist** (Hamilton, 1996, p. 33). It is also important to consider the fact that most of the *philosophes* came from the upper or professional classes of French society (Hamilton, 1996, p. 31). Yet, their ideas influenced those involved in the French Revolution. The violence following the French Revolution elicited reactions to and critique of the Enlightenment by conservative social thinkers of the time. These conservative thinkers influenced the rise of sociology as a "social science". Irving Zeitlin, for example, asserted that the development of early sociology was a reaction to the Enlightenment (as cited in Ritzer, 2000, p. 10). In general, the *philosophes'* influences on sociology were more negative and indirect rather than positive and direct (Ritzer, 2000, p. 10). That is, although we can define classical French sociology as rationalist, empiricist, "scientific", and change oriented, it, nevertheless, contained elements and ideas that were developed in reaction to the Enlightenment.

One of the most extreme reactions to the Enlightenment was proposed by Louis de Bonald (1754–1840) (Hadden, 1997). His solution to the French Revolution was a return to the old system and the assumed harmony and peace that he thought characterized the Middle Ages (Ritzer, 2000, p. 11). He argued that since God is the source of society, a focus on reason is inferior to traditional and religious beliefs and ideas. His logic was that if society is created by God, then people should not attempt to interfere with the divine plan and change any aspect of society, a holy creation (Ritzer, 2000, p. 11). For him, there had always been an authority higher than and superior to humans (Hadden, 1997, p. 24). The conservatives emphasized the importance of extra-individual entities, such as collectives or groups, which were central to the maintenance of what could be called humans (Hadden, 1997, p. 23). Traditional forms of society, such as monogamous family, patriarchal relations, and the monarchy, were viewed as central to reestablishment of social order (See Box 5.3 – Sociology, Conservative Reactions, and the Enlightenment). The critics of the Enlightenment were

BOX 5.3 - Sociology, Conservative Reactions, and the Enlightenment

Several major points arise out of the conservative reaction that informed the rise of classical French sociology:

First, rather than emphasizing individuals, sociologists began to focus on society and large-scale phenomena. Society was conceived as an entity above the individual (Ritzer, 2000, p. 12).

Second, society, rather than individual, was considered as the unit of analysis in sociological research. Society produces individuals and informs their identities through the process of socialization.

Third, society was conceptualized as a system that is made of different interrelated parts, such as statuses, roles, institutions, relationships, and structures. They argued that individuals come to fill these units and structures.

Fourth, society was made of parts that were interdependent on one another. It was assumed that change in one part of the system would result in the creation of instability in the system. As a result, it was argued that change must be introduced with extreme care (Ritzer, 2000, p. 12).

Fifth, they assumed that each part of society has a specific function for its reproduction. Each part satisfies specific needs of individuals. So, if social institutions were to be changed and altered, it would be the individual who will suffer the most. The end result of rapid and unplanned change would be disorder.

Sixth, due to their assumption that each part of the system has a function for the survival of society, they ignored the existing negative aspects of society, as a system, on individuals and groups.

Seventh, the family, occupational groups, and religious organizations were viewed as essential to the survival of the system.

Eighth, they also argued that industrialization, bureaucratization, and urbanization had negative and disorderly consequences for society. They maintained that there is need to develop ways of dealing with such negative consequences.

Ninth, the conservative highlighted the importance of nonrational aspects of life, such as rituals and worship, in the social world (Ritzer, 2000, p. 12).

Tenth, they also asserted that a hierarchical system of rewards and status is a necessary component of any society (Ritzer, 2000, p. 13). It is important to note that this view was questioned by Karl Marx, but it formed the basis of structural functionalism and their proponents' approaches to sociology.

characterized by antimodernist sentiments (Seidman, as cited in Ritzer, 2000, p. 11). Many of the thinkers reacting to the Enlightenment considered tradition, authority, and community as important sources of social cohesion (Hadden, 1997, p. 23). In contradistinction to the Enlighteners who privileged individualism, the conservative thinkers focused on society, as a collective entity informing human actions and thoughts. Society, they argued, was not reducible to its parts: individuals.

The conservatives were critical of the naïve rationalism of the Enlightenment by recognizing the irrational aspects of social life and by assigning them positive values (Ritzer, 2000, pp. 11–12). The conservatives asserted that traditional views, emotionalism, and religion were instrumental principles of social life. They were critical of disorder and chaos and wanted to reinforce traditional forms of social order. For them, the French and Industrial Revolutions were disruptive processes (Ritzer, 2000, p. 12). Social order was a central aspect of any society, an idea that is also a central to Émile Durkhiem's theories (Ritzer, 2000, p. 12). In general, sociology acquires its rationalist approach to society from the liberal thoughts of *philosophes*, but it also adopts from the conservative tradition its main focus and subject matter, an emphasis on society, community, tradition, and collective matters (Hadden, 1997, p. 24). In a sense, sociology is liberal due to its emphasis on progressive change and conservative due to its search for order and stability (Hadden, 1997, p. 25).

Society in Modernity

Sociology is often defined as the study of human societies. As the discussions in Box 5.3 – Sociology, Conservative Reactions, and the Enlightenment suggest, **society** emerges as the most important unit of analysis in modernity. Most contemporary authors who invoke the term "society" use it to refer to societies associated with the rise of modernity (Giddens, 1990, p. 13). As Hiller (2006, p. 7) maintained, traditional type societies were identifiable and distinguishable from each other because people in these communities lived in isolation and their social and cultural boundaries were discernible from one another. The introduction of industrialism and the breakdown of traditional forms of community resulted in the early sociologists to theorize about the complexities of society in modernity (Hiller, 2006, p. 7).

Giddens (1990, p. 13) asserted that although sociologists speak of society, this term is ambiguous and could refer to both "social association" and to a distinct system of social relations. Let us consider how some of the early sociologists during the nineteenth and early twentieth centuries conceptualized society. **George Herbert Mead** (we explore his ideas in more detail in the following sections), for example, viewed society as "the ongoing social process that precedes both the mind and the self" (Ritzer, 2000, p. 355). For him, society exists prior to the individual (Ashley & Orenstein, 2001, p. 400). It is society that provides the context and setting for the development of self. Yet, the existence of society is also contingent on social actors "to create social groups and structures" (Ashley & Orenstein, 2001, p. 400). He viewed human societies as processes of adaptation to the social environment through individual actions. Society gives birth to individuals; and society also emerges out of human interactions (Ashley & Orenstein, 2001, p. 400). The social reality of group structure emerges as individuals take on their roles in society and act upon the expectations associated with those statuses. For Mead, society functions as an adaptive mechanism that produces unity out of diversity (Ashley & Orenstein, 2001, p. 400). Society's existence depends on the actions of individuals who are reflective and possess *mind* and self (Ashley & Orenstein, 2001, p. 401). Yet, *mind* and self are developed only in the context of society. In general, Mead gave society priority over individuals; however, he also stressed that society evolves out of individual behaviours. That is, society emerges out of human communication, but it is also the end result of emerging structures of groups and institutions (Ashley & Orenstein, 2001, p. 402).

Émile Durkheim defined society in a number of ways (Ashley & Orenstein, 2001, p. 86). He, for example, viewed society as a supernatural entity to which individual members tend to show and display awe (Giddens, 1990, p. 13). He also viewed society as an entity that is composed of social parts, which work and function "together to maintain the existence of the whole organization or society" (Ashley & Orenstein, 2001, p. 86). That is, he perceived of society as a social organism (organic analogy). He viewed the emergence of modern societies from an evolutionary perspective in the form of a move from *mechanical* to *organic* type societies that exhibit different divisions of labour and adherence to the *collective consciousness*. In general, he considered society as a distinct aspect of reality that was external to individuals (Ashley & Orenstein, 2001, p. 86). He also believed that society exists both before and after an individual is born and died; yet, it is an external reality that individuals are aware of its existence (Ashley & Orenstein, 2001, p. 88). He viewed a person's self from a dualistic perspective as being composed of two parts: **social** and **individual** (Ashley & Orenstein, 2001, p. 90). Through socialization the **social part** that is "inborn and organic" is developed and is continued through life as a result of interactions with others and in the culture of his/her community/society (Ashley & Orenstein, 2001, p. 90). The social part aims at satisfying the collective goals and is altruistic in its orientation since it attempts to fulfill the social roles defined by society. In contrast, the **individual part** is self-centred and is concerned with satisfying the needs and wants of the individual that are egoistic. In "simple" societies, the social part is dominant. In modern societies, the individual part is dominant. Durkheim maintained that if we want to see a well-functioning society, the social aspect must be well developed and sustained in order to have happy and well-adjusted individuals (Ashley & Orenstein, 2001, p. 90). In short, society outlives the individual as an external force that determines and shapes the actions of individuals (Ashley & Orenstein, 2001, p. 87).

For Karl Marx, society is the outcome and the expression of individual subjectivity; and it is not a system that is alien and impersonal but an aspect of the everyday relations (Ashley & Orenstein, 2001, p. 195). **According to Marx, humans make their own history. He viewed society as a reflection of human labour: human history is the creation of human labour** (Ashley & Orenstein, 2001, p. 195). Marx maintained that human societies have gone through certain stages of development. He promoted an evolutionary understanding of changes in the economic, social, and political structures of human societies. In pre-class Asiatic, Feudal, and Capitalist societies, the foundation and basis of the organization of human experience is the social regulation of labour (Ashley & Orenstein, 2001, p. 196). According to Marx, social and economic relations in society could result in human unhappiness. Yet, it is also within the confinement of society that humans can have an understanding of the "limits and potential of their own humanity" (Ashley & Orenstein, 2001, p. 200). He was critical of the idea of the autonomous individual and considered it as an absurdity (Ashley & Orenstein, 2001, p. 200). In the context of capitalist societies, he maintained, the individual loses his/her control over his/her future and destiny (Ashley & Orenstein, 2001, p. 201). It is in a communist society that the individual can truly be free to express and pursue his/her interests.

Max Weber was critical of an evolutionary approach to the development of societies based on general laws (Ashley & Orenstein, 2001, p. 232). He was also critical of the view that society was an abstract unit of analysis. Instead, he was interested in the actions of individuals as the focus of sociology (Ashley & Orenstein, 2001, p. 232). He wanted to find out how social actors conceptualize their actions in means-ends approaches (Ashley & Orenstein, 2001, p. 232). For example, in a bureaucracy, each individual in the system is assigned specific tasks and goals that must be met. In this way, the activities of individuals are organized by rules and norms that define and limit what a person should do and how to do it. These roles are assigned to individuals in the context of a hierarchical structure. They are the means to achieve the goals of the bureaucracy. These rules and norms make the world of work routinized and formalize the interactions of individuals in the bureaucracy (Ashley & Orenstein, 2001, p. 232). **In short, society for Weber referred to a network of social relations and roles as well as statuses that are the creation of individuals and given meaning by them** (Ashley & Orenstein, 2001, p. 237). Weber assumed that the individual and society could not coexist in harmonious ways and equilibrium (Ashley & Orenstein, 2001, p. 237). Bureaucracies, for example, act as iron cages dominating all aspects of life. For example, it is most likely that if you decide to cut a tree in your yard that is fully grown, you need to get permission from the city officials. If you want to build a house, you need a permit from the city's engineering office. If you want to travel with your daughter to the United States after having separated from your partner, it is likely that you need to have the proper paperwork showing that your ex-partner is aware of this and has given you the permission to take your child with you on reaching the border guards.

From the discussions above it is obvious that social thinkers have provided different and contradictory definitions and understandings of society over the years. To provide you with a general framework to think about society, we argue that what in fact most modern scholars mean by this term is the **nation-state** (Giddens, 1990). In the following section, we provide you with a general discussion about the rise of nation-states and national cultures in modernity.

Modern Nation-States

Modern nation-states are very different in their organization and effects than the premodern states (Giddens, 1990, p. 13). A **state** refers to a political organization or structure that has the power to govern the members of a society (Hiller, 2006, p. 7). The emergence of the modern state as the main institution with sovereignty over other institutions was an important development in modernity (Hiller, 2006, p. 7). A modern state is composed of the government, judiciary, and civil bureaucracies, such as public corporations and regulatory bodies, that aim at controlling the behaviour and actions of large numbers of individuals through the creation, enforcement, and interpretation of rules (Hiller, 2006, p. 7). As the modern states increased their control, they began to govern people with different ethnic, racial, religious, and linguistic characteristics that were very different from the dominant group that controlled the state (Hiller, 2006, p. 7). In modernity, one "nation" comes to control the power of the state and uses it to promote a single national identity based on the values of the dominant cultural, ethnic, racial, and religious group. In this sense, the state and nation are fused and form a whole.

In the **modern era**, a central concern of politicians and social scientists is how to form and create a sense of belonging amongst people; how to construct and perpetuate a sense of nation-hood; how to link people of different backgrounds who speak different languages and have different ethnic allegiances by imposing upon them a unified identity that surpasses any other form of identity, and how best to establish and construct a single political entity that meets the needs of all members of a society.

In contrast to premodern societies, nation-states are characterized by roundedness. There are clear geographical and political boundaries that divide between people who are identified as Italians, Iranians, Brazilians, etc. However, premodern societies did not have clear boundaries and were not as well-integrated and bounded as modern nation-states (Giddens, 1990, p. 14). Agrarian societies had frontiers, but neither they nor smaller agricultural societies and hunting-gathering societies were territorial in the same ways as the state-based societies (Giddens, 1990, p. 14). The disintegration of traditional societies required exploring new ways of integrating people with different backgrounds into a single political entity (Hiller, 2006, p. 7). For example, the term South African society implies that such a society can be distinguished from others based on some semblance of shared characteristics and internal sense of coherence that brings people of various African ethnic backgrounds, White British settlers, and the Boer people (descendents of Dutch colonialists) together (Hiller, 2006, p. 1).

In the context of nation-states, a **society** is a collection of people living as collectives, separate from other people and groups. For example, members of a society share a common language and culture. The Farsi language is the national language of Iran and Shi'a version of Islam is considered as its official religion. And, Iranian New Year is celebrated by its citizens as an important national holiday. In this sense, society refers to people living in a limited or confined territory demarcated by visible or invisible boundaries who share common beliefs, values, and material objects, referred to as **culture**.

The **national culture** in each nation-state reflects the values, norms, and beliefs of the dominant group in that society. However, all modern societies are multicultural and multinational. There are many nations and **subcultures** with different values, norms, and belief systems that reside within any given national society. Even after the establishment of nation-states, due to war, economic interrelationships, expansion of population, the breakdown of feudal societies, colonialism, and industrialization, these societies have become more diverse, which has resulted in an increase in complexity of life in modern societies. For example, American and British cultures have been influencing Canadian society and culture in a number of ways. Canadian political system is based on a British approach to politics. Canadians watch American media and our identities are informed by those cultural values that are reflected in the movies and TV shows produced in America and from their perspectives. At the same time, many British Columbians, especially Indo-Canadians, watch Bollywood movies that are influenced by, for example, Hindu cultural norms and values produced in India and various other parts of the world by Indian artists. Italian-Canadian immigrants and citizens purchase ethnic music produced in Italy (such as in Calabria region in Italy) and continue to be involved in cultural practices that define their identities as both Canadian and Italian.

Despite such influences, the term, "Canadian society", also implies that Canadians are different than the members of other societies due to cultural, linguistic, racial, ethnic, historical, and various other relations, structures, and factors (Hiller, 2006). It is assumed that there are certain characteristics that distinguish Canada from other societies. These characteristics define what it means to be a Canadian and who is a Canadian, establishing categories of "Us" versus "Them". Yet, there are divisions within Canada that undermine the "imagined" internal coherence that is assumed by the term, "Canadian society". For example, "Québec society" is different than Atlantic and Western regions. In Québec, the majority of its residents are Catholic and identify themselves either as French or Québécois.

Characteristics of Modern Societies

Modern societies are characterized by several core features (Hiller, 2006). The first characteristic is the issue of **locality**. A society is formed based on a common territory. In this common territory, people belonging to diverse groups form a cohesive unit. This is due to the fact that living in a shared environment has the potential to result in the creation of feelings of affinity amongst those living in that territory (Hiller, 2006, p. 2). In Canada, due to the country's vast territory and the effects of immigration and settlement of various ethnic groups, many regional cultures and subcultures have emerged with their own distinctive economic and demographic characteristics. Despite the feelings associated with being Canadian, the members of Canadian society tend to view their fellow citizens living in various regions as competitors rather than as compatriots (Hiller, 2006, p. 3).

The second characteristic of society is its levels of **organization.** The survival of a society depends on how well it organizes itself in order to provide for the needs of its communities and members, for example, meeting educational needs, employment requirements, and/or transportation require-ments. There is need for organizations and institutions that create interdependencies. There is also the need for guidelines, laws, and provisions of responsibilities and roles in various areas, such as transportation, broadcasting, and the arts, that must be established for the smooth operation of society (Hiller, 2006, p. 3). An organized set of relationships must be present that not only account for, but also create interdependence between people and regions within a territory. A sense of belong-ing and shared values and norms needs to be established in order to ensure the survival of society. In Canada, different regions provide different goods and services that perpetuate interdependencies. For example, grain is produced in Saskatchewan; Ontario is home to major investment firms and banks; and Atlantic Canada "possesses fishing stock and fishing technology" (Hiller, 2006, p. 3). The Canadian government has also historically enforced regulatory policies, such as tariffs, laws that promoted economic relations between provinces rather than economic relations between provinces and their American neighbours to the south (Hiller, 2006, p. 3).

Another characteristic of a society is **durability.** The relationships between members of a society need to be relatively permanent and durable and cannot be simply based on an ad hoc basis. There is need for a sense of common heritage based on common and shared behavioural patterns and a sense of national coherence. The establishment and reproduction of common reference points are paramount for the reproduction of society to facilitate societal interactions at both macro and micro levels (Hiller, 2006, p. 5). The **discourse of multiculturalism** is one policy the Canadian government has implemented to reinforce a sense of belonging and ensuring the durability and reproduction of society. The education system also plays an important role in promoting a cohesive national identity and the inculcation of national identity in the minds of Canadians.

The fourth characteristic of society is related to issues of **self-identity** (Hiller, 2006, p. 7). The creation and development of a sense of uniqueness (being different from others) promotes societal cohesiveness and endorses shared sentiments that bring people of different regions and ethnic and religious backgrounds within a society closer to one another. Members of a society must develop and have a sense of awareness of their commonality and society. They also need to develop a sense of belonging and attachment to it. This is often achieved through sharing symbols, customs, and heroes and an understanding of the history of the nation. For example, developing a sense of national ident-ity is an important criterion for the reproduction of Canadian society. In Canada, the Québécois have been critical of the formation of a national society, which is viewed as a policy to incorporate and assimilate the French culture into the dominant Anglo-culture of Canada. Canadians also tend to identify with more than one identity. Many Canadians construct their identities as hyphenated-citizens, as both Canadian and something else, such as Italian-Canadian, German-Canadian, and Indo-Canadian. It is important to note that this type of identification is also reinforced by the fact that members of the dominant society may also perpetuate the existence of hyphenated identities, in order to **otherize** them as "foreignness" and to exclude them from full Canadian citizenship. In general, "ideas of nationhood and nationality are used to evoke the broader political coherence of groups as a nation. This coherence produces what Benedict Anderson calls an '**imagined community**', an imagined communal organization that gives a group a sense of their ideal citizenship, but also, in turn, acts as a way of making state power cohere effectively" (emphasis added, Gedalof, Boulter, Faflak, & McFarlane, 2005, p. 28).

We share many national symbols that define us as Canadians. The national anthem is one such symbol. The national flag and the maple leaf also define us as Canadians and separate us from other nationalities. When Canadians travel across Europe, the flag on their bags denotes their Canadian heritage and distinguishes them from American tourists. They also view themselves as firm believers in liberty, equality, peace, pluralism, acceptance, and tolerance. Canada is constructed and construed as a multicultural society in which its citizens are free to be who they want to be. However, the cultural, norms, values, and laws of the country reflect the French and English traditions dominant in Québec and in the rest of Canada, respectively.

Part Two
. . . .
Identity Construction in Modernity

In modernity, social scientists and philosophers began to view and conceptualize human beings differently than in the traditional type societies. "Humans" were no longer viewed as **objects** but, as **subjects** who were rational and had the capacity to think and to determine their own roles and functions within the social life. As Powers (2004, p. 113) explained, "how we have come to view ourselves as **objects** does influence how we interpret and respond to situations [as **subjects**]" (emphasis added). These scholars were interested in interrogating why and how individuals viewed and constructed their identities differently than in traditional type societies due to the consequences of changes that were affecting European societies, such as the rise of the nation-state (i.e., national identity) and the increasing status and roles resulting from the industrialization and specialization at work.

By **identity construction,** we refer to those processes and structures through which we develop conceptions of who we are, how we present ourselves to other people, and how other people view us. Our identities are influenced by multiple factors, such as "race", social class, status, gender, sexuality, ideology, religion, ethnicity, ability, and age, as we interact with other people in institutions, such as the family, economy, and education system. **Identity** refers to our membership in a group or category, including gender, ethnicity, and religion (Powers, 2004, p. 112).

Identity is important because people often react to us because of our membership in categories to which we belong: for example, if one belongs to (or assumed to belong to) the category gay or lesbian, individuals who are homophobic may shun such an individual and discriminate against him or her. How people interact with such an individual has nothing to do with the actual individual characteristics of the person: whether or not this person is a nice individual, is a cheater, or discriminates against others. As Powers (2004, p. 112) stated, "identity captures how we have come to expect to be treated because of our appearance or our memberships, without regard to the true nature of our individual beliefs, actions, or performance".

Identity is socially constructed (Kelly, 1998). Identity construction is affected by the process of **identification**, which refers to a process of constructing who one is that is ongoing. For example, Black identity is not a static sense of **self** (Kelly, 1998, p. 10). The extent to which a person identifies with Black identity depends on whether or not one is recognized and acknowledged as a Black person by non-Black communities (Kelly, 1998, p. 10).

In contrast, **self-concept** refers to those qualities that are essential to our characters as individuals "or reflective of our own current performance potential as individuals" (Powers, 2004, p. 112). It refers to seeing oneself as an **object**. It is about those qualities that one thinks he/she possesses, such as how attractive or smart one is (Powers, 2004, p. 112). **Self**, then, refers to "what makes us unique in [contrast] and comparison" to other people who are "otherwise very similar" to us, for example, in the case of the above example, other Black-Canadians. Yet, it is important to note that there is a socially common aspect to the construction of self that is affected by how society views Black individuals. That is, individual aspects of the self are intertwined with the social aspects of the self that may be shared with others.

According to Hall (1996, p. 597), we can distinguish between three different conceptions of identity in modernity:

1. the *Enlightenment subject*,

2. the *sociological subject*, and

3. the *postmodern subject*.

During the Enlightenment, human subject was perceived as a unified, fully centred, reasoning, active, and sovereign individual. The inner core of the subject was assumed to be present at birth "and unfolded with it" but remained essentially the same throughout the individual's existence (Hall, 1996c, 597). For the Enlighteners, society was composed of the aggregate of individuals. Society was the end result of individual actions and interactions. The unit of analysis was the individual rather than the social structure. These views were debunked by the conservatives and antimodernists in their reactions to the Enlightenment.

For Émile Durkheim, for example, in modern societies, individuals were confronted with the consequences of *anomie*, especially when there are no sufficient moral constraints to curb their desires and wants (Ritzer, 2000, p. 82). As we previously mentioned, because of the rise of *organic solidarity* and the division of labour, individuals become isolated and involved in highly specialized tasks, resulting in *anomic suicide* since social actors become detached from others around them. *Anomic suicide* is the consequence of the "decline in collective morality and the lack of sufficient external regulation of the individual to restrain his or her passions" (Ritzer, 2000, p. 82).

Beginning in the early to mid-1900s, however, some sociologists argued that the inner core of individuals was not something that was autonomous or self-sufficient. The Identity of an individual was a process and the end result of human relations. It was formed in relation to how and when we interact with **significant others** (Hall, 1996c, 597). Significant others are those individuals who play an important role in our embryonic and formative years during the process of **primary socialization**. Primary socialization involves learning the basic elements and knowledge that are deemed necessary for social interaction in society, whether intentionally or unintentionally. Learning language is considered as the basic and the most essential aspect of primary socialization. The family is the main and the most important agent of primary socialization. **Charles Herbert Cooley** argued that the basic unit of society was the primary group, which he identified as those associations that are characterized by face-to-face interactions, associations, and cooperation (Turner et al. 2002, p. 448). Parents, grandparents, caregivers, and teachers play the role of significant others. They inform our conception of **self**. Self is considered as a dimension of **personality**. Personality is defined **as the individual's consistent pattern of attitudes**, **needs**, **behaviours**, **actions**, **thoughts**, **reflections**, and **sentiments**. The self, then, refers to an individual's self-awareness and self-image. It differentiates us from other individuals. It is a dynamic social product. In short, the self is related to society and must be understood in the context of social relations and interactions.

In general, our sense of self is developed as a result of our interactions with significant others and other members of society at work, in schools, the media, the legal system, and others. We first learn about values, norms, and social mores prevalent in our societies in the context of family relations. The main function of the significant others is to transmit the meanings, symbols, and values that are deemed important in the culture to the next generation. This is the view that is put forward by **symbolic interactionism**.

According to **G. H. Mead** and **C. H. Cooley**, two of the most influential symbolic interactionists, the important element in the construction of identity and self is the role of human relations and interaction. This view argues that identity is the outcome of interaction between self and society. Although the subject still has an inner core or essence which could be conceptualized as the "real me", but the sense of self emerges as a result of "a continuous dialogue with the cultural worlds 'outside' and the identities which they offer" (Hall, 1996c, p. 597).

This sociological concept of identity accounts for both "inside" and "outside" factors; that is, between the interactions of the personal and public worlds (Hall, 1996c, 597). We adopt the range of cultural identities that are available to us and internalize their meanings and values by making them part of ourselves, which allows us to coordinate our subjective feelings with the material and objective positions we occupy in the societies in which we live. The function of identity is then to link or stitch "the subject into the structure[s]" of the society (Hall, 1996c, 597–598). In this way, both the subject and the social world are made more stable and predictable. As Mead maintained, a person has a personality, "because he belongs to a community, because he takes over institutions of that community not his own conduct" (Mead, 1961, p. 167).

The sociological conception of the subject assumes it has "a unified and stable identity" (Hall, 1996c, 598). This view is now being questioned by **postmodern thinkers** and theorists, a topic which will be discussed in more detail in Chapter Nine. For now, suffice it to state that the postmodern conception of the subject views it as something that is made of different and contradictory elements. They posit that the self is not a unified and stable entity. Rather, it is fragmented and variable. The postmodern subject lacks any "fixed, essential or permanent identity". In other words, in current societies, we no longer view ourselves based on generalized and essentialized categories: our class position (i.e., as members of working classes) or sexuality (i.e., as gay or lesbian individuals). Who we are is a combination of these identities that are drawn upon during different times and in different places as the basis for our actions. Identity becomes a "movable feast". Who we are is comprised of a series of senses of self that are contradictory and provisional (Hall, 1996c, 598). Who we are is constantly being shaped due to the effects of global and local cultural, political, economic, social, and environmental changes. Postmodernists highlight the fact that we are historically situated, and our conceptions of selves are not determined by our biology. Our identities change during different times and in different spatial conditions: they are not constructed around a unified and coherent sense of self (Hall, 1996c, p. 598). If we think that our selves have coherence to them, this is because of the narrative devices that we use to talk about ourselves, rather than because of the inherent characteristics of self. In the postmodern world, we are confronted with a range of possibilities that we could identify with at any time, "at least temporarily" (Hall, 1996c, p. 598).

Symbolic Interactionism: George Herbert Mead and Charles Horton Cooley

As mentioned, **George Herbert Mead** (1863–1913) and **Charles Horton Cooley** were influential figures in theorizing identity formation and construction in modern societies. They were influenced by the ideas prevalent in the fields of psychology and philosophy. They were interested in understanding how human action reproduces social structures. They explored how face-to-face and micro processes of interaction between individuals integrate and connect individual social actors to the macrostructures of society (Turner et al., 2002, p. 434). Mead, for example, asked: "how do people adjust to one another in face-to-face interactions" (Powers, 2004, p. 109)? They contended that individuals create and recreate their social world through small-scale interpersonal **interactions** and **symbols**; Mead's and Cooley's ideas form the basis of **symbolic interactionism**.

Symbolic interactionism questions the **structural determinism** of structural functionalism and conflict theory, which argue human actions and relations are affected and determined by the social structures in society (Powers, 2004, p. 172). Symbolic interactionism, in contrast, focuses on the agency or the power of individuals to shape their social relations and to redefine shared meanings prevalent in society. It does not deny the effects of structures on individuals; it accounts for them. However, they also look at the role of individuals in redefining these structures of society or in reproducing them through their individual and collective actions.

Symbolic interactionism attempts to answer the following questions:

1. How are society and individual connected and linked?;

2. How do individual acts and social structures influence one another?;

3. How are societies reproduced through the actions and interactions of its individual members?; and

4. How are the thoughts and actions of members of society influenced by the social structures of society (Turner et al., 2002, p. 434)?

These are the questions that scholars, such as Durkheim, Weber, and Marx, did not explore in detail.

Symbolic interactionism is based on three main principles. **First**, it focuses on the interactions between social actors and the world. **Second**, symbolic interactionists are critical of those who consider social structures as static. They conceptualize the actor and the world as dynamic processes (Ritzer, 2000, p. 338). **Third**, symbolic interactionism views social actors as capable and involved in actively interpreting the social world around them (Ritzer, 2000, p. 338).

There are certain principles that are shared by various symbolic interactionists. They are (Ritzer, 2000, p. 357):

1. Humans are able to think abstractly.

2. Our ability to think abstractly is influenced by social interaction.

3. It is through our participation in social interactions that we learn the symbols and meanings that are required to exercise our capacity to think.

4. The fact that we are able to become involved in interactions with others is due to the shared meanings and symbols.

5. Humans can alter the meanings of the symbols they use in actions and interactions since they can interpret situations differently.

6. We are able to make changes and modifications to symbols because we are able to interact with ourselves, which enables us to evaluate and consider possible courses of action, gauge their comparative advantages and disadvantages, and then select one (Ritzer, 2000, p. 357).

7. The systematic and interrelated patterns of action and interaction result in the development of groups and make up society.

In the following section, we explore the main ideas of Mead who is considered as the father of symbolic interactionism.

George Herbert Mead

George Herbert Mead was influenced by several key theoretical and philosophical traditions, such as **utilitarianism**, **evolutionism**, **pragmatism**, **behaviourism**, and **Cooley's** conception of the *looking-glass self* (Turner et al., 2002, p. 435).

Utilitarianism was a popular discourse of analysis during the eighteenth and nineteenth centuries. The utilitarian ideas were promoted by individuals, such as Adam Smith and David Ricardo. They assumed that human action was influenced by **self-interest**. Human nature dictated that humans seek to maximize their 'utility' or benefit in a free and openly competitive marketplace.

Mead adopted three elements of these ideas in developing his theories of social action:

1. actors seek rewards;

2. actors attempt to modify their actions and thoughts to competitive contexts and situations; and

3. actors are goal oriented and their behaviours are influenced by instrumental approaches to social action (Turner et al., 2002, p. 436).

Utilitarianism also assumes that human action is rational. That is, in deciding their actions or judgments, individuals base them on the relevant information that has been gathered; consider the consequences of various types of conduct; and choose the action that will yield the most utility and benefit (Turner et al., 2002, p. 437). Mead's conception of the human mind was influenced by these arguments. He viewed the human mind as a reflective process of thought through which alternatives are weighed and considered.

Mead's ideas were also affected by the ideas of **Charles Darwin**. Mead asserted that at birth an infant is asocial and not yet human. It is through adapting to a social environment that an infant is able to develop behavioural capacities that are unique to humans (Turner et al., 2002, p. 437). He asserted that an infant's humanness is developed through a process of selection. In order for an infant to survive, he/she must adapt to his/her environment, which is composed of people who use language and possess mind and conceptions of self.

Pragmatism was concerned with how the process of thinking inclined individuals to act in certain ways and how actions of individuals had consequences for the thought processes of individuals (Turner et al., 2002, p. 438). Pragmatists viewed thought as a process that enabled humans to adapt to their social environments and to achieve their goals. Pragmatism, then, is concerned with symbols, language, rational thinking, and how the world is affected by the mental capacities of humans (Turner et al., 2002, p. 438).

Mead adopted the emphasis of pragmatism on language and symbols in thought and self-control (Turner et al., 2002, p. 438). Thought, in its lay or scientific forms, is considered as an instrument that is drawn upon to achieve goals (Turner et al., 2002, p. 439). Pragmatists argued that as humans we are constantly adjusting and adapting to our environment (social or physical) and thought is the main means of adapting to our environments. Pragmatists also highlighted the fact that we use our experiences as a way to check our thoughts and conceptions. That is, social actors are **reflective**. In fact, sociologists maintain that **social experience** enables individuals to learn, to think, and to develop behavioural patterns that are also meaningful to others. These ideas were central to the development of Mead's conception of self. He agreed that the adaptation of individuals to their environments was influenced by a constant process of verifying thought and action based on experiment (Turner et al., 2002, p. 439).

In general, **pragmatism** influenced Mead in several ways. **First**, pragmatism assumed that what we consider reality is not an objective phenomenon that actually exists in the real world, as external to us out there. Reality is the outcome of human relations and the end result of humans acting in the world (Ritzer, 2000, p. 338). **Second**, people act upon the world (in the world) based on their experiences that highlight what has worked in the past. They would alter their actions based on what they think no longer works (Ritzer, 2000, p. 338). As Powers (2004, p. 110) explained, "Pragmatism stresses doing what works rather than sticking to failed models of the past". For example, Dewey stressed that lecturing as a method of teaching has failed students. He introduced new methods of teaching, such as field trips and the importance of hands-on experience (experiential learning), that formed the basis of his **child-centered pedagogy** (Powers, 2004, p. 110). **Third**, humans define the objects that they encounter in the world based on their use for them. **Fourth**, the best way to understand who and what individuals are is to observe how they act in the world and in their social relationships with others (Ritzer, 2000, p. 338).

John Dewey's ideas also influenced the symbolic interactionist approach to understanding **mind**. For Dewey, mind was not a structure. Mind was a thinking process that was composed of several stages. The **first** stage involves defining the object. The **second** stage involves delineating possible means of conduct (Ritzer, 2000, p. 338). In the **third** stage, social actors consider and imagine the consequences of the different actions that are open to them. The **last** stage includes choosing the best way of action that is optimal (Ritzer, 2000, p. 338).

John Dewey is labelled a **nominalist pragmatist**. Nominalists do not reject the existence of macrostructures in society. However, they argue that these macrostructures do not determine the consciousness of social actors. Social actors are conceived as being endowed with free wills, "who accept, reject, modify, or otherwise define the community's norms, roles, beliefs" based on self-interests and preconceived plans (as cited in Ritzer, 2000, p. 338). In contrast, Mead's ideas about the self, some critics maintained, was more influenced by **philosophical realism**, which claims that the emphasis of analysis should be on society and the extent to which society determines and influences the mental processes of social actors (Ritzer, 2000, p. 339). In this view, social actors are not really free agents but their ways of thinking and actions are influenced by their communities (Ritzer, 2000, p. 339).

Another pragmatist who also influenced Mead's ideas was William James. James argued that thought enables the individual to deal with the external world, and it is selective as it emphasizes some objects and excludes others (Turner et al., 2002, p. 444). Mead, as a result, conceived of the mind as a process that selectively denotes objects and responds to them (Turner et al., 2002, p. 444). Self and mind are dialectically related to one another (Ritzer, 2000, p. 351). The body becomes self only after a mind has been developed. The self and its ability for reflexivity are also central to the development of mind. However, the self is not simply a mental process but also a social one (Ritzer, 2000, p. 351).

Mead also argued that we can have and develop different self-feelings and act differently depending on the contexts of our social interactions. That is, our **self-concepts** are influenced by how we see ourselves in various social contexts and interactions (Turner et al., 2002, p. 445). For example, a person may be viewed as a cooperative individual in the religious organization he/she belongs to, or as a mediocre student at school. So, he/she may construct his/her self-feelings as a cooperative individual in one context and as a "bad" student in another. This is due to the **reflexive** aspect of the self. **Reflexivity** implies the capacity to place ourselves consciously into others' positions and to behave, view the world, and act as they normally do (Ritzer, 2000, p. 351). It is the ability of the self to think about itself. The self enables individuals to become involved in conversations with other people since one is aware of what one is saying and as such one is able to screen what is being said and to control what is going to be said next (Ritzer, 2000, p. 352).

Mead was also influenced by **behaviourism**. He developed the field of **social behaviourism** as a way to debunk the ideas of **radical behaviourists**, such as John B. Watson. Radical behaviourists focused on observable behaviours (Ritzer, 2000, p. 339). Mead wanted to analyze those covert aspects of behaviour that are not observable. Mead wanted to study these covert behaviours by applying the principles of empiricism and science to them. Mead pointed out that humans have the capacity to think and use language in their interactions in order to decide how to respond to a stimulus (Ritzer, 2000, p. 340). Mead maintained that both covert and overt behaviours must be understood and analyzed through the capacities and abilities of individuals to adjust to society (Turner et al., 2002, p. 439).

In general, Mead's ideas were influenced by an emphasis on the process of thinking and rational conduct (utilitarianism and pragmatism), the importance of competition and struggle and selection of attitudes (Darwinism and utilitarianism), and the importance of adaptation and adjustment to understand human thought and action (Turner et al., 2002, p. 441). He synthesized these ideas into three main propositions:

1. self is the outcome of the process of viewing oneself as an object "in the stream of conscious awareness";
2. self is constructed differently from one experiential situation to another; and
3. there is also unity and stability that informs self in different situations (Turner et al., 2002, p. 445).

Mead and Cooley: the concept of 'looking-glass' self

Cooley's conceptualization of identity and his approach to sociology was a central aspect of Mead's understanding of self and mind (Turner et al., 2002, p. 446). Cooley maintained that society emerges out of reciprocal interactions. Interaction, according to him, is the exchange of gestures, whether facial, bodily, vocal, or linguistic, in groups. He argued that the self is the outcome and the end result and permits the preservation and reproduction of patterns of social organization (Turner et al., 2002, p. 446). That is, social organization is the outcome of people's attachment to groups. These groups link individuals to the larger existing institutions in society (Turner et al., 2002, p. 446). Society consists of and is constructed from small groups and larger social institutions (Turner et al., 2002, p. 446). It is in the contexts of groups that the self originates (Powers, 2004, p. 111). The capacity of humans to interact and to share ideas is the glue that holds society together (Turner et al., 2002, p. 446). Human interactions are possible because individuals are able to use gestures and language to communicate with one another.

According to Cooley, the most important aspect of interaction is the ability of people to assign shared and common meanings to gestures and the ways in which they interpret other people's gestures (Turner et al., 2002, p. 447). Social relations are established due to this ability of humans to communicate through symbols and gestures. Mead adopted this view of social organization as something that is constructed through gestural communication (Turner et al., 2002, p. 447).

According to Mead, human interaction and organization is a process of interpreting signs, imagining and viewing oneself from the position of others, and altering one's behaviour in order to cooperate with others (Turner et al., 2002, p. 447). The self, then, is the most important aspect of creating and maintaining society that emerges from the formation of patterns of communication and interaction.

Another important argument by Cooley was his assertion that humans are able to have **self-consciousness**, which is the end result of communicating with others in groups. This enables people to organize themselves in society (Turner et al., 2002, p. 447). Cooley also argued that the self is the outcome and the capacity to see oneself and **acknowledge oneself as an object**.

We construct who we are based on how we see ourselves through the gestures of others. He asserted that "the images people have of themselves are similar to reflections from 'looking-glass', or mirror; they are provided by the reactions of others to one's behaviour. Thus, by reading the gestures of other humans, [they] see themselves as ... object[s]" (Turner et al., 2002, p. 447). Individuals come to have specific self-concepts of themselves "in ways that mirror how they believe" they are seen by others (Powers, 2004, p. 111). For example, when one is called stupid or slow by others, one may develop self-feelings that may result in having less self-confidence in the future (Powers, 2004, p. 111).

Like seeing an image of ourselves in the mirror, as we also see (imagine) images of ourselves and our appearances and manners in the minds of other people's thoughts, we become affected by them (Cooley, as cited in Turner et al., 2002, p. 447). That is, as we see reflections of ourselves in the "looking-glass of other people's gestures",

1. "we imagine this appearance in the eyes' of others,

2. [we] sense the judgment of others, and

3. [we develop] self-feelings about [ourselves]" (Turner et al., 2002, p. 448).

In other words, self-feelings and self-conscious is the outcome of the process of interaction with others. For example, male Black students are often viewed by their teachers as good athletes rather than as good students (Kelly, 1998, p. 71). This view may inform the self-concept of male Black students negatively about their abilities to become successful academic students and excel in subjects, such as math and sciences. Before immigrating to Canada, many Iranians viewed their identities as White Aryans. However, upon arrival in Canada and after living in this country for a period of time, they may begin to view themselves as non-Whites and visible minorities since the dominant society in Canada views and constructs them as non-Whites. Their racial self-concepts become a reflection of how they imagine other people see them, and they act based on that image in social interactions with other Canadians, not as White people but as "people of colour". In short, the way we come to be aware of ourselves is the outcome of the ways in which other people have responded to us, which influence the ways in which we adjust in our day-to-day interactions with others (Powers, 2004, p. 111).

The availability of stable sets of self-feelings provides human actions stability and predictability and enables cooperation with others (Turner et al., 2002, p. 448). That is, cooperation with others in society is made possible due to the fact that we begin to see ourselves as objects that can be reflected upon because we have the ability to perceive the dispositions of others towards us in the context of developing understandings of the perspectives of a broad 'public' or 'community' (Turner et al., 2002, p. 448). In short, self-concept results from seeing ourselves as an object (Powers, 2004, pp. 111–112).

To recap, self-feelings emerge and are maintained due to the *looking glass* gestures that are emitted by individuals who form our primary groups (Turner et al., 2002, p. 448). The self emerges in the context of face-to-face organized activities in primary groups (Turner et al., 2002, p. 449). In conclusion, Cooley influenced Mead in three distinct ways:

1. the self is the outcome of "the looking-glass of other people's gestures";

2. the self emerges as a result of human interactions in groups; and

3. the self is the basis for social organization (Turner et al., 2002, p. 447).

Play and Game Stages in Child Development and Development of Self

As we have been arguing, Mead (1961, p. 163) was concerned with how the **self** emerges as an object. Mead argued that the self develops in childhood through two stages. Mead explained that children develop their self-concepts and self-feelings through **play** and **game stages**. It is in the first stage (play) that children learn to **take roles** (the idea of **role-taking**). The play stage helps children to develop their personalities by taking on the roles (i.e., expectations associated with a status) of others and imagining the personalities that are associated with statuses, such as parent or teacher. That is, children play as if they are someone else (as cited in Ritzer, 2000, p. 352). For example, many people in North America may have played "Indian" and Cowboy or Teacher and Student. As children, we take on the role of an "Indian" and act accordingly in such a way that we reproduce an image of an "Indian" and his/her actions that are understood by all (although we do it based on stereotypes about how Aboriginal people should act that we have learnt from movies and the literature).

In this way, a child learns to be both a subject (acting like {as} an "Indian") and an object (reproduce an image of the "Indian" that is also shared by others). When we play with other children and take the role of a parent, we learn to evaluate ourselves as our parents would. For example, imagine that a child who plays the role of a parent tells another playmate who is playing the role of his/her child to go and wash her/his hands before eating lunch. In this case, the child evaluates him/herself based on the expectations that his/her parent has of him/her. As a mother or a father, he or she imagines how a mother or a father should behave and say in such a situation. At the play stage, thinking is quite rigid and thus the child can only play one role at a time; he/she cannot assume the roles of multiple actors at the same time. For instance, in a Little League, the child will invariably throw the ball back to the teammate who threw it to him/her; he/she cannot imagine that he/she could also throw the ball to other members on the team.

The second stage is referred to as **game**. The difference between **play** and **game** is that in the context of a game, a child must take into consideration the roles of all other participants and act based on such an understanding. The child must have the attitudes of all the other social actors who are involved in the game (Mead, 1961, p. 164). When one plays baseball, one's actions, during the game, are based on an understanding and assumption of the actions of all others who are also playing the game in different positions. One behaves and acts according to the expectations associated with one's position in the game in relation to all other positions of the rest of the players as they are defined by the rules in the game of baseball. All of these roles associated with different positions in the game also have specific relationships with one another. In a sense, the actions of a player are controlled and determined by him/her being aware of everyone's responsibilities on the team, "at least in so far as those attitudes affect his[/her] own particular response" (Mead, 1961, p. 164).

According to Mead, organized personality arises out of the game (Mead, 1961, p. 165). Mead maintained that "self-consciousness refers to the ability to call out in ourselves a set of definite responses which belong to the others of the group" (Mead, 1961, p. 168). When a child takes "the attitude of the other and allows that attitude of the other to determine the thing he[/she] is going to do with reference to a common end, he[/she] is becoming an organic member of society" (Mead, 1961, p. 166). Mead referred to this common end as the **generalized other**.

The *generalized other* refers to "the organized or social group which gives the individual his[/her] unity of self". In other words, "the attitude of the generalized other is the attitude of the whole community" (Mead, 1961, p. 165). The prerequisite to develop a full sense of self is not just to account for the roles of others in respect to him/herself or to the other members of society, but also to "take their attitudes towards the various phases or aspects of the common social activity in which … they are all involved" (Mead, 1961, p. 164). It is through the *generalized other* that society influences its members and exercises control over them (Mead, 1961, p. 165). The *generalized other* refers to the general norms, values, and mores that are prevalent in and promoted by the culture in which one lives.

In order for us to develop an organized personality and the ability for abstract thinking, we need to take the role of the *generalized other* rather than of discrete others (Ritzer, 2000, p. 353). In other words, to develop a sense of self, we must become members of a community and our actions be directed by the attitudes common to the community to which we belong (Ritzer, 2000, p. 353). This is also a requirement for the development of a community. A community requires its members to behave in accordance with the expectations and attitudes of the *generalized other*. Mead also maintained that although individuals' sense of self shares common characteristics, the self of each person is different from others. He acknowledged that there are many *generalized others* in society since there are many groups in society. For example, we may belong to a specific ethnic/racial group (Arab), a religious group (Orthodox Christianity), sexuality (i.e., gay), and professional organization (i.e., Canadian Sociological Association). He also argued that because humans are capable of thinking, they are also able to change their communities.

Components of self: The "I" and "Me"

According to Mead, the self is composed of two "parts" or phases. The first "part" or phase is labelled *I*, which is the "immediate response of an individual to others" (Ritzer, 2000, p. 354). The *I* is the creative aspect of the self that is unpredictable and spontaneous. The actions of the *I* are not known to individuals in advance of the actions. The actions of *I* surprise us and it is only after the action that we become aware of the *I*. Mead maintained that changes in society are achieved through the actions of the *I*. The self emerges as the result of the interaction between the *me* and the *I*. The *I* is the unsocialized self. The **me** is the socialized aspect of the self. The self is the outcome of juxtaposition of the two (Ashley & Orenstein, 2001, p. 395).

Mead's concept of the self implies that we are both subjects and objects to ourselves. As **subjects**, the *I*, we think, feel, and know ourselves. As **objects**, the *me*, we are capable of evaluating and responding to ourselves. Our social experiences involve the interactions between *I* and *me*: the *I* is spontaneous, active, and experiencing; and the *me* is the conformist, reflective, and experienced (having learned through experience) aspect of the self. The *I* often responds and reacts to the *me* (Ritzer, 2000, p. 355). It is through the *I*, as the creative and imaginative aspect of the self, that new lines of action are suggested.

The *I* provides subjects ways of behaving and actions in and reacting to new social circumstances (Ashley & Orenstein, 2001, p. 404). The *I* is the knowing and self-conscious aspect of the self. When we are involved in situations that are riddled with conflicts, for example, it is the *I* that is aware of the situation that needs to be resolved. The *I* exists at the present time and enables us to reflect on the present situations; it is not "known or reflected on" (Ashley & Orenstein, 2001, p. 404).

The known or the part that is reflected on is the *me* phase. This is the part that has life experiences. The *I* is aware of the *me*, which forms the basis of who the person is. That is, the *me* is the part that contains all the past experiences of the person and what he/she has learnt (Ashley & Orenstein, 2001, p. 405). It contains the knowledge of all the roles and situations that the individual has experienced in the past. The *me* part is aware of the social norms and expectations that are placed on him/her by the society and groups to which the individual belongs. The *me* part is also aware of the consequences of the different actions that are open to the individual (Ashley & Orenstein, 2001, p. 405). Subjects reflect on the *me* part: they are conscious of it. In short, the *me* provides the subject with consistency "by references to social roles and values" prevalent and dominant in society (Ashley & Orenstein, 2001, p. 405).

The *me*, then, refers to the "organized set of attitudes of others which one himself assumes" (sic) (Mead, as cited in Ritzer, 2000, p. 355). The *me* is a reflection of the *generalized other*, or cultural norms and values. The *me* is a reflection of the habitual individual who is conventional and acts according to the expectations of one's society and culture (Ritzer, 2000, p. 355). That is, society dominates and controls the behaviour of individuals through the *me*. Social control happens when the *me* dominates the *I*. The *me* "allows individuals to live comfortably in the social world, while the 'I' makes the change of society possible" (Ritzer, 2000, p. 355). The *me* is involved in self-criticism based on the societal and cultural expectations.

In general, the *me* could be viewed as the judgmental part of the self that is concerned with self-censorship and determining how to act (Ashley & Orenstein, 2001, p. 405). For example, after an exam in which you think you have done very well, the *I* part of yourself wants to announce it to the whole world: "I am so smart. I am going to get an A in my Calculus exam". As you are approaching your friends who also took the same exam, you notice that their faces are "sad" and as you listen to the conversations you note that they all think the exam was hard and that they most probably failed the exam. At this moment, the *me* part of the self appears and based on the accepted social conventions of the *generalized other* (general cultural norms) that teaches one should be sensitive to the feelings of other people deters you from expressing the emotions that the *I* part of the self wants so desperately to act out. In this sense, Mead viewed self-criticism as a reflection of social criticism "and behaviour controlled socially" (Mead, as cited in Ritzer, 2000, p. 355).

In conclusion, Mead (Powers, 2004, pp. 113–114) argued that,

1. Individuals are capable of observing other people's gestures and what they mean.

2. As individuals make sense of the meanings associated with the gestures of other people, they take the role of the other person to determine what the gestures actually mean.

3. As we account for the views of others in social situations, we are also involved in self-reflection since we consider how other people react to us. We consider how we appear to others.

4. We become engaged in considering how to react in a situation based on a series of actions that are open to us, our analysis and understanding of the above stages, and the outcome we want to produce.

5. "Having gone through these various mental exercises based on the interpretation of the actions of others, we must then take the step of modifying our own contact as we continue the interaction".

Conclusion

Sociology has been influenced by the ideas of the Renaissance and the Enlightenment. The ways in which society and individuals are conceptualized are the outcomes of how these views have been critiqued, revised, and synthesized into various theories and perspectives. It is in this context and the rise of modernity that sociology analyzes how society affects individuals and how individuals reproduce society. Sociological theories, such as symbolic interactionism, have been influenced by ideas and theories developed in other disciplines. In this sense, sociology is truly a multidisciplinary approach to understanding human relations and social structures. In the next two chapters, we explore the institutional characteristics of modernity.

Chapter Review Questions

1. What are some of the historical epochs that influenced the rise of modernity?

2. What were the consequences of the Renaissance for the rise of modern societies? Explain.

3. Define humanism.

4. Explore the ideas of Niccolò Machiavelli.

5. Explore the key principles of the Enlightenment. How did they influence sociological theories? Explain.

6. How did the Scientific Revolution influence the ideas of the Enlighteners?

7. Explore the ideas of Adam Smith.

8. What are the four general principles of Enlightenment's ideas? Explain.

9. Discuss and explain how reactions to the Enlightenment thinking and ideas influenced sociology.

10. How did the conservative reaction inform the rise of classical French sociology?

11. Explain and explore how George Herbert Mead, Émile Durkheim, Karl Marx, and Max Weber viewed modernity, society, and individuals.

12. Define modern nation-states and explore their characteristics.

13. In the context of nation-states, what is meant by the term society?

14. What are the main characteristics of modern societies? Explain.

15. Explain what is meant by the Enlightenment subject, the sociological subject, and the postmodern subject. What are the similarities and differences among them?

16. Define the term significant others.

17. Explore the main assumptions and characteristics of symbolic interactionism.

18. How did utilitarianism, evolutionism, pragmatism, behaviourism, and Cooley's conception of the looking-glass self influence Mead's conception of the self? Explain.

19. Discuss the importance of the play and game stages in child development and development of the self.

20. Define the term role-taking.

21. Define the term generalized other.

22. In detail, discuss the ways in which the components of the self complement one another.

Critical Thinking Questions

1. To what extent are national identities important aspects of identity construction in contemporary societies?

2. To what extent are Mead's ideas and theories applicable to how social actors construct their identities in non-Western parts of the world? Explain. Are his ideas and theories Eurocentric?

3. Explore how people construct you and behave towards you in your daily interactions.

4. Is your self-perception and identity a reflection of how other people view you? Explain.

5. Do your ethnicity, "race", gender, age, and social class affect the ways in which people view you?

CHAPTER SIX

∙∙

Industrialization, Political Revolutions, Urbanization, Capitalism, Militarization, and Modernity

Introduction
∙∙

Modernity and modern societies are characterized by four distinct institutional dimensions that are not found in traditional societies (Giddens, 1990, p. 55):

1. Capitalism;
2. Industrialism (i.e., economic development);
3. Surveillance (i.e., control of information and social supervision); and
4. Military power.

In this chapter, we examine the history of **capitalism** and **industrialization** and the rise of the military-industrial-complex. We explore terms and concepts, such as **feudalism**, **guilds**, the **New Deal**, **Taylorism**, **Fordism**, **post-Fordism**, **liberalism**, **welfare state**, **conservatism**, **neoliberalism**, **neoconservatism**, **postindustrialism**, **de-industrialization**, the **Enclosure Act**, **political revolutions**, and **Keynesian economic policies**. Our aim is to provide you with a comprehensive historical account of the economic and political changes that have shaped modern societies.

Modernity's social order in terms of the economy is influenced by the rise of capitalism and industrialism, which have had both positive and negative consequences for groups and peoples around the world. They introduced structural changes to societies that transformed the ways in which people's activities were organized and how work was conceptualized in modern societies. They altered the structure of politics as well as the class structure in Western and European parts of the world and non-Western societies. Although capitalism and industrialization are two distinct processes, they are interrelated. As such, it is important to understand the rise of capitalism and industrialization and their effects on human societies intersectionally.

The accompanying changes in how people produced items of consumption, consumed goods, lived their lives, and interacted with one another became the main focus of research and inquiries by sociologists and other social thinkers of the time. They argued that the changes that were introduced during the Industrial Revolution are important factors in better understanding the development of modern societies (Morgan, 1999, p. 1). In fact, these changes also shed light on why and how sociology developed as a "science" of society (Ritzer, 2000).

Sociologists trace the beginning of industrialization to the period between 1750 and 1825, during which the application of mechanical principles, including steam power, to manufacturing was accelerated. In general, **industrialization** refers to a period of history "when there was a structural change in the economy from ... rural, agricultural setting, with some manufacturing and trade and modest rates of population and economic growth, to a more urbanized, industrial country with a significant demographic upsurge and annual rates of economic growth of about 2 or 3 percent" (Morgan, 1999, p. 3).

The rise of capitalist modes of production and organization also played significant roles in the formation of modern societies in light of the changes in politics, the role of the state, and technological innovations. Fredric Jameson (1991) divided capitalism into three abstract stages, each with their corresponding aesthetic forms. First, **market capitalism** was characterized by steam-driven motors; and *realism* was its aesthetic form. Second, **monopoly capitalism** relied on electric and internal combustion motors to produce goods and commodities; and its aesthetic form is expressed through *modernism*. Third, **consumer capitalism** emphasizes marketing, selling, and consumption of commodities by moving away from an emphasis on the production of goods and services; and *postmodernism* highlights its aesthetic form.

This chapter is divided into three parts. In Part One, we examine how the rise of industrial relations affected European societies in the context of political and demographic changes. In Part Two, we explore the effects of capitalism on modern societies with a focus on **merchant** and **industrial capitalism**. We also discuss **Taylorism** and **Fordism** and their consequences on the structure of work in factories. In Part Three, we offer the reader an examination of the characteristics of the **Keynesian State/Corporate Capitalism**, the **militarization of the world**, and **neoliberalism**. We end this section with a discussion of **Post-Fordism** and **postindustrial** societies.

From Preindustrial to Industrial Societies

Just as we established that modernity presupposes premodernity, the industrial age was also preceded by the preindustrial periods. We can identify three main shifts in **paradigms** that characterize human history: the **first** is "the pre-modern period or the Neolithic Revolution and is dated from about

1000 B.C.E. to 1450 C.E." (Slattery, 1995, p. 18). This period is "characterized by a slow-changing and reversible concept of time rooted in mythology and an artistic culture with integrated artistic styles" (Slattery, 1995, p. 18). The **second shift** is referred to as the modern period or the Industrial Revolution "and is dated from about 1450 to 1960" (Slattery, 1995, p. 18). This period is "characterized by a linear concept of time, called the arrow of time, [and] a bourgeois mass-culture of dominant styles" (Slattery, 1995, p. 18). The **third shift**, which is the focus of Chapter Nine, is the postmodern era that is characterized by the process of globalization, mass/popular culture, and media images.

In preindustrial societies, people lived mainly in the countryside and worked on farms. All members of the family worked together. Food production was carried out by human and animal labour and was the main economic activity. Preindustrial societies were small, closely-knit, and territorially-bounded communities based on kinship relations. Sociologists and anthropologists have delineated four preindustrial societies based on their levels of technology and methods of producing food: **hunting and gathering** (societies typically consisting of between 60 and 100 people whose main occupation was the daily collection of wild plants and hunting wild animals); **pastoral** (societies that live nomadic lives foraging for food for their animals); **horticultural** (mainly sedentary societies in which members are "growers of fruits and vegetables" in garden plots and cleared forests); and **agricultural** (completely sedentary societies in which the main occupation is food production with more complex tools).

Industrialization implies a shift in the ways products are made based on machine production powered by wind, water, and later coal, rather than handmade products using human or animal power (Kelleher & Klein, 2009, p. 8). Industrialization occurred when the place of production shifted from the home and small craft shops to large factories (Perry, Globa, Weeks, Yoshida, & Zelinski, 2007). Industrialization and its attempts to revolutionize the production process through introduction of new technology resulted in the making of new and more efficient and cheaper ways to produce goods (Giddens, 1990, p. 60). During this period, societies transitioned from largely agrarian economies to a machine-based manufacturing of goods and services.

The most significant characteristic of industrialization is the replacement of individual labour and craftsmanship by mechanized mass production and the assembly line. Industrialization was based on specialization of work as well as organizational and intellectual changes in production. It involved the application of mechanical power on a large scale to the process of production. Industrialization revolved around two important principles: division of labour and the use of mechanical, chemical, and power-driven production. **Machinery** plays a central role in the production process in industrial type societies (Giddens, 1990, pp. 55–56). A **machine** is an instrument through which certain predetermined set tasks are accomplished by employing inanimate power as the means of operating the machines (Giddens, 1990, p. 56). Two factors distinguish modern manufacturing from the previous systems: **1)** as a result of the introduction of machinery we notice a decline in the need for labour and skills to work in the factories and **2)** machinery also wrestled control over the nature and pace of work away from the workers (Allen, 1996a, p. 285).

Industrialism also required the regularization of the social organization of production and coordination of human activity, machines, and the production of raw materials and manufactured goods

(Giddens, 1990, p. 56). As a result, workers were grouped together in factories using concentrations of capital equipment that were more efficient in producing goods. The primary objective of industrialization was to reduce real cost per unit of production of goods and services.

Industrialism also had effects not only on the workplace but also on how goods were transported, how humans communicated with one another, and the ways in which they organized national life (Giddens, 1990, p. 56). By the 1750s, for example, the river systems were improved and played an important role in moving goods and products across England. Technological improvements, such as new system of smelting iron, had also had positive impacts on the industrial production (Morgan, 1999, p. 2). During this period, middle-classes and artisans experienced a rise in their incomes due to the growth of domestic markets. In general, England had more developed manufacturing sectors in comparison to other European countries, such as Germany, that were mainly agrarian and rural (Morgan, 1999, p. 2; Seidman, 1994a).

One of the most important impacts of the commercial and industrial revolutions was the weakening of the old economic order in Europe (Turner, et al., 2002, p. 4). The Industrial Revolution resulted in the transformation of many European societies from predominantly agrarian to industrial ones. But, this transformation was not the end result of a single event. Rather, it consisted of a number of interrelated forces and developments (Ritzer, 2000, p. 6). The rise in rationality, the Scientific Revolution, political revolutions, cultural ideals, and technological advancement were central in the rise of the Industrial Revolution and the changing structure of European societies (Pampel, 2007, p. 7). In the era of the Industrial Revolution, commerce and trade were combined with recent scientific and technological advancements that changed the nature of life, first, in England and, then, in other parts of the world.

As mentioned, the introduction of large-scale industry resulted in and required the reorganization of European societies. It is, however, important to note that the structure of most European societies during the eighteenth century was based on the ownership of land. In these societies, the landed gentry (i.e., the land-owning class) was very powerful, both economically and politically (Hamilton, 1996, p. 32). This structure was the end result of the social, political, and economic factors that grappled Europe due to the collapse of the Roman Empire. After the collapse of the Roman Empire in the sixth century, European societies experienced the process of devolution and could be considered as economically "backward" in comparison to other countries and regions in Africa and Asia. Nevertheless, between the sixth and sixteenth centuries, these societies began incorporating techniques and knowledge produced in other parts of the world in order, for example, to increase agricultural production. By incorporating new agricultural methods, the peasantry was able to increase agricultural yields. For instance, starting in the sixth century, a new design of plough in Eastern Europe found its way westward and resulted in an increase in productivity (Harman, 2008, p. 142). The implementation of such techniques and technologies resulted in an increase in the wealth of the landlords, who could then buy luxury items produced by merchants and artisans in the cities.

During the Middle Ages until the end of the eighteenth century, the European social structures were influenced by the Roman socioeconomic practices. Until, the tenth century, the barons and landlords adopted the Roman practice of slave-labour to cultivate the land. With the introduction of new technologies and farming techniques, the relationship between the landlords and peasants also changed. Starting around the tenth century, the barons began the practice of **serfdom**. According to this new arrangement, the peasants were given "control" over parcels of land, and in return, they paid taxes and tribute to the landlord. As a result, the serfs had a reason to incorporate new techniques and increase the yield of the land. This had a positive ripple effect on wealth accumulation in Europe: the landlords were able to increase their economic power.

The landlords also forced many free peasants into **serfdom**. As a result, a new system of **feudal serfdom** became a central defining feature of European system (Harman, 2008, p. 144). Those who controlled and owned the extra food and agricultural products could exchange it for goods brought over by travelling "merchants". The landlords and barons were able to exchange these products for weapons and silk or other products, such as iron and sickles, that could be provided to peasants to increase their productivity and produce more cash crops, which could, then, be sold in the market. These changes resulted in the rise of wealth in rural areas and the growth of cities. It is important to note that after the collapse of the Roman Empire most of the towns in Europe were small or non-existent. Most towns functioned as administrative centres for religious centres and bigger barons (Harman, 2008, p. 141). Nevertheless, within cities, the power of small artisans grew. As the power of cities increased, walls were erected to protect the townspeople from outside intrusions. These artisans also established urban militias to further protect themselves from outsiders and landlords (Harman, 2008, p. 144). In contrast to rural areas, where ancient customs were still central to the organization of life, "a new evolving 'law of merchants' regulated much of the commercial activity" in the towns (Heilbroner, 1989, p. 31). Although the growth of cities was a slow process due to lack of roads and efficient means of transporting goods and labour, during the 1000 years of the Middle Ages, about 1000 towns were erected in Europe, which became the basis for the commercialization of Europe.

The rise of cities and the travelling and itinerant merchants were two of the factors that were responsible for the development of a market economy in Europe. The travelling merchants played an important role in the rise of urbanization of medieval life (Heilbroner, 1989, p. 44). During most of this period, the fair, which consisted of travelling merchants, would move from one region to another during specific times that often coincided with social holidays or religious festivals to sell goods that were not produced locally (Heilbroner, 1989, pp. 31–32). They often stopped at local castles or burgs, which resulted in the establishment of permanent trading posts. These burgs were eventually transformed into the inner cores of small towns. They were not part of the manor and had strange and apprehensive relations to the manorial world (Heilbroner, 1989, p. 44). In contrast to the manorial systems, these burgs were independent units and "outside the main framework of power" (Heilbroner, 1989, p. 44). They developed independent codes of law, mores, and institutions of governance that eventually replaced the power structures of the feudal systems. By the twelfth century, for example, the commercial burg of the Bruges had overtaken the manor in terms of size and economic power and importance. In the towns, we also find the first stages of the development of centres of medieval "industrial production", such as "glaziers and masons, expert armorers and metal workers, fine weavers and dyers" (Heilbroner, 1989, p. 32). The lack of usage of common coins and a common law, however, made it more difficult for merchants in different parts of Europe to become involved in economic activities with one another.

In general, during the Middle Ages, the towns were alternative sources of power in Europe. They were dependent on trade, commerce, and manufacturing. They had developed independent systems of rules or *charters* that set them apart from estates and manorial feudal systems of power. During the thirteenth and fourteenth centuries, for example, communes or city-states were becoming the dominant form of sociopolitical organizations in northern Italy and Flanders. Some of the best known cities were Venice, Florence, and Siena in Italy (Held, 1996, p. 64). In these cities, artists and scholars like Dante began producing regional literature in the local idiom that was later drawn upon as the source of national language. Starting in the thirteenth century, kings also began to increase their power over the barons by establishing "universal" and national systems of courts that partly undermined the power of barons. The kings also increased their power by providing towns more independence and by using them as counterforces to the power of local barons.

The rise of urban traders and their eventual transformation into small and large merchants also required new written methods of keeping accounts and business contracts. Rather than relying on the legal decisions made by the lords in the villages, which were ad hoc, these merchants established a legal system and written laws (Harman, 2008, p. 145). Many of the urban merchants also began to become literate in their own local vernaculars. This eventually resulted in the decline of the power of Latin as the "official" written language. The power of monasteries also declined since priests were no longer the "only" literate people and the importance of Latin as the language in which knowledge could be preserved and communicated was declining (Harman, 2008, p. 144). At the same time, the importance of universities that were established in cities like Paris increased. These new institutions of learning and their tutors that replaced monasteries and their instructors produced knowledge outside the control of the Church and religious authorities. University tutors were also able to earn a living as tutors. Many of them travelled to Moorish Spain, Syria, and other parts of the Middle East to have access to Greek and Arabic translations of Classical Greek texts. They studied these nonreligious texts and synthesized these ideas and reintroduced them to Europeans (Harman, 2008, p. 145). At first, these scholars focused on generating new ideas based on these texts. Abelard, for example, in the twelfth century, emphasized the importance of reason and stated that the task of scholars and scholarship is to understand the origin of hidden things through the application of reason (as cited in Harman, 2008, p. 145). These ideas and individuals were viewed as dangerous since they questioned and subverted the power of the Catholic Church. Abelard's ideas were attacked due to his insistence that through human reason a person could "comprehend God altogether" (as cited in Harman, 2008, p. 146). A lot of practical knowledge was also produced starting in this era. For example, Roger Bacon was the first person in the West to come up with the formula for gunpowder and designed magnifications of mirrors and lenses (Harman, 2008, p. 146). The "new" knowledge gained from the translation of Arabic, Greek, Chinese, and Roman texts was also used by millwrights, blacksmiths, artisans, and others to improve the tools of their trades. This was a great impetus in the creation of innovative tools and more new knowledge. As Herman (2008, p. 146) also pointed out, "the spinning wheel and the compass arrived from the Far East in the twelfth century, and the rudder replaced the steering oar in the thirteenth century, enormously increasing the reliability of sea transport". The introduction of the cannon in 1320 also transformed warfare. These innovations were central in the early colonial exploration of the world and the domination of local people by Spanish and Portuguese "explorers".

During the fourteenth century, however, as a result of many wars fought in Europe and elsewhere, innovation and technical advances were severely hindered. The feudal lords' lifestyle was based on consumptions of luxury goods and military honour gained through waging wars. For example, many of the legends during this period mythologized the efforts and policies of those who waged wars on Moslems who controlled Jerusalem (i.e., the Crusaders). There were also wars between Norman Kings who attempted to control Scotland, Wales, and much of England. As well, there were wars between 'German 'Holy Roman' emperors and French Kings allied with the pope" (Herman, 2008, p. 147). During this time period, the popes also attempted to centralize their control over abbeys and bishoprics, "so as to impose a near-theocratic structure on the whole of Europe" (Herman, 2008, p. 147). The Church aimed at establishing itself as the dominant force in society. It also attempted to create peace between the warring lords (Herman, 2008, p. 147). At the same time, the Church promoted the Crusade and persuaded the kings and knights to invade the Middle East and destroy property and rape women of both Moslem and non-Catholic Christian backgrounds. The other negative aspect of papal ambitions was the devastating wars between the popes and French Kings and the European emperors (Herman, 2008, p. 148).

The power of the Church and the kings and knights were very much intertwined during this period and was based on a commonsense approach to religious texts. The Church and the kings were considered as God's representation on earth. In fact, the Cathedrals and other religious icons that were built were manifestations of the strength and power of these elite groups in society. The introduction of new ideas and Greek knowledge to the society was viewed as a dangerous element by the Church and the papacy. The belief in reason was counter to the belief in superstitious and religious ideas that promoted the interests of the elites. Beginning in the thirteenth century, the Catholic Church began the process of silencing those who were promoting "revolutionary ideas". By the fourteenth century, the Inquisition started and the Church practiced burning of people for promoting unorthodoxy and heresy (Herman, 2008, p. 148). At this time, the emphasis of scholars was on textual analysis of texts that did not question the authority of the Church and the European elite groups.

Beginning in the fifteenth century, we also notice a slow amalgamation of European states and their economies into large units (Heilbroner, 1989, p. 47). That is, the compartment and isolated units of government in Europe were now being organized into larger and more powerful political units. During this time, the city burghers also began to support the monarchies and "disassociated themselves from the local feudal lords" (Heilbroner, 1989, p. 47). That is, both the monarchs and the occupants of towns (bourgeois) combined their powers to "bring about the growth of centralized governments" in Europe. The rise of centralized governments in Europe from the tenth to sixteenth century not only resulted in the unification of law and money, but it also resulted in stimulation of business and commerce in Europe. In fact, the establishment of larger and stronger political units brought about a slow but steady growth in commercialized economic life. One of the effects of this political organizational remapping of Europe was the standardization of money, laws, units of measurement, and the reduction in the cost of moving goods from one area to another within a region, which made commerce more efficient. For example, during the fourteenth and fifteenth centuries, there were a number of toll stations within a region, and a travelling merchant would have to travel through a number of different sovereignties in order to sell his goods. The centralization of power made it easier for merchants to travel from one region to another. The significant point here is that the association between monarchs and bourgeois brought significant economic and political changes to life in Europe. Not only the growth of monarchies resulted in the demand for luxury items that then stimulated the need for manufactured goods, but the rise of centralized governments and larger political units also resulted in the development of (mercenary) armies (standing armies) and modernization of weaponry. Centralized governments also played an important role in funding European expeditions into various parts of the world, starting in the fifteenth century (i.e., the era of colonialism).

Despite such changes, however, by the eighteenth century, there were still no economically defined modern social classes. The society still consisted of **orders**. In eighteenth-century France, for example, these orders were represented as three **estates** (i.e., the clergy, the nobility, and the 'Third Estate', which included all other individuals, including wealthy bourgeois and poor peasants) (Hamilton, 1996, p. 32). Despite variations in their powers, landowners formed one of the most important and powerful groups in most European states (Hamilton, 1996, p. 32). Below this 'order' was a class of traditional professional 'orders', such as the lawyers, clerics, and state officials (Hamilton, 1996, p. 32). The traditional merchant 'order' of feudalism was placed below the traditional professional 'order', consisting of urban craftsmen "from the wealthy goldsmiths, perfumeries or tailors who worked for the nobility, through to an assortment of printers, furniture makers, or carriage makers, down to modest shoe makers or masons" (Hamilton, 1996, p. 32). At the bottom of this social hierarchy was "a structure of small labourers or gentry farmers" (Hamilton, 1996, p. 32). We can also add to this list the emerging middle-class, whose members invested in new forms of manufacturing and "a large class of domestic servants and a small urban working class" (Hamilton, 1996, p. 32). We can safely state that the majority of the population was classified as peasants or small landholders who occupied the bottom of the social hierarchy. These societies were characterized by strong forms of social control, and there was very limited social mobility between classes.

By the advent of the French Revolution with its emphasis on liberty and parliamentary politics, moreover, the landed aristocracy in France had lost much of its power and wealth (See Box 6.1-Political Changes: liberalism, individual rights, and justice). As the nobility faced economic hardship, the newly emerging bourgeoisie purchased their land. By 1789, they bought their way into the titles and ranks of the nobility since the financially constrained monarchy wholesaled titles to these upwardly mobile classes and families (Turner, et al., 2002, p. 5). The monarchy was very much dependent on the financial support of the bourgeoisie. The actual power of the monarchy by now laid in the hands of the professional state bureaucrats and administrators, most of whom were enlisted from the emerging bourgeoisie class (Turner, et al., 2002, p. 5). Taxes were also collected by independent financiers who were given the right to collect the taxes by the monarchy in return for a fixed amount

BOX 6.1 - Political Changes: liberalism, individual rights, and justice

Two main political revolutions brought about major changes in how people came to think of themselves as individuals with rights and responsibilities. The French Revolution in 1789 and the American Revolution (1776) were symbols of breaking away from traditional forms of government by introducing new forms of political ideology. Howard Zinn (2003, p. 58) asserted that it was through the language of liberty and equality that American elites were able to unite the population of the American colonies, especially the White population, to fight against British colonialism without actually ending inequality or slavery. The United States, as a legal entity and as a nation, was a means through which a group of rich White men in America were able to legitimize their control over the land and its resources (Zinn, 2003, p. 59). The English, after defeating the French, were in need of revenues to pay for the war. They looked to their colonies in North America to achieve this goal. The economic activities in the colonies had become an important aspect of the British economy. In fact, by 1770, it was estimated to be worth 2,800,000 pounds (Zinn, 2003, p. 60). American leadership, such as lawyers and merchants, which was excluded from benefiting from the British colonial rule after the defeat of the French, organized caucuses that attempted to form and mobilize lower-classes for their own purposes (Zinn, 2003, pp. 60–61).

The revolutionary leadership had to rely on a political and moral language that could downplay the tension between upper and lower classes. This language needed to be vague enough to soften the existing class differences amongst the revolutionary groups and the general population and general enough to bring people of diverse backgrounds together and focus their anger and criticism against the British (Zinn, 2003, p. 68). The basis of this language was provided by Tom Paine's speeches, which questioned the idea that kings have a divine right to rule. The *Declaration of Independence* signed and ratified on July 4, 1776 provided the discourse that ended the colonial rule of Britain over its American colonies: "***We hold these truths to be self-evident, that all men are created equal, that they are endowed by their Creator with certain unalienable Rights, that among these are Life, Liberty and the pursuit of Happiness***. That to secure these rights, governments are instituted among Men, deriving their just powers from the consent of governed, that whenever any Form of Government becomes destructive of these ends, it is the Right of the People to alter or to abolish it, and to institute new Government" (emphasis added, U.S. National Archives and Records Administration, 2013; Zinn, 2003, p. 71).

However, many Americans were excluded from this document: women, Blacks, poor Whites, and "Indians" (Zinn, 2003, p. 72). A paragraph in the *Declaration of Independence*, in fact, demonized "Indians": "[The King] has excited domestic insurrections amongst us, and has endeavoured to bring on the inhabitants of our frontiers, the merciless Indian savages, whose known rule of warfare is an undistinguishable destruction of all ages, sexes and conditions" (as cited in Zinn, 2003, p. 72). This view of the "Indian" considered him/her as "uncivilized" beings. In fact, in 1755, Penobscot Indians were referred to as "enemies" and "traitors" and the legislature of Massachusetts set a bounty of twenty to forty pounds for every scalp of "Indian" men, children, and women killed. Also, Thomas Jefferson's paragraph about Black slaves was omitted from the *Declaration of Independence* since many of those involved in the revolutionary leadership did not want to end slavery. This is not to say that the ideas promoted by these men and their attempts to bring about equality should be ignored. The point here is that despite the consequences of such ideas on the "evolution" of human societies across the globe, we must also understand how the Declaration, or for that matter, any other political treaty and document, have functioned to organize and mobilize specific groups while ignoring and excluding others (Zinn, 2003, p. 73).

The *Declaration of Independence* and its emphasis on equality was not a new idea. In fact, since the 1600s, many scholars and philosophers like Thomas Hobbes (1588–1679), John Locke (1632–1704), and Adam Smith (1723–1790) emphasized individual liberty and rights in their writings. This is a major defining characteristic of modernity that highlights the change away from an emphasis on one's moral duties to the king (i.e., political rulers) and to God in traditional societies. These scholars and philosophers promoted an understanding of individuals that emphasized self-interest, individual rights, liberty, and justice. The American *Declaration of Independence* was also influenced by the ideas of John Locke expressed in his *Second Treatise on Government*. His ideas were formed during the English uprisings in the late 1600s to set up parliamentary governments. Locke believed that in setting up governments, individuals did not give up their natural rights to any government authority (Perry et al., 1995, p. 58). He argued that the founders of the state should aim at preserving the natural rights of individuals and to account for the will of the people (Perry et al., 1995, p. 90). What Locke is pointing out here is that the origin of the state is based on a social contract (McCullough, 2010, p. 10). His other assumption is that "human nature is rational and self-interested" (McCullough, 2010, p. 10). He distinguished between the *natural liberty of man* and the *liberty of man in society*. The former refers to the fact that individuals are free from any superior power "and [are] not to be under the will or legislative authority of man, but to have only the law of nature of his rule" (as cited in McCullough, 2010, p. 10). Locke maintained that in a **state of nature** human actions and relations are determined by "consent in commonwealth" (as cited in McCullough, 2010, p. 10). Unlike Hobbes, he did not view the *natural state* as brutish and poor. Rather, the *natural state* refers to a state in which there are no common judges to protect individuals' rights of property, life, and liberty (as cited in McCullough, 2010, p. 10). What is lacking in the *state of nature* are: "a settled and known law ... secondly, a known and indifferent judge, with authority to resolve disputes according to established law; and thirdly, the power to execute the judge's sentence when right" (as cited in McCullough, 2010, p. 10). Locke, however, did not question the prevalence of inequalities in property and wealth in his writings (Zinn, 2003, p. 73). In fact, his revolutionary ideas about individual rights supported the "free development of mercantile capitalism" in England and beyond (Zinn, 2003, p. 73).

Even in the *Declaration of Independence*, the term "people" refers to the capitalist class, the merchants, and the country gentlemen. This document supports the economic activities of the elite classes in society. Consider, for example, the fact that the majority of the leaders of the American Revolution and those who signed the Declaration had held colonial offices under the British (Zinn, 2003, p. 74). After the signing of this document, moreover, the rich were excluded from being drafted into the military and could substitute someone else by paying these individuals to enlist in the army instead of them (Zinn, 2003, p. 75). In Maryland, according to the new constitution of 1776, to be elected for the governor position, one needed to have 5,000 pounds in property; to run for the senate office, one needed to have 1,000 pounds in wealth. That is, the majority of the American people at the time could not run for such offices and were excluded from political decision making processes (Zinn, 2003, p. 82). Even when one looks at the processes of land distribution after the British Loyalists fled the United States, it becomes apparent that most of the land was given to the revolutionary leadership (those men who were already powerful and wealthy) and the rest was given to small farmers: creating one of the richest ruling elite in history and giving enough to the emerging middle classes to act as a buffer between the rich and the poor (Zinn, 2003, p. 84). In short, despite the emphasis of the revolutionary leadership on equality, the American Revolution replaced the old British oligarchy with a new class of colonial White men and excluded the poor Whites and tenant farmers from sharing the wealth of the nation (Zinn, 2003, p. 86).

The *Declaration of Independence*, nevertheless, provided Black elites an avenue to demand freedom and the abolition of slavery. They wanted equal rights for Blacks in the United States. They, for example, demanded public money to educate their children, to be able to testify in courts, and the right to vote (Zinn, 2003, pp. 87–89). However, the Constitution of 1787 ignored the rights of Blacks, "Indians", and women (Zinn, 2003, p. 73). In fact, the majority of the politicians who drafted the Constitution were members of the elite rich White Anglo-Saxon groups. They wanted a strong federal government: the manufacturers were asking and pushing for protective tariffs; the moneylenders argued that the government should not use paper money to pay off debts; the land investors demanded protection as they took over "Indian" lands; slave owners wanted the support of the federal government against slave revolts and runaways; bondholders demanded that the government raise money through a national tax system in order to pay off those bonds (Zinn, 2003, p. 91). The constitution was not reflective of the interests of many peoples since women, men without property, slaves, and indentured workers were excluded from participation in drafting this document (Zinn, 2003, p. 91). It is important to note that the phrase ***Life, Liberty and the pursuit of Happiness*** was also replaced with ***Life, Liberty and Property*** (Zinn, 2003, p. 98).

As the above arguments point out, the political concerns were intertwined with economic considerations. The Constitution, then, is not a document to establish order in society, but a manifesto by certain groups in society to protect and enhance their economic interests and privileges (Zinn, 2003, p. 97). Also, those in power had the privilege of interpreting the law.

For example, the First Amendment of the Bill of Rights that was passed in 1791 clearly stated that the government must protect the freedom of speech and press by not passing laws that would infringe upon them. However, in 1798, the Sedition Act limited the freedom of speech during a time period when Irish and French people in the United States were viewed as perilously radical due to the recent French Revolution and Irish rebellions (Zinn, 2003, p. 100). This act made any comments or expressions that questioned the government of the United States as a criminal act, punishable by law: ten individuals were imprisoned because of this act (Zinn, 2003, p. 100).

Another important political event was the French Revolution, which also emphasized *liberty*, *equality*, and *fraternity* (Perry et al., 1995, p. 88). As Emmanuel Sieyès (1748–1836) maintained, the dominant social orders in France controlled the state and used it to privilege their positions within the nation, which he defined as "a body of associates living under common laws and represented by the same legislative assembly" (Sieyès, 1995, p. 89). The revolution attempted to democratize social relations in France. The French National Assembly adopted the **Declaration of the Rights of Man and of Citizen** in August 1789. This document maintained that the people are the source of sovereignty of the state and political power (Perry et al., 1995, p. 89). It also stated that all "men" are born free and have equal rights. The role of the government, according to this document, is to protect the "natural rights of the individual" (Perry et al., 1995, p. 89). These views were in opposition to the ideology of the aristocracy and the clergy that controlled the political system in France at the time. The rights of men were defined as "liberty, property, security, and resistance of oppression" (*Declaration of the Rights of Man and of the Citizen*, 1995, p. 90). The nation was also defined as the source of all sovereignty and the law was viewed as "an expression of the will of the community. All citizens have a right to concur, either personally or through their representatives, in its formation" (The Constitution Society, 2012; *Declaration of the Rights of Man and of the Citizen*, 1995, p. 90). Freedom of thought, press, and expression was also enshrined in the law: "every man may speak, write, and publish freely, provided he is responsible for the abuse of this liberty in cases determined by the law" (The Constitution Society, 2012; *Declaration of the Rights of Man and of the Citizen*, 1995, p. 91). One of the articles in this document also explicitly stated the rights of individuals to property as inviolable and scared: "no one ought to be deprived of it, except in cases of evident public necessity, legally ascertained ..." (The Constitution Society, 2012; *Declaration of the Rights of Man and of Citizen*, 1995, p. 91).

The ideas promoted by these revolutions are important because of their global implications and influences. The American and French revolutions played important roles in the rise of social movements in various centres of the world that attempted to introduce constitutional monarchies and democratic governments in non-Western parts of the world. These ideas were adopted by anticolonial politicians and reformers that attempted to establish modern nation-states in Asia, Africa, and South America.

of money. These financiers collected much taxes from the population, which resulted in an increase in the general populations' resentment of the monarchy. These financiers became the major bankers of the time that almost anyone looking for loans (i.e., the monarchy, nobility, monopolistic corporate manufacturers) went to them for financial support (Turner, et al., 2002, p. 6).

The modern class structure in industrial societies was partly the outcome of the reorganization of the agricultural system due to the implementation of **parliamentary enclosure** (Morgan, 1999, p. 17) (See Box 6.2-The Enclosure Movement). As a result, large landowners were able to create large estates during the early Industrial Revolution "at the expense of owner-occupiers who were already being squeezed [out] by the mid-eighteenth century" (Morgan, 1999, p. 17). Consolidation of land

BOX 6.2 - The Enclosure Movement

The enclosure movement in England was "a by-product of the monetization of feudal life" (Heilbroner, 1989, p. 55). Beginning in the thirteenth century landlords began to view their estates not simply as ancestral land but as a potential source for generating cash revenues (Heilbroner, 1989, p. 55). So, in order to generate more cash, landlords began to enclose pastoral land that was more or less considered as common land. The communal land was now exclusively claimed to benefit the lord or the landlord. They were turned into sheep pastures. This is due to the fact that there was an increase in demand for woollen cloth, which made raising sheep very profitable (Heilbroner, 1989, p. 55). During this period, many landowners moved away from farming and turned their lands into pastures to produce more wool for the textile mills and factories that were growing in the cities. This push factor in addition to the fact that factories had become the main source of work (pull factors) resulted in the movement of large numbers of people into cities.

By the eighteenth and nineteenth centuries, the enclosure process reached its engulfing climax (Heilbroner, 1989, p. 55). By this time, more than two million acres or half of the arable land of England were enclosed. As the land was enclosed, it was harder for the tenant farmers to support themselves (Heilbroner, 1989, p. 56). These processes were central in the "dissolution of feudal ties and the formation of a Market society" (Heilbroner, 1989, p. 56). As a result of "dispossessing the peasant, it created a new kind of labour force–landless, without traditional sources of income, however meagre, impelled to find work for wages wherever it might be available" (Heilbroner, 1989, p. 56). With the rise in agricultural proletariat, we also notice a rise in urban proletariat, which is associated with the transformation of **guilds** into more "'business like' firms" (Heilbroner, 1989, p. 56). This period also witnessed a power struggle between traditional landlords and guild masters and manufacturers. Traditional landlords and guild masters fought against the invasion of their protected trades by manufacturers who introduced new machinery as part the established modes of production (Heilbroner, 1989, p. 57). In short, in the course of the eighteenth century we see increases in population, food production, and people involved in the paid labour force, all stemming partly from the effects of the enclosure. In fact, England was now facing the problem of "wandering poor".

through the **Enclosure Act** and other means resulted in the creation of larger farms and enhanced the power of landlords. In fact, during the sixteenth and seventeenth centuries, the rise of commercial agriculture rather than subsistence farming had resulted in the improvement of economic position of England (Morgan, 1999, p. 2).

The structure of the European class system was also being altered thanks to technological innovations and the introduction of new techniques. These innovations had significant consequences for the social and economic organization of rural life in Europe. For example, "in the early nineteenth century the replacement of harvest time of the sickle by the scythe [a much larger tool] saved 40 percent of the labour in harvesting an acre" (Morgan, 1999, p. 19). The rise in agricultural output "in the early Industrial Revolution was [also] accompanied by innovation in cereal cultivation use of fodder crops and livestock breeding" (Morgan, 1999, p. 19). It is also important to note that most of these landlords were absentee landlords, meaning they were not involved in the daily operation of the land and lived in the cities most of the year. In general, the fixed capital was provided by the landowners, and they relied on income accumulated from renting the land to tenant farmers "who were responsible for many agricultural improvements" (Morgan, 1999, p. 17). Morgan pointed out that, for example, "more was achieved in the diffusion of these new techniques by tenant farmers and estate stewards than by the large landlords" (Morgan, 1999, p. 20). As a result, agricultural production more than doubled during the period between 1750 and 1850 (Morgan, 1999, p. 16). In fact, this rise in the agricultural output was an important impetus for the early industrialization (Morgan, 1999, p. 17). At the same time, the changing organizational structure of the agrarian society hardened the social relationship connected to the land, "with a gulf opening between the great landlords and the rural proletariat" (Morgan, 1999, p. 19). In fact, at the bottom of the agricultural ladder were farmworkers, servants, day labourers, and increasingly landless rural proletariat, all of whom relied on wage labour (Morgan, 1999, p. 18). In general, the introduction of new technology and the amalgamation of land in the hands of large landlords resulted in the creation of a landless working class that moved from one region to another looking for employment. Farm workers were no longer in demand and workers were fired and hired according to short-term and seasonal needs (Morgan, 1999, p. 19).

Although the trade expansion of the seventeenth century had already eliminated much of the feudal order, the economic activity in the eighteenth century was still being dominated by the **guilds** (See Box 6.3 - Guilds), "which controlled labour's access to skilled occupations, and by chartered corporations, which restrained trade and production" (Turner, et al., 2002, p. 4). The first industry to undermine the control of the guilds and the power of chartered corporations was the cotton industry (Turner, et al., 2002, p. 4). The eighteenth century was characterized by the rise in more competitive manufacturing (Turner, et al., 2002, p. 4).

In short, the impact of industrialization transformed rural communities (*gemeinschaft*) into more complex social systems based upon association, or *gesellschaft*. By this time, more people were working in the factories than in the agricultural sectors. For example, consider the fact that until the 1810s, most people worked in agricultural settings in England than in mining, manufacturing, and industry; but, by the 1850s, more people were working in mining and various types of industries (Morgan, 1999, p. 16). In 1851, 42% of the labour force worked in industry, manufacturing, and

BOX 6.3 - Guilds

In the towns, **guilds** were formed that acted as the business institutions of the Middle Ages. One had to belong to a guild to be able to set up a business. Guilds were a form of a union of managers rather than workers (Heilbroner, 1989, p. 32). They were highly hierarchical and acted as the regulators of production and social contracts (Heilbroner, 1989, p. 33). The **function of guilds** was not to ensure making money but to "preserve a certain orderly way of life" that made making a comfortable living possible for the master craftsmen (Heilbroner, 1989, p. 33). Rules and regulations of guilds protected the members from the creation of monopolies.

During this period, "economics was a subordinate and not a dominant aspect of life" (Heilbroner, 1989, p. 33). The most important and influential guiding principle was religious faith, and the Church "constituted the ultimate authority on economics" and all other matters (Heilbroner, 1989, p. 34). The making of money was viewed negatively, as prevalent in the views of the Church regarding usury, or lending money and gaining interests from this transaction. This was constructed as a "mortal sin" (Heilbroner, 1989, p. 36). For example, during the thirteenth and fourteenth centuries, the usurers were viewed as outcasts and pariahs of society. In general, "medieval economic organization was conceived of as a means of reproducing, but not enhancing, the material well-being of" people (Heilbroner, 1989, p. 36). During the period between 1723 and 1790, as the result of the control of guilds, "no master hatter in England could employ more than two apprentices; in the famous Sheffield silver trade, no master cutler could employ more than one" (Heilbroner, 1989, p. 61).

In short, economic activities based on the organization of guilds did not promote progress. As mentioned, during the Enlightenment, progress had become the focal point of European social thinkers and the guiding force behind the development of European societies' economic expansions. The guilds were now in the way of economic development and the efforts of free and self-interested individuals (i.e., capitalists and industrialists).

mining and the number of workers in the agricultural sector, forestry, and fisheries fell to half of the numbers of workers during the previous periods (Morgan, 1999, p. 16).

The Industrial Revolution was also an important factor in promoting colonial expansion into other parts of the world in search of natural resources as well as markets for the goods produced in Europe in which to be sold (Kelleher & Klein, 2009, p. 8). The expansion of trade and commerce during the seventeenth and eighteenth centuries were also influential in the accumulation of capital in European states, which was the end result of "an aggressive search for new markets" with the consequence of tapping into "the wealth of a much larger area of the world than the Mediterranean land accessible to earlier generations" (Perry, 2001, p. 349). Colonial control of much of the resources of Africa, the Americas, and other parts of the world helped fuel the growth of the economies in Western European states. For example, the growth in Atlantic trade and the increase in rural manufacturing, coupled with political stability in England were important factors in the growth of economic power of England in comparison to the rest of Europe (Morgan, 1999, p. 2).

Part Two
···

Capitalism: an overview

In general, we can distinguish between four stages of capitalist development: merchant, industrial, corporate industrial, and corporate capitalism. Each stage corresponds to different:

1. levels of technological advancement and social relations of production;
2. forms of international exchange relations; and
3. levels of state responsibility.

Mercantilism-Merchant Capitalism (1500–1770s)

The seventeenth century is often considered the era of **mercantilism** (Robbins, 2008, p. 81). During this period, trade and commerce resulted in capital accumulation. This period also corresponds to the rise of the merchant class to power in European societies. Scholars have attributed "the development of capitalism … to an increase in the power of the merchant class" (Robbins, 2008, p. 85). The merchant class competed with the ruling classes, such as the landlords, for power. The class struggle between the old and new elite classes ended up in the increase of the power of the merchant class. By the seventeenth and eighteenth centuries, the merchants were the most influential players in the rise and development of capitalism (Robbins, 2008, p. 85). Merchants were not involved in producing goods. They bought goods at a lower price from one group (i.e., silk from China) and sold them for profits to other groups (i.e., "consumers" in England and other parts of Europe).

The mercantilist offered an economic explanation of society that emphasized the importance of gold in producing wealth and promoting economic activities. This economic explanation also adorned the function of merchants as the source of wealth due to their economic activities that brought "treasures" from other parts of the world and sold them goods produced in the respective nation of the individual merchant (Heilbroner, 1989, p. 60). As we mentioned, John Locke's ideas promoted mercantilism as a righteous economic system. Adam Smith (1723–1790), however, criticized his ideas and was critical of mercantilism as a system in which: "the wealth of nation consists in gold and silver, and those precious metals could be brought into a country which lacked mines only by balancing trade and by exporting more than was imported" (McCullough, 2010, p. 19).

The mercantile ideas were also criticized by another school of thought popular in France, the **Physiocrats**. These theorists argued that the source of wealth is not the activities of merchants. Rather, they argued that wealth is produced due to the productive labour of farmers. That is, wealth is produced from land, or nature's bounty (Heilbroner, 1989, p. 60). They considered the efforts of merchants and manufacturers as insignificant to the production of wealth in comparison to wealth produced by the farmers (Heilbroner, 1989, p. 61). In this regard, Adam Smith disagreed with the Physiocrats. He did agree with their general assertion that the wealth of the nation is created as a result of "consumable goods actually produced by the labour of that society" (McCullough, 2010,

p. 20). However, he disagreed with their claim that the only productive labour is the one that is employed upon the land (McCullough, 2010, p. 20).

This period also corresponds to the rise of nation-states in European societies. During this era, the European states passed laws and legislation to expand industries; to protect their industries from competition from foreign firms; to control trade; to prevent wealth in the form of gold and silver to leave their countries; and to ensure the existence of cheap supply of labour and subsidizing select industries (Robbins, 2008, p. 81). In this system, the aim of the state was to encourage exports and restrain imports. Adam Smith was also critical of the creation of monopolies that enabled certain "charted companies" to control the economic activities in a mercantile system of capitalism, "such as the trades with the East Indies" (Heilbroner, 1989, p. 61) (See below). The role of the state, according to Smith, was threefold:

a) to protect society from external forces and invasions;

b) to protect individuals within society from the efforts of others that undermine their right to liberty and property; and

c) to establish public institutions that individuals are incapable of forming on their own (McCullough, 2010, p. 20).

This view forms the basis of **liberalism** with its emphasis on liberty as a sacred economic right (McCullough, 2010, p. 20). In short, for Adam Smith, more wealth is produced in countries that "encourage a steady rise in the productivity of its labour". That is, wealth creation was associated with an increase in the production of goods due to the rise in the ability of workers to manufacture more goods (Heilbroner, 1989, p. 62).

During this period, **colonialism** served as a way of exploiting the resources of other parts of the world. The establishment of colonies in other parts of the world was partly due to the need for gold and silver. The resources in other countries became the main sources of wealth production and power in European societies. The resulting capital accumulation from colonial exploitation paved the road for the next stage of capitalism, the rise of **industrialism**. In the mercantile system, trading or joint stock companies were created that combined trade and armed forces to promote the extraction of wealth from other parts of the world (Robbins, 2008, p. 81). These trading companies were state-sponsored initiatives. These companies consisted of a group of investors who were given a charter by the government that entitled them to "monopolistic trading privileges" in specific parts of the globe (Robbins, 2008, p. 81). An example of this type of company is the British East India Company (originally called the Company of Merchants of London) that was given exclusive rights to trade with the East Indies in 1600 by the British government (Robbins, 2008, p. 81). The proliferation of charter corporations, such as the Virginia Company in 1606 and the English Amazon Company in 1619, resulted in the incorporation of various groups and parts of the world into a global economic order. For example, slaves and deerskin were sent from the American colonies to England and other British Colonies, for example, East Indies. The West Indies shipped sugar and tobacco to the other parts of the "British Empire". Rum produced in North America from molasses imported from the West Indies in exchange for North American lumber was also exported to other parts of the world.

Colonialism and mercantilist global trade had devastating consequences for local cultures and groups. For example, by 1710, more than 12,000 American "Indians" were sold and exported as slaves. The political and economic structure of the Cherokee was also disintegrated. Their economy was transformed from a focus on producing food and other resources for internal usage to a focus on producing goods that were needed by the colonialists. The Cherokees also amassed debts arising from the advances given to them to purchase European goods, which resulted in the selling off of the communal landholdings by the Chiefs who were chosen by the British colonialists: about 57 percent of the Cherokee land was privatized and controlled by White settlers (Robbins, 2008, pp. 82–83). The introduced economic "incentives" also affected the social structure of life in the Cherokee land. Men were no longer involved in agricultural endeavours and this task was performed by women only. The introduction of European goods also resulted in the decline of traditional crafts and skills amongst the Cherokees.

As mentioned above, during most of the period between 1500 and 1770s, the structure of European society was based on traditional and agrarian settings, where relations were based on face-to-face interactions. Tradition played an important role in connecting past, present, and future. These societies had few statuses (Giddens, 1990, p. 102, Table I). There were few recognized social positions available to individuals, and they were often fixed and ascribed (i.e., mother, chief, landlord, peasant, or serf). These societies were characterized by few manufacturing products, since the economy was based on agriculture. The unit of production was the family. The main agent of socialization was also the family or the extended relatives. Kinship relations functioned as the foundation of social ties "across time-space" (Giddens, 1991, p. 102, Table I). Local communities, because of their familiar settings, were the few places where people were able to communicate and interact with one another. Giddens (1990, p. 102, Table I) maintained that religion and religious cosmologies informed the worldview of people in these societies and were the sources of interpreting social and political relations. These societies were also characterized by a high infant mortality rate and low life expectancy. The majority of the population lived in rural rather than urban centres. Population density was extremely low. Education was also reserved for the elite groups. In these societies, the state usually did not control its periphery, the outlying areas of the country.

Industrial Capitalism (1770s–1860s)

Industrial capitalism refers to the period characterized by "the development of market economies based on manufacturing in the wake of industrial revolution" (Leicht & Fitzgerald, 2007, p. 31). This period is marked by the onset of the **Industrial Revolution**, during which new methods of wealth accumulation were introduced. The existing class structures were also transformed due to structural changes, the new conceptions of wealth, the ways in which wealth was accumulated, and how work was organized. In this period, the unit of production became the factory, in which mechanized machinery was used. This resulted in an increase in productivity and material goods/products. During this period, the role of the state was redefined in the wake of the emergence of **laissez-faire policies**, which reduced the power of the state by limiting the state's regulations over industries. The laissez faire doctrine, advocated by scholars, such as Adam Smith, in his book

The Wealth of Nations, promoted the principles of free trade. By free trade, these thinkers pointed to the "liberation of economic production [structures and relations] from all limiting regulation" and "leaving individuals' economic activities to their own devices", or the *invisible hands* of the market (Perry et al., 1995, p. 119).

During this period, many more peasants moved from rural areas to cities and became incorporated into the working class (See Box 6.4 - Urbanization). They lived in poverty and worked in factories or mines under dangerous working conditions. We also witness the specialization of work and the rise in wage labour. In reaction to the exploitation of labourers in factories, workers began to organize themselves and establish unions through which they demanded better working conditions and wages. We will explore the characteristics of this period in more detail below.

Industrial Capitalism: a historical-theoretical analysis

For Karl Marx and all those social thinkers that have been influenced by his ideas, such as the conflict theorists and Marxists, the most important single aspect of change that characterizes modernity is capitalism (Giddens, 1991, 11). According to Marx, in capitalism many material goods and human labour power become **commodified**, that is they come to have an **economic value** that can be **exchanged** in the marketplace (Giddens, 1991, p. 11). Marx argued that capitalism emerged prior to industrialization (i.e., mercantile capitalism) and "provided much of the impetus to its emergence" (Giddens, 1990, p. 61).

In contrast, Émile Durkheim attributed the changes in modernity to the consequences of **industrialism**. He argued that modern social relations were influenced by the emerging division of labour in industrial societies (Giddens, 1991, p. 12). Max Weber singled out capitalism as the main driver of modernity. However, he, unlike Marx, focused on the consequences of **rationalization** (influencing the organization of all human activities) and technology in the form of bureaucracies and their consequences on society (Giddens, 1991, p. 12). According to Weber, the Western form of capitalism was

---

BOX 6.4 - Urbanization

Due partly to the effects of the Industrial Revolution, large numbers of people began migrating from rural areas to major urban centres in search of jobs (Ritzer, 2000, p. 9). The rise of urban centres coincided with the creation of major social, cultural, and economic problems, such as overcrowding, noise, traffic, poverty, and pollution (Ritzer, 2000, p. 9). Homelessness, as well as poverty and alienation, were influential factors in the growth of sociology as a discipline, as many scholars were interested in applying "scientific" methods to understanding the causes for such problems and providing remedies for them. Scholars, such as Max Weber, Karl Marx, and George Simmel, were concerned about these issues. In addition, the Chicago School, which can be singled out as the first major school of American sociology, "was in large part defined by its concern for the city and its interest in using Chicago as a laboratory in which to study urbanization and its problems" (Ritzer, 2000, p. 9).

a way to "organize work and production in a rational manner", the same way "science" was a rational way of controlling nature (Perry, 2001, p. 486).

Despite these different interpretations, capitalist societies are one of the distinct forms of societal organization in modernity (Giddens, 1990, p. 56). One of the characteristics of the capitalist system is the production of goods for competitive markets (Giddens, 1990, p. 55). **Capitalism** is defined as "a system of private enterprise" (Perry, 2001, p. 274). That is, in this system, the central economic decisions ("what, how much, where, and at what price to produce, buy, and sell") are made by private individuals, especially the owners of firms and their managers (Perry, 2001, p. 274). Capitalism, then, refers to a system of economic relations that emphasizes commodity production. It is based on the relationships between wage labourers who are propertyless (they only have their labour to sell in the marketplace) and the propertied or those who own the capital (who can purchase the labour of workers to work in their factories and enterprises). The relationship between the owners of the capital and workers, which is based on **exploitation**, forms the main "axes of class system" in modernity (Giddens, 1990, p. 55).

Starting in the mid-1700s England, **capitalism**, "or private production for a market in pursuit of profit, combined with new forms of industrial organization", resulted in the creation of immense wealth that brought a number of changes to societal organization (Pampel, 2007, p. 7). Many scholars have pointed out that capitalism resulted in the creation of social problems and more misery than goodness for the majority of the population in various parts of the world. In contrast, as a result of new innovations in the production processes a number of new products, such as clothes, household goods, and food, were also produced at cheap prices, which resulted in the improvement of hygiene, life expectancy, and a better standard of living, accompanied by the lower mortality rates, for the population (Pampel, 2007, p. 7). For example, by 1850, life expectancy rose from about 33 years in the Middle Ages to 43 years (Pampel, 2007, p. 7).

The **Industrial Revolution** and technological advancement also resulted in the creation of new forms of wealth and the rise of the middle-class in England. Ralf Dahrendorf (Giddens, 1982, p. 38) argued that **industrialization** "refers to the mechanized production of goods in factories or other enterprises". An **industrial society**, then, refers to a type of society in which **industrialism** is the most central defining element of the economy (Giddens, 1982, p. 38). During the Industrial Revolution, the middle-class or the bourgeoisie was able to take advantage of the advances in technology, industry, and the "material prosperity" associated with industrialization. The middle-class was composed of "bankers, merchants, factory owners, professionals, and government workers" (Perry et al., 1995, p. 108). Due to their investments in the factories that produced commodities that were then sold in local or global markets, these groups were able to accumulate immense amounts of wealth.

The ideals associated with individual characteristics that were promoted during this period assumed that national development and progress was attributable to the overall efforts of industrious and energetic individuals. In contrast, national stagnation was considered to be the end result of "individual idleness, selfishness, and vice" (Smiles, 1995, p. 109). Selfish indulgences, wastefulness, and vanity were viewed as vices which retarded the progress of nations and the thriftless person was viewed as the enemy of the public (Smiles, 1995, p. 110).

p. 402). The National Labour Relations gave unions legal status and provided mechanisms to listen to them and settle some of their concerns. That is, it attempted to moderate work dissatisfactions of the labourers by channeling their energies into voting. At the same time, the unions became a vehicle through which workers' dissatisfaction and their oppositional energy could be channelled into concerns over contracts, negotiations, union meetings, and trying to reduce and decrease the number of strikes (Zinn, 2003, p. 402). As a result, unions actually lost most of their power. In fact, during the Great Depression, before they were organized into unions, factory workers had their greatest influence in the factory. Their influence and power during the Depression stemmed from not in their ability to organize, but to disrupt the running of factories (Cloward and Piven, as cited in Zinn, 2003, p. 402).

The start of World War II helped the American economy to recover since there were now more demands for American made military equipment and ammunition in Europe and by the United States armed forces. This stimulated economic growth and the recovery of corporations that were involved in the war effort (Ferguson, 2006, pp. 527–528). In fact, many of the largest US corporations were producing war materials and equipment rather than consumer goods during this period (Ferguson, 2006). In various stages of the War, corporations, such as General Motors, General Electric, Boeing, and others, were able to take advantage of the war efforts to increase their profits (Ferguson, 2006). However, it was not until the end of World War II that the incongruity between the volume of goods produced and effective capacity of the population to consume them was to be resolved in any concrete way (Allen, 1996a, p. 286). The war also resulted in the weakening of the old labour militancy prevalent during the 1930s. The war effort put almost everyone to work. It also achieved one other thing: through patriotic feelings it united all classes to fight a common enemy. In other words, during the war, it became much more difficult to organize the workers and channel their anger against the corporate elite, which would have been viewed as un-American and unpatriotic. In fact, the CIO promised to call no strikes during the war (Zinn, 2003, p. 402).

After the Great Depression, government policies and programs, such as industrial regulation, public projects, social insurance programs, and welfare programs became central and important policies in promoting economic stability in liberal Western capitalist societies. It is also important to note that not all Americans benefitted from the *New Deal*. Most Black people were ignored by the system. Black people who were tenant farmers, farm labourers, migrants, and domestic workers did not qualify for the unemployment insurance schemes, minimum wage laws, social security, or farm subsidies (Zinn, 2003, p. 404). Black workers faced discrimination: they were hired last but fired first. It was not until the possibility of a massive march on Washington in 1941 by the Sleeping-Car Porters Union (majority Black workers) that the Fair Employment Practices Committee was established with no power to enforce the policy. In Harlem, people continued to live in rat infested buildings, unemployment was high amongst its population, and in the Harlem Hospital in 1932 twice as many patients died as in Bellevue Hospital located in a White neighbourhood (Zinn, 2003, p. 404). Nevertheless, the *New Deal* like policies continued to inform American and Western approaches to economic development until the 1970s through the expansion of trade unions, regulatory bodies,

The Industrial Revolution and technological advancement further contributed to the displacement of rural populations, as new technologies, such as new techniques of crop rotation, new strains of crops, and new-seed-planting and harvesting machines, were implemented in agriculture and replaced the need for the labour of farm workers (Pampel, 2007, p. 8; Ritzer, 2000, p. 7). Although during the Middle Ages, the majority of the population lived in rural areas in farming communities, or they were involved in small scale manufacturing production. By the end of the eighteenth century, due to the introduction of new forms of energy, such as coal and steam, manufacturers were able to "operate large scale machines in mills and factories", which required the need for workers to work in large-scale factories in cities, such as Manchester.

The industrialization of society also accompanied the rise in economic bureaucracies that provided the many services that were needed to operate large-scale factories and satisfy the needs of the "emerging capitalist economic system" (Ritzer, 2000, p. 7). The structure of work was also changing in industrialized societies (Ritzer, 2000, p. 7). This is the beginning of the era during which a new class of individuals, who worked for the owners of factories in order to make a living, were formed. Karl Marx referred to this class as the **proletariat**. Their only means to provide for themselves and their families was by selling their labour in return for wages to the capitalist class, or the **bourgeoisie** who controlled the **means of production**, such as the machines, knowledge, factories, and land. Due to the fact that many people were moving into cities in search of employment, factory owners were able to pay low wages to male workers and even lower wages to women and children. That is, they were able to **exploit** the workers.

Although the roles of women and children in the process of industrialization and the rise of capitalism are often ignored, it is important to note that they made significant contributions and their work/labour was a crucial factor in raising productivity during this time period (Morgan, 1999, p. 4). During the early stages of industrialization, in the cotton industry, for example, about 40 to 45 percent of the labour force was made of children and young people under the age of eighteen. The hiring of children as wage labourers was due to the prevailing views of the bourgeoisie that the younger generations were more inclined to adjust to the new forms of factory discipline than the adult population "who were used to traditional handicraft routines" (Perry et al., 1995, p. 113). Since children were employed in the mills and factories, this resulted in them being away from their parents and families, which also undermined their socialization and family life. Their health was also affected because of the unsanitary conditions of factories. Children worked from 5:00 in the morning until late at night, at times until 11:00 P.M., with only two 40 minute breaks in between (Sadler Commission Report on Child Labour, 1995, p. 114). Children were also employed in various industries in Canada. In the mines, children were employed as trappers, whose job "was to open and shut the doors in the mine so that the coal cars could pass" (Cruxton, Wilson, Francis, Harrison & Johnson, 2008, p. 204). They earned 25¢ a day for this job. It was not until 1884 and the passing of the Factory Act in Ontario that employing children under the age of 12 became illegal and no child could be employed for more than ten hours. In 1908, the Child Labour Act prohibited children under 12 to work in stores and children under 14 to work in factories (Cruxton, et al., 2008, p. 204). In general, during this period, the life chances of individuals were more and more affected by the market forces over which the working classes had no control (Pampel, 2007, p. 9).

The factory also required new ways of organization based on rational approaches to production that promoted efficiency and punctuality. The factory workers needed to be disciplined workers. They needed to be socialized into the new culture of work. In 1844, The Foundry and Engineering Works of Royal Overseas Trading Company enforced the following rules upon the workers (The Foundry and Engineering Works of Royal Overseas Trading Company, 1995, p. 111). The workers had to start work at 6 A.M. and had to be at the factory five minutes before the start of their work. Those arriving late by 2 minutes would lose half an hour's wage. Workers could not leave their place of employment and tasks without permission. Workers were also expected to be searched before leaving the workplace, so they would not steal from the factory. Conversation amongst workers was frowned upon and prohibited. Insubordination to and disobedience of management and foremen were punished by firing and dismissal (The Foundry and Engineering Works of Royal Overseas Trading Company, 1995, p. 112). These rules were in contradiction to the mores of most workers who were recent migrants from rural areas who lived in face-to-face and closely-knitted communities. The rise of this form of factory production and work environment resulted in the loss of tradition and weakening of the importance of the family as the main source of support, as many individuals had to leave their communities and settle in cities (Pampel, 2007, p. 8). In Canada, similar rules and regulations also informed the relationship between workers and the owners of capital. Owners of capital could fire workers as they saw fit and reduce their wages (Cruxton et al., 2008, p. 202). In the 1870s, workers in Quebec were paid an average of $185 a year, and, in Ontario, they earned $245 a year, which was not enough to pay for the cost of living of a family. As a result, many working families had to rely on the income of more than one member of the family to pay for the cost of living (Cruxton et al., 2008, p. 201). In addition, many workers lost income for talking at work, for not working as fast, or for making errors. In general, workers did not have any job security. If they were injured at work, they were not compensated and did not have access to pension or medical insurance.

Racism also affected the working conditions of workers. In Canada, Irish immigrants who immigrated to Canada after the 1840s and found jobs working on the construction of canals in Montreal were mistreated and viewed as menaces to society. The Irish were viewed as "irrational, emotionally unstable and lacking in self-control" (Bleasdale, 2006, p. 28). They formed a large reserve labour that was used as a justification to pay low wages to other workers. These Irish immigrants were not even employed by Anglo farmers on their farms, as they believed that these new immigrants of peasant background were not familiar with the farm skills of British technology (Bleasdale, 2006). Company stores were also charging exorbitant interests on credits to workers to purchase goods to satisfy their basic material needs, such as food and clothing. Some even paid their workers in credit tickets that were only redeemable in company stores, which became another source of profit for the capitalist class. As a result of low wages and these other practices, the Irish canallers were kept in a perpetual state of poverty (Bleasdale, 2006, 32).

The industrial process and the factory system also resulted in the creation of new problems, such as overcrowding in cities, that "had poorly constructed housing [and] few sanitation facilities"

(Pampel, 2007, p. 8). The condition of life in the urban centres during this period has been described as poor and unsatisfactory. These cities were polluted by the smoke from the factories. There were also poor sewage systems and facilities. Most poor people lived in proximity to animal waste. Friedrich Engels (Engels, 1995, p. 117) described the conditions of working classes in England as miserable, resulting in the stunting of their full capacities as human beings. British towns and cities were filled with slums that housed the workers in deplorable conditions (Engels, in Perry et al., 1995, p. 118). These districts were characterized by high rates of crime, poverty, disease, and pollution. The slums were unplanned and the population lived in overcrowded housings that were built back-to-back. These buildings lacked adequate ventilation. The streets were not paved and were filled with many potholes. They did not have gutters or drains either; as a result of which, the streets were filled with "animal and vegetable refuse", resulting in unsanitary living conditions (Engels, in Perry et al., 1995, p. 118). In fact, Morgan stated that, "it is difficult to accept that the mortality rate could have been improved by changes in hygiene or the state of the environment" (Morgan, 1999, p. 10). Despite the fact that there was more consumption of soap and better washable clothing was available at the time, most of the soap was consumed by the industries rather than in the homes. It is also very difficult to account for how frequently people washed their clothing. Although, better diet and nutrition have been identified as the reason for the rise of population and reduction in the death rate, it is important to note that "it has not yet been proven that better nutritional standards were diffused through the English population before the late nineteenth century" (Morgan, 1999, p. 11).

Although many historians associated the rise of population during the process of industrialization to the falling mortality rates, the research by the Cambridge Group suggested that higher birth rates resulted from greater marital birth fertility (Morgan, 1999, p. 13). That is, the changing economic conditions of the era in terms of rising real wages over time (despite the exploitation of labour by the capitalist labour), higher family income, and a greater proportion of the population living in urban centres resulted in the creation of the condition for many people to have access to the means to marry in a more urbanized, industrial environment (Morgan, 1999, p. 13). As more people moved to the cities, more and more people were involved in industrial work and relied on wage-labour to make ends meet. In fact, "paid work was regularly available in industry and many worked in family groups, with income supplemented by the labour of women and children" (Morgan, 1999, p. 13). The growth of wage labour stimulated family consumption. This was also fuelled by a rise in consumer revolution that promoted purchasing household goods, which resulted in the size of the domestic market to increase drastically (Morgan, 1999, p. 13). In fact, Morgan (1999, p. 12) argued that the larger number of people marrying seems "closely related to the growth of the industrial economy and the proletarilization of the work force".

As previously discussed, the capitalist system in the context of industrialized workplaces was an exploitive system since it provided few incentives for the workers. The work conditions were unsafe and workers worked long hours without any benefits. As a result, there were a number of riots and oppositions by the workers against the system (Ritzer, 2000, p. 7). They were simply demanding better wages and working conditions. These riots were also triggered by the government's prohibition of workers to form unions. In England, the government did not protect the rights of workers.

It "provided little help or protection to vulnerable factory workers. To the contrary, an English law passed in 1800 banned trade unions from representing workers" (Pampel, 2007, p. 39). In fact, it was not until 1833 when laws preventing employing children under the age of 9 and "limiting the employment of older children for more than 12 hours a day" were enacted (Pampel, 2007, p. 39). In Canada, unions were also illegal. It was not until the late 1870s when the government of Canada passed a law making unions legal. In 1872, Ontario workers marched in Toronto to demand a nine-hour work day. Many of the leaders of the unions that organized the event were arrested. But, this event led to the government passing the aforementioned law (Cruxton et al., 2008, p. 200). Workers also resisted the exploitive aspect of the capitalist system in many other ways. For example, a group of workers known as **Luddites** (also defined as individuals who oppose technological advancement) aimed at destroying machines that were thought to have enslaved them. These movements and the attempts of workers to organize themselves was a reflection of the fact that only a small proportion of the population directly benefited from the capitalist system: the capitalist class aimed at increasing its rate of profit by paying the workers less.

In general, there were two broad reactions to these events and processes. English economists, such as **Adam Smith**, argued for free markets unfettered by government control and restrictive policies (Pampel, 2007, p. 10). As mentioned above, they argued that such a system combined with an emphasis on economic competition and individual self-interest would bring efficiency and wealth for all (Pampel, 2007, p. 9). Their assumption was that left on their own devices, individuals "pursuing their own interests would contribute to the economic well-being of all members of society" (Pampel, 2007, p. 10).

In contrast to this view, a number of French writers and Karl Marx promoted the idea that capitalism needs to be replaced with a socialist/communist system in which the means of production are communally owned. They proposed the abolishment of private property. In fact, an important factor that played a role in the development of sociology and sociological theory was the fear of socialism as a solution to the negative consequences of capitalism and industrial problems (Ritzer, 2000).

In general, several important changes can be identified during this time period. First, labor was released and separated from the land [and] wealth and capital became independent of the power of the large noble estates (Turner, et al., 2002, p. 4). The urbanization of the population accelerated as a result of the industrialization process and the creation of large-scale industries. The competitive nature of large-scale industries also resulted in the development of new forms of technology, which resulted in the increase in production of goods. This, in turn, resulted in and stimulated the expansion of worldwide markets and trade in order to secure raw resources for the industrialists and to sell manufactured goods (Turner, et al., 2002, pp. 4–5). The expansion of secular economic activity had an effect on the power of religious organizations to control people and their needs and wants. Family structures were also affected as more and more people moved to the cities in search of industrial jobs. New laws were enacted to promote the interest of the emerging bourgeoisie (Turner, et al., 2002, p. 5). During this period, the emerging capitalist economic system resulted in the destruction of the last fragments of the feudal and the transitional mercantile orders that promoted restrictive guilds and chartered corporations (Turner, et al., 2002, p. 5). The new system had various and interrelated consequences for how people organized their lives and how people thought about themselves and their society due to the fact they affected how people lived and satisfied their material needs. The economic changes caused the formation of new class relations and social classes: the **bourgeoisie** and the urban **proletariat**. They also resulted in the rise of a revolution of ideas, as well as corresponding political revolutions (Turner, et al., 2002, p. 5). The mixture of these economic, "scientific", technological, and political changes explains how sociology emerged as a "science" of society.

Corporate Industrial Capitalism (1860s–1930s)

During this period, small enterprises gave way to larger and more powerful business groups. The ownership of **the means of production** became concentrated in the hands of the few capitalists who controlled the existing corporations. As Zinn (2003, p. 323) stated, by 1900s business was now concentrated in the hands of a few financiers and manufacturers; due to the effects of technology and as corporations were becoming larger, "they needed more capital, and it was the bankers who had this capital. By 1904, more than a thousand railroad lines had been consolidated into six great combinations, each allied with either Morgan or Rockefeller interests". That is, individual ownership of factories and corporations was being transformed into corporate ownership. In the United States, for example, Morgan and Rockefeller and their financial associates sat on 341 directorships in 112 corporations. In 1912, moreover, these corporations had an asset of $22,245,000,000, which was more than the value of all assets "in the twenty-two states and territories west of the Mississippi River" (Zinn, 2003, p. 323). This period is characterized by the institutionalization of capital accumulation in large corporations. In general, local/national markets became saturated, which, coupled with a lack of local investment opportunities, led to the internationalization of capital.

The need for raw materials by the industrialists in the West also resulted in a new era of colonialism and imperialism. European corporations in various countries began competing for raw materials, markets, and investment outlets in other countries. Relying on the military power of their respective countries, other non-Western "countries" were colonized after 1875, resulting in the availability of new markets for the goods produced in European and Western factories. This imperialist incursion into other parts of the world that resulted in the creation of new markets/places for European and Western capitalists to invest their surplus value (profit) without fear of losing their investments had devastating consequences for local industries in non-Western parts of the world. These changes and the competition between different Western nations to dominate the rest of the world culminated in World War I. This era also signalled the end of the British Empire and the Beginning of American Imperialism.

Fordism and Taylorism

The main mode of production during this period is referred to as **Fordism**. Prior to the introduction of Fordism as a mode of production, **scientific management approaches** to the organization of work had already transformed the workplace in the late nineteenth century. The success of this system has a lot to do with the desire of the capitalist class for "regularity, stability, and predictability" in the workplace (Zinn, 2003, p. 323). By 1907, the profits of the capitalist class were not as high as they wished for and the industry was not expanding as fast as it could, which forced the industrialists to look for ways to reduce the costs associated with running their corporations, mills, and factories (Zinn, 2003, p. 323). The **Taylorism** approach to management was one way of achieving these goals. Frederic W. Taylor applied two principles to reorganizing the work place:

1. the production process could be divided into smaller, specialized, and discrete parts; and

2. the relationships between these different tasks could be scientifically and rationally structured by analyzing the production process in the factory (Allen, 1996a, p. 283).

Taylor was a steel foreman who closely analyzed all jobs in the mill and developed a blueprint for a well detailed division of labour at work, "increased mechanization, and piecework wage systems, to increase production and profits" (Zinn, 2003, p. 324). Thanks to Taylor's principles, management was now able to closely control all aspects of labour. Harry Braverman pointed out that the main goal of *Taylorism* "was to make workers interchangeable, able to do the simple tasks" that the new system of division of labour required of them. In this system, workers are treated like standardized parts of a machine: they are easily replaced and exchanged as commodities (Zinn, 2003, p. 324). This system was considered to fit the new auto industry very well. It was also the perfect system for many other industries that hired immigrant labourers, many of whom were illiterate and unskilled. Taylorism not only simplified the production process, it also deskilled workers, thereby making the employment of unskilled and illiterate workers an attractive and profitable option for employers (Zinn, 2003, p. 324).

Fordism denotes the ways in which modern manufacturing is organized (Allen, 1996a, p. 282). It coincided with the beginning of the era of **mass consumption** (Teeple, 1995, p. 18, Footnote). Fordism, then, refers to a period of industrialization that is characterized by mass production of standardized goods for mass consumption (Allen, 1996a, p. 282). It was made possible by interventionist state policies that provided people with the purchasing power to become involved in large scale consumption of goods (Allen, 1996a, p. 282). It is a system of mass production based on semi-automated assembly lines through which commodities are cheaply mass produced, resulting in the expansion of domestic and foreign markets (Teeple, 1995). Mass production of goods was made possible by the introduction of:

1. "moving assemble lines,

2. specialized machinery,

3. high wages, and

4. low cost products" (Allen, 1996a, p. 283).

During the early decades of the last century, Henry Ford with the help of skilled mechanics developed machines that could be operated by unskilled workers to produce uniform parts. The work was arranged in a sequence of putting together parts in order to produce, for example, cars. Ford was able to refine the American process of repetitious manufacturing developed by companies, such as the Singer Sewing Company, as the foundation upon which the "techniques of continuous-flow and assembly-line production rests: the standardization and simplification of the product, the use of special purpose equipment together with the interchangeability of parts, and the reduction of skilled workers" (Allen, 1996a, p. 283). Fordism operates on a hierarchical and complex system of national labour market, which is proven to be highly efficient and productive.

Taylorism and Fordism: What are the Differences and Similarities?

Ford's approach to the reorganization of factory work was different than Taylor's approach in a number of ways. **First**, Taylor attempted to organize the work and labour of the worker around machines. In contrast, Ford replaced the labour of the worker with machines (Allen, 1996a, p. 283). **Second**, the goal of Taylor was to increase the efficiency of the worker by reorganizing the process of work in the factory. Ford, on the other hand, used the available technology and mechanized the workplace (Allen, 1996a, p. 284). **Third**, in the context of the scientific approaches to organization of work, the pace of the work and speed of production was still set by the worker or the supervisor. For Ford, the pace of work was set by the speed of machines. Despite these differences, both systems resulted in the fragmentation of work and the formation of a more comprehensive division of labour (Allen, 1996a, p. 284). Under the Fordism model, however, the skills needed by the worker to do a job under the craft production were no longer needed. This was due to the fact that fixed-speed and moving assembly-lines resulted in breaking down of tasks and the further simplifications of the type of work. A worker needed to have no skills or very limited skills to do the job. In fact, many of the workers in Ford's factories were European immigrants who had arrived from rural parts of Europe.

Ford's approach to production had a number of negative consequences: higher "turnover rate of labour", higher levels of nonattendance, and general discontent with work and labour relations at his plants (Allen, 1996a, p. 284). Due to the increased levels of labour unrest in Detroit, Ford introduced higher wages to his workers, which played no small role in the rise of the system of mass consumption. Ford introduced the **Five-Dollar Day**. This policy doubled the income of Ford's workers (not all of the workers qualified for the profit-sharing scheme, but those who were willing to change their private lives and cultural values by setting aside their home cultures and meeting the standards laid down by Ford's new Sociological Department that promoted the Americanization of immigrant workers and their assimilation into the American culture) (Allen, 1996a, p. 284). Ford's policies resulted in the creation of the **mass worker** who was highly paid but unskilled.

Another aspect of the system of mass production that was initiated by Fordism is a low-price strategy in the system of manufacturing. Ford's aim was to produce cheaper cars than his competition in order to increase the sales of his cars. According to Allen (1996a, p. 285), Ford achieved workplace efficiency through high-volume production, which decreased the cost per car as production rose. This system and method of mass production became the basis of production in manufacturing in several other fields, such as various consumer goods industries, housing, and furniture factories (Allen, 1996a, p. 285). However, during this period, the consumption level of the mass of the population was limited, which in conjunction with "the sharp increase in the productivity growth of the industry … brought about what many considered to be a crisis in the very functioning of capitalism itself" (Allen, 1996a, pp. 285–286).

In general, Fordism can be conceptualized in four distinct but interrelated ways:

1. Fordism refers to a specific labour process involving assembly-line mass production that uses semi-skilled labourer who performs limited tasks at a pace that is determined by the speed of the production line.

2. Fordism is considered as the main growth sector, able to influence growth in other sectors of the economy thanks to its dominant role in the mass production of goods and services until the 1970s. The car industry, for example, resulted in the growth in steal, rubber, and glass industries. The overall growth of these industries could be referred to as the **Fordist growth**.

3. Fordist style management and organization of the workplace and factories is hegemonic. The Fordism approaches to organization became pervasive and influenced other industries. The management style promoted by Fordism was also adopted by non-mass production sectors of the economy. Other aspects of Fordism were also adopted by other industries, such as the "collective bargaining procedures, contracts on a rate-for-the-job basis, management hierarchies which leave little discretion to the workforce, or the technical innovations of mass production". "In this sense, the Fordist influence may be regarded as a widespread theory of the economy".

4. Fordism can also be viewed as a model of regulation in economic, cultural, social, and political terms. (Sayer, as cited in Allen, 1996a, pp. 286–287)

During this era, progress was understood as mass-making of things: the capability to turn raw materials and transform them into physical and material goods in unparalleled quantities and volumes (Allen, 1996a, p. 297).

The Great Depression and the New Deal: from *laissez-faire* economy to planned economy

Although from 1900 to 1929, western and European societies experienced economic boom; in 1929, the market collapsed, resulting in the **Great Depression**. The US and global economy was devastated as a result of the Great Depression. The Great Depression started with the collapse of the stock market in 1929. Half of the banks in the United States closed and had to declare bankruptcy. Lack of confidence in the economy led to a decrease in the levels of consumerism and demand for manufacturing products, which made the economic situation direr. Many people lost their jobs and unemployment rates rose across the globe. In the United States, for example, unemployment rose to 25 percent (Leicht & Fitzgerald, 2007, p. 37). By 1933, in Pennsylvania, only two-thirds of the working population were working in full-time jobs and more than one million people were unemployed (Leicht & Fitzgerald, 2007, p. 37).

The Great Depression also affected many countries in Europe, especially those that were in debt to the United States because of the loans given to them after the end of World War I to rebuild their countries. As a result of the Great Depression, many countries introduced protective measures to guard their industries from outside competition by introducing high tariffs, which reduced the levels of international economic interaction and negatively affected global markets (Kelleher & Klein, 2009, p. 11).

The Great Depression also resulted in political changes across the world. Depression resulted in the rise of extremists forces in Europe. In Germany, for example, Adolf Hitler with his Nazi ideology rose to power (Kelleher & Klein, 2009, pp. 11–12). The Nazi government introduced publicly funded projects that in conjunction with the expansion of military production resulted in the end of the Depression in the mid-1930s (Ferguson, 2006, p. 246).

During this period, scholars and politicians began to rethink the role of the state. The Great Depression was interpreted as a sign that when the market is left to its own devices and without regulation, it can have devastating consequences. Many argued that the state should regulate and intervene in the economy to make sure that another 'Great Depression' would not occur in the future (Leicht & Fitzgerald, 2007, p. 37). In the United States, for example, Franklin D. Roosevelt who was elected President in 1933 (Bakan, 2004, p. 85), used the power of the state to increase government spending in the form of large publicly funded projects to downgrade the effects of the depression. He instituted a set of regulatory laws and government agencies that attempted to increase the federal government's control over corporations and banks (Bakan, 2004, p. 86). This policy is known as the **New Deal**.

The New Deal was composed of a series of policy intervention schemes, such as the National Industry Recovery Act, the Social Security Act, and the Works Progress Administration (Leicht & Fitzgerald, 2007, p. 37). The assumption was that government expenditures in social programs and road constructions, for example, would result in stimulating economic growth. Government intervention and regulations, it was argued, would remedy some of the **contradictions of capitalism** (i.e., to decrease labour cost, produce more commodities, sell more products, and increase the rate of profit). The New Deal did not resolve the economic problems, but it reduced the consequences of the crises. This law institutionalized "new rights and protection for workers, debt relief for farmers, and fairness and transparency guarantees for investors" (Bakan, 2004, p. 86).

However, it is important to note that the introduction of these new laws and acts were not necessarily implemented as the result of an ideological desire to promote equality for the workers. For example, when the Wagner Act was passed in 1935, this act was opposed by the capitalist class and major companies, such as Republic Steel and Ford Motor Company and other huge companies in the fields of electrical industries, rubber, and meat packing (Zinn, 2003, p. 401). This law was challenged in the courts, but it was found to be constitutional. The implementation of this act was partly due to the fact that the government wanted to provide stability in commerce. In fact, during this period many sit-down strikes were organized by the workers outside the control of the unions. These wildcat strikes were viewed by the state as hurting the interstate commerce. The unions were more controllable than these wildcat strikes by the ranks and files of workers. In fact, the leaders of the Congress of Industrial Organizations (CIO) claimed that "A CIO contract is adequate protection against sit-downs, lie-downs, or any other kind of strike" (as cited in Zinn, 2003, p. 401). What conspired through the implementation of the Wagner Act and the National Labour Relations is the role of bureaucracy and the government in regulating and controlling direct labour action (Zinn, 2003,

and extensive social programs and services for the elderly, unemployed, and the poor (Bakan, 2004, pp. 20–21).

The ideological justification for this policy was put forth by a British economist, **John Maynard Keynes** (1883–1946) (Leicht & Fitzgerald, 2007, p. 37). He argued that the government is responsible to ensure full employment and productive capacity by sustaining the levels of **aggregate demand**. By *aggregate demand*, economists mean, "the amount of goods and services" that businesses and consumers are able and willing to buy (Leicht & Fitzgerald, 2007, pp. 37–38). The aim of government policies should be to lower **inflation** (which refers to the upward increase of wages and prices) and unemployment and to promote **economic growth** (referring to the increase in the economic output as a whole) (Leicht & Fitzgerald, 2007, pp. 35–36). The basic argument of the Keynesian economics is that economic difficulties could be solved through political solutions (highlighting the role of the state).

As mentioned above, this approach was the main economic policy that influenced government policies until the 1970s. According to this school of thought, economic problems arise from problems associated with *aggregate demand*, and it is possible to stimulate *aggregate demand* "through income maintenance programs such as unemployment insurance, social security benefits, and other government spending programs" (Leicht & Fitzgerald, 2007, p. 38, Box 3.2). The aim of these programs is to provide money to people to spend on goods and services. It assumes that these people have a *high propensity to consume*; that is, rather than saving or investing the money, they would spend it on purchasing manufactured goods, which would then stimulate *economic growth*. This is in contrast to other policies and economic theories, such as **supply-side economic policy**, that assume money should be given to those who have a *high marginal propensity to invest*: those who save or invest a large proportion of "their increases in income" (Leicht & Fitzgerald, 2007, p. 38, Box 3.2). Under the Keynesian system, people are given tax cuts and the government is involved in public works jobs. In short, raising *aggregate demand*, it is assumed, would raise employment rate by creating more jobs.

Part Three

Keynesian State/Corporate Capitalism (1930s–1970s): the era of intense social, cultural, economic, and political changes

The period between the 1930s and 1970s is characterized by the economic growth and prosperity in Western countries. The Second World War changed the workings of international relations between nation-states (Kelleher & Klein, 2009, p. 11). Several trends characterize the postwar period:

a) the rise of the United Sates as a superpower,

b) the establishment of the Soviet Union as the "**other**" of the West,

c) the rise of nationalist movements in various parts of the world and the end of colonialism, and

d) the globalization of the world (Kelleher & Klein, 2009, p. 11).

The consequences of the war also resulted in the establishment of new international organizations or the reform of the existing ones. The United States used its hegemonic power to establish two kinds of institutions:

a) economic (i.e., the World Bank) and

b) political (i.e., the United Nations).

The aim was to restructure international relations in order to promote global economic prosperity and to eliminate those states whose ideology and policies would undermine global economic prosperity. Three main institutions were organized in order to promote and regulate economic relations:

1. International Governmental Organization (IOGs),

2. the World Bank (WB), and

3. the International Monetary Fund (IMF) (Kelleher & Klein, 2009, p. 12).

These institutions are also referred to as **supranational organizations** that dictate national economic, social, cultural, and educational policies in various parts of the world. The goal of the International Governmental Organization was to stabilize the economic order and promote growth by coordinating national policies. The task of the **World Bank** was originally to assist European countries that were devastated by the war to rebuild their economies through economic loans aimed at improving the infrastructures within those countries (i.e., schools, roads, and dams). As Europe prospered and many ex-colonial countries became independent, the mandate of the World Bank also changed and it started to provide financial assistance and loans to the newly independent countries to industrialize and modernize (Kelleher & Klein, 2009, p. 12).

The goal of the **International Monetary Fund** was to give loans to "restore international confidence in a country's currency if its value plummet[ed]" (Kelleher & Klein, 2009, p. 12). The problem with these institutions has been that those members that contribute the most to their financial well-being (the donors) determine and control policy initiatives and have the voting power to influence policy directions. In short, Western countries have dominated these institutions and their policies have tended to benefit capitalist societies and Western corporations (Kelleher & Klein, 2009, p. 12). Other examples of newly established supranational bodies include **The General Agreement on Tariffs and Trade,** which has since changed its name to **World Trade Organization** (WTO). The aim of WTO is to lower tariffs globally in order to promote and improve interstate economic relations. The initial plan focused on what has come to be known as *most-favored-nation status,* which promoted the creation of economic agreements between two nation-states to decrease tariffs for specific products or categories. The WTO has tremendous power and uses a variety of ways of enforcing these policies. Due to its efforts, the general tariffs around the world have decreased, which has resulted in the ease in the movement of capital and investment around the world, benefitting the corporations (Kelleher & Klein, 2009, p. 12).

The task of the **United Nations** that was established in 1945 was to deal with security threats. However, its mission and functions have expanded since then. The *General Assembly* of the United Nations provides a forum for all members to discuss issues pertaining to them. The *Security Council* deals with those events and issues that threaten peace globally. The five permanent members of the fifteen member council (the United States, the United Kingdom, France, Russia, and China) have the most power and can veto policies and resolutions that they deem against their interests.

Militarization of the World: military industrial complex, educational security state, national security state, and industrial-consumer society

In addition to the establishment of various supranational bodies, soon after the end of World War II, the United States also introduced the **Marshall Plan** to rebuild Europe, fight Communism, and stop its expansion across the world. The *Marshall plan* provided economic aid to European states as a way to provide American corporations with a network to control economic structures globally (Zinn, 2003, p. 438). The $19 billion aid in four years aimed at providing markets for American goods produced by corporations in Europe. It was also a way to exert pressure on politicians in certain countries in Europe to make sure that communist and socialist candidates in, for example, Italy and France would be kept out of cabinet posts (Zinn, 2003, p. 438). Since 1952, the American aid to the rest of the world emphasized building up military power in non-Western parts of the world to fight "communism". From 1952 to 1962, for example, out of $52 billion in aid, only $5 billion was geared toward nonmilitary development (Zinn, 2003, p. 438). Even when President Kennedy introduced his Alliance for Progress programs for Latin America that aimed at social reforms, the majority of help was military assistance to keep right-wing governments in power (Zinn, 2003, p. 438). An important characteristic of this era was also the space "war" between the Soviet Union and the West. In general, the Americans intervened in the political affairs of many countries to assert their economic and political interests. In 1953, for example, Americans ousted the democratically elected government of Iran through a CIA sponsored *coup d'état*. The Americans soon influenced the design and implementation of economic modernization programs that changed the structure of social, economic, and cultural life in Iran through the introduction of the *White Revolution* programs. These interventions had economic bases. In Guatemala, for example, the left-wing government of President Jacobo Arbenz had confiscated and nationalized 234,000 acres of land owned by United Fruit, an American company. Although he compensated this company, it was deemed as unacceptable by the company directors. As a result, with the assistance of the United States, mercenary forces trained by the American armed forces invaded this country and put into power Colonel Carlos Castillo Armas who "gave the land back to United Fruit, abolished the tax on interest and dividends to foreign investors, eliminated the secret ballot, and jailed thousands of political critics" (Zinn, 2003, p. 439).

The period from the 1930s to the 1970s also corresponds to the role of World War II in the rise of a **warfare economy** and *military industrial complex*. According to Giddens (1990), one of the most important institutional characteristics of modernity is the process of **militarization**. Scientific knowledge, technology, and systems of management have been used in military conflicts around the world to inflict the most damage on both civilian and non-civilian populations. World War II was very instrumental in the success of the capitalist class in the United States. In 1944, for example, corporate profits had risen to $10.8 billion from $6.4 billion in 1940 (Zinn, 2003, p. 425). Charles

Wilson, the president of General Motors, for example, suggested that business and military should continue their alliance and push for "a permanent war economy" (as cited in Zinn, 2003, p. 425). It is at the time after the war that the Soviet Union is constructed as the "enemy other" that needs to be controlled. Through public opinion campaigns hysteria was promoted that demonised communism. The military budget was increased and more war-related products were purchased, justified as a means to stimulate the economy (Zinn, 2003, p. 425).

The leadership of social movements in other countries that aimed at bringing independence and equality were also constructed as puppets of the Soviet Union and as communist sympathizers to expand their control over world politics. For example, a right-wing government was in power in Greece during the World War II. Soon after the war, its power was challenged by the left-wing National Liberation Front, which was crushed by British intervention (Zinn, 2003, p. 426). A strong guerilla movement started soon after with a strong support amongst the population. The British asked the Americans to intervene and help to curb the movement. President Truman responded by giving $400 million in military and economic aid to Greece and Turkey (known as the **Truman Doctrine**) (Zinn, 2003, p. 426). The United States provided financial aid and military advisors to the Greek government to end the insurrection by 1949. The American military advisors implemented a policy of removing thousands of Greek civilians in rural areas to isolate the guerrillas, whom the United States had labelled as "minorities" who wanted to impose their will on the majority (Zinn, 2003, p. 426). What is striking about the Greek uprising is that they did not receive any help from the Soviet Union since this country (the Soviet Union) had promised Britain Greece, in exchange for their control of Poland, Romania, and Bulgaria (Zinn, 2003, p. 426).

The military industrial complex is related to the rise of the **educational security state** through which the government aims at directing the learning of students and its citizens for economic and military purposes (Spring, 2006, p. 3). The rise of the *educational security state* was due to the globalization of economy and its competitive nature (Spring, 2006, p. 5). The aim of such a system is to emphasize science and math in addition to teaching economic and political/religious ideologies that are central for the processes of industrialization, militarization, patriotism, and cultural assimilation of diverse ethno-national groups into the dominant national culture (Spring, 2006, p. 3). For example, during the Cold War era both the Soviet Union and the United States, as well as Canada, introduced more science and math courses into their curriculum to get ahead in and win the "space war" (Spring, 2006, p. 4; Wotherspoon, 2009).

The core of the *educational security state* is based on a **consumer model of industrialization.** The aim of the **industrial-consumer society** is to produce more items of consumption. That is, economic growth is measured through the level of services and goods consumed by the population (Spring, 2006, p. 4). According to the **industrial-consumer paradigm**, personal satisfaction is achieved through the purchasing of products and their consumption at an individual level (Spring, 2006, p. 4). This paradigm is drawn upon as an indicator of economic well-being and has several characteristics (Spring, 2006, pp. 239–240). **First,** it is fearful of the possibility that industrialism would create more leisure time that could "corrupt workers and make them more difficult to control". **Second,** it purports that the aim of industrialism must be to constantly produce new products and promote their consumption through the "psychological techniques of the advertising profession". **Third**, advertising must create new needs for people as consumers and to impel them to work for the sake of purchasing these items. **Fourth**, it is through consumption of products that individuals can fulfill their personal desires. **Fifth**, "planned obsolescence, particularly by changing the design of products and adding new features, is to heighten the desire to continually consume" (Spring, 2006. P. 240). **Sixth**, high end brand names are tools for individuals to construct and achieve higher status and new personal images.

Mass consumption is an important element of the capitalist system. People must be persuaded to buy and consume goods, and advertisement plays an important role in creating wants and desires in consumers. In the United States, representations of the perfect 'American life' have been used to influence the public opinion (Spring, 2006, p. 59). Since 1922, psychological methods and techniques have been used to shape mass opinion about economic, political, cultural, and social issues. During the 1920s, Walter Lippmann (in his book *Public Opinion*) believed that people act based on irrational impulses (Spring, 2006, p. 59). As we have discussed previously, individuals were perceived as rational beings by many theorists since the era of Enlightenment. However, people like Stanley Roser, a pioneer in advertising, and others rejected such a view. They claimed that advertising can draw upon irrational emotions of people to encourage them to buy consumer products. In fact, the same methods were used by the Committee for Public Information during World Wars I and II to create posters and advertisements for the war effort that "appealed to emotions rather than reason" (Spring, 2006, p. 59). Lippmann believed that "mass behaviour could be manipulated by influencing the public imagination" (Spring, 2006, p. 61). Advertising campaigns and public relations schemes began to manipulate people's emotions and desires instead of their reason. Public opinion could be controlled through images and symbols in schools, the media, clubs, and community organizations.

The *educational security state* is also an element of the **national security state**. The aim of the *national security state* is to use all the available institutions of society, such as schools, the media, the economy, and popular culture, for military purposes and preparedness (Spring, 2006, p. 5). In such a system, who we are and how we define our status within society is determined by brand loyalty and the types of items we consume (i.e., purchasing a BMW) (Spring, 2006, p. 4). In general, in the context of these systems, there is a tendency to construct internal groups, outsiders, and other states as the "**other**" and as enemies that need to be feared and controlled (Spring, 2006, p. 7). After the Russian Revolution of 1917, which institutionalized the communist ideology as the state ideology, for example, American politicians introduced the "100% Americanism" policy in schools. This policy aimed at controlling and limiting the growth of socialist ideas in America and required the implementation of patriotic school activities, censorship of textbooks, and firing of teachers who were viewed as having subversive (socialist) ideas or tendencies (Spring, 2006, p. 7). Also, during the 1950s, the ideas of John Dewey and other progressive educators were labelled dangerous. Their views were considered subversive by many patriotic organizations, such as the American Legion (Spring, 2006, p. 18). Ironically, Dewey's ideas on education also influenced Chinese educators during the 1920s; however, on the advent of communist control of the state in China, these ideas and the American system of education that were already implemented in China were critiqued as capitalist in nature and undermining the socialist effort to equalize society (Spring, 2006, p. 25).

What we notice in this era is the increased power of the elite in Western societies. C. Wright Mills in his book *Power Elite* argued that the military forms one of the elite powers in society in addition to politicians and corporate elites (Zinn, 2003, p. 438). C. Wright Mills employed Marxist and Weberian analysis in his study of mass society. He argued that mass society is the outcome of the process of rationalization. In a mass society, the power elites consist of business, political, and military leaders who govern our lives (Wotherspoon, 1998, p. 25). In such a society, formal education and colleges are mechanisms for access to positions of power, enabling the elite to foster their solidarity and control of important institutions in society. Schools and colleges reproduce a body of experts in technical knowledge and are also based on practices that promote "rational processes of planning and management" (Wotherspoon, 1998, p. 25).

The Rise of the Welfare State

The growth of economy based on Fordism during the 1950s and 1960s in Western European centres and the United States was achieved due to what has been often referred to as **managed capitalism** (Allen, 1996a, p. 286). *Managed Capitalism* is based on a large-scale management of the economy and other sectors of life. In this system, governments took central roles in regulating and directing national economies (Allen, 1996a, p. 286). For example, in the United Kingdom, the introduction of welfare payments raised the spending power of the people, which helped to sustain the growth of the market (Allen, 1996a, p. 286). The period between the 1930s and the 1970s was also characterized by the emergence of the **welfare state**, which is a form of capitalist society (Teeple, 1995). Gary Teeple (1995, p. 15) defined the *welfare state* "as a capitalist society in which the state has intervened in the form of social policies, programs, standards, and regulations to mitigate class conflict and to provide for, answer, or accommodate certain social needs for which the capitalist mode of production in itself has no solution or makes no provision". As Harman (2008, pp. 549–550) explained, this system allowed the capitalist class to use the "labour union and political intermediaries (social democratic politicians in Europe, 'liberal democrats' in the US) to buy the consent of a workforce which was potentially much stronger than it had been before the war".

Teeple (1995, pp. 15–16) maintained that the *welfare state* intervened in four areas of social life:

1. education and health, resulting in the physical reproduction of the working class and preparing it for the labour market;

2. labour market control, providing a labour supply for the capitalist class by introducing regulations that determined the minimum wage and controlled immigration levels;

3. the point of production, "the point of contact between workers and the representatives of capital and the point at which labour has submitted to the dictates of capital" through conflict resolution and collective bargaining; and

4. providing unemployment, social assistance, and retirement insurance for those dealing with chronic unemployment and life after employment (i.e., retirement).

In terms of labour supply, for example, soon after the war, as a result of the reconstruction of Europe and due to the shortage of workers in Europe, many migrant workers were brought to Germany from Turkey and from French colonies in Africa to France to work in the factories and on other economic projects (Harman, 2008, p. 550). In England, Caribbean health workers and textile workers from the Punjab region were brought over as migrant workers (Harman, 2008, p. 550).

The rise of the *welfare state* was a way to socialize the cost of reconstruction of the economy after World War II. That is, the public paid for the cost, but the capitalist class reaped the profits. What is important to note is that the introduction of welfare policies or **Keynesian Welfare State** was partly due to fear of Marxist, socialist, and working class politics that it was assumed could topple the capitalist system in various parts of the world and in Europe (Teeple, 1995, p. 17). The success of the *welfare state* was dependent on several factors, two of which are:

1. the expansion of a **consumer culture** after the war and

2. the process of **decolonization**, which resulted in the creation of new markets and a large labour supply (Teeple, 1995, p. 18).

In general, the aim of these policies was to humanize capitalism by integrating the working class into the capitalist structure. By the 1960s, however, European markets and the Japanese economy posed challenges to American control of the marketplace. High government expenditure resulted in high deficits. These debts helped the multinational companies to grow (i.e., military and space race). The establishment of OPEC and the oil crisis of the 1970s also added to the instability of the international capitalist system. All these factors resulted in the formation of a new economic ideology and system championed by multinational companies.

Neoliberal/Corporate Capitalism (1960s-present)

The recessions of the 1970s as well as high inflation and rising unemployment caused many economists to question the validity of Keynesian economic policies (Leicht & Fitzgerald, 2007, p. 39). In their place, many focused on solutions provided by modernists and supply-side economics (Leicht & Fitzgerald, 2007, p. 39). The new capitalist discourse since the 1960s and 1970s is based on the **neoliberal and neoconservative philosophies** and **ideologies** that aimed at lowering trade barriers. It was a way out of the economic crisis of the 1970s in the West based on mobilizing certain powerful elements in the class structure (Allen, 1996b, p. 552).

Neoliberalism is an offshoot of **liberalism**. According to Giroux (1994, p. 158), *liberalism* views individuals from the perspective of humanism, which asserts, "there is a unified subject" and this subject is the source of all action. As such, the government must maintain social structures that enable individuals to achieve their goals (i.e., welfare programs). According to *liberalism*, the market is a self-regulating mechanism that is based on the most efficient way of allocating goods and services. The market is considered as naturally moving towards equilibrium and any interference with the "natural efficiency of competition" is assumed to lead to social stagnation (Steger, 2003, p. 40). In other words, according to *liberalism*, a free economy that is unimpeded by the regulative laws of the government "is as important as political freedom to the well-being of individuals and the community" (Perry, 2001, p. 362).

In contrast to *liberalism*, **conservatism** assumes that individuals have been assigned economic, political, and social roles in the hierarchy of the social structure. From this perspective, culture is considered to be unified and stable. However, culture is viewed from the perspective of elites. *Conservatism* also promotes the view that society is a unified entity. The role of the state and the government is to reproduce the existing social order and preserve the hierarchal nature of social relations and structures. **Neoconservatism** promotes moral and political agendas. It is critical of excessive individualism and focuses on family, legal, and sexual issues, and criminal activities. According to Giroux (1994, p. 157), *neoconservatism* functions from the perspective of structural functionalism. It, for example, assumes that the role of the education system is to develop certain capacities in students that fit into the existing social order and forms, such as schools, the workplace, and the state (Giroux, 1994, p. 158).

Neoliberalism

Neoliberalism emphasizes the importance of individual liberty and negatively sanctions any state interference in the lives of individuals. *Neoliberalism* promotes: "privatization of public enterprises; deregulation of the economy; liberalization of trade and industry; massive tax cuts; 'monetarist' measures to keep inflation in check, even at the risk of increasing unemployment; strict control on organized labour; the reduction of public expenditures, particularly social spending; the down-sizing of the government; the expansion of international markets; and the removal of controls on global financial flows" (Steger, 2003, p. 41).

In general, we can delineate five characteristics of neoliberalism:

1. it promotes **deregulation** (i.e., getting rid of laws protecting the environment and workers' rights);

2. **liberalization** (i.e., opening up the nation-state to investment by foreign capital, which results in the free movement of capital and investment and an increase in foreign ownership of national corporations and natural resources);

3. government **fiscal responsibility** (i.e., cutting government expenditures to reduce the deficit);

4. a **free market** without regulations and government interventions; and

5. **privatization** of public assets (Leicht & Fitzgerald, 2007, p. 42).

Under neoliberal policies, everything must become privatized: land, education, health, welfare, prisons, water, state owned industries, and, in the case of Canada, crown corporations.

Neoliberalism is an ideology that attempts to apply free market principles to all spheres of human activities. It emphasizes "contracts of short duration, including employment contracts [i.e., part-time work]; constant assessment and the continual production of performance information [i.e., how teachers' performance and their employment is gauged and determined by how well their students do on standardized tests]; the growth of the financial services sector and the expansion of financial exchanges divorced from the production of actual goods and services; and the relentless outsourcing [of jobs] … goods and services" [i.e., relocating call centres to countries such as India due to the availability of new communication forms] (Leicht & Fitzgerald, 2007, p. 43).

The aim of neoliberalism is to "'harmonize' the world of national capitals and nation-states, creating a global system of internationalized capital and supranational institutions" (Teeple, 1995, p. 2). For example, the deregulation of industries that have been witnessed in the United States since the 1980s have also been fully or partially implemented in other parts of the world. In the United States, limitations in interest rates were eliminated for banks and financial institutions (they can now give the lowest interest rates and returns to their customers). Airlines are no longer required to provide mandatory services to smaller markets and have no route restrictions and requirements. For electric companies, they are now able to sell the surplus electricity across regions since governments have reduced environmental restrictions (Leicht & Fitzgerald, 2007, p. 42, Table 3.1). Such harmonisations across regions and nations are enforced by organizations, such as WTO (World Trade Organization), the World Bank (WB), and the International Monetary Fund (IMF), that have partly replaced the power of national states. The "leaders" of these supranational organizations are not democratically elected by the citizens of the world. Yet they develop policies that are enforced across the world and limit the type of plans/policies that national governments can implement in terms of economic, educational, and social strategies that meet the needs of their populations and citizens rather than the global capitalist class. In fact, beginning in this period and as a result of the neoliberal polices, corporations have the freedom to move around the world in search of cheap labour, tax breaks and incentives, lower regulations, and rudimentary labour and environmental laws. Their aim is to reduce labour and other costs in order to maximize profits for their shareholders. National governments compete with one another to attract these corporations to invest in their respective countries by limiting the power of the unions to organize and deregulating their economies. In this system, we tend to work more hours for less pay and benefits while there are many ways for the investors to make money in ways that "do not involve making anything, providing any services, or employing anyone" (Leicht & Fitzgerald, 2007, p. 43).

One of the main features of the neoliberal policies in Western countries has been an attack on the welfare programs for marginalized peoples. During the Reagan administration, beginning in the 1980s, for example, financial help to single parents with children was reduced in such a way that for many people on welfare, they were now receiving $500 to $700 a month, below the poverty level of $900 (Zinn, 2003, p. 578). Their access to food stamps and health care was also reduced or eliminated. These cuts affected Black children more than Whites since they were four times more likely to be on welfare (Zinn, 2003, p. 578). People on welfare were viewed as lazy individuals who were taking advantage of the system. What the public was not informed of was that the military budget (welfare for the corporations) was more than the budget geared for the welfare programs.

These ideologies formed the basis of Ronald Reagan's and Margaret Thatcher's policies in the United States and Great Britain, also known as **Reaganism** and **Thatcherism**, respectively. These policies, dubbed **Reaganomics** in the US, emphasized and directed that government incentives should be geared towards individuals and corporations that have a higher propensity to invest and save. Also termed "Trickle Down Economics, it was presumed that tax cuts for the wealthy and big corporations would trickle down in the form of investment in the economy translating into jobs for the unemployed. Corporate welfare (as it is now called) for the rich and big corporations, it was argued, would increase and inflation would decrease, unemployment would be reduced, and "tax revenues [would] rise" (Leicht & Fitzgerald, 2007, p. 41). These policies assumed that due to the rise in productivity and productive capacities in comparison to wages, inflation would drop. The rise in international competition would also result in keeping prices down. Government revenues would, moreover, rise because of the new taxes that are gained as a result of the increased economic activities.

Post-Fordism and Postindustrialism

The period since the 1960s is characterized by a move from semi-automated production to automated production based on microelectronics and the application of computers. Since the 1960s, Fordism as the dominant of mode production has been replaced with **post-Fordism**. *Post-Fordism* as the main form of manufacturing does not signal the end of *Fordism per se*, but a move beyond it (Allen, 1996b, pp. 546, 551). It is simply a newer form of industry. It highlights a "break in the mode of regulation" and "a shift in the organization of production and consumption" (Allen, 1996b, p. 551). *Post-Fordism* is considered as the economic form of the **postmodern culture** (Allen, 1996b, p. 546). *Post-Fordism* signifies a new era and the coming of the information age (Allen, 1996b, p. 552). In fact, some scholars also argue that this period is characterized by the rise of **postindustrial society**. *A postindustrial society* is a society "in which service sector work and knowledge are coming to supersede industrial world and manufactured goods as the core foundation of economic development" (Wotherspoon, 2009, p. 179). One of the most striking changes in Industrially Advanced Societies (IACs) has been identified as the decline in the manufacturing sector and an increase in the service sector jobs (Braham, 1996, p. 308). More white collar jobs and service occupations have been available since the end of World War II than manufacturing (Braham, 1996, p. 308).

In fact, it has been argued that many Western capitalist societies have experienced **deindustrialization**. Manufacturing jobs have been moved to other parts of the world, where there is an abundance of cheap and unskilled workers. Moreover, we have also witnessed a rise in part-time jobs in comparison to full-time occupations (Braham, 1996, p. 308). In the context of *postindustrial* societies, such as the United States and Canada, corporations began investing in other parts of the world due to the higher cost of labour in North America. As a result of branching out, many of the unionized jobs have disappeared. Instead, as mentioned above, there has been a rise in the service sector jobs, which are often low paying and part-time. During this period, underemployment and unemployment increased with devastating effects on "minority" members of society. The changes in immigration laws have also resulted in the creation of an underground economy, through which corporations and other business organizations hire undocumented workers (and women) to work in sweatshops or as pieceworkers at home.

In general, there are several differences between postindustrial and industrial societies. Work has been reorganized due to downsizing (corporations have reduced their labour force), outsourcing, and temporary work, which have made it more difficult for people to find steady jobs and have careers (Leitch & Fitzgerald, 2007, p.32). The relationship between large corporations and cities have also changed as cities now compete to attract corporations by providing them with tax cuts, lower regulations, and deregulating labour laws (Leitch & Fitzgerald, 2007, p.32). This makes it more difficult to maintain and determine who is responsible for job creation and welfare for the population (Leitch & Fitzgerald, 2007, p.32).

Under *post-Fordism* two things happen: "transformation of the labour process" and "the global shift in the organization of production" (Allen, 1996b, p. 550). In this system we notice increased automation at the workplace and the introduction of new computer-integrated manufacturing systems that resulted in the reduction in the need for labour power to produce goods (Allen, 1996b, p. 550). In the context of *post-Fordism* there is "a shift in control ***away from machine operators to skilled technicians***, and, above all, a greater flexibility in production scale without increasing further substantial costs" (emphasis added, Allen, 1996b, p. 550).

Another characteristic of *post-Fordism* is the ability to move away from mass production to "smaller-batch production" due to the availability of new technologies. In this system, flexible manufacturing plays an important role (Allen, 1996b, p. 551). One major consequence of this type of new production was that "greater decentralization of production [was made] possible" (Allen, 1996b, p. 551). This has allowed larger firms and corporations to move parts of their production processes to other countries and peripheral locations in the world (Allen, 1996b, p. 551). At the same time, the search for new mass markets to keep the same productivity levels was also another reason for moving manufacturing industries out of the West into various parts of the world in search of cheap and nonunionized labour. This move was a solution to the crisis of *Fordism* in the West (the centre of economic growth). Instead of manufacturing industries in the West, there has been a rise in new technologies that have resulted in the formation of a "highly skilled, technical elite" and unskilled workers due to the process of automation (Allen, 1996b, p. 551). The mass of unskilled workers are also mainly unemployed. In the periphery, on the other hand, the dominant modes of production rely on routinized and labour intensive work (Allen, 1996b, p. 551).

A number of scholars have argued that under *post-Fordism* there are new opportunities for reskilling the workers, despite the ongoing process of deskilling labour.

Some of the examples of production changes during the era of *post-Fordism* include: "change in product life and product innovation, with shorter, flexible runs and a wider range of products on offer, changes in stock control, with just-in-time methods, removing the need to hold large amounts of costly stock [e.g., print-on-demand methods by publishers]; and changes in design and marketing in response to an increasingly diverse pattern of consumer demand" (Allen, 1996b, p. 552). In the post-Fordist market, the consumers' tastes are changing and there has been a shift from standardized styles of Fordism in order to account for the existence of difference and plurality in the West (Allen, 1996b, p. 552). Post-Fordism is also characterized by de-emphasizing Keynesian economics and a shift toward neoliberal economic policies.

In general, this period is believed to result in the concentration, centralization, and internationalization of capital. Corporations become the dominant forms of governance as political power is placed in the hands of corporations. The role of the state is to adapt their policies based on recommendations of supranational organizations, such as promoting low corporate taxation laws, and to reduce the deficit by cutting social programs (i.e., unemployment insurance). In reference to the education system, for example, these policies aim at introducing measures to "contain cost [limit the right of teachers to collective bargaining], ensure accountability [if teachers want their jobs, their students must do well on standard tests that are written by corporations], outline explicit performance indicators [for educators]" and turn education into a private commodity and good that is sold in the market free of regulations (e.g., the rise of learning centres for K-12 students) (Wotherspoon, 2009, p. 181). In this light, education is no longer a public good. Instead, it is viewed through a discourse of productivity, quantifiable measurements, and return on investments (Wotherspoon, 2009, p. 181).

Capitalist Stages: similarities and shared characteristics

Despite the differences between various forms and stages of capitalism, Giddens (1990) maintained that capitalist societies are characterized by the following four features:

1. They are competitive and expansionist. In these systems, technological innovations are both pervasive and constant (Giddens, 1990, p. 56). The aim of capitalism is to increase the rate of profit through production of new forms of consumer items and by expanding its control over all aspects of life in various parts of the world. For example, many corporations have been providing free samples of their products to villagers in the Global South, such as India, to increase their sales in these "untapped" markets.

2. The economic sphere is very much insulated and distinct from other institutions of modernity, such as political institutions (Giddens, 1990, p. 56). This is not to say that the economic and political spheres are not interrelated or connected. The point here is that economic decisions are made in the boardrooms of corporations and involve the owners, investors, and managers of these corporations. For example, although a lay person cannot influence the policies of corporations, the "owners" of the Microsoft Corporation influence educational policies in the United States and other parts of the world.

3. As Giddens pointed out, "The insulation of polity and economy ... is founded upon the pre-eminence of private property in the means of production" and "the ownership of capital is directly bound up with the phenomenon of 'propertylessness'—the commodification of wage labour in the class system" (1990, p. 57). That is, an important characteristic of capitalism is that property, knowledge, land, and technology must be owned by private individuals and labour power is a commodity that can be sold in the market in exchange for wages.

4. The state's autonomy "is conditioned, although not in any strong sense determined, by its reliance upon capital accumulation, over which its control is far less than complete" (Giddens, 1990, p. 57).

Conclusion

Modern societies have gone through major changes since the 1750s. This period and the accompanying transformations have been the focus of theoretical and empirical studies by the early and contemporary scholars. Economic, social, and political changes have been central to the transformation of local and global spaces. In this sense, modernity is indeed a globalized world. The effects of industrialization and capitalist relations are central to the rise of sociology. Central to the understanding of modernity is the rise of capitalism and the changes from industrial to postindustrial societies. In the next chapter, we explore the rise of nation-states in modernity and its consequences.

Chapter Review Questions

1. What are the four distinct institutional dimensions of modernity? Explain and explore two of them in detail.

2. Define industrialization. What are its characteristics?

3. According to Fredric Jameson, what are the three abstract stages of capitalism and their associated cultural forms? Explain.

4. What are the three main shifts in paradigms that sociologists have been concerned about and studied? Explain.

5. Define the term "machinery".

6. What are some of the consequences of industrialism on the workplace? Explain by providing two examples.

7. Examine the characteristics of European societies during the Middle Ages. How did political, demographic, capitalist, and industrial relations affect/change these societies?

8. By references to the United States and France, critically explore the consequences of political changes and liberalism on individual rights and conceptions of justice in modernity.

9. What were the consequences of parliamentary enclosure? Explain by references to the Enclosure Movement.

10. What were some of the characteristics of guilds? Were they conducive to capitalist development and expansion? Explain.

11. What are the four stages of capitalist development? Explore and examine each stage by references to their:
    1. levels of technological advancement and social relations of production;
    2. forms of international exchange relations; and
    3. levels of state responsibility.

12. Define mercantilism.

13. What is meant by the term "the laissez-faire policies"? Explain.

14. What were the consequences of urbanization on European societies?

15. Define capitalism.

16. Offer a historical-theoretical analysis of industrial capitalism.

17. Briefly explain how Karl Marx, Émile Durkheim, and Max Weber viewed capitalism and industrialization in modernity.

18. Define exploitation.

19. Define the terms "proletariat" and "bourgeoisie".

20. What is meant by the term "means of production"?

21. Define Luddites.

22. What are the characteristics of "corporate industrial capitalism"?

23. Define and distinguish between Fordism and Taylorism.

24. What were the consequences of the scientific management approaches in factories and workplaces?

25. In what ways was Ford's approach to the reorganization of factory work different than Taylor's? Explain.

26. Define and conceptualize Fordism by references to its characteristics.

27. What were the consequences of the Great Depression for the implementation of the New Deal policies? Explain.

28. Explore the main ideas of John Maynard Keynes.

29. Define the following terms: aggregate demand, economic growth, and supply-side economic policy.

30. What have been the consequences of supranational organizations? What are their roles in the global capitalist expansion?

31. Explore and examine the significance of the military industrial complex, national security state, industrial-consumer society, and educational security state in the development of modern societies.

32. Explore why mass consumption is considered as an important element of the capitalist system.

33. What is meant by the term "managed capitalism"? Explain.

34. In what ways has the welfare state intervened in and influenced social life?

35. Distinguish between liberalism, conservatism, neoliberalism, and neoconservatism.

36. Examine the five characteristics of neoliberalism and their consequences.

37. What are the basic elements and characteristics of post-Fordism and postindustrialism? Explain.

38. What are the similarities and shared characteristics of the four stages of capitalism? Explain.

Critical Thinking Questions

1. Critically explain why you would or would not want to live in a "welfare state".

2. Critically examine the ways in which the welfare state was a hegemonic tool in the hands of the elite groups.

3. How can you resist the impacts of neoliberalism? Explain.

4. How have the military industrial complex, national security state, industrial-consumer society, and educational security state affected your life chances and experiences?

5. What are some of the consequences of living in a post-Fordist and postindustrial society for different social categories?

6. Do you live in a free and democratic society? Critically explain.

CHAPTER SEVEN

....

Capitalism, State, Nation-States, Surveillance, and Violence

Introduction
....

As we mentioned in Chapter Six, modernity has four distinct institutional dimensions that are absent in traditional societies (Giddens, 1990, p. 55). These dimensions highlight the discontinuities between modern and premodern societies. We discussed capitalism and industrialism in the previous chapter. In this chapter, we examine **surveillance** (i.e., control of information and social supervision), military power, and the use of **violence**. We also explore the relationship between the economic system of capitalism and the rise of **nation-states**, which, as we argued in previous chapters, is one of the main characteristics of modernity that also distinguishes it from traditional societies. **Modern states** in Europe and other continents are current phenomena. In fact, many of the current *nation-states* did not exist one thousand years ago. Prior to the eighteenth century, Europeans, for example, did not construct themselves as people with a shared common history, value system, and culture (Held, 1996, p. 69). As Kelleher and Klein (2009, p. 4) asserted, "trace history far enough, and all states disappear". In fact, modern states only appeared in Europe since the sixteenth century as a result of the centralization of violence and militarization of society (Held, 1996, p. 57).

The process of the *industrialization of warfare* is central to understanding modernity. As we maintained in Chapter Six, the growth of **militarism** in modern societies was influenced by the industrialization process in terms of its organization and the weaponry at the disposal of the elite groups (Giddens, 1990, p. 58). Modernity coincides with the expansion of weapons of mass destruction and how knowledge and technology were used to produce more efficient and effective ways of destroying lives. The military was used as a force that "was directed towards other states" and acted as a "remote backup to the internal hegemony of the civil authorities" (Giddens, 1990, p. 60). The consequences of militarism were evident during World War I, during which destructive new weapons and military tactics were used by all sides in the conflict.

The power of the *state* has also been used to put down **ethnic nationalist movements** that attempt to secede from existing *nation-states* in order to establish their own *national states*. *State* violence has also affected other "minority" groups that have been trying to assert political rights within existing national structures. They are often viewed as "outsiders" and "dangerous enemies", which cannot be trusted and must be dominated. In short, modernity is informed by the ability of the *state* to use violence in a systematic and efficient way against its citizens and other peoples and nations. In other words, *modern nation-states* are militaristic and informed by institutionalized forms of control and violence.

The **modern era** is also characterized by concerns over several interrelated questions of how to:

1. form and create a sense of belonging amongst people;

2. construct a sense of nationhood;

3. link people of different backgrounds; and

4. construct a single political entity (Hiller, 2006; Hall, 1996b).

As we explained in Chapter Five, **society** refers to a group of people who think of themselves and are thought by others to be different due to the fact that they share a common language and culture. We argued that modern societies have several characteristics (Hiller, 2006):

1. **Locality**: refers to a common and shared territory in which people of various groupings live together as a cohesive unit, resulting in the creation of feelings of affinity amongst those living in that specific territory;

2. **Organization**: the survival of a society depends on how well it organizes itself in order to provide for the needs of its communities and members. There is need for guidelines, laws, and provisions of responsibilities and roles to create order and cooperation in various areas, such as transportation, broadcasting, and the arts. That is, an organized set of relationships must be present, accounting for and creating interdependence between people and regions within a territory;

3. **Durability**: relationships between members of a society need to be relatively permanent and durable. There needs to be a sense of common heritage based on common and shared behavioural patterns and a sense of national coherence. Establishment of common reference points results in societal interactions at both macro- and micro-levels; and,

4. **Self-identity**: this requires the creation of a sense of uniqueness and being different from other people living in other territories. This necessitates developing a sense of awareness of one's society, which must also be accompanied by the development of a "sense of belonging to it" through the internalization of shared symbols, customs, heroes, and a common national identity (Hiller, 2006).

This chapter is divided into three parts. In Part One, we discuss and explore the functions and types of political systems. We examine terms, such as **power** and **politics**. In Part Two, we examine how structural functionalism and Marxism view and analyze the state and its elements. We focus on **institutional**, **instrumental**, and **structuralist approaches** and analyses of the role and functions of the state. In Part Three, we examine the history of the rise of *nation-states* and their characteristics. We explore the consequences of the nation-building processes in terms of **violence**, **surveillance**, and **genocide** across the globe, with a focus on European societies.

Part One

∙∙∙

Power and Politics

In discussing the rise of the *nation-state* in modernity, we are also studying the roles of the **political system**. *Political system* refers to those structures, relations, and institutions through which the goals of a society are achieved (i.e., allocation of "valued resources"). National, state, provincial, and regional social, economic, cultural, and environmental policies are decided in the context of the *political system*.

Central to a discussion of the *political system* is the role of **power** in modernity. *Power* is often defined as the ability to exert one's will over another. Max Weber defined this term as "the chance of a man[/woman] or of a number of men[/women] to realize their own will in a communal action even against the resistance of others who [are participating] in the action" (as cited in Olsen, 2011, p. 24). This definition influenced Robert Dahl's understanding of the term: "A has power over B to the extent that he[/she] can get B to do something that B would not otherwise do" (as cited in Olsen, 2011, p. 24). *Power*, then, is the ability to achieve preconceived and desired goals in spite of opposition from others, groups, and institutions. Thus, *power* is the desire and ability to act on people and make them do what is wanted (Howard, 1993, p. 386; Kelleher & Klein, 2009, p. 165).

Politics is compared to a machine that regulates which groups and individuals are given control over others when, and how. *Power* is conceptualized as what "fuels [that] machine" (Brym, Lie, Nelson, Guppy, & McCormick, 2003, p. 325). *Politics* refers to the institutions that distribute *power* as well as formulate society's agenda and make decisions. It is a system through which individuals, international bodies, groups, and institutions bargain and negotiate in the context of the processes of decision making (Kelleher & Klein, 2009, p, 178). *Politics*, then, involves "competition for power" (Howard, 1993, p. 386). It is closely related to the **economy**.

Power is everywhere. It is an influential resource that is unevenly and inequitably distributed in society (Olsen, 2011, p, 23). It informs human interactions at face-to-face relations, for example, between parents and children and between a wife and a husband. College instructors have *power* to determine the extent to which they should focus on certain aspects of the chapter and ideas and also determine what kinds of assignments students must do in order to receive credit for the course. *Power* is also an important aspect of abusive relations. In this sense, *power* is coercive. It must be noted that power is not a zero sum game. Those who are dominated also have access to oppositional *power* to resist their oppressors. *Power* also undergirds all social institutions. Those who control the education system have the *power* to determine which kinds of knowledge are considered useful. They determine the content of the official knowledge that students must know. For example, students in many parts of the world do not learn about the ways in which their national leaders have exercised their *power* to practice **genocide** against "minority" groups. The privately-owned corporate media uses its control over dissemination of information to instill a specific view of the world onto its readers/viewers and direct and control the public discourse about specific social issues, such as tax cuts and welfare reforms. For example, the media often constructs people on welfare as "cheaters" and "lazy" people (Mosher, 2002).

Public policy and laws are also reflections and manifestation of *power* inequalities and stratification in society. *Power* is an important criterion in any discussion of social inequality (Olsen, 2011, p. 23). For example, a sociologist may ask what have been the outcomes of the *Safe Street Act* that was introduced in Ontario, Canada on marginalized groups. In answering this question, a sociologist may rely on research produced by criminologists, social workers, legal scholars, youth advocates, social geographers, and researchers in the fields of Aboriginal, Legal, Youth, Urban, and Gender Studies, which are themselves also manifestations of *power* (i.e., knowledge as *power*). By analyzing this act from a legal perspective, it may become apparent that the *Safe Street Act* does not allow certain activities to be performed in public spaces, such as "begging" and solicitation for money (Mosher, 2002, p. 50). These activities are considered "illegal" and "deviant", which actually defines what the dominant society means by acceptable types of behaviour in public spaces.

As David Schneiderman (2002, p. 85) pointed out, "the dominant purpose revealed by the Act as a whole has more to do with regulating behaviour found to be offensive by some … [and considered] 'threatening and harassing behaviour' than the regulation of streets and sidewalks". However, when we analyze the conceptualization of, for example, the squeegee kids from a legal perspective, we notice that they are actually viewed by some legal experts as "commercial solicitors offering an identifiable service to public", which is in contrast to how they were depicted by the media (Schneiderman, 2002). During the late 1990s, the *Toronto Sun* portrayed the squeegee kids as "herds of locusts who have made it almost impossible for ordinary taxpayers to drive downtown without having their cars descended upon" (as cited in O'Grady & Bright, 2002, p. 23). One politician in Toronto even stated that he would like to "wipe out street corner squeegee squads in Toronto" (O'Grady & Bright, 2002, p. 24). In fact, in the summer of 1996, more than 150 monthly summonses were issued to squeegee youth. In 2000, the *Safe Street Act* made this activity illegal (O'Grady & Bright, 2002, p. 24). Since then, many squeegees had reported that the police force was involved in their **surveillance**: taking photographs of them, jotting down their names, and identifying any "tattoos, scars or piercing for future reference" (O'Grady & Bright, 2002, p. 24). They were, in other words, under the **gaze** of the police.

Scholars and activists have pointed out that this Act emphasizes disorder as a tool to view poverty and various "expressions of social and economic inequality in the context of the criminal justice, law and order" (Hermer & Mosher, 2002, p. 16). Those who controlled the government (i.e., controlled both the machine and the fuel: *politics* and *power*) in Ontario were able to implement **neoconservative** laws to construct certain marginalized groups as "disorderly" (Hermer & Mosher, 2002, p. 16). Their ideology is reflected in the law that treats certain people in contempt of the law and as "criminals" instead of seeing and understanding the social and economic causes of their marginalized situations.

This Act is also an attempt to commodify crime, which is central to the **neoliberal ideology** of the neoconservatives in North America (Hermer & Mosher, eds., 2002, p. 19; Martin, 2002, p. 95). Crime is a valuable commodity for politicians (Martin, 2002, p. 95). The fears associated with "crime are now being marketed for political purposes" (Martin, 2002, p. 95). In their ads, politicians often promise orderly and safer streets, fight against crime, and tougher laws against repeat offenders. As a result, an emphasis on fear of crime in the media and politics turns people's attention away from more pressing national and international issues that have real and more important consequences on their lives, than, for example, the actions of squeegee kids (Martin, 2002, p. 96).

The Act stipulated that the best way to deal with these individuals is through:

1. increasing **policing** and *surveillance,*

2. placing them in the for-profit private prison-industrial complex systems that are managed by multinational corporations in the form of mega jails, and

3. decreasing parole (Martin, 2002, p. 97; Moore & Hannah-Moffat, 2002, pp. 105–120).

This Act is an "aggressive example of anti-homeless and panhandling legislation that has [also] become popular in the United States" (Hermer & Mosher, 2002, p. 11). The recent welfare reforms in Ontario and the establishment of new laws, such as the *Safe Street Act* by the Conservative government in that province on January 31, 2000, has resulted in constructing the poor "as undeserving, lazy and frequently criminal. In addition, [these] **discourses** and practices have pitted the poor against the public" as dangerous elements who must be controlled and be placed under *surveillance* (Mosher, 2002, p. 50; Martin, 2002, pp. 92–94).

As mentioned above, the media, particularly tabloids, such as the *Toronto Sun,* have misrepresented the squeegee kids as troubleshooters causing disorder (O'Grady & Bright, 2002). So, in order to protect the public from these "unwanted" elements within society, laws have been passed to criminalize their behaviour. In this sense, the views of the dominant members of society found reflections in the dominant media and through their control of the *state* (i.e., government); such constructions of nondominant groups also became reflected in the laws that were enacted. A critical analysis of the laws that are supposed to protect the citizens of a country would reveal that such acts and regulations have had negative consequences for certain groups in society. Through such acts and regulations the elite exert their *power* over the rest. An important point that emerges is that those who have *power* have been able to control the economic, cultural, and political spheres in such a way that they use their influences to disseminate ideas, enact laws, and use the coercive elements of the states (i.e., police) to benefit them.

The construction of those on financial assistance and welfare programs as "cheaters" has also been a powerful tool to implement laws to regulate the activities of the poor and marginalized people in Western capitalist societies. To combat welfare frauds, the state has now changed laws to accommodate it in achieving this goal. According to the *Ontario Works Act,* if you are a single parent and on welfare you need to be wary of having relations with any other person since, according to the Act, "persons of [the] opposite sex residing in the same dwelling place [are] presumed to be spouses" (Mosher, 2002, p. 46). This means that single parents (mothers) who cohabit with other persons are now considered as "cheating the system" and the system has implemented measures to catch them and deny services to them. Recipients, for example, are required to complete questionnaires "about their spousal status". The officials are also given legal rights to gather information about these single parents. They can visit their homes without notice or enter it with a warrant if they have evidence that these people are cohabiting. If one refuses entrance, this action could be used as justification for denial of the benefits (Mosher, 2002, p. 47). In this sense, single parents are controlled and their lives are under the *surveillance* of the *state* and its officials, which reinforces their construction in the media as "promiscuous" and "shiftless". They are the disorderly **others,** who must be despised and who have caused economic hardships for the rest of **us** (i.e., law abiding, married, and not on social assistance) by cheating the system. What is the solution? Reduce and eliminate the welfare system and privatize the services: Long Live Corporate Canada!

Types of Resources and Three Models of Power

For Karl Marx, it is the ownership of property that confers *power* on people and determines how goods, services, and wealth are distributed in society (Olsen, 2011, p. 23). For Max Weber, it is through classes and status groups that *power* is distributed in society (Olsen, 2011, p. 23). Despite their different approaches, for both, *power* plays a central analytical role in understanding society and how its resources are distributed.

In modern capitalist societies, there are three main significant types of resources:

1. **material resources** in the form of wealth, income, and property;

2. **normative** and **ideological resources** in the form of the media and the education systems; and

3. **political resources** in the form of control over the *state apparatus* (Olsen, 2011, p. 178).

Despite the control of the **means of persuasion** (the media), **means of production** (the economy), and **means of coercion** (the police and other security and law enforcement agencies) in the hands of a few, many groups and individuals, nevertheless, have attempted to organize themselves and use their collective *power* to bring about equality and equity for marginalized peoples and workers. Research based on the **power resources theory** has shown that when people organize themselves, they can influence change (Olsen, 2011, p. 185). They highlight two types of resources that can be drawn upon "to begin to shift the power balance in society": **organizational/associational** and **political resources.** Workers can, for example, organize unions and other grass roots organizations to insert their rights. *Rethinking Schools*, the Occupy Wallstreet, and the *Idle No More* movement are such examples. In the case of *Rethinking Schools*, dedicated groups of educators have organized themselves and others against censorship and antilabour practices, and have been very successful in their attempts. The existence of alternative left-oriented political groups are also great incentives for workers and marginalized people to bring about more social programs that benefit a larger proportion of the population (Olsen, 2011, pp. 187–189). Such educators and progressive organizers realize that, despite the fact that the "upper reaches of the state have been 'colonized' by the capitalist class" and that their members have also assumed positions of power in various levels of the government (i.e., the Bush Family members as state governors, CIA directors, and Presidents of the United States) and the media (enabling them to influence public opinions), there is still hope to bring about social justice (See Olsen, 2011, p. 182). Indeed, the **power elites** (i.e., political, economy, and military) in society can be challenged.

We can conceptualize *power* based on three ideal models. It can be **coercive**, through which *violence* and force is used to achieve predetermined goals rather than through consensus and collaboration. *Power* can be exercised through **influence**. In this form, **persuasion** is central to the exercise of *power*. The aim here is to achieve consensus. *Power* can also take the form of **authority**, which is institutionalized *power* that is recognized by people as legitimate. That is, one has the right and not simply the desire or ability to control and to command obedience. This type of *power* lies outside the individual and is related to the social position(s) that the individual occupies. It is an **institutionalized power**. That is, "the norms and statuses of social organizations govern its use" (Brym et al., 2003, p. 325). In other words, norms and statuses "define how authority should be used, how individuals can achieve authority, and how much authority is attached to each status in the organization" (Brym et al., 2003, p. 325).

Power: Its forms and levels

We can also analyze *power* by focusing on its **levels** and **forms**. There are three main **levels of power**:

1. **situational**,

2. **institutional**, and

3. **systemic/societal**.

The **forms of power** are: **economic**, **ideological**, and **political**, which are distinct yet interrelated (Olsen, 2011, p. 177). The *forms* and *levels* of *power* are interrelated to the main *types of resources* that are unequally distributed in society and we discussed previously.

Situational power refers to the extent to which social actors in specific situations and settings have access to *power* (Olsen, 2011, p. 178). Powerful individuals may also have access to the political *power* of the *state* and the legal system to impose their will on others (Olsen, 2011, p. 178). Social actors can force upon their subordinates in social institutions "options" that reflect their interests through use of force, coercion, *violence*, and other channels, such as persuasion and propaganda. For example, few people assign income inequalities to the effects of structural inequalities in society (i.e., the fact that one does not have access to the means to improve one's life or women make less income than men due to the effects of sexism). Rather, most people assume that income inequalities are caused by individual actions and inactions, choices or lack thereof, whether or not individuals have worked hard, applied themselves, and taken advantages of opportunities that are equally available to everyone. Thus, a poor person, who thinks and explains his/her situation in this manner, has internalized the views of the power elite as explanations for inequality.

Through schooling and the mass media, we are bombarded with the mantra "hard work is virtuous" and that when we work hard, we can achieve our goals. For example, many White Americans point out how their fathers and mothers after World War II worked hard, saved, and built middle class lives for themselves and their children without accounting for how the system might have assisted many of them to join the ranks of the middle class. They fail to consider the fact that the same system might have been working against the benefit of other groups, such as African Americans and women. For example, soon after World War II, returning soldiers in the United States qualified for the GI Bills to continue their education and find employment as white collar workers in high income full-time occupations.

During the postwar period, there was also a surge in building colleges and universities to accommodate the number of GIs (General Infantry for WWII veterans) who were taking advantage of the GI Bill and attending postsecondary education. At the time, college education was the main tool to enter the Protestant elite positions in the ranks of the middle class (Brodkin, 2002, p. 42). The GIs were also offered grants to buy homes in the suburbs that were expanding after the war. This urban renewal in the suburbs resulted in the construction of a new White-American identity, as many European ethnic neighbourhoods in the inner cities became vacant since their residents moved to the suburbs (Lipsitz, 2002, p. 65). Ethnic differences amongst White Americans became a less dividing factor, but rather a passport for inclusion into the White race. In their place, "minorities" of non-White backgrounds moved into some of these areas of the inner city, looking for cheap and affordable housing (Lipsitz, 2002, p. 65). As a result of many Ethnic Europeans moving away from the inner cities, there was a reduction in the amount of taxes that inner-city governments could collect to pay for various services, such as educational facilities.

As White Americans moved to the suburbs, so did industries, businesses, and corporations. Also to follow suit, were white-collar jobs. For example, consider the proliferation of many electronic companies at the Silicon Valley in California. These companies created many white-collar jobs and were involved in the design of semiconductor electronic parts. In fact, their products were mainly purchased by the different government bodies and the military. This industry needed trained white-collar workers, positions that were filled by White men who were able to train in local colleges using their GI benefits (Brodkin, 2002, p. 42). At the time, as mentioned above, many poor whites, migrants, immigrants, and Black individuals were also moving into the inner cities in the United States in search of better lives and work. However, they faced unemployment and poverty and lack of equal educational services for their children in the inner cities.

In the case of World War II Black and White female veterans, moreover, they were not provided with GI Bill benefits and many African American people did not qualify for loans to buy homes in the suburbs either. For example, between 1934 and 1962, less than 2 percent of the housing in the suburbs was made available to non-White families, and those who relocated into suburbs often lived in segregated neighbourhoods (Lipsitz, 2002, p. 65). In fact, the GI Bill of Rights could be considered as a form of *affirmative action* for White people that benefitted from the programs afforded to the veterans of World War II and the Korean War, preparing them for the types of jobs that the growing economy and industries needed workers to fill (Brodkin, 2002, p. 41). Throughout the 1950s and 1960s, African Americans continued to face discrimination in housing and education. Also, many of them could not enter white colleges and black colleges were too overcrowded to deal with their needs (Brodkin, 2002, p. 42).

As the above examples suggest, one cannot assume that African Americans did not work hard. They were not provided with the same privileges that the system had given to certain Whites. Here we notice the consequences of **racism** (ideas and policies that justify the unequal treatment of individuals and groups based on racial assumption that result in privileges for other raced groups) and **discrimination** ("the unequal treatment of different groups") on the life chances of individuals that are due to structural factors (Olsen, 2011, p. 33, end note 20).

Ideological power is often accompanied by presenting specific views about social relations, economic structures, and political systems as the "truth" about the world (Olsen, 2011, p. 180). For example, the term **free trade** has become an unproblematic criterion that influences how people come to think about economic, social, and political issues and policies. This discourse assumes that businesses are better positioned to manage the economy and provide services to people in the most efficient ways without any wastes, in such ways as to offer consumers more options for their buck. So, for example, government-managed health care is viewed as inefficient. The media often points to the wait lists without analyzing or problematizing the fact that there are wait lists because of the cuts to the medical services and hospitals in the last three decades. The solution to wait lists, proponents of *free trade* claim, is to privatize the system and allow for private insurance companies to enter the market. Health care is no longer a right: it has been turned into a privilege. It is not a social service, but considered as a valuable commodity to be sold to us costumers. Those who have access to private insurance can receive services. Others, who do not, are blamed for their lack of hard work and not taking care of their health and bodies.

The **antitax discourse** in the media has also constructed tax as a burden (Olsen, 2011, p. 180). When people buy into this discourse, governments are able to cut taxes to the wealthy individuals and corporations without any objection from the masses. For example, it is interesting to note that the local media in British Columbia, Canada often interviews the spokesperson for the *Canadian Taxpayers Association* about such issues. This organization "is a federally incorporated, not-for-profit citizen's group dedicated to lower taxes, less waste and accountable government" (Canadian Taxpayers Federation [CTF], 2013). The language of tax cuts employed by this organization (*lobbying group*) is very similar to the discourse of **neoliberals** who also promote accountability and a reduction in the size of the government.

In the wake of the *Idle No More* protests by Aboriginal peoples since early 2013, calling for the end of poverty and inequality, the *Canadian Taxpayers Association* (CTF) has been interviewed and consulted as an expert by the media to reflect on the situation. It stated in a news release, *CTF Proposes to End Aboriginal Poverty*, posted on its Website that CTF encouraged the Prime Minister of Canada to introduce major changes to the government's aboriginal policies by consulting grass roots, business organizations, and Aboriginal peoples who live on reserves to put an end to poverty amongst the Aboriginal population. CTF proposed a new approach that treats all Canadians equally and provides Aboriginal peoples with occupations and other opportunities. The CTF proposed five policy recommendations to advance better conditions for aboriginal people. One of their recommendations asserted that all Canadians should be treated the same:

> While abiding by treaty contracts and the constitution, phase out non-treaty laws
> and programs that single out aboriginal people. (CTF, 2013)

Central to this news release is the demonization of social programs, and the assumption that Aboriginal people have more access to services than other Canadians. In this news release that calls for an end to race-based laws and programs there is no mention of more than 500 years of discriminatory laws that have devastated Aboriginal communities and/or the effects of contemporary racism and discrimination on Aboriginal societies and individuals. Thus, the CTF has become the mouthpiece for the *power elite* and their organizations to promote a language that when adopted by the lay person promotes the interests of the corporate elite, in particular those endorsed by neoconservative and neoliberal policies. This is another example of *institutional* and *systemic power*.

Power is also "inscribed in the dominant institution of society", which is referred to as *institutional* and *systemic power* (Olsen, 2011, p. 183). For example, when and how workers could organize themselves and take action(s) against their employers is often determined by the laws that are set by the government. In the last two decades, in many parts of the United States, there has been a push to limit and eliminate collective laws that had been inscribed previously. Teachers' rights to collective bargaining in many states in America, for example, have been curtailed by neoconservative governments, such as Scott Walker's government in Wisconsin. As the editors of *Rethinking Schools* in their editorial, *This Is What Solidarity Looks Like*, maintained, assaults on public sector unions are not just affecting working people in Wisconsin and Ohio, but they are also being implemented in all states in America. The aim of all these attacks in the form of legislations and laws is to undermine and forbid collective bargaining over, for example, health care and pensions for all public employees, such as police and firefighters:

> The governors of Wisconsin, Michigan, Ohio, and a handful of other states hope to replicate and expand the policies of Indiana Gov. Mitch Daniels, who eliminated collective bargaining for state employees six years ago through executive order. New Jersey Gov. Chris Christie is refusing to negotiate with state workers over health and benefits, and has proposed eliminating tenure, seniority, and civil service protections for teachers while imposing a mandatory test-based evaluation system not subject to collective bargaining. (Rethinking Schools, 2011)

However, teachers across the United States have been organizing to assert their rights and to fight against such draconian laws and cuts to the education system that affect the poor and "minority" students more than others. They are also using their **oppositional power** or what is also called **counter-hegemony** to assert their will and to oppose these new antiunion laws.

Social and Economic Power and Power Structure Models

From a **political economy perspective**, in order to understand how society operates, one needs to study and analyze its economic structure and its influences over all other institutions (i.e., political). From this perspective, the most important group constitutes the capitalist class (See Box 7.1 - Critical Political Economy). Those who have economic, political, and ideological *power* have access to mechanisms that direct the decision making processes (Hiller, 2009, p. 114). The term **elite** refers to those

BOX 7.1 - Critical Political Economy

Although there are several different approaches to political economy, from liberal to Marxist, we subscribe to the **critical political economy** perspective. It looks at the interrelationships between cultural, social, economic, and political spheres (Wotherspoon, 2009, p. 15). It examines the integrative relations between and within factors, such as "race", gender, sexuality, social class, age, and ability. That is, it accounts for the intersection of the effects of racism, sexism, classism, homophobia, and other forms of inequalities at both micro- and macro-levels. It analyzes how society is organized and critically examines the existing social inequalities and ideologies prevalent in society in terms of, for example, distribution of goods, services, and opportunities. Critical political economists argue that inequality is a reflection of *power* differential in society. They also maintain that the dominant class plays a hegemonic role in society as it demands and perpetuates obedience from dominated classes (Wotherspoon, 2009, p. 33).

Critical political economy also asserts that in order to understand social reality, there is a need to also understand/examine how people produce and reproduce both the material and symbolic conditions of their social existence collectively. Social analysis cannot only focus on macrostructural analysis but also on how people make sense of their social experiences in the context of opportunities and constraints within the social structures of society.

Theorists of the critical political economy persuasion maintain that economic power translates into social *power* and **social capital** that are unavailable to less privileged and deprived groups. As such, they analyze the economic basis of class relations in both the public and private spheres. According to these theorists, those who control the economic system also "control" and influence other institutions within society. They contend that class ideology and *power* ideology are interrelated. That is, *power*, class, and ideology are mutually intersecting and influencing. *Power* in this sense, has both **economic** (i.e., wealth differences) and **political** (i.e., power differences in social relations, arising out of the economic process) **dimensions**.

Critical political economy also argues that globalization has eroded the *power* of labour to organize, and highlights the extent to which concentration of economic *power* in multinational corporations has affected different social categories due, for example, to the introduction of **deregulation** and **privatization** policies by neoliberal and neoconservative governments. For example, the proponents of this theory point out how in the context of neoconservative and neoliberal agendas families are now responsible for many provisions previously covered by the state.

individuals who have considerable amount of *power* and as such control important decision-making positions in the economy, civil society, and state. Elites are found in every sector of society: the economy, culture, media, and politics. The *power* of elites can be overt, for example, when they support political candidates during the elections with similar economic and ideological views. It can also be covert, for example, in the form of economic *power*. The economic elites' *power* can be formalized through the election of select individuals to governmental positions of authority. When their *power* is invisible they are often referred to as ***unelected economic rulers***, who have tremendous *power* in/over society (Hiller, 2006, p. 114).

According to the **pluralist model**, *power* is "shared" by many competing **interest groups**. *Interest groups* refer to associations of citizens and members of corporations or grass-roots organizations that attempt to influence socioeconomic and political policies of the state. These groups organize political action committees (PACs) that support/oppose other political, social, and cultural groups or policies of the government. The assumption of this model is that these various groups form alliances amongst and between themselves and make compromises that promote their varied interests. They also act as veto groups and attempt to make sure that the opposition does not achieve its goals. Another assumption of this model is that political *power* is diffused. That is, there are **plural elite groups** that are formed according to various economic, political, labour, bureaucratic, and ideological factors/relations.

In contrast, the **power elite model** asserts that *power* is concentrated among the rich who act as self-conscious cohesive units. *Power elites* are divided into several main categories of military, government, media, labour unions, corporate sectors, and other groups in the economy. According to this theory, a few groups have power and control the economy. The super-rich control society since these elites have *power* both inside and outside the government. For example, few capitalist families control much of the economy, the media, finance institutions, and the commerce (i.e., they own the means of economic and ideological productions). *Economic elites* influence the direction of the capitalist society in a number of ways. Their members are highly educated and are mainly from middle and upper classes. Until the 1960s, for example, they were mainly from the dominant British ethnic group. Since the 1960s, the ethnic base of this group has expanded to include Quebecois and other European ethnic groups as well as visible minorities (Hiller, 2006).

In general, it can be stated that soon after the Confederation, the Canadian capitalist class opted to focus on finance, commerce, and transportation rather than investing in industries (Hiller, 2006, p. 114). This led to a lack of extensive industrial development of Canada outside Quebec and Ontario and the development of an extensive economy focusing on extraction and export of natural resources (See Box 7.2- The Staple Thesis). Accordingly, there has been an antagonistic relationship between Canadian merchant and industrial capitalists. The merchant capitalist (i.e., the bankers) saw it in their best interest to develop a staple economy that undermined industrial development. As a result, Canadian industries developed partly because of the influences of American branch plants. However, Richardson has shown that the Canadian *economic elite* belonged to both factions and "considerable capital integration existed within the elite" (Hiller, 2006, p. 114).

Analysis of Elite Groups in Canada

The Canadian sociologist, John Porter, in his book the *Vertical Mosaic*, stated that *power* refers to the "general social need for order" (Hiller, 2006, p. 115). He maintained that despite differences between various elite groups, they work towards establishing and maintaining societal equilibrium.

BOX 7.2 - The Staple Thesis

As a political economist would argue, in order to understand the Canadian economy, there is a need to analyze it in the context of the industrialisation process in other countries, such as the United States, which viewed Canadian resources as commodities needed for industrial developments in their countries. The **staples thesis** states that an emphasis on natural resources as the main focus of economic activities has resulted in the export of labour-intensive industrial jobs in Canada.

Harold Innis, proponent of the staples thesis, maintained that the foundation of Canadian society was based on the establishing of **staple industries** for export "to empire societies" (Hiller, 2006, p. 49). That is, Canada tends to export fish, lumber, minerals, or agricultural products to other countries. This has resulted in the development of the Canadian hinterland; and Canada's resources have been exploited by external markets. That is, Canada has developed, what is referred to as, **resource-based communities**, which are based on extractive industries.

In Canada, there are many small single-industry towns that are resource based, where the majority of jobs are found in a single industry. Fluctuations in the global market in terms of prices and changing demands for these products often have had devastating consequences for the labour force in these small towns, resulting in unemployment, suicide, poverty, and displacement (Hiller, 2006, p. 49). The problem with this type of industries is that they are capital intensive and most of the capital is provided by other core countries, such as the United States and Japan, resulting in higher rates of foreign ownership. Another problem with this type of economy is that it hampers diversification of the labour force. It also impedes the general industrial growth of the country, in that most workers in this sector are unskilled or semiskilled blue-collar workers. In addition, as Canada exports its natural resources, the country is also exporting labour-intensive industrial jobs (Hiller, 2006, p. 50). These jobs tend to add more value to products and lack of such jobs and the related industries result in, what is referred to as, the **staple trap**.

The end result of this resource-based economy has been making Canada a **shadow society**. The independence and exceptionality of a *shadow society* is undermined by the influences of other industrialized countries in the form of "foreign ownership, the importation of skilled labour and cultural penetration" (Hiller, 2006, p. 51).

He identified several forms of elite, such as economic, media, and bureaucratic. Porter looked at the extent to which these groups were interconnected. He also accounted for the extent to which their members crossed boundaries and formed coalitions (Hiller, 2006, p. 115).

During the early 1950s, the *economic elites*, according to Porter, consisted of a few White men (985 in total) who controlled management positions, owned the means of production and investments, and "hold directorship in 170 corporations" (Hiller, 2006, p. 115). During this period, there was a clear concentration of power in the hands of a few people who were well connected. Several factors characterised this group. **First**, members of this *economic elite* sat on each other's various boards of directors and formed **interlocking directorship**. **Second**, few famous and powerful families dominated the *economic elite*. **Third**, most of the members had obtained high levels of education. **Fourth**, they were mainly of British background with few Catholic and Quebecois families. That is, they were mainly White. **Fifth**, they were also members of exclusive elite private clubs and were also involved on the boards of charities, educational institutions, and trade associations (Hiller, 2006, p. 115). As such, they could influence policy directions in these other institutions that reflected their economic interests.

In contrast, the **elite of organized unions**, according to Porter, consisted of members who were mainly foreign born and had lower levels of educational attainment. Most came from working class backgrounds (Hiller, 2006, p. 115). The **political and federal bureaucratic elites** had a higher proportion of Canadian born members. They were mainly from British, Protestant, and professional backgrounds and had obtained university education. Many of them also resided in the province of Ontario. The **mass media elites** were smaller in size. Most of the industry in the English speaking parts was controlled by a few families. The **intellectual and religious elites** were less homogenized than the other groups.

Wallace Clement and His Analysis of Elites

Wallace Clement argued that in order to better understand the nature of the Canadian economic system, there is a need to approach such an analysis from a continental perspective (i.e., in reference to American influences). He pointed out that *interlocking directorship* was still an important characteristic of the Canadian *economic elites* that he characterized as **corporate elites** (Hiller, 2006, p. 116). For example, the most significant interlocking aspect of corporations could be found in the Canadian Imperial Bank of Commerce, the Bank of Montreal, Royal Bank, the CPR, and Sun Life (insurance). He showed that by the 1970s there was more concentration of power and control over the economy by a few corporations.

Clement also argued that there is also a close relationship between American and Canadian economic *power elites*. He identified three main elite groups: the **indigenous elite**, controlling Canadian corporations in finance, transportation, and utilities. The **comprador elite** refers to those Canadian-born individuals who controlled the managerial and directorship positions in foreign-controlled corporations that operated in Canada in the manufacturing and natural resources sectors. The **parasite elite** refers to those individuals who controlled the multinational corporations that were based outside Canada but operate in this country. Clement focused on the role of *corporate elites* (Hiller, 2006, p. 116). In fact, he pointed out that as a result of a rise in subsidiaries in Canada, there had been a corresponding decrease in the number of corporations from 170 to 113 (Hiller, 2006, p. 115).

Clement also emphasized the extent to which the *economic elites* have extended their control over other institutions due to the role of corporations in Canada. He asserted that there are links between the *corporate elites*, the *media elites*, and the *government elites*. Through participation in various forms of advisory committees, the *economic elites* are able to exert their influences over future public policies and economic policies of the *state*. Clements questioned the validity of a ***pluralist conception*** of *power* that Porter put forth in his book, *Vertical Mosaic*.

William Carroll and His Analysis of Elite Groups

William Carroll offered an understanding of the ***corporate elites*** based on three types of corporate power (Hiller, 2006, p. 117). He argued that the boards of directors consisted of individuals who have access to three forms of *power*. **First,** *operations power* refers to the *power* of the management to control the process of labour. **Second,** *strategic power* refers to the *power* that aims at establishing business strategies that are characterized by those who own the majority of corporate shares. **Third,** *allocative power* refers to the *power* that is controlled by those who are in charge of finance and the line of credit. The board of directors, he pointed out, is composed of representatives from all these forms.

According to his research, there is more diversity amongst the members of the boards of directors. For example, women now consist of about 10 percent of the *corporate elite*. There is also greater ethnic diversity amongst the boards of directors (i.e., more Jewish and French-Canadian backgrounds); despite the fact that those with British descent continue to be overrepresented. In addition, elites no longer join elite clubs as a way of distinguishing between themselves and others. The *economic elites* are now older and have more educational credentials.

Due to the fact that the size of these boards has decreased, *interlocking directorships* have also shrunk from 123 to 80. Yet, the boards of banks remain highly centralized and their members tend to have multiple board memberships in other corporations. Nevertheless, families, such as Watson and Bronfmans, continue to have control over corporations in which they own the majority of shares. At the same time, some ***nonproprietary interests***, such as insurance policy holders, workers' unions, and federal and provincial governments, are now members of the ***controlling shareholder*** category.

In general, Carroll argued that it is important to distinguish between those who control the boards of directors and those managers who control the operation of the corporations. It is also significant to distinguish between ***core elites***, or those who have inherited wealth and status, and ***strategic elites*** who have achieved important roles and functions in various corporations. He also concluded that the *corporate* and *economic elites* have become more transnational. In this sense, "the Canadian corporate elite can no longer be understood purely in nationalist terms" (Hiller, 2006, p. 118). It should be noted that the Canadian corporations do not play a major role in global economic activities, but the largest corporations are transnational with an emphasis on global market trends and relations (Hiller, 2006, p. 119).

States and Types of Government

Political sociology studies the modern institutions and *states* that are means and sites for the exercise of *power* and authority. A modern *state* is an administrative and political unit (Fleras, 2010, p. 109). It is an institutional order that deals with the perpetration of political *power*, and is concerned with promoting social stability and order through the exercise of authority (Knutilla, 1998, p. 9).

A *state* has four general characteristics: "territory, government, a loyal population and the recognition of other states" (Kelleher & Klein, 2009, p. 9).

The *state* consists of the **executive branch** (i.e., government; for example, the Office of the Prime Minister introduces laws and implements them), **legislature branch** (i.e., the House of Commons makes laws), and the **judiciary branch** (i.e., courts interpret the laws of the country and apply them to specific situations) (Olsen, 2011, p. 182). These institutions form the *state*, through which formulates and carries out the laws and public policies of a country that regulates the lives of its citizens in the **civil society** (Brym et al., 2003, p. 326).

Civil society refers to all aspects of social life that are organized by voluntary and private arrangements between individuals and groups outside the control of the *state* (Brym et al., 2003, p. 326). It consists of **political parties** that provide alternative social policies; **lobbies** (for example, *interest groups* that help shape *state* policies); the **mass media**, which keeps an eye on the government and informs **public opinion**; and the **social movements**, or those collective actions that aim at changing society, the political systems, and social order (i.e., student movements, feminist movements, and Idle No More Movement) (Brym et al., 2003, p. 328).

Narveson (2008, p. 10) defined the *state* as "a society with a government". A ***government*** is "a political entity that is empowered with making and administering of laws and the creation of 'institutions' under its [control]" (Narveson, 2008, p. 10). It is a formal organization that aims at regulating and directing the political relations in a nation. That is, a *government* has the legitimate claim to have authority and control over a specific territory and its people (Kelleher & Klein, 2009, p. 9). Legitimacy is a central aspect of modern *governments* for ruling the country effectively (Kelleher & Klein, 2009, p. 9). Legitimacy of the *government* is achieved when the people think it is a justified institution and represents them in democratic ways. That is, political participation (i.e., voting) makes *governments* accountable to the people. The rules and laws that are designed and implemented by the *government* are obeyed and followed by its citizens, since they are thought to reflect the collective interests of the people (Kelleher & Klein, 2009, p. 9).

There are several forms of modern *states*. **First,** we have those *states* that are characterized by **constitutionalism. Constitutional states** refer to those *states* in which there are limits placed on political or *state* decision-making processes. *Constitutionalism* outlines the acceptable forms and confines of state actions (Held, 1996, p. 72). The goal of the *state* is to maintain and defend the rights and freedoms of citizens who are considered to be the ultimate judges of their own interest. As such, the *state* must also be limited in its scope and controlled in its practices in order to guarantee the maximum possible for all citizens (Held, 1996, p. 72).

Second, there are **liberal states**. In these systems, there is a private sphere that is independent and separate from the *state* and it attempts to reshape and influence the *state*. In such systems, there are attempts to make sure that *civil society* is freed from unnecessary interferences by the *state's authorities* (Held, 1996, p. 72). The basic building blocks of a *liberal state* are *constitutionalism*, private property, and free market principles. The rights of male-property-owning individuals are also celebrated (Held, 1996, p. 72). That is, the new freedoms were conceptualized mainly for the men of the new middle classes or the bourgeoisie (Held, 1996, p. 72). Most of the Western world was first liberal only after internal and societal conflicts that won universal franchise for all; they eventually became liberal democratic.

Third, we have **representative democracies**, which are systems of governance composed of elected officials whose actions are determined by the established rules and who represent the interests or opinions of their constituents and the citizens of the *state* within the context of the "rule of law" (Held, 1996, p. 73). They take the form of elections to congress, parliaments, or similar national bodies. **Fourth**, there are **one party** or **single party polity**. In such a system, a single party is considered as the legitimate expression of the will of the people (i.e., the Soviet Union) (Held, 1996, p. 73).

Accordingly, we can also distinguish between several types of *government*. **Monarchy** is a system in which the transfer of power from one generation to another occurs within one family. We can distinguish between two types of monarchies: **absolute**, in which monopoly over *power* is based on the idea of the divine right of the king/queen to rule over the people and a region; and **constitutional**: in this system monarchs play symbolic roles as the head of the *state*, and it is the elected officials who determine the *state's* policies and administer the country. In general, these types of government are characterized by **traditional authority** (also found in tribal and feudal societies). *Traditional authority* is based on ascribed legitimacy and historically held custom and accepted norms, which are practiced due to respect for long established mores (i.e., based on the idea that the right of tribe or family stems from the will of the God) (Ritzer, 2000, pp. 127–128). In such a system, legitimacy is not an individual issue and does not arise from personal merits.

Democracy is based on power shared by the people. In this system, *power* is given to the people as a whole and citizens in the *civil society* have greater degrees of control over the *state*. In **representative democracies**, authority is invested in the hands of elected representatives or politicians who are accountable to the citizens of the country. This system is based on **rational-legal authority** and personal liberty. *Legal-rational authority* (found in modern societies) refers to *power* that is legitimized by laws and regulations that are legally enacted and binding. For example, the Canadian Confederation Act of 1867 gave Canadian Parliament the power to "make policies and enact laws". In this system, the source of authority is found in the legal code of the country. Leaders are given certain power and authority based on these laws and regulations. In this system, political freedom is understood in the context of individual liberty. The globalization process, however, has led to the transfer of *legal-rational authority* from governments to corporations. The problem with this is that corporations are not accountable to the citizens who elect governments. As such, *state* authority is undermined by the power of transnational corporations (Macionis, Benoit, & Jansson, 1999, pp. 270–274).

Authoritarianist governments (i.e., Saudi Arabia and Kuwait, military juntas of Congo, Ethiopia, and Haiti) do not allow for popular participation in selecting the *government* and its rulers. Citizens in the *civil society* do not control the *state* since there are no free elections and no legal ways of removing the leaders from power.

Totalitarian governments are centralized *states* that attempt to regulate every aspect of life. In such systems, *power* is not shared and there are no means and avenues for free expressions of political oppositions. Citizens are required to show both outward and inward commitments to the central ideology. The mass media and the education system are controlled by the *government* and are involved in **propaganda** and **indoctrination** of the masses. (i.e., Nazi Germany and North Korea) (Macionis et al., 1999, pp. 270–274).

Part Two

••

Two Theoretical Perspectives: the state in modernity

There are various views of the *state* that explore its ideological *power* and authority differently (i.e., the ability to control and change peoples' perceptions). They can be grouped under three main headings:

1. **The institutional approach** assumes that the government is the arbiter between various groups with opposing and conflicting interests. The focus is on how laws, social policy, and rights are reflected in the constitution and legal documents as well as the structure of the *state* and *government*.

2. **The instrumental approach** views the *state* as an instrument of *power* in the hands of the capitalist class, promoting their interests. That is, *state* policies promote the needs of capitalism due to the fact the *state* is dominated by business interests (Hiller, 2006). According to this view, the capitalist class forms the ruling class and *power* resides in this class. The ruling *political bureaucratic elites*, it is assumed, are recruited from the ranks of the capitalist class (See McGrew, 1996a, p. 265).

3. **The structuralist approach** contends that the *state* is relatively independent of the capitalist system, but it reflects the assumptions of the capitalist system. Structuralists criticize the instrumentalist approach for its lack of attention to how the structure of the *state* (or structural factors) determines *state* actions. These structural factors aim at securing "the conditions for the continued reproduction of the capitalist society even when the necessary action conflicted with the short-term interests of the capitalist class" (McGrew, 1996a, p. 266). For example, the formation of the welfare state can be viewed as a necessary policy/structure in the long-term reproduction of the capitalist class.

It is also important to note that the *state* is also conceptualized as autonomous from the powerful groups in society. According to the neoliberalism and neoconservative philosophies "the state is not subordinate to the societal forces but can and does act quite autonomously" (McGrew, 1996a, p. 267). Despite the important role of rice farmers and their relative power in Japanese society, for example, the Japanese *government* liberalized the economy and permitted the importation of cheaper American rice into Japan, resulting in the mass bankruptcies amongst Japanese farmers (McGrew, 1996a, p. 266, See Hiller, 2006, p. 124). However, as the *political economy perspective* maintains, the *state* in terms of its educational policy, labour laws, and universal care programs uses tax payers' money to subsidize the capitalist class. For example, the capitalist class is subsidized since the state is responsible for the cost of training the workforce (i.e., K-12 education and postsecondary education).

As such, since they are not responsible for the cost of educating the workforce, this becomes a source of profit for the capitalist class.

In the following two sections, we explore in more detail the ways in which two main theoretical perspectives in sociology view the role of the *state*.

Structural Functionalism on State: the discourse of instrumentalism

Émile Durkheim was concerned with issues of social order during the period of great changes brought about since the French Revolution of 1789 and the industrialization and urbanization processes. Industrialization resulted in greater specialization, both at individual and institutional levels. In industrial societies, the new institutional arrangements needed to account for the consequences of the new division of labour and fragmentation on the applicability of traditional beliefs and values that were being undermined and could no longer be the basis for social order. Durkheim maintained that as the division of labour becomes more diverse, the occupational and corporate groups that emerge in modernity would play an important role in terms of consolidating and managing the many roles of individuals in society (Knutilla, 1998, pp. 9–10). These groups would play an important role as conduits between individuals and the polity: they communicate to the *government* the needs, concerns, and demands of the population, and inform the population and members of society about the actions and policies that are proposed and implemented by the *government* (Knutilla, 1998, p. 10). Durkheim's ideas influenced structural functionalism and Talcott Parsons.

Structural functionalism is based on diverse approaches that are based on sophisticated and abstract models, but, as we mentioned in previous chapters, certain general characteristics are shared by many of its theorists:

1. Society is understood as a system and compared to a biological system, such as a human body.
2. Every society has needs and faces problems that need to be solved.
3. For society to survive, these needs must be fulfilled.
4. For society to survive, there also must be in place certain arrangements that lead to the reproduction and redistribution of those goods and services that are necessary for, and central to, the biological survival of society as well as for its spiritual needs and the transmission of its culture from one generation to another, such as child care facilities, education system and schooling, and administrative social decision-making processes and structures (Knutilla, 1998, p. 10).
5. Society is composed of many complex and integrated parts. Structural functionalism looks at the functions of these subsystems for the reproduction of society and establishment of social order.
6. It argues that social institutions have functions: mainly to satisfy the needs of society or solve its basic problems.

7. It assumes that social systems are considered as stable and orderly due to the shared and accepted beliefs and values within society that act as a cement bringing people together (Knutilla, 1998, p. 11). That is, they assert that stability, equilibrium, and order are the normal conditions of any society.

According to Parsons, polity or political order functions as an institution that is responsible to make decisions for the entire society and to maintain order in the entire social system (Knutilla, 1998, p. 11). Despite diversity of groups and their interests in society, he argued that it is possible to establish a political order that can set goals and policies for the entire social system (society). Parsons' ideas were central in developing the theoretical perspective that is known as **pluralism**. Charles Merriam also defined polity "in terms of power" (Knutilla, 1998, p. 11). According to him, polity, *government*, and *political power* all deal with the development of a set of decision-making processes that arbitrate and normalize relations in society that is divided into social classes, ethnic groups, and other factions (i.e., the unions and the capitalist class) (Knutilla, 1998, p. 11).

Structural functionalists maintained that the best way to account for diversity in the context of an attempt to establish order and unity is the American approach to *government*: the **pluralist approach**. Robert Dahl, for example, argued that **polyarchy** is the "best" system of polity. In this system, the function of the *government* is based on "mediation and arbitration" processes through which consensus is reached between and among different groups (Knutilla, 1998, p. 12). This system is not the same as the **simple majority-rule** or an elitist system. It accounts for how to protect the rights of "minorities" by ensuring that their basic democratic rights of equity and consent are adhered to and protected.

A *polyarchy* is a complex system, characterized by institutional assurances that attempt to protect human rights and to guard citizens from arbitrary application of the *power* of the *state* (Knutilla, 1998, p. 12). In this system, legal and constitutional procedures have been developed to determine the legal *powers* of both *government* and citizens of a *nation-state*. At the same time, it is recognized that the *government* also has the right to use *violence* to defend national interests, such as liberty and private property (Knutilla, 1998, p. 12).

Polyarchies often take the shape of constitutional formats that establish the criteria for the conduct of the *government*, such as "the selection of state official". According to *polyarchists*, despite income and educational differences between individuals, all individuals are equals and have the same power on Election Day. This belief is based on the assumption that in the Western electoral system, which is based on individual votes, everyone has the *power* and is capable to change or transform the political process. In such a system, groups also have the ability to influence *government* policy through **lobbying**. In fact, *lobbying* is another important characteristic of a *polyarchy* or pluralist society. In this system *interest groups*, such as doctors, nurses, teachers, students, ethnic groups, and the elderly, can form collective fronts and put pressure on the *government* (Knutilla, 1998, p. 13).

As Durkheim maintained, organized groups can intervene in the political process without disrupting the democratic decision makings (Knutilla, 1998, p. 13). In this system, no single or dominant centre of power dominates. That is, many centres hold *power*. They "compete" with one another in the electoral process and through *lobbying* influence *government* policies, as a result of which, thus, no one centre can become dominant. These theorists maintain that the exclusion of various *interest groups* in influencing the *government* may result in its demise during the next election (Knutilla, 1998, p. 13).

In a pluralist society, it is assumed that *government's* aim is to represent the will of the "majority", through mediation and "trade-offs". *Governments* act in such ways that their policies tend to create harmony and to establish social order. In this system, it is assumed that the need to solve social problems would result in *state* intervention. Social problems are viewed as normative, that is, they result from "some breakdown or dysfunction in the overall values and norms of society". The aim of the *government*, then, is to reestablish "a normative consensus or some new normative orientation" (Knutilla, 1998, p. 13). For example, issues of sexism and racism may be "resolved" by the introduction of educational programs that aim at changing the overall values and norm in society about "race" and gender in order to promote stability and order. However, social problems are often viewed in light of "individual pathologies" (Knutilla, 1998, p. 14). To deal with such pathologies, functionalists may offer policing, prison, rehabilitation, and medicalization of such individuals as solutions to protect the public.

In addition, structural functionalists argue, social problems may be due to the **dysfuction** (a term introduced by Robert Merton) of institutions that are not fulfilling their intended functions. *Dysfunction* refers to an element of society that disrupts a social system or causes societal instability. For example, as more women enter the workforce and the ideals of the nuclear family with a stay home mom is undermined; functionalists may argue that the family is no longer adhering to its function of socialization of children, so there is a need for more child care centres (Knutilla, 1998).

Structural functionalism assumes that the American political system is democratic and is fair. However, as Charles Lindblom pointed out, the *power* of business to influence *government* policy will have significant consequences for democratic societies in industrialized worlds. Business is concentrated in the hands of a few elites able to influence the political system thanks to their enormous *power* (Knutilla, 1998, p. 14). This has been especially the case as influential *corporate elites* have created and financed think tanks to shape government polices (i.e., the Fraser Institute, informing neoliberal approaches to economic issues promoted by the federal and provincial *governments* in Canada).

Marxism on State: the discourse of structuralism

In contrast to structural functionalism, Marxism uses a materialist perspective to analyze society. Marxists maintain that humans produce the goods and services to satisfy their material needs. They assume that culture is shaped by the economic system of a society. As Marx and Engels pointed out, "it is not the consciousness of men that determines this being, it is the social being that determines the consciousness" (as cited in Macionis et al., 1999, p. 48). **Materialism** asserts that a society's system of material production (i.e., capitalism) has a powerful effect on all aspects of life: our values and mode or manner of living reflect our economic systems and the way we produce goods through application of knowledge and skills (Knutilla, 1998, p. 15). Marx maintained that humans' basic material needs must first be met before they can engage in any social and political activity (i.e., providing food, shelter, and clothing). That is, our productive activities are considered as important in understanding our ways of living. They shape our characters. Marx argued that to understand material production of society, there is a need to analyze:

1. **social relation of production**, ownership of society's productive resources; and

2. **forces of production**, technology, knowledge, and skills or tools that aid material production.

He also maintained that social structures are determined and influenced by the mode of material production. In a capitalist society that is divided into social classes, these classes are organized based on their relations to the *productive forces*. Two main classes are prevalent in an industrial capitalist system: those who own the *means of production* and buy the labour of others and those who do not own the *means of production* and have to sell their labour power. The third class, the petite bourgeoisie, owns the *means of production* but does not buy or sell labour power (Knutilla, 1998, p. 15). The capitalist class is in a structural position to exploit the workers, which results in a social system based on conflict and contradictory interests. In this system, the capitalist class has the *economic power*, which leads to other types of *power*, including cultural and political. The relationships between social classes are understood in structural terms that include **alienation, domination**, and **exploitation**. These relations are characterized by poverty and unequal access to health care or in educational settings due to such structural relations of classes.

Marx was also critical of Hegel's view that assumed the *state* represent the general interests of all in modern societies. He asserted that the *state* reflects the particular interests of the ruling party and class (Knutilla, 1998, p. 16). From a Marxist perspective, then, the *state* must be understood in the context of material basis of society. In a capitalist society, the *state* is viewed as an instrument in the process of class domination. This is due to the fact that the structures of the economy are based on class relations. The *state* is in the hands of those who have *economic power* and those with *economic power* exert their interests over those they dominated (Knutilla, 1998, p. 16).

Neo-Marxists, such as Ralph Miliband, have developed more complex theoretical approaches to the role of the *state* in modern societies (Knutilla, 1998, p. 17). He, for example, criticized the *pluralist model* of the state. He maintained that large scale corporations control *political power*, and, as a result, should be considered as the ruling elite in capitalist societies. He viewed the *state* as having several distinct parts: elected government, bureaucracy, administrative apparatus, and military (Knutilla, 1998, p. 17). He maintained that those individuals who are in charge of the *state* and its components share the ideological position of the capitalist class (they are sympathetic to their values, lifestyles, networks, and tastes) or are members of the capitalist class. As such, *state* policies reflect the interests of the capitalist class. The *state* is not a neutral entity that mediates between different groups with equal amounts of *power*. He maintained that the term "national interest" is a discourse of power and is an ideological way to manipulate public opinion and legitimize the class domination that is prevalent in capitalist society (Knutilla, 1998, p. 18).

Nicas Poulantzas offered an alternative theory to the *pluralist approach* to the *state*. He was not interested in analyzing personal connections between the capitalist class and the *state*. He was interested in "the role and function of the state in the capitalist mode of production" (Knutilla, 1998, p. 18). His approach is labelled as a **Marxian functionalism** since he focused on the roles and functions of the *state* in promoting capitalism. He maintained that one of the defining characteristics of the capitalist *mode of production* is its division into competing and conflicting *interest groups* with various concerns. He argued that the role of the *state* is to alleviate the conflicts between these groups and stabilize the whole system. Although he agreed that the *state* promotes stability in the interest of the dominant society, this is achieved, he explained, only when "the state has considerable degree of autonomy from the capitalist class" (Knutilla, 1998, p. 18). Miliband also argued that there are four functions that the *state* plays in capitalist societies (Knutilla, 1998, pp. 18–19):

1. To preserve law and order,

2. To endorse value consensus,

3. To encourage economic stability, and

4. To maintain and promote the nation's interest in the world.

There is a general problem with these theories. They assume that the *state* reproduces the system that is needed for capitalist accumulation. These approaches have come be known as **structuralism** since the role of the *state* is understood in the context of the overall "structures, dynamics and logic of the capitalist mode of production" (Knutilla, 1998, p. 19). They are based on circular (tautological) explanations: "the assumption that the state performs functions for the survival of capitalist system is used as the explanation for the state actions", which simultaneously promotes the accumulation process (Knutilla, 1998, p. 19). These theories are also not based on empirical research and explanation.

In short, *structuralists* assume that the *state* works in the benefits of the capitalist class, which is then used as an explanation for the *state's* role in the system. In contrast to *structuralism*, others have looked at explaining how the *state* operates to promote the interest of the capitalist class by analyzing the similarities between the capitalist class and those who control the *state* in terms of personal, ideologies, and lifestyles. As mentioned above, this approach is referred to as **instrumentalism**. These two general approaches have been criticized by others. For example, Albert Szymansk has argued that the *state* is not totally controlled by the capitalist class, but the overall policies of the state tend to act in their interests (Knutilla, 1998, p. 19). According to him, social actors can affect and influence *state* policies through various mechanisms of *power* (Knutilla, 1998, p. 20), including:

1. Policies of the *state* can be influenced directly by having members of the capitalist class in the *state* and *government*.

2. *Lobbying* process can be used as a tool to influence the *state's* policies and directions.

3. "The state can be influenced through policy-formation process" since advice from organizations and industrialists can guide the actions of the *state* (e.g., the role of think tanks such as the Fraser Institute) (Knutilla, 1998, p. 20).

Szymansk also pointed out that there are several indirect linkages between the *state* and capitalist class (i.e., the use of *ideological power* to influence public opinion, use of *economic power* to withdraw investments when the capitalist class is in opposition to *state* policies, and through funding of political candidates, affecting the electoral process) (Knutilla, 1998, p. 20). In short, since economic resources are unequally distributed, it is the capitalist class that can exert its *power* over the *state*.

Part Three

••

The Rise of Nation-States

Modernity is characterized by the rise in *nation-states* and the ability of the *state* to control and monitor economic, social, cultural, and political activities of its citizens. As we explored in Chapter Five, a capitalist society is conceptualized as a society only because it is also a *nation-state* (Giddens, 1990, p. 57). According to Immanuel Wallerstein (as cited in Robbins, 2008, p. 114), the establishment of *nation-states* was the most important vehicle behind the globalization of the economy. As Tilly stated (as cited in Held, 1996, p. 59), there were no political bodies and structures resembling anything like a centralized national state that existed anywhere in Europe. By the late 1500s, however, a number of independent political units controlled many parts of Europe, numbering more than 500 (Held, 1996). In contrast, only about twenty-five political units were in control of Europe by the early 1900s (Held, 1996).

Premodern *states* were not in control of their entire territory, especially its peripheries, and did not actively promote economic interactions and trade. In fact, it can be stated that in many ways the ancient *states* actually inhibited trade and economic growth by taxing the merchants and reducing their profits, thus limiting the extent to which they could reinvest in their businesses (Robbins, 2008, p. 113). Prior to the development of *nation-states*, **feudal systems** of organization were the dominant forms of political, economic, and social organization in many parts of Europe. The fall of the **Roman Empire** coincided with the rise of *feudal societies*. The period between the collapse of the Roman Empire and the end of the Renaissance, or the Middle Ages, is an epoch of warfare "among feudal lords, and the rigid dogmas of religion" (Turner, 2003, p. 1; Heilbroner, 1989, p. 26).

In modernity, existing *states* needed to transform themselves in such a way as to facilitate the creation and observance of uniform rules that led to an integrated **interstate system**. By the nineteenth century, the new capitalist *states* were faced with two major problems:

1. how to integrate various regions into an economically viable unit, and

2. how to deal "with crisis of political legitimacy" in the wake of the downfall of the doctrine of the divine right of kings and absolute state" (Robbins, 2008, p. 114).

As Robbins (2008, p. 114) maintained, the capitalist system "required for its operation an integral division of labour, along with guarantees regarding the flow of money, goods, and services". Although *states* were free to impose constraints on these rules, they could only do so in the context of a set of rules that reflected the interests of the most dominant *states* that were enforced collectively (Robbins, 2008, p. 114).

In general, we can isolate five general forms of *state* that governed Europe after the collapse of the Roman Empire. They are:

1. "traditional tribute-taking empires; up to 5th BC";

2. "systems of divided authority, characterized by feudal relations, city-states and urban alliances; with the Church (Papacy) playing a leading role";

3. "the polity of estates";

4. "absolutists states";

5. "modern nation-states, with constitutional, liberal democratic, or single party politics" (Held, 1996, p. 59).

In the following sections, we offer the reader a short history of the rise of the *modern nation-state* in Europe.

The European World Prior to the Establishment of Nation-States

Empires

After the collapse of the Roman Empire, European societies experienced disintegration and chaos and many centres of power were created in various parts of Europe. These societies experienced many internal conflicts and Europe was constantly invaded by outsiders. In 410 AD, for example, the city of Rome was invaded by the Germanic people and by 476 the last emperor of the Western Roman Empire was eliminated, but the Eastern part of the Empire continued its control of parts of the territory as the Byzantine Empire throughout the Middle Ages until 1453 when it was defeated by the Ottoman Empire (Held, 1996, p. 58).

During the Middle Ages, no centralized power was able to control the entire or parts of Europe (Held, 1996, p. 58). The political system of the Roman Empire was replaced with smaller units of political outfits. During this period, no single unifying language, national identity or political allegiances, system of law and order, or currency reigned supreme over vast parts of Europe. Many barons controlled various parts of Europe. These areas were administered separately from one another. Each area produced many of the materials needed for its survivor internally. Although it is difficult to generalize about the conditions of life in this period due to diversity of societies and systems of governance, it can be stated that on average, most people did not see more than two or three hundred people in their lifetimes and many did not have a knowledge of more than six hundred vocabulary words (Heilbroner, 1989, p. 27). The people relied heavily on the products of land to feed and clothe themselves. The diet of many peasant societies was limited to bread and gruel, and clothing was spun out of rough wool and flax (Harman, 2008, p. 140). Many of the peasants worked for the lord of the land for free, which means that most of their labour was unpaid work (Harman, 2008, p. 140).

Beginning in the fifth century, the population of major Western European cities declined. For example, the population of Rome fell from 1,500, 000 to about 300,000 (Heilbroner, 1989, p. 27). It was not until the twelfth century that European towns began expanding again. Many people also lost their lives to diseases, famines, and epidemics. In 1348, for example, the Black Plague (Death) resulted in the death of one-third to two-thirds of the urban population (Heilbroner, 1989, p. 27). This period also corresponded with a decrease in economic interactions between various parts of European societies as anarchy and chaos made the movement of people and commodities unsafe and hazardous (Heilbroner, 1989, p. 27). A few products, such as salt, iron, and weaponry, however, were traded (Harman, 2008, p. 140).

In 1000 AD, although the Papacy, the Holy Roman Empire, and the Byzantine Empire were in control of most of the territory of Europe, their power and claims were questioned and contested by local authorities and by a number of city-states, such as Florence (Held, 1996). Emperors, dukes, kings, princes, and bishops controlled many parts of Europe independently as military victors and conquerors, exacting tribute and rent to support their endeavours/expeditions (Held, 1996, p. 59). They did not rule as the heads of *states* who governed clearly demarcated territories based on universal and formal legal systems (Held, 1996, p. 59). Empires used military force to expand their territories, which were not fixed but were based on ever-shifting borders due to rebellions, invasions by outsiders, and other forms of conflict (Held, 1996). The territories that were controlled by the emperor were also ethnically and culturally diverse. In fact, many *nations* resided in a single political structure. These *nations* did not have any allegiances to the emperor, but to their own clans, ethnic backgrounds, or leaders. As such, empires were not governed. Rather, they ruled the *nations* within them (Held, 1996, p. 63). That is, empires lacked a centralized administrative power to control their far-reached territories based on regularized administrative bodies (Held, 1996, p. 63). The economic needs of the empires were often met through extracting tributes form the conquered people. This tribute was often used to "buy off threatened assaults if military power fell short" (Held, 1996, p. 63).

Feudalism

After the collapse of the Roman Empire, **feudalism**, as an example of divided authority and a decentralized "political" system, dominated European politics from about the eighth to the fourteenth centuries (Held, 1996, p. 63). The *feudal system* is based on a network of interlocking small autonomous units (Held, 1996, p. 63). *Political power* was localized but no single ruler had supreme control over a single territory. In fact, wars and tensions were common aspects of European history during this period. The emphasis was to become self-sufficient, which brought with it localized systems of **manorial-estates** (Heilbroner, 1989, p. 27).

The feudal system was influenced by Roman practices and the militaristic characteristics of the Germanic tribes. In such a society, the leader, due to his militaristic and leadership skills, gained the trust of his tribe's warriors, known as *vassi* or "servants" (Held, 1996, p. 63). The warriors expressed their loyalty to the leader in exchange for protection and privileges. By the late seventh century, the idea of *vassalic* bond was extended to "the governing of territories" (Held, 1996, p. 63). Rulers provided their *vassals* with land that they had control over in return for their loyalty, military support, and tributes in the form of taxes (income). At the bottom of this hierarchy were the majority population. They (the majority population) were ruled, but they did not act as the "subject of political relationships" (Held, 1996, p. 64). This system was based on contractual obligations between the feudal king and his lords. The king was obligated to consult and negotiate with the lords on important issues; and in return, the lords were supposed to provide the king with military support. This resulted in the creation of somewhat autonomous lords, who could use their military power against the king. For this, and other reasons, the nature of *feudalism* was based on disintegrative tendencies (Held, 1996, p. 64).

As mentioned above, *feudal states* were characterized by the *manorial-estates*. The *manorial-estate* consisted of a large tract of land that was often controlled ("owned") by a feudal lord, temporally or in kind (Heilbroner, 1989, p. 27). The manor should not be viewed as an economic unit and property only. It was also a social and political unit. The lord of the manor not only acted as a landlord but also as the protector of the peasants and the administrator of the manor. Although there were hierarchies among the landlords within a region, the feudal noble was considered the lord of the land in the context of his own manor (Heilbroner, 1989, p. 28). The population of the manor was divided into free, unfree, and half-free serfs, who belonged to the landlord. Even if you were a free person, you were still not able to sell your land, since the land belonged to the lord of the manor (Heilbroner, 1989, p. 29). A serf, or a peasant, was very much tied to a specific place and piece of land (See Box 7.3 - Peasant, Serfdom, and Sharecropping). The serf needed permission to leave his plot of land and move to another place. The serf often owed the landlord money for the services he provided to the serfs and for taxes they had to pay to the landlord. Most of the fruits of the labour of serfs also belonged to the landlord. At the same time, the landlord had obligations towards his serfs: he would feed them during harsh economic times and protect them against outsiders. Within this system of economic and political relations, economic development was lacking and the role of tradition and custom was paramount in the reproduction of societies during this period (Heilbroner, 1989, p. 30).

Beginning in the fourteenth century, however, the power of feudal lords began to decline. It can be stated that by the sixteenth century, *feudalism* as the main political system governing various parts of Europe faded away and was replaced by the **Holy Roman Empires**, **polity of estates**, and **absolutist states**.

BOX 7.3 - Peasant, Serfdom, and Sharecropping

Although we have been using the terms peasant and serf interchangeably, it is important to distinguish between them. **Peasants** were agricultural workers who were not able to leave the land that they were cultivating without the consent of the landlord. They paid the landlord "payments in the form of crops and labour in exchange for access to land and the right to grow crops to feed their families" (Leicht & Fitzgerald, 2007, p. 12, Box 1.4). **Serfdom** refers to those *peasants* who were tied to a specific land by the landlords, and who were required to provide military service for the landlord and to work on his land "in exchange for land grants" (Leicht & Fitzgerald, 2007, p. 12, Box 1.4). **Sharecropping** refers to when the landlord leases his land to **tenant farmers,** who were required to provide the landlord with a share of the crops as payments to be able to work on the land (Leicht & Fitzgerald, 2007, p. 12, Box 1.4).

Holy Roman Empires

During the Middle Ages, European societies could be generally referred to as "Christendom". This European Christendom found its source of unity in the power of the Papacy and the Holy Roman Empire. The history of the Holy Roman Empire can be traced from the eighth century to the early nineteenth century (Held, 1996, p. 64). The Roman imperial title was resurrected in 800 AD by Pope Leo III and was given to the King of Franks. The Holy Roman Empire was an attempt to unite Western Europe through the efforts of the Catholic Church. The aim was to organize the fragmented European political organization into a "united federation". The regions, which were unified under the Holy Roman Empire, "spread from Germany to Spain, Northern France and Italy" (Held, 1996, p. 64). However, the extent to which the Holy Roman Empire was able to exert its control over various regions was always contingent upon the nature of feudal power systems. There were frictions between feudal lords and the Catholic Church that limited the power of the various Holy Roman emperors.

In fact, the Catholic Church was one of the sources of power contention as were the medieval feudal lords and city networks. The goal of the Catholic Church was to impose spiritual power over secular power in Western European societies. The source of power and authority were shifted from "this-worldly to other-worldly representatives" (Held, 1996, p. 65). In medieval Europe, the theocratic positions of popes and the Holy Roman emperors were deemed supreme. This political order was based on the assumptions that the main characteristic of European societies was Christianity, and these societies "look[ed] to God for the authority to resolve disputes and conflicts" (Held, 1996, p. 65). Thus, the political ideology of Christendom was based on a religious doctrine. The power of the Catholic Church, however, was challenged by the rise of the Reformation movement and the rise of *national states*.

The Polity of Estates

Due to the demands of the various social groups or "estates", such as the nobility, clergy, and leading townspeople or burghers for political privileges, especially the right of representations, new forms of political relations were drawn by some rulers that defined their relationships with various elements within society in new and innovative ways. Beginning in this period, rulers were not simply feudal lords, but also acted as holders of higher powers that were now being conferred upon them through sacred ceremonies, such as "consecration of a king" (Held, 1996, p. 65). The representatives who acted as counterpart to the rulers were not individuals, but bodies that represented the interests of groups, such as "local assemblies of aristocrats, cities, ecclesiastical bodies and corporate associations" (Held, 1996, p. 65). Each one of these groups was an "estate" that promoted the interests of different collectivities and regions. The rulers or kings could rule legitimately as long they were to uphold the customs and interests of these "estates" and consulted with them in the form of gatherings and assemblies (Held, 1996, p. 66).

Absolutist States

Absolutist states became a powerful form of governance from about the fifteenth century to the eighteenth century. The changes in political transformation of *states* in Europe has a complex history and is the end result of several interrelated factors, such as the struggles between kings and barons, peasant rebellions, the effects of the Reformation, the rise of trade and commerce, the effects of technological changes, the rise of militarism, the flourishing of the Renaissance movement in cities, such as Florence, and the amalgamation of monarchies in places, such as England, France, and Spain (Held, 1996, p. 66). We can distinguish between two forms of monarchies during this era: the **absolutist monarchies** of France, Prussia, Spain, and Russia and the **constitutional monarchies** of England and Holland (Held, 1996, p. 66).

One of the consequences of the rise of *absolutist states* was the increase in the power of a professional and centralized administrative system and bureaucracies. Prussia can be singled out as one of the first countries that developed a number of "ministries" that enabled monarchs to rule their territories, enact laws, and consolidate power in the hands of the central government (Held, 1996, p. 68). Several changes occurred during this period:

1. the amalgamation of territories;

2. the development of universal and uniform systems of law and rule;

3. the development of new forms of law-making and law-enforcements;

4. "the centralization of administrative power"; and

5. the rise of diplomacy and diplomatic institutions as instruments to formalize relations among *states* (Held, 1996, p. 68).

These changes resulted in the reduction of tensions within *states* in terms of social, political, cultural, and economic relations and they also "expand[ed] the variation among them" (Held, 1996, p. 68).

The rise in the *state's* ability to administer the country was partly due to the extent of its ability and capacity to practice **surveillance** against its populations and subjects. The *states*, beginning in this era, gathered and stored knowledge and information about their "citizens" and as such were able to oversee and supervise their subject populations (Held, 1996, p. 68).

The *absolutist states* increased the power of the kings and rulers through the amalgamation of smaller and weaker power groups into a somewhat united, larger, and stronger political structure with a universal set of rules and laws throughout a rigid territory. *Absolutist rulers* viewed themselves as legitimate powers who had the right to decide over *state* affairs; this power was assumed to be driven from the law of God and based on divine rights. The *absolutist ruler* was at the top of the power ladder and based on a new system of rule, "which was progressively centralized and anchored on a claim to a supreme and indivisible power: *sovereign authority*" (Held, 1996, pp. 67–68).

As a result of these changes, it was no longer possible for the *state* to enforce its control over the population and its various regions through force alone. It also required the participation of people in the management of the *state's* affairs. There also developed reciprocities between those who were governed and those who governed. As such, marginalized groups within society were provided with more opportunities to influence politics and their rulers (Held, 1996, p. 68). Due to these changes, the *absolutist states* were transformed into constitutional forms that put limits on the power of the *state* by the most powerful groups in society. *Absolutist states* were, nevertheless, **despotic states**; yet, at the same time, they were involved in the coordination of activities between various powerful strata of society, such as the merchants, bourgeoisie, and the nobility.

The sovereignty of the *state* that implied a *state* has control over its territory and the people that live within its borders also implied the recognition that other *states* also have the same rights. That is, there developed an international conception of *inter-state relations*. In other words, *states* granted one another rights of jurisdiction, which implied that each *state* was independent and had rights to self-determination (Held, 1996, p. 69). This international law is known as the **Westphalian model**. This model, which was named after the Peace of Westphalia of 1648 and which put "an end to the Eighty Years War between Spain, the Dutch and the German phase of the Thirty Years War", points to the emergence of an international community of independent *states* that "settle their differences privately and often by force" (Held, 1996, p. 69). These *states* put their own interests above others.

This model was popular from 1648 to 1945 and is characterized by the following principles (Held, 1996, pp. 69–70):

1. Sovereign *states* compose the world and they do not recognize any other superior authority.

2. These *states* are responsible for making laws and enforcing them. The dominant form of logic in these *states* is the idea of "the competitive struggle for power".

3. Differences between independent *states* are settled through military confrontations.

4. "Responsibility for cross-border wrongful acts are a private matter concerning only those affected".

5. The *states* are deemed equal before the laws.

6. International law attempts to establish minimal rules for co-existence and allow for military objectives of single *states* to be met.

7. "The minimization of impediments on state freedom is the 'collective' priority" (Held, 1996, p. 70).

8. This model assumed that the *states* are autonomous "individuals" that pursue their own interests and use their coercive power to achieve their goals.

In general, during the sixteenth and seventeenth centuries, the European *states* and Japan started to play active roles in the promotion and protection of trade (Robbins, 2008, p. 113). It was assumed that the success of the *state* and its wealth depended on the success of its traders, merchants, and manufacturers. Protective tariffs were introduced to limit the importation of goods from other parts of the world. These *states* also drew upon their military forces to open up new markets for their economies. They gave trading rights to national firms, such as British and Dutch East India Companies. In fact, the creation of colonial empires also resulted in the creation of non-Western **Others** who were to be feared and treated as objects to be controlled and civilized. The British colonial experiences, for example, "proved Britain's providential destiny, that God had chosen them to rule over other peoples, and to spread the Gospel" (Robbins, 2008, p. 116). The construction of the *Other* permitted the members of European *nations* to distinguish themselves from those deemed as outsiders, "inferior", and undeveloped.

Several factors played important roles in the imperialistic success of Europeans, including paternalistic missionary zeal, **patriotism,** and their ensuing chauvinistic prides in the *nation-state.* The rationale for colonial practices was often expressed in religious and Christian terms: the Europeans simply brought civilization to the pagan and "heathenish" peoples of the world and salvaged their souls (Kelleher & Klein, 2009, p. 8). Informed by their racist and Eurocentric worldviews, they assumed that Anglo-Saxon (Western) European cultural, moral, economic, social, political systems and relations were superior to the subaltern and indigenous **Others.** The Europeans also judged the cultural norms and practices of non-Europeans based on their own values and ethical considerations, which they held to be "superior". These racist and Eurocentric ideas were used to justify the exploitation of the world and subaltern peoples of Africa, the Americas, and Asia.

The *states* also invested in the infrastructures within their *nations,* such as canals, roads, and ports and eventually subsidized railroad constructions. These investments resulted in better communication means and smooth movements of people and goods from rural areas into major urban centres and vice versa. In fact, "the nineteenth-century revolutions in transport and communications typified by the railway and the telegraph tightened and routinized the links between central authority and its remote posts" (Hobsbawm, 1990, p. 81). The *state* also began to organize and direct institutions, such as banking and other financial organizations, which "ensured the ready availability of capital" for investors and capitalists (Robbins, 2008, p. 114). The *state* was also a major consumer of goods that were produced by the rising bourgeoisie class who controlled the factories and trading companies. This is especially the case for the military that purchased weapons, ammunition, equipment, clothing, and food to organize and develop national armies. Although the goal of the development of a national armed force was to protect the country against foreign invasions, they were often used in expanding colonial control and maintaining domestic order (Robbins, 2008, p. 114).

Opposition to and reforms of *absolutism* resulted in the creation of secular and national systems of rule in many parts of Europe, Asia, and Africa. An important factor that also explains the European dominance over the world is the rise of **nation-states.** In general, *absolutist states* had less control over *civil society.* Prior to the rise of *nation-states,* people in an empire or a kingdom did not define their identities on the basis of the ethnic identity of the emperor or the king and/or did not have to pledge loyalty to the ruler. Only the governing elite were required to have these obligations and attitudes. Yet, modern *nation-states* have also behaved like an *absolutist state* due to the fact that they have not always been bounded by and followed the basic propositions in their constitutions.

Modern Nation-States: definition and characteristics

Nation-states define the limits and characteristics of all *modern states.* According to Max Weber, the *nation-state* is a rational form of *government* that has a written constitution; laws that are based on rational approaches to norms; and is staffed with trained bureaucrats who administer the everyday running of the government based on rational regulations (Perry, 2001, p. 486). As Weber argued, although reason and rationality may have resulted in self-liberation of human beings, it has also resulted in an "iron cage" that depersonalizes life due to bureaucratic control (Perry, 2001, p. 487).

That is, humans become controlled by bureaucracies. In fact, no other form of *state* in the history of humankind was able to achieve the same level of administrative control and coordination that was developed in the context of *nation-states* (Giddens, 1990, p. 57).

Modern nation-states have several distinct characteristics:

1. the territories of each *state* are fixed (*territoriality*);

2. beginning in the nineteenth century, with the pacification of the population and silencing the rival centres of power within the *state*, the *nation-state* began to monopolize and justify the right to have monopoly over the *control of means of violence* (such as the police or army);

3. governments are administered by *impersonal structures of power*; and

4. in *modern nation-states*, the ruler does not control the *state* and the country because of "divine right" or "state right".

In fact, such ideas were being challenged and the rulers were now obliged to win the consent of the population in order to rule. They needed to "prove" that their powers were legitimate and reflected and "represented the needs and interests of [their] citizens" (Held, 1996, p. 71).

We can, then, define *nation-states* as those political institutions that are:

1. distinct from both rulers and ruled;

2. have jurisdictions over a specific fixed boundary;

3. have access to a monopoly of using coercive power; and

4. enjoy a minimal level of support and loyalty from their citizens (Held, 1996, p. 71).

A *modern state* consists of a number of institutions that frame and carry out the laws and public policies in a country. In other words, the *modern state* has legitimate *power* to govern a specific region. It is a political organization and structure that has jurisdiction over the organization of social, economic, cultural, and political activities in a society. As mentioned above, the *state* consists of several parts:

1. government,

2. judiciary, and

3. civil society.

The *state* regulates and determines the lives of its citizens in *civil society*. The extent to which the *state* exerts control over social, political, and economic relations and structures has increased, which reflects the rise in the bureaucratic functions of the *state*. The aim of the *modern state* is to create a sense of belonging; to control the behaviour of the citizenry by enacting and enforcing laws, rules, norms, and regulations.

In general, the *modern state* has three distinct functions:

1. to instill obedience in the population and "gain a monopoly on force with legitimate violence";

2. to control economic activities, such as control over the production and distributions of goods, and "to take for itself a share of the national income to pay for its expenditure"; and

3. "to participate in spiritual or religious life and derive additional strength by using religious values or establishing a state religion" (Robbins, 2008, p. 113).

As Norene Pupo stated, *states* shape and inform our personal and social lives, and they play contradictory roles: they are sources of protection and justice and they also promote inequalities (Knutilla, 1998).

Modern Nation-States and Surveillance

Closely related to the administrative aspects of the *modern nation-state* is its ability and capacity for **surveillance** (Giddens, 1990, p. 57). *Surveillance* can take shape in direct forms (such as in prisons and schools) or indirectly through the control of information (Giddens, 1990, p. 58). *Surveillance* is the ability to supervise the activities and behaviours of the population or subjects in political and other spheres of life (Giddens, 1990, p. 58). Policing is a good example of the extent to which modern societies are *surveillance* societies. As an important aspect of *modern nation states*, policing is a "specialized, coordinated, proactive, and hidden" form of *surveillance* (Rejali, 1994, p. 56). Police officers confirm "suspicious and register possible future dangers" (Rejali, 1994, p. 56). The Police "coordinates its *surveillance* for bureaucracies, ensuring that decisions at the center are performed at local level" (Rejali, 1994, p. 56). Police officers are not simply involved in protecting the public, enforcing laws, and punishing criminals. They are also involved in surveying society and fortifying and examining it (Rejali, 1994, p. 56).

The Police regulate the activities of citizens within society. Different types of police forces are developed to increase the power of the different bureaucracies. The armed forces have their own police force. The border guards survey the population as they enter and exit the country. The Canadian Intelligence Security Service (CSIS) and the Central Intelligence Agency (CIA) gather intelligence information on both citizens and noncitizens, in order to promote national interests of Canada and the United States, respectively. The Transit Police enforces and monitors the local transit systems in various cities. The police also controls and spies on bureaucracies and bureaucrats. In Iran, for example, during the period of modernization from about the 1850s to the 1970s, "the new police officers were posted at crossroads, registering legal infractions, examining circumstances surrounding accidents, and enforcing modern dress codes. They moved in mobile units, investigating crimes, drafting pastoral nomads and rural peoples into military service, enforcing health and sanitary regulations, destroying squatter settlements, and inspecting schools, baths, and brothels" (Rejali, 1994, p. 57). The goal of policing is to strengthen the *state* apparatus.

In Canada, as Daniel Francis (1997, p. 30) argued, the images and the narratives of the Mountie provide a storyline through which Canadians come to believe that they actually peacefully subdued the Aboriginal people and made the West safe for settlement. This discourse of the Mountie affirms our sense of being a "civilized, orderly society, a 'peaceable kingdom'" (Francis, 1997, p. 30). The police, in fact, represents "British justice" and the power of Western civilization (Francis, 1997, p. 33). The myth of the Mountie asserts that even the "Indians" came to realize that the actions of the Mounties were for their own good: the Mounties protected them from other White people and

Whisky smugglers (Francis, 1997, p. 34). In contrast to Americans, who had to deal with the 'Wild West', in Canada, the absence of a "Wild West" was no accident, but due to the efforts of the Mounties (Francis, 1997, p. 34). The Mounties were an instrument of nation-building, "laying the groundwork for civilization" (Francis, 1997, p. 34).

The Mounties protected the nation from the influences of unwanted and dangerous elements that sought the dismantling of free democratic liberal capitalist Canada. During World War I and the Russian Revolution of 1917, for example, there was a Red hysteria in Canada. The elite groups were concerned about the rise of a communist revolution in Canada (Francis, 1997, p. 36). In order to circumvent any possibility of such a revolution, the government passed draconian laws and placed "strict press censorship [in addition to] banning various political organizations, intercepting mail, deporting so-called 'troublemakers', and putting together an extensive network of undercover agents to spy on anyone who supported radical social change" (Francis, 1997, p. 36). The Mounties played an important role in this process.

The war effort and the campaign against the "Reds" were interconnected. Any activity that undermined the war effort was considered as a seditious act and needed to be confronted: workers who opposed conscription and those labour organizers who wanted a more equitable society were considered as subversive forces (Francis, 1997, p. 37). Labour rebellions and strikes, or anyone who dared to criticize the *status quo*, were blamed on foreign elements and their efforts to change the system in Canada. In fact, it became illegal to speak and use "alien enemy" languages in public; and those writing in these languages were jailed. A Public Safety Branch was also established to control the activities of these "foreign" elements (Francis, 1997, p. 37). With their new powers extended to them by the *state*, the police force jailed, interrogated, and spied on Canadian citizens. The police also played an important role to silence anyone who wanted to offer "a counter narrative to the Red Scare" (Francis, 1997, p. 39). Police officers infiltrated unions and sent damning reports about union activists whom they accused of wanting to revolutionize Canada. When the unions in March 1919 voted to form One Big Union, this action was interpreted as the first stage towards the "Red Revolution" (Francis, 1997, p. 39). One undercover police agent went so far as to suggest kidnapping and making these agitators disappear (Francis, 1997, p. 41), which is now a popular approach to dealing with innocent Moslem citizens of Western countries by their own governments. The police also attempted to influence the types of information produced and disseminated by university professors, churches, and clubs. For example, E. J. Chambers wrote to university presidents asking them to write to newspapers, exposing the fallacy of the "Red Revolution" and socialist ideas (Francis, 1997, p. 42). These examples, in addition to the role of the police, at both federal and provincial levels, in crushing peaceful strikes by the workers, points out the extent to which the *state* used means of *violence* to create and enforce order and the *status quo* through *surveillance*. The fear of the **Other** played an important role in **demonizing** some Canadians (i.e., union members, the "Indians") and in **idealizing** others (i.e., the ruling elite and the police).

We continue to live in *surveillance* societies. Information and knowledge about citizens and their activities are used to control their behaviours. As Michel Foucault (1926–1984) maintained, modern societies are like **Panopticon** structures of prisons. As Ritzer (2000, p. 599) maintained,

"A Panopticon is a structure that allows officials the possibility of complete observation of criminals. In fact, officials need not always be present; the mere existence of the structure (and the possibility that officials might be there) constraints criminals". In general, a *Panopticon* takes the form of a tower in the middle of a prison that the guards use to control all the activities of prisoners since they can see into all the cells surrounding the tower (Ritzer, 2000, p. 599). This structure then becomes a very important source of *power* for the prison officials. It provides them with the ability for total *surveillance*. As a result, the prisoners come to police themselves and control their behaviours. They refrain from activities that would consider them as breaking the rules and label them as bad prisoners (Ritzer, 2000, p. 599). A *Panoptican* structure is a laboratory for gathering vital information and knowledge about people (Ritzer, 2000, p. 599). It is the central aspect of modern disciplinary societies. In fact, the computer and the internet could also be considered as forms of *Panopticon* that are used to spy on people and put their activities under the control and view of officials, employers, and corporations (Ritzer, 2000, p. 599).

To illustrate the importance of *surveillance* and the *Panopticon* like structures and relations, consider two people driving a car at nighttime in downtown Vancouver, Canada. The passenger of the car notices a parked police car and comments to the driver, "Police! Police!". The driver right away slows down despite the fact he/she was not driving above the speed limit. As they pass the police car, they notice that there is no police officer in the car. Their behaviour changed and they adjusted their driving habit (although there was nothing wrong with it to start with) to resemble and follow the norms and laws of driving.

Schools also play an important role in the *surveillance* process, and control the behaviour of students belonging to various ethnicities, sexualities, abilities, and racialized backgrounds. In their book, *Get that Freak: Homophobia and Transphobia in High Schools*, Rebecca Haskell and Brian Burtch (2010) argued that high schools for gay, lesbian, and transgendered students function as a form of *surveillance society*. In the high school, sexualities of students are scrutinized in light of the of **heterosexual-homosexual dichotomy**, with the aim of identifying and disciplining the "deviant" homosexuals.

Hegemonic masculinity defines the appropriate actions of male students. A critical approach to this term points to the fact that some men in society are more privileged in respect to others and enjoy higher status: men are not monolithic. *Hegemonic masculinity* refers to the ideal forms of maleness that might also be associated with being abled-body, White, athletic, heterosexual, middle class, and other attributes (Haskell & Burtch, 2010, p. 29). Those who do not conform to these measures of *hegemonic masculinity* are viewed and treated as subordinates, and, as a result, marginalized in society (Haskell & Burtch, 2010, p. 29). In high schools, sexualities of students are monitored and controlled.

In schools, *power* serves as ways to regulate and subvert expressions of gender and sexuality considered abnormal and unacceptable (Haskell & Burtch, 2010, p. 90). We tend to internalize the norms of society regarding sexuality and proper gender roles. As we internalize these norms, we take them for granted and are unable to notice how they inform the ways in which we police ourselves and other people's behaviours and condition ourselves and others to act in ways that society wants us/them to act. As such, it is important to note how *power* insets itself into the body of the individual and defines peoples' dispositions and beliefs (Haskell & Burtch, 2010, p. 91). Discriminatory views about homosexuals, homophobia, act as "lessons" about acceptable behaviours and as tools in forcing social actors to accept heterosexual behaviours that are valued in society. That is, *power relations* in society are reflected in how we manage our expressions and the way we perform our roles.

During the eighteenth century, according to Foucault, torture as a form of corporal punishment was used to monitor people's behaviours in society. Pain on the body of individuals who were considered as criminals and labeled as abnormal was a way of deterring others to engage in certain activities and actions deemed to undermine social order (Haskell & Burtch, 2010, p. 93). In modern societies, **discipline** takes a different form than through this type of "spectacle". In the nineteenth century, according to Foucault, "there is a shift from the 'spectacle' of physical violence to the 'surveillance society'" (Haskell & Burtch, 2010, p. 93). That is, modern societies are disciplinary societies, characterized by *surveillance* (Weeks, 1992, p. 230).

Power in modern societies is not something negative that prohibits an act/action ("thou shall not"). Rather, *power* should be viewed "as a positive force concerned with administrating and fostering life ('you must not do this or that')" (Weeks, 1992, p. 230). For example, the conception of sex based on biological differences became a tool to regulate "individual bodies and the behavior of the population ... as whole" (Weeks, 1992, p.230). That is, for example, if you have a penis, then, you must act like a man. If you have a vagina, then, you must behave like a woman. Foucault argued that there is a link between *power* and knowledge. He highlighted the fact that "the sharpening definition of 'true' male and female characteristics is allied to a new zeal in defining what is 'normal' or 'abnormal' in judicial, medical and political discourse" (Weeks, 1992, p. 229).

Foucault pointed out to the discourses that define for us what sexuality is and what sex is. These discourses come to influence how we come to think about our and other people's bodies, and how we define our and other people's identities as men and women. So, discourses, such as the masturbating child and the pervert, especially the homosexual, are regulative means of controlling the individual and his/her body. In this way, discipline is not administered through corporal punishment; rather, discipline becomes invisible and takes the form of **symbolic power** (Haskell & Burtch, 2010, p. 94).

Pierre Bourdieu (1939–2002) defined *symbolic power* as 'a power of constructing reality ... [That is,] the immediate meaning of the [social] world" (as cited in Haskell & Burtch, 2010, p. 94). *Symbolic power* asserts that certain forms of sexuality are more valued than others, and assumes that social hierarchies are natural and normal. This form of *symbolic power* results in **symbolic violence**: when one considers that heterosexuality is the only normal and proper way of expressing oneself, one shuns and rejects any act deemed as "homosexual". *Symbolic violence* happens when the histories and stories (myths) about gay, lesbians, and tanssexuals are denied expressions in school curriculum (Haskell & Burtch, 2010, p. 94). Those who try to question the normative constructions of sexuality are *stigmatized* and harassed for daring to make themselves visible and to identify as homosexuals. To protect oneself, one tries to hide from the gaze of society and act normal. As Bourdieu maintained, through our dispositions, our ways of gazing at people and showing our disapproval, or even through making fun of a person, we exercise *power*; for example, by telling a boy that, "he runs like a girl" or calling him "Nancy".

For Black students in Canada, their colour of skin in this White dominated society also marks them as different since it is through the discourse of Whiteness that "we" define normalcy. As such, being Black "highlights their presence and reinforces a sense of 'otherness'" among them (Kelly, 1998, p. 17). They become highly visible and under the gaze of school authority. This process of **othering** is used as a technique of monitoring Black students' usages of social space and their bodies. For example, when in groups, Black males are often under the suspicion of police; and, if a Black person enters a store or malls, he/she is often followed and watched (Kelly, 1995, p. 18). Black male students are also often viewed by their teachers as good in sports rather than in academic subjects (Kelly, 1998). Being under the **gaze** makes Black students both visible and invisible. They are often viewed as "troublemakers", "school skippers", or "criminals" (Kelly, 1995, p. 19).

The aim of the *gaze* is to make sure that those under it would want to make themselves invisible. It makes one to slip into the corner, to remain silent, to accept the lot, so no one notices him/her (Fanon, as cited in Kelly, 1998, p. 19). As Foucault maintained, *gaze* is a process through which one attempts to control people through immersing them "in a field of total visibility where the opinions, observation and discourse of others would restrain them from harmful acts" (as cited in Kelly, 1998, p. 19). That is, one becomes subjugated and dominated through "social illumination". They, then, end up policing themselves. They start self-censuring themselves when in contact with White people. There is no need for force or violence. An inspecting *gaze* would suffice. This is not to say that people under the *gaze* do not resist these constructions (For example, see Kelly [1998, p. 20–24] for how Black students **glare** back at the *gaze*). The point, here, is that *surveillance* affects us all and social control happens through discourses and social organizations that regulate our behaviours and our bodies by defining who is abnormal and what normal is.

Modern Nation-States and Violence

As we have emphasized in this chapter, another important feature of modernity and the *nation-state* is the ability "to control the means of violence" (Giddens, 1990, p. 58). In premodern societies, the "central governments", monarchs, and princes were not able to amass military force for a long period of time and did not often have a monopoly over the usage of *violence* and military force (Giddens, 1990, p. 58). The military *power* of the ruling elite was always the result of alliances with other centres of *power* and with other princes or warlords in the region. Such alliances were short-lived, as the *power* of the king and his sovereignty were often questioned and challenged by those allying with him (sic) (Giddens, 1990, p. 58). The *modern nation-state* signals the successful monopolization of *violence* in the hands of a centralized *government* that is fully in control of all parts of the country (Giddens, 1990, p. 58). In fact, war and military conflicts have been important tools in the process of *nation-building*. Related to the *monopoly of violence* by the *state* is its ability to develop modern secular codes of criminal law and its "supervisory control of 'deviance'" (Giddens, 1990, p. 59).

As Pierre L. van den Berghe (1990, p. 1) pointed out, *states* have and "claim a monopoly of the legitimate use of violence". As structures of *power* that practice mass murder, *modern states* display three main characteristics. **First**, the *state* has access to an industrialized machinery of mass killing. Killing involves the incorporation of sophisticated knowledge and science of management (van den Berghe, 1990, p. 2). For example, the Nazi government used technologies, such as Hollerith tabulation machines produced by the IBM, to manage its labour and concentration camps and efficiently kill millions of people (Bakan, 2004, p. 88). During the 1930s, General Motors also invested in the car manufacturing sectors in Germany, which produced military vehicles for the German armed forces. The entire *military industrial complex*, such as the transportation system, research institutional, and universities, are involved in this process. Mass killing is an aspect and a foundational characteristic of *modern states* (van den Berghe, 1990, p. 2). For example, during the era of the construction of railways in Europe and other parts of the world, the *state* considered them as tools of moving armies and equipment from one region to another when needed for military purposes (van den Berghe, 1990, p. 3).

Second, the *modern state* is not only involved in external killing but there has also been a shift towards internal mass killing and *violence* (van den Berghe, 1990, p. 3). For example, a study looking at *violence* since 1945 concluded that "two-thirds of all people killed by states have been internal victims of genocide, or what I call 'politicides'" (van den Berghe, 1990, p. 4). The main internal events causing mass killing have been in the Soviet Union, China, Indonesia, Pakistan-Bangladesh, Kampuchea, and Afghanistan. There were also the victims of colonial and civil wars, such as the Indochina War and the Nigerian Civil War. These two wars resulted in 3.13 megadeaths (van den Berghe, 1990, p. 4).

Third, the *modern state* kills in the name of **nationalism**. Since the French Revolution, *nationalism* has become the main "basis of legitimation for state power" (van den Berghe, 1990, p. 5). *Nationalism* has been a critical force in the development of *nation-states* and has been "linked to the administrative unification of the state" (Held, 1996, p. 78). *Nation-state*, as a concept and practice, often includes prescriptions for cultural destruction of those considered as dangerous and outsiders through assimilation policies. The *state* is the architect of ethnic and religious suppression (van den Berghe, 1990, p. 6). The main tool in this effort has been the education system and reliance on a single national language. In many Latin American countries, for example, the Spanish- and Portuguese-speaking elite groups view(ed) Aboriginal peoples as "ignorant", "primitive", and "backward" in light of a discourse that "equates[ed] progress, enlightenment, and civilization with the acquisition of the 'national' language and culture" (van den Berghe, 1990, p. 5). In fact, **ethnic nationalism** has been a pervasive aspect of the *nation-building* in, even, countries, such as Canada, that officially promote policies of multiculturalism.

In addition, another central factor that has led to the formation of *nation-states* and their rise was the ability of *states* to wage war against one another to secure resources and territories. That is, the ability of the *states* to "organize the means of coercion (armies, navies) and to deploy them when necessary" (Held, 1996, p. 76). In fact, during the seventeenth and eighteenth centuries, we notice a rise in the expenditure of coercive *power* in comparison to the minimal expenditures on nonmilitary goods (Held, 1996, p. 74). Due to the rise of warfare, more developed and permanent armed forces were established; as a result of which, the size of the *states* also began to increase in relation to the size of the *civil society* (Mann, as cited in Held, 1996, p. 76).

The survival of the *state* depended very much on the maintenance of coercive capabilities at its disposal (Held, 1996, p. 76). The competition between *states* was a reflection of the structure of the international system of *power* since, as individual *states* would prepare themselves for war in pursuing their own securities, this would lead to creation of insecurities in other *states* (Held, 1996, p. 76). However, it is important to note that there were very few people in many *states* who were willing to sacrifice their lives for the country. This resulted in *states* implementing and developing extensive *state* structures, such as administrative, bureaucratic, and coercive structures, to assist them in the coordination and control of their subject populations (i.e., police force and schooling) (Held, 1996, p. 76).

The rise of the *nation-state* is not a uniform process. In **capital-intensive** European societies, we notice the rise of *power* of the capitalist class. In contrast, in **coercive-intensive** societies, such as the Russian Empire, the landlord class came to dominate the political system (Held, 1996, p. 77). In general, the rise in warfare, in addition to its reliance on technological and administrative, as well as industrialisation and an increase in commercial activities between *states*, led to the ascendancy of the *nation-states* (Held, 1996, p. 77). As people were required to fight for the *state*, this also provided the impetus for members of nation-states to ask for democratic rights and demand "a right to a fair share in governing" (Held, 1996, p. 78). However, these same rights were denied to the nondominant *nations* within the *state* and in the colonized world (Held, 1996).

Violence, Genocide, and Nation-States in Modernity

As explained above, one of the main characteristics of *modern nation-states* is their control over the means of *violence*. One way *modern states* have controlled their populations and political affairs within their respective countries has been through the practice of **genocide**. *Genocide* refers to the systematic "mass destruction of racial, ethnic, or religious groups" (Kuper, 1990, p. 20). This definition does not allow us to make distinctions between **pogroms** (referring to organized persecution of, for example, an ethnic group) or **communal massacres**. An example of *genocide* is the massacre, annihilation, and total destruction of Aboriginal peoples and communities across the world, especially due to the effects of colonialism in countries, such as Canada and the United States. Another example of *genocide* is the European trade in African slaves or the Trans-Atlantic Slave Trade, during which millions of Africans were killed in slave raids or thrown overboard from ships en route to the Americas either because the slaves were too ill to survive the journey or were rebellious. *Genocide* can also happen due to political conflicts within a *nation-state*, for example, when a group, such as an ethnic community, attempts to assert its independence from an existing *state*, to separate, and exert its self-determination. In Africa, in the last fifty years, we have witnessed the destructions of lives through *genocide* and mass killings (i.e., in Rwanda and Congo).

The United Nations **Convention on the Prevention and Punishment of the Crime of Genocide** defines *genocide* as acts that have the intent to "destroy, in whole or in part, a national, ethnical, racial or religious group". It includes acts such as:

1. "killing members of the group;

2. causing bodily or mental harm to members of the group;

3. deliberately inflicting on the group conditions of life calculated to bring its physical destruction in whole or in part;

4. imposing measures intended to prevent births within the group; and

5. forcibly transferring children of this group to another group" (Kuper, 1990, p. 20).

Although there are problems with this definition, such as what is meant by *whole or in part*, this definition is a useful **ideal type** (See Box 7.4 - The Ideal Type) that can be applied to comparative analyses of *states'* policies towards their "minority" populations.

It is important to note that in most cases of *genocide* those who are affected, those who kill, and those who are killed are often from different religions, classes, and racialized and ethnic backgrounds. There are differences and disparities in how "minority" groups are integrated into the dominant society. These "minority" groups often experience structural inequalities. There are often physical separation and occupational differentiation between members of the dominant society and those deemed as "minorities". An example of this type of physical separation is the isolation of Aboriginal

BOX 7.4 - The Ideal Type

An *ideal type* is "a hypothetical construct or intellectual standard that can be used as heuristic [and empirical] device to compare and classify empirically observable types" (Olsen, 2011, p. 35, endnote 37). It is an abstract construct that is not found in the real world. For example, social scientists have developed the *ideal type* of a **bureaucracy**, but this framework is not considered "to be perfect and normatively desirable" (Olsen, 2011, p. 35, endnote 37). For example, according to Weber, modern societies are dependent on the role of *bureaucracies* for mass administration of the country (Ritzer, 2000, p. 126). Education system is a *bureaucracy* that controls all aspects of learning and teaching in schools. In order to study a *bureaucracy*, social scientists have developed a general model of how it would look like and organized: an *ideal type*. An *ideal type bureaucracy* is characterized by several factors. **First**, it is made of many interconnected offices bound by rules. **Second**, each office is also bound by a set of internal rules and goals that must be achieved; and it has the authority to do so. **Third**, these offices are hierarchically organized and each is responsible for different aspects of work. **Fourth**, in order to work in these offices, participants must have the required education, training, and certification. **Fifth**, the means used by the employers of a *bureaucracy* are not owned by them but by the organization. **Sixth**, "the incumbent is not allowed to appropriate the position; it always remains a part of the organization"; that is, **nepotism** has no place in bureaucracies (Ritzer, 2000, p. 126).

communities into reserves that are usually located in remote peripheries of the society (Kuper, 1990, p. 22). In short, *genocide* entails a history of conflict between groups that is expressed in **historical memories** (or collective memories) of groups that construct other groups in dehumanizing and hostile ways. **Collective memory** refers to a shared knowledge of one's history and contemporary and historical experiences (Kelly, 1998, p. 17). Yet, in many cases, these groups had lived in close proximity with one another and had been involved in various social, economic, and cultural relations. Their relations were altered due to the *power* imbalances introduced as a result of the processes of *nation-building*, colonialism, and neocolonial relations.

Although, many theorists have asserted that the *modern nation-state*, such as the liberal system, are emancipatory and based in the ideals of democracy and freedom, *states* have been **genocidal** entities. The Stalinist regime (1929–1953) is an example. This *state* created the famine in the Ukraine (1932–1933); repressed the rise of nationalism in Ukraine, and expelled many ethnic "minorities", including Koreans, Kurds, Crimean Tartars, and Chechens in conditions that were not suitable for survival. This *state* also massacred peasants and 'kulaks' as well as the bourgeoisie and the old elite members of the Tsarist regime (Kuper, 1990, p. 23). Another example of a *genocidal state* is Nazi Germany. This regime employed an extensive bureaucracy and used the existing technologies to systematically destroy Jews, Gypsies, communists, and other "unwanted" elements of society, such as homosexuals. The usage of gas chambers and fatal injections exemplify the use of modern technologies in mass-killing of "minority" groups (Lifton, as cited in Kupper, 1990, p. 40). The German Nazis introduced and put into practice euthanasia programs, or "the deliberate destruction of unworthy life" (Kuper, 1990, p. 23). The Nazi's racialized ideology was central in promoting *genocide*. This ideology idealized the German people as a "race" "superior" to other raced groups, such as Slavs, Gypsies, and Jews. This ideology intended to purify the "Aryan-Germanic race" from its corrupting influences and polluting elements (Kuper, 1990, p. 31). The hatred towards Gypsies and Jews has a long history in Germany and other parts of Europe. The anti-Jewish stance reflects the Christian anti-Semitic ideology that identifies Jews as "polluting" and "threatening" features within society, who are thought to be involved in world conspiracy to overthrow Christianity by controlling the banking system (Kuper, 1990, p. 31), a view to which Henry Ford, the American industrialist, also subscribed and promoted in his editorials published in one of his newspapers. During its brief control of Cambodia, the Khmer Rouge regime (1975–1979) also killed many hill "tribal" people, Chinese, Muslim Chams, Buddhists, Vietnamese, and Thai ethnic groups. Cambodians considered to be enemies of the revolution were placed in camps with a sole purpose of reforming them, but, in reality, to destroy them (Kuper, 1990, p. 31).

In general, Kuper (1990) identified three forms of *genocidal states*:

1. the endemic,
2. the ethnocratic, and
3. theocratic.

The **endemic genocidal states** arise due to the introduction of radical revolutionary changes to society and how the *state* is governed. The Khmer Rough's control of Cambodia is an example of this type of *state*. Their revolutionary ideology called for the elimination of various groups that were viewed through the lens of **xenophobia** (fear of foreigners). Their aim was to rid the current society from the previous regime's elite groups and "minority" groups who were viewed as "inferior" to the assumed racial superiority of the "Khmer race" (Kuper, 1990, pp. 26–27).

The **ethnocratic genocidal state** highlights the killing of ethnic groups that attempt to secede from an existing *state* as a solution to end discrimination against them, or seek better political rights within the *state*. An example of this type of *state* is Sri Lanka. During the colonial era, the British colonialists formed a single colonial unit by bringing together the two distinct populations of Sinhalese and Tamils under one administrative unit (Kuper, 1990, p. 33). They also introduced Tamil workers to Ceylon (Sri Lanka) to work in the coffee and tea plantations of British colonialists. When Sri Lanka became independent in 1948, the Sinhalese majority took control of the government and enacted laws that denationalized Tamil workers in the plantations. They also made Sinhalese the official language of the country in 1956. All economic development projects aided the Sinhalese to improve their economic positions within society. The Tamil people were discriminated against in employment, especially in universities and civil servant positions. In 1972, Buddhism became the state religion. The introduction of Prevention of Terrorism Act in 1979 also resulted in the reduction of the political power of the Tamil United Liberation Front, since it refused to "abandon its aspirations for an independent Tamil state" (Kuper, 1990, p. 34). This political consolidation of *power* coincided with a large-scale massacre of Tamils.

Such examples of ethnic *violence* are also evident in many non-Western countries that went through the process of decolonization. The fact remains that modern ethnic divisions stem partly from the consequences of colonial policies and practices that arbitrarily grouped people together or divided the land mass between colonial powers. The consequences of the artificial partitioning or forcible groupings of different ethnic groups for postindependence *states*, which sometimes capitalize on and manipulate the colonially-created ethnic differences, have been tremendous (i.e., the situation in Rwanda and Burundi). The *genocide* of Armenians after the collapse of the Ottoman Empire by the Young Turks in today's Turkey is another example of systematic annihilation of a people by the dominant group. The chauvinistic attitudes and the ultranationalism of Young Turks to create a *modern state* out of the ruins of the Ottoman Empire in 1915 were significant ideological reasoning for eliminating the Armenians (See Kuper, 1990, pp. 39–40).

In **theocratic genocidal state,** religious differences, at times, are the source for *genocide*. The religious values of the dominant society may provide the basis for stereotyping "minority" religious groups as traitors, outsiders, and elements that should be policed and not trusted. An example of this form is the efforts of Sinhalese Buddhist monks in Sri Lanka that drew upon the fear of Indian invasion to inflame divisions between Tamil and Sinhalese populations. Another example is the condition of Iranian Baha'i, whose rights as the largest religious "minority" are not protected under the Islamic Constitution. In fact, since the inception of this religion in the nineteenth century, they have been used as scapegoats and blamed for colonial interventions in Iran (Kuper, 1990, p. 42; Mirfakhraie, 2008). Although the persecution of Baha'i members since the 1900s has not resulted in their physical *genocide*, the fact remains that they have been facing *religious* and *cultural genocide*.

Nation-States and Constructions of Imagined Identities and Invented Traditions

The *nation-state* is a modern phenomenon constructed through social engineering and the creation of *imagined solidarity* and **invented traditions** (Robbins, 2008, p. 114). In modernity, people are socialized to see themselves in light of a common *national identity* and as members of a *nation*. At the beginning of the nineteenth century, for example, few people in England, Germany, and France considered themselves British, German, and French, respectively. In fact, only about 25 percent of the population in France spoke French and the *states* of Germany and Italy did not even exist (Robbins, 2008, p. 114).

Due to cultural, ethnic, religious, and class differences in many *states*, their populations had to be convinced or forced to "share certain features, such as language, religion, ethnic group membership, or a common historical heritage" (Robbins, 2008, p. 115). In the case of Britain, "British Protestantism allowed the English, Scots, and Welsh to overcome their cultural [differences] to identify themselves as a nation" (Robbins, 2008, p. 116). There was also weak economic integration within European states. Not only did many people speak different dialects and languages; they also used different currencies and had different standards of measurements. *State* officials were also very much resented in many part of the country (Robbins, 2008, p. 114). Workers were paid different wages for the same type of work and prices also varied from one region to the next. There were also no unified standards of vocational training.

The solution to all these problems was to turn *states* into *nations* (Robbins, 2008, p. 114). In a sense, one of the characteristics of modernity and the rise of *nation-states* has been the harmonization of standards and creation of uniformity across societies. This uniformity was also conceptualized in terms of who was deemed a member of the *nation* and who would be excluded. As mentioned above, the constructions of *nation-sates* were bureaucratic endeavours that required national infrastructures that would serve to unite the people. The education system has played a central role in this regard (See Box 7.5 - Modern Education Systems).

To form unity between ethnically, linguistically, culturally, and religiously diverse populations within a national territory, *nation-states* often construct false continuities between present and past and invent social practices that are then considered and viewed as aspects of tradition and part of the heritage of the *nation*. For example, the beret as the symbol of the French identity became popular only after the 1930s. In fact, it was only worn by the Basque people during the 1920s. However, by 1932, around 23 million berets were manufactured for the French population as the symbol of France and French nationalism (Robbins, 2008, p. 118).

In Iran, during the 1930s, the government also established a law that required all Iranians wanting to work for the *state* bureaucracies to dress in Western clothing and wear Western style hats that came to be known as the Pahlavi Hat. In fact, Reza Shah's "dress reforms … reflected his Europeanizing policies. All of Iranians, including Persians were forced to wear versions of European dress" (Beck, 1990, p. 206). This royal decree regarding clothing reinforced and exacerbated the division between the modernized/westernized and "the rest of the society, which resented the intrusion in their lives"

BOX 7.5 - Modern Education Systems

The modern education system and its development must be analyzed in the context of "the wider process of state formation" (Whitty, 1995, p. 277). The education system as part of the *state apparatus* plays an important role in the reproduction of dominant ideologies in society (Whitty, 1995, p. 276). Education is also an important tool in the process of constructing the *national identity*. The construction of the *national identity* has been a major force "to gain or enhance state power" (Held, 1996, p. 79). The *state* relies on the education system to shape the shared *national identity* of students (for example, making them into the subjects of the *state* by instilling in them a sense of being, for example, Canadian, Iranian, and German). It also plays an important economic purpose: as a tool in training people for different types of jobs and occupations and economic progress of the country (Kubow & Fossum, 2007, p. 3).

Education is about both the education of citizens and the training of students as future workers (Whitty, 1995, p. 276). In Canada, the history of public education suggests that the role of the education system was to socialize the children of the poor based on the ideology and culture of the dominant society (Prentice, 1977, p. 121). The goal of the education system was to eliminate class distinctions and class conflict, but not the existence of a class structure (Prentice, 1977, p. 121). The aim of the early school promoters was to fight **pauperism** in society, and education was viewed as an effective tool in producing a "respectful class of labouring people" (Prentice, 1977, p. 122). Their assumption was that as the poor and working classes internalize the views of the dominant society, class conflicts would also be eliminated (Prentice, 1977, p. 124). Schools, then, served ideological and economic purposes.

In their analysis of the American education system, Samuel Bowles and Herbert Gintis analyzed the relationship and connection between the capitalist economy and schooling from a Marxist perspective (Whitty, 1995, p. 274). For them, capitalism and its structure are at the root of inequality, not the education system (Barakett & Cleghorn, 2000, p. 31). They criticized liberal reforms for their lack of promoting an egalitarian society. They questioned the conservative ideology that claims educational inequality is due to differences in individual abilities and intelligence levels. Bowles and Gintis argued that inequality "is rooted in the class structure of capitalism" (Wotherspoon, 1998, p. 31). As such, educational reforms cannot simply fix socioeconomic inequalities. In order to create a more democratic society, there is a need to restructure capitalism and to account for how economic considerations reproduce inequality and class differences. In Western societies and totalitarian states, schools limit democratic participation in order to "maintain material and ideological conditions to generate profit" and reproduce a docile working class. In fact, Louis Althusser also argued that the main goal of schooling has been to submit working class (and "minority") students to the ruling ideology and to use the ruling ideology "as agents of manipulation and repression" (as cited in Whitty, 1995, p. 274).

Bowles and Gintis put forth the idea of the **correspondence principle**. They were concerned with the social relations of schooling, not simply its content. They maintained that schools are hierarchical structures, and are based on an overall ideology that promotes competition. Schools, like a factory, mass produce "common educational experiences [that are] marked by authoritarian relations and centralized planning and rigid organization" (Ball, as cited in Whitty, 1995, p. 274). This ideology informs both the relationship of workers in industrial societies and school participants (i.e., wages and the grading system). The *correspondence principle* suggests that schools socialize students of different socioeconomic classes according to a set of values that are predetermined and expected of such individuals. Thus, working class children who are assumed to end up in subordinate positions are placed in high schools/programs/courses that train them for vocational and general education. Such high schools/programs/courses emphasize close supervision and acceptance of authority. On the other hand, students from middle class and affluent groups are educated for university tracks. Such schools/programs/courses teach leadership and decision-making skills, which correspond to their future roles as leaders in industry. Bowles and Gintis maintained that schools are institutions that affirm inequality by promoting the **meritocratic ideology**, rewarding personality types that best suit the capitalist relations and structures and serving the interest of the dominant groups and training them in the skills needed to dominate other groups in society (Barakett & Cleghorn, 2000, p. 31). The **discourse of meritocracy** assumes that we achieve our positions in society due to the levels of our hard work and based on our own aptitudes and levels of intelligence. That is, failure and lack of success in schools and the types of programs one studies are blamed on individual failings and characteristics, not the effects of racism, sexism, classism, or ableism.

According to Bowles and Gintis, the American education system has been affected by three main historical shifts. These changes in schooling reflect the wider changes that have taken place in the capitalist economy. **First**, during the period 1850–1900, there was a need for disciplined wage labour that corresponded to the rise of public schooling in the United States. **Second**, between 1890 and 1930, there was a need for a diversified workforce at the time that corporate capitalism emerged, which corresponded to the implementation of school bureaucracies and promotion of standardized curriculum, testing, and systemic control. **Third**, the need for professional and white-collar workers after the end of World War II corresponded with the rise in postsecondary education (Wotherspoon, 1998, p. 33). In their analysis, Bowles and Gintis argued that educational trends and issues reflect conflicts in the economy; and, the role of schooling is to maintain social order and smooth the progress of capitalism. In other words, schools systematically reproduce social inequalities.

As good as their explanations sound, there are three problems with the Bowles and Gintis analysis that are discussed by Livingstone (Wotherspoon, 1998, p. 34). **First**, schools do not only reproduce capitalist knowledge, they also produce other forms of knowledge. **Second**, capitalist production and relations are not the only factors determining the content and the form of schooling. **Third**, their analysis does not offer an overall explanation as to why racial, ethnic, and gender inequalities happen in schools. Their theory tends to emphasize the functions of schooling. That is why their approach is also referred to as **critical functionalism** (Wotherspoon, 1998).

In Canada, scholars, such as George Martell, have also pointed out that schools reinforce class inequalities and include corporate values and strategies for profit making as part of the curriculum: "Canadian education system has been infused with class-based ideologies and practices" (Wotherspoon, 1998, p. 35). It is important, however, to refrain from too much emphasis on the role of schools in economic reproduction and to account for the extent to which schools can be sites to challenge corporate values and as spaces in which the interaction between educators, community members, students, and others can lead into practices that attempt to democratize society and the process of schooling.

Schools have also played an important role in the process of nation-building and have been a tool in the hands of the *state* to control the types of information and knowledge that students learn about themselves and others. In Iran, the education system has also played similar roles and goals. Sadiq (1931, pp. 83–84), the Minister responsible for education, in justifying the need for a centralized education system in Iran, maintained that Iranians "desire to have a country strong and independent to preserve this entity and their national life. They wish to have a Persia prosperous through scientific development of their natural resources in agriculture and mines, and through exchange of those products with other countries. They aspire that Persia have a place of honour among nations of the earth by constituting the country's best to the culture of the world". Sadiq (1931, p. 84) also argued that the aim of the education system should be to provide students with a cultural capital that would enable Iran to enter the age of modernity as a powerful contender in the region. He (as cited in Banani, 1961, p. 109) proposed for a nationalistic education system that was also based on the principles of progressive education with a strong base in science and technical knowledge. Iranian education system was "to create in the minds of the people a living consciousness of the past by showing the great achievements of the race; … to train boys and girls to become good citizens of modern Persia; … to teach the rural people and the tribes to live, make a home, … prepare food and clothing, … [and] prevent disease …." (as cited in Banani, 1961, p. 109).

In general, according to Fleras and Elliott (2002, p. 200) and Kubow and Fossum (2007, p. 78), the education system has three main goals:

1. To transmit and teach knowledge and skills,

2. To prepare students for citizenship and employment by selecting and differentiating among students, and

3. To foster intellectual growth through a selective approach to knowledge transmission and production.

In Israel, the main purpose of schooling is to promote dominant religious, labour, and political ideologies. In Israel and other societies, such as the United States, schools function in the **indoctrination** of students into the dominant and hegemonic ideologies. *Indoctrination* refers to denying "students relevant and developmentally appropriate information and choices by teaching them *content* known to be false or using instructional *methods* that disrespect students, such as inappropriate rewards and punishments" (Snook, as cited in Kubow & Fossum, 2007, p. 113). In Israel, schools teach Zionist ideology that ignores the histories and identities of non-Jewish people in that country, especially Arab-Palestinians. That is, schools' goals and functions are political, economic, social, and cultural. For example, in Iran, the goals of the education system in 1988 were conceptualized as: "[helping] students discover the mysteries of the cosmos and the cause-and-effect relations of natural phenomena";"[protecting] the sacredness of family relations based on Islamic faith"; and "[accepting] the absolute role of God over the world and human beings and unite Muslim nations" (as cited in Mohsenpour, 1988, p. 85; See also Shorish, 1988, p. 60, 2002, p. 232; Matini, 1989, pp. 48–49; Mohsenpour, 1988, p. 77; Siavoshi 1995, pp. 203–204). The ideal citizen favoured by Iranian educators is a person who is materialistically and spiritually mature. These national and global goals are juxtaposed against the other main goal of the *state* to indirectly intervene in the private affairs of Iranians, as reflected in the policies of the *state*, by dictating how families should be organized and how relations should be played out in light of the socialization of students in family settings.

As the examples above point out, schools have served the interest of the *state* and the dominant ruling parties (Fleras & Elliott, 2002, p. 201). Schools function based on "standardized norms, values and practices". Schools are sites for the socialization of students as members of the *nation-state*. They are agents of socialization. In other words, schools are involved in the processes of:

1. transmitting the dominant culture;

2. development of identity or self-development based on the characteristics of the dominant national identity, values, and norms; and

3. job training based on the economic needs of the capitalist class (Fleras & Elliott, 2002, p. 200).

Schools in many parts of the world and in Canada are based on the principles of a **monocultural perspective** that attempts to assimilate students into the dominant society and to "forge social cohesion according to the standards of [the] nineteenth-century elites" (Fleras & Elliott, 2002, p. 201). In this sense, schools are not free of cultural and political biases (Fleras & Elliott, 2002, p. 201). As we mentioned previously, **assimilation** is a process of change through which individuals or groups adapt to the culture of another group. As James Banks (2001, p. 95, Table 5.2, Multicultural Education Paradigms) maintained, US assimilationists believe that teaching about ethnic identification would result in the **balkanization of society**, separation of ethnic groups into distinct and unconnected associations. And, it would hinder academic achievements of ethnic students. The aim of the education system, they claim, should be to "free [students] of their ethnic characteristics and enable them to acquire the values and behaviors of the mainstream culture" (Banks, 2001, p. 95, Table 5.2, Multicultural Education Paradigms). In English-speaking Canada, this policy has promoted a universal image of being "Canadian", which is based on Anglo-values and norms. Schools, as agents of assimilation, perpetuate the power of the elite groups and reproduce the existing class differences/inequalities. The values of the dominant culture are reflected in the curriculum and school structure. "Whiteness" (read Euro-Western-ness) is privileged "as the standard by which all cultures are judged" (Fleras & Elliott, 2002, p. 201).

In contrast to *assimilationist approaches*, **cultural pluralism**, in the form of **multicultural education** or **antiracism education**, has been offered as a solution to educational issues and concerns. These perspectives assume that students must be free to pursue their ethnic cultures and racialized identities. And, their identities must be reflected in school cultures, programs, and curriculum. Their aim is to "liberate ethnic groups and to educate them in such a way that will not alienate them from their home cultures" (Banks, 2001, p. 95, Table 5.2, Multicultural Education Paradigms).

Despite the success of these theories and approaches, as Banks (2003, p. 8) has maintained, attacks on ethnic and racial "minorities" have increased since the 1980s and the 1990s in the United States, Germany, and the United Kingdom. As discussed, this period coincides with massive economic changes and restructuring that took place in the West as a result of the implementation of economic liberalization/globalization policies. Yasmeen Abu-Laban and Christina Gabriel (2002, pp. 19–20) argued that the "globalization [of economy and information] is a discourse (or framework of language, ideas, references, and understanding which shapes power relations)", which is informed by the ideology of neoliberalism. This ideology stresses efficiency and "global competitiveness" rather than "global responsibility".

Studies and research have shown that neoliberal policies have resulted in the creation of high retention rates in schools. These policies promote individualism in the form of individual expectations, such as hard work, behaviour, self-discipline, and motivation. Schools now offer fewer electives and more math, science, and computer courses. Supporters of neoliberal policies argue for a longer school year. They have also promoted national goals that must be measured by quantifiable data, such as standardized test results (Calvert, 1993). These policies assume and attribute the rise in poverty to individual behaviour and lifestyles. Their supporters claim that more educated high-tech workers are needed, a claim that is greatly exaggerated (i.e., economy has generated nine new cashiering jobs for every one computer programming job) (Calvert, 1993).

The goals of neoliberals are also to set *state legislatures* as *super school boards* and to establish educational goals nationally and use tests and other indicators to determine if the goals have been met. However, while setting goals centrally (nationally), "accountability" for meeting them is considered to be the responsibility of local school boards that were not involved in setting up these goals. They also promote and increase the role of the private sectors in the education system. These policies have resulted in:

1. Decreases in educational funding levels;

2. Elimination of social programs, affecting quality of students' school experiences;

3. Undermining the collective bargaining rights of teachers;

4. Privatizing and liberalizing the delivery of educational services; and

5. Creating unequal schooling based on factors, such as region, locality, "race", income, ethnicity, gender, and social class (Calvert, 1993).

Standardization across provinces/*states* and regions within the United States and Canada has resulted in the **harmonization** of the educational services. Harmonization is sought by powerful *lobbying groups* that are set up by transnational corporations. In Canada, corporations have formed US copycat organizations, such as *Business Council on National Issues* (BCNI) and *Conference Board of Canada* (CBC). CEOs of Canadian branches of transnational companies have supported the Free Trade Agreement (FTA) and North American Free Trade Agreement (NAFTA). They have influenced public policy based on the American policy initiatives. They have substantial behind-the-scenes power (Calvert, 1993, pp. 89–92).

BCNI is an example of direct lobbying of the *government* by top business leaders. BCNI takes preemptive positions based on extensive biased research as the basis for their specific recommendations, often already drafted as laws, attempting to set the overall framework or direction of *state* policy. For example, BCNI commissioned a study by Harvard University's Michael Porter (the $1.5 million cost of this study was picked up by the Canadian taxpayers, courtesy of the federal government), which suggested that national educational standards must be created. This study also recommended that provincial governments must agree to testing mechanisms to meet the standards. It maintained that universities must promote economic development. The aim of organizations, such as BCNI, is to assist business and education leaders to collaboratively promote the development of an education system that will prepare Canada's workforce for tomorrow's world economic needs (Calvert, 1993).

Conference Board of Canada (CBC) also established a subsidiary, the *National Business and Education Centre*, with its own secretariat and researchers with the goal of assisting business and education leaders work collaboratively to implement educational programs that will prepare Canada's youth for tomorrow's world (Calvert, 1993). Common themes promoted by these organizations include: establishing business-education partnerships to allow business leaders to bring their messages directly to education decision-makers; implementing curricular revisions in the fields of science and math; and setting national goals and testing that are considered as needed and required (Calvert, 1993). The common theme of these polices is an emphasis on **business-education partnerships (private-public)**. For example, at the University of British Columbia, the university accepted a $15 million grant to build a genetics research centre "in return for the university's support of the controversial drug patent bill" (Calvert, 1993, p. 125). In general, the common goal of these organizations is to increase the employable skills profile of the population. In this view, they perceive students as future workers who must develop competencies and maximize their productivity by meeting the current and future needs of the employers for skilled entry-level employees (Calvert, 1993).

> The federal government responded to the demands of these corporate interest groups by issuing a policy paper, entitled *Learning Well … Living Well*, as part of the government's prosperity initiative (Calvert, 1993, pp. 95–97). This policy paper concluded that educational programs need to be restructured in order to meet the needs of transnational corporations. There should be less emphasis placed on social and cultural elements of education and more emphasis put on economic aspect. In this light, education is only valued when it influences and impacts individuals' incomes and national prosperity as envisioned and promoted by transnational corporations (Calvert, 1993).
>
> In short, education is not innocent; it is about *power* and *politics* and is influenced by the ideas and needs of those who control the *state* and *supranational* bodies.

by the *state* (Chehabi, as cited in Keddie, 2003, p. 100). Reza Shah's dress policy was also viewed by "minorities" as a way for the *state* to enforce its policy of Persianising the ethnic population by stripping them from traditional forms of clothing as indicators of cultural/ethnic membership and identity. This policy was as a racist *state* approach to ethnic diversity in Iran based on cultural assimilation assumptions that assumed Persians are "superior" to the rest. This policy aimed at getting rid of ethnic symbols that distinguished between Iranians at the same time as distinguishing between modern and traditional Iranians.

Construction of National Identity: the discourse of nationalism

When we look at the meaning of the word *nation*, we note that it originally meant one's place of birth or one's descent or origin (Hobsbawm, 1990, p. 15). In Spain, the words *patria* or *tierra* ('the home land') were used to refer to the place and township one was born in or "any region, province or district of any lordship or state" (Hobsbawm, 1990. P. 15). It was not until 1884 when the term *tierra* was attached to a *state*. It was not until 1925 when the term *patria* came to be defined in terms of patriarchal emotions as "our own nation, the sum total of material and immaterial things, past, present and future that enjoy the loving loyalty of patriots" (Hobsbawm, 1990, p. 15).

The modern meaning of *nation* identifies it as "the body of citizens whose collective sovereignty constituted them a state which was their political expression" (Hobsbawm, 1990, pp. 18–19). That is, through mass participation in political affairs and through their choices, members of a *nation* desire to be under the same *government* that is made of them (John Stuart Mill, as cited in Hobsbawm, 1990, p. 19). The new definition of *nation* linked it to *state* and equated it with the people. As the French Declaration of Rights in 1795 stated, "Each people is independent and sovereign, whatever the number of individuals who compose it and the extent of the territory it occupies, This sovereignty is inalienable" (as cited in Hobsbawm, 1990, p. 18).

At the time, language and ethnicity were not considered a criterion of membership into the *nation*. Yet, since the French Revolution, language and ethnicity have become central aspects of defining who is a member of the *nation* and who is considered the *enemies within*. As Hobsbawm stated, it was not the French language that defined a person as French, as many people even did not speak it, but the willingness to learn the language. In this sense, in France, both Sephardic Jews who spoke medieval Spanish and Ashkenazi Jews who spoke Yiddish (which according to Richard Böckh, is a German dialect derived from Medieval German) could be considered as equal Frenchmen as long as they accepted the conditions of French citizenship and started speaking French (Hobsbawm, 1990, p. 22).

In general, during the eighteenth, nineteenth, and twentieth centuries, a common conception of French people, Germans, and Italians needed to be manufactured (Robbins, 2008, p. 115). In 1831, Giuseppe Mazzini (1805–1872) established the Young Italy Society, which aimed at uniting Italy (Perry et al., 1995, p. 145). In 1815, Italy was ruled by a number of diverse entities. It was a fragmented *nation* (Perry et al., 1995, p. 144). Lombardy and Venetia in Northern Italy were ruled by the Hapsburg Empire; the Kingdoms of Two Sicilies in the south were governed by the Bourdon King; Hapsburg princes, who were under the control of Austria, administered the duchies of Tuscany, Parma, Modena; and the "papal states in central Italy were ruled by the pope" (Perry et al., 1995, pp. 144–145). The centre of the Italian *nationhood* was constructed on the House of Savoy, an Italian dynasty that administered the Kingdom of Piedmont. The whole *nationalist* movement was inspired by past Italian histories of the Roman Empire and the Renaissance, which were used as ideological tools to manufacture a shared history and invented traditions that were, then, employed to unify various parts of Italy (Perry et al., 1995, p. 145). Mazzini and others who were involved in the struggle for Italian *nationhood (Risorgimento)* imagined this model as a framework for other European nations to form their *nation-states*.

According to Mazzini (1995, p. 145), "Young Italy is a brotherhood of Italians who believe in a law of Progress and Duty, and are convinced that Italy is destined to become one nation". The aim of this society was to reconstitute "Italy as one independent sovereign nation of free men and equals" (Mazzini, 1995, p. 145). In fact, when Italy was formed, as a result of uniting a group of provinces by Garibaldi in the nineteenth century, he asserted that now that he has created Italy, he needs to construct Italians out of the diversity of languages and cultures in these provinces (Robbins, 2008). At the time, less than 3 percent of the population spoke Italian and considered it their native tongue (Robbins, 2008, p. 114). German language was also arbitrarily chosen by Joseph II as the national language of Germany (Robbins, 2008, p. 114). The fact that many people spoke different dialects and languages in various *nations* in Europe was considered a menace to:

1. administrative unity and

2. ideological unity (Robbins, 2008, p. 117).

In general, one way to homogenize the existing cultures within a *nation* was to homogenize the language spoken by the majority of people. When one loses one's language, with it comes a loss of cultural knowledge, values, and norms that would define a person's identity. At the same time, with the opening of geographical spaces to influences from outside regions "local cultures began to be replaced" and dress and preferences became homogenized and standardized. In France, moreover, people were molded into the *nation* administratively.

The French language was brought to the countryside, where the majority of people did not speak French and did not view themselves as "Frenchmen" (sic):

1. through building roads that eased the conditions under which people could move from one region to another;

2. by increasing the masses' access to the national media, which provided them with news from other parts of the country and introduced them to political affairs in faraway places that would have effects on their lives; and

3. by incorporating a national system of education that was used to teach a shared history, culture, attitudes, norms, and values to the culturally and ethnically diverse population of France (Robbins, 2008, p. 117).

Central to the rise of *nation-states* in Europe and across the world is the ideology of **nationalism**. It is pertinent to note that as Anthony Giddens pointed out, "what makes the nation integral to the nation-state ... is not the existence of sentiments of nationalism [*per se*] but the unification of an administrative apparatus over precisely defined territorial boundaries (in a complex of other nation-states)" (as cited in Held, 1996, p. 76). For example, although Kurdish people in Iran, Syria, Iraq, and Turkey are incorporated as part of the *nation*, these groups do not necessarily share and promote the dominant nationalist discourses in these countries. Kurdish people may be considered the citizens of these countries, but they also view themselves as distinct from the dominant societies in these *nation-states* (Tilley, as cited in Held 1996, p. 71).

Nevertheless, during the era of **nation-building**, the ideals of **nationalism** and **patriotism** were fused. In this sense, people of different ethnic backgrounds came to relate to and identify themselves in light of a single and all-encompassing *national identity* (Kelleher & Klein, 2009, p. 10). As Kymlicka (1995, p. 13) pointed out in his book *Multicultural Citizenship*, we should distinguish between *patriotism*, the feeling of allegiance to a state, from *national identity*, which is the sense of membership in a national group. In other words, *patriotism* refers to identification of people with *modern states* (Kelleher & Klein, 2009, p. 10). *Nationalism* is defined as the feelings associated with one's identification with a specific **ethnic group**, or a cultural group that shares a number of characteristics, such as a language, history, and religion (Kelleher & Klein, 2009, p. 10). It is important to note that "distinguishing between ethnic nationalism and state patriotism help[s] clarify one of the most significant causes of current conflicts": mainly, the clash between these two forces occurs because one ethnic group tends to control the government, as the most important administrative unit within any given *state* (Kelleher & Klein, 2009, p. 10).

The nineteenth century is the beginning of the era of *nationalism*. Fleras (2010, p. 108) argued that, "Nationalism constitutes the political expression of a nation whose peoples claim a common ancestry and shared destiny to govern themselves in a place they call homeland". *Nationalism* is a form of ideology that justifies dividing the world into separate administrative political communities by a group of people who define themselves as a *nation* (Fleras, 2010, p. 109). In the context of *nation-states*, *nationalism* is grounded in a simple idea and assumption that membership in the *nation* is exclusive. The group that is considered as the source of *national identity* is considered as culturally, economically, and intellectually more "superior" to others. It promotes the idea that there must be collective loyalty to the *nation-state* against outside threats and forces (Fleras, 2010, p. 108). For example, the painting of Sir David Wilkie, *Chelsea Pensioners Reading the Gazette of Battle of Waterloo*, symbolized the importance of defending the *nation* against outsiders and forged the *British nation* "by uniting [the diverse population of Britain] against a common enemy" (as cited in Robbins, 2008, p. 116). It is during this time period that countries, such as Germany, were established as *national states*. Germany was perceived to belong to only Germans by excluding Jews, Slavs, and Gypsies from being considered as legitimate members of the German *nation*. They were considered "unwelcomed residues from past empires" (Fleras, 2010, p. 108). In short, *nationalism* rests on the politics of exclusion. It assumes that a group has the right to self-administrate a geographical area that is considered as the homeland "as self-governing entities (nation-state) or subunits within society (nations)" (Fleras, 2010, p. 109).

We can identify two types of *nationalism* based on how membership into the *nation* is conceptualized. As already discussed above, a *nation* consists of people who think they are essentially different than others and have the inherent right to self-determination to determine their social, cultural, economic destinies and "propose political autonomy on these grounds and claim to speak the language of nation-hood" (Fleras, 2010, p. 109). Membership in a *nation* is determined on the basis of one's place of birth (birthright) and one's descent from a common ancestry. As a member of a *nation*, one's loyalty is to the group that defines the *nation* and one is obligated to defend the homeland. Loyalty is not defined based on one's commitment to the *state*, to specific social classes, or ethnic "minority" groups (Fleras, 2010, p. 109). This imagined political community needs to be defended against internal and external enemies.

Ethnic nationalism defines the *nation* on the basis of ascriptive characteristics, such as kinship relations and blood ties. The process of *nation-building* is to promote the interest of the ideal "people" at the expense of others who are defined as outsiders. The key point is the emphasis on shared attachments to the nation rather than attachments to the key institutions that define the *state*. **Civic nationalism** "bases its appeals on loyalty to a set of political ideals, rules of law, the principles of inclusiveness, and institutions that are perceived as just and effective" (Fleras, 2010, p. 109). Despite one's "race" or ethnicity, as long as individuals believe and subscribe to the values and norms of the constructed notion of the political community of *nation*, they are accepted as insiders and a member of the *nation*.

National Identity and the Discourse of Binary Polarization

National identity is a modern phenomenon and reflects the *power* and political desires of the dominant society within a *nation-state* to enforce their cultural values and norms upon others. *National identity* is a construction that brings people together and creates a sense of belonging. The creation of a *national identity* was central to the formation of *modern states*. If and when people under the control of the *state* began to see themselves as one with shared heritage and culture, then, the *state* and those in control of its institutions "could claim to represent them" (Robbins, 2008, p. 115). *National identity* is a homogenizing and essentializing identity that erases *differences* in terms of culture, ethnicity, "race", and social class. It is an all-encompassing category that highlights *similarities* and *sameness*. The *national identity*, Canadian, does not account for the extent to which our identities are often determined by the regions in which we live or by our ethnic and cultural as well as religious beliefs. For example, in Quebec, many people identify with **Quebecois identity** as their *national identity* rather than as Canadians (Hiller, 2006). The **discourse of national identity** is based on the exclusion of the historical memories of subaltern peoples and "minorities". It erases, omits, and silences their experiences.

National identity implies the process of **Othering** or   placing people outside the structures of *power*. To highlight who is an insider and a member of the *nation*, it is important to determine who is an outsider and should be excluded from membership into the category "us". One of the most powerful discourses of *Othering* is the **discourse of binary polarization**. This is a hegemonic dualist conception of the world that results in the depiction of people and cultural, ethnic, and racialized groups from problematic and highly racist perspectives. This discourse, as Henry and Tator (2010, p. 11) argued, is used to differentiate between insiders and outsiders in such a way as to exclude certain people from membership into the category *nation*. It is a discourse of domination, which "attempts to explain, rationalize, and resolve differences between people based on dominant values of equality, tolerance and liberty" (Henry & Tator, 2010, p. 11). This discourse attempts to explore the relationship between "us" and "them" in light of the dominant values in relation to "minority" values and norms. In Canada, the "us" category is defined in terms of the **discourse of Whiteness**, which assumes that White people are simply the norm. Everybody else is different and abnormal. These **Others** must change their attitudes, values, and norms according to the expectations of the dominant cultural group. The "them" category possesses characteristics and as such are labelled as the *Other*, who must be feared, controlled, and policed. The "us" category is viewed as "law-abiding, hard-working, decent, and homogenous" (Henry & Tator, 2010, p. 14). The *Other* is viewed as "irrational", "mystical", in need of change, and even pathological. The *Other* is depicted by invoking stereotypical images that place them outside the category of *nation* and exclude them from *nationhood*.

The *Other* is often not given citizenship rights. In Canada, until the 1960s, there had been a concerted effort to exclude non-White people from accessing citizenship rights. Since the 1960s, however, Canadian citizenship rights are open to new immigrants who are qualified according to the citizenship requirements. Membership in the *nation*, however, does not translate into racial and ethnic equality. Many Canadian *visible minorities* face discrimination in employment and education (Hiller, 2006).

In contrast to Canada, in Germany, citizenship is based on ancestry (based on the principle of *jus sanguinis*), whereas in France, citizenship is based on the principle of place of birth (Berezin, 1994, p. 99). Ethnic "minorities" face discrimination in Germany by not being given citizenship rights. In France, despite the fact that second generation Arab Maghrabi are given citizenship rights, discrimination also limits their access to positions of power (Berezin, 1994, p. 99). In Iran, citizenship issues regarding Afghan asylum seekers have been a central concern since the invasion of Afghanistan by the Soviet Forces. The Iranian government has been involved in devising plans to return Afghan expatriates living in Iran, ignoring the citizenship rights of Afghan children born in Iran to Afghan or Iranian parent(s).

According to a study sponsored by United Nations Children's Fund (UNICEF), a majority of respondents disagreed with granting citizenship rights to Afghan children (Bazarnegar Co., 2001, p. 170). In fact, only about 10 percent of respondents agreed to grant citizenship if: one of the parents was Iranian, "the child [himself or herself is] Moslem"; "the children [are] physically and morally healthy"; and "the children be known to them" (Bazarnegar Co., 2001, p. 170). Even in regards to granting birth certificates to Afghan children born in Iran, 65 percent were opposed to this policy. However, the lower one's income level and education, the more one opposed such policies. According to the authors of this study, "more than half of the respondents in this study were positively against supporting the schooling of Afghan children in Iran". Also, "more than half of the respondents ages 18–36 and 37–55 respectively also asserted that Afghan children should never be supported" (Bazarnegar Co., 2001, p. 166). In contrast, "only 34% of respondents declared their approval. Opposition was mainly held by younger age groups (18–36 years old) and lower educated groups" (Bazarnegar Co., 2001, p. 165). Many of the respondents also believed that Afghan children (i.e., Afghan street children) should never be supported financially. Those with higher education were more likely to support the idea of helping and assisting Afghan children than those with less than high school diploma. Nevertheless, almost 50 percent of those with high school or higher education asserted that such children should not be financially assisted. When asked if they would allow their children to play with Afghan children, 69 percent claimed that they would never allow them to play with these children (Bazarnegar Co., 2001, p. 167). The majority of those making less than 120 thousand Tomans ($80, CAD) replied "never" in comparison to 56 percent of those making more than 250 thousand Tomans ($166, CAD). In terms of supporting needy Afghan children, a majority of the supporting views were from urban groups, with higher levels of education and income (Bazarnegar Co., 2001, p. 169).

As it can be stipulated, "us" and "them" divisions affect how we view and treat *Others*. The exclusion of *otherness* is an international problem that affects many countries in both Western and non-Western parts of the globe.

Conclusion

The history of the modern world is characterized by a desire to reproduce order and resolve conflicts that have resulted in mass murder and destruction of life. Modern *nation-states* are not innocent entities. Their histories highlight exclusion based on political, economic, and social considerations that reproduce inequalities. One's *national identity* is a product of historical relations between *states* in the context of local, national, and international structures. The history of the modern world is characterized by *violence* and *surveillance*.

Chapter Review Questions

1. Define the following terms: power and politics.

2. Explore the relationship between power and politics by references to one or two case studies.

3. In modern capitalist societies, there are three main significant types of resources. Describe and explain each.

4. What are the basic arguments of the power resources theory? Explain.

5. Offer several conceptualization of power based on three ideal models.

6. Discuss and analyze power by focusing on its levels and forms.

7. What is meant by the term oppositional power?

8. Define and explain critical political economy.

9. What are the basic arguments of the pluralist model?

10. Define interest groups.

11. Explore the significance of the power elite model for analysis of political systems.

12. What are the basic arguments of the staple thesis?

13. Define staple trap.

14. What is meant by the term shadow society?

15. Compare and contrast John Porter's, Wallace Clement's, and William Carroll's analysis of elite groups in Canada.

16. Define political sociology.

17. Define state and discuss its different elements.

18. Define civil society and discuss its various elements.

19. Define government and explore its functions.

20. What are the different forms of modern states? Compare and contrast.

21. Distinguish between the different types of government.

22. There are various views of the state that explore its ideological power and authority differently. Compare and contrast them.

23. What are the basic assumptions of structural functionalism? Explain what is meant by the discourse of instrumentalism?

24. What are the basic assumptions of Marxism? Explain what is meant by the discourse of structuralism.

25. Compare and contrast the following forms of state that governed Europe: the Holy Roman Empires, the polity of estates, absolutist states, and empires.

26. What was the significance of the Westphalian model for the rise of nation-states? Explain.

27. What are the characteristics of modern nation-states? Explain.

28. Closely related to the administrative aspects of the modern nation-state is its ability and capacity for surveillance. Explain what this statement means by references to appropriate examples.

29. As Michel Foucault (1926–1984) maintained, modern societies are like Panopticon structures of prisons. What did he mean by this? Explain.

30. Define hegemonic masculinity.

31. Define symbolic power.

32. What is meant by the term "othering"?

33. As structures of power that practice mass murder, modern states display three main characteristics. What are they? Explain.

34. Define nationalism and ethnic and civic nationalism.

35. Explore the consequences of genocide in modernity.

36. What is meant by the term collective memory?

37. Kuper identified three forms of genocidal states. Compare and contrast them.

38. Explore the main argument of the correspondence principle.

39. What are the roles and functions of modern education systems? Critically explain.

40. Define the following terms and ideas: discourse of binary polarization, meritocratic ideology, indoctrination, and discourse of national identity.

41. Critically examine how national identities are constructed.

Critical Thinking Questions

1. Critically explore the ways in which Canadian national identity has been constructed and consumed.

2. Offer innovative and practical ways through which you can become involved in ending genocide.

3. Explore the extent to which you may "suffer" from historical amnesia.

4. Critically explore the ways in which states and governments promote the interests of all their members.

5. Can pluralism be the answer to social, economic, and political inequalities? Explain.

6. How are your life chances affected by neoliberal policies? Explain.

7. Critically analyze your views about the poor, people on welfare, and the homeless people.

CHAPTER EIGHT

. . . .

Colonialism, Imperialism, and Postcolonial Relations

Introduction

. . . .

In this chapter, we examine how **colonialism** and **imperialism** have affected the political economy of the world since the fifteenth century. Colonial relations and imperialist incursions across the world are two of the defining elements of modernity that are related to the rise of industrialism, militarism, nation-states, and capitalism. We explore the history of *colonialism* and its effects by references to European interventions in Asia, Africa, South America, and North America.

Why did we choose to dedicate a chapter to the consequences of colonialism in the world? We believe that a historical approach to European exploitation of the world enables us to understand the exact processes and structures that informed and were shaped by *colonialism* and *imperialism* and resistance to them that are also now "leading the world today to a crisis that promises a foreseeable future of mass starvation, deprivation, and untold hopelessness" (Sotisisowah, as cited in Mackey, 2010, p. 13). There is continuity between capitalist and colonial racial, classed, and gendered practices and current neoliberal policies in terms of the racialization and feminization of poverty in both Western and non-Western countries.

More specifically, new and old racial forms of inequality link colonial periods to the contemporary neoliberal world (Mackey, 2010, p. 3). They are criteria of *difference* through which Western societies are able to build, develop, and normalize forms and structures of domination across the globe. **Neoliberalism** is the continuation of liberal ideology that was associated with the emergence of industrial capitalism since the eighteenth century. Liberalism undermined the citizenship of non-White peoples and excluded them from participation in the political system (we are not referring to White as a sign of the colour of skin but how and why one is considered as White and what are the consequences of such categorizations). As more racialized and other "minority" groups need to have access to government services, free education, public health system, affordable public transportation, increase spending in social services, more involvement of the state "as mediator of social conflicts", more extensive legal protection, better labour laws, and increase participation in unions, we are experiencing a reduction in such services. Neoliberalism promotes smaller governments, fewer social services, introduction of laws that undermine unions and their advocacy of workers' rights, privatization of goods, and liberalization of the economy (Mackey, 2010, p. 3). To understand the consequences of **neoliberal** policies and resistance to them by marginalized peoples, we need to develop a broad comprehension of colonial and postcolonial practices and their structural effects. An approach to how marginalized groups, such as the Aboriginal and Indigenous peoples who have been at the forefront of fighting the effects of colonial relations and the power of supranational institutions and their attempts to once again steal their resources and deny them their rights to "life, liberty, and property", points to the continuities and discontinuities between the past and present.

By having a good understanding of the history of *colonialism*, *imperialism*, and **postcolonialism**, we can also begin to think critically about the ways in which we talk about and discuss contemporary approaches to the nation-building process in Canada; for example, the **discourse of multiculturalism** and the ways it is practiced. By looking at the world through critical lenses, which enable us to question and subvert racialized ideologies and colonial ways of thinking, we can begin to interrogate and confront our ***historical amnesia*** that perpetuates the general belief that Canada is the best place on earth. We need to remember that our histories have been marred by genocide, inequalities, and domination (Mackey, 2010, pp. 13–14). Official and historical narratives (or what we call ***hegemonic narratives***) of nations across the world exclude images, representations, and contributions of those considered the **Other**. In order to deconstruct these *hegemonic narratives*, it is important to analyze them in the context of colonial and postcolonial relations and account for how the categories of "race", gender, ability, and sexuality are incorporated or excluded in constructing nations and their histories (Mackey, 2010, p. 14).

In order to analyze and study the experiences and life chances of racialized and marginalized peoples in Canada also require us to apply analytical frameworks that explore the overall and cumulative effects of *colonialism* and *postcolonial* relations and structures and the *discourse of Whiteness* in contemporary Canadian society. "Race" and racism have been effective discourses through which the dominant society has constructed many immigrants and racialized groups as "inferior". As Eva Mackey (2010, p. 3) argued, the experiences of Indigenous peoples are the first examples of the processes of **racialization** through which the dominant White settler societies imagined and labelled the Indigenous peoples as the **Other** of Europeans in order to justify the dispossession of their lands and the domination of their cultures.

It is in this light that we examine colonial and imperialist interventions in the context of global capitalism and its consequences in different parts of the world. In this chapter, historical and contemporary issues of diversity, language, and political rights are discussed from a *critical political economy* perspective. This chapter is divided into five parts. In Part One, we conceptualize *colonialism*, *imperialism*, and *postcolonialism*. We explore the ideologies and discourses of Eurocentrism and racism that informed European *colonialism*. In Part Two, we offer a general history of colonial and imperialist expansions into various parts of the world by looking at the two distinct periods of *colonialism*. We end this section with a general overview of postcolonial relations, the rise of independence movements across the globe, and their consequences. In Part Three, we analyze the effects of *colonialism, imperialism*, and capitalist relations through the lenses of three theories: modernization, dependency, and world-system. In Part Four, we examine the effects of *colonialism*, empire building, racism, and nation-building in Canada, with a focus on Aboriginal peoples. In Part Five, we explore the colonial and postcolonial nation-building processes in Canada by examining how immigration and multiculturalism have been used to construct different images of Canada throughout its history.

Part One

Conceptualizing Colonialism, Imperialism, and Postcolonialism

Colonialism as a Eurocentric Process and a Period

Colonialism is both a **process** and a **historical period**. As a *process*, it refers to European expansion into various parts of the world and their control over these parts that resulted in *mass murder, genocide*, and exploitation of labour and natural resources. Colonial powers invaded many parts of the world and ruled these regions, either directly or indirectly. There are many examples of European *colonialism*, such as plantation communities in North America and the Caribbean, mining and ranching in Latin America, and tea plantations in India. Britain, for example, ruled India, South Africa, Egypt, and North America as colonies. Italy controlled Ethiopia and Libya. France colonized Algeria and Mali. Spain and Portugal controlled many parts of South and Central America as well as parts of Asia and Africa (i.e., Spain in the Philippines and Portugal in Angola).

As a *time period, colonialism* refers to the events beginning in the 1500s until the 1960s and 1990s, when many colonial parts of the world became independent, often as a result of anticolonial and nationalist movements in colonized countries (Hall, 1996b, p. 190). As mentioned, *colonialism* entails foreign powers dominating Indigenous and subaltern groups by appropriating land and exploiting labour and the natural and material resources. Due to the exploitation of people and resources, it resulted in the "underdevelopment" of non-Western parts of the world. In short, *colonialism* connotes settlements of distant satellites, and is the consequence of *imperialism* (Said, 1994, p. 9).

Colonialism and *imperialism* are deeply imbued with Eurocentric views. **Eurocentrism** or **Eurocentricity** is a universal characteristic of *colonialism* and colonial relations (See Box 8.1 - Eurocentrism: The Ideology of Colonialism). According to this worldview, Western European-Canadian-American and their cultures define humanity and are considered as the centres of the universe. In general, *colonialism* expresses the superiority of Anglo-Western-European civilizations and their value systems. It assumes that western Knowledge is superior to other forms of knowledge. Since the era of *colonialism*, European and Christian values, norms, popular culture, and science have dominated other forms of worldviews. As we have mentioned in previous chapters, the Western

BOX 8.1 – Eurocentrism: The Ideology of Colonialism

Colonialism is driven by *Eurocentric* views and racist ideologies and discourses. As mentioned in Chapter One, *ideology* refers to those ideas and values that explain, justify, legitimize, and perpetuate the social, cultural, economic, and political oppression of marginalized groups. *Ideology* provides a framework that guides behaviour, and it allows people to make sense of the world. *Ideology* imparts specific meanings to life that are used to explain social, economic, cultural, and political situations. It also instils a common bond among group members that brings their members closer to one another (Henry & Tator, 2010, p. 382; Glossary).

As an *ideology*, *Eurocentrism* or *Eurocentricity* assumes that the cultural values, norms, and ethics of European and Western societies are "superior" to other forms of cultural practices. Western European cultural norms and values are viewed as the main vehicles to achieve progress, liberalism, and democracy. It also undermines and diminishes the roles that Europeans played in maintaining the oppressive systems of *colonialism* and racism (Henry & Tator, 2010, p. 381, Glossary). An example of *Eurocentrism* is the theory of **Social Darwinism**, which was a *racial ideology* that developed towards the end of the nineteenth century and institutionalized the assumed Western European "superiority", and was used as a justification to dominate non-Western and colonized people (Fleras, 2010, p. 40).

Samir Amin (2006, p. 97) asserted that *Eurocentrism* is expressed in everyday economic relations, politics, and information and knowledge about society and culture. From a *Eurocentric* point of view, the West is viewed as the symbol of progress, power, democracy, and freedom (Amin, 2006, p. 98). Within a *Eurocentric* knowledge base, progress is seen within the prism of European history of technological advancement. *Eurocentrism* requires and uses Europe and European history as the **ideal types** to measure everything else against them: it judges everything else by references to Europeans norms and values (Mehmet, 1995, p. 11). *Eurocentric* views about the economic policies of Western-European countries in Africa and Asia, for example, claim that the world is a better place because of the influences of Western countries around the world and their attempts to develop and modernize non-Western countries.

Ozay Mehmet (1995, p. 8) defined *Eurocentricity* as a 'European-centred worldview in which the interest or benefit of Europeans and their descendants is pursued at the expense of others, while justifying this worldview by paradigms or ethical norms that proclaim universal benefits for all'. It is based on the supremacy of the dualist thinking of Westerners that assumes the world is made of rational/irrational, citizen/barbarian dichotomies. As mentioned, it is related and linked to racially biased views, such as *Social Darwinism*, that assumed "the social life is a competitive struggle" in which "the fittest [group] will be best able to 'survive' and prosper" (Turner et al., 2002, p. 437). Social Darwinists borrowed the ideas of Charles Darwin, mainly the notions of the "struggle for survival" and "survival of the fittest", as the philosophical basis and justification for colonializing "peoples of colour" across the world (Fleras, 2010, p. 40). According to this perspective, the world is envisioned as a competitive place where groups compete over scarce natural resources and those who are better adapted and more able would ascend to the top of the evolutionary ladder (Fleras, 2010, p. 40). Thus, *Social Darwinism* was a defence for capitalist exploitation of the world as the best and most advanced system achieved by Europeans. As such, the Europeans and Westerners were not considered as morally responsible for the exploitation of colonized peoples: this was a natural phenomenon (Fleras, 2010, p. 40). According to this theory, those individuals who have access to social privileges deserve them "because they are the most fit, whereas those who have the least wealth are less fit and worthy" (Turner et al., 2002, p. 437). That is, for example, the inequalities and struggles of the "people of colour" and the working classes during the era of Industrial Revolution and *colonialism* were merely manifestations of the "survival of the fittest". The most advanced groups and nations "moved to the top", "while the weakest and least able fell to the bottom" (Sernau, 2011, p. 21). In fact, Edward Long in his book, *History of Jamaica*, stated that Africans were of a different species and were "brutish, ignorant, idle, crafty, treacherous, bloody, thievish, mistrustful, and superstitious" (as cited in Mehmet, 1995, p. 9). Such characteristics were due to their natural dispositions, which explained their lack of progress and "backwardness".

Eurocentricity is a way of analyzing the world: through this discourse, scholars study non-Westerners and their societies as objects to be gazed at by the knowledgeable and scientifically oriented Westerners (Mehmet, 1995, p. 11). That is, as Said (1978, p. 228) maintained, "only an Occidental [a White middle class male Anglo-European] could speak [with authority and certainty about] Orientals [darker skin non-European Middle Eastern groups]". Said referred to this body of knowledge produced about the Middle East by Europeans during the eras of *colonialism* and *imperialism* in scientific journals, manuscripts, history books, art projects, and literature as **Orientalism**. *Orientalism* is another example of *Eurocentrism*. It refers to the "western style for dominating, restructuring, and having authority over the Orient [i.e., the Middle East]" (Said, 1978, p. 3).

Eurocentrism permeates all facets of life in Western societies. For example, it informs Western education systems and the ways in which future generations are educated and provided information and knowledge to think about and imagine themselves in relation to the rest of the world. This knowledge base is not produced by Black Africans, Arab Africans, Asians, or Middle Easterners about themselves, but by Europeans and Westerners about them, which is used to politically, socially, and culturally dominate and control non-Western peoples (Mehmet, 1995, p. 10). *Eurocentrism* assumes that knowledge produced through Western European scientific lenses is "superior" to and more rational than knowledge produced through other means and perspectives. For example, during the British rule over India, Lord Macaulay asserted that "a single shelf of a good European library is worth the whole native literature of India and Arabia" (as cited in Mehmet, 1995, p. 9). Such belief systems and statements ignore the contributions of Indian and Moslem scholars to the development of science in Europe.

Eurocentrism also informs school curriculums and the types of knowledge students learn about national identity and the history of the nation. For example, in learning about the Aboriginal peoples in the United States, their histories in the textbooks are often discussed as appendages to European history or by references to them being "discovered" by White people (Henry & Tator, 2010, p. 203). For example, topics, such as *The New World* and *The European Discovery of America*, exclude the legitimacy of First Nations peoples of North America to the land and ignore and deny their political existence in this part of the world (Banks, 2001, p. 11). Another example of *Eurocentric* knowledge is reflected in a unit in the fifth grade American history texts, the *Westward Movement*, that explores the migration of European Americans from eastern United States to the western part of the country. Such lessons and units ignore the fact that the Lakota people were already living in the West at the time. From the perspective of Lakota peoples, the unit might as well be called: the *Invasion from the East by Racist Europeans* (Banks, 2001, p. 62). In general, the US history is told through an unilinear European-centred approach that follows the movement of European people across the Atlantic and into different parts of the United States (Banks, 2001, p. 237). The other groups are only mentioned in the context of their contacts with European settlers of North America (Banks, 2001, p. 237).

Official school knowledge about Europeans and Westerners also ignores the perspectives of other non-aboriginal and non-White groups and their experiences. For example, in the textbooks used during the 1980s in the United States, Black Americans were always mentioned in the context of discussions about Civil Rights Movement and slavery. In fact, when discussing the Civil Rights Movement, the textbooks failed to mention the oppression that Black Americans were facing at the time during the 1950s (Sleeter & Grant, 1991, p. 80). Even when issues of oppression were discussed, they were mainly portrayed from "a White point of view". The textbooks did not explore in detail the problems that "people of colour" faced due to the effects of racism, sexism, and classism (Sleeter & Grant, 1991, p. 86). As such, these people became and were rendered **invisible** or invisibilized. Lack of knowledge about a group or willful ignorance is another way of **silencing** it, which is a very powerful tool of domination (Wotherspoon, 2009).

Eurocentric curriculum and textbooks serve the interest of the White ruling elite and aid in social control (Sleeter & Grant, 1991, p. 80). They legitimize the *ideology* of the ruling elite by enforcing the idea that there are no alternative educational, cultural, political, or economic solutions or systems to the existing system of power. For example, those who promote and perpetuate a Eurocentric American culture in schools have historically campaigned for an English-only educational policy, which discourages educators to take advantage of the mother tongues of students who communicate in languages other than English as pedagogical tools to teach "minority" language students English and various other subjects in schools (Banks, 2001, p. 280). This policy prevails despite the fact that research has shown if their mother tongues are used in schools for the first five years of their education, "minority" students would perform better in schools (Nieto, 2000).

In Canada, *Eurocentrism* has also been an important characteristic of schooling and curriculum, which has negatively affected the experiences of both "minority" and "majority" students. Francis (1997, p. 53) argued that it was in the classrooms of Canadian schools during the first six decades of the twentieth-century where students were **indoctrinated** in the *ideology* of *imperialism*. In fact, students learned that they were members of the British Empire as much as they were citizens of Canada. One of the central aspects of the narrative of the nation was the assumed "superiority of the British form of government" (Francis, 1997, p. 54). Aboriginal peoples were also constructed and discussed in the textbooks used since the Confederation from highly stereotypical ways. The "Textbook Indian" was a racist and *Eurocentric* construction (Francis, 1997, p. 71). This image was created in order to justify British-Canadian hegemony over First Nations peoples. In one textbook used in Ontario during the time of Confederation, for example, only about eight pages were devoted to "Indian tribes", and the author indicated to the teachers that they could omit this section at their discretions (Francis, 1997, p. 71). In fact, most textbooks until the 1920s did not even include any sections on Aboriginal peoples. And when they were covered, the curriculum focused mainly on what they lacked in terms of cultural values and economic and political systems (Francis, 1997, p. 72).

In contrast to the construction of Anglo-Saxon culture and peoples, textbooks portrayed the Aboriginal people as nonmodern since they had no laws and no written language, did not live in houses, did not have access to sophisticated technology, and, of course, had no religions (in a book edited by the well-respected contemporary US educator, E. D. Hirsch [2001], *What Your Third Grader Needs to Know,* he also portrayed the Aboriginal peoples of the United States at the time of contact between the Aboriginal peoples and the White settlers in a section entitled, *English Colonies in North America* [2001, pp. 140–146], as individuals who lived in the forest and had no houses, churches, and government). One Canadian textbook also stated that "As they were Heathens, of course, they knew not the true God of Christians" (as cited in Francis, 1997, p. 72). In general, when Aboriginal peoples were discussed in the textbooks, it was always in reference to European expansion in North America. As Francis (1997, p. 72) maintained, history was taught as if it only happened to White people. Interestingly, in the lessons dealing with post-1885 events, the majority of the textbooks did not mention the "Indians" at all. In general, "textbook Indians" were constructed as "vicious" and "sinister" characters with no history or culture. According to these textbooks, Aboriginal peoples lived as "wild animals" in the forest and had no "civilization". They were depicted as a "strange race" whose members could endure cold, hunger, were "cunning" in behaviour, and stealthy in war (as cited in Francis, 1997, p. 73). In general, the Aboriginal peoples were depicted as warlike, "savages", "bloodthirsty", and "ruthless" individuals who inflicted pain and misery on White settlers (Francis, 1997, p. 74). In American social studies textbooks used during the 1980s, Native Americans were also viewed as mainly historical artifacts and their issues and histories were not discussed in the context of contemporary political economy of the United States (Sleeter & Grant, 1991, p. 80).

Racism and its consequences are also not discussed in many Canadian textbooks. Prior to 2000, for example, the subject of racism was discussed in only two of the twenty-two books approved by the ministry of education in Ontario. This is significant, in that due to the effects of cuts to the education system in that province in the last three decades many school districts are unable to purchase new textbooks that include information about the nondominant groups in Canada (Henry & Tator, 2010, p. 203). As such, students are socialized according to a curriculum that does not discuss the consequences of racism in Canada; thus, constructing Canada as the land of opportunity and a racism-free country. In this light, racism only occurs somewhere else, mainly in the United States. And, Canadians are not racist, but are tolerant of other cultures. In this light, a *Eurocentric* curriculum only explores the history of the nation through the examination of the accomplishments of European men and women, while excluding the contributions of non-Europeans (Nieto, 2000). It only explores the worldviews of Europeans as important sources of knowledge (Nieto, 2000). From the discussion so far, it is clear that schools are hegemonic spaces that disseminate knowledge that promotes the *ideology* of the ruling elites (this is not to say that schools and the education systems cannot be sites of resistance, empowerment, and emancipation).

worldview is based on a dualist approach that separates between mind and body, male and female, and reason and emotion, and assumes that the first category always is "superior" to the second. In this light, cultural forms of European *colonialism* have devalued non-White cultural norms, such as multiple Afrocentric values and Indigenous knowledge bases.

Colonialism is the direct political, social, cultural, and economic control of one country by another (See Box 8.2 - Colonialism: an overview). It refers to the practice of dominating the world by White Western Europeans who assumed that their racial characteristics, religious beliefs, and level of progress since the sixteenth century had given them the moral and intellectual right to rule the world. Cecil Rhodes (1853–1902), who was one of the most ardent supporters of British *colonialism*, for example, believed England should form colonies across the globe. Rhodes, who was the owner of DeBeers Consolidated Mines, Ltd, which controlled and still controls over 90 percent of the world's diamond resources, and who was influential in undermining the Boers' (Dutch settlers) control of South Africa and played an important role in the inclusion of Rhodesia as part of the British Empire, envisioned a world where England and English people, which he believed were the most honorable "race", must control the resources of the world (Perry et al., 1995, p. 226). During the colonial period, England and other European powers competed with one another to establish colonies in various parts of the world.

An example of the European colonization saga in Africa is the case of *South West Africa* (known today as Namibia, which became independent in 1989). In 1915, it was colonized by the *South African* forces that were fighting on behalf of the British Empire during World War I and defeated the German forces. Germany colonized the region and called it *German South West Africa*, which "formally designated it as a colony in 1884" (Kelleher & Klein, 2009, p. 87). During the occupation

BOX 8.2 - Colonialism: an overview

One way of understanding *colonialism* is by exploring the nexus of power, control, and exploitation. *Colonialism* is a discourse of domination, and a system of exploitation and political and cultural control (Peterson, 2002, p. 38). In the context of *colonialism*, the West is assumed to represent "humanity", "civilization", "progress", and economic growth. The colonialists pushed their ideas and values on those whom they captured and controlled. Western countries and their "native" agents in various parts of the world deprived societies of their freedom to rule themselves and control their wealth. *Colonialism* undermined Indigenous and local non-Western approaches to knowledge, morality, cultural values, and systems of governance (Gage & McNair, 2002, p. 37). However, this process was not without resistance and opposition to the colonial and imperialist forces. Despite such resistance movements and their success to assert independence, the postindependence governments did not necessarily promote the interests of all groups. In fact, the leadership cadres of many of these movements were made of educated elites, landlord families, and local capitalist classes from specific ethnic and religious backgrounds whose interests set them against the peasants, labourers, workers, and members of other religious and ethnic groups (Harman, 2008, pp. 449–462; pp. 551–562).

The European powers controlled their colonies through military force and destruction. Through force they were able to take over them politically, socially, culturally, and economically. *Colonialism* has had many devastating consequences for non-European nations, even after their independence from colonial powers (Gage, 1991a, 1991b, 1991c). In fact, one of the most important reasons for the prevalence of poverty and economic "underdevelopment", as well current ethnic conflicts in the world, is the consequences of colonial policies. The colonizing countries exploited the resources of the colonized countries for their own industrial and economic benefits without any regard for the needs of the colonized. As one British colonialist in Southern Africa stated, "We must find new land from which we can easily obtain raw materials and at the same time exploit the cheap slave labour that is available from the natives of the colonies. The colonies could also provide a dumping ground for the surplus goods produced in our factories" (as cited in Galeano, 2002, p. 44).

The colonies produced wealth for the colonial powers and this wealth was not spent on their "development" and the expansion of infrastructures in these countries, unless it was needed for the movement of goods and military equipment and personnel. The wealth gained from the colonies was not reinvested to increase productivity and industrial growth or to improve the lives of their inhabitants either. In colonies, such as the Philippines, India, Dutch East Indies (now Indonesia), Ceylon (now Sri Lanka), and Malay (now Malaysia), rich in natural resources, the raw materials and agricultural products were extracted and exported to European and Western countries. The colonialists used their newly and forcefully acquired lands to grow export crops, such as rice, rubber, sugar cane, and opium. They introduced these export crops into various colonies and as a result replaced the existing crops that were locally grown for internal consumption. In India, for example, tea, jute, and cotton were grown. In Malaya, the main crop was rubber, and in Ceylon tea became the main crop that was exported to various parts of the world. The wealth produced from the sale of these crops was used to pay the imposed colonial taxes on the colonized nations and peoples. In addition, since the prices for these crops were set by the colonial powers and were meager, the growers and farmers were not able to earn enough money to pay for their expenses and to feed their families (Gage & McNair, 2002, p. 35). This perpetuated poverty and social and economic problems for these populations.

In contrast, the *colonization* of the rest of the world played an important role in the economic growth of Europe. Many of the European landmarks were paid by the gold and other valuable minerals that were stolen from South American empires. The establishment of colonies in various parts of the world also resulted in economic stimulus and industrial growth in Europe, as these regions became markets for goods produced in Europe and the source of cheap raw materials for European industries. In fact, the source of almost all European colonial governments' operating budgets was the wealth gained from and produced in the colonies. Between 1850 and 1872, one-third of the budget of the Netherlands, for example, was provided by the Dutch East Indies, which enabled the Dutch to pay back their debt and to invest in the construction of the Dutch State Railways (Gage & McNair, 2002, p. 35).

Colonialism changed the character of life in many parts of the world. In Brazil, for example, before *colonialism*, "the lush land belonged to all just like the sun and water. The people live[d] in a golden age and [did] not surround themselves with ditches, walls, or hedges" (Pitro Martire d'Anghiera, 1500, as cited in Kempf, 2002, p. 34). Peter Vaz Caminha, in a letter to King Manoel I of Portugal in 1500 wrote that, "People are stronger and better fed than we are. They are well cared for and very clean and in this way they seem to me rather like birds. Their bodies are so plump and so beautiful that they could not be more so" (as cited in Kempf, 2002, p. 34). Another colonialist wrote of Brazil as a terrestrial paradise and a "delighted land with brightly colored birds, ever green trees … and an infinite variety of fruits" (as cited in Kempf, p. 34).

After years of *colonialism* and the exploitation of Brazil for its labour and resources, Nancy Scheper-Hughes, based on her research completed in 1990 (as cited Kempf, 2002, p. 34), concluded that, the Northeast region of Brazil is considered as one of the poorest regions in the world. She pointed out that, "Scenes of hunger, disease, and child death are commonplace. Two-thirds of all rural children suffer stunted growth from inadequate food. Hunger has made the population lean, nervous, and desperate. The Brazilian press refers to this region as 'the Valley of Death'. The country's rivers are 'spoiled brackish, salty, putrid and contaminated by pollutants. Their fish is gone. Children search through piles of garbage for food. Every four minutes two children less than a year old die in Brazil from starvation and disease" (as cited in Kempf, 2002, p. 34). The "underdevelopment" of the colonized world paid and paved the road for the development of Western European societies.

of Namibia, the German colonialists implemented a policy that "legalized land confiscation for European settlement" (Kelleher & Klein, 2009, p. 87). German occupiers forced the Indigenous peoples onto reservations and passed laws that prohibited the movement of people in the country without authorization (Kelleher & Klein, 2009, p. 87). This policy was developed after the defeat of the Herero and Nama nations that had resisted German occupation. The aim of this policy was to annihilate the Herero people: "Inside German territory, every Herero tribesman, armed or unarmed, with or without cattle, will be shot" (as cited in Kelleher & Klein, 2009, p. 87). In fact, between three-quarters and half of the populations of Herero and Nama people are estimated to have been exterminated as a result of this policy.

After the defeat of Germany, the *South African* government continued the German policy of forced relocation of the indigenous populations and their placement into reservations that led to the total **segregation** of White and non-White populations. The majority of the Black population was relegated to live in *reserves* in the regions with marginal land, which created a large pool of unemployed labourers ready and willing to work in the mines and commercial farms of White ruling elites (Kelleher & Klein, 2009, p. 87). This White supremacist system of racial segregation came to be known as **apartheid.** One of the consequences of *colonialism* and colonial policies was that the economy of Namibia became integrated with that of *South Africa*. Few infrastructures were built in the country by the colonial powers outside of the Northern region, most of which were developed due to the economic needs of the White Settlers or the war effort. This resulted in the "underdevelopment" of the country. In terms of educational attainment, for example, most educated people were of White background with a small number of non-Whites who "were able to receive formal education" (Kelleher & Klein, 2009, pp. 87–88).

As result of *South Africa's apartheid* policy and exclusion of the majority of the Black population from attaining basic and higher education, Namibia today is in desperate need of elementary and high school teachers and knowledgeable people in the fields of medicine and engineering to provide medical services and to participate in major development projects (Kelleher & Klein, 2009, p. 90). *South African* policies denied the Namibians to develop the skills and knowledge necessary to administer a modern economy and society (Kelleher & Klein, 2009, p. 90). The lack of educated personnel has undermined the efforts of the government, for example, to reduce the infant mortality rate (i.e., in 2001, 112 out of 1000 infants died before their fifth birthday) (Kelleher & Klein, 2009, p. 90). In addition, to become educated also requires Namibians to learn English or one of the other colonial languages. Knowledge of colonial language has become a source of power. In fact, the elite groups in Namibia speak English, Afrikaans, and German, the languages of the colonialists (Kelleher & Klein, 2009, p. 89). Due to the fact that many people in this country speak many different dialects and languages, English has become the official language, a testimony to the lingering colonial legacy of postindependence countries in the tri-continents of Africa, Asia, and Latin America and other parts of the Global South, and the fact that English has also become the language of commerce and politics, globally. The knowledge of these ex-colonial languages and the fact that the majority of the elite groups speak them fluently in comparison to the majority of the population has also resulted in exacerbating differences and inequalities in the postcolonial countries (Kelleher & Klein, 2009,

p. 76). In an ironic way, to become active in government and effect change and reforms, one needs to master the colonial "master's" language.

As the above discussion suggests, the contemporary history of the world must be contextualized against the backdrop of European colonialist interventions, most of which were through brute force and genocidal acts. A critical look at European *colonialism* and *imperialism* reveals a sordid tale of *mass killing*, the theft of land and natural resources, such as gold, diamonds, and timber, and exploitation of labour. This history also needs to be analyzed in the context of postindependence political economy of non-Western parts of the world and the ensuing ethnic and regional conflicts that have also resulted in the process of domination and resistance, including economic inequality, ethnic strife, and *genocide*.

Colonialism, "Race", and Racism

Central to the imperial and colonial expansions of Western powers was the concept of "**race**" as a tool and **racism** as an *ideology* to differentiate between White Europeans and non-White populations and to justify the exploitation of the people that they were encountering, especially since the seventeenth century (Castagna & Dei, 2000, p. 22). It is important to note that there is no one pure "race" in the world. The division of humanity into different "races" is misleading. It is not based on scientific proof. That is, "race" is not a biological reality. Antiracist feminists and other postcolonial thinkers have argued that RACE DOES NOT EXIST IN ANY BIOLOGICAL SENSE, BUT RACE IS REIFIED (to reify: to think of an abstract idea as a real thing, Henry & Tator, 2010, p. 25). It is a **social construct** that is given meanings in the context of political, social, and economic relations and structures. In the newspapers and magazines of the early decades of the twentieth century, for example, "race" was portrayed as a biological concept that was associated with certain qualities that could be used to distinguish between those who were suitable for citizenship in Canada and those who were not (Kelly, 1998, p. 42). For instance, the ability of Black women to produce future citizens of Canada who would "conform to conceptions of the 'Ultimate Canadian' bred of the 'best stock that could be found in the world'" was questioned by individuals, such as Cooke in 1911 (as cited in Kelly, 1998, p. 42). As a *social construct*, "race" has been drawn upon to describe and explain certain patterns of physical and genetic variation (Liodakis & Satzewich, 1998, p. 107). However, the usage of this term does not account for its history and consequences, such as unequal distributions of power and opportunities in societies for different racialized groups. During the colonial era, for example, "race" and ethnicity were *ideological constructions* that arose from the need to dominate and control peoples of colonized countries by the colonizing nations (Ng, 1993, p. 51).

Although "race" is not real, as Castagna and Dei (2000, pp. 19–36) maintained, there are "material, ideological and political consequences to race". That is, although "race" is a *social construct*, the effects of **racism** are real. Racism points to those systems of domination that involve subordination of specific groups through the imposition of certain discriminatory practices that are directed at marginalized groups and not others (Ng, 1993, pp. 51–52). In other words, conceptualization of peoples and groups based on the category "race" has had real economic, social, and political consequences in terms of lower educational attainment, lower health standards, denial of voting rights, and higher infant mortality rates. For example, when Africans from the United States immigrated to Canada after the American Revolution and the War of 1812, many of them settled in Halifax and faced discrimination due to their skin colour. In fact, in the 1840s, a section of Halifax became known as **Africville**, where many African-Canadians resided outside the White dominated neighborhoods in order to shelter themselves from the discriminatory views of the dominant society (Kelly, 1998, p. 30). This community was socially and politically isolated and neglected. The city council of Halifax, for example, did not provide basic services to its inhabitants. In fact, many factories that were considered as unsuitable for other White dominated parts of the city due to factors, such as pollution, were permitted to operate in Africville without any regards for the health of its residence. This practice is referred to as **environmental racism** (Kelly, 1998, p. 30). Eventually, however, the city council decided to "raze the community". As one resident of the city lamented, "If [the residence of this area] had been white people ... the city would have been in there assisting them to build new homes, putting in water and sewer and building the place up ... There were places in Halifax worse than Africville was and the city didn't do to them what they did to Africville" (as cited in Kelly, 1998, p. 31).

Environmental racism continues to affect "minority" peoples in the postcolonial era. In Houston, Texas, for example, more than 75 percent of municipal garbage incinerators and all the city-owned garbage dumps are located in Black neighbourhoods (Lipsitz, 2002, p. 67). Even when companies that pollute are fined, those polluting near white dominated neighbourhoods are fined about 500 percent higher than those that pollute near "minority" areas (Lipsitz, 2002, p. 67). In Los Angeles, 71 percent of African Americans and 50 percent of Latinos lived in polluted areas in comparison to 34 percent of Whites (Lipsitz, 2002, p. 67). It is no wonder that in 1988 among children of low income families, 68 percent of Black children were dealing with excess lead in their bloodstreams in comparison to 36 percent of White children (Lipsitz, 2002, p. 67). As the above arguments point out, "race" is not real, but its consequences are real and unequal.

Racial discrimination in the form of *residential segregation* was also considered as legally enforceable in Canada "through the use of racially restrictive covenants attached to deeds and leases" (Henry & Tator, 2010, p. 59). Black people were commonly refused services in taverns, restaurants, and other public places in Canada. Although Black Canadians challenged these forms of discrimination in the courts, the provincial courts as well the supreme court of Canada often held that racial discrimination was legal and "not contrary to public order or morality in Canada" (Henry & Tator, 2010, p. 59). In Ontario, separate and segregated schools were also established for Blacks.

Racialization, Whiteness, and Domination: from colonial conceptions of "race" to different forms of contemporary racism

It is important to note that our reference to and usage of the term "race" does not stem from "a need to categorize" (Castagna & Dei, 2000, p. 21). Instead, the aim is to understand and find ways of eliminating "racially constructed power-relations" in the world (Castagna & Dei, 2000, p. 21). In the past, for example, it was believed that "Whites" (read Europeans) should rule the world (**Manifest**

Destiny) and certain "races" were to be subservient to the "White race" (Castagna & Dei, 2000, p. 24). These ideas were accompanied with scientific theories that legitimated the social order and structure of society (Castagna & Dei, 2000, p. 25). Although "race" has no biological basis, instead of rejecting the term, **antiracist** and **critical race** theorists have argued that it is significant to talk about the processes of **racialization**. *Racialization* is understood as the ways in which social relations are affected by the "signification of human biological" and sociocultural characteristics, resulting in different ways of defining and constructing "social collectivities" (Castagna & Dei, 2000, p. 21).

We approach and apply the term "race" in the context of the history of colonial and postcolonial relations and not as a "biological essence" and as the basis to classify the world population into neat and well-defined groups (Castagna & Dei, 2000, p. 21). In talking about "race", we recognize that we are discussing "racial formations" and not indispensable "races" that are always the same and eternal (Castagna & Dei, 2000, p. 21). This current understanding of the term "race" and the process of *racialization* acknowledges that there are multiple forms of racism, such as **democratic** and **polite racisms** (See Box 8.3 - Different Forms of Racism).

BOX 8.3 - Different Forms of Racism

Individual racism "is a form of racial discrimination that stems from conscious, personal prejudice" (Henry & Tator, 2010, p. 382; Glossary). This form of racism does not account for how power and privilege are parts of the structures of society (Fleras & Elliott, 2002, p. 238). It occurs at the level of interpersonal relations, and can take the form of **hate racism**, **polite racism**, and **subliminal racism** (Fleras, 2010, pp. 72–76).

Hate racism could be considered as old-fashioned racism that assumes, for example, White people are "superior" to others, and non-White groups are "subhuman". The number of hate groups in the United States has risen since 2000 (Fleras, 2010, p. 73). In Canada, the Aryan Nation and Western Guard are examples of hate groups. **Islamophobia** is an example of *hate racism*. *Islamophobia* denotes discriminatory attitudes and practices against people and groups of Moslem or Moslem extraction, faith, and identity. Such attitudes and practices stem largely from exaggerated fears and anxieties and mistrust of the Islamic religion and Moslems. In recent times, particularly in the post-9-11 era, *Islamophobia* has become institutionalized in the form of knowledge produced by certain think tanks and university professors who demonize Islam and Moslems by constructing and miscasting them as "enemies" of Western liberalism (Fleras, 2010, p. 73). The result is that Moslems, such as Iranian-Canadians, are generally viewed as *enemies within the nation* and perpetual *outsiders* (Fleras, 2010, p. 73).

Polite racism is a covert form of racism, reflecting the attitude of individuals who are racist but do not express their racism outwardly. It is a "contrived attempt to disguise a dislike of others through behaviour that outwardly is non-prejudicial in appearance" (Fleras, 2010, p. 74). Such individuals believe in the general liberal conceptions of equality, yet they decide to refrain from becoming involved with "people of color" outside public societal contexts, such as in schools and workplaces. A **polite racist** individual treats the **other** fairly at work, but chooses not to invite him/her to his/her home and avoids contact with the racialized *other* outside conventional settings. The aversive feelings towards the *other* are not expressed through obvious forms of hatred and hostility but through avoidance and rejection (Fleras, 2010, p. 74). In contrast, **subliminal racism** refers to unconscious forms of dislike that are not apparent to the individual but are expressed in "principled statements" (Fleras, 2010, p. 75). It is a reflection of what people think and say and what they actually do (Fleras, 2010, p. 75). For example, such individuals may in fact oppose discrimination against racialized "minorities", but do not do anything about it: a person who is subliminally racist may not support the inclusion of **employment equity programs** based on the belief that such programs make the playing field unfair for White people and men.

Systemic racism refers to impersonal and largely unconscious forms of bias (Fleras & Elliott, 2002, p. 238). It is practiced through policies and practices that are rooted in established institutions, resulting in the exclusion or promotion of certain groups of people. It takes two forms. First, it manifests itself in the form of **institutional racism**, referring to "racial discrimination that derives from individuals carrying out dictates of others who are prejudiced or of a prejudiced society" (Fleras & Elliott, 2002, p. 238). Hiller (2006, p. 185) defined *institutional racism* as those "systematic and legal social practices that are rationalized by the belief in the superiority or prefer ability of one group over another". Examples of *institutional racism* are: excluding groups from certain occupations, denying people the right to vote, limiting certain groups to jobs that are low-paying, and paying members of specific groups according to an unequal pay-scale because of their presumed "racial" "inferiority" (Hiller, 2006, p. 185). *systematic racism* also takes the form of **structural racism**, or those forms of inequalities that are entrenched in the systematic operation of a society, which exclude large numbers of particular groups from meaningful participation in important social institutions (Henry & Tator, 2010, p. 384, Glossary). In general, *systemic racism* is an aspect of institutions, and it is built into them without social actors noticing how it operates and affects certain peoples and not others (Fleras & Elliott, 2002, p. 238). It is based on the application of rules and laws that seem to be universal and treating everyone the same, but their consequences often result in inequality. The intentions or motives are not of concern here. It is the context and consequences that are highlighted (Fleras & Elliott, 2002, p. 238). For example, consider the requirement of "having Canadian experience" and "Canadian credentials" as criteria for getting jobs in Canada that although may be well intentioned, exclude many immigrant "minority" people from getting "even low-paying entry-level jobs" in their professions (Fleras & Elliott, 2002, pp. 238–239). These people become **marginalized** as their credentials and work experiences are devalued due to the fact that standards and expectations are set too high (Fleras & Elliott, 2002, p. 239).

Cultural racism is replacing colour racism (Fleras, 2010, p. 66). That is, it emphasizes cultural "inferiority" rather than racial "inferiority". *Cultural racism* is entrenched in the values, norms, and beliefs prevalent in a society (Henry & Tator, 2010). It highlights the danger that foreign cultural practices have on the unity of the nation and cultural coherence within the country (Fleras, 2010, p. 66). It is based on sets of an unspoken network of beliefs and values that perpetuate and rationalize discriminatory and prejudiced beliefs, "actions, behaviours, and practices" (Henry & Tator, 2010, p. 380, Glossary). The dominant culture is considered as normal and more preferred over the cultural practices of subordinate groups. For example, Moslems are viewed as dangerous because of the values that are associated in the media to "radical Islam" that undermine democratic principles in the West (Fleras, 2010, p. 67).

Democratic racism refers to the coexistence of two competing value systems that are not compatible. On the one hand, one believes in the principles of equality and fairness that are central aspects of liberal democracy. On the other hand, one has prejudiced views towards members of specific racial or ethnic groups, and acts on these negative attitudes and discriminates against them (Hiller, 2006, p. 185). *Democratic racism* reduces the tension between commitments to democratic society motivated by egalitarian values of fairness and equality and the negative feelings one has towards "people of colour" (Driedger, 1996, p. 258). *Democratic racism* promotes British/White culture as the norm without references to "crude ideas of biological inferiority/superiority". For example, in democratic societies, individuals and organizations are "motivated" to ensure equality, but, in practice, "we" are more involved in promoting services, laws, and programs that "stabilize or increase" the power of the elite (Driedger, 1996, p. 258).

It is also important to differentiate between people who hold racist ideas and "the actual practice of racism with significant material consequences for people" (Castagna & Dei, 2000, p. 21). For example, in 1942, the United States removed all Japanese people living in the East Coast of the United States and placed them in internment camps. Both Japanese immigrants (referred to as Issei) and American-Japanese (referred to as Nisei) born in the United States were viewed as alien enemies. According to General John Dewitt, "In the war in which we are now engaged racial affinities are not severed by migration. The Japanese race is an enemy race and while many second and third generation Japanese born on United States soil, possessed of United States citizenship have become 'Americanized,' the racial strains are undiluted ... The very fact that no sabotage has taken place to date is a disturbing and confirmation indication that such action will be taken" (as cited in P. A. Thomsen, 2007, p. 74). Such a racist view was reflected in the laws of the country that were implemented and affected the Japanese-Americans.

Racially-biased views about Black people also made them vulnerable in medical studies and treatments. For example, in the Tuskegee Syphilis Study conducted in Alabama between 1932 and 1972 illiterate Black male sharecroppers were recruited to participate in this study of the treatment of syphilis. At first, the aim of the study was to observe how the disease was affecting these men without treating them for a period of six to eight months and then to treat them and observe the changes in the later phase (B. Thomsen, 2007, pp. 252–253). None of the participants were informed of the consequences of participating in this study. They were not given an **informed consent**, knowledge necessary to make a sound decision based on facts presented to individuals. None of the men were told that they could pass the disease to their offspring and partners. They were not also told that the disease was fatal. For a variety of reasons, the study never followed its original direction and purposes/goals. However, the study continued without providing a treatment phase to the Black men who were participating in this study, even though by the late 1940s a cure was available. This study was not terminated until 1972 when its existence was leaked to a reporter who wrote about it in the *Washington Star* (B. Thomsen, 2007, pp. 254–255). Only twenty-seven of the men were alive when the program ended. Twenty-six had died of the disease; and more than one hundred died as a result of syphilis related complications; forty of their wives also contracted the disease; and nineteen of their children were also diagnosed with the disease. This is not only an example of racism but also of a breach of medical ethics (B. Thomsen, 2007, p. 255).

Racial issues, moreover, are not non-White issues alone. The language of "race" has been an important aspect of political discourse in Canada before and after 1867; for example, "race" was used to distinguish between the British and French in 1837: "Canadian problem [was conceptualized as a] racial problem between French and British"; and Irish people in Canada and the United States were also viewed as non-White groups and a separate racial group (as cited in Satzewich, 1994, p. 40; Ng, 1993, p. 51). In this light, **Whiteness** is a source of power with certain privileges that are not extended to others. **White privilege** is the flipside of racism that is rarely discussed (Rothenberg, 2002, pp. 1–5). "Race", as a concept, has often been used to refer to only subordinate groups; White people are excluded from this category. The assumption is that Whites are "raceless", just people. (Roman, 1993, p. 71). For example, in Canada, White people often fail to recognize themselves as members of a racialized category (Schaefer, 2003, p. 210). Moreover, in the context of the **discourse of multiculturalism**, the term, "people of colour", treats the White culture as the hidden norm of society and as the *ideal type* upon which all other forms of culture are measured and compared (Roman, 1993, p. 71). When the so-called "people of colour" are asked when they noticed their characterization as a "person of colour", they often cite a specific moment and experience in their lives when their *difference* was highlighted for them. When White people are asked the same question, they tend to have no answer: White people associate *difference* with people who are not like them (Rothenberg, 2002, p. 2). In an interesting way, White people are not different than Indo-Canadians. It is always Indo-Canadians who are different than White people (Rothenberg, 2002, p. 2).

Colonialism, Modernity, and Racial Discourses

As mentioned earlier, central to *colonial* and *imperialist* expansions in modernity has been a racialized *ideology* that justified the actions and policies of Euro-Westerners. Rhodes (1995, p. 227), for example, stated that "why should we not form a secret society with but one object the furtherance of the British Empire and the bringing of the whole uncivilized world under British rule …". During the eighteenth and nineteenth centuries, the concept of "race" was interpreted in light of the biological theories that assumed "race" is an objective and scientific category that could be utilized to distinguish between people, what is referred to as **biological determinism** (Castagna & Dei, 2000, p. 23). In this way, people of the same racial backgrounds were assumed: to be the same, share specific intellectual and moral characteristics, and to be entitled to different political rights. "Race" in this context was imbued with power relations of domination and subordination (Castagna & Dei, 2000, p. 23).

Two general discourses were essential in the formation of colonial rules around the world: the **Manifest Destiny** (the idea that White people are destined to control the world) and the **Hamitic Rationalization** (the idea that some people are destined to be subservient and dominated) (Castagna & Dei, 2000, p. 24). In these discourses of power, *Blackness* was conceived as a sign of "immorality", "evil", "sin", and criminal behaviour; and *Whiteness* was depicted as its opposite (Castagna & Dei, 2000, p. 24). That is, in these discourses, the *other* was presented as something that should be feared, controlled, and avoided. The power of colonial knowledge lies in its ability to defer upon the *other* images of fantasies that were then used to depict an innocent construction of the **self** that also elevated it as the symbol of a civilizing culture. Contradictory images of men and women of different racial backgrounds were incorporated that in their **discursive formation** (in the ways that they come together and form a homogenized image and framework to think about the **self** in relation to multiple forms of *otherness*) provided a systematic structure that was hierarchical and positioned various types of groups and individuals within a single narration, enabling the dominant groups to control the *other* and reap the benefits for themselves only (i.e., Whites at the top and other groups at the bottom of the social, economic, and political ladder).

Consider, for example, that in the colonial discourses, colonized men were often depicted both as less masculine (as females) in relation to the dominant White males, and as dangerous bodies whose hypersexuality was a threat to White women, undermining the strict racial purity boundaries between Whiteness and *otherness*. Black men's sexuality was (is) considered as a threat to White women's safety and to the reproduction of the White race. White women in this discourse were divested of agency and conceived of as properties of White men. The woman was projected as the symbol of the nation whose purity was reflected in the types of racialized offspring they could reproduce for the nation.

As feminized men, Black men "were seen to have too little of some masculine characteristics, such as responsibility and stability" (Pettman, 2006, p. 147). At the same time, their sexuality was depicted as "savage, violent, [and] voracious" (Pettman, 2006, p. 147). In fact, the need to protect White women from the "rapist" Black men often coincided "when colonial authority [was] questioned, and Black/colonized men [were needed to] be put down" (Pettman, 2006, p. 147). In contrast, colonized women were often eroticized (i.e., viewed as sexual beings). However, unlike White upper class women, it was thought that they could not control their sexuality. As a result, they were often viewed as seducing White men. This seductive sexuality was either attributed to "their men's brutish nature or [considered] saveable through Christianizing and domesticity" (Pettman, 2006, p. 147). As Black men's and White women's bodies were gendered and racialized and controlled through these discourses, White men were able to transgress these socially constructed boundaries "and use, abuse or even care for colonized women" (Pettman, 2006, p. 148). However, the children of such "unions" often stayed with colonized mothers and in this way the racialized boundaries of the colonized world were maintained.

As the above discussions point out, "race" needs to be read and understood in the context of other factors, such as class and gender. In the era of *colonialism*, we witnessed a distinction made between different types of men and women based on highly racialized discourses (Pettman, 2006, p. 148). On the one hand, the colonized and colonial women were depicted along the vectors of bad/good mother and bad/good woman (Pettman, 2006, p. 147). Although, lower class White women were often depicted as bad mothers/women, White women were, generally speaking, constructed as "pure, non-sexual, mothers, [and having] civilizing influence on 'their' men" (Pettman, 2006, p. 147). In contrast, colonized women were depicted not only as nymphomaniacs, incapable of controlling their sexuality, but also as "temptresses" and amoral (Pettman, 2006, p. 147).

In general, colonial women benefitted from the colonial relations as the *"inferior" gender within the White society* who also belonged to *the "superior" race in relation to other racialized non-White groups* (Pettman, 2006, p. 146). For example, in Australia, many Aboriginal women were trained as domestic helpers in White households. They were used as cheap labourers and were supervised by the state, but their rights were not protected by the state agencies, such as the Aboriginal Protection Boards (Pettman, 2006, p. 146). Many of them were taken away from their own families to take care of White children, relieving White women of domestic work. Many of these Aboriginal women's children were also removed from their supervision because they were deemed unfit mothers, yet they could take care of the children of White women. In general, non-White women were viewed as "promiscuous" and "exotic" beings (Pettman, 2006, p. 146). And, colonizing women played an important role in the process of domestication of colonized women (Pettman, 2006, p. 145). In this way, White women were involved in the reproduction of the colonial order based on hierarchical and evolutionary perceptions of gender and racial hierarchies prevalent in society (Pettman, 2006, p. 145).

Monogenetic and Polygenetic Theories of Racial Differences: Scientific racism, eugenicism, and the discourse of Whiteness

During the early periods of contact between White and non-White peoples in North and South America, the Europeans were encountered with a moral problem: how to conceptualize Aboriginal peoples? Were they descendants of Adam and Eve? If so, how were they to explain the "Indian" in relation to White Christians? That is, one of the social elements that the early European explorers in South America were confronted with was how to explain "the natives' differences" from European cultural norms and values (Hall, 1996b, p. 212). For example, when the "natives" gave gifts to the so-called "explorers" upon initial contacts, this gift giving, which was a reciprocal act from the perspective of the "natives", was constructed by the Europeans in light of a discourse that claimed/assumed the "nice natives" bearing gifts recognized the "superiority" of European culture (Hall, 1996b, p. 212). In general, the Europeans viewed the Aboriginal peoples in dichotomous "friendly natives" versus "fierce natives" terms. This dichotomous depiction of the "natives" had an additional element to it: they were at once one with nature, thus, free; but without culture, thus, "uncivilized".

In accordance with the Christian faith, Europeans first approached these issues from the **monogenetic** interpretation that assumed all people were the same and had the same human potentials

(Mackey, 2010, p. 19). According to this view, all human "races" formed a single biological species "with a common origin and physical differences [were only] produced [due to] natural agents over time" (Erickson, 1998, p. 29). Until the late eighteenth century, it was assumed all humans were capable of civilization. As colonial powers established themselves around the world by the mid-seventeenth century, monogenetic ideas were replaced with a **polygenetic ideology**. At this time, it was believed that only certain "races" were able to achieve civilization, which was defined based on the evolution of European societies and their industrial and technological achievements (Mackey, 2010, p. 21).

Polygenists assumed that different raced groups belonged to separate human species. It was supposed that differences in terms of physical features were "unalterable and racially innate" (Erickson, 1998, p. 29). In this sense, White people formed the centre of humanity and their cultural, moral, and philosophical stances informed the basic characteristics of humans. They were placed at the top of the social pyramid. Their supposed "superior" qualities were proved through "scientific" measures, such as craniometry and intelligence testing (i.e., the IQ testing) that were manipulated to prove European assumptions about their supposed "superiority" (Castagna & Dei, 2000, p. 25).

Scientific racism assisted Europeans to justify their actions to dominate the world. *Scientific racism* refers to those dogmatic explanations that guise themselves as "scientific", and were used to justify the domination of people and their unequal positions in society. In the United States, for example, these views were popular during the turn of the twentieth-century when many Black migrants moved from south to north and a large number of immigrants from Southern and Eastern Europe arrived in the United States (Fleras, 2010, p. 41). *Scientific racism* is based on the idea that we can measure and evaluate people's racial capacities for thinking. The Americans used the IQ test that was originally not developed to measure intelligence of people by Alfred Binet, a psychologist at Stanford University, and applied it as an objective "scientific" measurement of intellect to all groups of people.

The IQ test was used during World War I to select those who would be suitable for leadership positions in the Army. Since these tests were racially biased, most Black people did very poorly on them, and many Whites became officers while Blacks were recruited as foot soldiers (Fleras, 2010, p. 41). The fact that Blacks on average fared worse than Whites was used to prove Whites' intellectual "superiority" over Blacks (Fleras, 2010, p. 41). However, certain results of these tests were ignored. For example, the highest and lowest scores for each group were similar. Also, 15 percent of Blacks scored higher than the average for Whites, which would suggest that many Black people were more intelligent than Whites (Fleras, 2010, p. 41). Such ideas have been reproduced in contemporary racist and white supremacist theories, which continue to be utilized to offer racial explanations of intelligence and social and economic problems and inequalities. For example, Charles Murray and Richard Herrnstein in their book, *The Bell Curve: intelligence and class structure in American life*, published in 1994, explained that low levels of intelligence of certain racial groups are "real, measurable by IQ tests, inherited, predictive, and resistant to modifications" (Fleras, 2010, p. 41). Others have also argued that genetics can be used to explain the differences in intelligence between racial groups. The problem with these explanations is that they use biology to explain poverty, dysfunctional elements of society, and crime rather than economic factors, class inequality, and political power differences as the causes of poverty. Also, the proponents of these theories maintain that since Blacks are not genetically inclined and suitable for the type of professional jobs that are "scientifically" orientated and require academic education then it is better to educate them according to their intelligence for the types of jobs that suit them. That is, let us eliminate programs that attempt to improve their educational attainment levels in fields, such as engineering, medicine, and physics, since Black people are biologically incapable of achieving the same ends as other racial groups, such as Chinese and Whites.

The **eugenics movement** that emerged at the turn of the twentieth century is another example of a racialized discourse that assumed it is possible to improve the mental capacity and behaviours of individuals through selective manipulation of their genetics and hereditary characteristics (Fleras, 2010, p. 40). According to this discourse, it is possible to improve the human condition by purging and eliminating the undesirable elements within human societies: the mentally ill, the deaf, the blind, homosexuals, and racial and religious minorities, such as Jews and Gypsies. These people could be sterilized, so they would not reproduce and "contaminate" the population and its genetic makeup (Fleras, 2010, p. 40). The *eugenics movement* has been popular in various forms in the United States, Canada, Germany, and England. This discourse was used to limit immigration to the United States from those countries whose citizens were considered as less fit to become absorbed into the dominant US culture (Fleras, 2010, p. 40). In Canada, a **Sexual Sterilization Act** was passed in Alberta in 1928 that paved the way for the sterilization of 3,000 women, the majority of whom were either poor or Aboriginal. This act was only repealed in 1972 (Fleras, 2010, p. 40).

As it can be inferred from the above examples, *colonialism* as a *process* was racist: it was based on a set of racial ideologies that assumed certain groups are culturally, socially, economically, and politically more superior to other cultural, ethnic, racial, and national groups. Spring defined **racism** as "prejudice plus power" (2007, p. 6). That is, when power is used to attend to and act upon feelings of *prejudice* (i.e., generalized views about a group that tend to describe the whole group based on specific criteria) one group has about others (i.e., the creation of segregated schools for Mexican Americans in the Southwest of the United States that resulted in their unequal **assimilation** into the American political and economic structure), then, this practice is a **racist act** and an example of **discrimination**.

Colonialism expressed the racial dominance of (Anglo) Western European civilization(s) and value systems through citizenship laws, education, economic relations and systems, and court rulings. By the nineteenth century, for example, in Canada, it was assumed that Native people were "incapable" of "civilization" and were destined to perish. By the twentieth century, it was assumed that Aboriginal populations needed to be protected from the evils of modernity and become assimilated into the dominant White Canadian society. *Colonialism* is based on the **discourse of Whiteness**. This is a very powerful racialized discourse that assumed certain White Europeans were more "superior" to other cultural and national groups. It assumed that **Whiteness** defines who and what is considered as "normal" and "human". European and Christian values, norms, popular culture, and science(s) were assumed to be more dominant than other forms of worldview.

As we have mentioned in this and previous chapters, beginning with the arrival of Columbus in the Americas, Europeans viewed the world through the prism of the discourse of "us" and "them" that divided the world's population into "civilized" and "uncivilized" and Christian and pagan (Spring, 2007, p. 2). It was assumed that Western knowledge is "superior" to other forms of knowledge. As we explained previously, the Western worldview is based on a dualist approach that separates between mind and body; male and female; reason and emotion; "developed" and "underdeveloped"; and "civilized" and "uncivilized". It purports that the first category always is "superior" to the second category. In this light, cultural forms of European *colonialism* devalued those cultural norms that were not based on dualist ways of thinking, such as multiple Indigenous knowledge forms. The British colonizers, for example, viewed all "native" people they encountered as the **other** and labelled them as different in terms of basic human qualities in comparison to themselves (Spring, 2007, p. 1). They were constructed as "uncivilized savages" and "pagans" who needed to be controlled and brought into the circle of "humanity" and Christianized (Spring, 2007, p. 1). In fact, Western expansion into various parts of the world was considered a necessary step in civilizing the world. For example, the Spanish viewed the world as their sovereign domain. They justified this through religious views of the time and the proclamation of Pope Alexander XI in 1493, which gave explorers and colonialists the right to occupy and claim all the land that they "discovered" through their voyages across the globe (Spring, 2007, p. 3).

The *colonialism* of the world was also a joint venture between the Christian Churches and the state. The relationship between the Church and state can also be observed in British colonial attitudes towards non-British and Aboriginal peoples. As economic Protestantism grew in England, English (Anglo-Saxons) began to view themselves as more "superior" to Catholic nations and countries, such as Ireland, Italy, and Spain (Spring, 2007, p. 4) (See Box 8.4 - Calvinism and the Protestant Ethic).

BOX 8.4 - Calvinism and the Protestant Ethic

As mentioned in the previous chapters, since the sixteenth century, the power of the Catholic Church was undermined with the rise of Protestantism and the Reformation. The Catholic Church was against usury and had strict principles regarding financial and economic gain that were not conducive to the growth of capitalism (Heilbroner, 1989, p. 49). The Church emphasized the afterlife and it "strove ... to denigrate the earthly activities to which an all-too-weak flesh succumbed" (Heilbroner, 1989, p. 49). The ideas of John Calvin (1509–1564) were influential in changing the general attitudes regarding "the zest of wealth making" (Heilbroner, 1989, p. 49).

In general, the Calvinist doctrine preached predestination, the idea that whether a person is going to end up in hell or heaven had already been decided by God, and there is nothing one could do to change this outcome. Calvinists promoted a life based on values, such as rectitude, severity, and diligence. Later, they sanctified and approved human endeavour as a kind of spiritual worth. As a result, "the idea of a man [sic] dedicated to his work" became the basis of the discourse of individualism in European and Western societies (Heilbroner, 1989, p. 50). That is, a "man" dedicated to "his" profession was not considered as unholy. In contrast, the more successful a "man" was in "his" worldly endeavours, the more worthy "he" was of salvation. In other words, Calvinist ideas were instrumental in creating an atmosphere that legitimized wealth seeking.

The other important impact of Calvinism was its emphasis on rejecting indulgence. They also influenced how wealth was going to be used. Unlike the Catholic merchants who believed that the aim of success was to make the earthly life luxurious and easy, the Calvinist believed that one must be thrifty (Heilbroner, 1989, pp. 50–51). Calvinism "made investment, the use of saving for productive purposes, an instrument of piety as well as profit" (Heilbroner, 1989, p. 51). Calvinism questioned the old belief of knowing one's place in the hierarchy of the world, and "brought respectability to an ideal of struggle, of material improvement, of economic growth" (Heilbroner, 1989, p. 51). This **Protestant ethic** played a central role in the growth of economic *ideology* of capitalism. It is important to note that countries like England and the Netherlands with their Puritan *ideology* were the ones that prospered first in the economic race of the time (Heilbroner, 1989, p. 51).

It was also assumed that it was the main destiny of Western Europeans to civilize the non-Christian peoples. For the English, the dispersion of Anglo-Saxon civilization and Protestantism provided the justification for English *imperialism* to increase its control over the rest of the world (Spring, 2007, p. 4). As already stated, they also believed that it was their destiny to save the world by imposing their culture, values, faith, and language upon the rest of the world (Spring, 2007, p. 4). They assumed that it was their "divine mission to spread doctrines of political liberty" (Spring, 2007, p. 4). It is important to note that the racialized conception of English "superiority" in terms of cultural and moral values was intertwined with their concepts of political liberty that were not equally applied to the peoples and cultures that they encountered and dominated. This remains a central aspect of the attitudes of Western *imperialism* towards the rest of the world. During the early Christian empires, "pagan or non-Christians were deemed less than human" (Spring, 2007, p. 3). The task of Christians, they assumed, was to make these pagan peoples pious and virtuous (Spring, 2007, p. 3). For them, piety implied "compliance with religious laws and loyalty to the family. Virtue meant a willingness to sacrifice oneself for the good of the Christian community" (Spring, 2007, p. 3). In fact, Spanish exploitation of the Americas was also based on the assumption that they were being virtuous and bringing those labelled as "inhuman … into the realm of humanity" (Spring, 2007, p. 3). As Said maintained, the assumption was that "distant territories and the native peoples should be subjugated" and it was their right and obligation to "rule subordinate, inferior, or less advanced people" (as cited in Spring, 2007, p. 3).

Colonizing Aboriginal Peoples in North America

We can trace the early period of *colonization* to the twelfth century when the English invaded Ireland; an act that was justified by their assumed cultural and religious "superiority" over the Irish Catholics.

In fact, the British viewed the Native peoples of North America in the same light as they viewed the Irish: "wild" (Spring, 2007, pp. 4–5). Both the Irish and Aboriginal peoples could be saved if they would only adopt the values and norms of English colonizers. It was only through **assimilation** that the "savage" and inferior" nations could be saved and brought into humanity and made human.

Similarly, two main views were central to British policies in North America in respect to the Aboriginal peoples. One view stated that the only solution to the "Indian problem" was to annihilate them. That is, the most extreme solution was *genocide*. This racist and supremacist policy was reflected in the views and comments about the Aboriginal peoples by individuals, such as General Philip Sheridan, who in 1867 stated, "The only good Indian I ever saw were dead" (as cited in Spring, 2007, p. 5). This comment has become popularized in the movies and popular culture: 'the only good Indian is a dead Indian".

The Americans adopted this British attitude towards Aboriginal people, and their policies reflected the general view that North America was to be for White people only (Spring, 2007, p. 5). Benjamin Franklin, for example, was adamant that there were many more Africans and Asians in the world than White European. He considered and imagined North America as geographical space to "increase the White race" (Spring, 2007, p. 5). He also proclaimed that the English were the main group of White people that should populate North America. In fact, he was concerned about the growing number of German populations in Pennsylvania (Spring, 2007, p. 5).

The organizations and structures of Aboriginal "tribes" were also viewed as something that was less "civilized" and less "superior" to the European social and economic organization. The Anglo-Saxon culture in North America, for example, emphasized the importance of the *Protestant ethic*, which was closely related to their conceptions of childrearing. The *Protestant ethic* highlighted the centrality of hard work and accumulation of property as defining elements of a civilized culture. Hard work was viewed as an activity that went against sinful acts. By focusing on work, it was assumed that individuals would not have time to think about evil acts. Idleness was considered the Devil's weapon. Accumulation of wealth was also viewed as a sign of God's blessing: "hard work and the accumulation of wealth were considered outward signs of a godly life" (Spring, 2007, p. 11).

In contrast, the Aboriginal cultures believed in communal ownership and sharing of property. Moreover, "there was no concept that work was good in and of itself" (Spring, 2007, p. 11). In these cultures, the time used to hunt and gather food was a central aspect of cultural celebrations and rituals, which integrated individual members into the fabric of society and linked them with nature and cosmos. The fact that Indigenous peoples did not use their time to accumulate wealth and property was used as a justification to characterize them as "lazy" and "uncivilized". The *Protestant ethic* impressed on people to sacrifice pleasure for work and wealth. For the Aboriginal communities, for example, personal pleasure in the form of sexual pleasure was important, which terrified the New England Puritans. They also did not have the same conceptions of sin as the Christian colonialists had regarding repression of sexual desires. In fact, Aboriginal peoples were viewed as "dirty" and "filthy". However, this reference to "filth" was not an allusion to uncleanness of the Aboriginal people. Rather, as Spring (2007, p. 12) pointed out, it was a reference to the "seemingly unrepressed sexuality [of Aboriginal peoples] and not for their inattention to bathing".

The Aboriginal childrearing practices were also viewed with suspect. The English/American emphasis on order, discipline, and authority was in opposition to "Indian" ways that emphasized "indulgence and permissive attitudes toward their children". The general view, expressed in the words of Reverend John Edwards in the late 1880s regarding the Choctaws peoples, was that, "there is very little order and discipline in the family. Each does what is pleasing in his own eyes. A parent may beat a child in anger, but seldom he chastise him with coolness and in love" (as cited in Spring, 2007, p. 11). The Aboriginal childrearing practices did not attempt to break the will of the child, to make sure that he or she obeys his or her "mother, father, government, church, and God" (in the ascending order) (Spring, 2007, p. 11).

Related to the childrearing practices was the role and position of women in many Aboriginal communities. Women tended to have more power than European women. The Aboriginal clans were not based on patriarchal values and system of hierarchy. The aim of the colonialists was to impose the social organization of nuclear family on clan-based systems of Aboriginal communities. In this system, many women had political powers. For example, among the Cherokees, there were women leaders, and women participated in wars as warriors. Women had their own councils and they influenced the decision of the tribes in which they lived. "Clan-mothers had the right to wage war" and had power to decide about the fate of their captives (i.e., to release them) (Spring, 2007, p. 13). In fact, White women who were captured by Aboriginal communities continued living amongst them, mainly due to the fact these women enjoyed more freedom than they did in European colonial settler societies. As one White woman recalled her experiences: we "… had no master to oversee or drive us, so that we could work as leisurely as we pleased" (Mary Jemison, as cited in Spring, 2007, p. 13). The European colonialist enforced the patriarchal system over the Aboriginal communities through the education system and laws, such as the Canadian **Indian Act**, ensuring the subordination of women to male authority. In fact, in Canada, until very recently, if an Aboriginal woman married a White man, she and her children lost their Indian status. However, if a white woman married an Aboriginal man, she and her children gained Indian status (Fleras, 2010).

The assumption of the colonizers was that these non-European people were "culturally retarded in their attitudes, customs, and technical abilities" (Parenti, 2002, pp. 64–65). This is one of those myths that reinforced the idea that the task of Europeans and Westerners was to assist Aboriginal people to develop and help themselves. The myth of "**cultural backwardness**" was a powerful notion in justifying the *colonization* of the world. This myth gave the impression that Western European powers were "civilized" and "modern". However, historical data suggests that during the period between the fifteenth and nineteenth centuries European societies "were 'ahead' in such things as the number of hangings, murders, and other violent crimes; instances of venereal disease, smallpox, typhoid, tuberculosis, plagues, and other bodily affliction; social inequality and poverty (both urban and rural); mistreatment of women and children; and frequency of famine, slavery, prostitution, piracy, religious massacres, and inquisitional torture" (Parenti, 2002, p. 65). In comparison to European societies, many other peoples across the world were technologically more "superior" and "advanced" than them. Many important techniques in fields, such as midwifery, architecture, fishing, and medicine, were developed in various other parts of the world.

This myth of "*cultural backwardness*" was promoted in light of the discourse of biological racism, which assumed that the colonized people were genetically less evolved than Western Europeans. Such ideas informed the imperialist attitudes towards non-White peoples in North America and across the globe.

Imperialism

The basis of colonizing ideas was informed by general theoretical and philosophical positions that can be subsumed under the heading of *imperialism*. Kelleher and Klein (2009) defined *imperialism* as a form of direct and/or indirect cultural, social, and economic control of one country by another. That is, *imperialism* refers to formal or informal relationships that result in political, economic, social, and cultural domination of one state by another (Said, 1994, p. 9). The *imperialist* power does not have to be present in a country to dominate it. This can be achieved through establishment of puppet governments that promote the interests of the imperialist powers, such as the Pahlavi Dynasty (1921–1979) in Iran that promoted the interest of American *imperialism* in the Middle East from 1945 to 1979. As Edward Said (1993, p. 9) observed, *imperialism* is about "the practice, the theory and the attitudes of a dominating metropolitan centre ruling a distant territory" (Said, 1994, p. 9).

Imperialism then is a discourse or set of ideas and frameworks about how to dominate **otherness**. It is practiced through a set of plans and policies. It is about controlling different nations, states, and peoples, as imagined collectivities, highlighting the importance and "superiority" of the cultural values of the dominant Euro-Western groups. *Imperialism* is "the process and or policy of establishing or maintaining an empire through which imperial powers exercise political, cultural, and economic control over other nations and states" (Said, 1994, p. 9). As a policy and *ideology*, *imperialism* reproduces the dominant position of the *imperialist* states by asserting how things ought to be.

Imperialism, for example, takes the form of cultural control. Cultural or symbolic forms of *imperialism* have resulted in the assimilation of nondominant groups into the dominant Western society. As Western cultural practices and products are sought by non-Westerners, Indigenous and local cultures have become marginalized and devalued. This aspect of *imperialism* has a homogenizing effect. It has resulted in the process of **deculturation**. However, it is important to note that many non-Western groups around the world have also resisted colonial and imperialist domination and have strived towards political, economic, social, and cultural independence.

> **Imperialism** has reproduced the dominant positions of the *imperialist states*. **Symbolic imperialism** has resulted in the assimilation of nondominant groups into the dominant Western culture and the promotion of **Whiteness** as a desired identity.

Imperialism also refers to a global stage of capitalism that is characterized by the dominance of corporate monopolies. According to Lenin, *imperialism* is a specific stage within the capitalist development, highlighting the crisis that occurred in capitalist profitability during the early decades of the last century (Webster, 1984, p. 81). Lenin pointed out that one of the ways of increasing the rates of profit for the capitalist class was by expanding into other parts of the world. This would have allowed the capitalist class to have:

1. access to global sources of cheap labour and resources, and

2. control over global markets (Webster, 1984, p. 82).

According to Lenin, capitalism and *imperialism* are related in four distinct ways:

1. export of capital to colonies was central to maintaining the profitability of capitalist classes;

2. due to their military strengths, Western and European countries were able to gain and demand favorable terms for raw materials from non-Western countries;

3. the need for capital, in the form of loans which were needed to be paid back with interest, to invest in the construction of railroads and ports in non-Western parts of the world to serve the capitalist expansion in the colonized countries also benefited the growth of capitalism in Europe; and

4. the above factors have led to the concentration of power in multinational firms (Webster, 1984, p. 82).

As such, *imperialist ideology* assisted capital to seek cheap labour across the globe. In this light, the primary export of Western countries is considered to be capital in the form of investments rather than manufactured commodities.

There are problems with Lenin's theory of *imperialism*, however. For example, capital was not invested in many parts of the world, but mainly in countries where White people settled. Nevertheless, Lenin also assumed that "capitalist expansion would have a progressive affect on those non-capitalist societies it penetrated" since it would have resulted in the development of industrial capitalism in these parts of the world, a view that is critiqued by post-Lenin thinkers (Webster, 1984, p. 83).

Neocolonialism, Internal Colonialism, and Postcolonialism

By the 1960s, one by one colonized countries became independent. However, the road to independence was an arduous journey and one that, many scholars argue, has led to **internal colonialism** and **neocolonial relations**. *Internal colonialism* refers to the treatment of "minority" groups within modern nation-states that are based on colonial-like relations. More specifically, it is a term that highlights and explains "the process of settler control and domination of Indigenous groups" (Fleras & Elliott, 2002, p. 271). In Canada, for example, Aboriginal people experienced direct colonial relations and *internal colonialism* after the establishment of the Dominion of Canada. According to the *internal colonialism* model, Aboriginal people in Canada are not an ethnic group but nations whose experiences of inequalities are colonial in nature (Fleras, 2010, p. 19). In the context of *internal* *colonialism*, Aboriginal peoples have been forcefully incorporated into the dominant system in order to control their land and resources. This system has three main characteristics:

1. Aboriginal peoples' political and social involvements in the process of nation-building are limited and constrained,

2. their cultural values and norms are weakened, and

3. their needs, political demands, and economic wants are controlled through imposed bureaucratic structures that are controlled by the dominant society (Fleras & Elliott, 2002, p. 271).

Their independence as political units is undermined and they are pushed to the margins of society since, for example, they occupy the "most menial occupations" in society (Fleras, 2010, p. 19). They are dominated through the establishment of bureaucracies, such as the Department of Indian Affairs, that control all aspects of their lives, including education, governance, and economic development (Fleras, 2010, p. 19).

Neocolonialism, a concept coined by Nkrumah (1965), refers to the dependence of the newly independent countries on the expertise and material goods produced in the former colonial countries. It is the end result of the "'deliberate policies of the industrialized [Western] nations to maintain their domination' through 'foreign-aid programs, technical advisors, publishing firms, or other means'" (Kelly and Altback as cited in Kubow & Fossum, 2007, p. 53). Nkrumah also asserted that "the essence of neo-colonialism is that the state which is subject to it is, in theory, independent and has all the trappings of international sovereignty. In reality, its economic system and thus its internal policy is directed from the outside" (Nkrumah, 1965, p.1). Proceeding from his central premise that the West, responding to the success of national liberation movements, first in Asia and then in Africa, shifted its tactics from *colonialism* to *neocolonialism*, Nkrumah posited that "[w]ithout a qualm it dispenses with its flags" and "claims that it is 'giving' independence to its former subjects, to be followed by 'aid' for their development" (Nkrumah, 1965, p.2). Behind the façade of such rhetoric, however, he maintained, the West "devises innumerable ways to accomplish objectives formerly achieved by naked colonialism" (Nkrumah, 1965, p.2). The *neocolonial* powers pursue their grand imperial scheme under the aegis of the United Nations by using its Breton Woods' agencies: the World Bank and the International Monetary Fund. These agencies, set up after WWII, were controlled undemocratically by the Euro-American West.

Nkrumah described the actions of the West as a neo-colonialist trap on the economic front, and observed that these actions couched as multilateral aid is dispensed through international organizations, such as the International Monetary Fund, the International Bank for Reconstruction and Development (known as the World Bank), the International Finance Corporation, and the International Development Association. Significantly, all these international agencies are backed by US capital. These agencies impose various restricting conditions on the would-be borrowers, such as supplying information about their economies, submitting their policy and plans to review by the World Bank, and accepting agency supervision of their use of loans.

Neocolonialism, Nkrumah suggested, is as profitable, if not more than, *colonialism*. He described how Western monopolies controlled the prices of commodities as a way to increase their wealth.

Western monopolies extracted some $41 billion in profits from 1951 to 1961 in the tri-continents of Africa, Asia, and Latin America. Also they profited from high rates of interest. He noted: "While capital worth £30,000 million was exported to some 56 [African, Asian, and Latin American] countries between 1956 and 1962, it is estimated that interest and profit alone extracted on this sum from the debtor countries amounted to more than £15,000 million" (Nkrumah, 1965, p.2).

Among the innumerable ways of *neocolonialist* exploitation, Nkrumah delineated and emphasized the economic and political consequences of the following for non-Western countries:

1. commerce and navigation treaties;

2. agreements for economic cooperation;

3. the right of Western aid agencies to meddle in internal finances, including currency and foreign exchange and to lower trade barriers in favour of the donor country's goods and capital;

4. protecting the interests of private investments;

5. determination of how the funds are to be used;

6. forcing the recipient to set up counterpart funds;

7. supplying raw materials to the donor countries; and

8. using the funds to buy goods from the donor nation (Quist-Adade, 2013, p.74).

Nkrumah argued that *neocolonial* conditions apply to wide-ranging entities, agriculture, shipping and insurance, the political military industrial complex, and the knowledge industry. Nkrumah described invisible trade as what "furnishes the Western monopolies with yet another means of economic penetration and exploitation. Over 90 percent of World Ocean shipping is controlled by the imperialist countries. As for insurance payments, in 1961 alone these amounted to an unfavorable balance in Asia, Africa and Latin America of some additional $370 million" (Nkrumah, 1965, p.26). *Neocolonial* exploitation, Nkrumah noted "operates not only in the economic field, but also in the political, religious, ideological and cultural spheres" (Nkrumah, 1965, p.26). We can conceptualize current neoliberal policies as a continuation of 20th century *neocolonialism* (Quist-Adade, 2013, p.75).

The continuation of the dominance of Western countries after the independence movements in many parts of the world is partly due to the fact that during the era of *colonialism*, the European and Western powers were able to impose an "international system of laws and regulations covering prices, currency dealings and banking systems" that benefited the West and imposed restrictions on how newly independent nations could function in the context of global economic relations (Webster, 1984, p. 79). That is, it is within this system that newly independent nations had to function. During the 1950s and 1960s, for example, US multinational corporations (MNCs) took advantage of this situation and invested in many parts of the world, exploiting the labour and raw resources of the newly independent countries. In this sense, MNCs are the main features of *neocolonial* relations. The MNCs exemplified the extreme "*concentration* of capital and the *integration* of production on world scale" (Webster, 1984, p. 80). The introduction of other **supranational** bodies, such as the European Economic Community (EEG), was also a political approach to ensure the right of

European corporations and to maintain political contact and trade with their ex-colonies in various parts of the world (Webster, 1984, p. 80).

Postcolonialism is a set of theories and perspectives that have been proposed by non-Western and Western scholars of White and non-White backgrounds to explain the legacies of *colonialism* and its effects since the independence of many colonized nations (Glesne, 2011, p. 13) (See Chapter Ten). It analyzes and examines the consequences of *colonialism*. It looks at how Western countries, their agents, and capitalist structures have and continue to subjugate(d) racialized peoples and nations in various geographical spaces. Scholars of the postcolonial orientation seek to address a number of questions, including the following:

1. How can we rewrite history to account for the perspectives of non-Western populations?
2. What would be the impact of such a rewriting of history on contemporary analyses and categories?
3. How can we develop a non-oppressive academic discourse?
4. Can the subaltern speak using Western perspectives?
5. Can Western scholarship speak for 'other' cultures?
6. Why are the concerns and views of Western scholars and policy-makers taken more seriously than those thinkers from the non-Western parts of the world?
7. What is the long-term legacy of the imperial era (i.e., in terms of political, cultural, and economic consequences)?
8. How meaningful is independence?
9. Who writes the history of *colonialism*? Whose version of *colonialism* should inform analysis of political and economic events and structures?

Postcolonialism is a perspective that analyzes and examines the varied and multiple intersections of factors, such as "race", gender, language, values, customs, power, and space. It problematizes how *colonialism* continues in the form of *imperialism*, affecting the lives of racialized people in both the West (North) and East (South), as more and more colonized people migrate to Western parts of the world. It attempts to produce knowledge that is based on the experiences of marginalized peoples and to replace Western hegemonic approaches to knowledge production. *Postcolonialism* gives voice to the marginalized peoples and communities to resist and challenge Western hegemony (Glesne, 2011, p. 13) (See Chapter 10). Edward Said's conception of **Orientalism** is an example of postcolonial approaches and studies.

Orientalism: the discourse of Western hegemony and domination

Edward Said (1978, p. 1) defined **Orientalism** as a discourse of power, and "a way of coming to terms with the Orient [i.e., the Middle East] that is based on the Orient's special place in European Western experience", starting in the eighteenth century. It is a "Western style for dominating, restructuring, and having the authority over the Orient" (Said, 1978, p. 3). During the post-Enlightenment period, we witness the creation of Orient as a geographical space, composed of peoples and cultures that became the object of European gaze and the subject of their "scientific" lenses (Said, 1978, p. 7). As a discourse, it is both a set of ideas (i.e., they are less "civilized" than us) and practices (i.e., it is our moral obligation to "civilize" them).

Orientalism is a collection of "scientific" theories and practices about the Orient and Orientals, which find expressions in colonialist interventions by the West in the East. *Orientalism* is about having the power to produce knowledge about non-Westerners: it "lives on academically through its doctrines and theses about the Orient and the Oriental" (Said, 1978, p. 2). Said (1978, p. 2) posited that "anyone who teaches, writes about or researches the Orient… is an Orientalist". As such, *Orientalism* is a form of hegemonic knowledge that is used by the West to dominate the rest of the world, especially the Middle East. Thus, it is a form of cultural leadership exercised by the West (Said, 1978, p. 7).

In order to describe and represent the Orient (i.e., Iran), there is a need for a strategy to envision the Orient. *Orientalism* was this strategy that produced the "orient" as a field of knowledge (Hall, 1996b, p. 205). To write about the Orient, however, requires prior knowledge about it. This knowledge "affiliates itself with other works, audiences, institutions, with the Orient itself" (Said, 1978, p.20). *Orientalism* is a set of contemporary and historical ideas that define the West against all those labelled as non-Westerners and non-Europeans (Said, 1978, p. 7). It is a discourse that defines the **other** as "backward" and in need of development and progress (Said, 1978, p. 7). In other words, it constructs a specific view of the Orient in the minds and imaginations of Westerners. Through *colonialism* the Orient was "discovered [and made and submitted to be] Oriental" (Said, 1978, pp. 5–6). In this sense, as mentioned above, *Orientalism* is about having power to generate knowledge about the Orient that can be used to dominate it.

Orientalism is a framework of describing and evaluating the **other** based on both "scientific" and nonscientific discourses. It is constructed based on an archive of information, which includ(ed) both facts and fantasies about the Orient, such as classical knowledge, religious and biblical sources, and knowledge about geography reinterpreted in the context of the bible, mythology, and travellers' tales, (Hall, 1996b, pp. 206–207). The goal of all these discourses and sources of knowledge in the context of *Orientalism* has been to deliberately contain the Orient through the applications of structures and methods of representations that are assumed to be objective.

Orientalism is a construction that distinguishes between the East and the West. It produces theories, policies, and economic and social reform programs *for* and *about* the East. Said maintained that all those who accept the basic distinctions between the West and the Orient (or the Middle East) are **Orientalists**. *Orientalism*, as a set of institutions (i.e., colonial administrations, universities, scientific journals, and think tanks), not only reproduces knowledge about **otherness** through a racialized typology, but also functions as a universal explanation for the behaviour of the **other** that simultaneously needs to be contained (Said, 1978, pp. 5–18, 203, 211). It is in the context of modern forms of relations that *Orientalism* emerges as one of the many discourses that define the West in relation to the rest of the world as more "superior".

Said (1978, pp. 1–5) defined *Orientalism* in three different ways:

1. as an academic field,

2. as a style of thought about the distinctions between the Orient and the Occident (imaginative), and

3. as an institutional authority about the Near East that makes statements about it, describes it, teaches it, and rules it.

the Orient is approached systematically, as a topic of learning and a discovery. It is a way of having authority about/on the Middle East and the East. It is a knowledge base and a "scientific" category/discipline that deals with the Orient as an object, which needs to be studied and evaluated. It is an institution that deals with the Orient by making statements about it that are then considered as the truth about the Orient. The assumptions of Europeans about the Oriental **other** are then used to explain the behaviours of Orientals. That is, *orientalism* constructs a mentality that is then applied to Orientals. For example, the Middle East is often constructed as a "mysterious" space, "strange", and "violent" in movies and popular accounts and newsreels. As such, *Orientalism* justifies the domination of the East by the West. The East is constructed as an "unchanging other", which lacks subjectivity or "internal variations". In this light, it puts a limit on how social actors come to imagine the Orient.

It generalizes about Orientals. Through *Orientalism* non-Western cultures are constructed as "exotic" and different that need to change.

Colonialism as an attitude and *Orientalism* as a way of viewing a group of people in light of supposed "superiority" of the colonial "man" make up a great deal of Western pre-understandings of the modern and postmodern Middle East. Said pointed out that the colonialist attitude, "his" novels, and "his" travelling accounts of "exotic," "wild," and "untamed world" all had and continue to have political and ideological connotations and significance. As Said (1978) pointed out, the politics of representing *otherness* and *difference* in its various forms has been biased and has been a reflection of colonial politics and the projects of rule and domination. But Said does not account for the existing constructions of **otherness** within the Middle East, which sprang within the region and demarcated imagined boundaries between the peoples of the Middle East based on factors, such as ethnicity, language, and religious beliefs. Although such constructions have been affected by the forces of modernity and the emergence of rational science as their safeguard, one cannot avoid taking note of the same "colonial-like" relationships that have constituted the everyday interactions between the peoples of the Middle East.

As such, it is important to apply his definition of *Orientalism* to those Middle Eastern scholars whose works on philosophy, society, law, and family have centred on the same basic assumptions about the distinction between "us" and "them". That is, *Orientalism* is not only the construction of Western institutions, but it also finds expressions in the works of those Middle Easterners who historically have argued for modernization of the Middle East based on various European models of development since the late eighteenth century. Although the Europeanization and later the Americanization of the Middle East has also faced opposition at local, national, and regional levels, the question that begs to be explored is how many years of Europeanization and Westernization have constructed an imagery of the West that reaffirms Orientalist assumptions about the Middle East and the rest of the World in the minds of non-Westerners. That is, it is significant to assess how because of cultural, economic, social, and political influences of the West in the region, Middle Easterners have come to think of and imagine other ethnic "minorities" or other nationalities from the perspectives of colonial and imperialist powers. Ideas about ethnic or religious "superiority" are also the products of internal conflicts and class struggles. So it is imperative to interrogate how **Westernism** reinforces prejudice and at times racist views prevalent in the societies of non-Western countries, such as those in the Middle East.

In short, Said maintained that *Orientalism* is a powerful figment of western imagination and a tool of domination. *Orientalism* creates "the very reality [it] appear[s] to describe" by references to such universal categories, as Iranian or Arab mentalities, and binary oppositions, such modern (European) and traditional (the Middle East) (Said, 1978, p. 94). *Orientalism* invokes binary oppositions that give meaning to the idea of the Orient as something "real" and experienced. As a **metanarrative**, it has also come to redefine the Oriental's view of himself or herself in light of knowledge that has been produced to dominate the East and create authority over it by invoking specific constructs and meanings and associating them with the Orient as a geographical area. The Orient is reified as an object of investigation and subjects of study by White middle class males, colonial administrators, social scientists, and popular culture products, such as novels and travellers' accounts of the so-called Orient. The fact that the **Oriental other** was an influential actor in the formulation of the **Western/European self** is ignored in the construction of Europe or the West as the originator of modernity and rationality.

Having said the above, it seems that *Orientalism* is more a discourse about the West than about the East; it tells us more about how the West thinks and acts than how the East really is. Through *Orientalism*, Westerners were able to define the Orientals by references to essentialized characteristics that fixed the Oriental as what the West was/is not: "dogmatic", traditional, needy, "uncivilized", and in need of **tutelage** and **salvation**.

Part Two

Colonial and Imperialist Expansions: two distinct periods

Goldthorpe (1996, p. 47) observed that the era of European expansion can be divided into **two distinct periods**. The **first period** spanned from the fifteenth century to the early decades of the eighteenth century. And the **second period** lasted from the middle of the eighteenth century to roughly the 1960s.

The First Period

Despite the domination of the world by European and Anglo-Saxon societies during the era of *colonialism*, before the fifteenth century, many of the continents/countries that were eventually labeled by Europeans during the latter centuries and the eras of *colonialism* and *imperialism* as "underdeveloped", "despotic", and "uncivilized" were in fact more "complex" and "advanced" than the European societies of the Middle Ages (Kelleher & Klein, 2009, p. 4). The Chinese, for example, had produced significant scientific and technological achievements. They had developed nautical knowledge and were aware of shipbuilding techniques that were unknown to Europeans (Kelleher & Klein, 2009, p. 4). Gunpowder was also another innovation of Chinese civilization that Europeans adopted and used in innovative and destructive ways. The usage of gunpowder by Europeans for military purposes drastically altered the balance of power between European states and non-Europeans. The development of compass and stern rudders also resulted in the transformation of European economic life as they were able to travel the world through the open ocean and bypass land-based trade routes that were controlled by the Middle Easterners or North Africans.

By the fourteenth century, Arab, African, and Middle Eastern societies were also economically and scientifically more "advanced" than European societies. These societies were centres of cultural, moral, and artistic fusions. By the 1350s, for example, trade activities had resulted in the growth of African civilization, such as the city of Timbuktu, which was the centre of commercial relations and learning within the Mali Empire (Kelleher & Klein, 2009, p. 5). There were a number of universities in the Mali Empire and to the south there was the city of Zimbabwe that was another advanced trade centre dealing with Middle Eastern merchants and importing goods from Asia through its well-established systems of market (Kelleher & Klein, 2009, p. 5). In the Americas, the Mayans had also developed a very complicated calendar and achieved great astronomical and mathematical knowledge.

In the Middle East, during the Umayyad period (661–750), moreover, the imperial culture was modeled after cultural elements of Byzantine and Sasanian (Iranian) artistic and literary expressions (Lapidus, 1988, p. 82). The Umayyad mosques were influenced by Christian and Byzantine decorative and iconographic symbols that were fused with Moslem concepts and ideas. The Umayyad also promoted debates between Moslem and Christians, which resulted in the adaptation of Hellenistic concepts into Moslem *ideology* (Lapidus, 1988, p. 82). During this period, the Islamic world was filled with many flourishing urban centres, integral irrigation systems, and social services, such as universities, pharmacies, piped water, and a well-established banking system with letters of credit (Kelleher & Klein, 2009, p. 5).

Moreover, Moslem contributions to mathematics, astronomy, medicine, chemistry, and zoology went beyond the influences of Greek and Persian cultures (Lapidus, 1988, p. 96). According to Cleveland (1994, p. 25), Moslem mathematicians played an important role in promoting algebra and trigonometry. Moslem astronomers, physicians, and chemists wrote significantly in these areas that became the basis for the development of natural sciences in Europe in the later centuries (Cleveland, 1994, p. 25). One of the most important contributions of Moslem societies to European development, as Lapidus (1998, p. 123) maintained, was the fact that the Hellenistic philosophy and "science" was preserved by Moslems and their dynasties "for future confrontations and interactions ... and for future transmission to Christian Europe". In fact, during the twelfth and thirteenth centuries, the Christian rulers of Spain stimulated the translations of Greek philosophical works from

Arabic into Latin. Paper manufacturing also found its way to Spain through Moslem civilizations (Cleveland, 1994, p. 25).

By the middle of the fourteenth century, the Ottoman Empire had just began exercising its control over most of the Islamic world and eventually threatened Europe and controlled many parts of Eastern and southern Europe, as well as North Africa. In 1453, the Ottomans invaded the Byzantine capital (Eastern Roman Empire) and put an end to "Constantinople's role as the symbolic centre for eastern Christendom" (Cleveland, 1994, p. 41). In fact, over the next two centuries, a large part of southern Europe came under the direct control of the Ottoman Empire (Cleveland, 1994, p. 40). By the sixteenth century, the Ottomans had added new European territories to their domain. In 1522, the Ottomans controlled the Island of Rhodes in the Mediterranean Sea, and in 1570 they occupied Cyprus (Cleveland, 1994, p. 41). By the end of 1529, the Ottoman Empire was in control of Belgrade and Budapest and laid siege on Vienna, the capital of the Hapsburg Empire. Although the Ottomans were able to control Hungary and Serbia, they were unable to seize Vienna.

From the seventeenth century to the twentieth century, the Ottoman power declined due to several factors. One the most important factors was the effects of the penetration of European merchants into the Ottoman Empire, which gave rise to the exchange of Ottoman raw materials for the manufactured goods produced in Europe (Cleveland, 1994, p. 50). This resulted in the rise of inflation; and the state was unable to raise enough revenue to pay for its expenditure. Starting in the 1500s, the Ottomans signed Capitulation treaties with European states that allowed European merchants to freely do business in the Ottoman land and be exempted from paying taxes and tariffs. After the shift in military power to Europeans, the Capitulation treaties became significantly profitable for the European merchants who now had the support of the military might of their respective states (Cleveland, 1994, p. 50). By the 1690s, the Ottomans lost successive wars with the Hapsburg Empire, the Russians, and Austria. These defeats sounded the death knell of the Ottoman Empire.

Africa had also been home to a number of historical kingdoms and civilizations, such as the Kingdom of Monomotapa in Zimbabwe, the Kingdom of Kush that predated the coming of Christ, and the Christian Kingdoms of Nubia and Axum with their extensive monasteries and churches (Gage, 1991, p. 5). In addition, in 969 AD, the Shi'a Fatimid Dynasty controlled Tunisia, seized Egypt, and ruled Sicily and many parts of North Africa for about 200 years. The Moorish people also had controlled Spain. It was also through them that Europeans were introduced to the Greek "science" and philosophy via Moslem scholars. During most of the medieval period, most African governments were more egalitarian and representative than their European counterparts (Basil Davidson, as cited in Gage, 1991, p. 5). Although there were also wars between African Kingdoms, they were not as costly and did not result in as much destruction as the wars in Europe (Basil Davidson, as cited in Gage, 1991, p. 5). In the universities of Timbuktu, Moslem and Christian intellectuals were also involved in the production of knowledge (Thomas Hodgkin, as cited in Gage, 1991, p. 5). As mentioned in previous chapters, this introduction to Moslem scholarship was the impetus for the Renaissance that had significant consequences for the progress and development of Europe. It was the Arab scientists who introduced Greek thoughts and Indian mathematical discoveries and knowledge through their synthesis of these ideas to Europeans. For example, Europeans were introduced to the number Zero. European scientists also began to adopt the medical knowledge of Islamic scholars.

Despite these advances and level of progress in various non-European parts of the world, starting in the fifteenth century, due to the effects of the Industrial Revolution, militarism, *colonization*, European exploration of the world, and disruption of well-established land trade routes, first Spain and Portugal, and later Western European states were able to exert their control and power over other peoples and political organizations in various parts of the world. In fact, it is the ways in which Europeans applied "scientific" knowledge and technology in the next four hundred years that drastically shifted the relations of power in the world.

As discussed in previous chapters, prior to the sixteenth century, Europe was a divided society and was plagued by many wars, such as the Hundred Years War (1337–1453) between French and English monarchs that weakened it, politically and economically. Moreover, many Europeans lost their lives to epidemics and plagues, such as the *Bubonic Plague* or *Black Death* that killed millions of people. By the end of the following century, European societies had transformed and they began establishing centralized political systems. More specifically, during the sixteenth century, Europe was going through major social, political, and economic changes. Europeans experienced the Reformation wars, economic growth, and advances in technology (Kelleher & Klein, 2009, p. 7). The power of the feudal system was not only being questioned as a result of the growth of cities, expansion of mercantile activities, and the consequences of *colonialism*, it was also undermined by the rise of nation-states and religious strife in Europe, which highlights the consequences of changes in political structures in Europe and values, beliefs, and worldviews of Europeans (Heilbroner, 1989, p. 49). The power of the Catholic Church was also being undermined during this period. With the help of technological innovations in transportation and weapons of war, European countries started their journey into centuries of exploitation and dominance over other non-Western parts of the world (Kelleher & Klein, 2009, p. 6). In fact, the period after the fifteenth century was marked by European control over the ocean routes through their military power, which enabled them to regulate vast parts of the Americas, occupying a number of islands, and establishing a number of posts and enclaves in African and Asian coasts (Goldthrope, 1996, p. 47).

It is in this context of political, cultural, and economic changes in Europe that many European explorations of various parts of the world took shape, mainly in search for gold and spices. Gold was needed to pay for the internal and interstate wars affecting European states. According to the Mexican Indigenous leader, Cuaicaipuro Cuautémoc, between 1503 and 1660, 185,000 kilos of gold and 16,000,000 kilos of silver were shipped from the Americas to Europe (Gage, 1990a, p. 39). As a result of forcefully confiscating this vast amount of gold and silver from the Aboriginal groups in South America, a small number of people in Europe became affluent. Cuautémoc (2002, p. 93) offered a very interesting interpretation of this exploitation of natural resources by the European powers. He considered the resources that Europeans took from the Americas as a loan that now needs to be paid back. He called this loan the ***Marshalltezuma Plan*** that was provided by the people of the colonized world to the colonialists (similar to the *Marshall Plan* of the United Sates that provided loans to European states to rebuild Europe after World War II). He maintained that the European states had plundered this wealth and has wasted it in the last 500 years. European and Western societies and their economies, he maintained, have been subsidized by non-Western peoples. He argued that since contemporary Europeans now believe in **neoliberal ideology** that asserts a subsidized economy does not function efficiently, it is time "to claim the repayment of capital and interest which we have so generously delayed reclaiming for all these centuries" (Cuautémoc, 2002, p. 93). As this argument points out, development in Europe was linked to the depletion of resources and wealth not only in South America, but also in other parts of the Global South.

The other reason why Europeans wanted to establish direct routes to Asia was the fact that the prices of spices imported from the Indies were too high and expensive. These spices were important ingredients for Europeans who used them in food preservation and in the production of medicine (Kelleher & Klein, 2009, p. 6). By dealing directly with the merchants of these goods in India and China, Europeans were able to bypass dealing with Arabs and other middlemen merchants and increase their profits. In fact, Spain, Portugal, and the Netherlands, in addition to controlling the spice trade, also wanted to gain converts to Christianity, and acquire new territories by extending their jurisdictions in Asia and the Western Pacific (Kelleher & Klein, 2009). For example, according to Leibo (1999, p. 7), the first European to reach Asia was a Portuguese by the name of Ferdinand Magellan. He acted on behalf of Spain to establish trading routes in these parts of the world. In 1513, Vascodo Balboa reached the Pacific Ocean and in 1519 another Spanish sailor reached the Philippines by travelling around South America (Kelleher & Klein, 2009, p. 6). Spain, from its bases in the Americas, eventually invaded and colonized the Philippines in the 1570s and controlled this country for about three hundred years, before the American invasion of the Philippines (Leibo, 1999, p. 7).

The Portuguese were also involved in slave and gold trades in coastal Africa. The Portuguese used their military power and strong armies to set up ports on the coasts of Asia and Africa in order to control the spice trade and the countries that were very well self-sufficient and did not have a need for many of the Portuguese goods, besides metal pots and guns that the Portuguese were not too eager to trade with them. As a result, the Portuguese used their superior armies to force these people to trade with them and plundered and destroyed the port cities on the East coast of Africa (Gage, 1990c, pp. 38–39). Within a few decades, the well-established centres of commerce and social activities were reduced to ruins. The Portuguese also attacked Islamic merchant ships that were involved in trades between Africa and Asia. They were able to control the ocean trade routes between Asia, Africa, and Europe. They established trading posts along the coast, and became involved in trading and exchanging slaves, ivory, and gold that were brought from the interior regions of Africa (Gage, 1990c, p. 39). The establishment of ocean routes to various parts of Asia and having access to its spices and other riches resulted in the decline in the might of Middle Eastern powers. The economies of Middle Eastern nations "slowly shrivelled without the trade lifeblood" since goods from Asia were no longer reaching European cities overland through central Asia and the Middle East (Kellher & Klein, 2009, pp. 4–5). In general, the sociocultural, economic, and political landscapes of many Middle Eastern and North African societies, dynasties, and communities were negatively affected.

Queen Isabella of Spain also funded Christopher Columbus to find similar routes to Asia and undermine the supremacy of Portuguese trade with Asia. Columbus unwittingly reached the Caribbean Islands between 1492 and 1502 and claimed these lands for Spain. In many of the tropical islands, large-scale plantations were established, which were the main source of economic activities for European colonialists (Goldthrope, 1996, p. 47). Columbus introduced the sugarcane into the area. Sugar was a highly prized pharmaceutical item of consumption in Europe. Arawak and other local Aboriginal peoples were forced to work in these sugarcane plantations. This is the beginning of the era of colonial expansion that was fueled with racist ideas about non-Europeans. Not only did the Europeans exploit; they also Christianize the "heathenish" non-Europeans, in order to benefit "their eternal souls" (News Article in Los Nuevos, July 1, 1501, as cited in Gage, 1991a, p. 4).

The Spanish conquerors suppressed the economy of the Caribbean Islands and exploited the labour of local people in their farming and mining endeavors. They used Indigenous people as slaves and overworked them in the mines and farms, a practice that resulted in the extermination or near-extermination of many of the Indigenous people of the region. The effects were compounded by the consequences of epidemics that were brought over by the Europeans to these regions. For example, the exploitation of the Arawak people resulted in killing of all 250,000 of Aboriginal populations in Haiti by 1650 due to "overwork in the mines and on the plantations, suicide, and European diseases" (Gage, 1990a, p. 3). As the Spanish conquered various peoples of South America by 1521, colonialists, such as Hernando Cortes, also destroyed books and artifacts that they considered heathenish according to their Christian (Catholic) views (Kelleher & Klein, 2009, p. 6). Their aim was to Christianize the natives whom they viewed as "uncivilized". As mentioned, the resources of South American civilizations, such as gold, were used to enhance the power of Spain in Europe with devastating consequences for the economies of Eastern European states, the Ottoman Empire, and other Middle Eastern societies (Kelleher & Klein, 2009, p. 7).

To replace the labour of Aboriginal people in these plantations, which had dwindled due to European *genocide*, the Spaniards began to bring slaves from Africa, which had begun in 1442 by the Portuguese who transported slaves from Western ports of Africa to Europe. In 1442, the Pope gave the practice the seal of religious approval and granted the slave traders forgiveness for all their sins (as cited in Gage, 1991a, p. 5). By the seventeenth century, the Europeans mainly relied on the slave trade to provide labour for their plantations in the West Indies and South America. Natural resources were transported from the West Indies to Europe, and goods (especially guns) manufactured in European factories were exchanged for slaves in Africa. African trade in other products but slaves was discouraged by the colonialists. Agricultural development in Africa was also affected and halted. African groups began raiding one another to capture slaves for the European markets. This is not to say that Africans did not practice slavery before or that they did not resist the slave trade, but the eventual consequence of European slavery was the economic downturn in Africa. In fact, in 1751, the British Board of Trade, in reaction to the efforts of the governor of Cape Coast Castle in West Africa who was encouraging the plantation of cotton, stated that "the introduction of culture and industry among the Negroes is contrary to the known established policy of this country, there is no saying where this might stop, and that it might extend to tobacco, sugar and every other commodity which we now take from our colonies [in the 'New World']; and thereby the Africans, who now support themselves by wars, would become planters" (as cited in Gage, 1991c, p. 8). The end result of colonial rule and its policies also affected the local industries, as they could not compete with cheaply made clothing that were produced in European factories by machines and were flooding the markets in various parts of coastal Africa (Gage, 1991c, p. 8).

The French and English monarchs, although less successful than the Spanish and Portuguese, nevertheless also established themselves in North America and claimed these lands on their behalf (Kelleher & Klein, 2009, p. 7). During this period, they also practiced *genocide* against the Aboriginal peoples of North America. As mentioned, in North America, the dominant European societies also characterized Native Americans as their **other** and viewed them as "uncivilized", "savage", "pagan", and "simple". That is, cultural differences were viewed in light of racial differences. "Indians" were compared to "Wild Irish" and conceived as "subhuman\barbarians with no cultures" and no "civilizations". In this sense, the act of civilizing them implied domination. **Civilization**, then, was a discourse that justified and promoted cultural domination and forced social, economic, cultural, and political change (Spring, 2007, p. 3). The enslavement of Native Americans was justified by the presupposition that servitude is a natural characteristic of these groups: to dominate and enslave them was for their own good. In addition, in the United States, *genocide* was considered as one of the solutions to deal with the "Indian problem" (Spring, 2007, p. 5). Civilizing the natives was a joint venture between the Church and the state, as exemplified in the case of Spain and Pope Alexander XI. North America was envisioned as the land that should be occupied by White English people. The rest of the world was conceived as being inhabited by non-Whites and non-English Whites. The division between Anglo-Saxon and other Europeans based on religious denominations (i.e., Catholic and Protestant) was also an ideological tool to distinguish between English and other Europeans, itself also based on the assumed superiority of the English over the Irish and non-Europeans. This racial superiority of Anglo-Saxons also found contemporary expressions in the ideology of the Nazi Party and the KKK (Spring, 2007).

In general, by the mid-nineteenth century, Spain and Portugal had lost much of their power in Europe, but kept some of their colonies in Asia, Africa, and South America. In contrast, France, England, and the Netherlands experienced intense economic growth as a result of the wealth of their colonies and a rise in their commercial classes (Kelleher & Klein, 2009, p. 7). During the first stage of colonial expansion, slaves were bought from West Africa and shipped to the West Indies and later to the Southern United States; natural and agricultural goods, such as sugar, cotton, and coffee, were exported to the European cities; and goods manufactured in European cities, such as guns, were exported from England to "West Africa, to pay Arab slave traders for the slaves" (Gage, 1991c, p. 4). In this way, Europeans were able to have access to the natural resources and to sell their manufactured products in other parts of the world. It is estimated that about 12 million African slaves out of 48 million who were captured arrived to work on plantations in the Americas; that is, the rest died on their way to the Americas (Gage, 1991c, p. 4). By the eighteenth century, the European powers were involved in various forms of plantation that exploited the labour of Black African slaves in the Caribbean and in North America. They continued exporting natural resources, such as lumber and fur, and importing finished goods from their respective home countries. Rum, slaves, and tobacco were the main sources of "goods" that brought immense wealth to European countries through the control of their colonies (Kelleher & Klein, 2009, p. 7). This economic growth was at the expense of Aboriginal peoples in North America who were either decimated and/or pushed out of their land.

The Second Period: modern consequences of colonialism and imperialism

As mentioned, *colonialism* is defined as the direct administration of a distant territory, and *imperialism*, which includes *colonialism*, is an indirect way to rule local and Indigenous peoples by outsiders (Kelleher & Klein, 2009, pp. 7–8). This was often justified by the assumption that local people were "incapable" of governing themselves since they were at a lower level of development than European societies. During the era of *imperialism*, many parts of the world were considered as the 'protectorate' by European colonial powers (Kelleher & Klein, 2009, p. 8). That is, the main political, social, cultural, and economic decisions and policies were decided by the colonial powers, which were then implemented by local authorities either of colonial origin or by local elite groups within a region or a country. Britain, for example, controlled Iraq in this manner soon after the collapse of the Ottoman Empire at the end of World War I.

After the British passed the India Act, which made India a colony of England, the era of *colonialism* and *imperialism* "reached its maturity during the late nineteenth and early twentieth centuries" (Kelleher & Klein, 2009, p. 7). In 1776, Britain also lost its control over the American colonies, and the American colonies themselves became a contender of power and a major player in imperialist and colonial policies in North, Central, and South America. They began to assert their power across the globe and to exploit peoples and resources through their capitalist investments and activities. In 1871, for example, an American investor built a railroad in Costa Rica and experimented with banana production, which led to the creation of the United Fruit Company in 1889 (Robbins, 2008, p. 91). This company produced more than 2 billion bunches of bananas in the next thirty-five years. It purchased land in various Central American countries. In fact, it purchased more land than it could use at any time (Robbins, 2008, p. 91). This resulted in the relocation of Indigenous populations and the creation of landless "peasants" who had no other ways of satisfying their basic needs but to work in the banana plantations. As we discussed in Chapter Seven, this company played a major role in disposing the government in Guatemala with the help of American armed forces in the 1950s.

In 1898, the United States also signed the peace treaty with Spain, and the Philippines, Guam, and Puerto Rico officially came under the control of the United States for a payment of $20 million (Zinn, 2003, p. 312). President McKinley justified his decision to take over the Philippines by asserting that "we could not turn them over to France or Germany, our commercial rivals in the Orient—that could be bad business and discreditable. That we could not leave them to themselves—they were unfit for self-government—and they would soon have anarchy and misrule over there worse than Spain's was; and that there was nothing left for us to do but to take them all and to educate the

Filipinos, and uplift and civilize and Christianize them, and by God's grace do the very best we could by them, as our fellow men for whom Christ also died" (as cited in Zinn, 2003, p. 313).

The Filipinos revolted against American imperialism and after three years of insurrection the Americans were able to crush the rebellion through military force, killing many innocent people (Zinn, 2003, p. 313). In 1900, Albert Beveridge speaking in the Senate of the United States bragged that "The Philippines are ours forever … And just behind the Philippines are China's illimitable markets. We will not retreat from either …. We will not renounce our part in the mission of ours race, trustee, under God, of the civilization of the world" (as cited in Zinn, 2003, p. 313). Many people in the southern Luzon region of the Philippines were massacred by the US Army: "One-sixth of the native of Luzon have either been killed or have died of the dengue fever in the last few years … It has been necessary to adopt what in other countries would probably be thought harsh measures" (an American general in 1901, as cited in Zinn, 2003, pp. 315–316). The criticism against the brutality of the War by the Anti-Imperialist League in the United States was undermined by the Secretary of State who commented that the war in the Philippines was conducted by the American army without any regards for the rules of war and human rights (as cited in Zinn, 2003, p. 316).

During this period, Western and European colonizers continued to see themselves as the chosen people whose task it was to bring civilization to the world. The goal of Christians was to sacrifice themselves for the "good" of Christianity and its community (Spring, 2007). This view functioned as an *ideology* that justified the exploitation of resources and the destruction of various Indigenous and non-Western European civilizations (Spring, 2007). *Colonialism* in the nineteenth century was also a solution to economic depressions in American and European capitalist societies (Robbins, 2008, p. 90). *Colonialism* became an approach to expand markets, find new sources of raw materials, and provide new opportunities for investment for the capitalist class in parts of the world that had not been influenced by European economic relations. In fact, one of the most important characteristics of European and Western expansions into various parts of the world was the creation and rise of the trading companies that began in the previous centuries and helped them secure their control over global trade and commerce (Robbins, 2008, p. 81).

As mentioned in the previous chapter, the beginning of the seventeenth century marked the rise of what economists refer to as **mercantilism**. During this period, the aim of the European states was to protect their select internal industries from competition from foreign firms. In this way, they ensured that gold and silver would not leave their states' coffers, which were deemed sources of power and wealth. During this period, we also notice the rise of the trading companies. These companies ensured that merchants were able to increase their rates of profit since they were "sophisticated instruments of state-sponsored trade" (Robbins, 2008, p. 81). In 1600, for example, a royal charter was issued by the British crown to the merchants of the Company of Merchants of London that was trading with the East Indies. This company later became known as the British East India Company, which also faced competition by the Dutch East Indian Company (established by the Dutch government). The aim of these two colonial companies was to monopolize Asian trade in the name of Britain and the Netherlands (Robbins, 2008, p. 81). During the seventeenth century, the Dutch had a vast army and navy protecting its ports and trading posts in India. The British East

India Company eventually defeated the Portuguese troops in India and was able to achieve trading concessions from the Mughal Empire. By 1757, the British had controlled the Bengal region and eventually controlled most parts of India (Robbins, 2008, pp. 81–82). *Mercantilism* also paved the road for the creation of export markets in many parts of the world (i.e., raw materials). The development of export markets in the colonies was thought to benefit these exporting countries since they lacked industrialized economies. However, this type of economy resulted in what is referred to as *unequal exchange*. Although these countries gained currency from selling their raw materials, they also had to spend this currency to buy industrial goods from European nations. These goods were more expensive since they required additional labour to produce. So, if a country exported lumber, but did not have the facilities to process it and make, for example, finished lumber products, then this country had to import these products from those countries that had the mills that process these raw resources into finished goods (Robbins, 2008, p. 92).

Colonialism and its expansion oversees was also an important tool in creating peace at home in Europe. The rise in riots by the unemployed and the attempts by the working classes to improve their conditions required new solutions to the existing internal national problems. As Cecil Rhodes maintained, "My cherished idea is a solution for the social problem, i.e., in order to save … the inhabitants of the United Kingdom from a bloody civil war", England must acquire new lands for the settlement of its unwanted surplus population and for its industrial goods (as cited in Robbins, 2008, p. 90).

Colonialism was not an ad-hoc approach to domination. It was based on a set of concerted, systematic, and contradictory efforts by Europeans to dominate the world. For example, although the slave trade was the main factor that had resulted in the increased prosperity of the colonial powers, by the end of the nineteenth century, many people began to see slavery as a morally reprehensible act (Kelleher & Klein, 2009, p. 8). In the face of an antislavery movement, European states, especially after the slave trade became illegal in 1833, continued carving Africa as their colonies, but this time systematically. In 1882, at the British Conference, European powers devised a plan to divide sub-Saharan Africa among them. However, the conference organizers claimed that their main goal behind controlling and dominating Africa was to bring an end to the practice of slavery and "establishing free navigation and trade in the Congo River basin" (Kelleher & Klein, 2009, p. 8). Sir George Goldies through his company, United African Company, annexed West Africa as part of the British Empire. Other explorers, such as Henry Stanley who worked on behalf of King Leopold of Belgium, were also involved in colonizing various parts of Africa in the colonial competition to control the resources of Africa and limit the power of other colonial powers to capture and invade African lands (Gage, 1991c, p. 11). During the Berlin African Conference in 1884–1885, moreover, the Europeans developed other plans to divide and administer various parts of Africa amongst themselves; and by 1914, they had achieved their goals, except in Ethiopia, which had defeated the Italians in 1896, and in Liberia, which was ruled by freed slaves (Gage, 1991c, p. 12). The "King of Belgium established the Congo Free State … and began to rule it as a personal possession" (Kelleher & Klein, 2009, p. 9). The Belgians used force and genocidal policies to control most of the region. Belgian companies were given administrative rights to exploit the resources of this part of Africa. The exploitation of the resources of the Congo met the needs of the capitalist class and industrialists in Europe. From 1885 to 1908, for example, when cars and bicycles were becoming popular in Europe, the price of rubber increased and also the need for rubber, which was produced in plantations in the Congo. Labourers in Congo lived under harsh conditions and were violently exploited. For example, those refusing to gather enough rubber were punished by cutting their hands. In fact, as a result of such policies and practices, the population of the Congo fell from 20 million to 10 million (Gage, 1991c, p. 14).

At the Berlin Conference, central and Western Africa were added to the possessions of the European colonial powers. As a result, Africa was divided into major jurisdictions under the control of a specific European power: by 1902, for example, South Africa was under the control of Britain after a bloody war with the Boer people, the descendants of Dutch settlers. By the early twentieth century, Italy, Germany, France, Belgium, Spain, and Portugal had decided that Africa belonged to them (Kelleher & Klein, 2009, p. 9). As a result of colonial interactions and power, Christian missionaries were also able to convert millions of people, and had assisted in spreading European cultural values, which highlights the religious and cultural forms of *colonialism* (Kelleher & Klein, 2009, p. 9).

The European powers imposed high taxes on Africans. They also provided them with loans to pay for the colonial expenditures, which these countries were obliged to pay back. This perpetuated the economic downfall of African countries and made their economic situation direr. In the final analysis, the Africans ended up paying for colonial explorations of their continent (Gage, 1991c, p. 15). Agricultural lands were bought or taken over by the colonialists and were converted to grow cash crops, such as Coffee. In Kenya, for example, Lord Delamere purchased 100,000 acres of land for 1 cent an acre and produced coffee for the British market. This resulted in less food being produced for internal markets with devastating consequences (Gage, 1991c, p. 15). Africans then became reliant on agricultural goods produced in other parts of the world, while they exported food. The European powers were also involved in depleting the natural resources of Africa. For example, between 1933 and 1953, the British mined all the gold of Chunya, in what is now known as Tanzania, and thereby impoverishing the region (Gage, 1991c, p. 17). The development of infrastructures in Africa, such as roads and railroads, were based on the colonial, economic, and military needs of European countries. The purpose of such development projects was to connect various parts of Africa to the main ports for the export of their natural resources. That is, rather than developing roads that would be useful to Africans, connecting the various parts of Africa to one another; the roads were used as part of the colonial plan to exploit Africa (Gage, 1991c, p. 17). Moreover, the Europeans used their influences over local leaders as their colonial agents to control the local peoples. This resulted in the creation of African elites that became alienated and dissociated from the rest of the population. In the French colonies, this group was known as *Beni Qui Oui* (the "Yes, Yes, Men") (Gage, 1991c, p. 18).

In general, one of the consequences of colonial expansion and imperialist attitudes was the transformation of non-Western parts of the world into cash-crop producing nations and countries. Rather than producing for themselves, they were now producing for markets far away from themselves; and, as a result, were forced to import those goods and services that were produced by Western capitalist nations. This was an exploitative situation, which led to the rise of poverty and the "underdevelopment" of non-Western parts of the world. In other words, the so-called "underdevelopment" of the colonized parts of the world and "Third World" countries has been due to policies that were imposed on the colonized countries and peoples. In 1810, for example, India was exporting more textile to England than England was exporting to India. By 1830, the situation had reversed. The British had introduced tariffs on Indian goods, which made them more expensive, and "were dumping their commodities in India, a practice backed by British gunboats and military force" (Parenti, 2002, p. 65). Within a few years, there was a drastic decline in the number of manufacturing centres of textile in places, such as Dacca and Madras. India had become an exporter of cotton to be used in British textile factories (Parenti, 2002). One of the consequences of such changes was also the rise of India's debt to about £53 million by 1850. As Parenti (2002, pp. 65–67) informs us, "From 1850 to 1900, [India's] per-capita income dropped by almost two-thirds. The value of the raw materials and commodities the Indians were obliged to send to Britain during most of the nineteenth century amounted yearly to more than the total income of the 60 million Indian agricultural and industrial workers". Mass-scale poverty in India was not the precolonial characteristic of that country, and an issue with which people had to face. Rather it was an imperialist manufactured reality by first limiting and stopping development and then making the country "underdeveloped".

India's case is not unique. In the early nineteenth century, China also had a trade surplus. European societies had a difficult time trading in China. Although tea was a popular item of consumption in England, there were not too many products that the Chinese wanted or needed that were made in Europe. The British and other Europeans used their military power to change the trade surplus in their favours. For example, at the time, most of the Opium production was organized and controlled by the *British East India Company*. American and British merchants were involved in the illegal importation of opium into China, which was illegal in China, but a highly sought product. When in 1839, the Chinese government attempted to enforce its laws against the sale of opium by the British merchants in Canton, British troops intervened, resulting in the Chinese government to refrain from enforcing the law. Additionally, the British, using their military force, were able to gain several more trade rights in China, which led to the importation of more opium and British textiles into China. In fact, it has been stated that British colonial expansions into various parts of the world was paid by the opium sales in China. In addition, many Chinese became addicted to opium, with devastating social and economic costs to the country and its peoples. As a result of colonial, military, and capitalist interventions in China and India, by 1873, British exports to these countries had increased to 50 percent in comparison to 6 percent of total British exports in 1815 (Robbins, 2008, p. 92).

Related to the "underdevelopment" of the colonized world is the fact that *colonialism* was also responsible for the creation and manifestation of a **global division of labour** in which certain countries were compelled to produce agricultural goods and export their natural resources. It facilitated the creation of the global system of economy in which Western European countries concentrated on industrialization, while exporting their finished products to other parts of the world. It was assumed that it is in the best interests of the countries to concentrate on the economic activities for which they were best suited: that was their economic advantage. However, for many of the colonized countries and the so-called "Third World" countries that were not directly colonized, but nevertheless affected by colonial and capitalist relations, the emphasis on exporting natural resources, such as minerals, also coincided with importing industrialized goods and other products that were made in Western industrialized countries. These imports competed with locally produced products by internal and national "industries", craftspeople, and manufacturers. Craftspeople were heavily taxed by the colonial rulers. In addition, the colonial powers limited the import of European machinery into their colonies, and assumed that Asians, for example, were not able and were incapable to operate the machinery produced in European countries to improve production of goods in Asia. The end result was the destruction and crash of local crafts production and manufacturing in Asian countries and the deskilling of their workers (Gage & McNair, 2002, p. 35).

Another significance of *colonialism* was the arbitrary division of the geographical spaces that the colonialists occupied. One of the consequences of this division of geographical places was the separation of cultural groups that shared similar cultural, linguistic, "ethnic", "tribal", and religious characteristics into different regions, administered by different colonial powers. After creating a colony, people "with little in common were chucked together or those with a lot in common had a line drawn between them" (Gage & McNair, 2002, p. 36). For example, many Aboriginal peoples in the United States and Canada were separated from one another due to the creation of national boundaries between Canada and the United States. The colonial powers also drew upon the **discourse of divide and rule** to differentiate between groups. The colonialists were successful in dividing the people and ruling them by putting one group against another. In Malaysia, for example, the Anglo-Saxon colonizers "tried to assimilate the Chinese into [their] culture by providing them with an English education while attempting to control the Indigenous Malay population by denying them an education" (Spring, 2007, p. 7). In this way, they ensured that this Indigenous population would remain hunter and gatherers and not threaten the British colonial rule.

This *policy of divide and rule* can also be observed in what is today known as Rwanda. As Rwanda became a colony of Belgium by the end of World War I, after being controlled by the Germans since 1894, the divisions between the Tutsi and Hutu groups became more entrenched as a result of the *racist ideology* of Europeans that informed their policies, and was also adopted by local African leaders. Ethnic and cultural differences were being reinterpreted in light of *racialized ideologies* that were being developed in Europe at the time. Internal cultural differences became institutionalized due to the application of the "race science". According to the **Hamitic hypothesis**, for example, it was assumed that "all culture and civilization in central Africa had been introduced by the taller, sharper-featured people, whom [Hanning Speke] considered to be a Caucasoid tribe of Ethiopian origin, descendants from the biblical King David, and therefore a superior race to the native Negroids" (Gourevitvch, 2006, p. 198). According to this theory, Tutsi "tribe" was labelled as part of this "superior" "race", despite their darker skin, which was considered to be the result of years of intermarriages with local people (Gourevitvch, 2006, p. 199). This group was labelled as the lost Christians that could be re-Christianized through European education and reintroduced to the "superior White race". By the end of World War I, Tutsi and Hutu were perceived as two historically distinct groups, a view that ignored their long history of interactions and mutual economic and social relations. During the German reign, the Tutsi elites "exploited the protection and license extended to them by the Germans to pursue their internal feuds and to further their hegemony over the Hutus" (Gourevitvch,

2006, p. 200). The Belgium colonialists continued exploiting this division after they took control over the region. Through "scientific" explorations of the population characteristics of Rwandans, mainly by measuring their cranial capacities, the myth of the Tutsi people as a "superior race" was reinstated as a proven fact. The Tutsi elites abused the power given to them and exploited the Hutu population. In 1957, in reaction to the exploitation by the Tutsi people, a group of Hutu intellectuals published their Hutu manifesto, which stated that if the Tutsi people were foreign invaders, as the Hamitic hypothesis stipulated, then Rwanda was naturally a Hutu nation. By the end of 1962, and as a result of the violent events of 1959, when Rwanda was given its independence, there was a shift of power and the Hutu were now in control of the country. During the events of 1959, for example, a large number of Tutsi people were massacred and the Tutsi monarchy was abolished in 1961, as Belgians switched "ethnic" sides and supported the Hutu politicians who led the revolution against Tutsi elites (Gourevitvch, 2006, pp. 203–204). The ethnic violence of this era was reenacted during the 1994 genocide in Rwanda when more than 800,000 Tutsi and other moderate Hutu were also massacred. As the above examples point out, *colonialism* is a racialized construction of national identity that was used to eliminate a group depicted as outsiders and nonmembers from membership into the nation. Colonialism engendered violence and *genocide* with devastating consequences for economic, social, political, and cultural relations and structures in Africa and other parts of the world.

In general, the colonizers manufactured divisions between local peoples and "encouraged distrust between different groups" (Spring, 2007, p. 7). Rather than uniting against a common "enemy" and rising up against colonial powers with a cohesive front, these groups began to view one another in light of modern discourses of "us" and "them". In the Dutch East Indies, for example, the Ambonese people were used as soldiers to suppress the other Indonesian peoples. They were educated in Christian schools and served as officers in various capacities in the Dutch administration and army. In fact, after the Independence of Indonesia, the majority of the Ambonese people had to leave Indonesia and settle in Holland due to their involvement in the colonial administration of the country and violent acts against Indonesians on behalf of the Dutch colonial government (Gage & McNair, 2002, p. 36). European colonialists used their military might to keep one ethnic and religious group in power as the leaders, assisting them to administer their colonies. This resulted in the formation of divisions and hierarchies within the colonies, which became objectified through the institutionalization of such ethnic, racial, linguistic, and cultural differences in political, economic, cultural, and educational structures.

Related to the above discussion and one of the other consequences of *colonialism* has been the movement of various groups of people across the globe, and the creation of **transnational populations** that have multiple loyalties to two or more nation-states and connect these states through nongovernmental organizations and bodies, such as ethnic organizations, political parties, and religious institutions (For example, Sikh organizations in India, England, the United States, and Canada). This has led to the creation of many **diasporas** across the world. *Diaspora* means the forceful relocation of people or inducing the movement of people from their homeland and their resettlement in other parts of the world (Spring, 2007, p. 40). Examples of Diaspora are Black populations in the West Indies and the Americas that were formed as result of the slave trade. The British colonial power also relocated a large number of "free labour" from their colony in India to various parts of the world to work in mines and plantations; thus changing the demographic characteristics of many Islands and various countries across the world (Spring, 2007, p. 40). In Trinidad and Tobago which were colonies of Spain until 1797, the Spaniards introduced slaves into these islands to work in the plantations. The British controlled these islands by 1815. After the British outlawed slavery in 1834, they had to deal with the shortage of workers needed to work the fields. The British first brought Chinese **indentured workers** who were later considered too expensive. Indian *indentured workers* were a much cheaper solution to the labour shortage. As a result, many Indians were brought over to work on the cacao and sugar plantations.

The population of Singapore was also transformed due to the colonial practices. Singapore, which was also a colony of Britain, became independent in the 1950s after Malaysia gained its independence from Britain. In 1810, this port city was "purchased" by the *British East India Company*. The British brought Chinese migrant workers to work in the tin mines. By the end of the nineteenth century, the British introduced the Brazilian rubber tree into this region. The British brought Tamil-speaking Indians to the Malaysian plateau to work in the newly established rubber tree plantations. In a span of a few decades the population of this part of the world was transformed due to colonial policies and the capitalist need for indentured labour. The establishment of rubber plantations in Asia also resulted in the devastation of the rubber industry in Brazil, a situation which did not improve until World War II when the Japanese army controlled many parts of Asia, leaving the Western world to export its needed supplies from Brazil (Heyck, 2002, pp. 25–30).

Colonialism and Domination: assimilation, deculturalization, segregation, and educational denial

Colonial powers used a variety of practices to deal with the subjugated cultural groups and nations. For example, the colonial powers imposed policies, such as **deculturalization**, **segregation**, **assimilation**, and **denial of educational opportunities** in order to control, divide, and rule them. **Acculturation** occurs when two equal cultural groups come into contact with one another and each one keeps its own identity and dynamic and successfully integrates and assimilates the foreign element of the other culture as part of its own (Latouche, 1996, p. 54). In contrast, *deculturalization* refers to those policies that aim at replacing the culture and values of a group with that of the dominant society. It is a way to destroy a group's culture. It is a form of **cultural genocide** or **ethnocide** (Latouche, 1996, p. 55). The introduction of Western values and their conceptions of phenomena, such as science, technology, economics, development, and mastery of nature, served as the bases for *deculturalization* (Latouche, 1996, p. 54). The aim of *deculturalization* was to **assimilate** the marginalized group into the culture of the dominant society. For example, in the United States, it was assumed that only the Anglo-Saxon culture should be taught in schools since it supported and promoted the ideals of capitalism and republican and democratic institutions (Spring, 2007, p. 7). The language of the dominant society was used as the language of instruction in schools to ensure that the new generation of "minority" groups lose their cultures (hence, language is an important element of culture and central to its survival). Similarly, the British used their schools to impose their culture and language on the people and residences of their colonies. Today for example, English is the official language of Trinidad and Tobago (Spring, 2007, p. 40).

Segregation refers to dividing the population based on racial and cultural factors and placing them, for example, in different educational institutions with different and unequal resources. *Segregation* can also take the shape of forcing people to live in specific geographical locations and regions within the country and city. For example, Aboriginal peoples of North America were forced to live in *reserves* and Chinese were segregated into specific residential neighborhoods, known as Chinatowns, due to discrimination and racism of the wider society against them. These policies are/ were imposed on "minority" populations as ways of subjugating them and making them into the *other* (Spring, 2007, p. xi).

Assimilation requires the integration and absorption of "minority" groups into the dominant culture (Spring, 2007, p. 8). The dominated group is forced to lose its culture and adopt the culture and language of the dominant society without, at times, being structurally incorporated as equals to the members of the dominant society. The colonial powers in the Americas attempted to destroy the cultures of Aboriginal groups through the implementation of educational, economic, and cultural policies based on the cultural and religious values of the European settler groups. As mentioned in Chapter Seven, education has played an important role in the process of *cultural genocide*. In the United States, Puerto Ricans and Mexican Americans also experienced *cultural genocide* (Spring, 2007, p. 7). In South and North America, the Aboriginal people were prohibited from practising their rituals and observing their cultural norms. These policies were intended to change these cultural groups by making sure that they could not transfer the knowledge of their cultures from one generation to another. *Assimilation* in North America has promoted **Anglo-conformity** (Hiller, 2006, p. 215). *Anglo-conformity* is a type of assimilationist practice in which "minority" groups are pressured and forced to conform to the norms, values, and cultural practices of the Anglo "majority" (Hiller, 2006, p. 215). This can take the form of learning about the history of the nation from the perspective of the dominant Anglo-society, ignoring the history of "minority" groups, and excluding them from the national historical narrative.

Education based on European values and norms was also a very powerful means of **social control**. Through the imposition of European styles of modern education systems, the colonizers were successful in replacing the regional, ethnic, and local cultural practices. As Chief Kabongo of the Kikuyu tribe of Kenya asserted, "the young men are learning new ways, the children make marks which they call writing, but they forget their own language and customs, they know not the laws of their peoples and they do not pray to Ngai. They ride fast in motorcars, they work fire-sticks that kill, they make music from a box. But they have no land and no food and they have lost laughter" (Chief Kabongo, 2002, p. 49).

In Africa, schooling provided by the missionaries was also a powerful tool to socialize African children and mould them into good Christians and modern individuals. The colonial education systems in Africa were not based on the needs of Africans and did not reflect their natural environments and cultures. The main goal of these imposed educational systems, which inculcated the *ideology* and values of the colonizers in African students, was to train them as future lower rank administrators and as staffs of private capitalist firms that were owned by Westerners (Rodney, 2006, p. 123). As Rodney (2006, p. 123) noted, the colonialists were selective in terms of which groups were to receive European education, as colonial education was not equally available to everyone. Educational facilities in Africa were more available in urban centres than in rural centres. They were also more accessible in regions where the colonialists had economic interests. For example, in Gold Coast, now Ghana, the Northern Territories were neglected since there were no products that could be exported by the European companies from this region (Rodney, 2006, pp. 122–123). The Southern region of Sudan also experienced the same fate as did the region of Tanganyika, now part of Tanzania, where educational facilities were more accessible and available in regions with the most coffee and cotton plantations (Rodney, 2006, p. 123). It is important to note that secondary education was not often afforded to Africans, since too much education was deemed as dangerous for junior clerks and messengers. The majority of high school and higher education was reserved for only European children in Africa. As late as 1959, in Uganda, for example, "186 pounds was spent on a European Child's education in comparison to 11 pounds per African student" (Rodney, 2006, p. 123).

As we mentioned previously, the education that most Africans received was also influenced by religious concerns. In fact, religious missionaries played an important role in the process of *colonization* in Africa. They were influential agents of *colonization*: the role of the Church was to "preserve the social relations of colonialism" (Rodney, 2006, p. 124). They emphasized "humility, docility, and acceptance" (Rodney, 2006, p. 124). These religious schools were forms of social control. The Churches did not teach the message that in the eyes of God everyone is equal, but they taught "turning the other cheek in the face of exploitation, and they drove home the message that everything would be right in the next world" (Rodney, 2006, p. 124).

These schools also socialized pupils in the capitalist discourse of **individualism**. In terms of land ownership, *individualism* translated into an emphasis on **private ownership**, which went against the communal conceptions of land ownership amongst many African nations and groups (Rodney, 2006, p. 124). The proliferation of such views undermined egalitarian concepts and structures in Africa. As such, "in Africa, both the formal school system and the informal value system of colonialism destroyed social solidarity and promoted the world form of alienated individualism without social responsibility" (Rodney, 2006, p. 125). During the era of postindependence in Africa, moreover, many of these educated Africans also became involved in the administration of African nation-states. In other words, colonial relations did not end with independence as colonial ideas and views came to be institutionalized and incorporated into the culture of the elite groups.

Anticolonial Resistance and Neocolonialism: postcolonialism

The resistance against *colonialism* has a long history. African slaves, for example, revolted in the colonies of England in North America and in the southern United States after its independence (Zinn, 2003). Here we can only pay a cursory attention to this rich history. In this section, we focus on the events in Asia and Africa since the twentieth century. In Asia, for example, the invasion of various parts of the continent by the Japanese imperialists was an awakening time for many Asian "nation-states" and peoples. The Japanese claimed that their objective was to mobilize Asia to get rid of Western imperialism (Spring, 2007, p. 41). As the first Malaysian leader maintained, "Under the Japanese I learnt that an Asian is just as good as a European ... [The Japanese] were brutal too, but they inspired us with a new idea of what Asia might become" (as cited in Spring, 2007. p. 41; Latouche, 1996). The ideal of "Asia for Asians" championed by the Japanese inspired many local nationalist liberation movements to fight for independence from European *colonialism* and subjugation.

The call for **decolonization** and contraction of colonial rule and an end to foreign rule in many parts of the world came to fruition during the twentieth century (Goldthorpe, 1996, p. 70). This fight/struggle has not ended. Many Aboriginal peoples, for example, continue to engage in the *decolonization* processes, attempting to reverse the dehumanizing effects and processes of *colonialism* (Hiller, 2006, p. 187). The *ideology* of *decolonization* rests on the premise that non-White people are equal to Whites, and are entitled to democratic representation and to rule their own countries and nations. *Decolonization* also involves the process of rethinking epistemic systems of knowledge creation and mechanisms and logic of the construction of *otherness in dominant* and *subordinated* and *non-white* and *white relationships.*

As increasing numbers of scholars from the colonized countries obtained their education in Europe and became familiar with the Western ideals of liberty, justice, and equality, they began to demand these rights for them and their fellow compatriots. In 1945, for example, African leaders, intellectuals, or their representatives, such as Kwame Nkrumah (Ghana), Jomo Kenyatta (Kenya), Nnamdi Azihiwe (Nigeria), gathered at the 5th Pan-African Congress in Manchester and devised plans to move towards independence. Since 1945, more uprisings and struggles ensued that resulted in independence of many countries, starting in 1951 with Libya. From 1957 to 1967, 32 African countries became independent. The last country that became independent was Namibia on November 7, 1989 (from South Africa) (Gage, 1991, p. 20).

The independence of many of the Asian and African countries has not been without violence. Both during and after independence, many people lost their lives, and many more people were forced to flee their homelands to seek asylum in the former colonial metropolises. In general, World War I played an important role in the *decolonization* process. As Asian and Africans were used as soldiers and labourers in the war effort by the colonialists, they were more fully reincorporated into the capitalist system (Herman, 2008, p. 453). At the same time, due to the increase in colonial taxes, the masses of the people were now affected by the burden of the war in Europe. For example, "war taxes and loans meant 100 million pounds flowed out of India to swell the imperial finances—paid for out of increased taxes and price rises, which hit the workers and poorer peasants alike" (Herman, 2008, p. 454).

The First World War also resulted in the rise of industries in the colonies as access to Western goods and resources were undermined due to the effects of the war (Herman, 2008, p. 454). As a result, the number of working classes in various parts of the colonized world increased. The intellectuals, students, and the middle classes in these countries could now rely on the political power of the capitalist and working classes to demand independence from colonial powers (Herman, 2008, p. 454).

By the end of the First World War, there were many revolts across the world that undermined the legitimacy of colonial powers and their control over their colonies. Many people in India, China, and Egypt participated in strikes and demonstrations. In China, for example, student demonstrations in 1919 resulted in the civil war of 1926–27 (Harman, 2007, p. 449). Many of these movements were led by the new classes of elites in the colonized worlds, who were partially or fully incorporated into the Western capitalist system. Many of them were very familiar with European systems of governance and were educated in European style education systems. In fact, it could be stated that many of them were Westernized.

During this period, the domestic native capitalist classes were concerned with the formation of governments that would promote their interests. In India, for example, the anticolonial sentiments were expressed in various demonstrations and strikes during the period between 1918 and 1920, when many people lost their lives as a result of violence by police and the army. The role of the working classes in the strikes and their relative power was not only a sign of stress for the British but also for the membership of the nationalist movement and the Indian Congress Party whose members were connected to the Indian capitalist class that wanted a protected Indian market. Ghandi was also concerned with the growing militancy of the movement that might have focused on the Indian capitalist class instead of the British colonialist, which led to his decision to discourage militant agitations throughout the early periods of resistance (Herman, 2008, p. 455). Fearing that anti-British sentiments of the workers and their militancy could easily be transformed into anti-Indian capitalist sentiments, Ghandi and others emphasized peaceful, disciplined, and non-cooperation with authorities (Herman, 2008, p. 455). Ghandi did not support the initiative of nonpayment of general taxes since this policy could result in the nonpayment of rent to the Indian landlords by the peasants (Herman, 2008, p. 455). As violent clashes between the police and British army and the protestors escalated, Ghandi eventually called off the movement due to the level of violence, which resulted in giving the British time to reorganize and arrest many members of the Congress, including Ghandi. This also resulted in the exacerbation of the division between Moslems and Hindus during the 1920s.

In India, due to the British division of the province of Bengal into two areas, Moslem and Hindu, we notice the creation of a division between the Moslem and Hindu populations. During the 1920s and 1930s, religious differences and classes became more pronounced and each group attempted to secure their own interests. The real power of the anti-imperialist movement, nevertheless, remained in the hands of the right wing faction of the Indian Congress Party, with connections to the capitalist class close to Ghandi (Herman, 2008, p. 552). The British creation of Bengal also resulted in bringing together the political organization of the Indian National Congress (INC) and radical elements of Hindu society. The INC was composed of English speaking middle class elements of the Indian society who were from professional backgrounds (Harman, 2007, p. 450). Their nationalist ideology was now combined "with a willingness to countenance 'terrorist' methods with the encouragement of upper class Hindu antagonism towards Moslems on the grounds that Hinduism was the 'authentic' Indian tradition" (Harman, 2007, p. 450). Religious strife increased between Moslems and Hindus, as each group blamed their conditions on landlords of the other group. By 1943, England had conceded that it would need a significant military presence to control India. However, England soon realized that this was not a viable option and decided to instead use the Moslem League in India as a counterweight to INC (Herman, 2008, p. 552). At this time, the Moslem League was given control over several provinces. By this time, the leader of the Moslem League was calling for a separate Moslem state, which he had opposed in the previous years. The Hindu and Moslem groups were now viewed as two distinct groups and nations. Yet, it is important to note that it was impossible to simply draw a line on the map to determine the boundaries of the two nations without mass expulsion of members of both groups from one region to another. Although, on 15 August 1947, India became an independent country, signalling the fall of the British Empire (Herman, 2008, p. 551), we also notice the rise of ethno-national violence within this newly independent nation-state. Eventually, the Indian subcontinent was divided into two parts by drawing an arbitrary line between Bengal and Punjab and separating these heterogeneous regions along the dividing lines of Moslem, Hindu, and Sikh. The result was mass deportation and *genocide* in both parts. By 1971, Pakistan was also divided and partitioned into two countries of Bangladesh and Pakistan, but not before the massacre of Bengalis.

In general, internal class differences also affected the political formations of the newly independent nation-states. For example, Nkrumah's socialist policies in Ghana after the independence movement were opposed by the national capitalist class, whose members deposed his government and replaced it through a military coup, which was sponsored by the US Central Intelligence Agency (C. I. A.) in 1966 (Webster, 1984, p. 79).

In short, after independence, many African and Asian states had to deal with economic inequalities and emerging national and ethnic strives. Due to colonialists' policies and their arbitrary approaches to dividing Africa and Asia and choosing their colonial agents, nation-building in many African and Asian societies had to rely on colonial languages as a tool to unite people and provide an avenue to communicate between the different peoples, speaking different languages and dialects. In this sense, colonial influences remained through language *colonization*. In addition, the reliance of many national elites on their sense of nationalism that excluded many other groups from participation in the political reconstruction of various states in African and Asian countries resulted in ethnic/national uprisings, which were met with force by the newly-independent governments.

Part Three

• •

Theorizing the Effects of Colonialism, Imperialism, and Capitalist Relations: Modernization, dependency, and world-system theories

One of the assumptions prevalent among many people living in the Western parts of the world is that "underdevelopment" in the "Third World" countries is caused by the inherent conditions prevalent in non-Western countries. This myth was further promoted by the **modernization theory**, a **structural functionalist** approach to analyzing the global economy. According to this theory, lack of development in non-Western parts of the world was the end result of "a deficiency in appropriate modernizing values" within those nation-states. The *modernization theory* assumed that "exposure to advanced industrial countries could only be a positive benefit to the Third World" (Webster, 1984, p. 84).

In contrast to this theory, the **dependency theory** and the **World-System theory** argued that the cause of poverty is explained in terms of the "Third World's" dependency on Euro-western economies and societies (Webster, 1984, p. 84). According to this theory, the dominant colonial powers have exploited the labour and resources of non-Western regions. The colonized people have been constructed and treated as the *other* who needed to change their attitudes and cultural values to become developed. In general, these theories asserted that *colonialism* as a practice and a set of values (i.e., *Orientalism* as a way of viewing a group of people in light of the supposed "superiority" of the colonial "man", Said, 1979) make up a great deal of Western assumptions about "Third World" countries.

Modernization Theory

The *modernization theory* was influenced by the ideas of Talcott Parsons, whose ideas influenced the theoretical perspective of structural functionalism. It was developed in the context of the decline of the colonial empires (Webster, 1984, p. 49). It was an approach to show that ex-colonial countries could achieve development under the auspices of the West rather than the socialist Soviet Union (Webster, 1984, p. 49). This theory assumed that economic development was dependent on changes in human attitudes and aptitudes and political structures in these societies (Bauer, as cited in Webster, 1984, p. 50). These theorists distinguished between traditional societies and modern ones. In traditional societies, they claimed, tradition makes people oriented to the past and incapable to adjust to the introduced changes in modernity. Traditional people are "irrational" and "have an emotional, superstitious and fatalistic approach to the world" (Webster, 1984, p. 50). In contrast, modern people are willing to engage those aspects of their cultures that undermine social cohesion and social progress.

Modern people, these theorists argued, are future-oriented and forward-looking as well as innovative (Webster, 1984, p. 51). As Parsons argued, modern societies are characterized by **achievement orientation**, as the most likely choice of action for people in the economic sphere because it is more rational (Webster, 1984, p. 50). In such a system, occupations are distributed based on the **achieved status** and skills of individuals rather than on **nepotism**. This level of achievement is considered to be a reflection of the levels of entrepreneurial activities and innovations within the society (Webster, 1984, p. 50).

Modernization theorists maintained that the process of modernization in non-Western parts of the world could only occur through diffusion of European style social structures and urbanization, "based on nuclear family households"; education, literacy, and training; the expansion of mass media to "educate" people about new ideas, values, and norms necessary for modernization; participation in the democratic processes; and replacing traditional values with a system of law based on "representational national government" that is rational (Webster, 1984, p. 54). Such ideas, in fact, influenced the basic assumptions and approaches of the development agencies that were involved in the modernization of the 'Third World' (Webster, 1984, p. 56).

According to this theory, global inequality is explained by references to technological and cultural differences between nations. *Modernization theory* pioneers, like Durkheim and Weber, placed premiums on the values and norms that influence the societal relations in the newly independent nations of the colonial world (Webster, 1984, p. 50). They argued that diffusion of technological advancement from Western countries to non-Western countries would result in better standards of living. They claimed that most countries until very recently were poor. In order to promote prosperity, then, it was important to account for how affluent societies emerged. They contended that affluence is the result of economic and cultural changes in Europe since the Middle Ages (i.e., the liberalization of Catholicism and the fact that material affluence was viewed as the sign of personal virtue). Factors, such as trade, exploration, innovation, and industrialization, were viewed as the reasons for such affluence in Europe. According to this theory, industrialization was the answer to poverty. In other words, a modern society was viewed as an industrialized nation.

They maintained that technological changes must accompany cultural changes. That is, people in non-Western societies must change their attitudes and values in order to become modern. To become modern, these countries must promote the *ideology* of *individualism* and **political rights**. According to the *modernization theory*, a transition from tradition to modernity must be a central aspect of any development project based on Western styles of government and capitalist and industrial economic systems (Theobald, 1990, p. 47). A modern and developed society is characterized by a "highly differentiated and functionally specific system of governmental organization, a high degree of integration within governmental structure and the prevalence of rational and secular procedures for the making of political decisions" (Theobald, 1990, p. 47).

Lack of development was thought to be intrinsic to the internal history of these societies. Economic inequality, modernization theorists argued, has nothing to do with *colonialism* and its aftermath (Webster, 1984, p. 55). According to this model, "the development of industrialization in the West [should be a model and] the blueprint for development throughout the world" (Webster, 1984, p. 54). The lack of development was viewed to be the "fault of socio-economic systems that created obstacles to modernisation and encouraged little ambition or incentive in pursuing commercial production and enterprises in commerce" in the "Third World" countries (Webster, 1984, p. 55). According to W. W. Rostow, for example, low levels of development in "Third World" countries were due to "low levels of capital in particular" (Kubow & Fossum, 2007, p. 37).

Critics have pointed out that Rostow's approach to development was a justification for economic aid and investments by Western industrialized countries in "underdeveloped" countries with disastrous consequences (Kubow & Fossum, 2007, p. 37). Rostow theorized that all societies "pass through similar stages of development", culminating in a consumer society resembling the structure of society and economy in the United States during the 1950s (Kiely, 2005, p. 121). The proponents of this view claimed that modern schools play an important role in the implementation and normalization of modern attitudes and values. Schools, they maintained, also play an important function in the maintenance of other modern institutions that are necessary for the process of modernization.

This theory draws upon an evolutionary perspective that was based on a **culture of poverty** explanation of "underdevelopment" (Kubow & Fossum, 2007, p. 37). As a process, modernization was envisioned as Western style social, cultural, economic, and political structures and relations that promoted rationalism, professionalism, and the incorporation of "cutting edge technology" (Kiely, 2005, p. 121). These characteristics, modernization theorists pointed out, were lacking in "Third World" countries, and their "poverty" in cultural attitudes and knowledge explained their "underdevelopment".

One of the main proponents of this theory was W. W. Rostow. Based on his study of British industrial development, he proposed European countries passed through four main stages of development:

1. **traditional stage,**

2. **take-off stage,**

3. **drive to technological maturity stage**, and

4. **high mass consumption stage** (Webster, 1984, p. 53).

The traditional stage is characterized by strong cultural tradition and resilient community and family relations with little individual freedom. During the *take-off stage*, people begin using their talents and imaginations, prompting economic growth and the development of the market system (i.e., Great Britain reached this stage by the 1800s). In the *drive to technological maturity stage*, people desire a higher standard of living within the context of a diversified and industrialized economy. During this stage, industrialization erodes traditional family and community life and we witness the rise in urbanization, specialization, and *individualism*. *The high mass consumption stage* refers to the stage during which there is an increase in industrial technology and standards of living. During this stage, **mass production** results in *mass consumption*.

Modernization theorists assumed that the role of Western countries in the modernization of the "developing" world is manifold:

1. assisting in population control (i.e., through the introduction of birth control technology),

2. increasing food production (i.e., through the introduction of high tech farming, such as the "Green Revolution"),

3. introducing industrial technology, and

4. providing foreign aid (Webster, 1984, p. 56, pp. 145–168).

The aid is provided to these countries because it was assumed that many of them lacked sufficient capital to instigate the *take-off stage*. Aid would provide these countries with the adequate foreign currencies needed for manufacturing and agricultural investments (Webster, 1984, p. 151). However, as previously mentioned, Western aid agencies, such as the International Monetary Fund (IMF), the World Bank (WB), and others, have only been assisting those countries that have been considered as "friendly" by Western capitalist nations. Countries that promoted socialist and/or revolutionary ideologies were excluded from the Western aid assistance (Webster, 1984, p. 149). For example, in the 1960s, the United States introduced the Alliance for Peace program that aimed at providing assistance to Latin American countries in order to make sure that Cuban revolution would not be exported to these countries. That is, these programs were viewed as ways of ensuring that socialist governments could not be established in Latin America. One of the results of this program has been the reliance of almost all Latin American countries on investments, loans, imports, and grants from the United States (Kamrava, 1993, p. 40). Because of this overreliance, the economic recession in the United States during the 1980s had ripple effects in Latin America. For example, from 1980 to 1988, Argentina's rate of inflation averaged at 88.6 percent and Mexico's at 73.8 percent (Kamrava, 1993, p. 40).

In addition, much of the aid was not free, but in the form of loans to be repaid by the recipients. This has resulted in situations where "Third World" countries have become more indebted to Western countries, exacerbating poverty in their countries (Webster, 1984, p. 152). In addition, the aid money is used to pay for the **expert systems** that are often provided by Western countries. The problem with these Western experts was/is that many of them did not (do not) have full knowledge of the countries in which they work(ed) (Webster, 1984, pp. 152–153). These experts were/are paid from the same aid money, thereby taking away precious resources needed for investing in projects that could (have) actually benefit(ed) the population. For example, the average cost of a British expert to assist in a development project in a "Third World" country was about $150,000 (Webster, 1984, p. 153).

Furthermore, a good portion of aid to developing countries has also been in the form of food aid. This is a problematic policy since it has actually benefited Western capitalist societies, and has resulted in the destruction of agricultural development in many developing countries. For example, after World War II, the American farmers, due to the introduction of new technology and machinery, produced more grain than could be consumed internally. The farmers did not want to release their products into the market since it would have resulted in the decline in the value of the dollar and lower prices for their commodity in the international market. The grain, then, was given in the form of aid to developing countries that could purchase it in their own currencies (Webster, 1984, pp. 153–154). These countries, nevertheless, had to pay back these loans in American dollars. In general, food aid and expert aid were forms of postcolonial relations that have had negative consequences for non-Western countries.

Mehran Kamrava (1993, p. 35) argued that those aligned with the *modernization theory* often focused on political modernization instead of technological and industrial development. As such, this theory is more apt for analysis of the political systems of non-Western countries. According to this school, political stability is viewed as central to industrial development (Kamrava, 1993, p. 35). The *modernization theory* also assumed that the path to capitalism and industrial development is a linear evolution from simple to complex societies (Kamrava, 1993, p. 36). Lack of industrial development was considered to be the end result of a lack of well-developed political structure and a capable leadership to guide the nation (Kamrava, 1993, p. 36). It was also assumed that, in order to promote industrial development, the policies that are implemented must not threaten the position of existing economic elites in non-Western countries. As a result, the implementation of *modernization theory* led to industrial and economic policies that were promoted by dictatorships in many non-Western countries (Kamrava, 1993, p. 36).

This theory is criticized as a defense of capitalism. Critics argued that modernization has not taken place in many countries; for example, industrialization has been occurring unevenly in various parts of the world. In fact, Western countries have often blocked the path to industrialization for "Third World" countries. This theory is based on Eurocentric standards that assumed that all countries must follow the paths of Western countries to achieve development. To reiterate, the cause of poverty was erroneously thought to be intrinsic to traditional societies due to a lack of the prevalence of capitalist values.

This theory did not account for the fact that the development of the West has been at the expense of "Third World" countries (Kamrava, 1993, p. 37). Critics have pointed out that "underdevelopment" must be understood in the context of *colonialism* and postcolonial relations. Many have argued that the so-called "Third World" countries fared better before colonial relations. In fact, it was due to the effects of *mercantilism* and *colonialism* that many non-Western countries began to develop specialized economic systems in the "Third World", such as exporting raw materials to Western industrialized nations. This has been partly due to the consequences of private Western elite's control of colonies and the expansion of a bureaucratic approach to colonial exploitation of the "Third World".

Before we switch to the next theory, it is germane to comment on two terms employed in the preceding analysis: "underdevelopment" and "developing countries". These terms have been criticized for their racist and Eurocentric connotations. The term "underdeveloped" implies some people have lacked the capacity to achieve and evolve the same conditions of development as Europeans have had. It is also pertinent to note that the term "underdeveloped" is a social construct. It takes one country to make another "underdeveloped". "Underdevelopment" is not a natural condition. At one point in history, all countries, including the so-called advanced capitalist countries, were "undeveloped". In other words, "un-development" could be considered a natural stage through which all nations pass. "Underdevelopment", however, is an artificial state; the so-called "developed" capitalist countries caused the "underdevelopment" of the so-called "developing" countries. The term "developing countries" is also a problematic construction. It assumes that these countries are on their way to become modern, as they emulate standards set and imposed by Western countries and their agents, such as the World Bank and International Monetary Fund. This term assumes that poverty is intrinsic to the cultural values of the "Third World" people. It also implies that they are improving their lot when the reality points to how global capitalism has induced poverty through neoliberal policies and imperialist incursions (Parenti, 2002, p. 66). Also the term "Third World" has been criticized for its assumption that people in these countries are "Third Class". The preferred terms to describe peoples in the Western countries and those in the non-Western nations are "**Global South**" and "**Global North**". Although these designations are not entirely accurate descriptions of these countries, (for example, Japan is included in the advanced capitalist category, but it is not located in the *Global North*), all the Western countries, with the exception of Australia and New Zealand, are located in the Northern Hemisphere; and all the non-Western countries are situated in the Southern Hemisphere.

To reiterate, as Parenti (2002, p. 66) stated, *imperialism* has created what he has termed as **maldevelopment**. The term, *maldevelopment*, highlights the fact that "underdevelopment" is itself a form of "development" that was imposed by Western imperialist powers. *Maldevelopemnt* refers to ideals of "development" that emphasize "modern office buildings and luxury hotels in the capital city instead of housing for the poor, cosmetic surgery clinics for the affluent instead of hospitals for the workers, cash export crops for agribusiness instead of food for local markets, highways that go from the mines and *latifundios* [land grants given to Spanish and Portuguese colonialists in South and Central America] to the refineries and ports instead of roads in back country for those who might hope to see a doctor or a teacher". *Malevelopment* highlights the transfer of wealth form non-Western parts of the world to Western capitalist countries, which is considered as necessary, normal, and natural. Through such a system, non-Western countries are "denied the freedom of trade and the opportunity to develop [their] own natural resources, markets, and industrial capacity" (Parenti, 2002, p. 66).

Dependency Theory

Dependency theory explained global inequality in terms of historical exploitation of "Third World" countries by Western countries. It focused its analysis on the economic failures in Latin American societies (Webster, 1984, p. 84). The *dependency theory* critically evaluated the role of Western *imperialism* in dominating non-Western countries and regions. Theorists, such as Andre Gunder Frank, were critical of the *modernization theory* and their assertion that the road to modernization was through emulation of Western societies (Webster, 1984, p. 84). They maintained that poverty was caused by the economic and political influences of Western countries in the 'Third World'. They argued that as long as "Third World" countries were subjected to the control of their economies and political systems by imperialist societies, poverty would persist in these societies (Webster, 1984, p. 85). According to Frank, "poverty in the Third World is a reflection of its dependency" on Western societies (Webster, 1984, p. 85).

This theory argued that the exploitation of the "Third World" countries was achieved as a result of the consequences of *merchant capitalism*, *colonialism*, and *neocolonialism*. More specifically, Frank maintained that these factors resulted in the specialization of "Third World" countries in primary export oriented economies, which required unskilled cheap labour (Webster, 1984, p. 85). The end result of these factors were manyfold: creation of elite groups in various parts of the world that were no longer connected to the masses of people in their countries, and their political and economic interests were dependent on commerce with Europe; introduction of European currencies that undermined local currencies; and making various parts of the world dependent on the products, technology, and expert systems manufactured and produced in Europe (Webster, 1984, pp. 71–73).

As we mentioned previously, *merchant capitalism* refers to the accumulation of capital through trade and plunder during the sixteenth century to the late eighteenth century (Webster, 1984, p. 70). For example, the merchants purchased slaves in Africa, sold them to plantation owners in various parts of the world, bought the agricultural goods produced in these plantations and sold them in Europe for profits, which were refined in Europe, thus, contributing to the process of industrialization in Europe, and bought goods produced by the industries in Europe and traded them with African chiefs for slaves. The main effect of *merchant capitalism* in the context of colonial rule was establishing a pattern of economic development in non-Western parts of the world that revolved around export of natural resources and raw materials (Webster, 1984, p. 73). The economic activities in the colonies, in terms of production of sugar, cocoa, or coffee, that were not suitable for the climates in Europe did not compete with the industrial and agricultural production in the colonial empires. The emphasis on such activities in the colonies had the negative consequence of not developing other industries, such as manufacturing (Kubow & Fossum, 2007, p. 51).

Between the 1750s and 1914, with the growth of colonial bureaucracies in the colonies to manage these parts of the world, we also notice the formalization of the dependent relationship between colonized countries and colonial powers in the form of state-to-state affairs that enhanced the control of the **centre** (or **core**) over the economic activities in the **periphery**, promoting the privileges of the *core* nations (Kubow & Fossum, 2007, p. 51). The effects of the Depression and the crisis of capitalism during the period between 1914 and 1940 resulted in a decrease in demand for the goods produced in *periphery countries* that had the consequence of an increase in foreign investment in these countries, which resulted in an increase in foreign debt as these countries borrowed more money from Western countries to invest in natural and agricultural resources.

As critics of the *modernization theory* pointed out, the proponents of dependency theory posited that social and political independence since the proliferation of nationalist movements in many non-Western parts of the world have not accompanied **economic independence**. This is despite the fact that the nationalization of industries by many independent nations was considered by many of the revolutionary leaders of newly independent "Third World" countries as an effective way of promoting industrialization in their respective countries. It was thought that through **statism** (a system in which the government plays the role of the main manager of industrial development) the nation could become self-sufficient in producing many of the goods necessary for internal consumption. However, these policies were often ill-advised and were opposed by international bodies and creditors that wanted strict government control over industries to be relaxed, a process that was accelerated by the 1980s with the rise of neoliberal policies (Kamrava, 1993, p. 42).

Frank also argued that the elites of the "Third World" have been incorporated into the world capitalist system with little power to effect change in the system (Webster, 1984, p. 85). The *dependency theory* also analyzed the role of the "Third World" elites in the exploitation of resources and "underdevelopment" of these countries. They have pointed out that the activities of these elite groups (*comprador*, interpreter) and their lifestyles have become more and more intertwined with the economic policies of the elite groups in Western countries (metropolitan countries). According to Frank, the solution to "underdevelopment" in the "Third World" is for the working classes to unite and change their conditions through socialist revolutions (Webster, 1984).

According to this theory, colonial relations and patterns of domination are also reflected in postcolonial interactions and relations between the North and the South. *Neocolonial* relations and *imperialism* are viewed as inimical to industrial development (Kamrava, 1993, p. 36). They contended that the colonies were too important to the colonial powers and their economies to become truly and one hundred percent independent from colonial powers. That is, they were too dependent on the economies of their colonial "masters" for them to be able to completely eliminate or relinquish such ingrained and exploitive relations (Kamrava, 1993, p. 37). They also pointed out that new methods and means of domination were applied by Western governments to continue the exploitive nature of the colonial relations. These new methods included international loans and assistance programs that aimed at achieving capital exportation and exploitation of resources in non-Western parts of the world. Western countries provided agricultural loans, food loans, technical (industrial) equipment, know-how knowledge, and *expert systems*, as ways to influence development projects and enforce their power (Kamrava, 1993, pp. 37–38).

The aims of these programs were not to increase the availability of the infrastructure, such as roads, railroads, dams, bridges, hospitals, and schools, necessary for industrial development in these countries. Rather, the goal of these programs was to provide a market for the manufactured goods in the West and importation of expert knowledge into these countries. These policies stemmed from the effects of the rise of monopoly capitalism that required the creation of new markets in order to "mitigate problems arising from over production [in Western industrialized countries]" (Kamrava, 1993, p. 38).

The proponents of the *dependency theory* argued that no real development could be achieved if the main export of the majority of Global South countries remained to be raw materials and agricultural goods. This specialization in the export of raw materials has had a negative consequence for the development of industrial growth since the demand for these products and their prices are determined by fluctuations in the international market that are decided by Western governments, banks, and investors (Kamrava, 1993, p. 38; See Nkrumah, 1965).

The economic inequalities between Western countries (the *core*) and "Third World" countries (the *periphery*) have also resulted in the creation and manifestation of class structures in the *periphery*. In this sense, dependency is the outcome of class differences within and between nations (Kamrava, 1993, p. 38). The economic growth of non-Western parts of the world has only benefitted a small proportion of the population, mainly the elite capitalist class. The existing power relations have created a small group of international elite made of big corporate-financial interests that exist above the mass of poor, disenfranchised, and marginalized people (Kamrava, 1993, p. 39). In this theory, the Marxist analysis of class privileges of the bourgeoisie and the exploitation of the working class is replaced "by a parallel [analysis that looks at] globalized pattern[s] of exploitation and oppression" between the have and have-not nations (Kubow & Fossum, 2007, p. 51). That is, the countries in the *centre/core* exploit the countries in the *periphery*. However, it is important to note that the internal elite groups within "Third World" countries that have been labeled as "**Lumpenbourgeoisie**" and "comprador capitalists" function to benefit themselves as well as the Western capitalist class. The function of internal class structures in the *periphery* are explained in terms of the global capitalist relations (Kubow & Fossum, 2007, p. 53).

The problem with this theory is that it did not focus on other countries but on Latin American societies. It also focused on those countries that had been colonized. So the question that arises is to what extent is this theory applicable to countries, such as Iran or Turkey, that were not colonized.

The proponents have argued that even those countries that were not directly colonized are now affected by neo-colonial polices (Kamrava, 1993, p. 41). Another criticism of this theory is that it also focused on the consequences of external factors and ignored the effects of internal factors (Kubow & Fossum, 2007, p. 53). Another criticism leveled against this theory is its bias against capitalism and the lack of attention paid to the conditions of socialist states that were also quasi-imperial and in many cases also characterized by exploitation (Kubow & Fossum, 2007, p. 54). This theory has also focused on historical analysis rather than developing general theoretical dispositions. Furthermore, it lacked any real approaches to offering alternative paths for the development of "Third World" countries (Kubow & Fossum, 2007, p. 54).

The Modern World-System Theory

Immanuel Wallerstein, who is a conflict theorist, argued in *The Modern World-System* that the growth of capitalism depended on the incorporation of the colonized world into a system of exploitation in which **core countries**, such as Spain, the Netherlands, Britain, and the United States, exploited the resources and labour of the **periphery countries** in the Caribbean, South and North America, Africa, and Asia. The *periphery countries* provided cheap labour and natural resources for the manufacturing sectors of the *core countries* that were by the nineteenth century more industrialized than the rest of the world (Lemert, 2005, pp. 52–53). Wallerstein maintained that the slave trade became the basis for the modern world capitalist economy. Slaves were used to produce coffee, cotton, spices, and sugar that were exported to Europe and sold; and the money was then used to purchase more slaves that were brought to the Americas and the Caribbean to work in the farms and mines (Lemert, 2005, p. 53). He also pointed to the existence of a third category of nation-states: the **semiperiphery** that refers to those regions that have characteristics of industrialized nations and also rely on exploitation of their natural resources, mainly countries, such as Canada (Ritzer, 2000, p. 299).

Wallerstein's unit of analysis was not workers, classes, or states. Rather, he focused on the **world system** (Ritzer, 2000, pp. 298–299). This system is made of parts that are inherently in opposition to one another. He argued that we have had two main world systems: the **world empire** and the **capitalist world-economy** (Ritzer, 2000, p. 299). The first form of empire is based on military domination and the other relies on economic domination. The capitalist system is assumed to be more stable because: it encompasses more states; it promotes ways to ensure economic stabilization; and the states absorb economic losses, and benefits are distributed to private hands (Ritzer, 2000, p. 299). The important point to remember is that to him "the international division of exploitation is defined not by state borders but by the economic division of labour in the world" (Ritzer, 2000, p. 299).

In general, Wallerstein analyzed the rise of the capitalist world system starting in the 1400s. He proposed that three factors were necessary for the development of a capitalist world system:

1. geographical expansion (*colonialism*),
2. worldwide division of labour, and
3. development of core states.

The expansion of European control over the rest of the world is considered the prerequisite for the development of the other two factors. In the world capitalist system different regions of the world "specialize in specific functions—breeding labour power, growing food, providing raw materials, and organizing industry" (Ritzer, 2000, p. 300). *Colonialism* also imposed a system of law and order that benefitted the colonial powers (Webster, 1984, p. 77). The colonialists often relied on the Indigenous elites to impose and implement the laws and customs of the colonial powers. For example, the British introduced the Permanent Settlement Act, which gave the local landlords private ownership rights, which they did not enjoy under traditional forms of ownership (Webster, 1984, p. 77). As the different parts of the world capitalist system began to develop different specializations in producing different products, we also notice the development of different types of workers in various parts of the world, starting in the seventeenth century. That is, the world capitalist system is characterized by the internal division of labour, which in its original form coordinated with different modes of labour control (See Ritzer, 2000, p. 300). The expansion of the capitalist system also involved the rise of nation-states and how various economic groups used the state and its infrastructure to advance their interests (Ritzer, 2000, p. 300). Wallerstein maintained that the incorporation of a nation-state into the world capitalist system required their incorporation into the interstate system and their acceptance "to act in accord with the dictates of the capitalist world-economy" (Ritzer, 2000, p. 302).

Wallerstein's approach has been criticized for not focusing on relations between classes prevalent within the nation-states. Critics have argued that the focus should not have been on the *core-periphery* international division of labour, but on internal class divisions and their consequences. Bergeson, for example, has argued that *core-periphery* relations are not just about the unequal exchange relations between *core* and *periphery* regions, but are also affected by global class relations (Ritzer, 2000, p. 302). These exchange relations are also power-dependent relations (or class relations) that need to be accounted for in the analysis of world capitalism.

The post-World War II policies and the Cold War also had implications for the world capitalist system. **First**, the United States, according to Wallerstein, became the hegemonic power from 1945 to 1990 (Ritzer, 2000, p. 302). **Second**, under the hegemony of the United States, capitalism flourished. **Third**, the anticolonial policies in the "Third World" were dealt with in such a way as not to upset and affect the "world political and economic status quo" and the hegemony of capitalist order (Ritzer, 2000, p. 303). Although Wallerstein argued that the American economic power is declining, he nevertheless has maintained that the United States will keep its military power and use it in its advantage.

In short, the capitalist system in which the *core countries* exploit the *peripheral* ones is considered to be responsible for world poverty. "Developed" countries have benefited from capitalist relations, and "underdeveloped" countries have, as result, become dependent on Western countries. Global inequality is due to colonial processes that have resulted in the development of the West and "underdevelopment" of the "Third World" countries. However, the world economic system has been going through structural changes due to the division and differences between the

North (i.e., capitalist and industrialized nations) and South (seeking egalitarian restructuring of the world system).

The theories of development and modernization that we have so far discussed have also informed how knowledge about "development" and "underdevelopment" has been communicated to students in various school textbooks across the globe. The *ideology* of the ruling elite in control of the state apparatus determines how these theories are expressed and discussed in the official knowledge. In the next section, we explore how political changes in Iran have influenced the ways in which economic development issues are portrayed in Iranian school textbooks of pre- and post-revolutionary textbooks (See Box 8.5 - State Ideology, Modernization and Dependency Theories, and School Textbooks: the case of Iran).

BOX 8.5 - State Ideology, Modernization and Dependency Theories, and School Textbooks: the case of Iran

Siavoshi (1995) explored the theoretical assumptions of both pre- and postrevolutionary Iranian textbooks in terms of their portrayal of economic relations. The prerevolutionary textbooks (pre-1979) promoted an approach to economic, political, and social development that was based on the theoretical assumptions of the *modernization theory* of Rostow. As mentioned, according to Rostow, development required the transformation of traditional institutions and their replacement with modern institutions based on principles of industrialization, the utilization of science and technology, and the promotion of investment and savings (Siavoshi, 1995, p. 206). During the Pahlavi regime (1925–1979), which was a pro-Western government and influenced by the policies of the United States, the textbooks highlighted that religion and politics should be separated. **Secularization**, as the main characteristic of modernity, was considered and emphasized as the most important element of and requirement for economic, social, and cultural growth and development (Siavoshi, 1995, p. 204). Prerevolutionary textbooks were critical of any form of religious interference in the affairs of government. In fact, during this period, the authors of the Iranian school textbooks also informed students that the prerequisite for economic development demanded a desire and an attempt to change one's attitudes and values (Siavoshi, 1995; Higgins & Shoar-Ghaffari, 1995). In the textbooks, students were informed that religious and traditional values were the causes of "underdevelopment" of the "Third World" and "developing" countries, as well as for the increase in the birthrates, which was assumed to exacerbate "underdevelopment" (Siavoshi, 1995, p. 204). In other words, the discourse of **culture of poverty** was employed to blame the Islamic/traditional culture of Iran as the source of the problem rather than presenting students with an analysis of global structural factors as the causes of poverty and "underdevelopment".

These textbooks did not offer any real critical analysis of the effects of *colonialism* and *neocolonial* relations and did not examine how "underdevelopment" was affected by the role of international political, social, and economic institutions and global capitalism (Siavoshi, 1995, p. 206). In general, Western Europe and the United States were portrayed in a positive light and discussion about Iranian welfare programs praised the Shah for his economic and social policies, known as the "White Revolution", which were designed based on the principles espoused by the *modernization theory* (Siavoshi, 1995, pp. 206–207). In these textbooks, political stability was viewed as central to economic and cultural development. Political stability, the textbooks argued, attracted foreign investments needed for development. As such, anyone or any group that undermined the legitimacy of the state, controlled by the king of Iran and his elite groups, were viewed as dangerous elements that needed to be swiftly dealt with through violence.

The assumption in these textbooks was also that Iran needed the assistance of Western countries to develop. As Rostow pointed out, the reason for "underdevelopment" in the "Third World" countries was due to lack of cultural values and emphasis on traditional values that devalued and inhabited modern development. That is, it was assumed that "underdevelopment" in Iran was intrinsic, the end results of its cultural forms, and due to the *cultural poverty* of its citizens. This theory also invoked the old *colonialist* assumption that it is the "white man's burden" to assist the non-Western people to modernize. This is an example of the **discourse of imperialist fantasy**. This discourse is also a racialized framework that allows us to think and approach non-Western countries from a Eurocentric perspective that ends up promoting the position of imperialist and capitalist nations.

In contrast, after the Revolution of 1978–79, when the pro-Western government of Iran was deposed, the revolutionary elite conceptualized the Pahlavi's approach to modernization and modern education as hegemonic structures and processes of Americanization. Siavoshi (1995, pp. 206–207) maintained that the postrevolutionary high school textbooks reflected the revolutionary elite's views and explained global relations by references to the ideas of the *dependency theory*. According to *dependency theory*, the lack of development in the non-Western parts of the world was not the end result of "a deficiency in appropriate modernizing values" (Webster, 1984, p. 84). As mentioned, this theory is critical of the assumption of *modernization theory* that argued "exposure to advanced industrial countries could only be a positive benefit to the Third World" (Webster, 1984, p. 84). The current textbooks analyze the effects of *colonialism* and explain the inequality in the world due to the hegemonic role of Western countries (Mirfakhraie, 2011, 2008). However, these textbooks do not critique the consequences of capitalism (Mirfakhraie, 2011, 2008). That is, they are critical of the roles of Western countries, *colonialism*, and *neocolonial* policies but not of the effects of capitalist and economic exploitation. This is due to the pro-capitalist nature of the postrevolutionary elite's *ideology* and their anti-Western stances/*ideologies*.

Part Four

• •

Colonialism, Empire, Racism, and Nation-Building: the case of Canada

During the early decades of the last century, Canadians believed that they are part of the British Empire and their future is linked to the success and power of Britain (Francis, 1997, p. 63). R.B. Bennett, in 1914, stated that, "We are the only colonizing race that has been able to colonize the great outlying portions of the world and give the people the priceless [benefit] of self-government and we have educated men year after year until at last those who were once subjects became free, and those who were free became freer, and you and I must carry our portion of that responsibility if we were to be true Imperialists we should be ..." (as cited in Francis, 1997, p. 63). For many of these politicians, to be a Canadian was another way of saying that one was a Briton (Francis, 1997, p. 64). The Premier of Ontario, for example, in 1900, stated that "there is no antagonism between Canadianism and Imperialism. The one is but the expansion of another" (as cited in Francis, 1997, p. 65). Canadians, especially the Anglo-Saxons, viewed themselves as "superior" to others. This view was reflected in how they perceived and treated non-White immigrants and Aboriginal peoples in Canada. For example, the processes of *colonization*, *internal colonialism*, and *postcolonial* relations have been affected by how knowledge about Aboriginal people and other racialized groups have been communicated and told by the so-called academic experts, who claim to offer unbiased and objective views of the past and present about the non-White communities.

How we think about the **nation** is often understood in light of the official **national narrative** or **discourse.** This **narrative** relies on specific ideological and normative discourses to inform the citizens of a nation about their history and identity. In **settler societies**, such as Canada, through "scientific" accounts and "objective" narrations, *colonization* has been normalized. For example, native history is told through "accounts of specific intervals of 'contact', accounts which neutralize processes of *genocide*, which never mention racism, and which do not" discuss the implication of past policies in contemporary contexts (Lawrence, 2010, 38). In the following sections, we expose this history and provide a different reading of Canadian political economy and racialized constructions.

Hans Kohn (1965, p. 9) defined *nationalism* as "a state of mind, in which the supreme loyalty of the individual is felt to be due the nation-state". *Nationalities* are the products of historical events and are never rigid (Kohn, 1965, p. 9). As Enakshi Dua (2000, p. 55) maintained, *nationalism* and **racism** in Canada are articulated in two main ways. **First**, they are aspects of how we imagine what we mean by nation and how it is imagined and constructed. **Second**, they influence how the state through its policies recruits labour from across the globe for the needs of the capitalist class. Nation-building is a two-fold process. It involves managing the population and the creation of national identity (Mackey, 2010, p. 17). As we mentioned in Chapter Seven, *nationalism* involves imagining a mythical narrative of a cohesive and united nation that has an origin in the past and progressively moves toward a better future (Mackey, 2010, p. 17). As Mazzini (1965, p. 119) stated in regards to Italy in 1861, the Italian "nation has not as yet existed; therefore, it must exist in the future … the history of our people and nationality … has yet to be written". The Canadian *nationalism* and national identity is also work in progress; their construction and meanings have changed over the years.

One of the main assumptions of Canadian *nationalism* is the supposition of tolerance. The **discourse of tolerance** is an important defining characteristic of Canadian national identity. Canadians are told that they are tolerant of *difference* and diversity due to, for example, their recognition of Quebec's distinctiveness (i.e., The Quebec Act of 1774) and recognition of the rights of Aboriginal peoples to self-governance (i.e., the Royal Proclamation of 1763) (Mackey, 2010, pp. 17–18). The *discourse of tolerance* is a complex and contradictory process of both inclusion and exclusion of various forms of *otherness* that are either depicted positively or negatively (Mackey, 2010, p. 18). Although we acknowledge that we should be accepting of the cultural practices of groups, the main premise of the *discourse of tolerance* remains the assumption that the dominant culture is "superior" and accepting (Henry & Tator, 2010, p. 15). The dominant culture defines which practices of other groups are acceptable and which ones are not. Too much tolerance is considered to result in dissent and disharmony, undermining the desired Canadian principles (Henry & Tator, 2010, p. 15). This *discourse of tolerance* leads to the **discourse of denial**, which feeds the naïve notion that racism did not occur in Canada and has not been part of the ways Canadians have and continue to view themselves.

The assumption behind the *discourse of denial* is that racism was not a structural element of Canadian political economy and hence not institutionally practiced in a "democratic" Canada. In this sense, racist acts are considered not as emanating from structural factors and institutionalized practices, such as laws and policies. Rather, they are considered stemming from individual actions and belief systems (Henry & Tator, 2010, p. 11). The *discourse of denial* tends to erase history and create **historical amnesia**. In fact, during most of the history of Canada, the popular media, indeed the "knowledge industry" as a whole, has assumed and propagated the idea that in comparison to the experiences of Aboriginal peoples in the United States, Aboriginal people in Canada did not face the same brutal polices visited upon their counterparts in the United States in the American quest to conquer the "Indians" (Mackey, 2010, p. 18). Canadian historians explained the destruction of Aboriginal cultures as the end result of epidemics and intertribal wars in Southern Ontario and Quebec that left the land "unoccupied" for the White settlers to occupy. In this sense, the White settler society in Canada is constructed as an innocent, nonracist bystander (Mackey, 2010, p. 18).

As Yasmeen Abu-Laban and Christina Gabriel (2002, pp. 37–43) have also pointed out, since the colonial era, Canada has been constructed and thought of as a White settler society despite the presence of non-White groups in Canada (i.e., the Aboriginal peoples). Related to viewing/constructing Canada a White country is the historical amnesia and the denial of racist immigration laws that have existed. In Canada, factors, such as culture, "race", ethnicity, and religion of would-be immigrants, were important criteria for acceptance of immigrants. For most of the Canadian history, the immigration policy has favoured the migration of White British Protestant males. Immigration policies were based on economic and political expediencies. Economic considerations and the labour needs of the Canadian capitalist class or political consideration of the state (i.e., to settle the West) were the prime motives behind decisions to grant entry to non-White and non-British groups. Chinese, for example, were brought in to work on the railroad. Yet, their further immigration to Canada was limited due to anti-Chinese sentiments and policies, such as the head tax and the eventual ban on Chinese immigration to Canada. For example, as late as 1947, the Prime Minster of Canada, McKenzie King, maintained that "Large-scale immigration from the orient would change the fundamental composition of the Canadian population. Any considerable oriental immigration would, moreover, be certain to give rise to social and economic problems of character that might lead to serious difficulties in the field of international relations" (as cited in Abu-Laban & Gabriel, 2002, p. 40). In addition, Chinese women were excluded and not permitted to enter Canada (Abu-Laban & Gabriel, 2002, p. 38). The fear was that women of these "lower races" would reproduce and dilute the essence of what it meant be Canadian. The dominant view during the late nineteenth century and the early twentieth century constructed Blacks and Asians as "morally deprived"; and thus as undesirable citizens (Abu-Laban & Gabriel, 2002, p. 38). In contrast, White British women were encouraged to immigrate to Canada. Most of the White women were recruited for domestic type work and they were conceived as the "mothers of the nation". It was assumed that **Whiteness** can only be reproduced through White women as the "Daughters of Empire" and "Mothers of the Nation". Their task was to be the builders and civilizers of the nation. Although they were discriminated against, they had more rights than women from the less desired classes. For example, they "could change employers, exit domestic work for other types of work, or marry" (Abu-Laban & Gabriel, 2002, p. 38).

The racist and gendered aspects of nation-building were also central to the settlement of the West. The Canadian authorities allowed Eastern and Southern Europeans to enter the country: the men were viewed as hardworking agriculturalists and the women as breeders of future Canadians. However, immigration of free Blacks from Oklahoma to the Prairies was discouraged by the Canadian officials (Abu-Laban & Gabriel, 2002, p. 39). Their move into the nation was depicted in the media as the "Invasion of Negros". In fact, the Athabasca Landing Board of Trade stated that, "Canada is the last country open to the white race. Are we going to preserve it for the white race, or are we going to permit blacks free use of large portions of it" (as cited in Abu-Laban & Gabriel, 2002, p. 39).

In addition to racist and sexist policies, ideological and political concerns were influential in determining who was accepted into Canada as would-be Canadians and as future ideal citizens. The Bolshevik Revolution of 1917 and the rise of unionism propelled the state to deny entry to members of entire groups, such as Russians, Fins, and Ukrainians who were considered to have subversive (anti-capitalists) ideas (Abu-Laban & Gabriel, 2002, pp. 39–40). During the Cold War era, those deemed to be communist sympathisers also were not allowed to immigrate to Canada or the United States. In general, until the early 1960s, factors, such as "race", nationality, ethnicity, gender, occupation, and class, were influential in deciding who entered Canada; in addition, "unsuitability with regard to climatic, economic, social and educational … requirements" were also considered as important factors in considering whether or not the would-be immigrant could become assimilated into the dominant White Anglo Canadian society (as cited in Abu-Laban & Gabriel, 2002, pp. 40–41).

As the above discussion points, the **discourse of Canadian nationalism** was based on the assumption that certain peoples and racialized groups were better suited for citizenship than others (Dua, 2000, p. 55). Social and racial "purity" were interconnected factors in determining who would become part of the nation. Social "purity" implied that Anglo-Saxon Canadians were morally and intellectually "superior" to many other groups, including White Americans. Canada, as John A. Macdonald asserted, was to remain "a white man's country" (as cited in Dua, 2000, p. 57). However, the needs of industrial and agricultural capitalists at times required the temporary immigration of Asians. During the mid- to the end of the 1800s, for example, more than 50,000 men from Asia were permitted into the country (Dua, 2000, p. 57). The dominant view at the time was that Asians were unsuited and incapable of assimilating into the White settler society (Dua, 2000, p. 58). They were temporary residences who would go back to where they came from after there was no need for their labour.

The temporary status of Asian men was due to the implementation of immigration laws and provincial legislations that limited their freedom and prohibited them from voting, holding property, and bringing their wives into Canada (i.e., through measures such as the **head tax**, they had to pay amounts ranging from $200 to $500 to be eligible to enter Canada; **continuous passage**, in order to come to Canada, South Asian men had to travel directly from their home country [India] to Canada, which at the time was not possible since no steamships sailed from ports in India to Canada) (Dua, 2000, pp. 58–59). Single and married South Asian women were also prohibited to enter Canada, which points to the gendered and racialized aspects of Canadian immigration. South Asian women were also viewed as "dangerous," in that their presence would eventually and inevitably lead to the creation of ethnic communities and the reproduction of their members (Dua, 2000, p. 61).

The proliferation of ethnic "minority" non-White communities was thought to undermine the social order based on the **discourse of Whiteness**. This discourse is a powerful ideological tool employed by the power elite to institutionalize racism and racist beliefs. It is more than just a descriptive category; it is also a set of beliefs, ideas, practices, and institutions that materialize a hierarchical formation and systems of domination that result in marginalization and discrimination (Henry & Tator, 2010, p. 6). The culture of White people is the hidden aspect of the normative elements against which cultural and value differences of other groups are judged (Henry & Tator, 2010, p. 6). The presence of ethnic communities, reproduced through the bodies of non-White women, was seen as a threat to the nation-building process in Canada by politicians and the Canadian public at large. In this sense, as mentioned above, the only way that Canada was to reproduce itself was through the bodies of White women (Dua, 2000, p. 62).

Although there were those Canadians who argued that there is a need to apply the principles of fairness to the immigration of Hindu women into Canada, their arguments revolved around the rights of Hindu men to have families (a patriarchal argument) and the fear associated with South Asian men's sexuality to copulate with White women and the creation of unwanted hybrid cultures (a racist conception) (Dua, 2000). In this sense, Whiteness is not simply a reference to one's skin colour but it is also reflective of power, gender, and economic inequalities (Henry & Tator, 2010, p. 6). For example, the intersection of Whiteness with class, gender, ability, and age produces different forms of Whiteness that may or may not experience discrimination (i.e., White single mothers on welfare, homeless/unemployed White males and women) (Henry & Tator, 2010, p. 36).

The *discourse of Whiteness* was a central aspect of imagining Canada. In 1869, the Canada First Movement provided a powerful discourse to distinguish between Canadians and other "races", including the Americans. Canada was considered as being settled by the Northern "races", which symbolized masculinity, self-reliance, health, and unity (Mackey, 2010, p. 23). In contrast, Southern "races" were perceived to be characterized as decaying and "effeminacy … disease", and division (Mackey, 2010, p. 23). Northern "races" were the champions of freedom and liberty. The Southern "races" were depicted as degenerates. The aim was to keep the North uncontaminated by the southern elements. In fact, it was thought that the climate of Canada would assist in the process of keeping the "Negro race" out, which could assist Canada to avoid the "Negro problem" that had plagued the United States (Mackey, 2010, p. 23). Canada stood as the epitome of the 'White Race" since its composition had not been diluted by the effects of Southern climate and immigration of non-Whites. In this discourse, even the French Canadians were ignored since it was assumed that they would cease to exist within generations (Mackey, 2010, pp. 23–24).

The power of the *discourse of Whiteness* is evident in the lack of knowledge about Black Canadians. As Sylvia Hamilton (2010, p. 61) has argued, there are Black communities in Nova Scotia, but you would not learn about them in most history textbooks. Black people in Nova Scotia have a long and rich history in Canada. However, they are even absent in tourist guides and official provincial advertisements, displays, and brochures. The first Black person who arrived in Canada in 1605 was Mathiue da Costa, who acted as the interpreter for Sieur De Monts translating from Micmac to French (Hamilton, 2010, p. 61). By the 1700s, 3,000 Black Loyalists, who were free, came to Nova Scotia during the American War of Independence. There were also other Black people who arrived in Nova Scotia during the same time period with White Loyalists as "servants for life" (Hamilton, 2001, p. 61). There was, furthermore, a small population of Black slaves who were forcefully brought to Nova Scotia from Africa. After the War of 1812, 2,000 more Blacks arrived in Nova Scotia as refugees, who were former slaves in the United States. In 1796, about 500 Jamaican Maroons "immigrated" to Nova Scotia, who waged war against the British colonialists in this province (Hamilton, 2010, p. 63).

One of the main experiences of Blacks in Nova Scotia has been racism and discrimination. They were segregated into different schools. They had to sit in the balconies of movie theatres. Their skin colour was a marker of their status within society as outsiders and those who did not belong. The Black loyalists who were promised agricultural land in Nova Scotia received smaller parcels of un-arable land in comparison to their White counterparts (Hamilton, 2010, p. 63). As a result, 1,200 of them decided to migrate to Sierra Leone in West Africa in 1792 in order to build a better life for themselves and their children. The Maroons also left Canada to the same place in 1800. In fact, the present legacy of Blacks in Nova Scotia began with the arrival of Black refugees after the War of 1812. In addition, many ministers owned slaves and they separated mothers from daughters when unruly behaviours occurred (Hamilton, 2010, p. 62). These slaves were not able to purchase their freedom and remained the property of their "masters". Even after the death of the owner, they were divided amongst the living relatives of the "master". Although many slaves escaped to secure their freedom, slave owners advertised rewards for their return in the newspapers.

Not only do Canadians not learn about this history of Black "immigration" to Canada, the history of Black women is also untold. Black women were involved in more than just working as domestic helpers in their "masters'" homes. For example, Sylvia who served in the house of Colonel Creighton, helped to supply ammunition to the colonel and his forces during the American attempt to invade Nova Scotia in 1782. She saved the life of his son and made sure that his valuables were hidden in a well when his farm was under attack by the American forces. However, her efforts were not recognized, yet her master was given cash payments for his bravery from the country's land taxes (Hamilton, 2010, p. 62). Slave women's histories are also untold. Many of them became mistresses of influential White colonialists. Free Black loyalist women "endeavoured to provide a livelihood for themselves and their families while at the same time labouring to establish communities" (Hamilton, 2010, p. 62). They acted as teachers instructing children. For example, thanks to the efforts of some, a tradition of Black women teachers was established in 1787, which has been upheld and continues to flourish. These stories and histories are silenced and do not find reflection in the official discourses about Canada.

Aboriginal Peoples, Colonialism, Internal Colonialism, and Schooling: Total institutions and resocialization

In order to better understand the effects of schooling on Aboriginal peoples, it is important to explore and analyze how the conflation of political, social, and economic factors have been impinged on their lives after contact (Dyck, 1994; 1995, p. 31). The processes of *colonization* and *internal colonialism* have adversely affected the Aboriginal groups thanks to the implementation of a welter of policies and laws, including the **Indian Act** of 1876. The reservation system is an example of *internal colonialism*, which was imposed on Aboriginal peoples (Frideres, 1998, p. 3). It is important to note, however, that the *reserves* are also conceptualized by Aboriginal peoples as their homelands that provide them spaces where they can practice their cultures and resist the dominant Anglo/French-societies). **We can delineate six general areas of the effects of the colonial process. First**, it is about the taking over of the land and geographical space. **Second**, it has had social and cultural effects as White colonizers destroyed the systems of politics, culture, kinship, and religions of Aboriginal peoples.

Third, it is the imposition of external political structures on the Aboriginal peoples by turning them into wards of the state. For example, until 1940, Indian Affairs officials decided whether or not Aboriginal people could leave their reserve land (Frideres, 1998, p. 4). The *Indian Act* also gave the state the power to arrest Aboriginal peoples living in *reserves* other than their own (Henry & Tator, 2010, p. 107). Although Aboriginal bands are "allowed" to elect their own chiefs, these bodies play an advisory role and have no real powers; Aboriginal "council recommendations continue to be subjected to acceptance or rejection by government of Canada" (i.e., the Department of Indian Affairs and Northern Development) (Frideres, 1998, p. 4). In addition, only men were given the right to vote in band election. This sexist policy was only changed in 1951 when Aboriginal women were given the right to vote in selecting members of their councils (Henry & Tator, 2010, p. 107).

The **fourth** element is the creation of economic, social, political, and cultural dependency on the dominant society for various services and provisions. The dependence of Aboriginal communities and *reserves* is due to the fact that the White society treats *reserves* as "geographical and social hinterlands [peripheries] for" corporate and capitalist exploitation (Frideres, 1998, p. 5). The ***Indian Act*** for example enabled the government in the late 1890s to take over the "Indian" land considered "idle" and "surplus" and handed them over to White settlers. However, the Act also prohibited the sale of Aboriginal agricultural products without official permission by officials (Henry & Tator, 2010, p. 107); a policy that ensured their products would not compete with White farmers' agricultural yields. This was a discursive practice aimed at displacing the political sovereignty of Aboriginal peoples through a system of control and segregation, intended at separating them from the dominant society (Henry & Tator, 2010, p. 107). This was also a way to control them through the **discourse of tutelage**, a paternalistic means of infantilizing Aboriginals by treating them as children who were to be under the supervision of the state (Henry & Tator, 2010, p. 107). By 1911, the changes to the *Indian Act* also allowed the state to take over the *reserve* land to be used for road and other public projects by municipalities (Frideres, 1998, p. 5). Historically, the federal policy has also streamed Aboriginal peoples toward agricultural occupations and jobs in primary industries, which have limited their access to positions of power (Frideres, 1998, p. 5). In addition, Aboriginal peoples were not permitted to vote in provincial elections, a policy which ended as recently as after World War II. They were federally enfranchised in 1960.

The **fifth** element of *colonization* has been "the provision of low-quality social services" for the Aboriginal peoples. The **sixth** element of ***colonization*** is the pervasiveness of racist views and how Aboriginal peoples are treated. All these elements are interrelated and will be discussed in the context of the effects of residential schools on Aboriginal societies.

DID you know that ...?

Although education is a provincial responsibility, Aboriginal educational policies are the responsibility of the federal government. In fact, "jurisdictional disputes ... have restricted educational funding and services for the First Nations people and produced considerable variations in the nature and quality of educational servicers" for various Aboriginal groupings (Wotherspoon, 2009, pp. 248–249). As a result, on/off-reserve registered Indians, Metis, non-status Indians and Inuit have been facing discrimination. This discrimination is compounded by the fact that the teaching materials that are used in the education system are not culturally sensitive and the majority of teachers working with/in Aboriginal students and communities are not trained to teach in these settings and communities.

As the above points out, White conceptions of White-Aboriginal relations are informed by the *ideology* and *discourse of* **Social Darwinism**. Aboriginal peoples have been treated and viewed as objects of paternalist policies based on the concept of wardship (Henry & Tator, 2010, p. 97).

This discourse has a long history, beginning with the first contact between the two groups of people. We can divide this history of contact into four distinct periods. During the **first period**, from the sixteenth century to the late seventeenth century, this relationship was characterized by "mutual tolerance and respect" (Henry & Tator, 2010, p. 98). The **second period**, during the eighteenth century, the relationship between Whites and Aboriginal groups was characterized by trading and military alliances as France and England competed to dominate the region (Henry & Tator, 2010, p. 98).

The **third period**, beginning in 1780 and ending in the 1870s, is dominated by assimilationist policies that resulted in the displacement of many Aboriginal peoples. During this period, the relationships between the colonizers and colonized was characterized by expropriation, theft, and extreme regulation (Henry & Tator, 2010, p. 98). At the time when Southern Ontario was being populated by White settlers, for example, three main options were open to native peoples: **extermination**, **amalgamation** with the internal colonists, and "enforced civilization in communities isolated from whites" (Canada's response) (Dyck, 1995). During this period, the state began institutionalizing its approach to Aboriginal peoples based on economic considerations, which informed the creation of the *reserve system* (Henry & Tator, 2010, p. 102). **Segregation** of Aboriginal peoples into the *reserve system* coincided with **assimilationist policies**, such as the "1857 Act to Encourage the Gradual civilization of the Indian Tribes", which required Aboriginal peoples to be of good character, to let go of their Indian Status in order to become enfranchised. This policy was resisted by the Aboriginal people, as they viewed it as a way for the state to attack and undermine the "land base of Aboriginal communities" (Henry & Tator, 2010, p. 105). Several elements informed the administration of "Indian" affairs in Canada:

a) legislation, including the *Indian Act* and the Canadian constitution;

b) administrative structure in the form of the Department of Indian Affairs;

c) *system of reservation*, and special status; and

d) knowledge about "Indians" (Dyck, 1995).

All these forms have been used to dominate and control the Aboriginal lives and their access to goods, services, and economic, educational, social, and political opportunities. This system was forced upon them. They did not have the option of not accepting it and/or altering it based on their own needs and views.

The **fourth period** has been a continuous process that was "accelerated after publication of the federal government's *White Paper on Indian* Policy in 1969" (Henry & Tator, 2010, p. 98). The government of Canada and many other right-wing groups, in fact, have been trying to get rid of the *Indian Act*, but Aboriginal peoples have been resisting their attempts (See Chapter Seven). This is not to say that Aboriginal people do not criticize the Act and its components. For example, in 1946, the president of North American Indian Brotherhood condemned the Act "as an imposition" and an authoritarian and bureaucratic system (as cited in Haig-Brown, 1988, p. 32). The Aboriginal people have been arguing for **self-government** as the main way to achieve equality and control over their lives. However, the voices of Aboriginal peoples have often been silenced or not heard. In 1946, for example, rather than accepting the recommendations of the North American Indian Brotherhood, the government opted for the inclusion of the recommendation of Diamond Jennes who, in 1947, offered his plan for "liquidating Canada's Indian Problem within 25 years" (Haig-Brown, 1988, p. 32). He argued for the abolition of the *reserves* and an integrated education system as the basis for *assimilation*. However, amendments to the Act did allow Aboriginal students to attend provincial schools, which marked the beginning of the elimination of residential schools by the late 1980s (Haig-Brown, 1988, p. 32).

As above discussions make clear, the *Indian Act* has been amended many times, which points to the "contradictory approach to [allowing Aboriginal peoples and bands to affect policy]" (Haig-Brown, 1988, p. 30). But in reality, the actions of the government to give Aboriginal people a say in influencing, for example, Aboriginal educational policy has often been couched in a language that predetermined what kinds of schools should be established and who should be teaching in them (Haig-Brown, 1988, p. 31). In general, the Act and its amendments have served the interests of the state. By 1920, the Act was amended to include compulsory school attendance of Aboriginal students; a policy that was enforced by the RCMP officers gathering children and sending them to boarding or industrial schools. By this time, the aim of the *Indian Act* and polices it promoted, in the words of Deputy Superintendent General, Duncan Campbell Scott, was to ensure "that Indian cultures as such were to be eliminated" (as cited in Haig-Brown, 1988, p. 31). He stated, "Our objective is to continue until there is not a single Indian in Canada that has not been absorbed into the body politic and there is no Indian question, and no Indian department, that is the whole objective of this Bill" (as cited in Haig-Brown, 1988, pp. 31–32).

Moreover, in 1967, anthropologist Henry B. Hawthorn, who was commissioned by the government to look into the economic, social, and cultural needs of Aboriginal peoples, provided another assimilationist framework to deal with their educational failures and to enhance their upward social mobility (Schissel & Wotherspoon, 2003, p. 56). In his report, Hawthorn maintained that Aboriginal people need to become productive citizens by being schooled in the industrial ways of the White society (Schissel & Wotherspoon, 2003, p. 56). His assumption was also that the cultural values of Aboriginal people stood in their ways of personal and social progress (Schissel & Wotherspoon, 2003, p. 56). He viewed the ideal citizen as a middle class White Canadian who "Indian" children should emulate (Schissel & Wotherspoon, 2003, p. 56). He blamed the cultural values of Aboriginal peoples, such as noncompetiveness, lack of independence, as the sources of the problem. In other words, he used the discourse of **culture of poverty** to explain their lack of success. The solution was for these children to refute their cultures and change their perspectives and attitudes (Schissel & Wotherspoon, 2003, p. 57). This report problematized and pathologized Indian cultures and values. They are the ones who are ultimately responsible for their educational, economic, and social failures. This policy legitimized the historical assumption of the Canadian state that it has had been necessary to remove Aboriginal children from the "backwards" influences of their cultures and communities. In summary, all laws pertaining to Aboriginal peoples have attempted to "hide and conceal what [White Settlers] did and what they continue to do" to Aboriginal peoples (as cited in Schissel & Wotherspoon, 2003, p. 55).

As the above points out, **there are four main discourses that determine and characterize Aboriginal and White relations in Canada**. **First**, the **discourse of nationality** stated that only British identity was to form the basis of the ideal citizen and that all other "ethnic" groups were to become "White British" (Henry & Tator, 2010, p. 116). **Second**, the **discourse of paternalism** drew upon the discourses of **manifest destiny**, **scientific racism**, **social Darwinism**, and **Christian theology** to "civilize" Aboriginal peoples. **Third**, they were deemed "childlike" "creatures" in their "primitive" and "backward" cultures who needed the help of fatherly Whites to grow up and to be modernized. The **discourse of blame the victim** faults Aboriginal peoples for their problems while ignoring the effects of years of domination, tutelage, and oppression on Aboriginal peoples. **Fourth**, Aboriginal relations and peoples are viewed in light of the **discourse of a monolithic "other"**, which fails to consider the complexities of Aboriginal languages, cultures, and political systems and economic consequences of *colonialism* on Aboriginal peoples.

In order to develop a critical and comprehensive anti-hegemonic understanding of the history of Aboriginal and White relations in Canada, we first need to question our taken-for-granted assumptions about the roles of modern institutions, such as the education system and the state and their responsibilities towards citizens of the nation. For example, many of us may believe that central to the ideology of education in the modern world are the axiom and belief that any state has the moral obligation to provide its citizens equal opportunities (Schissel & Wotherspoon, 2003, p. 48). However, what we may fail to understand is that education can actually be used as a tool of domination and **cultural genocide** by the state and its agents. In Canada, one of the philosophical justifications for educating the Aboriginal peoples was that morality and education are inextricably intertwined. The role of schools was to save the "soul" of Aboriginal pupils, which was invoked as a justification to involve the Churches in government plans to school and "educate" the Aboriginal peoples (Schissel & Wotherspoon, 2003, p. 48). Before the establishment of **residential schools**, the earliest forms of schooling were established by the missionaries and religious orders. The main goal of these schools was to replace Aboriginal knowledge systems and cultural values "with European concepts of morality and consciousness" (Wotherspoon, 2009, p. 58). Aboriginal peoples were often viewed the prisms of two main discourses, the *discourse of the illiterate* and the *discourse of the noble savages*, which functioned to romanticize Aboriginal life as peoples in harmony with nature, and at the same time to undermine their cultural knowledge systems and ways of life (Wotherspoon, 2009, p. 58).

The Canadian state policies and the effects of *colonial* and *internal colonial* relations and structures have resulted in the fragmentation of Aboriginal societies. The various Aboriginal educational policies promulgated by the state were institutionalized forms of domination with destructive consequences for Aboriginal communities, families, and peoples. In 1847, the Province of Canada published a policy paper that drew on the ideas of Egerton Ryerson, who promoted the establishment of public schools in Canada, as the basis of government's approach to Indian education (Haig-Brown, 1988, p. 29). The document explicitly stated that the aim is to "raise [the Indians] to the level of the whites, and the ever increasing pressure to take control of land out of Indian control" (as cited in Haig-Brown, 1988p. 29). At the same time, the aim of the state was to protect Aboriginal people from the influences of White society, which were considered evil by isolating them from the dominant society (Haig-Brown, 1988, p. 29). This document recommended that Indians affairs, such as establishing *reserves* and manual schools for them, be the responsibility of the Crown rather than the provincial governments (Haig-Brown, 1988, p. 29). At this time, cultural oppression became written into the laws of the state. The aim of Aboriginal education was not simply to train their minds, "but of weaning [them] from the habits and feelings of their customs, and the acquirements of the language, arts, and customs of civilized life" (as cited in Haig-Brown, 1988, p. 29).

Through the imposition of modern schooling Aboriginal peoples were told that their cultures and values were "inferior" to that of European and Western cultures. The organization and structures of schools and where they were located also resulted in the "separation of children from their [cultures], families, and communities (Wotherspoon, 2009, p. 58). Residential and boarding schools, bureaucratic institutions formed in the 1870s, were employed to deal away with the so-called "Indian problem" (Dyck, 1995). The aim of these schools was to replace the cultural knowledge necessary for life in Aboriginal communities with European cultural, religious, and educational knowledge. In residential schools, for example, children were punished for speaking their native languages, and they were prohibited from interacting with other family members in the school.

As Haig-Brown (1988, p. 28) stated, the Oblates who aimed at saving the souls of Aboriginal peoples in British Columbia viewed their migratory lifestyle as primitive and considered "settlement into an agrarian lifestyle as a positive step for Native people". To teach Aboriginal peoples farming techniques and skills was seen as introducing progress to these people and bringing them into "line with White European standards" (Haig-Brown, 1988, p. 28). In fact, by 1869, residential schools were believed to be effective tools for teaching Aboriginal people agrarian lifestyle, and, as a result, "assimilating them into a 'superior', European society" (Haig-Brown, 1988, p. 29). According to their survivors, residential schools were mainly involved in exploiting students' labours. In many schools, students were put to work, performing manual labour on the farms and in schools. In most cases, schools and their farms were maintained by exploiting the labour of students "at the expense of their education" (Schissel & Wotherspoon, 2003, p. 50). In these schools, academic/curricula contents of education were compromised as a result of the emphasis placed on "the philosophies and morality of labour" (Schissel & Wotherspoon, 2003, p. 53). It was thought that moral redemption could only be achieved through labour. The goal of the Department of Indian Affairs was to encourage the development of manual skills and "to remove prejudice against labour and to give courage to compete with the rest of the world" (as cited in Schissel & Wotherspoon, 2003, p. 53). The focus was on vocational education, which eventually resulted in the formation of half-day schools "in which education accounted for half-day and labour occupied the other half" (Schissel & Wotherspoon, 2003, p. 53). However, rather than imparting skills, Aboriginal students were used as free-labour (Schissel & Wotherspoon, 2003, p. 54).

The schooling of Aboriginal people in Canada and the establishment of residential schools also highlight the global aspect of colonial domination, since these schools were modeled on the similar types of boarding schools already established in the United States by Major J.S. Pratt. After the establishment of the *Indian Act* in 1876, the government commissioned N.F. Davin to study the American industrial schools. These schools were the end result of American policies of *aggressive civilization* introduced by President Grant in the United States.

Davin recommended that Indian education must be controlled by the Churches for two main reasons. **First**, it would have been unrealistic to take away Aboriginal ways of thinking and acting upon the world without replacing them with "civilized" and "positive and uplifting" sets of belief systems that were not simple like the Indian mythology (Schissel & Wotherspoon, 2003, p. 49). **Second**, it would have been a lot easier to find "teachers" with values and virtues that would not cost the government as much money. He believed that the Aboriginal children did not possess the same "inherited aptitudes" as White pupils due to their "semi-civilized" nature (as cited in Schissel & Wotherspoon, 2003, p. 49). Education and schools were, then, viewed as the solution and panacea for cultural *inferiority* of Aboriginal children (Schissel & Wotherspoon, 2003, pp. 51–53). These children were considered morally "inferior" (Schissel & Wotherspoon, 2003, p.50). As Randy Fred (1988, p. 24) maintained, "the objective of these schools was the total integration and elimination of all Indian cultures, like the Canadian objectives".

Central to the implementation of residential schools was the **discourse of tutelage** (Dyck, 1995). This discourse was a powerful tool used in dominating Aboriginal peoples in Canada. It is based on the assumption that individuals must change their attitudes to changing social conditions, but they are often incapable of doing it themselves. They therefore need the help of a tutor in order to achieve their goals. Informed by this assumption, government officials acted on the premise that the state knows what is good for the "Indians" who were thought to be incapable of coping with the effects of colonial contact and could change their attitudes. The discourse of the "noble savage" constructs the "Indians" as individuals who live in "primordial" and "unspoiled natural" order that preceded Western civilization. This image of "noble savage" is constructed in opposition to the harsh conditions brought about by the industrialization and urbanization processes by the Europeans. Such an image also assumed that Native peoples were "incapable of coping with the changes triggered by the coming of white people" (Dyck, 1995, p. 33). This discourse provided the ideological justification for controlling "Indian" land. As mentioned above, the reservation system was also another solution to avoid costly military campaigns against the "Indians". In fact, by the 1820s, the administration of "Indian" affairs was transferred from the military to civilian authorities (Dyck, 1995, p. 37).

It is in this light that Fred (1988), in his forward to *Resistance and Renewal: Surviving the Indian Residential School*, stated that the effects of *colonialism* and *neocolonial* relations everywhere have been the same: these policies have resulted in "displacement and elimination of indigenous culture[s]" (Fred, 1988, p. 15). He asserted that the colonialists drew upon two methods of *genocide* to achieve their goals: **intentional** and **unintentional**. The *intentional genocide* was in the form of laws and policies, such as the *Indian Act* and the establishment of residential schools. The *unintentional forms* were the introduction of diseases that decimated a large portion of Aboriginal populations across the world. In fact, this approach has been dubbed "the first form of germ warfare". One of the most effective ways of achieving **cultural genocide** was the elimination of Aboriginal languages, and their replacement with English, French, or Spanish.

Residential schools functioned as a form of **total institutions** that attempted to resocialize Aboriginal peoples by replacing their norms and values with the culture of the dominant White-Settler societies (Wotherspoon, 2009). Erving Goffman delineated five types of total institutions that tend to target specific groups of people. **First**, there are those institutions that care for those individuals who do not pose any danger to society and who are considered as not being able to take care of themselves, such as "the homes for the blind, the aged, the orphaned, and the indigent" (Goffman, n.d., p.1). **Second**, there are also those institutions that care for individuals considered a threat to society and incapable of taking care of themselves, such as "TB sanitariums, mental hospitals, and leprosarium" (Goffman, n.d., p.1). **Third**, there are those total institutions that house individuals considered dangers to society, such as "jails, penitentiaries, POW camps, and concentration camps" (Goffman, n.d., p.1). **Fourth**, other institutions are established "to pursue some technical task and justifying themselves only on these instrumental grounds", such as army camps and barracks, boarding schools (residential schools), work camps, colonial compounds (Goffman, n.d., p.1). The last form of total institutions are training facilities for religious groups, such as monasteries and convents (Goffman, n.d., p.1).

Resocialization refers to a process of socialization that is deliberate and aims at changing and altering the personality of individuals and their identities. It is a process that promotes relearning new values, norms, and ethics. The goal is to alter the personality of those involved through controlled measures within confined and specific environments. *Resocialization* often occurs in the total institutions, such as prisons, mental asylums, boot camps, and residential schools.

Total institutions are bureaucratic spaces and settings in which individuals are separated from the rest of society. In these institutions the personalities and behaviours of individuals are under the scrutiny and gaze of the staff of such institutions. The staff has authority over the individuals and determines all the activities in which they are supposed to participated. The staff is involved in manipulating the individuals who are isolated from the wider society to perform tasks with the goal of achieving the objectives of the administrative staff. As Goffman (n.d., p. 2) pointed out, total institutions are informed by four main characteristics. **First**, all activities take place in the same space and under the authority of a single entity. **Second**, "each phase of the member's daily activity will be carried out in the immediate company of a large batch of others, all of whom are treated alike and required to do the same thing together" (Goffman, n.d., p. 2). **Third**, all activities are forcefully scheduled, and are logically arranged in a sequence by authorities following explicit formal norms and rules. **Fourth**, the purposes of the activities and their contents reinforce the overall rational plan designed to achieve the official aims of the institution.

Although the staff in total institutions is supposed to consist of trained individuals knowledgeable in specific areas of expertise, this was not the case in many residential schools. The majority of the teachers in these schools were clergy or nuns with no teacher training. In these institutions activities were regimented and performed by all individuals whose lives were affected by the same circumstances and events. The types of activities promoted in the residential schools were decided by those in charge of these institutes, and the aim of all activities was to satisfy the needs and functions of the institution. In these institutions, staff attempted to undermine the individual's autonomy and to established new conceptions of self-identity through what sociologists call **degradation ceremony**, humiliation, and abasement of the old self. The new sense of self was constructed through the establishment of a series of methods that manipulated individuals to accept the new identities by rewarding those who complied and punishing those who resisted.

Goffman also argued that in total institutions there is a split between the staff and those who are supervised by the staff (e.g., inmates in a prison, and Aboriginal students in residential schools). As Goffman (n.d., p. 2) stated, members of both groups perceive one another in stereotypical and hostile ways. Staff considers themselves more "superior" to, for example, inmates, who are constructed as "untrustworthy". In contrast, the inmates view the staff as mean spirited and biased. There is also a distinct social boundary and distance between the staff and "inmates" that cannot be crossed. In the case of residential schools, however, these distinct social boundaries between the staff and students were already created due to, and influenced by, the existing *racial ideologies* and long years of colonial relations. They were, nevertheless, also institutionalized in the context of residential schools as total institutions.

An important process of resocialization in total institutions is the **mortification processes**. Total institutions are not about acculturating or assimilating individuals. Goffman (n.d., p. 3) observed that "they effectively create and sustain a particular kind of tension between the home world and the institutional world and use this persistent tension as a strategic leverage in the management of men [and women]". In total institutions, the conception of the self already developed by the individual is questioned, and their perceptions of the self are systematically and intentionally **mortified**, (i.e., **shamed**). They face "abasements, degradations, humiliations, and profanations of self" (Goffman, n.d., p.3). Their personal identities are reconfigured. For Aboriginal people, this meant that they could not use their "Indian" names to refer to one another. They could not speak their languages and could not practice their rituals. They could not dress in their cultural attires: their hair was cut short and they were to dress in European clothing.

In residential schools, as total institutions, a hierarchy of authority also existed that undermined Aboriginal cultural norms based on respect and mutual understandings. Authority system in total institutions has three distinctive characteristics that were also found in residential schools. **First**, any member of the staff had the right to discipline Aboriginal students for minor infractions of institutional norms and values. **Second**, the power of the authority to impose positive and negative sanctions for accepting or undermining institutional rules happened constantly and were directed to various issues and matters. **Third**, misbehaviours in one area affected the life of the individuals in other areas.

The consequences of residential schools on Aboriginal students have been manyfold. The survivors of these institutions were "tortured by their teachers for speaking" their mother tongues, by for example, punishing students using needles that were pushed through their tongues (Fred, 1988, p. 16). Those who were punished for speaking their languages "chose" not to teach their children how to speak Aboriginal languages for fear that they too would be tortured and punished when they would attend residential schools later on. Residential schools were also similar to prisons, where there is a hierarchy amongst prisoners. In residential schools, younger kids were forced by older kids to wash their socks, with refusal eliciting harsh retributions from the older kids (Fred, 1988, p. 19). The structural-hierarchy of the school and student-body "did not always follow the pattern of tribal affiliation or family" amongst Aboriginal peoples (Fred, 1988, p. 19). In these institutions family and tribal members were set against one another. In residential schools, many students were also given inadequate nourishment necessary for the normal development of body and mind. Religion and religious studies were the main core of the curriculum. Students were forced to attend church every morning; and the principals of many of these schools were mainly priests and minsters who were not trained as teachers and educators. As a result of attending residential schools, many students did not get to know their families. These institutions took away the opportunity for these students to be socialized by their families according to the cultural norms of their nations (Fred, 1988, p. 20). Students were also sexually abused by the school supervisors and teachers, some of whom were sadists and had been kicked out of the RCMP or retired from the armed forces (Fred, 1988, p. 20). As Fred reminded us, "Homosexuality was prevalent in the school. I learned how to use sexuality to my advantage, as did many other students, Sexual favours brought me protection, sweets (a rarity in the school), and even money to buy booze. But this had its long term effects … including alcoholism, the inability to touch people …" (Fred, 1988, p. 21).

The residential schools negatively affected the self-perceptions of Aboriginal peoples. For example, as these students read about themselves in their school textbooks, they were always portrayed as the "enemy", pagans, and "uncivilized" (Schissel & Wotherspoon, 2003, p. 53). Being "Indian" was regarded as undesirable". **Whiteness** was imposed as the normal state of being. Not only were these schools involved in *cultural genocide* and what we call "**genocide of authentic selves**", residential schools were also an effective way of stealing their land and resources. The aim was to eliminate, dismantle, and rectify the "Indian Problem" by socializing First Nations youth as "non-Indians". The role of the state in "educating" First Nations children was an attempt to integrate them into the Canadian society, not as equal partners in rebuilding Canada, but as unequal **others**. Lack of knowledge about familial relations, understanding one's culture, and incorporation into Euro-Canadian society as unequal citizens have resulted in social, economic, and cultural problems that have affected First Nations peoples to this day. The end result of residential schools has been the miseducation of Aboriginal youths. For example, between 1890 and 1950, the majority of students did not advance past Grade 3 (Schissel & Wotherspoon, 2003, p. 54). In 1930, out of one hundred students, only three went past Grade 6.

DID you know that …?

From the 1940s to the 1980s, residential schools were viewed as child-care centres, assuming that the parents of these children were incapable of socializing their kids. In the files of these students, during this period, one can read comments, such as the child has "shiftless fathers" "unmarried mothers", and "live in poor homes" without supervision (Schissel & Wotherspoon, 2003, p. 58). Social problems affecting Aboriginal kids were blamed on "parental moral shortcomings" (Schissel & Wotherspoon, 2003, p. 58). In fact, during the 1960s and 1970s, more than 50 percent of Aboriginal children in residential schools were institutionalized because it was thought that "their parents had neglected them or they were not equipped and capable of taking care of them" (Schissel & Wotherspoon, 2003, p. 58).

The educational inequalities facing Aboriginal peoples have continued since the establishment of residential schools in the form of reserve-based school and provincial school systems. The Canadian education systems have continued to contribute to the marginalization and experiences of failure of Aboriginal students (Wotherspoon, 2009, p. 247).

During the mid-1990s and 2003–4, the number of registered "Indians" between ages 6 and 16 living on-reserve who were enrolled in full-time K-12 programs "declined from 87 per cent to 80 per cent" (the rate for the general population of the same age category was over 95 per cent) (Wotherspoon, 2009, p. 247). At the postsecondary education level, Aboriginal peoples are also less likely to be enrolled in university and college courses and programs than the general population. In the late 1990s, only 6.6 percent of the registered Native Canadian population between the ages 17 to 34 enrolled in postsecondary full-time university programs. In contrast, the rate for the general population during the same period was 11.4 percent education (Wotherspoon, 2009, p. 248).

In Saskatchewan, where 13.2 percent of the population is of Aboriginal backgrounds, only 2 percent of all students who graduated from postsecondary studies in 2003 were Aboriginals. In Canada as a whole, in 2006, 53.5 percent of those identifying as having Aboriginal identities "had high school equivalency or less", where as 39.4 percent of the general population were categorized in this group (Wotherspoon, 2009, p. 248). In contrast, 22.9 percent of the general population had university degrees, whereas only 7.5 percent of Aboriginal peoples had such degrees and certification (Wotherspoon, 2009, p. 248).

DID you know that ...?

In addition to the consequences of residential schools and the inherent racist policies of the Canadian state, the fact that Aboriginal people have not been involved in the process of educational decision-making and curriculum development have also been influential in the under-representation and underachievement of Aboriginal people in educational institutions. The dominant educational policies continue to promote Anglo-conformity (Wotherspoon, 2009, p. 248).

In spite of the negative consequences of years of colonial and postcolonial relations for Aboriginal peoples, it is important to resist from viewing them as "victims" and people without agency. In fact, Aboriginal people have been actively involved in effecting change and influencing the education of their children. They have historically organized themselves to effect policy changes, to improve the educational experiences of their students, and enhance their socioeconomic positions. The education system, at the same time, is envisioned by Aboriginal leaders and Elders as a tool to support Aboriginal interests and improve their life-chances in society. For example, in 1972, the National Indian Brotherhood published a position paper, *Indian Control of Indian Education*, arguing that it is important for Aboriginal nations to take control of their education as part of the general approach to self-determination and self-government initiatives. As a result, the numbers of schools operated by

Indian bands have been on the rise, with "three out of five on-reserve registered Indians" now attending such schools at various levels. Aboriginal communities and educators have also been involved in producing curricular material that is attentive to their needs and accounts for their history of domination and resistance. Although these initiatives have resulted in more Aboriginal students to graduate from these programs and attend postsecondary education since 1972, the numbers of have been declining since the 1990s (Wotherspoon, 2009, p. 250).

In general, for Aboriginal people living off-reserve, their attainment of higher educational credentials has been translated into better economic positions and status, overall; however, "Aboriginal people pursuing post-secondary studies remain relatively under-represented in the most prestigious or highly skilled fields, focusing instead in such areas as human services, trade and construction, and technologies for men and commercial and human services and clerical programs for women" (Wotherspoon, 2009, p. 252). In fact, it can be concluded that registered Indian women tend to have a weaker labour market participation and success than registered Indian men. Both groups are also highly concentrated in specific fields and occupations that are not highly skilled (Wotherspoon, 2009, p. 254). We can also conclude that "considerable evidence points to the reality that Aboriginal people in general are more likely than other Canadians to experience a diminished relationship between education and social and economic opportunities" (Wotherspoon, 2009, p. 254).

Part Five

Nation-Building, Immigration, and Multiculturalism: the case of Canada

Rethinking the Mosaic Metaphor

In popular accounts of the narration of nation, Canada is often viewed as a **mosaic** in which a number of different ethnic, religious, and racial groups live in peaceful coexistence and appreciate the characteristics and contributions of all other groups to the multicultural image of Canada (Francis, 1997, p. 80). The metaphor of the *mosaic* was used as an instrument by John Murray Gibbon, a publicist hired by the Canadian Pacific Railway (CPR), to construct how Canadians should live together, which would set them apart from the Americans. This usage of the term was very different from its original conceptualization by Victoria Hayward in 1922, who used the term to refer to the "patchwork nature of exotic churches erected by the many different religions" in the Canadian prairies (Francis, 1997, p. 80). In fact, Gibbon popularized this term as a way to offer a new image of a postcolonial Canada that replaced the identification of Canadians with Britain (Francis, 1997, p. 81). Gibbon's book, *Canadian Mosaic*, celebrated the cultural diversity of Canada; however, it failed to mention the existence of non-White groups in Canada, which might have been to the general view of the time that these groups were not capable to assimilate into the White culture of Canada (Francis, 1997, p. 82).

In general, there are several points that need to be considered when studying the history of the term, *mosaic*, in Canada. It was promoted by White-Euro-Canadians that only celebrated diversity and did not discuss or account for the inequalities based on factors, such as ethnicity, gender, and "race". It was a way to promote Canada's culture to tourists across the world: the pristine cultural groups in their traditional clothing practicing folk cultures were employed as a marketing tool to sell Canada to the rest of the world. This discourse was based on a folk-arts approach to cultural diversity and *difference* that depicted Canada as a more desirable place in which to live. It is this image that became the precursor to the official multiculturalism policy in Canada (Francis, 1997, p. 83).

Multiculturalism in Canada

Canadians distinguish themselves from Americans in many ways. For one thing, the American system of **cultural pluralism** is termed **melting pot**. That is, American culture is considered to be a mixture of all cultural groups who have equally contributed to its production over the years. America is a place where people let go of their cultural idiosyncrasies and adopt the American way and cultural norms. In this light, ethnic groups are amalgamated. **Amalgamation** is a process through which all ethnic groups contribute to the construction of the nation's culture and in the process lose their ethnic identities as a new national identity is formed (Hiller, 2006, p. 216). However, in both the United States and Canada, there has been a pressure on "minority" ethnic groups to assimilate into the dominant culture by groups that espouse **nativism**. *Nativism* is an *ideology* that claims new groups pose threats to the national identity and stability of the nation and therefore policies must be put in place to ensure their exclusion or *assimilation* (Hiller, 2006, p. 216). In fact, *nationalists* and *nativists* in Europe claim multiculturalism is a defunct policy and call for the protection of the cultures of the dominant societies in Europe from the dangers of immigrant groups, mainly Moslem immigrants in England, Italy, Germany, and the Netherlands.

Officially, the three goals of Canadian approach to multiculturalism were:

1. to assist the government construct a new national identity,
2. to enhance civic participation of all members, and
3. to promote social justice.

We often view Canada as a *mosaic* consisting of different colourful equal tiles. This image is misleading since these tiles are not equal in worth. In fact, "some are raised while others are lowered, reflecting differences in social status and unequal contribution to society" (Fleras & Elliott, 2002, p. 41). Such a reality, notwithstanding, multiculturalism preaches inclusiveness. The assumption is that a commitment to equality will enhance structural integration of diverse groups into the national identity.

The **discourse of multiculturalism** thereby assumes that Canada practices tolerance, is sensitive to other cultures and their needs, and achieves harmony through *difference* and diversity (Henry & Tator, 2010, p. 15). It is a powerful *ideology* that informs the way through which Canada is perceived around the world. Multiculturalism is a discourse (the law for that matter, as enshrined in the

Multicultural Act of 1988) that actually elevates English Canadian culture as the norm upon which every other culture is considered as multicultural (Henry & Tator, 2010, p. 317; Case Study 12.2). **It is a way of locating who is *different* and who is not willing to assimilate** (Henry & Tator, 2010, pp. 317–318; Case Study 12.2). However, as Augie Fleras and Jean Leonard Elliot (1992) pointed out, multiculturalism is a multifaceted term. It means different things to different people with different perspectives and experiences. Goli Rezai Rashti (1994, p. 76) also maintained that after two decades of multiculturalism in Canada, "the meaning of the term and its implications for education remain obscure and problematic".

The discourse of multiculturalism is related to the concerns about immigration but it was originally developed as a result of the intersections of three interrelated factors: the rise of French nationalism that undermined Canadian federalism during the early 1960s, the anti-hegemonic discourses of "minority" cultures that questioned their exclusion from being considered as important actors in the process of nation-building in Canada (i.e., Ukrainians); and "the aggressive state intervention in social policy" (Ghosh & Abdi, 2004, p. 103). The multicultural Act was the end result of opposition to the findings and recommendations of the Royal Commission on Bilingualism and Biculturalism, which assumed that the founding nations of Canada are the French and British, thus, ignoring the role of the Aboriginal groups and their status as other founding nations of Canada (Ghosh & Abdi, 2004, p. 104). In fact, Henry and Tator (2010, pp. 116–117) maintained that the discourse of multiculturalism reflected the desire of the Federal government to get rid of the *Indian Act* and its legal and treaty obligations to Aboriginal peoples by treating them as "ethnic minorities" in Canada, without any legal rights outside the **Canadian Charter of Rights and Freedoms** and *Multiculturalism Act. Multiculturalism Act* is a controversial concept and policy, which attempts to deal with diversity and accommodate pluralist aspects of liberalism. In general, we can conceptualize this policy in three general ways. **First**, as a **discourse of social organization**, legitimizing and narrating the place of "minority" cultures in relation to French and British elite groups (Ghosh & Abdi, 2004, p. 104). **Second**, it is a form of **political ideology** that has enabled Canada to define its identity along a pluralist framework, distinguishing Canada from the United States. **Third**, as a **policy**, multiculturalism establishes a set of consensus about equality and equity in Canada that builds upon the notion of "unity within diversity" (Ghosh & Abdi, 2004, p. 105). The main objectives of the multicultural policy were:

1. to help all cultural groups to contribute to the process of nation-building and to grow within the context of the framework of Canada as a nation-state;

2. to help "minority" groups to break barriers that undermine their socioeconomic positions in society;

3. to entice intergroup relations and interactions; and

4. to assist "minority" peoples to learn one of the two official languages (Ghosh & Abdi, 2004, p. 105).

Multiculturalism is also a **descriptive** term that points to actual and "real" cultural diversity and *difference* without accounting for power-inequalities in ethno-racial interactions and relations

(Fleras & Elliott, 1992, pp. 68–69). Often, in both public and media discourses, the term "cultural diversity" refers to "immigrant" cultures mainly those of non-European and/or non-White backgrounds. In this sense, multiculturalism is a discourse based on the idea of "race," which is expressed through **discourses of cultural differences**. It is a way of constructing **otherness** within the context of postcolonial and imperialist relations without discussing and considering the effects of racism (Fleras & Elliott, 1992, pp. 68–69). It attempts to delineate "minorities'" statuses, positions, and rights sociologically, psychologically, and legally in public/private and "scientific" discourses within the context of the **discourse of liberalism**.

Multiculturalism is also a discourse that reflects Easterners' (non-Westerners') desire and non-White populations to create a dialogue about the effects of inequalities and to implement change in Western parts of the world. It is an ideological tool, which is perceived to be different from the goals and consequences of **assimilationist** and **melting pot** approaches to cultural diversity. Multiculturalism, then, is not only a tool in managing diversity, but it is as well a process through which diversity is politicized and "minority" rights are acknowledged (Fleras & Elliott, 1992, pp. 68–69).

Multiculturalism is a set of liberal ideas about *difference*. It is knowledge about *difference*, which is produced and maintained by the elites in the West, mainly male, middle-class, heterosexual, and Christian. As such, it is a source of power. It manages diversity through existing socioeconomic relations and structures. It is a local/national way of dealing with the effects of globalization of the economy, information, and "immigration"/"migration" issues.

That is, multiculturalism is a discourse of managing how various ethnic groups should be living in harmony with one another in society. It assumes that people have the right to belong to their own cultures in the context of dominant culture. For example, the two "main" functions of *Multiculturalism Act* were:

1. to reduce tension in Quebec: French language became one of the official languages of Canada; and

2. to promote the integration of "minority" cultures into the political sphere since "minorities" were viewed as exercising tremendous voting power due to their concentrations in major urban centres of Canada.

However, Quebecois and the First Nation groups have criticized the government of Canada for introducing multiculturalism as a federal policy. They argued that the distinct characters/cultures of Quebec and the First Nations and their historical roles in the nation-building process are not recognized within the context *Multiculturalism Act* (Fleras & Elliott, 1992, p. 120). Their issues, it is claimed, are about power inequalities, group rights, and self-government, which cannot be reconciled within the context of a policy that aims at solving "issues pertaining to integration and cultural diversity" (Fleras & Elliott, 1992, p. 120).

Multiculturalism, it seems, actually refers to multiple forms of bicultureness, in which all cultural forms are constructed and valued against dominant values and norms. Multiculturalism has been criticized for its lack of analysis of power relations. More important, there has been a lack of initiating programs, for example, aiming at integrating multiculturalism into school curriculum and "everyday educational activities" (Rezai-Rashti, 1994, p. 76). Multiculturalism has also been criticized for its lack of attention to gender issues (sexism), racist views, and class differences and inequalities. Over the years, however, multiculturalism has been influenced by an **antiracist perspective**, which aims at introducing antidiscriminatory practices to promote equity (Ghosh & Abdi, 2004, p. 106). The Multiculturalism Act of 1988 introduced nine principles, most of which deal with eliminating racial discrimination at individual and institutional levels. It is in this context that critics claim multiculturalism should be understood and practiced. However, as Himani Banerji maintained, it is difficult to conceive of Canada as a multicultural society when, in fact, "all the power relations and signifiers of Anglo-French White supremacy are barely concealed behind a straining liberal democratic façade" (as cited in (Henry & Tator, 2010, p. 318). The Act's approach to racial discrimination is "symbolic" and "non-coercive" (Henry &b Tator, 2010, p. 319).

Four Different Meanings of Multiculturalism: a recap

As we mentioned above, multiculturalism means different things to different people. In general, we can distinguish four distinct definitions of multiculturalism. **First**, multiculturalism is understood as a discourse that highlights Canada's demographic reality. Many different ethno-cultural and linguistic groups live in Canada. Although Canada has always been diverse, since the 1970s, immigration from non-European and non-Western countries has added to the diversity of cultures in Canada. Canada's diversity reflects both regional divisions and ethnic constellations. Canada's regional division is termed **regional multiculturalism**. In order to better understand the history of Canada, we need to apply a regional analysis and consider the differences and similarities between the different regions within Canada.

Despite the globalization of economy, economic clout or power is unevenly distributed. One way to understand this phenomenon is to explore how **regions** within a country relate to one another. By the term **region**, we mean that areas within a country have unique economic, physical, and political dimensions that distinguish them from other parts. Those who live in a *region* often develop a *regional* culture and *society*. *Region* refers to a range of symbols, sets of institutions, behaviours, values, and ideas that arise from people living in a specific **space** that defines their conceptions of the *self* and identity, such as identifying oneself as a Vancouverite living in Ontario. As *regions* are politically transformed into **regionalism**, a sense of belonging and collective consciousness arises. For example, consider the fans of Rough Riders who live in Vancouver, British Columbia and support their team whenever they play B.C. Lions in Vancouver. Their support of this team is a demonstration of their **regional identity** from Saskatchewan, for instance. When *regional identity* is formed through the politicization of regional traits into concrete and experiential phenomena, sociologists speak of *regionalism*. *Regionalism* refers to a dynamic process of politicization of a *regional identity* in relation to other *regional identities* within a nation-state (Hiller, 2006, pp. 137–138). *Regionalism* is a conceptual and analytical tool used to understand Canadian socioeconomic and cultural structures and relations. *Regionalism* has a psychosocial dimension comprising *objective factors*, such as languages spoken, ethnic identity, occupation, industries, and *subjective factors*, such as how people identify themselves, how they feel about their region, which is a reflection of their shared attitudes.

Dreidger (2003) argued that Canada is characterized by **multicultural regionalism**. In fact, there are distinctive regional cultures with different ethnic and linguistic characteristics in Canada. Our identities are influenced by our home and regional cultures. For example, our mother tongues and languages spoken at home and regions inform and shape our world views and values and ways of behaviour. That is, ***ethnic identity*** formation and language are closely related, since in order to pre-serve cultural/ethnic identity, language plays an important role in this process. Although the ethnic and linguistic demographics conform very well to the official bilingual national policy of Canada, Canada's regions are ethnically diverse: Aboriginal majority in Northwest Territories; French major-ity in Quebec; British majority in Newfoundland, Prince Edward Island and Nova Scotia; non-charter and multiple responses majority in five westerly provinces and Yukon. As such, we can identify six distinct Canadian **ethnic regions**: Northlands; Atlantic Region; Quebec; Bilingual belt in the Prairies; Upper Canada; and the West. That is, Canada's different regions are mainly **unicultural/ monocultural** in the east, **multicultural/multilingual** in the northwest, **Aboriginals** in the North, **'other' ethnic groups** in the West, **French** in Quebec, and **British** in the East.

It is important to note that in order for *differences* between *regions* to become objectified and noticed by their inhabitants, people must become aware or conscious of their *differences* from other people who preside in other regions within a country. Several factors explain the growth of *region-alism* in Canada:

1. uneven development,
2. state policy,
3. elite control of economy and capital flows,
4. political structures, and
5. North-South linkages (Hiller, 2006).

Uneven economic development between different regions is a major force behind *regionalism* in Canada. For example, 75% of all corporations and 85% of all financial institutions have been located in central Canada, predominantly in Ontario since the end of the Second World War (Hiller, 2006). At the same time, the two cities of Montreal and Toronto (also referred to as ***primate cities***) have benefited from this concentration more than any other major urban centres in Canada. The con-centration of power in Toronto has also resulted in the formation of ***megalopolis*** centres, stemming directly from the creation of major industrial centres in cities, such as Oakville and Mississauga, resulting in the linkage of cities like Toronto and Hamilton. Evidently, the development of these centres has been at the expense of other regions, which have been "underdeveloped" and thus exac-erbating the regional power differentials and gap between the hinterland [*peripheral* regions] and *core* regions (Hiller, 2006, p. 140).

The other factor that has also played a role in the importance of *regionalism* in Canada is ***state policy***, which has had both indirect and direct consequences for different regions. The fact remains that government policies are not neutral. For example, the protective tariff policy of 1879 resulted in the industrialization of central Canada, the deindustrialization of Maritimes, and turning the West into a raw materials trove for industries in central Canada. During the period from 1930 to 1950, state policies encouraged American direct investment in order to promote strong economic growth in Canada. Although the government aimed at promoting growth in regions other than Ontario through its regional development and equalization grants, the policy inevitably resulted in an increase in the power of the *core* regions in relation to hinterland. The free trade agreement promoted by the Canadian government has also been blamed for the exacerbation of regional disparity especially in light of transfer payments that some argue resulted in the encouragement of people to stay in their regions rather than to migrate to other regions in search of jobs and better economic opportunities. Multicultural policy woefully fails to adequately address regional differences and the concomitant power asymmetries and competing *regionalisms* in dealing with economic, political, ethnic, and racialized schisms. In this light, multiculturalism has turned out to be a **hegemonic policy**.

Second, **multiculturalism** is an integral part of the **dominant pluralist ideology**. As an *ideology*, it is a set of ideas, objectives, and beliefs about what multiculturalism *should be*. It defines Canadian national identity in such a way that it sets it apart from the American **melting pot** ideals. Multiculturalism promotes survival of ethnic identities and subcultures, and also promotes equality and equity between groups. According to Fleras and Elliott (2002, pp. 37–38), multiculturalism is an ideologically-based discourse since it functions as a description about "how Canadian society ought to work in its social organization". It is based on the idea of accepting and "taking difference seriously". **Diversity** is considered desirable and the basis for developing a national identity, unity, and achieving socioeconomic progress (Liodakis & Satzewich, 1998, p. 97). In this context, all cultures are deemed equal. It assumes individuals have the desire to view themselves as culturally and ethnically different, and allows for self-identification in terms of cultural identities. However, as an *ideology*, "it privileges some perspectives as natural, normal and superior" (Fleras & Elliott, 2002, p. 35), and "it shapes what we see, how we think, what we experience and how we relate to the world at large" (Fleras & Elliott, 2002, p. 35). As a *dominant ideology*, it privileges certain positions (those promoting the interest of the ruling classes) "through its capacity to dominate debates over what is acceptable or normal" (Fleras & Elliott, 2002, p. 36). Cultural diversity is not viewed as divisive. In fact, the idea behind the slogan *Diversity within Unity* assumes that individual affiliations "must be first with the state" (Fleras & Elliott, 2002, p. 38).

Multiculturalism is based on the notion of **cultural relativism** and not **ethnocentric** views (Liodakis & Satzewich, 1998, p. 97). Cultural relativists suggest that individuals should not judge other cultures based on their own cultural standards, but on the "evaluative criteria" within that specific culture. That is, in order to evaluate a culture, we need to base it on the values and norms internal to that culture rather than using external cultural standards to evaluate a culture (Liodakis & Satzewich, 1998, p. 97). In this view, knowledge is historically determined and "socially constructed" (Fleras & Elliott, 2002, p. 38). The main assumption is that there are no standards that are universal: "All cultures are equally good and right" (Fleras & Elliott, 2002, p. 39). However, it is important to note that *cultural relativism* implies *tolerance*, which is different from *acceptance*. The assumption is that by becoming active in accepting others and promoting diversity, we are paving the road for others to accept those who are culturally different. In this sense, multiculturalism "promotes intergroup tolerance on the assumption that 'the more someone experiences his[/her] own way of life as fulfilling, the more likely he[/she] is to welcome … others'" (Fleras & Elliott, 2002, p. 40). However, this perspective does not account for the fact social actors choose to be *tolerant* towards certain groups and not others. That is, we need to ask who has the power to define certain practices as *tolerable*.

Third, multiculturalism is an avenue for people to raise their discontent and struggle for economic, social, and political access. It can also be regarded as an arena of competition between various groups for "access to valuable economic and political resources". It is a **discourse of conflict resolution**. It was developed as a response to the "third force" (i.e., Ukrainian-Canadians) and other cultural "minorities" (visible minorities). These groups criticized the government for its "bicultural" policies that only reflected the Anglo-French cultural elements. Many "minorities" argued that multiculturalism as a policy would endorse and open up "economic opportunities" and would put an end to discrimination in employment (Fleras & Elliott, 2002:46). As such, Fleras and Elliott (2002, p. 46) argued that multiculturalism has empowered non-White men and women to demand equality of opportunities.

Fourth, multiculturalism is defined as a set of government policies and programs. It is a federal state policy in Canada, but it did not originally aim to deal with "the historical legacy of racism, discrimination, and prejudice" (Liodakis & Satzewich, 1998, p. 97). It only gave the impression that changes were occurring. As a policy, it is a way of "uniting all Canadians without actually redistributing power in any fundamental way" (Fleras & Elliott, 2002, p. 42). However, as mentioned, the policy was developed as a response to the critique of the *Royal Commission on Bilingualism and Biculturalism* report of 1963–69 by groups, which argued that their contributions to the nation-building process in Canada was not recognized in the aforementioned report. Multiculturalism is also viewed as a ploy of the liberal government during the 1960s to woo ethnic voters in urban areas, such as Toronto, at a time when ethnic "minorities" were dissatisfied with the federal government. However, it only modified "minority interests to suit the national agenda" (Fleras & Elliott, 2002, p. 42). Multicultural policy also undermined the Quebecois' claims "for equality with English within Canadian confederation" (Fleras & Elliott, 2002, p. 42; Liodakis & Satzewich, 1998, pp. 97–98).

The Four principles and Three Phases of Multiculturalism

There are **four basic principles** that informed the development of multiculturalism as a state policy. As already mentioned, the goals of the government were to assist ethnic groups to: **1)** maintain their cultures; **2)** overcome cultural barriers in order to equally participate in Canadian society; **3)** promote cultural exchanges between groups as a way to enhance national unity; and **4)** assist individuals to learn one of the official languages as a way to ensure their integration into Canada (Liodakis & Satzewich, 1998, p. 98). The assumption was that the era of Anglo-conformity was now a part of the past, and, as mentioned, all cultures are now equal to coexist within one nation.

The development of multiculturalism can be divided into three distinct stages (Fleras & Elliott, 2002; Liodakis & Satzewich, 1998, p. 98). **Folkloric multiculturalism** was the first stage through which the focus was on "celebrating our differences" (Liodakis & Satzewich, 1998, p. 98). The Government of Canada would assist all cultural groups to maintain their traditions and to overcome cultural barriers in order to fully participate in the Canadian society. The government would promote cultural interconnectedness. The federal government would also assist immigrants to learn one of the official languages. Keeping one's culture is viewed as a matter of personal choice. It is assumed that cultural diversity defines "our" identities as Canadians (Fleras & Elliott, 2002).

Economic Framework, the second phase, was more concerned with the institutionalization of multiculturalism as an Act in 1988. The constitution was repatriated during this time to account for the introduced changes. That is, multiculturalism was turned from a *de facto* to a *de jure* and legal framework (Liodakis & Satzewich, 1998, p. 98). During this period, multiculturalism reflected business and economic factors of the time. The idea of "multiculturalism means Business" was a popular slogan during the 1980s (Fleras & Elliott, 2002, p. 42). The argument was that our culturally and ethnically diverse population could be a very useful tool in enhancing Canada's economic relations with other countries. Multiculturalism became a "valuable resource" (Fleras & Elliott, 2002, p. 42). In this context, the aim of the government to "fight" racism and consider it as a problem was not because of its dehumanizing consequences, but due to its consequences in terms of "inefficient use of human resources" (Liodakis & Satzewich, 1998, p. 108). Although racism and discrimination are considered important issues that need to be dealt with, they are largely perceived as irrational features of a system that otherwise is "rational, peaceful, and harmonious" (Liodakis & Satzewich, 1998, p. 109).

Multiculturalism as an *ideology* is also used "to attract members of transnational elite associated with global capital" (Fleras & Elliott, 2002, p. 44). Canadian culture is constructed as a fair, tolerant, and equal entity (Liodakis & Satzewich, 1998, p. 99). This image is also considered as an important characteristic of Canadian national identity. Multiculturalism is regarded as an asset that establishes Canada as an ideal country worthy of emulation by various countries. This image is advertised in the world (i.e., Canada could assist other countries to establish/implement multicultural programs). This discourse implies that in Canada, a fair and friendly country, racial and ethnic differences do not affect one's position in society. However, **multiculturalism as business** is defined by the business elite and for the purpose of economic growth and is envisioned in the context of the globalization of capitalism and **neoliberal policy** without accounting for their negative unequal consequences (See Chapter Nine).

Civic Multiculturalism, as the name suggests, deals with civic issues (Fleras & Elliott, 2002, pp. 67–68). Some of the elements of the first and second stages were reconsidered and reformulated in the context of the citizenship education that promotes society building through fostering a sense of common identity by promoting antiracist policies (Liodakis & Satzewich, 1998, p. 104). In this stage, the focus is not to foster ethnic cultures, but rather the aim is to incorporate ethnic cultures into the national identity. The goal is tp develop core values of equality, mutual respect, and diversity regardless of one's background (Fleras & Elliott, 2002, p. 68). The aims are to foster a society in which everyone feels a sense of belonging, is able to participate in shaping Canada's culture, and is treated fairly and equally (Fleras & Elliott, 2002, p. 68). The question that arises is the following: "who has the power to define the values and norms upon which the national culture or identity is defined?" (Fleras & Elliott, 2002).

Problems Associated with Multiculturalism

Multiculturalism has been criticized by a number of scholars and groups. For example, it has been argued that multiculturalism is supported only in the context of those values and norms that do not question the legitimacy of the dominant culture. It has **depoliticising** effects: it concentrates on issues such as "song and dance". It does not deal with political, economic, and cultural inequalities and their causes. It has not been fully incorporated due to lack of leadership and funds. It results in the deterioration of intergroup relations. It is, then, a threat that undermines unity and stability of Canada (Liodakis & Satzewich, 1998, pp. 98–105):

1. **It produces stereotypes.** Multiculturalism tends to solely focus on cultural events and attempts to define culture based on the lowest common denominators. It emphasizes *what* people are rather than *who* they are. In its current manifestation, it views cultures and people based on problematic conceptions of food and dance that do not account for diversity and *difference*/inequalities *between* and *within* ethnic groups. For example, Iranians in Canada are comprised of various ethnic groups, such as Persian, Arab, Baluch, Kurd, and Turkish backgrounds. Within this community, Persian category tends to dominate (Mirfakhraie, 1999). In this sense, multiculturalism tends to essentialize *difference* and ignore diversity *within* diversity (Fleras & Elliott, 2002, p. 102).

2. **It promotes cultural relativism.** Critics have pointed out that multiculturalism undermines Canadian values. It eradicates the centre and promotes "everything goes mentality". It does not promote a general and cohesive sense of community but divides ethnic groups, leading to the **Balkanization of society** (See Liodakis & Satzewich, 1998, pp. 101–103). Multiculturalism, it is argued, "fosters an inward-looking mentality" that makes it difficult to promote and construct a national identity in the context of the proliferation of ethnic tribalism (Fleras & Elliott, 2002, p. 99). However, it is important to note that not all cultural practices and customs are accepted in the Canadian brand of multiculturalism. Although female circumcision is practiced by a number of cultural groups around the world, this practice is proscribed in Canada; it is thought to violate human rights of women and "offends notions of equality, human integrity, and other core values prevalent in Canada" (Liodakis & Satzewich, 1998, p. 103). Critics of this law maintain that although this practice is illegal, many women in the West go through breast and other types of body augmentations, practices that equally harm and violate the female body, yet are deemed acceptable and legal.

3. **It ghettoizes ethnic issues.** It results in the treatment of inequalities in the context of approaches to cultural differences. For example, rather than dealing with the internment of Japanese in the context of the Justice Department, it was dealt with by the Ministry of

Multiculturalism. Such issues are justice issues and the consequences of racism and not ethnic issues of dance and food (Liodakis & Satzewich, 1998, p. 103). It is also important to note that there is no minister of multiculturalism in Canada. In fact, multiculturalism is now the responsibility of the Ministry of Canadian Heritage, which symbolizes the extent to which multiculturalism itself is being ghettoized (Liodakis & Satzewich, 1998, p. 104). Multiculturalism is also considered to result in marginalizing ethnic "minorities". The fact that we emphasize their hyphenated identity as, for example, Indo-Canadian, results in their exclusion from being considered as fully Canadian (Fleras & Elliott, 2002, p. 100). In addition, cultures are now **commodified** and are used as marketing tools: visit Toronto where you can experience cultures from across the world (Fleras & Elliott, 2002, p. 103).

4. **It undermines the First Nations' and Quebec's issues**. Multiculturalism weakens Quebec's *nationalism*, as it reduces their concerns to that of "ethnic" issues (i.e., their issues are considered to be cultural dilemmas and not due to political factors). This process is referred to as "minoritizing" Quebecois identity (Liodakis & Satzewich, 1998, p. 104). As already mentioned, it also undermines First Nations' aspirations and demands for self-governance. In this light, they are not viewed as part of the founding nations of Canada, but as ethnic groups (Liodakis & Satzewich, 1998, p. 104).

5. **It depoliticizes social inequality**. From a *political economy perspective*, too much emphasis is placed on cultural factors to the point that inequalities based on structural factors are not considered and problematized, mainly because such cultural views do not question the *status quo* and the legitimacy of the liberal White system. That is, multiculturalism functions as a discourse that gives the impression everything is fine. It assumes that the government is dealing with social issues, such as ethnic economic inequalities. As such, it tends to neutralize people's antagonism toward the state and the ruling classes. Multiculturalism is hegemonic, promoting and exacerbating hierarchies and inequalities along class, gender, and "race" lines and fails to address in any appreciable manner the consequences of racism, sexism, classism, and ableism. Canada's many divisions are glossed over and the country is projected as a "community of communities" whose citizens live in harmony with one another and differ only in terms of cultural and linguistic values (Liodakis & Satzewich, 1998, p. 105).

The discourse of multiculturalism masks the extent to which people and groups have been affected by racism and discrimination, and the extent to which Canadian immigration policy has been a racist discourse designed to keep Canada a White nation. But there is an official ambiguity towards immigration. While immigration is viewed as essential to the nation-building process in Canada, it has been at the same time treated with apprehension, because of its potential to undermine efforts to develop and maintain a White society (Mackey, 2010, p. 24). This ambiguity has informed immigration policy throughout the history of Canada, whereby both "race" and culture have been used to determine who comes in and who is shut out and who is included and who is excluded (Mackey, 2010, p. 25).

Immigration, State Policy, and Discrimination: a historical-sociological overview

Canada is an **immigrant society**. *Immigrant societies*, such as the United States, Australia, Argentina, and Brazil, have devised multiple active approaches to immigration and immigrants. There are four characteristics that define an *immigrant society* (Fleras, 2010). While these characteristics do not always direct official policy, they nevertheless inform the principal approaches of governments to immigration and immigrants:

1. there are policies and rules regulating the entrance of immigrants;

2. programs and services are available for immigrants, assisting them to settle and integrate into society;

3. immigrants and native-born citizens are equal before the law; and

4. immigration is an important aspect of and source for the nation-building process (Fleras, 2010, pp. 248–249).

An *immigrant society* differs from other societies' approaches to immigration. In Germany, for example, despite the existence of a large population of "migrant" groups, Germans do not view themselves as an *immigrant society*. These countries tend to view themselves as **complete societies** (Fleras, 2010, p. 249). In Germany, due to acute labour shortage in the wake of World War II, large numbers of Turkish migrant workers were admitted into the country; however, they were by and large denied permanent settlement and citizenship rights (Fleras, 2010, p. 249).

In the **popular discourses of immigration**, Canada is often depicted as an open country that has always welcomed immigrants. However, we have not been (are not) always open to immigration of specific types of nationalities and cultural backgrounds into this country. The discourse of immigration in Canada constructs the country as the land of opportunity that is open to diversity. Immigration is an important plank in an assumed liberal Canadian society built on the pillars of "'the fairness of British institutions', and now by the 'civility of state sponsored pluralism in the form of official multiculturalism'" (Mackey, 2001, p. 25). Canada is a multicultural society because of its liberal immigration policy. Despite the rich history of immigration to Canada from various parts of the world, it is important to note that "Canadians" viewed themselves as British subjects until the implementation of Citizenship Act in 1946. The current Canadian flag that replaced the Union Jack was only introduced in 1965. The current national anthem also became incorporated only in 1967 (Francis, 1997, pp. 85–86). Despite these changes and the official Multiculturalism Act, racism towards Aboriginal groups and non-British and non-White immigrants has been a central defining aspect of Canada's history. Canada and Aboriginal peoples, whose land was confiscated by force, were colonized through immigration.

From a critical perspective, immigration is both a labour and citizenship policy that defines who is eligible to become a member of the nation and which groups are not entitled to citizenship rights (Mackey, 2010, p. 24; Abu-Laban & Gabriel, 2002; Ghosh & Abdi, 2004). Immigration as a discourse in the nation-building project highlights the connection between politics, culture, and economy (Fleras, 2010, pp. 242–243). It is influenced by both *ideology* and economic considerations. It also defines the relationship between a citizen and a noncitizen: as mentioned, immigration laws determine who is allowed in and who must stay out. Immigration has been sought as a solution to: an aging population, shortage of skilled workers, decrease in birth rate, improving the GDP through induced consumerism, attracting foreign investment, and contributing to Canada's global economic position, enabling it to exploit resources and labour (Fleras, 2010). In contemporary Canada, it continues to be a way of thinking about **otherness** and how we want to practice *tolerance* and multiculturalism. However, it is important to note that until the reforms of the late 1950s and the early 1960s, Canada preferred immigrants from mainly Western-European nation-states. Yet, despite introducing the **points system** to effect changes to the racist aspects of the past policies, current immigration policy continues to discriminate against women, the working classes, and immigrants from South/Central America and Africa (Abu-Laban & Gabriel, 2002). In addition, despite changes to the immigration policy in the last six decades, economic and labour needs of Canada have been influential factors in deciding who should be allowed into this country (Abu-Laban & Gabriel, 2002; Ghosh & Abdi, 2004).

Until the late nineteenth century, immigration was based on informal and discretionary policies. The early attempts to develop policies reflected the ideological considerations, political concerns, international obligations, and colonial requirements of a hinterland economy (based on agriculture and natural resources) (Fleras, 2010, p. 250). Several factors determined the types of policies that were devised and implemented: racism, agricultural concerns of the early nation-building process, the private, capitalist, industrialist, and business interests, Canada's membership in the British Empire and its Commonwealth obligations; and out-migration to the United States (Fleras, 2010, p. 250).

The early periods of immigration resulted in different responses by various groups, often with diverse and conflicting approaches. For example, as industrialists argued that growth requires a steady migration of labour, unions and organized labour called for restrictions on immigration to protect their wages, jobs. Many lay Canadians also viewed immigrants as undermining their standard of living (Fleras, 2010, p. 251). In general, the initial policies of immigration had an economic base/bias and were based on pragmatic approaches (Fleras, 2010, p. 252).

Since the implementation of the first Immigration Act in 1896, satisfying the economic and labour demands of the Canadian labour market and capitalist classes and the requirement for the nation-building process has been determined and affected by an *ideology* that has defined the ideal citizen based on discriminatory views about "race", ethnicity, nationality, religion, occupation, skills, class, and the ability to speak one of the two official languages. Since the early 1980s, moreover, the discourses of immigration, citizenship, and equity are informed by the *ideology* of **neoliberalism** that emphasizes free market practices, efficiency, competitiveness, and individualism (Abu-Laban & Gabriel, 2002). *Neoliberalism* views citizenship in light of a framework that proposes limited access to social services; promotes erosion of social rights; considers success in the market as the main determinant of one's status; and institutionalizes attacks on various forms of social solidarity and collective political action (Abu-Laban & Gabriel, 2002). In the context of globalization of the economy, information, capital, and labour, *neoliberalism* promotes a limited role for the state and emphasizes the importance of self-sufficiency. In this context, "various aspects of policy-making are [partially] influenced by factors outside national territorial boundaries" (Abu-Laban & Gabriel, 2002, p. 23).

Throughout Canadian history, specific immigrant groups, such as Italians during World War II or Ukrainians during World War I, have been singled out and constructed as "dangerous aliens" who were to be feared. Immigrants have been viewed as problematic elements within society; they are believed to have a proclivity for criminal behaviour and engaged in all manner of criminal activities, including prostitution, extortion, global crime, and, most recently, global terrorism (Fleras, 2010). They are blamed for undermining the moral and ethical values of the Canadian society and introducing vices into society. The **discourse of moral panic** constructs a group as dangerous and associates social, economic, political, and cultural problems existing in a society to an ethnic, racialized, gendered, and political group as the source of the problem. The *discourse of moral panic* often regulates when, how, and which groups of immigrant are permitted into the country. For example, by constructing asylum seekers in Canada as illegal immigrants who break the rules and abuse the system, the government and political groups have been able to introduce new laws that have toughened up immigration refugee rules, enabling the state to expel them from the country (Fleras, 2010; Abu-Laban & Gabriel, 2002). The *discourse of moral panic* is a strong tool of domination, especially in the context of lack of information about the extent against which immigrants have been discriminated.

An important element in the discourse of multiculturalism is the *historical amnesia*. It has been official practice in Canada to ignore or minimize the extent to which the so-called "visible minorities" and First Nations Peoples have contributed to the development of the country. Let's take the enormous sacrifices, toil, and sweat of Chinese Canadians in the construction of the Pacific Railway as an example. One cannot imagine Canada as a modern nation without the contributions of the Chinese railroad worker. Yet, the discourse of multiculturalism merely pays lip service and perfunctory attention to the role Chinese Canadians and other non-European migrant groups have played in the development of the country. The discourse of multiculturalism also excludes the experiences of racism from the historical narrative about national-building. This is hardly surprising. As we mentioned in previous chapters, Canada has had a 'White Canada Policy" that was reflected in its immigration policies that "drew upon an essentialist racism … excluding Black and Asians in the grounds that they were unfit to the cold climate of Canada" (Mackey, 2010, p. 25; Fleras, 2010). Throughout most of the history of Canada, the preferred immigrants had been White northern Europeans (Mackey, 2010, p. 24).

The history of Canadian immigration can be divided into six general phases (Abu-Laban & Gabriel, 2002; Ghosh & Abdi, 2004; Fleras, 2010). During the **first phase**, from the confederation to the first decade of the twentieth-century until the 1860s, three factors influenced immigration: racism, economic consideration, and commonwealth obligations (Fleras, 2010; Ghosh & Abdi, 2004, p. 95). During this period, Canada admitted immigrants of the "*White race*" (British first and then other groups) and rejected non-White *others*. The Immigration Acts of 1869–1910 excluded certain groups from immigrating to Canada. The list of the "unwanted aliens" included: Chinese, mentally ill people, South Asians, criminals, inassimilable nationalities (such as Blacks), and Japanese

(Fleras, 2010). *Scientific racism* and *eugenics* explanations were used to justify the ban on Asians and Africans, as well as mentally ill people (Ghosh & Abdi, 2004). However, due to the need to settle the prairies many Ukrainian peasants were admitted to Canada. This was partly due to the fact that during the nineteenth century the United States was a more attractive destination for immigrants; and as a result, Canada had a harder time attracting British immigrants and other Northern Europeans to settle in the country. As mentioned, the need to settle the West as well as to bring labourers to meet the demands of the capitalist class resulted in the immigration of Slavs from the Austro-Hungarian Empire (Mackey, 2010, p. 24). Yet, they were viewed with suspicion during the First World War, when many of them were labeled as the "fifth column" and considered "enemy alien", and placed in internment camps. During this period, the desired immigrants were British and Northern Europeans. In 1907, laws were passed to disenfranchise non-White immigrants, such as Indians already living in British Columbia (Ghosh & Abdi, 2004, p. 96). Japanese and Chinese also experienced social and economic discrimination, culminating in the Race Riots of 1907 in Vancouver.

As the above examples point out, although immigration laws were flexible, they were also very much racialized, which is "exemplified in Canada's treatment of Chinese labourers" (Mackey, 2010, p. 25). For example, as Slavic people were being encouraged to come to Canada, the Chinese were treated not as potential immigrants, but as temporary indentured labourers who were brought on to work on the Canadian Pacific Railway (CPR) and such were denied citizenship rights (Mackey, 2010, p. 25). As Prime Minster Macdonald stated, "until we find white workers to replace the Chinese, it is better to bring Chinese labourers than having no workers at all" (as cited in Mackey, 2010, p. 25). During the mid-1850s, Chinese indentured workers were viewed as useful and important to the development of British Columbia until the economic hardships paved the stage for the rise of **anti-Orientalist sentiments**. By the 1870s, the news-media in its depiction of the Chinese blamed them for all the ills of society and criminal activities and constructed them as culturally "inferior". Soon after the completion of the railway, between 1878 and 1899, more than 26 bills were passed in British Columbia to halt and restrict Asian settlement in the province (Mackey, 2010, p. 25).

British Europeans constructed themselves as "superior" to the Chinese and other non-White groups (Li, 1998). For example, in British Columbia, the "Chinese race" was viewed as less "intelligent" and "inferior" to the White "race". In fact, middle class British Columbians viewed the Chinese as "unclean" and morally "corrupt". Such a in 1907 was central in passing laws limiting the freedoms of Chinese-Canadians (Li, 1998). Starting in 1885, many laws were enacted in British Columbia that limited the freedom of Chinese (Li, 1998). In 1875, for example, British Columbia disenfranchised the Chinese; thus taking away their legal rights. In 1876, the law prohibited them to work in government sponsored work projects, which affected their income and economic well-being. They were excluded from holding office and professional jobs or from working on crown timberlands. Since they were not British subjects, in Saskatchewan, the Chinese were also disenfranchised in 1908. Federally, however, no Anti-Chinese bill was completed before the completion of the CPR. The first federal law that was directed at the Chinese was passed in 1885 in the form of a *head tax*. Despite such legislations, Chinese workers were deemed a solution to the economic needs, labour demands and supply, and population trends (i.e., migrations trends) of the period (Li, 1998). During the recession of the late nineteenth century, there was a lack of able-bodied workers. During boom times, there was a shortage of labour. The population of British Columbia was also in decline and there was out-migration from Canada to the United States, which resulted in shortages of labour. During this period, the **Chinese were constructed as machineries with use-values**: they could be called upon when other sources of labour were not available (Li, 1998). Although, the Chinese were viewed as "undesirable" and inassimilable due to their cultural and social "peculiarities", their labour was needed in industries, such as canning and railroad construction when white workers were unwilling to work in such jobs. That is, while the Chinese were not viewed as ideal Canadian citizens, they were seen as transient cheap labourers who would migrate back to their country of origin after the expiration of their employment contracts. Chinese workers were also paid less than White workers (Li, 1998). As such, Chinese workers were viewed by White workers and unions as undercutting their wages, resulting in Unions and White workers demanding the exclusion of the Chinese. The Chinese were blamed for economic recessions and social woes of the period. There was a strong *anti-Oriental sentiment* affecting the life experiences of Chinese migrant workers. As an ideology, *anti-Orientalism* viewed the West as "normal" and the East as "abnormal" and in need of change. Chinese were viewed as "aliens" who came from a "backward" country. As mentioned, the Chinese also faced riots and attacks in 1887 and 1907 in Vancouver. These riots occurred with the approval of the provincial government and city officials. In general, no distinctions were made between Chinese-Canadians and Chinese immigrants. *Anti-Orientalism* benefited the government and employers and also served the interest of unions and politicians. Unions in BC were weak and attempted to capitalize on *anti-Oriental sentiments* towards Chinese as a weapon to attract membership/popular support. In short, **anti-Orientalism scapegoated** the Chinese and blamed them for the social, economic, and cultural problems in society that were caused by **modern social structures** (Li, 1998).

During the **second phase** (also known as White Dominion), from 1911 to 1945, Canada continued accepting immigrants for agricultural expansion of the West. However, fewer immigrants were admitted due to the effects of World War I and economic recession (the Great Depression). During this period, non-White immigrants continued to face discrimination. In 1917, Chinese were excluded from civil jobs. By 1920, the Chinese were also excluded from voting in federal elections since they were not eligible to vote in provincial elections, and they were not British subjects. In 1923, the Chinese Immigration Act was passed, prohibiting immigration of Chinese people (Ghosh & Abdi, 2004). During this period, only diplomats, children born in Canada to Chinese parents, students, and merchants were allowed to enter Canada. Chinese residents had to register with the government or pay a fine of up to $500. This act stopped Chinese immigration and "legalized the inferior status of those already in the country" (Li, 1998, p.35). The Chinese were also indirectly affected by the implementation of other laws, such as the Factories Act of 1922. The Chinese, nevertheless, had to pay taxes like all other Canadians (Li, 1998). Racial discrimination intersected sexist and patriarchal forms of discrimination. For example, upon marrying a Chinese male immigrant, Chinese women who were citizens of Canada lost their citizenship.

As the above examples point out, Canadian immigration policies and provincial and federal laws are forms of **structural** and **institutional** forms of **racism**. The withdrawal of citizenship rights, exclusion from immigration and restriction on occupational selection "were legally sanctioned and… formally institutionalized" (Li, 1998, p.37). In institutional form, racism is "articulated as both a racist theory and a discriminatory practice" (Li, 1998, p.37). In this context, "race" is viewed as a legitimate way of treating people differently and unequally. *Institutional racism* helps to facilitate the exploitation of labour and diverts the cost of the reproduction of labour. By reducing or limiting a group's civil rights their bargaining power is also limited. This leads into a **split labour market**, where two different wages are paid for the labour of two racially different groups performing the same task. In this system, menial and low-paying jobs are performed by marginalized groups in society. The low economic status of the group reinforces their social marginality. The ideology of viewing a group as "inferior" is essential in "rationalizing racial exploitation" (Li, 1998, p.38).

Beginning with the **third phase**, from 1946 to 1967, immigration was based on the needs for industrial semi-skilled and skilled labourers and professionals. Several factors, such as "low birth rate during the Depression, industrial growth, and economic expansion after the war, and a general shortage of workers", were influential in encouraging immigration from other countries (Ghosh & Abdi, 2004, p. 98). A 1947 immigration policy highlighted several categories of preferred immigrants: 1) British and American individuals (read White) with good character, 2) those qualified/ willing to work in the resource industries, 3) family members of European immigrants already in the country, and 4) refugees and other displaced persons of World War II in Europe (Fleras, 2010, p. 252; Ghosh & Abdi, 2004, p. 98). As it can be inferred, the *discourse of Whiteness* (based on the supremacy of the Anglo "race") remained the defining factor in choosing immigrants during most of this period. However, in 1947, the federal government repealed the Chinese Immigration Act and more displaced people from Southern and Eastern Europe were selected as immigrants (Ghosh & Abdi, 2004). Moreover, the government of British Columbia also enfranchised all Chinese and South Asian residents in 1947 and, by 1949, the Japanese-Canadians were also reenfranchised (Ghosh & Abdi, 2004, p. 98). Yet, racial quotas limited the immigration of non-Whites to Canada. In 1951, for example, an annual quota was set, "allowing 150 independent immigrants from India (this was doubled in 1957), 100 from Pakistan, and 50 from Ceylon (now Sri Lanka)" (Ghosh & Abdi, 2004, p. 99). It was not until 1962 when Canada became the first country to implement policies that chose immigrants solely on their personal merits and assumed/perceived contributions to the nation-building process. Despite deracializing its immigration policy, class and economic consideration remained one of the main factors in selecting immigrants. Labour market needs determined what kinds of immigrants (read workers) were to be admitted to Canada.

With the implementation of the *Immigration Regulation* in 1962, Canada no longer chose immigrants on the basis of ethnicity, religion, region, language, or political affiliations, but rather on non-discriminatory criteria, such as the level of education, job prospective, and language abilities (Fleras, 2010, p. 255; Table 9.3, pp. 258–59). This policy ended the official White Canada policy (Jakubowski, 1997, p. 17). The principle of this policy was reinforced in the *White Paper* of 1966 that stressed all immigrants coming to Canada would be chosen based on the same entrance standards that were no longer based on racist, ethnocentric, and discriminatory factors, such as religion, or place of birth (Jakubowski, 1997, p. 18). One of the reasons for the implementation of this policy was due to the international pressures on Canada to end its racialized immigration policy and Canada's obligations to the Commonwealth countries after their independence from Brittan (Jakubowski, 1997, p. 18; Ghosh & Abdi, 2004).

Canada officially introduced the *points system* in 1967. As discussed, prior to the introduction of the *points system*, the *discourse of Whiteness* was a central defining element of the immigration policy in this country. It was based on historical racialized conceptions of "us" and "them". It also excluded certain types of people, such as mentally ill, prostitutes, and those who were not considered to be able to assimilate into the White culture (Fleras, 2010, pp. 251–252). Canada's immigration policies were racist, classist, ableist, and sexist. In contrast, the *points system* was thought to be an objective way of assessing whether or not an immigrant would successfully be integrated into the Canadian system, based on factors, such as level of education, knowledge of French or English, employment opportunities where the immigrant intended to settle; arranged employment; and whether or not the immigrant had relatives who could assist him/her to settle in the country (Jakubowski, 1997, p. 18). Although the system seems to be non-racist, the racism of the system was now subtle and covert. For example, although the criteria were now universal, the fact remained that the number of overseas offices that could process immigration applications remained few and were not equally available in many parts of Asia, South and Central America, and Africa. Moreover, in the last three decades, the government has introduced the **Right of Permanent Residence Fee**, which excludes many poor people (many of them of racial and working class backgrounds, including single women and female headed families) who cannot afford the fee to apply for and become landed immigrants in Canada (Fleras, 2010, p. 273). The discriminatory aspects of the immigration policy are no longer overtly racist, classist, or sexist, but they are now incorporated in the form of laws and regulations that seem to treat everyone the same. In general, with the introduction of the *points system*, Canada began to view immigrants as **commodities** (Abu-Laban & Gabriel, 2002).

Since 1962, we can conceptualize the types of immigrants being accepted under three broad criteria:

1. **economic**, which has become a major source,
2. **refugee** (i.e., asylum seekers in Canada; convention refugees that are selected outside Canada; and assisted refugees who are sponsored by various organizations and churches), and
3. **family** (under the points system, they were either accepted as "dependents" under the "independent category" or under the "family reunification" program).

From 1968 to 1993 (the **fourth phase**), immigration was influenced by an emphasis on family reunion and refugee obligations of Canada. The immigration policy during most of this period was affected by the iintroduction of the *points system*. The Immigration Act of 1976 officially and explicitly ended racial discrimination in immigration (which became a law in 1978). The emphasis during the early periods was on recruiting immigrants from developed Western countries (Jakubowski, 1997, p. 19). However, by this time, Canada needed educated and highly skilled immigrants (in comparison to semiskilled or unskilled manual labour during the previous eras). The traditional sources of immigrant producing countries were no longer viable and adequate sources since Europe was now experiencing postwar economic restructuring and Europeans were no longer "willing" to immigrate. The policy now was to recruit immigrants from other countries, such as from the "Third World". This period is characterized by an increase in the number of non-European immigration entering Canada. From 1967 to the mid-1970s, "Third World" immigration increased by 40 percent (Ghosh & Abdi, 2004, p. 100). For example, by 1978, more than 90, 000 people from Lebanon, Syria, and Egypt were admitted into the country. The selection criteria emphasized **human capital** and **investment** criteria and it was **occupation based** (i.e., medicine, computing science). That is, the policies emphasized the skills of immigrants that suited the Canadian labour market needs (Jakubowski, 1997, p. 18).

From 1993 to 2001 (the **fifth phase**), there was a greater emphasis placed on job experiences and language proficiency of the would-be immigrants. Immigration was viewed in the context of globalization and border security issues. Immigrant communities and individuals were considered to be "responsible" for providing and distributing services to immigrants. Since 2001 (the **sixth phase**), security measures and terrorism dominate immigration issues (i.e., Bill C-36): the emphasis is on establishing more restrictions, choosing those immigrants who can easily become integrated (i.e., middle-class, modern, and "liberal minded"). This period is characterized by a move away from the *points system*. It places more emphasis on the labour needs of Canada and security issues. In 2003, for example, the Minister of Immigration, Denis Codere stated that,

> Our strategy is designed to strike a balance between attracting workers with flexible skills, reuniting families and being tough on those who pose a threat to Canadian security, all the while maintaining Canada's humanitarian tradition of providing a safe haven to people in need of protection. (as cited in Fleras, 2010, p. 254)

Since the 1980s, immigration issues have been politicized by the Right Wing groups that problematize alleged refugee claimants' abuse of the refugee policies of Canada, the abuse of the welfare system by the immigrant population, and the cost associated with immigration that is absorbed by taxpayers. They use the *discourse of moral panic* to instill fear in the population of the negative consequences of immigration. As a result, certain changes have been introduced into the immigration law; for example, raising the selection criteria for accepting immigrants; enforcing the obligations of family members who sponsor relatives to cover the cost of immigration. The fact that at times sponsors may default on their obligations is drawn upon to construct and stigmatize them as abusers of the system. This should not be seen as a reflection of immigrants' and their sponsors' willful desire to cheat the system; many sponsors default on the obligations because of the consequences of harsh economic reality and high unemployment rates.

The discourse of immigration now has more than ever an economic focus that portrays the ideal citizen as one who "has the skills" to contribute to the economic growth; who is self-sufficient; and does not use the social services historically provided by the state (Abu-Laban & Gabriel, 2002, p. 65). The current immigration policy and law emphasizes the **human capital theory**. This theory has become the deciding factor in the selection of immigrants with greater emphasis placed on would-be immigrant's job experience and language abilities (Abu-Laban & Gabriel, 2002, p. 65).

This theory posits that people's skills and knowledge are important factors, just the same way as investment, in economic growth. It assumes that productive capability increases when individuals throughout their lifetime invest in retraining themselves and in their formal education. The *Human Capital theory* asserts that increases in educational expenditure results in important returns for society. Education is viewed as a form of investment in human capital. Economic development is not simply based on technological advancements. It also requires highly qualified individuals who are motivated and skilled (Wotherspoon, 1998, p. 20). To be competitive in this world, Canada needs to make sure that schools train highly motivated individuals who are innovative and who can contribute to the development of technology and economy. Many jobs and positions require specific types of knowledge. As such, many governments (including the Canadian government) have invested in the education system, developing a strong science and technical education. In terms of the curriculum, sciences and mathematics have been emphasized. More institutions of higher learning were established since the 1960s. The assumption is that in order to stay competitive in the world we "need to match skills with jobs" (Wotherspoon, 1998, p. 21). Retraining workers to increase productivity is an important consequence of such a theory. In (post)industrialized societies, such as Canada, it is often assumed that there are many opportunities for social mobility. Individuals can take advantage of the education system and graduate with credentials that would help them to enjoy a better standard of living. Choosing immigrants who are skilled is a way to **externalize the cost of training**. Other countries spent their capital to educate people and when they immigrate to Canada, Canada becomes the beneficiary of such investments in other countries. This is referred to as **brain-drain**, which also affects Canada, as many educated Canadians emigrate to the United States and other parts of the world in search of jobs. According to the *human capital discourse*, these types of immigrants are accepted thanks to their abilities and skills. It is assumed that these immigrants would pay higher taxes since they "tend" to earn higher income levels (although this is not the case since many of their credentials are not recognized and a large number cannot find jobs in their professions due to the lack of having Canadian job experience). In short, under the current system of immigration, the ideal immigrant settles quickly and contributes to Canada, pays higher taxes than others, connects "his" employers to other parts of the world, and brings knowledge and skills to Canada. However, women continue to be considered noncontributors to the economy since most of them are accepted under the family reunion criterion.

In fact, policy papers and immigration Acts since 2000 (such as, **Bill C-11** and **Immigration and Refugee Protection Act**) have been labelled as sexist and biased. For example, the aim of the *Immigration and Refugee Protection Act* has been to limit and restrict immigration (Fleras, 2010, p. 254). The focus has been on immigrants who can better integrate into the Canadian society and workplace. That is, Canada seeks those immigrants who have the Western cultural capital that are regarded as normative and essential. There has been also a shift to accept immigrants who already have extensive knowledge of English or French. The overemphasis on the ability to speak French or English discriminates against those who do not have the resources to learn English in their own countries or pay for English language courses in Canada, services which have been cut since the

1990s. Finally, this Act requires immigrants and their families to pick up the cost of the settlement of the would-be immigrants (Fleras, 2010, p. 254). The idea that the cost of the integration of immigrants must be paid by the immigrants is a neoliberal policy that attempts to privatize these costs. In other words, this equals to the privatization of the social costs that should be paid by all Canadians: paying for the cost of "immigration" is now the responsibility of individuals and their families; hint, the importance of the **discourse of individualism** and a move away from an emphasis on collective social responsibility.

The changes to the immigration policy have also promoted *institutional discrimination*. For example, the Right of Landing Fee (ROLF) privileges the rich and well-to-do in both Canada and in other parts of the world (Abu-Laban & Gabriel, 2002). Canadian immigrants are now responsible to pay for the processing of immigration application, which is a cost-cutting measure. This cost, it is argued, should not be covered by all taxpayers. This approach ignores the fact that immigrants pay taxes and they contribute to the economic growth, regionally and nationally. In addition, this policy ignores the fact that most "people and women of colour" in the South cannot afford the cost of ROLF. "Race", gender, and class continue to be factors that affect the types of immigrants that are accepted. For example, the increase in the number of immigrants under the independent and investment categories also privileges people who are well-off and excludes the poor and working classes in other parts of the world. In this sense, sexism, racism, and classism as criteria of selection are externalized (Abu-Laban & Gabriel, 2002, pp. 66–68).

The desirable immigrants are those with "transferable skills" that are portable and applicable to many other jobs and occupations, such as communication skills, analytical skills, data collecting, and interpersonal skills, and "skilled technical workers" with appropriate human capital attributes (Abu-Laban & Gabriel, 2002, p.79). Moreover, the move away from the occupation based model to an emphasis on transferable skills discriminates against those in seasonal work that happen to be women and racialized workers from Mexico and Jamaica. As such, the "independent immigrants" continue to be highly preferred; they are selected and identified by the labour needs of the private economic sector. In these policy papers and Acts, citizenship is not viewed in the context of its roots in "institutional reform, in the welfare state", but it is reconceptualized in the context of an emphasis on "charity, philanthropy and self-help" (Abu-Laban & Gabriel, 2002, p.73). **Citizens are now perceived as consumers and clients**.

As it can be seen from the above discussions and analysis, the changes to immigration and citizenship rights must be viewed in the context of global factors and the extent to which in the context of the **globalization** process (which is explored in more detail in Chapter Nine) the role of the Canadian state is changing. In the context of **neoliberalism**, which professes "competitiveness, individual self-sufficiency … and cost recovery" certain issues are accentuated, such as what it means by belonging, *difference*, and national identity (Abu-Laban & Gabriel, 2002, p. 61). Despite the attempts to make the system fairer, in contemporary Canada, the ideal immigrant is conceptualized as a male, highly skilled individual whose wealth and knowledge promotes the global interests of Canada.

Conclusion

Modern social, economic, political, and cultural relations have been affected and influenced by colonial, neocolonial, and postcolonial events. The process of nation-building in Canada and other parts of the world have been marred by racism, sexism, and classism, with devastating consequences for marginalized peoples. Through a comprehensive analysis of the history of *colonialism*, *imperialism*, and *postcolonialism*, we can develop our sociological imaginations, accounting for the intersections of historical and contemporary issues and their cumulative effects, locally and globally.

Chapter Review Questions

1. Define Eurocentrism. In what ways is Eurocentrism manifested in colonial and postcolonial societies? Explain.

2. Define the term and offer an overview of colonialism.

3. What is meant by the following statement: colonialism as a process and period?

4. Explore the relationship between colonialism, "race", and racism.

5. Define and explain the following terms: racialization, Manifest Destiny, individual racism, hate racism, Islamophobia, polite racism, subliminal racism, systemic racism, institutional racism, structural racism, cultural racism, Hamitic Rationalization, and Democratic racism.

6. Distinguish between monogenetic and polygenetic theories of racial differences, scientific racism, Eugenicism, and the discourse of Whiteness. Explain their roles in the colonization of the world.

7. Define imperialism and distinguish between imperialism and colonialism.

8. Distinguish between neocolonialism, internal colonialism, and postcolonialism.

9. Why is Orientalism considered a discourse of Western hegemony and domination? Explain.

10. Offer a general historical account of the colonial and imperialist expansions.

11. Define Hamitic hypothesis. Provide an example.

12. Colonial powers used a variety of practices to deal with the captured cultural groups and nations. What are they? Explain.

13. How do sociologists theorize about the effects of colonialism, imperialism, and capitalist relations?

14. Compare and contrast modernization, dependency, and world-system theories?

15. How are modernization and dependency theories reflected in school textbooks? Explain.

16. Define culture of poverty.

17. As Enakshi Dua maintained, nationalism and racism in Canada are articulated in two main ways. Explain.

18. By references to Aboriginal peoples, explore the effects of colonialism and internal colonialism on their schooling.

19. In what ways were residential schools forms of total institutions? Explain.

20. Define resocialization.

21. We can conceptualize the effects of the colonial process in terms of six general areas. Explain them.

22. We can divide the history of contact between Aboriginal and White society into four distinct periods. What are they? Explain.

23. There are four main discourses that characterize Aboriginal and White relations in Canada. Explain them.

24. What is meant by the term aggressive civilization?

25. What is meant by the term discourse of tutelage?

26. What is meant by the term mortification processes?

27. What is meant by the term total institutions?

28. Explain the three goals of multiculturalism.

29. Critically explore the four different meanings of multiculturalism.

30. What are some the problems associated with multiculturalism? Explain.

31. Offer a critical historical analysis of the history of immigration by looking at the relationship between state policy and discrimination.

Critical Thinking Questions

1. To what extent does Canada remain a colonialist state? Explain.

2. How has Canada dealt with postcolonial relations?

3. In what ways do we continue to live in a world affected by racist and imperialist policies?

CHAPTER NINE

•••

Globalization, Postindustrialism, and Postmodernity

Introduction
•••

In this chapter, we explore three interrelated phenomena of **globalization**, **postindustrialism**, and **postmodernity**. We offer a general framework of how to analyze and understand the changes that have affected societies since the end of World War II. This chapter is divided into four parts. In Part One, we explore the main characteristics of *globalization*. In Part Two, we examine the ideology of *globalization*: **neoliberalism**. In Part Three, we discuss the changes form industrial type societies to **postindustrial** and **information society**. In Part Four, we offer a general overview of *postmodernity* and **postmodernism**.

Part One
•••

Sociology as a Discourse to Understand Globalization

Since the 1750s, societies in Europe and in other parts of the world have gone through major changes. **Modernity**, explained Giddens (1990), is a double-edged series of events and structural changes. It is inherently **globalizing**: connecting every corner of the world in political, social, cultural, and political ways. As a result, for example, economic recession in Asia will have economic consequences in North America. Political revolutions in other parts of the world will result in the movement of peoples as refugees and/or immigrants into other parts of the world. It is in this sense that Giddens (1990) argued *modernity* is instinctively globalizing. The question that arises is whether or not we are still living in a modern society or do we live in a society that is markedly different than modern society? Do we now live in a postmodern society? If so, can we still use modern theories of society to understand and analyze the social world? Or, do we need to develop different theories and ways of understanding the world around us?

Since the 1960s, many social scientists have argued that we have entered the age of *postmodernity*. **Postmodernists** question the basic arguments and assumptions of **modernist** thinking and worldviews about the social world. The change from *modernity* to *postmodernity*, many pundits have argued, is characterized by a number of institutional changes, such as a change from an economic system based on manufacturing to information and knowledge base (Giddens, 1990, p. 2). In this chapter, we explore the extent to which the **postindustrial world** is structurally different than the **industrial world** in which the emphasis was on manufacturing and production of material objects. A **postindustrial society** is characterized by "information technologies and networked offices rather than by coal or steam power and sprawling workshops" (Allen, 1996b, p. 534).

Today, many people in the West and other countries have access to personal computers, can communicate with others using programs, such as *Skype*, can access information about almost any topic and issue using the World Wide Web. We use email services to talk to one another and send personal communications via *Twitter* and similar programs. Many people have virtual presence on the web through their Facebook accounts. We can learn about events in other parts of the world instantly, and can organize for or against an issue, such as the effects of bullying, violence against women, torture, war, or homophobia, in various parts of the world without even leaving our bedrooms. The structure of work and how work is organized has also drastically changed since the 1960s. Knowledge and information have become commodities that are sold and manipulated to produce more wealth. Our identities are influenced by cultural manipulations of symbols in the media and advertising as ways to influence our consumer habits and purchasing powers. In Western countries, many people now work in part-time and low paying jobs rather than in manufacturing jobs. In this chapter, we explore these changes in the context of a discussion of *globalization*.

We approach sociology as a set of multidimensional "scientific" discourses of understanding the effects of *globalization*. *Globalization* refers to the dialectical relationship between distant localities that influence one another in various ways. As mentioned in previous chapters, sociology is a historical, multidimensional, and transdisciplinary field that analyzes social, economic, cultural, political, and environmental relations and structures at both local and global contexts. That is, sociology accounts for the dialectical relationships between local events and global contexts. In other words, sociological knowledge assists us to bridge the gap between global and local events and to understand the relationship between the two in light of **both/and** rather than **either/or** approaches and explanations. Sociologists explore how the intersections of local and global political, social, economic, and cultural factors affect the lives of individuals in different parts of the world, both similarly and differently, by accounting for the consequences of power inequalities. They explore and examine how factors, such as "race", gender, ethnicity, religion, or sexuality, intersect one another and result in various and at times conflicting consequences for different people across the world. Sociology is the study of global changes in modern societies since the 1700s, beginning with the process of industrialization.

Globalization refers to international networks of peoples, ideas, and capital that occur as a result of the stretching and widening processes of time and space in modernity (the processes of **distanciation** and **disembedding**) that we discussed in Chapter Four (Giddens, 1990, p. 64). As John Allen (1996, p. 534) asserted, there has been a "quickened pace and a wide scale of change". *Globalization* implies the increased access to various parts of the world for economic, educational, social, cultural, and political reasons (Hiller, 2006, p. 68). It is the intensification of relations between localities across the globe. *Globalization* highlights the extent to which new economic and political bodies are now determining and regulating economic, social, cultural, and political interactions between **nation-states** by managing, directing, and promoting the intensification of contacts between various localities, institutions, and social actors (Hiller, 2006, p. 68). Distant spaces are linked to one another in direct or indirect ways as events in one part of the world have consequences for social structures, peoples, and institutions in other parts of the world (Giddens, 1990, p. 64). In this context, *globalization* points to the extent to which there has been a transfer of power from *nation-states* to **supranational** bodies. In contrast, **glocalism** is a term that is used to refer to the ways in which local cultures, national issues, and economic factors are influenced by global factors, relations, and structures (Hiller, 2006, p. 41). It also highlights for us the fact that national identities are now questioned in light of the formation of transnational identities and localized identities. That is, national, international, and local identities are not static constructions and are influenced by events and policies beyond the borders of a specific *nation-state*. In addition, **glocalization** highlights the process through which local governments, such as provincial governments, become much more involved in direct economic, political, and social action and relations with other states and governments in promoting their various interests. That is, the government of British Columbia does not need to rely on the federal government and its structures of power to promote its economic survival. Local governments now form and establish trade agreements with other provinces and states, as well as federal/central governments, in other parts of the world to enhance the welfare of their citizens and economies.

The effects of *globalization* have been significant in terms of, for example, the rate of economic activities within Canada. In 1981, the majority of trade within Canada occurred between provinces. By the mid-1990s, the majority of the provinces were involved in exporting their goods and services to other parts of the world rather than to other Canadian provinces (Hiller, 1996, pp. 60–70). *Globalization*, then, implies the creation of new forms of interaction between international players that may not have had historical connections and considered as partners in economic, social, political, or cultural exchanges (Hiller, 2006, p. 71). In this sense, *globalization* enables social actors, organizations, and institutions to move away from old and established dependencies and to create new forms of dependencies with new partners in various parts of the world. It also enables various players in the international systems of exchange to reconfigure their old relationship in light of new policies and approaches to economic or political relations.

In understanding the consequences of *globalization*, it is important to distinguish between *globalism* and *globalization*. World history has always been affected by global relations. The term *globalization* refers to a distinct period of global relations in the histories of world civilizations.

Distinguishing between Globalism and Globalization

Globalization is not a new phenomenon and was preceded by the processes of *globalism*. In this section, we focus on the consequences of *globalism* on human interactions and the consequences of human agencies on the processes of *globalization*. We ask several interrelated questions: What are the effects of global relations on localities? How do non-Western societies and cultures influence Western ideals and conceptions of peace, war, beauty, knowledge, values, and norms? What are the effects of the movement of people across the world as immigrants, refugees, migrant workers, indentured workers, and "illegal aliens" in search of employment in both Western and non-Western parts of the world?

Globalism refers to historical processes that are influenced by **relations**, global capitalism, and flow of goods, services, information, ideas, capital, and people in the context of environmental, political, social, cultural, and religious structures (Hebron & Stack, 2009, p. 2). It is a set of well integrated networks of interdependence that bring localities that have historically been separate and distant from one another into direct or indirect contact with one another (Hebron & Stack, 2009, p. 2). *Globalism* is a historical phenomenon and has been a defining characteristic of world politics. We conceptualize *globalism* as an ideology, while *globalization* is a process. *Globalism* is an ideology that sees *globalization* not only as a natural process, but also as an inexorable (unstoppable) and inevitable (unavoidable) phenomenon. Thus, globalists believe that *globalization* is generally a positive process, and that its excesses should and can be controlled or contained. The question is not whether *globalization* is good or bad; the most important thing is to manage *globalization* in such a manner that it benefits the largest number of people.

Globalization refers to the intensification of the process of *globalism* since the 1960s. Hiller (2006, p. 68) defined *globalization* as "the increased access to all parts of the world for whatever purposes". It is the broadening and deepening of the processes of *globalism* (Hebron & Stack, 2009, p. 2). *Globalization* is affected by trade expansion and the processes of exploration, conquest, war, transmigration, colonization, and conservative and fundamentalist movements (Hebron & Stack, 2009, p. 2). In the context of *globalization*, social, political, and geographical distances are being shrunk on a large scale (Hebron & Stack, 2009, p. 2). National economies are more than ever affected by economic factors in other parts of the world and by the import/export of tradable goods and services, movement of investment, capital, knowledge, and information, as well as people and groups across national borders (Hebron & Stack, 2009, p. 3). *Globalization* has been a contentious process. Those who have been advocating *globalization* are only concerned with accelerating the process of global integration rather than questioning whether or not such an increase has had positive consequences and is worth pursuing (Hebron & Stack, 2009, p. 9). Those who support the *globalization* of economy based on a market ideology assume that production and pricing are most effectively managed and regulated by a market free of interventions by the government (Hebron & Stack, 2009, pp. 6–7). Those who are critical of the *globalization* of the economy point out that the rate and the intensity of the exploitation of labour and natural resources have had negative social and cultural consequences. In general, *globalization* brings into contacts and exchanges a number of diverse global, national, and local networks of groups and peoples with diverse interests in unpredictable ways (Hebron & Stack, 2009, p. 4).

We can identify four dimensions of globalization:

1. world capitalist economy,

2. *nation-state* system,

3. world military order, and

4. international division of labour (Giddens, 1990, p. 71).

In this light, *globalization* is a process that aims at creating a unified global economic culture and a new form of polity that not only influences smaller units but also results in merging them into the larger regional or global units (Hebron & Stack, 2009, p. 6). It is characterized by the creation and formation of new *supranational* organizations and **regulators**, such as the European Union (EU), the North American Free Trade Agreement (NAFTA), Arab-Maghreb Union, East African Community (EAC), Asia-Pacific Economic Cooperation (APEC), Free Trade Area of the Americas (FTAA), and Association for South Asian Nations (ASEAN). Critics point out that these organizations are not democratically elected, yet the policies that they promote have consequences for people in various *nation-states* (Hebron & Stack, 2009, p. 8; Hiller, 2006, p. 68).

At the same time and despite the fact that certain cultural norms, ways of thinking, and organizational skills (i.e., American popular culture and media images) are now adopted in many parts of the world, *globalization* does not imply that the world is becoming the same and homogenous. Yes, global structures and relations have consequences for how people organize their activities at local levels. But, global events do not necessarily constrain and predetermine the actions of individuals, locally. *Globalization* should not be understood as a uniform process with universal consequences (Hebron & Stack, 2009, p. 4).

Globalization has, for example, contradictory effects on *nation-states*. On one hand, it undermines the power of *nation-states* since they are not in control of social, political, and economic policies and structures in other parts of the world that affect their polices and citizens. At the same time, it has also resulted in the intensification of national ideologies across the globe since localities through an emphasis on nationalist agenda and ideologies attempt to protect themselves against the effects of global relations and structures (Giddens, 1990, p. 65). In the context of *globalization*, the *nation-state* has become "too small for the big problems of life and too big for the small problems of life" (Giddens, 1990, p. 65). In general, it can be stated that *nation-states* have lost some of their sovereignty and control over their own affairs (Giddens, 1990, p. 66). For example, they do not control all aspects of national life, such as economic policies, yet they still reserve the right to use violence against their citizens. Almost all *nation-sates* are also capitalist societies; that is, their main forms of production and consumption are capitalist in nature or influenced by global capitalist relations (Giddens, 1990, p. 70).

Since *globalization* highlights the coming to power of *supranational* bodies that are not elected by citizens of *nation-states*, the insulation of economy from the polity has become central in understanding the consequences of *globalization*. That is, transnational corporations have tremendous power over political decision making processes in various parts of the world. This is reflected in their budgets, which is more than the GDP of many *nation-states*, and power of investment to promote economic growth and progress in the countries in which they decide to invest (Giddens, 1990, p. 70). Despite the fact that a number of corporations have a home base within a specific Western *nation-state*, this separation of economy from polity (at least in theory) has provided the business corporates a lot of leeway in establishing markets in any part of the world (Giddens, 1990, p. 70). However, corporations do not control the means of violence. For this, they rely on the *nation-state*. It is in this light that *nation-states* continue to be the central actor in the global polity, and corporations are the hegemonic dominant agents within the world capitalist system (Giddens, 1990, p. 71).

We approach the process of *globalization* in light of Cornel West's (2004) arguments regarding the **three main dogmas** and social, cultural, and political relations that have had negative consequences for the regeneration of democratic values in the United States and across the globe. The **first** is the free market ideology, or **free-market fundamentalism**. He maintained that, "this glorification of the market has led to a callous corporate dominated political economy in which business leaders (their wealth and power) are to be worshiped" (West, 2004, p. 3). The **second characteristic** of the modern American political system that is having negative consequences on the future of democracy is the rise in **aggressive militarism**, "of which the new policy of preemptive strike against potential enemies is but an extension" (West, 2004, p. 5). The **third dogma** is identified as the rise in **authoritarianism**, which is rooted in fearing potential terrorists, fear of too many liberties, and distrust of one another (West, 2004, p. 6). He maintained that, "we have witnessed similar developments in our schools and universities—increasing monitoring of viewpoints, disrespecting of those with whom one disagrees, and foreclosing of the common ground upon which we can listen and learn" (West, 2004, p. 7). He argued that "the market-driven media—fueled by our vast ideological polarization and abetted by profit-hungry monopolies—have severely narrowed our political dialogue" (West, 2004, p. 7). The *aggressive militarism* is also found in the United States (and in other countries) in the form of "abusive police power in poor communities of color" (West, 2004, p. 9). An example of *free-market fundamentalism* is NAFTA or North American Free Trade Agreement. In fighting *authoritarianism*, he asserted that we need to emphasize that **democracy matters**. This requires us to account for the intimate relationship between domestic policy (local) and foreign policy (global). He maintained one of the ways to keep democracy alive is through questioning the dominant society through dialogue and debunking dominant ideologies. To do so, we need a broad knowledge of how the world has been changing since the 1960s. In the following sections, we explore some of these changes in more detail.

Globalization from the Above and Globalization from the Below

Globalization is not inevitable or unilinear. It can be resisted, and its consequences may be different in various parts of the world due to local reactions to the forces of *globalization*. Groups and social movements at local levels have undermined global and external forces and policies, and have introduced changes that have had global consequences. For example, neoliberal policies that are espoused by global suprastructures, such as the International Monetary Fund (IMF), are fought against by people in various parts of the world, with a number of success stories, such as the resistance to the privatization of water and other natural resources in South America by the Indigenous peoples. For this reason, it is important to explore social, cultural, economic, and political issues at the nexus of the interactions between **globalization from above** (macro-approach) and **globalization from below** (micro-approach). We draw upon the term **glocalization** to highlight the processes of the *globalization from above* and *globalization from below* and their interactions. *Glocalization* is closely linked to the process of **fragmegration**, which refers to the processes of fragmentation and community formations. That is, globalization can result in weakening of national relations, yet at the same time can also result in the formation of community and subnational organizations to be formed that aim at promoting the interests of localities in light of the effects of global capitalism and powerful *supranational* organizations (Crothers, 2007, pp. 15–26).

Globalization: economic, cultural, political, and social perspectives

From an economic perspective, *globalization* refers to a shift from national investment, production, and trade decisions to economic decisions that serve the world market (Abu-Laban & Gabriel, 2002, p. 16). This shift in focus is characterized by several processes: 1) the international expansion of markets, 2) an increase in the mobility of capital, as investors can easily move their finances from one country into another to invest in various economic projects, and 3) the internationalization of product production (i.e., an item of consumption produced in, for example, Turkey consists of parts that are produced in other parts of the world).

From a cultural perspective, *globalization* has cultural and technological implications (Abu-Laban & Gabriel, 2002, p. 17). There is a flow of information, ideas, and images from one part of the world to another that function as ways of connecting people across national borders and imagined geographical spaces (Abu-Laban & Gabriel, 2002, p. 17). Rap and Rock & Roll music are the mediums of expression for many youth across the world. Cell-phones are the common form of communication in many parts of the world. Wal-Mart and McDonalds, as cultural icons of America, are found in many parts of the world.

The Three Dimensions of Globalization

Globalization has three main dimensions:

1. **"the density of networks"**, which refers to the extent to which we are connected globally through systems of communication and linkages that defy localities and their characteristics;

2. **"institutional velocity"**, which is reflected in the ways that the division of labour is affected by the new technologies and the transnational networks of trade, capital, and social movements; and

3. **"transnational participation"**, which refers to the ways in which national and local issues are influenced by nonstate actors, reflecting the declining power of *nation-states* in promoting national (economic and social) policies (Hebron & Stack, 2009, p. 3).

Globalization can also be understood in light of the movements of immigrants, migrant workers, and refugees across the world. In this sense, it has resulted in the intensification of cultural, racial, ethnic, and religious diversity across the globe. Events in other parts of the world have had direct and indirect consequences for the social, economic, and cultural organization of localities (Abu-Laban & Gabriel, 2002, p. 17). Political events in Iran, the Iran-Iraq War (1980–1989), the lack of economic growth, and the lack of political freedom soon after the Islamic Revolution in 1978–79 have resulted in the exodus of a large number of Iranians to other parts of the world, including Canada (Mirfakhraie, 1999). For example, between 1980 and 1998, more than 69,000 Iranians immigrated to Canada, whereas from 1945 to 1978, less than 2, 500 Iranians had immigrated to Canada. As such, they have added to cultural diversity of Canada. For example, North Vancouver in British Columbia is now home to a growing and well established Iranian-Canadian community. In addition, due to the effects of *globalization*, new forms of cultural practices are created as people from diverse backgrounds interact and intermarry, forming **hybrid cultures** (Abu-Laban & Gabriel, 2002, pp. 17–18). As a result, the dominance of many national cultures is undermined and questioned in the era of *globalization*. The opposite is also true. Many national cultures are now concerned about cultural and moral decays of their societies (Kubow & Fossum, 2007). They are now attempting to deal with the consequences of cultural loss due to the effects of *globalization* and the influences of American and/or Western cultural norms and values. This has resulted in the rise of nationalistic policies that are not inclusive of regional and internal ethnic diversity and only promote the cultural and social interests of the dominant ethnic group in a nation-state.

Related to the cultural, economic, and social aspects of *globalization*, is the political perspective and the fact that *globalization* has also resulted in the lessening of the power of national governments (Abu-Laban & Gabriel, 2002, p. 18). At the same time, *glocalization* has resulted in the localities and local communities to bypass their national governments and to become economically more assertive since they are now linked directly to the world economy (Hiller, 2006, p. 68). For example, as mentioned, British Columbia's (BC) Provincial Government intensively seeks economic relations with Asian countries to promote investment in the province. Various Premiers of BC have traveled to various parts of Asia, such as India and China, to promote BC and its products. As Hiller (2006, p. 68) maintained, *nation-states* have been experiencing the "transfer of power and loss of control". In fact, "states no longer determine interactions between people and organization across state lines" (Hebron & Stack, 2009, p. 3). That is, in the era of *globalization*, "the site of authority, power, and politics is located outside the state" (Abu-Laban & Gabriel, 2002, p.18). This is exacerbated by the creation of *supranational* organizations. For example, the austerity measures that have been introduced in Greece and Spain in 2012 were imposed upon these countries by the European Union. The requirement of these policies is for the national governments to cut social programs and services, which will result in high unemployment and reduction in services available to their citizens.

Supporters of Globalization

Those who support *globalization* argue that it will result in:

1. better standard of living through consumerism and global production of goods and services;

2. promotion of democratic rights and values through spreading institutions that are based on democratic values; and

3. decreasing social, political, economic, and cultural conflicts due to the proliferation of global cosmopolitan values, implying that humans are citizens of the global village with similar aspirations, goals, and values (Hebron & Stack, 2009, p. 6).

The supporters of *globalization* maintain that the above characteristics further result in unifying the diverse populations of the world. They point out that due to the proliferation of mass communication more and more people have access to information and knowledge. As a result, politicians are made more accountable to their citizens. However, critics point out that the citizens of a *nation-state* are no longer isolated from their national governments (Hebron & Stack, 2009, p. 7). With more access to knowledge about other people and other cultural groups, for example, there will also be more tolerance toward and understanding of other countries and peoples. According to this view, an integrated global economy also leads to a much more efficient division of production between different *nation-states* as "capital and labour can be easily shifted to whatever country [that] offer[s] the most favourable opportunities" for investment (Hebron & Stack, 2009, p. 6). That is, supporters of *globalization* suggest that countries that have low wages should specialize in the type of work and production that are labour intensive, and those countries that have high wages can focus on capital and technologically intensive "productions" (Hebron & Stack, 2009, p. 6). In other words, certain countries can focus on producing agricultural products, exporting their natural resources, or become the hosts for mass-production of goods that are then exported to other countries for mass consumption. On the other hand, some countries should focus on research and development, which requires a highly educated and technical population. The problem with this type of argument is that such a division reproduces the already unequal power relations and inequalities between Western countries (with highly advanced technologies) and non-Western countries (that lack industrialization and high-tech corporations).

Detractors of Globalization

Unlike the supporters of *globalization*, the critics point out that *globalization* has also resulted in the intensification of poverty and widening the gap between the rich and the poor. The *globalization* process has also eroded democratic values and processes as economic, social, and cultural decisions and policies are decided by *supranational* organizations, whose members are not only not elected by civil society, but are also appointed by the most powerful people in the West. In this sense, IMF, the World Bank (WB), and the World Trade Organization (WTO) as well as Transnational/multinational corporations "reign supreme" (Hebron & Stack, 2009, p. 9). The end result is that citizens become marginalized and their concerns are moved to the margin of political, economic, and social decision-making processes. Despite the *globalization* of communication means and their usage by democratic forces and grass-roots organizations to push forward social justice policies and programs, the concentration of the ownership of these media networks in the hands of a few has weakened the free flow of ideas that are subversive and critical of *status quo*. For example, when discussing teacher unions, newspaper editors often use words such as "militant" that constructs them in a negative light. In fact, those who promote *globalization* of the economy and the rule of market, also promote antiunion policies, which have resulted in the passing of laws in various parts of the world that deny workers the right to form unions or to strike.

Critics also point out that *globalization* undermines the sovereignty of states. National governments can no longer determine their own political, economic, and social policies that address the needs of their populations. Despite the fact that countries are now economically interdependent, they do not have any global political influence over how such policies are devised or how they should be implemented. There are no social safety nets to protect the population against global economic fluctuations.

Globalization has also had dire consequences for political leaderships within *nation-states*, resulting in the overthrow of some leaders, thanks to global economic crises, such as the 1997–1998 Asian Financial Crisis that caused the ousting of President Suharto in Indonesia (Hebron & Stack, 2009, p. 9). *Globalization* is viewed as another way to "keep poor countries in a perpetual state of underdevelopment" (Hebron & Stack, 2009, p. 10). The adversaries of *globalization* remind us that although markets provide us with the products we want, they do not give us the types of lives based on social justice principles that many people across the world strive for (Benjamin Barber, as cited in Hebron & Stack, 2009, p. 10). The ideals of *globalization* (i.e., democracy and the free market) require the acceptance of (neo)liberal political cultural, social, and economic principles that are based on Westerncentric assumptions by non-Westerners (Hebron & Stack, 2009, p. 11). *Globalization* and marketization have also resulted in the institutionalization of the power of specific ethnic/national groupings and the further marginalization of ethnic "minorities" in various parts of the world. In other words, *globalization* fosters ethnic competition and instability (Hebron & Stack, 2009, p. 11). For example, it is criticized for its effects on the Indigenous cultures around the world, as they are forced with greater intensity to become assimilated into the dominant cultures of their respective *nation-states* and/or "into homogenized global monolith[s]" (Hebron & Stack, 2009, p. 11).

Part Two

The Ideology of Globalization: The neoliberal discourse

Critics of *globalization* argue that the process of *globalization* translates into global hegemony of capitalist relations. They point out that *globalization* is a discourse that promotes international trade, competitiveness, and cost-effectiveness. As a discourse, or "a framework of language, ideas, references, and understandings which shapes power relations", it is based on the **neoliberal ideology** (Abu-Laban & Gabriel, 2002, p. 19) that informs the perspective of the policy makers. They conceptualize *globalization* in the context of *neoliberalism*. Neoliberals assume that allocations of goods and services are managed better in the context of a market free of regulations. It is a set of policies that are devised and implemented by the West. *Neoliberalism* is influenced by an ideology that promotes the internationalization of public policy. Internationalization of public policy refers to "the extent to which national policies are influenced by outside factors in other parts of the world" (Abu-Laban & Gabriel, 2002, p. 23). As a result, national policies are more than ever influenced by Western socio-political-economic institutions. *Neoliberalism* emphasizes the role of the market and minimizes the role of government in economic decision-making.

Neoliberals argue for the transnational decentralization of production and services, resulting in the economies of various countries to become more than ever integrated into the global economy. Neoliberal policies promote and lead to the increasing economic specialization of nations in exporting food, natural resources, or industrial manufactured goods, perpetuating a tertiary division of economic development. Investment in local economies by multinational corporations has had devastating effects, namely the rise in unemployment and the movement of rural people into urban centres. This is especially the case since local firms and businesses cannot compete with multinational companies.

Neoliberalism argues that states must be less involved in monitoring economic policy. It promotes the downsizing of welfare programs. It is based on an ideology that promotes the idea that families and individuals must take responsibility for more of the services that were once offered by the government (Apple, 2007, pp. 15, 19). It promotes a limited role for the government, restricting the extent to which national governments should provide social services to their citizens. In fact, more emphasis is placed on individual self-sufficiency. Yet, neoliberals draw upon the state's power to implement their policies.

Neoliberalism endorses the idea that public firms, such as national airlines and utilities, must become privatized. It commodifies social services or programs, such as the education system, health services, and the prison system. Rather than thinking of Canadians as citizens, they are treated as clients and/or customers (Abu-Laban & Gabriel, 2002). As mentioned, it emphasizes global competition rather than the formation of global community or responsibility (Abu-Laban & Gabriel, 2002, p. 20). Neoliberals are also critical of the rights of social groups to organize and there have been "ideological attacks on social solidarity and collective political action" (Abu-Laban & Gabriel, 2002, p. 21). In this sense, *neoliberalism* is said to promote a narrow definition of citizenship.

Characteristics of Neoliberalism

Neoliberalism is characterized by a push towards the privatization and liberalization of the market. **Privatization** refers to a policy initiative that encourages governments to reduce their roles as managers and owners of business enterprises. Privatization "signifies the transfer by the state of public-sector enterprises to the private sector and/or liquidation of enterprises", and it can also take the form of "partnership between the private sector [and public sector] through joint ventures or partial sale of public-sector shares" (Harik, 1992, p. 1). An example of this is to turn various Crown Corporations into private hands as private enterprises, such as the sale of Air Canada. In general, privatization is influenced by the policies of the IMF and the World Bank. These international bodies also determine the extent and the nature of the liberalization policies.

Liberalization refers to those *laissez-faire* economic policies that aim at removing barriers to the movement of goods, capital, and services. Liberalization policies put limits on protective tariffs and other barriers to trade that can be implemented by national governments to protect their small industries from competition by bigger foreign firms. **Liberalization** as a process of opening of the national economy to foreign investments leads to extension of tax benefits to investors, which expands the freedom of private enterprises. Liberalization also results in the process of withdrawing from providing welfare and other social services by the state (Harik, 1992, pp. 1–13). Liberalization entails relaxing laws and regulations that protect the rights of workers and the environment. That is, it results in **deregulation**, as a way to attract foreign and national investment into the country or a specific region.

Are Neoliberal Policies Hegemonic?

A number of scholars have argued that neoliberal ideology results in racism, sexism, and classism, locally and globally. They maintain that neoliberal ideology is hegemonic (Giroux, 2012). **Hegemonic ideologies** are those dominant views and ideas that have become acceptable explanations of reality. They are presumed to promote the interest of all people. They are considered as normalized aspects of the everyday culture that should influence the social practices of social actors (**Social practice** refers to "what people say and do", McLaren, 1998, p. 178). Through hegemony, the most powerful classes in society win the consent of those classes that are oppressed (McLaren, 1998, p. 177). **Hegemony** refers to a process through which the oppressed classes unknowingly participate in their own domination (McLaren, 1998, p. 178). It is a form of moral and intellectual domination that is achieved not through coercion or force, but through "the general winning of consent of the subordinated class to the authority of the ruling class" (McLaren, 1998, p. 178). It is not a form of active coercion and domination. It is a process of structuring the culture, norms, values, and experiences of the subordinated groups and manufacturing their dreams and values in such a way that the dominant values and norms become aspects of the culture of the subordinated groups (McLaren, 1998, p. 178). According to Gramsci (as cited in Turner, 2003, 204), the ruling party (social class) is hegemonic since they determine and control not only the means of production and the political structure but also reproduction of ideology. Culture is propagated through the state's control over educational institutions, which promotes the ideas of the ruling class. *Neoliberalism* informs the global cultural, economic, social, and political practices and relations. As this ideology is normalized and internalized by the general populations, it forms the basis upon which they interpret the world and act upon the world. In this sense, it is hegemonic: it is a form of "cultural leadership exercised by the ruling class" (Ritzer, 2000, p. 275).

Part Three
From Industrialism to Postindustrialism

One of the most important characteristics of *globalization* has been its effects on *industrial development* across the globe. *Globalization* has also resulted in the **global division of labour** and the differentiations between those countries and regions considered as more or less *industrialized* (Giddens,

1990, p. 75). Modern industry has promoted divisions of labour not only in terms of the types of jobs and tasks that are needed to produce goods, but also in terms of the know-how knowledge, skills, natural resources (raw materials) used in the production process, and the types of industry (Giddens, 1990, p. 76). One of the consequences of *industrialism* has been the *globalization* of the usage of machine technology (Giddens, 1990, p. 76).

As mentioned, some sociologists have maintained that we now live in *postindustrial* and *postmodern* societies, as opposed to *industrial* or *modern* societies, where service sector economy dominates and images and popular culture are the most important aspects of the social world.

They have maintained that there are a number of discontinuities that distinguish the current historical epoch from the **industrial epoch**. We defined **industrialism** as an organization of society characterized by large-scale mechanized manufacturing industry using machines (Conley, 2010). As an economic system, *industrialism* signalled a radical shift from small-scale economic activities, such as farming, fishing, and craftsmanship mostly dependent on "manpower" and physical labour. As an ideology, *industrialism* promoted the idea that a movement away from back-breaking labour and small-scale production of goods and services is not only good for society, but inevitable and inexorable (unstoppable). In general, the terms *industrial* and *postindustrial* are used to mean technological and economic development, while the terms traditional, *modern*, and late modern have often been associated with the social and cultural changes that were induced by or caused economic and technological "progress" (Richmond, 1994, p. 37).

Daniel Bell argued that there are three successive phases of economic "progress" that have characterized modern societies: agricultural, manufacturing, and services (Allen, 1996b, p. 537). In contemporary Western societies, such as Japan, Canada, the United States, Germany, and France, more than half of the workforce is involved in a service oriented economic sector. In fact, since the 1750s, there has been a steady rise in the affluence of consumers, which has led to the purchase of more services than manufactured goods (Allen, 1996b, p. 537). This has resulted in the formation of a service economy. Bell argued that unlike in the *industrial* stage where the driving force beyond the economy was production and profit, in *postindustrial* societies the main driving forces are information and knowledge. Consider the fact that many companies, such as Yahoo, attempt to gather information about your behaviour on the web in order to use this knowledge to attract more and more companies to advertise on its web site and many services that it provides. Yahoo is not producing an item of consumption; it simply uses the existing technology to gather knowledge on its users and to sell the information as a way to make more profits. In other words, "it is the generation of knowledge and the processing of information that stimulate economic growth" (Allen, 1996b, p. 537).

Postindustrialism, Postindustrial Society, and Information Society

A *postindustrial society* is characterized by the production of services and information rather than material/manufactured goods. Since the 1960s, the Western world has experienced **deindustrialization**: many of the manufacturing companies have relocated to other parts of the world in search of cheap labour and less restricting environmental laws and regulations (Hiller, 2006).

Deindustrialization is one of the aspects and consequences of the *globalization* process (Hiller, 1996, p. 71). *Deindustrialization* highlights the new period of capitalism, in which capital has become global and mobile and moves with ease from one part of the world to another in search of increase in corporate profits (Hiller, 2006, p. 71). *Deindustrialization* signals the end of **Fordism** and the rise of **post-Fordism** in the West. As mentioned, in the context of *Fordist* production, manufacturing concentrated on the domestic market, and foreign countries were regarded as markets and places where, for example, Canadian industrial products could be sold for profits. In the context of *post-Fordism*, both capital and industries have relocated to non-Western parts of the world, where labour power is cheaply available. This has had the consequence of the decline of the industrial sector in countries, such as Canada. The other consequence has been the structural incorporation of the "Third World" countries into the capitalist world system.

Consider, for example, the fact that many of the items and products that we consume in our everyday lives are produced in places like Mexico, China, Pakistan, Indonesia, and Brazil. Most of our clothing is imported from non-Western parts of the world, where multinational corporations have set up shops and factories to exploit the labour of marginalized racialized groups. Even when the products are made and assembled in Western parts of the world, it is often the case that parts of the products were assembled or produced in other parts of the world in order to "minimize inventories and costs" (Hiller, 2006, p. 72). This is referred to as *vertical disintegration*. That is, certain parts of products are contracted out to factories and production units in other parts of the world in the form of "just-in-time-supply". In this way, corporations do not need to hold large inventories; thus, reducing their cost of production and increasing their rates of profit. Global communication has made this approach to production more readily available as managers and capitalists can transfer capital and place orders with a push of a button (Hiller, 2006, p. 72).

Popularized by Daniel Bell (1973), *postindustrialism* denotes a passing away of the *industrial* order and the emergence of a new era, where information, knowledge, and services are the dominant modes of production. In these types of societies, there is a shift in the types of work in which people are involved (Allen, 1996b, p. 538). Bell (1973) forecasted a shift from employment in primary and secondary industries into tertiary sector of the economy. According to Bell, as a result of the rise of affluence in Western countries amongst consumers, people began to purchase more services relative to manufactured goods and food products (Allen, 1996b, p. 537). That is, since the 1960s, Western societies have been moving toward **service economies**. As society shifted from agrarian mode of production to an *industrial* one, several structural changes occured. The changes include:

1. a shift from simple technology toward the application of "scientific" knowledge, creating more complex devices,

2. Human and animal labor are replaced with power-driven machines (mechanization),

3. Urbanization: increase in urban population, and

4. Family changes (i.e., in terms of economic activities, education, partner choices, more gender equality).

The following features characterize *postindustrial* societies:

1. the majority of the labor force is employed in services rather than agriculture or manufacturing,

2. white-collar employment is replacing blue-collar workers,

3. technical knowledge is considered as the key organizational feature of today's societies,

4. technical change is planned and assessed, and

5. reliance on computer modeling is found in all areas.

In general, **service sector** jobs are the main types of occupations available for people. In contrast to manufacturing jobs, these types of work are **nonmanual work**. This means that they involve some degree of social interaction and/or creativity (Allen, 1990, p. 538). In this type of work, we do not produce tangible products (i.e., a computer) rather we work with other people to deliver a service (i.e., a salesperson in a Department Store). For example, the Sylvan Educational Centres in British Columbia, Canada offer tutoring programs for K-12 students. They hire teachers and tutors whose main job is to offer educational services. These services are sold in the market for a price. Parents who think their kids need help with a specific subject, such as math, reading, and sciences, purchase them to enable their children to become successful in school (i.e., to get higher grades in their subjects, preparing them for university or college education that is necessary if they wish to obtain higher paying jobs in fields, such as medicine, law, computing sciences, and education). Lawyers, teachers, and nurses offer services. 7/11 workers and sales associates in various stores also offer some kinds of service to their clients. Service sector jobs tend to be part-time with no benefits, such as medical insurance or job security. Professional service sector jobs, on the other hand, are full-time, high paying, with a number of benefits. The changes in the types of work we do have resulted in changes in the structure of work: manual jobs are now replaced with white-collar and professional occupations (Allen, 1996b, p. 538). Most of these white-collar and professional occupations are characterized as **think work** since they involve using knowledge and information and their applications in the organization of the economy or the social world. In this type of society, we notice the rise of **knowledge elites**. They have control over and own the production and dissemination of knowledge and information (Allen, 1996b, p. 538). The *knowledge elites* or the **technical elites** are found in the universities, government institutions, economic bodies, and corporations (Allen, 1996b, p. 538).

There is also a tendency toward the bureaucratization of the work in which "knowledge elite" are involved through the processes of specialization and differentiation in their occupations (Allen, 1996b, p. 538). Bell "identifies a structural dislocation between the economic and the cultural realms of *post-industrialism* in which the Protestant value of economic efficiency and restraint, on the one hand, are undercut by a material sufficiency, on the other" (Allen, 1996b, p. 539). In this new society, there is a "desire among many to [be involved in] more individualistic and culturally expressive lifestyles" (Allen, 1996b, p. 539).

Alain Touraine also maintained that the new society is characterized by the "disposal of knowledge and the control of information" (Allen, 1996b, p. 538). He called this type of society a **programmed society** in which knowledge is an important and central defining element (Allen, 1996b,

p. 538). He used the term, **technocracy**, to refer to those agents of change who control knowledge production and its dissemination (Allen, 1996b, p. 538). According to him, there is a divide between technocrats and bureaucrats and "a renege of social groupings, including workers as well as students and consumers" (Allen, 1996b, p. 538). The main opposition is not between those who own the means of production or private property and the proletariat. The main form of opposition is in terms of "access to information and its uses" (Allen, 1996b, p. 538). This view contrasts with classical Marxist analysis, which argues the centre of conflict in modern societies is in the factory "and at the point of production" (Allen, 1996b, p. 539). According to Touraine, *postindustrial society* is "a setting in which the lack of power among certain social groups provides the basic new lines of social control and resistance" (Allen, 1996b, p. 539).

In the 1980s, a new term was introduced that is related to our discussion of *postindustrial society*: the *information society*. According to Bell, the proponent of the term, *information society* is a new expression of *postindustrial society* (Allen, 1996b, p. 539). *Information society* is about producing, disseminating, and selling images, knowledge, and information. The most important corporations, such as the IBM and Microsoft, produce services and knowledge that are sold in the form of programs and software that consumers use in their day-to-day interactions and workplace, globally. Whereas manufacturing jobs were located in the factories, workplace in the postmodern world is found in offices, shops, and for a number of people, in their homes. In this type of society, knowledge and information are the basis of innovation and they play important roles in the organization and administration of the economy. They (knowledge and information) are also the final product of the economic processes (Allen, 1996b, p. 537). That is, we use knowledge and information to produce more knowledge and information. They have become commodities that are sold in the marketplace for profit. Bell argued that "knowledge has replaced (productive) labour as the source of value which yields future profits" (Allen, 1996b, p. 540). He classified this as the "knowledge theory of value". That is, knowledge and how it is utilized are viewed as resources that have "the potential to transform … any kind of activity in an economy"; the new information technologies "have the potential to reshape the ways in which we produce and consume, as well as when we perform these activities" (Allen, 1996b, p. 540). For example, did you ever think that one day you would work for free for a grocery store when shopping there? Nowadays, due to the availability of self-serve checkout units in corporate grocery stores, we use these machines to process our purchases in the name of convenience. At the same time, we contribute to the loss of a number of jobs as only one person often manages these units in a store. Information is also a commodity, "which can be bought and sold in the marketplace" (Allen, 1996b, p. 540). The *information society* is led by "professional and technical workers, many of whom are concerned with the production, processing, or distribution of information" (Allen, 1996b, p. 540). Bell argued that these occupations have become central to the success of *postindustrial societies* (Allen, 1996b, p. 540).

Manuel Castell is critical of the term, *postindustrialism* (Allen, 1996b, p. 540). He maintained that *information society* should not be confused with "a service industry in which manufacturing sector has all but disappeared from the view" (Allen, 1996b, p. 541). He identified the new society not in terms of a particular sector of economy, but one based on the role of knowledge and the use of information (Allen, 1996b, p. 541). According to him, knowledge is used as a catalyst to produce new forms of knowledge that acts as a way to enhance economic development (Allen, 1996b, p. 541). The new technologies have enabled the corporations to operate in new and more footloose fashion (Allen, 1996b, p. 541). They have also resulted in the creation of "multiple networks between corporations" (Allen, 1996b, p. 541). He highlighted the fact there has been a move toward the creation of a *core-periphery* model of economic and labour market orientation. There is a high concentration of "information power" among the "knowledge elite" in the corporations and "the automation of low-skilled jobs" (Allen, 1996b, p. 542).

Andre Gorz argued that the introduction of new technologies has resulted in changing the nature and structure of employment in such a way that we now have social division between a class of aristocracy of secure and well paid workers and jobs in comparison to "a growing mass of unemployed" (Allen, 1996b, p. 542). Automation, he argued, has undermined the type of the jobs available to the working classes in terms of quality and status (Allen, 1996b, p. 542). Work for the majority of working class individuals has become an instrumental activity in order to earn a wage without substantial "satisfaction or skill content attached" (Allen, 1996b, p. 542). *Information society* is characterized by the "commodification of domestic tasks and their incorporation into the realm of economic rationality" (Allen, 1996b, p. 542).

In the context of *postindustrial society*, work for the majority of people involved in servile tasks lacks any dignity much the same as the jobs in mining and manufacturing during the era of industrialization (Allen, 1996b, p. 543). That is, *postindustrial* societies are marked by a growing social inequality (Allen, 1996b, p. 543). Although Bell pointed to the growth of white-collar occupations and the rise of the "knowledge elite", Gorz pointed to the rise of a deskilled working class who are made to serve the elites in *postindustrial society* (Allen, 1996b, p. 542).

In general, *postindustrial societies* are characterized by several features (Allen, Figure 16.1: Postindustrialism: dynamics and trends, 1996, p. 545):

1. At its core is the importance and centrality of "the role of knowledge and use of information".

2. Multinational corporations have promoted a system of centralized control over the decision making process, usually in Western countries, but have "decentralized production units" as products are made in different parts of the world.

3. There has been a relative increase in services in contrast to goods.

4. Social movements are no longer formed based on economic needs and class positions of the participants, but defined according to factors, such as "race", gender, sexuality, ability, etc. Examples of such new social movements are: the Feminist Movement, the Gay Movement, the Civil Rights Movement, which are based on "post-material needs".

5. There is an increasingly uneven global development characterized by "knowledge production in the advanced economies" and "industrial mass production at the periphery".

6. There is a rise in the polarization of the work force or an increase in the "new servile class".

7. There has also been a rise in the hierarchization of technical labour.

8. There has been a trend toward the "bureaucratization of scientific and administrative work".

9. There has been a push toward professionalization of work.

10. Information is considered as both a product and a process.

11. There has been a rise in the development of information networks and "wired" societies.

In summary, since the 1960s, some scholars have argued that we have been witnessing the disappearance of large scale mass production or the *Fordist* style manufacturing. The new economy is characterized by flexible forms of production that are then used in dealing with "the greater diversity of consumer demand and fragmented market tastes" (Allen, 1996b, p. 534). The shift from a mass to a more pluralistic kind of society is referred to as the rise of *post-Fordist* society. Those who propose that we have entered the *postindustrial* world see continuities between *Fordism* and the new social, economic, and technological arrangements. On the other hand, those who propose the *post-Fordist* thesis highlight breaks with *Fordism*. One thing that both of these theories have in common is their argument that "the ideas of progress that we associate with a modern *industrial* economy, especially those based on the methods of mass production, are also losing their relevance" (Allen, 1996b, p. 534). The industrial world was characterized by the notion that we can measure the transformation of nature through the application of technology and "science" in the process of making goods to be sold in the mass market. The *industrial* economy was a manufacturing economy that transformed raw materials into tangible goods. However, in *postmodern* societies, the majority of workers are not employed in factories and are not involved in the process of manufacturing goods that are then sold in the market (Allen, 1996b, p. 535). If the modern economy based on manufacturing was characterized by centralization and bureaucratization, the *post-Fordist or postindustrial society* is characterized by "more flexible, less hierarchical modes of economic organization" (Allen, 1996b, p. 535). There have been certain trends in the types of jobs that have been rising in importance since the 1960s. There has been a rise in service sector jobs and a decrease in manufacturing type jobs, partly due to the process of *deindustrialization*. Many of the factories in Western parts of the world have been relocating to other parts of the world in search of cheaper labour and lower standards of environmental protection in various parts of the world (or, in the Global South). Our lives today than any other time in the history of the world are dominated by a type of technology that is referred to as microchip. The composition of the workforce has also changed. In the past, many of the workers employed in full-time positions were men. In today's society, there has been a rise in part-time occupations that are mainly occupied by women and non-White "minority" groups (Allen, 1996b, p.536). A shift from manufacturing to service oriented economic system is influenced by "a generation of knowledge and information which act as the dynamics of change" (Allen, 1996b, p. 536). For example, consider how office work has been affected by the introduction of new technologies, such as email, fax, and instant messaging. In *postindustrial* societies this is characterized by an emphasis on knowledge and control of information (Allen, 1996b, p. 536).

Part Four

••

Postmodernity and Postmodernism

Postmodernism is a paradigm that is used by *postmodernists* to make sense of the changes that have affected the world since the 1960s. *Postmodernism* offers a critique of *modern* Western ways of thinking that is critical and radical in its orientation (Glense, 2011, p. 12). *Postmodernism* is a general term that is used to "describe the new aesthetic cultural and intellectual forms and practices which [have been] emerging [since the 1960s]" (Thompson, 1996, p. 569).

One of the main points that is expressed through the ideas of *postmodernism* is that it is no longer possible to distinguish between culture and society (Strinati, 1995, p. 223). The *postmodern* world is characterized by the centrality and power of the mass media, popular culture, and the ways in which the popular culture shapes and defines all forms of social relations (Strinati, 1995, p. 223). What we define as real and the truth about the world is more than ever determined and defined by the cultural forms, images, and signs we encounter in our every-day-livings (Strinati, 1995, p. 224). *Postmodernists* argue that the mass media does not reflect reality. Also, the mass media does not simply distort reality since this assumes that there is an objective reality out there (Strinati, 1995, p. 224). Rather, *postmodernists* point out that the mass media's constructions of reality are the only types of realities that are known to us (Strinati, 1995, p. 224) (See Box 9.1 – Postmodernism: the future is here?).

BOX 9.1 - Postmodernism: the future is here?

For *postmodernists*, the future is here. They contend that we no longer live in the *modern* world. Thus, *postmodernists* reject anything that relates to the *modern* project, including the search for grand theories or unifying explanations for social reality. Instead, they conceive *postmodern* social reality as heterogeneous, fluid, fragmentary, plural, unstable, and shifting.

Postmodernism connotes both a genre of artistic style and a set of theoretical and philosophical tenets. *Postmodernism* is characterized by extreme relativism, rejecting other theories, which can be tested according to rational, universal principles. It holds everything to ridicule (Wallace & Wolf, 2006).

Postmodernists challenge absolute truth, claiming there is no one truth but many truths; no one large story about the world; only small stories. They privilege multiple perspectives of class, "race", and gender. *Postmodernists* use subjugated knowledge to unmask and transform oppressive power relations. They insist that social reality is language games and insist that no one language is truer or "superior" to others. *Postmodernism* emphasizes the role of the unconsciousness, reinterpreting knowledge as socially constructed and historically situated instead of a timeless representation of the world by separate individuals. *Postmodernism* is a way to challenge the old *modernism* (Hall, 1996, p. 17). The intellectual roots of *postmodernism* have been traced to the writings of Foucault, Derrida, Lacan, Baudrillard, and Barth. Most of these thinkers became critical of Marxism. Some alleged that Marxism is too deterministic and reductionist, while others were disappointed by neo-Marxists who found it hard to come to terms with the collapse of communism. Foucault and Baudrillard maintained that theories, such as Marxism, are incapable of explaining current developments since the 1960s; however neo-Marxists, such as Harvey and Jameson, asserted that "postmodernist developments can be incorporated into renovated Marxist framework" (Thompson, 1996, p. 566).

Another related point argued by *postmodernists* is that it is now more difficult to distinguish between the economy and popular culture (Strinati, 1995, p. 224). That is, what we consume (the economy) is determined by the popular culture. For example, we buy cell-phones to communicate with one another. As we surf the Internet using our cell-phones, we receive advertisements that use cultural references and symbols that influence our purchasing and consumption habits. When we watch sitcoms, we may be influenced by fashion statements expressed through the characters of these sitcoms and purchase clothing and other fashion accessories that are worn by the characters in these sitcoms (or by characters in our favorite music videos). We may be also influenced by the product placements in such programs, such as the Brand of potato chips, soft drinks, and beer.

In the *postmodern* world, we increasingly consume products, images, and signs for their **symbolic values** rather than for their **use value**, usefulness. That is, in consuming goods, we are not concerned about questions of utility or value: they are ignored. For example, we purchase a Gucci watch not because we want to be able to tell time, but because a Gucci watch or purse denotes our positions in the hierarchy of society. As Strinati (1995, p. 225) maintained, "this is evident in popular culture itself when surface and style, what things look like, and playfulness and jokes, are said to predominate at the expense of content, substance, and meaning". We also experience reality through computer images and programs, such as virtual reality computer graphics (e.g., Grand Theft Auto video game). *Postmodernists* maintain that these images that are surface stimulations have the potential to replace real relations (Strinati, 1995, p. 225).

In the *postmodern* world, in addition, it is difficult to distinguish between popular culture and (high) art. Art has become a commercialized enterprise itself. It has also become increasingly incorporated into the economic world and the economy. Art is used to entice people to consume more due to the role it plays in the world of advertisement (Strinati, 1995, p. 226). "Another aspect is that *postmodern* popular culture refuses to respect the pretentious and distinctiveness of art" (Strinati, 1995, p. 226). *Postmodernist* thinkers also question the evolutionary and linear conception of time. History, for them, is not based on clear sequences of linear events that follow one another in a predictable and orderly manner (Strinati, 1995, p. 227). Unlike the *modern* thinkers, these scholars argue that the *postmodern* popular culture undermines our perception of a coherent sense of space and time and does not reflect it (Strinati, 1995, p. 227). The *postmodern* culture is one that is outside history (Strinati, 1995, p. 227).

As mentioned in the previous chapters, *modernity* refers to a historical epoch that changed the conditions of life for the population of the world drastically. *Modernity* refers to a historical period that is marked by the industrial revolution, the rise of the *nation-states* as a dominant form of political structure, and mechanization of society (Glesne, 2011, p. 12). *Modernity* is characterized by several factors: formal logic is thought to be a necessary aspect for reason, the process of the bureaucratization of society that refers to the process of rationalization and its effects on how humans organize their activities, and the belief that through application of technological innovation and "scientific" knowledge it is possible to solve all the ills of society and social and cultural as well as economic problems (Glesne, 2011, p. 12). *Modernity* assumes that there is a knowable objective world that is external to human subjectivity. "Science" was assumed to provide us with answers about the world and solutions to the world's problems, such as poverty: "Modern science and modernity have given us a great many benefits; better communication, better transportation, better roads, buildings, bridges, sewer systems and better housing. It continues to improve the means of production of food, shelter, clothing, and medicine. Yet, it has many problems in that it dismisses complexity; dismisses mystery; objects to surprize and is hostile to the emotions which expand the endpoints of human endeavor. It is an[*sic*] magician's apprentice which may well be misused with applications to war, to exploitation of people and environment as well as to the reproduction of its own lifeless, soulless, amoral approach to human knowledge and human frailty" (Young, 2012). A number of scholars have argued that we have now entered the age of *postmodernity* that is drastically different than the *modern* world. *Postmodernity* is a term that highlights a break with *modernity* (Glesne, 2011, p. 12). The change from *modernity* to *postmodernity* is also a subject of analysis for sociologists. *Postmodernity* refers to a historical epoch during which there has been a change from an emphasis on manufacturing to *information society*. Ritzer (2000, p. 223) maintained that there is a need to distinguish between *postmodernity* and *postmodern* social theory. He defined *postmodernity* as "a new historical epoch that is supposed to have succeeded the modern era, or modernity" (Ritzer, 2000, p. 223). *Postmodern* social theory or *postmodernism*, Ritzer asserted (2000, p. 223), is the way that we come to understand and conceptualize *postmodernity*. Loytard (as cited in Giddens, 1990, p. 2) defined *postmodernity* as "a shift away from attempts to ground epistemology and from faith in humanly engineered progress". The condition of *postmodernity* is believed to be distinguished by the loss of the importance of **grand-narratives**. *Grand-narratives* are those overarching 'story lines' through which humans "are placed in history as beings having a definite past and a predictable future" (Giddens, 1990, p. 2). *Postmodernism* is a shift in paradigm and how we come to think about the social world since the 1960s. We can label *postmodernism* as the third shift in paradigms about the world. The first shift in paradigm was characterized by "the move from isolated nomadic communities of hunters and gatherers to feudal societies with city-states and agrarian support system" (Slattery, 1995, p. 17). The second shift is characterized by the "move from the tribal and feudal societies to a capitalist industrial-based economy relying on scientific technology, unlimited consumption, social progress, unrestrained economic growth and rational thought" (Slattery, 1995, pp. 17–18). The third shift is the *postmodern* paradigm that "is characterized by fast-changing and cyclical concepts of time with sundry cultures and many genres of expression and is sometimes called the global international revolution" (Slattery, 1995, p. 18). The *postmodern* age is characterized by "a loss of rational and social coherence in favour of cultural images and social forms and identities by fragmentation, multiplicity, plurality, and indeterminacy" (Thompson, 1996, p. 566). *Postmodernists* claim that we have now entered a new, postcapitalist and *postindustrial* era. In short, *postmodernity* is characterized by the process of *globalization*. In this light, *globalization* is characterized by "the spread of information technologies and the fragmentation of nation-states" (Glesne, 2011, p. 12).

Giddens, however, argued that we have not entered the age of *postmodernity*. Rather, he posited that we are entering **late modernity**, where the effects of *modernity* are more pronounced and universalized (Giddens, 1990, p. 3). Giddens uses terms, such as "high", "radical", or "late" *modernity*, to refer to the world today. Ulrich Beck maintained that today's society is best described as a "risk society", whereas the classical stage of *modernity* is associated with *industrial* society. The central problem in new *modernity* is how to prevent, minimize, and channel risk (i.e., risk of nuclear disasters and war). Yet, the main concern remains the maximization of rationality in terms of both the system and the life-world (Ritzer, 2000, p. 222). Ritzer agreed that rationality is the key process of "high modernity". Ritzer introduced the concept of the **McDonaldization of Society** to highlight the increase in formal rationality in the late twentieth and early twenty-first centuries with its associated dangers of an "iron cage" bureaucracy (Ritzer, 2000, p. 222).

In short, *postmodernity* means several things (Giddens, 1990, p. 46):

1. "Nothing can be known with any certainty" due to the fact that modern "foundations of epistemology have been shown to be unreliable".

2. "History is devoid of teleology and consequently no version of progress can plausibly be defended".

3. "A new social and political agenda has come into being with the increasing prominence of ecological concerns and perhaps of new social movements generally".

Postmodernism makes several assumptions. **First**, since we now live in a postcapitalist/*postmodern* world, there is need for new social theories. The **second** assumption of *postmodernists* is that modern **grand theories**, such as feminism, Marxism, etc., do not offer adequate tools of analysis. The **third** argument of *postmodernists* is that the *grand theories* that define social reality in terms of dichotomies, such as male/female, human/machine, man/nature, nature/culture, self/other, primitive/complex, and capitalist/proletariat, are inadequate ways of viewing and understanding the world. These dichotomies are considered as myths that distort reality rather than represent or explain it.

As mentioned, *postmodernists* tend to reject those *modern* perspectives that were outlined by the early modern social theorists in understanding the world of politics, economy, and culture (Ritzer, 2000, p. 222). They, for example, reject the adequacy of the *grand-narratives* of classical sociological theories to explain and describe the world in its totality. Theories of Marxism and structural functionalism are considered as *grand-theories* or *grand-narratives*. In other words, *postmodernism* is characterized by the loss of the importance of *meta-narratives*, such as Marxism, structural functionalism, and the discourse of "science", which "make absolute, universal and all-embracing claims to knowledge and truth" (Strinati, 1995, p. 227). By this, it is meant that these theories were assumed to explain social, political, cultural, and economic relations and structures, in all parts of the world, and were considered as unified theories that could provide a single vision and paradigm to understand human relations and structures, both locally and globally. These modern theories attempted to explain "how societies work and how people develop and interact" (Glesne, 2011, p. 12). *Postmodernists* argue that one theory cannot explain the world and that "there are no universal truths to be discovered, because all human investigations are grounded in human society and can only produce partial locally and historically specific insights" (Delamont, as cited in Glesne, 2011, p. 12). *Postmodernists*, in fact, tend to prefer "more limited explanations or even no explanations at all" (Ritzer, 2000, p. 223). They are critical of putting boundaries between different disciplines, such as sociology as distinct from philosophical thinking or storytelling (Ritzer, 2000, p. 223). *Postmodernists* "are often more interested in shocking … the reader than they are in engaging in careful, reasoned academic discourse", which are the characteristics of modern theoretical thinking (Ritzer, 2000, p. 223). Instead of looking at how rationality or capitalist exploitation works in society, *postmodernists* are more interested to look at "more peripheral aspects of society" (Ritzer, 2000, p. 223). In this sense, *postmodernism* is a form of critical theory that questions the "scientific" and analytical aspects of sociology (Turner, 2003, p. 227). *Postmodern* social theory defines the *postmodern* world as a consumer society (Ritzer, 2000, 226). That is, consumption plays an important role in organizing society and people's behaviours and conceptions of reality. *Postmodernism* looks at micro-politics, power relations in various local contexts, and interrogates "discourses, language games, or interpretative communities" (Thompson, 1996, p. 570). As such, it tends to promote political change through multiple and local struggles.

To recap, according to Fredric Jameson (Ritzer, 2000, p. 223), *postmodernity* is viewed as: "a depthless and superficial world"; a world of simulation, that is, rather than experiencing a real jungle, we prefer to go to Disneyland's jungle cruise, which is a copy and "man-made" (sic) construction of the real thing; "a world that is lacking affect and emotion"; a world that one's place in history is lost, where it is difficult to distinguish between past, present, and future; a world where the productive and exploitive technologies of *modernity*, such as automobile assembly lines, are replaced with "implosive, flattening, reproductive technologies of television and visual culture". Thompson maintained (1996, p. 568), Baudrillard saw the *postmodern* world as one where culture is produced through an emphasis "on images (simulations) in which it is no longer possible to distinguish the 'real' from the copy that 'improves on the real'. In this new *postmodern* world, the hyper-real replaces the real. In this sense, Baudrillard defined *postmodernity* as a cultural period that highlights "the death of meaning" (Thompson, 1996, p. 568).

Postmodernity is an attempt to transcend *modernity*. Transcending *modernity* is achieved in eight distinct but interrelated ways (Slattery, 1995, p. 19):

1. We need to be critical of the view that we can and should control and exploit nature. We need to learn to live in harmony with nature and move away from a post-anthropocentric view.

2. We need to develop ways of promoting peace and harmony without resort to militaristic options.

3. We need to become critical of patriarchal views and seek to dismantle the ways in which we subordinate women by creating social structures that are inclusive of both masculine and feminine worlds equally.

4. We need to become critical of Eurocentric views that assume other cultures are "inferior" to European values and cultural norms or economic, political, and technological systems. We need to become inclusive of indigenous forms of knowledge as legitimate knowledge.

5. Scientific knowledge is not the only way to understand and approach the social and natural worlds. There are numerous other forms of moral, religious, and cultural intuitions that shed light on the truth about the world. These types of knowledge and ways of knowing must inform public policy formations.

6. We need to become critical of expert knowledge based on mechanistic perspectives of modern sciences that aim at controlling the universe. Rather, we should strive toward ecologically informed consensus that accounts for interdependency of various factors and structures.

7. We must become aware of the consequences of nationalism and nationalistic views and replace these ideas with a set of principles that promote the welfare of the world population.

8. The world needs to be conceptualized as an organism rather than a machine. The earth is our home rather than a possession of humans. We are interconnected souls rather than atomized individuals.

Due to its emphasis on diversity and *difference* rather than *sameness* (a characteristics of modernity), *postmodernism* is a paradigm that highlights the views of the less privileged in society. *Postmodernism* is critical of imperialism and focuses on the effects and legacies of colonialism and the ways in which colonial structures and relations subjugated other groups based on specific conceptions of "race", ethnicity, and nationality (Glesne, 2011, p.12). It analyzes how colonialism is practiced and continues to affect people by problematizing the multiple ways through which colonialism informs the lives of people across the globe (i.e., through language, values, customs, positions of power, and borders). It attempts to open up spaces for the voices of nondominant groups to talk about their experiences and to speak for themselves (Thompson, 1996, p. 570).

Postmodernism emphasizes micro-politics and local issues. It highlights how societies are fragmented by emphasizing on discontinuities between past, present, and future (Thompson, 1996, pp. 569–570). It questions the assumption that through the application of "scientific" knowledge and technological innovations reason will triumph over nature (Thompson, 1996, pp. 569–570). *Postmodernism* is critical of Western humanist and modernist ideals that have shaped how we think about the world around us (these ideas form the centre). It seeks to make the centre inclusive of the voices of non-Westerners (to make it more diverse). The goal is to forge a nonhierarchical view of the world, disrupting and debunking the conventional "superior-inferior" mindset prevalent in Western societies. It is a way of dismantling the hegemony of Western knowledge (Glesney, 2011, pp. 12–13). Edward Said, Gayatri Spivak, Homi Bhabha, and Arjun Appadurai are important figures who have attempted to theorize based on the experiences of marginalized people in the world and question the dualist thinking so prevalent in Western ways of thinking.

In general, *postmodernism* refers to a set of diffused sentiments rather than to a set of common doctrines. *Postmodernism* indicates that "humanity can and must go beyond the modern" (Griffin, as cited in Slattery, 1995, pp. 18–19). *Postmodernism* is a perspective that rejects the search for *grand theories* or unifying explanations for social reality, but instead it conceives of social reality as heterogeneous, fluid, fragmentary, plural, unstable, and shifting. It connotes both a genre of artistic style and a set of theoretical and philosophical tenets. *Postmodernism* is characterized by extreme relativism, rejecting other theories, which can be tested according to rational, universal principles. Although the world today is much different than the world that Marx, Weber, and Durkheim theorized about, a number of contemporary scholars argue that there are more continuities between the *modern* world and the so-called *postmodern* world that meets the eye (Ritzer, 2000, p. 222).

There are at least eleven different ways that *postmodernism* has been defined and understood (Slattery, 1995, pp. 15–16):

1. It is a historical period that signals the major changes taking place in the modern industrial and technological age.

2. It refers to a collection of aesthetic styles in art and architecture that are multiple and eclectic.

3. It is a framework that criticizes liberalism and communism as examples of unified and all-encompassing systems of political and economic organization.

4. It is a way to critique modern understandings of truth, language, knowledge, and power by exploring the internal contradictions of theories that attempt to explain social, economic, political, and cultural events (meta-narratives). It is a philosophical movement.

5. It is a cultural critique that highlights the negative consequences of *modernity* in terms of technological influences. In its place, it attempts to offer ways through which a holistic and ecologically sustainable global community could be constructed.

6. A radical approach to both the past and future that simultaneously criticizes and accepts, honors and subverts, embraces and limits, and constructs and deconstructs. It is a double-voiced framework of understanding the world after *modernity*.

7. It is a movement characterized by critique of the materialist conceptions of *modernity*.

8. It is a framework that not only celebrates other peoples and cultures but also acknowledges the histories and voices of women and racialized groups.

9. It is a revolutionary historical period during which the basic assumptions of the modern age and the cosmology of *modernity* are subverted and questioned.

10. It informs ecological and ecumenical frameworks and approaches that are not based on conceptions of dominance and control that define modern approaches to nature and the physical world.

11. It is a de-centring movement based on post-structuralism that focuses on the margins and borders of the social world. It questions the values and views of those who control the centre of power and knowledge and offer their understandings of the world as the truth about the world, ignoring the knowledge systems of those in the margins as unimportant or lacking objectivity.

A Critical Summary

There are as many criticisms as there are praises for *postmodernism* as a social theory. The critics fault *postmodernism* of its extreme relativism. They allege that for *postmodernism*, everything and anything goes, as there are no unifying moral values that can be applied universally. There are no conceptions of right or wrong. Despite such a criticism, it is important to note that the world is becoming more diverse and culturally plural and there are a number of competing ideologies and episteme (understanding of knowledge) that inform peoples' behaviours and actions (Slattery, 1995, p. 17). Thus, scholars sympathetic to the *postmodernist* paradigm see an emancipatory and empowering potential in this new perspective, in that it seeks to disrupt and decentre the existing oppressive and dominating structures in society. *Postmodernists* challenge any claim to absolute "truth", arguing that there is no one "truth" but many "truths". They maintain that there is no one all-encompassing story about the world that can explain it; there are only small stories that highlight the fragmented nature of life. They privilege multiple perspectives of class, "race", and gender of many other group affiliations. *Postmodernists* use subjugated knowledge to unmask and transform oppressive power relations. They insist that social reality is a form of language games. No one language (discourse) is "truer" or "superior" to others. *Postmodernism* emphasizes the role of the unconsciousness, reinterpreting knowledge as socially constructed and historically situated instead of a timeless representation of the world.

Conclusion

We now live in a world that is heterogeneous and relations and structures in one part of the world are affected by relations and structures in other parts of the world. Whether we live in a *postindustrial* or *information society*, the world is influenced by *neoliberal* policies that have had devastating effects on peoples across the world. This world is best understood through the prism of many theories and perspectives. In the next chapter, we explore the ideas and forces that drove and continue to drive transhistorical and global transition from *modernity* to *postmodernity* with the help of major sociological perspectives.

Chapter Review Questions

1. Define the following concepts and give an example for each: globalization, glocalization, neoliberalism, globalism, modernity, modernism, postmodernity, and information society.

2. How does Lyotard define postmodernity? What two major meta-narratives did he see in modern history? Do we still believe in either one?

3. According to Bell, what are the three main types of society found in human history? What sort of economy, technology, and social structure do we find in each?

4. What are the main elements of postindustrial society? Do we in fact live in such a society? Has Big Industry left our shores forever?

5. How does Castells define the information age and network society? Is our network society still capitalist? If so, how so?

6. What sort of time and space dominates Castells' information age? Give examples.

7. Outline Baudrillard's idea of simulacrum.

8. Outline the five key aspects of postmodern popular culture, giving examples of each from film, TV, music, and literature. Is most of popular culture today postmodern?

9. What are the neoliberal and social democratic approaches to the global economy?

10. Outline the five major characteristics of globalization. Give examples of how each has affected your own life.

11. What does Beck mean when he says that we live in a "risk society"? How is the "risk society" related to what he calls the 'post-traditional' order?

12. What does Ritzer mean by McDonaldization of society?

13. In what ways postmodernity transcends modernity. Explain.

14. What are the different ways in which postmodernism has been defined and understood?

Critical Thinking Questions

1. Are we moving toward post-postindustrial and postmodern types of societies and social, economic, political structures? Explain.

CHAPTER TEN

· ·

Classical and Contemporary Sociologists and Sociological Theories

Introduction

· ·

In this chapter, we introduce the reader to a number of classical and contemporary theoretical perspectives in sociology. The chapter is divided into seven parts. In Part One, we explore some of the terminologies and ideas that cut across all types of theory. We also introduce the reader to three different ways of conceptualizing the different types of theory. In Part Two, we examine the main social thinkers who influenced sociologists. In Part Three, the ideas of structural functionalism and conflict theory, as well as Durkheim, Marx, Weber, Hegel, and Gramsci are explained. In Part Four, we examine the ideas of poststructuralists, such as Foucault and Bourdieu. In Part Five, we highlight the main argument of different strands of symbolic interactionism. In Part Six, we focus on feminism and queer theory. Finally, in Part Seven, we offer the reader an overview of theories that focus on the process of racialization.

Part One

· ·

Sociology is a multidimensional and multidisciplinary approach to understanding human relations and behaviour and social organizations and structures. As we explained in Chapters One and Two, sociology is a field of study that offers controversial and at times divergent understandings of the same phenomenon. It is generally accepted that Émile Durkheim, Max Weber, and Karl Marx are the "fathers" of sociology. Each one has influenced sociology in a number of ways. Marx has influenced conflict theory and its focus on how inequalities are reproduced in capitalist societies.

Max Weber has influenced conflict theory, structural functionalism, and symbolic interactionism. Durkheim's analysis and arguments have also been influential in the formation of structural functionalism and post structuralism. In this section, we explore some of their main arguments and essential ideas.

We begin this section with a brief exploration into the definitions, functions, and characteristics of theories. We will then proceed to introduce the major sociological paradigms or theories. So what is a theory? In general terms, a theory is a set of ideas supported by facts. There are as many definitions of the concept of theory as there are scholars studying the phenomenon. But we will not inundate you with a variety or versions of definitions. Instead, we offer what we think is a simple and straightforward definition given by George Ritzer. He defined a theory as "a set of interrelated ideas or concepts that allow for the systematization of knowledge of the social world, and predictions about the future of the social world" (Ritzer, 2002, p. 2). Theories are derived from practical, everyday realities. Far from springing from nowhere, theories are based on empirical, observable, testable, and verifiable reality.

Theories perform a variety of useful functions in helping to better cognize, perceive, and understand our seemingly chaotic, complex, and information-rich world. Among the functions theories perform, are the following:

Prediction: Theories, as Ritzer (2002) notes, assist us in predicting future events. Sociologists and other social scientists have used a variety of theories not only to explain the causes of social problems, but also to make predictions about the probability of these problems occurring in the social world. For example, Karl Marx, studying the capit\alist system in the eighteenth century, predicted that, given the nature of the capitalist economy, the recession the world capitalist economy is now facing is inevitable.

Generation of ideas: Theories help communicate ideas. Any good theory generates new ideas for research and for understanding social, economic, political, and cultural issues and relations. This is the *heuristic function* of theories. A theory is said to have a heuristic value when it aids discoveries, in creating new ideas, "new research questions, new hypotheses, or new variables or concepts" (Littlejohn & Foss, 2008, p. 27). This means that an original theory provides the basis for the creation of newer and more comprehensive theories.

Control of events: Theories assist us to control current or future events. Good theories enables us to deal with social problems by pointing to the root causes, impacts of, and possible solutions to these problems.

Generating new ways of living: Theories have an inbuilt subversive and disrupting logic that challenge the *status quo*. Thus any new theory proposes the rejection of the old way of doing things and puts forth new ways of doing things. For example, feminist theories have not only challenged and disrupted the centuries-old patriarchal system built on the subordination of women, but also have proposed new ways of analyzing male-female relationships in our society. While women by and large still play the role of "nurturers" of young ones and homemakers, increasing numbers of men are staying home to take care of the children while their wives go to work as breadwinners.

Types of Theories

Descriptive versus Normative

Mann (2011) distinguishes between ***descriptive*** and ***normative*** theories. A *descriptive theory* "describes and explains the nature of a given society"; whereas, a ***normative*** theory "suggests what is right and wrong about that society and what needs to be done to change it" (Mann, 2011, pp. 2–3). Both of these types attempt to criticize aspects of a society, but *normative theories* seek to criticize and reform society, whereas *descriptive theories* attempt to avoid basing conclusions grounded on values. *Normative theories* are also known as ***value-conscious*** theories (Littlejohn & Foss, 2008, p. 27). Scholars who adopt this approach follow in the footsteps of Karl Marx, who not only insisted that the scholar cannot be value-free, but he or she must be an activist, vigorously participating in seeking practical solutions to problems that the oppressed peoples, such as the working classes, face in society. Marx advised that it was not enough for scholars to propound theories to identify, interpret, or explain problems facing the world; the scholar must do something about those problems. He wrote that until his time philosophers had only interpreted the world in various ways; the goal must be to change the world (See Box 10 - 1: Karl Marx and Praxis).

BOX 10 - 1: Karl Marx and Praxis

Karl Marx was raised during the reign of the Prussian state over the geographical space that is now known as Germany. Prussia was a repressive society in which organized religion supported the state's activities (Turner et al., 2002, p. 103). Anyone, like Karl Marx, who questioned the legitimacy of the religious order or the state was considered as the enemy of the state and labelled as subversive (Turner et al., 2002, p. 103). Marx was a member of a group called *Young Hegelians*. He also worked as a journalist and wrote critically about the experiences of wine growers and peasants "who stole timber to heat their homes in winter". He was critical of the repressive nature of other European governments. Because of his political activities and writings, Marx had to leave Germany and eventually settled in Paris, where he was introduced to the political economy of Adam Smith and David Ricardo (Turner et al., 2002, p. 104).

Like Durkheim and Weber, Marx was also concerned with abstract philosophical thought and concrete realities of the everyday life. He was an active agent of social change. He practiced what he preached. He believed in the idea of **praxis**. That is, he maintained that ideas and simply talking about issues or having knowledge about the conditions of life cannot in themselves result in social change. One must also act upon ideas and materialize them. Action is the source of social change: "Philosophers have only interpreted the world, the point is to change it" (Marx, as cited in Seidman, 1994a, p. 45). He was involved in many social movements. During the mid-1800s, many revolts took shape in Europe that aimed at changing the system, but all of them were defeated by oppressive forces, the army, and the European states. For example,

Paris "workers hold the city against the onslaught of the French army for six weeks" (Turner et al., 2002, p. 105). And, in 1864, the International Working Man's Association was established in London (Turner et al., 2002, p. 106). Through immersing himself in such movements, Marx attempted to demonstrate how theory and action could be united to bring about change through revolutionary movements (Turner et al., 2002, p. 106).

In contradiction to Marx's position, Max Weber insisted that the scholar should be neutral, taking no definite position on social issues. Unlike the scholar-activist who descends from an ivory tower into the real world to become involved in promoting change *with* and on behalf of the oppressed groups, Weber called for an armchair scholar who merely theorized about the world. This may not be an entirely fair assessment of Weber's ideas, because he did apply his theoretical knowledge in practical ways in his academic and public life. Mann (2011, p. 3) suggested that while both *descriptive* and *normative social theories* are applicable in social theory, it is "unlikely that we can actually achieve a full-fledged scientific objectivity in social theory".

How Do We Know What We Know?

As we pointed out in Chapter Two, social scientists answer the above question by using two different paradigms or approaches: **ontological** and **epistemological**. **Ontology**, simply defined, is the study of being or what *is* or what exists. It refers to theories concerning what 'exists' to be known. Thus, taking a particular ontological position articulates your assumptions about the nature of social reality and what is 'knowable' to the social scientist. The ontological perspective seeks to answer questions, such as: "What is society? What are its constituent parts and how are they related?" and What is the cause of social change? In answering these questions, social scientists who adopt the ontological approach deploy the positivistic method in carrying out research. In other words, some researchers answer the question by way of *positivism* and *empiricism*, the idea that sense perceptions are the only admissible basis of human knowledge and precise thought (Littlejohn & Foss, 2008, pp. 16–17). The term *positivism* was coined by French sociologist, Auguste Comte, who insisted that social scientists must use the same methods employed by natural scientists (i.e., observation, collection of data, analysis of the data, and drawing conclusions) to study human society. Just as the natural world is guided by natural laws, positivists contend that society is guided by societal laws, and the duty of the social scientist is to discover these laws, in order to properly understand the nature of the social world (Quist-Adade, 2012, p. 11).

Empiricism is an outgrowth from and an extreme form of *positivism* and emphasizes verifiable and observable phenomena. The central premise is that research should be driven by raw data drawn from objective, observable, and quantifiable social phenomena. In other words, the empirical and positive traditions in social research and analysis assert that only what is perceivable by our senses, sight, smell, touch, hearing, and taste, are worthy of our attention or study. Positivists seem to argue that "seeing is believing"; everything else is considered as speculation, conjecture, and wishful thinking, and does not count much in "scientific" research. From the positivist perspective, things are what they are ("what you see is what you get"). They exist outside of our consciousness. A tree is a tree, period; just as the mathematical formula 1 + 1 = 2 will hold true anywhere (say in Canada, Cambodia, or India). Knowledge is held to be universal and constant (Quist-Adade, 2012, pp. 10–11).

In the social sciences, two major **worldviews** help us to capture the essence of how we come to know what we know. The ontological paradigm falls under **Worldview I**. *Worldview I* adopts a positivistic, objective, and empiricist methodology in research and knowledge creation, and is based on the following assumptions:

1. Knowledge is created through discovery;

2. The world and its attributes are assumed not only to be external to the individual, but also conceived as *a priori* (already existing);

3. The world and its attributes are quantifiable, meaning each attribute can be studied separately and mathematically;

4. There is only one knowable "truth" about the world to be discovered. This "truth" is not constructed by human beings; rather it is a natural, objective reality, waiting to be discovered by the social scientist;

5. The "truth" is quantifiable (i.e., it can be objectively perceived and countered one by one); and

6. The point of academic research, then, is to discover the "truth". In short, the ontological approach informs empirical scholarship and quantitative research methodology, such as *the experiment* and *the survey* (Littlejohn & Foss, 2008; Quist-Adade, 2012, p. 12).

Epistemology is defined as the study of knowledge and how knowledge comes to be created. It is used to refer to theories about the ways in which we perceive and know our social world. An epistemological position thus states *how we know what we know*. Knowledge, from the epistemological position, is not *sui generis* (self-generating/of its own), something out there or *a priori (*independent*)*, but instead, a social and cultural construct. What this means is that human beings create their own knowledge about the world. What we know is simply our own creation through interpretations and understandings. Thus, for example, a tree is not a tree unless we call it so. This book you are reading is simply an object like any other human phenomenon until you call it so (i.e., a book). A Martian, for example, may call this book something else (i.e., flakes of wood with undecipherable "gibberish", perhaps) (Quist-Adade, 2012).

The epistemological paradigm falls under **Worldview II**. *Worldview II* is *interpretativist* and *constructivist*, and treats knowledge not only as a social, historical, political, and cultural construct, but also as value-loaded. Rather than being a fixed, universal, and natural phenomenon, knowledge is an ever-changing fluid reality bound by temporal (time/historical), spatial, political, normative, and cultural factors. Furthermore, since knowledge is constructed by human beings, it stands to reason that the "constructors" embed their values in the knowledge they construct. As is true that beauty lies in the eyes of the beholder, the "truth of any given domain is dependent on each individual's perception and conception of what constitutes the truth" (Quist-Adade, 2012, p. 12).

Worldview II adopts **qualitative** and **interpretativist** methodology in research and knowledge creation, and is based on the following assumptions:

1. Knowledge is arrived at by interpreting the world, meaning that the world exists outside the person but individuals conceptualize and interpret it in ways that make sense to them;

2. There is not one single and knowable "truth" in the world to be discovered, but rather multiple "truths";

3. The point of academic research therefore is to examine how and why different people construct, understand, and interpret the social world differently;

4. There is no objective and universal "truth"; and

5. Knowledge cannot be quantified or measured (Littlejohn & Foss, 2008; Quist-Adade, 2012, pp. 11–12).

This approach allows us to examine why and how different people construct messages from the same media text. Different people will have different understanding of the same newspaper text because media texts are conceived by social scientists who adopt the second worldview as embedded with multiple meanings, and, hence, are considered as polysemic or polysemous. Each individual filters the same media message through his/her cultural, "race", ethnic, gender, class, and religious lenses.

The Critical Constructivist Paradigm

The critical constructivist paradigm, which we may term the **Worldview III** is an offshoot of, and takes constructivism further. Its central assumption is that since knowledge is constructed to serve peoples' interests, we should look at whose interests are being promoted and for what ends. The following premises inform the critical constructivist paradigm:

1. It is not enough to discover or interpret the world;

2. Knowledge has power implications: it can be used to oppress people or be the source of resistance and anti-oppression movements; maintaining the *status quo* or challenging, subverting, or overthrowing the *status quo;* and

3. Dominant groups in society use their advantage of, and control over, knowledge to entrench their interests and values.

This approach emphasizes the need to get at the bottom of how social institutions, such as the media and the educational system and the power elite who dominate them, construct meaning for us; and how we, in turn construct meaning to suit our own needs. It directs our attention to the forces behind knowledge construction and dissemination, and sheds light on whose ideologies and values are embedded in knowledge, as well as problematizes who profits from such knowledge. In short, the *critical constructivist* paradigm focuses on the intersection of politics, culture, and the economy in light of the interactions of various social actors in multiple institutions, creating, shaping, and directing the social world (Quist-Adade, pp. 10–11; Heiner, 2010, p. 11).

Part Two

• •

The Social History and the Philosophical Roots of Classical Sociological Paradigms

In this section, we sketch a social history of sociological theories, beginning with their philosophical antecedents in the works of Hobbes, Locke, and Rousseau, followed by the "movers and shakers" of classical sociological theories, including Émile Durkheim, Herbert Spencer, Karl Marx, Max Weber, Talcott Parsons, and Robert Merton. We follow with an exploration of the main classical theoretical paradigms and finish with modern and postmodernist paradigms.

Thomas Hobbes (1588–1679)

Hobbes' most important writings are *The Elements of Law* (1640), *De Cive* (*The Citizen*, 1642), and *Leviathan* (1651). His overall objectives were to put moral and political philosophy on a "scientific" basis, and to contribute to the stability, peace, and welfare of "mankind". Hobbes felt that the majority of earlier thinkers had failed to achieve these goals because they based their theories of society on "mankind's" highest aspirations. He therefore sought to create a code of natural law as morally binding and determining the purpose of society. In other words, Hobbes sought to formulate a general law of ethics that would be universally binding. He started by separating his notion of natural law from human perfection. He then developed a psychology of human passions or interests (Delaney, 2004, p. 2; Quist-Adade, 2012, p. 88).

Hobbes believed he had uncovered the basis of human behaviour and human nature. He used these as assumptions to build his theory. Finally, he believed that people have competing interests, and this has implications for what he termed the "**state of nature**" (Westby, 1991, p. 24). The *state of nature* was a chaotic and lawless place of permanent war of all against all and was characterized by the vilest of human behaviour: selfishness, greed, brutality, and meanness. In this state, people lived in constant fear (Delaney, 2004, p. 2). Hobbes reasoned that to prevent chaos, society, through political and economic organization, must use force and coercion to hold society together. People ought to be willing to give up the same rights as they expect others to give up, and ought to be satisfied with just as much liberty with respect to others, as others have with respect to them. What Hobbes meant is that society operates on what we would term the *principle of surrendered freedom*. What we mean by this principle is that for any collective action to be successful, each member of the group or collectivity must forego at least one freedom. For example, our decision to write this book together involved each of us sacrificing some of our freedoms; the freedom to go on vacation, the freedom to read a book we long wanted to read, or the freedom to just rest. Your decision to be in your sociology class implies you have sacrificed your freedom to do other competing tasks. An agreement about the limits of one's and others' freedom by the members of society forms a **social contract**. In short, to secure their survival, people must mutually agree to set aside their hostilities and establish a government and appoint a central authority, which Hobbes called the **Leviathan**, to assure that they abide by their agreements.

Social Contract

The *social contract* is not between the citizens and the ruling power. Rather, it is a contract the citizens make with each other to accept the rule of central authority. The contract stipulates that the "minority" accepts the "majority" decision. Hobbes proposed that societies need to become united by forming a single political body, a commonwealth. In his book, *The Leviathan*, the ruler is the absolute authority or sovereign. Hobbes invested the following roles in the sovereign:

a) Enforcement of Law,

b) Legislative power, and

c) Judicial power.

The sovereign is not subject to the laws. Citizens retain certain "inalienable rights" or "retained rights". Hobbes asserted that for social rights to be attained, there must be a guarantee that people would obey and perform their parts as commanded by *social contracts*. For example, without respect for (private) property rights, everyone has a claim on everything, and chaos will ensue. He contended that justice is not based on equal outcomes, but rather it was based on the equality of process and equality of opportunity. In the *state of nature*, people share a kind of equality. Inequality is the product of civil law. Regardless, people perceive themselves as equals, and will enter into contracts willingly only under equal terms.

What are Hobbes' contributions to sociological thought and theorizing? Simmons (2013, p. 52) observed that "Hobbes' legacy with regards to the development of sociological theory is his assertion that individuals are the basic building blocks of society". Since human beings are "active, assertive and dynamic being[s]" (Yurdusev, 2006, p. 308), the appropriate role for government is to preserve the individual's ability to achieve self-interests (e.g., through the accumulation of wealth) while protecting everyone from others' natural and self-serving inclinations (Ravelli 2011, p. 40).

John Locke (1632–1704)

John Locke has been described as a **natural law** theorist. He is widely believed to be one of the chief inspirations of the American Revolution. His major works included *Essays on the Law of Nature* (1664), *Essay Concerning Toleration* (1667), *Two Treatises of Government* (1689), and *Essay Concerning Human Understanding* (1690). The key to understanding Locke's philosophy is his belief, set out in his *Essay Concerning Human Understanding* (1690), that people are born **tabula rasa** (a Latin term meaning "**blank slate**"), suggesting that there can be no knowledge independent of experience (see Gintis, 2006). Several assumptions underpin his theory of *natural law*. **First**, human society and morality is governed by God's will. **Second**, God saw human beings as rational agents, invested with reason. **Third**, God contended that there is an intersection of self-interest of the individual and general interests of society as a whole (Delaney, 2004, p. 6).

The central thesis of Locke's *law of natural rights* is that God has invested all people with fundamental rights to life, health, liberty, and possessions, and governments are formed to protect these rights. He postulated that God's will is the standard of morality in human society. However, humans do not need divine revelation to discover "his" will; they can figure it out by reason. Specifically, humans can infer God's purposes for human beings from the way "he" made them. Since God made humans essentially rational and social beings, "he" must had intended them to live lives centred around reason and sociability. He reasoned that if God had intended humans to have dominion over other humans, "he" wouldn't have given *all* humans the ability to think for themselves. So God must had intended for them all to have *equal* rights. He wrote: "Men are not made for one another's uses" (Delaney, 2004, p. 6).

As a product of his times, Locke did not think this *natural law* applied to all members of society equally. Thus, in response to the question 'does this apply to women too, or is this equality for men only?', Locke asserted that on the one hand, the existing subordination of women to men is the result of sin, not the decree of God. On the other hand, one could plausibly defend such subordination by appeal to biological differences. In other words, Locke did not give a straight answer; though later, Lockeans would argued that equality applies to both sexes. Locke's conclusion was that no one can legitimately exercise authority over another individual without his/her consent. Furthermore, governments must rest on consent of the governed, and may legitimately be overthrown if they overstep their authority (Delaney, 2004, p. 6).

Locke was an ardent opponent of the **divine right of kings,** a notion that the right to rule derives from God and the king's actions are answerable to God alone. He dismissed Robert Filmer's assertion that kings had **absolute rights** over citizens in the way that fathers have natural rights over their children. He questioned the assumption that fathers inherit their authority from the patriarchal authority of Adam. He maintained that even if God gave Adam such rights, it is not clear how these rights would be passed down to other generations. Locke also sharply disagreed with Hobbes' position on the *state of nature* and its laws. Contrary to Hobbes who saw the *state of nature* as warlike, brutish, and nasty, where men lived short lives, Locke posited that the *state of nature* was a pre-political, yet moral, society where humans were equal and bounded by divinely commanded laws of nature. He pronounced that the *state of nature* was a state of perfect freedom and equality. Locke argued that the world was never without political or social structure and that political and social structure arose naturally with humankind (Delaney, 2004, p. 10). In his view of the *state of nature*, peoples' relations were based on reason, and no higher authority could judge their actions. The fundamental *law of nature*, he suggested, was epitomized by ensuring that no harm is done to others with respect to life, health, liberty, or possessions. The responsibility for law and order is invested in individuals, not a supreme authority. Thus, lawbreakers are to be punished by citizens themselves; each person has the authority to punish those who break the *law of nature*. Finally, each member of society retains the right to life unless he or she forfeits it by violating the rights of others.

The Sanctity of Private Property

On property, Locke advanced the following arguments:

1. We create private property when we mix our labour with an object held in common;
2. Everything in the world first belonged in common to all humans, and one does not need to seek permission of others to use one's labour to alter common objects, such as natural resources;

3. God has provided virtually unlimited natural resources that we may acquire; and

4. Common Land could be acquired by individuals through the application of their labour to alter the common land, which was in virtually unlimited supply.

Locke proposed that private property was sacred and inviolable. He began with the assertion that every person owns himself/herself and his/her labour and that this is the foundation of all other property. He defined property as one that is acquired through just acquisition, earned through the application of one's labour to animate objects. In contrast, Robert Filmer, Locke's archenemy, had argued that all property in the realm belonged rightfully to the King. Filmer insisted that a citizen's farm, tools, and the clothes on his back were the King's property. In his critique of this view, Locke developed the theory of property rights. In this theory, he tried to answer the question: How do unowned things become rightfully owned? (Waldron, 2002)

Locke contended that God gave the entire earth to humankind in common. However, there is a dilemma in Locke's proposition: if the earth remained common property, human beings would have to get permission from all the other joint-owners (the entire human "race") before they could use any object. Locke's answer to the dilemma was that God would not have made humans with bodily needs if "he" didn't want them to satisfy the needs. Hence, God must have intended humans to appropriate, from the commons, goods for their own private use. His conclusion was that God favoured private property. Locke rationalized that by mixing one's labour with previously unowned objects and transforming them, human beings made them their own. This, he said, is permissible so long as people did not make others worse off by doing so.

The second dilemma Locke faced on his principle of private property is captured in the question: Does not *all* appropriation diminish the amount available to others and so make them worse off? He answered this question by insisting that since private land is more productive than common land, appropriation usually made society better off.

The final challenge to his argument in favour of private property over communally-owned property was expressed in the form of the following question: Why is private land more productive than common land? He argued that people were willing to put more effort into something if they knew they would get to reap the benefits. Locke argued that an individual created value through *homesteading* (to settle and farm land) previously unowned resources. The product was an extension of the producer's labour and so could not be appropriated, hence, he considered private property as *sacred*.

In his two treatises on government, Locke suggested that people form larger communities for the benefit of mutual protection, but, in exchange for this protection, they give up some of their liberty. Citizens must follow the will of the majority, which is the only basis of lawful government. In addition, Locke made the following propositions. He maintained, political power must:

1. be limited,

2. be based on majority rule, and

3. ensure the separation of powers between the various branches of government (i.e., the judiciary, the legislature, and the executive).

According to Locke, justice and rights did exist in the *state of nature*. The *social contract* created the state in order to define and defend the rights of individuals within it. He averred that humans have "**natural rights**", which entitled them to liberty (freedom) and private property. He argued that without government, humans would be in a "*state of nature*". Humans, therefore, invented government to ensure that they exercised their freedom (and sheltered themselves from arbitrary laws) and protected their property from theft. Locke thought capitalism was an ethical system based that protected individual rights, because it is based on liberty and private property. He saw government regulations as unethical, because they infringed on liberty and private property (Quist-Adade, 2012, p. 88).

Jean-Jacques Rousseau (1712–1778)

Jean Jacques Rousseau was one of the major social thinkers who influenced Western thought, and an important Enlightenment *philosophe* (Zeitlin, 2004, p. 23). Rousseau began his most important book, *The Social Contract*, with the following famous epigram: "Man is born free, and everywhere he is in chains. One man thinks himself the master of others, but remains more of a slave than they are" (Rousseau, 1762, p. 1). The epigram cogently expresses the central thesis of the book, which derives from his belief that "man" is naturally good, but corrupted by the ways of society. But more than capturing the core thesis of his work, this epigram reflects his optimistic views of humanity. To him, "man" in the *state of nature* lived a simple, free, uncorrupted, and fulfilling life. In rebuttal to Hobbes, Locke, and other Enlightenment scholars, he contended that "man" in the *state of nature* was not "selfish, brutish, in war against all" (Westby, 1991, p. 40; Zeitlin, 2004, p. 21), but instead, cooperative, and filled with sympathy for "his" fellow "men". It was society that corrupted "him"; it was society that created inequality and war. His optimism led him to conclude that human beings are perfectible (i.e. they can be changed from their corrupted ways through the right form of education).

Rousseau held the possibility of creating a better society, arguing that while people were now isolated in a *state of nature*, it was still possible to create society in the image of the *state of nature* through cooperation. Rousseau's desire was the creation of "a social order whose laws were in greatest harmony with the fundamental laws of nature" (Zeitlin, 2004, p. 17). This was achieved through the *social contract*, whereby individuals are absorbed into the common, general will, without losing their own will. In this new social arrangement, individuals lose nothing and gain in return the assurance that they would be protected by the full force of society against the encroachment of other individuals and groups. The individual is now a member of a society of equals and has regained equality not unlike the one he enjoyed in nature, but in a new form and on a higher level (Zeitlin, 2004, p. 25). According to Zeitlin (2004), Rousseau was a forerunner of sociology because he had a good grasp of the notion of culture, how people internalized it, and how it changed people for better or for worse. Rousseau also saw human beings as flexible, plastic, and malleable, who can be molded by society. He was one of the first to see inequality in society and in his writings thought that societal change could occur in a way that would remedy some of the inequalities. This view was revolutionary since many earlier writers had viewed social, political, and economic forms of inequality as natural and good.

Auguste Comte (1798–1857): the "Father" of Sociology

August Comte was a French eighteenth century social scientist and philosopher. Comte coined the term "Sociology" in 1838, and is regarded variously as "father" and "godfather" of sociology (it is important to note that he initially conceptualized "sociology" as "social physics"). He saw sociology as the "father" of all "sciences" (Mann, 2011, pp. 12–13). He conceived of sociology as a "science" that "discovers the universal laws that govern organization and evolution of humanity" (Seidman, 1994a, p. 29). He maintained that studying human relations based on physical sciences' methods would lead to a more rational human interaction. He wanted to explore how the world (society) is like, rather than how or what anyone thinks or assumes it should be like. Comte assumed that there are laws that govern our relations, and these laws can be studied and "discovered" through careful observation of the social world. He lived during the aftermath of the French Revolution (1789). His social thoughts were developed during an era in which France was influenced by both the views of those supporting the Enlightenment project and the "supporters of empire and monarchy" who argued the solution to social problems in France was a return to the old order of rigid class relations of feudalism (Seidman, 1994a, p. 26). As we noted in Chapter Five, early sociology developed as a result of the new streams of thought that grew out of the Enlightenment movement, and out of the conservative reaction to this movement. Early sociologists, such as Comte, were influenced by this conservative reaction. Comte maintained that France was in "turmoil" during the period between 1800 to 1850. Although he did not think that a return to the old order was possible either. He took some of the ideas of the Enlightenment and argued that social order could be preserved through social reforms. If Comte represented the first systematic social theory inspired by the reaction to the Enlightenment, it is Marx who was the first theorist to fully work out the implications of the Enlightenment ideas. While Marx grew up and wrote in Germany, where the Enlightenment did not have such strong effects as in France, Britain, or North America, Marxian thought can be seen as resulting partly from the Enlightenment (Wallace & Wolf, 2006).

Comte viewed the crisis France was experiencing as the outcome of unlimited human progress and as a "cultural one" (Seidman, 1994a, p. 27). He saw the industrialization process as inevitable and a sign of social progress. His vision of New France free of conflict was to be found in his new "science" of society. Comte also believed that social change must be envisioned in the context of tradition and custom. However, he emphasized the view that it is important to move from religious and metaphysical explanations of the world to a "scientific" one. He maintained that he has discovered a law regarding the progress of the human mind. He called it the **Law of Three Stages**. According to this law, the human mind goes through three stages of thought:

a) **Theological Stage**: Supernatural entities, such as spirits, divine beings, or God's will, are used to explain "the origin and the purpose of phenomena", such as the Christian worldview (Seidman, 1994a, p. 28).

b) **Metaphysical Stage**: Essences or abstract forces are used as explanations (i.e., "human reason or natural law" [Seidman, 1994a, p. 28]). Descartes' way of thinking would be an example of the metaphysical stage.

c) **Scientific Stage**: During this stage (referring to the era of modernity), it was assumed that society operates based on its own natural and social laws. The aim is to explain the interrelationships between facts and to discover those laws that govern human relations.

In this light, Comte claimed that sociology developed along three main general stages. The first stage, which he called *theological*, lasted until the end of the Middle Ages in Europe, when religious views were employed to explain society and people's relations with God. It was assumed that society is organized according to God's will and divinity. It was not until the Renaissance, that the *metaphysical approach* (the second stage) became popular, according to which, society was viewed as a natural phenomenon rather than a supernatural one (Macionis, 2008, p. 11). For example, as mentioned, Thomas Hobbes argued that that society did not reflect God's will, but was a reflection of the flaws of selfish human nature (Macionis, 2008, p. 12). The third stage, the *scientific stage*, coincided with the contributions of Nicolaus Copernicus (1473–1543), Galileo Galilei (1564–1642), and Isaac Newton (1642–1727). Comte appropriated the scientific methods and applied them to the analysis of society. In fact, Comte could be considered as the first positivist in sociology who assumed that society functioned and operated according to general discoverable laws. Although this approach has been criticized, (there are no common laws that affect all of us the same way), this view was revolutionary at the time. As we have mentioned, other social thinkers following Comte, such as Karl Marx, also conceptualized "sociology" not only as a science of society, but also as a framework to bring about social change (i.e., social justice).

As it can be stipulated, Comte's last stage exemplified a move from speculation to truth. According to this view, truth was viewed as liberating the human beings from dogma (Seidman, 1994a, p. 28). Each science (i.e., astronomy, mathematics, and Physics), Comte asserted, went through these stages. Sociology is the last one to have gone through such stages, because it was the most complicated since it dealt with social issues and facts. He argued that first views about nature must have been freed from religious and metaphysical explanations, and then views about the social world (i.e., it was only then that "scientific" approach could be applied to the social world). He viewed society as an organism, as a system "whose needs are met by the normal operation of its functionally interdependent parts" (Seidman, 1994a, p. 29). According to this view, society expands slowly and in a linear fashion. That is, society moves from the stage characterized by simple organization to more complex structures.

According to Comte, sociology consisted of two parts: **statics** and **dynamics. Social statics** attempted to describe, explain, and analyze the parts of the system, how the parts were interconnected and what were their functions (Seidman, 1994a, p. 29). It also attempted to develop generalizations about social stability (Erickson, 1998, p. 39). **Social dynamics** examined how the humanity has evolved; it looked at sources of change, its stages, and directions (Seidman, 1994a, p. 29). It was concerned with developing generalizations about social change (Erickson, 1998, p. 39). Unlike many of the Enlighteners, Comte did not view society as the sum of its parts: a collection of individuals. Society consisted of social relations, interactions, rules, and institutions, which were "independent of the psychology of individuals" (Seidman, 1994a, p. 29). Social statics attempted to explain the structure and functions of this realm. The main aim of sociology was to explicate social order in modern society (Seidman, 1994a, p. 29).

Comte's analysis and views influenced Émile Durkheim's approaches to sociology and his research as well as methodology. Durkheim is an important figure in sociology and influenced the ideas promoted by structural functionalism, which will be discussed in the next section. But before we do so, it is important to discuss the contributions of Herbert Spencer and the role of evolutionary thinking that influenced many of the early founding "fathers" of sociology.

Herbert Spencer (1820–1903): evolutionism and the survival of the fittest

According to Wallace and Wolf (2006, p. 18), the intellectual roots of structural functionalism can also be traced to the **organicism** of the early nineteenth century, which is one of the oldest and until recently the most dominant conceptual perspective in the social sciences. Herbert Spencer saw human society as an analogy to the human body. Herbert Spencer was a broad based social philosopher. He wrote multivolume treatises on ethics, biology, and psychology, all part of his **synthetic philosophy.** His aim was to unify the diverse realms of the universe under a common set of abstract principles. His major work on sociology was *The Principles of Sociology.* Spencer is best known for coining the term *survival of the fittest*, which implies that only the strong should survive, and for his application of the principles of biological evolution to human societies, referred to as **Social Darwinism** (See Chapter Eight, Box 8.1). After reading Thomas Malthus' *Essay on Population*, Spencer agreed that overpopulation would become more of a problem over time and believed that, as a result, people would be forced to compete over increasingly scarce resources. This led him to coin the term *survival of the fittest* ten years before Charles Darwin developed the idea of *natural selection* (Delaney, 2004, p. 41), the biologically based principle that environmental pressures allow certain beneficial traits to be passed on to future generations. Spencer argued that growing competition would mean that those individuals and groups who were better able to compete would survive, and those who could not would perish. What is important here is that while Darwin's concept of evolution explains how biological organisms can be selected for by environmental pressures, Spencer moved beyond the biological application of evolution and argued that societies can be selected for as well.

This resulted in Spencer's concept of *Social Darwinism*, which posited that societies evolve just as biological organisms do. Adherents of Spencer's views are today known as **social Darwinists.** *Social Darwinists* assume that some societies, raced groups, etc., are endowed with "superior" genes, while others inherit "inferior" genes. Those fortunate enough to have "superior" genes are better able to survive and thrive and control their social environments. *Social Darwinists* drew on the idea of struggle and survival as natural mechanisms for improving the "stock" of human beings (i.e., genetic characteristics). In fact, "inferior races" and societies, it was hypothesized, would "naturally" wither away. Any attempts to save them were in defiance of the laws of nature. One can see that Spencer was employing a structural functionalist approach by suggesting that societies evolve because there is a reason (function) for the changes (i.e., they need to survive). Spencer's approach became very popular in the United States, as it helped to explain why some in society were doing well and others were not. Some were simply more evolved or better adapted than others. And since this was a natural process, many believed that nature should be allowed to take its course and that to interfere would only make matters worse (Ritzer, 2000, p. 32). The belief that it is best to leave things alone and let them take care of themselves is called a *laissez-faire* approach, and it is often used by some economists to suggest not interfering with market forces (e.g., the government should not provide subsidies to companies or industries that cannot survive on their own). Spencer's views on social welfare programs, or any initiatives intended to help those who were not doing well, were clear: fostering the good-for-nothing at the expense of the good, is an extreme cruelty. It is a deliberate stirring-up of miseries for future generations: "There is no greater curse to posterity than that of bequeathing to them an increasing population of imbeciles and idlers and criminals…. The whole effort of nature is to get rid of such, to clear the world of them, and make room for better…. If they are not sufficiently complete to live, they die, and it is best they should die" (Spencer, as noted in Ritzer, 2000, p. 34, citing Abrams, 1968, p. 74).

Spencer's ideas were informed by the theories of two other important scientists and philosophers of his period: Charles Darwin and Adam Smith. Charles Darwin applied the Newtonian law of gravity to the law of nature, and concluded that it is not divine power that ruled the natural world. He applied his theory first to the animal and plant kingdoms and then to the human kingdom. Charles Darwin's book, On *Origin of Species*, is based on the premise that all plants and animals evolved from common ancestry through the principle of *natural selection*. Akin to the "law of the jungle", the most fit survived and reproduced, and the less fit died out. In 1871, Darwin's second book, *The Descent of Man*, was published. He applied the evolutionary principle to human societies, claiming that man had common ancestry in great apes. Herbert Spencer latched on to this aspect of Darwin's theory of evolution, combining Darwin's evolutionism with Adam Smith's *laissez faire* (free market forces) to propound his own theory of *Social Darwinism*. As we have already mentioned, Adam Smith's *laissez faire* economic theory proposed no government intervention in the economic affairs of individuals and promoted a free-market economy based on the 'invisible hands' of the market. Combining the principle of *laissez faire* with evolutionism's view of stratification, Spencer argued that rich men have risen to the top by virtue of their talents, the poor had remained at the bottom because of their inherent deficiencies. For example, he argued for need to examine the psychological differences between the sexes before deciding to give women the vote. Spencer's aim was to let the "natural laws" of the market take their due course, during which the "economically deficient" peoples would be weeded out and the "economically progressive" would thrive (Quist-Adade, 2012, p. 123).

For Spencer, sociology was the study of the evolution of societies. The central premise of his argument was that society is governed by objective *laws of nature*, and human actions are in concert with these laws. If human actions contradicted the *laws of nature*, no matter how well-intentioned, they would fail to achieve their aims. He saw the process of evolution as key to understanding all phenomena: organic, inorganic, and superorganic (society). He applied a **teleological approach** (social structures and practices can only be understood by reference to the ends or purposes those structural practices serve) to the study of society. For example, social institutions like marriage or religion exist because they contribute to the survival of the social system. Spencer conceptualized societies as having evolved from simple and primitive to complex states. He arranged primitive, ancient, and modern societies in a hierarchical order, reflecting the stages of evolution.

Spencer's evolutionary sequence involved simple, compound, doubly compound, and trebly compound societies. The major motors of change were twin processes of **integration** and **complexity**. Spencer observed that no tribe became a nation by simple growth; and no great society was formed by the direct union of smaller societies. Accompanying the process of growth or *integration* is a progressive **differentiation** of the various structures of society (e.g., the consolidation of small, dispersed groups into larger political units would lead to increasing political *complexity*). As structures differentiated; so did activities or functions among structures. This gave rise to a greater need for *integration* and coordination of mutually dependent parts of the social system in order to maintain harmony and equilibrium (Wallace & Wolf, 2006).

Spencer argued that increasing *complexity* and *differentiation* led to greater **specialization** of functions within the social organism. In the simplest societies, *specialization* occurred around:

a) matters of defence and offence against external enemies (i.e., human or animal, real or imagined) and

b) questions of general sustenance (i.e., provision of food). This process led to *differentiation* between, for example, warriors, cultivators, hunters, fishers, priests, etc.

But in addition, warriors must eat and cultivators must be protected. So as society grew and evolved, further *specialization* also took place. Finally, to complete the picture, society gradually developed a system of *regulation*, (i.e., a political function) designed to enable cooperation among differential parts. This function was the responsibility of political leaders and lawmakers who determined rules and governed the general polity (Wallace & Wolf, 2006).

Spencer maintained that the *regulative system* was like the neuromuscular system in organisms and took the form of the government-military apparatus in social systems. He spoke of contrasting characteristics of simple and complex societies: simple societies or less evolved were characterized as militant/militaristic and premised on coercive or compulsory *cooperation*, while complex or highly evolved were seen as industrial, and premised on voluntary *cooperation* (Wallace & Wolf, 2006). As it can be stipulated, Spencer offered an ideological premise for describing "developing and developed countries": the former characterized by political instability and the latter by political stability.

While Spencer is credited for his insistence on individual choice and agency and even applauded as the "father of liberalism", today most sociologists view his ideas with much skepticism for a number of reasons. **First**, these ideas provided justification for colonial expansion (See Chapter Eight). **Second,** Spencer's argument equated evolution with progress and assumed that over time human society would inevitably improve (Delaney, 2004, p. 53). However, can we really argue that given global warming, international state sponsored terrorism, and worldwide poverty and malnourishment, humanity is now better off today than 10,000 years ago? Are larger, more complex societies necessarily better than small, less complex ones? As Ravelli (2010) observed, while the majority of contemporary sociologists are uncomfortable with many of Spencer's ideas, it is important to recognize that his ideas were central to the development of sociology and sociological theories.

The Major Classical and Contemporary Sociological Paradigms

There are four main classical sociological perspectives that have paved the foundation for sociological analysis: structural functionalism, conflict theory, symbolic interactionism, and feminism. There are also other contemporary theories that have influenced sociological knowledge: postmodernism, poststructuralism, critical race theory, and neo-Marxism, which are also explored in this chapter.

Part Three

Structural Functionalism

We begin our survey of the major theoretical paradigms with what sociologists have described the "grand old man" of sociological theories, **structural functionalism.** According to Ravelli (2010), the origins of structural functionalism can be traced to the ideas of the Arab North African sociologist, Ibn Khaldun and the conservative reaction of some social thinkers to the ideas of the Enlightenment (See Chapter Five). First developed in Europe by pioneer sociologists Auguste Comte and Émile Durkheim, structural functionalism is a framework for building theory (a paradigm) that visualizes society as a complex system, consisting of different and interdependent parts, each of which plays an assigned role to ensure the smooth-working of society (Knutilla, 2008, p. 162). Durkheim provided an analysis of social structures and their functions with his groundbreaking work, *Suicide* (See chapter Two). Talcott Parsons and Robert Merton in the United States of America were other influential proponents of the structural functionalist paradigm. The ideas of Parsons and Merton were influenced by Max Weber's analysis of social action and his emphasis on social taxonomies or social ideals, of both subjective meaning and social structure. Robert Merton, for example, showed that social patterns can have many functions. However, functions differ depending on the point of view of specific categories of people. For example, traditional courtship may benefit society, encouraging new families, but the practice may also confer advantages on men, with disproportionate access to wealth and power, while limiting the opportunities of women who may forgo professional advancement in favour of raising a family.

Structural Functionalism: Assumptions and Premises

As we discussed in Chapter Seven, the central focus of the structural functionalist paradigm is how the different parts of the system work together to promote solidarity and stability. Structural functionalists, (functionalists, for short), see society as a complex system made up of different, but interdependent parts (**structures**), with each part playing (**functioning**) its given role to ensure the smooth operation of the entire system. This paradigm was influenced by the biological sciences. In what they termed *organismic analogy*, structural functionalists compared human society to, for example, the human body. The human body or organism is made up of different parts, such as limbs, lungs, heart, head, blood vessels, veins, ligaments, etc. Each of these parts is interconnected and interdependent with other parts, and functions cooperatively to ensure the survival of the person. In the same light, society is perceived as being made up of social structures or **social institutions**, such as the family, the educational system, the economy, the polity, religion, the mass media, etc. For society to survive and function smoothly, each of these institutions must play their roles well.

To grasp the meaning of structural functionalism, let's break the paradigm into its basic constituent parts: **structure** and **function**. *Structure* connotes a relatively stable pattern of social behaviour. It refers to practices and behaviours that people engage in repeatedly or ritualistically. Examples of *social structures* include family life, political systems, economic systems, the mass media, religion, norms, and values. Thus, functionalists hold that society as a system has certain needs, which its parts (i.e., its *structures*) must meet. The assumption is that it is the *social structures* that are satisfying these needs. This theory also assumes that as long as the *structures* are meeting society's needs, then they are *functional*, because they help society to run smoothly (to reproduce itself in an orderly manner from one generation to another). In addition, it is assumed that all the various *structures* are not only interconnected, they also grow and change in tandem or together. That is, for example, when the economy changes, other institutions also must change. When a social institution fails to change with the rest, the systems becomes *anomic*. For example, during the periods of economic development and labour shortages, economic elite may endorse the government to introduce new immigration laws, inviting skilled workers from other parts of the world to legally enter Canada as landed immigrants. When the birth rate is low and the family does not contribute to the reproduction of the population, the government may introduce tax and other incentives for families to have more children, or to encourage immigration of families from other parts of the world in order to ensure that population growth keeps up with the economic needs of the country. Changes in the economy and technological changes may also be accompanied with changes in schools and school curriculum to reflect the need for skilled individuals in fields needed by the corporations and the economy. Having said the above, it is important to note that contemporary functionalists tend to veer away from a focus on the structural aspect, arguing that it renders the theory tautological (circular reasoning) (See Wallace & Wolf, 2006 pp. 16–17).

Function implies the consequences of a *social structure* for the operation of society. Every society has certain needs that must be met if it is to survive. These needs run the gamut from food, shelter, and clothing to education, leisure, and reproduction. Briefly put, a *social function* is the outcome of a *social structure*. Let's use education to illustrate the link between *social structure* and *social function*. A student who attends postsecondary school for a number of years and receives a certificate indicates a successful completion and acquisition of requisite knowledge or skills that are deemed necessary for her or him to function in her/his intended occupation in society: The postsecondary school constitutes a *social structure*, while the certificate of completion of her/his education is a *social function*. Another example is sexual reproduction. Society must reproduce itself through the replacement of aging and dying members with new and young ones. The family becomes the *social structure* that allows this reproduction to happen. The roles of parents who nurture, socialize, and protect the newly-born and young members of society constitute the *social function* in the *structure-function* equation. Thus, if the family is the *structure*, mothering, for example, is its *function* (See Wallace & Wolf, 2012 pp. 24–41).

Structural functionalism is built on the following central assumptions. **First**, humans have constant and unalterable needs. **Second**, these needs are provided by social institutions. **Third**, the different parts of the system are interdependent. **Fourth**, society strives toward a "normal" state of affairs, or **state of equilibrium**, comparable to the normal or healthy state of an organism. **Fifth**, customs and institutions are positively functional in that they sustain and preserve social order. **Sixth**, "nonrational" aspects of human existence, such as rituals, ceremony, and worship, are crucial for the smooth running of society. **Seventh**, status and hierarchy are essential ingredients for the continuity, predictability, and the harmony of social relations. **Eighth**, all the parts of the system function to achieve equilibrium (See Wallace & Wolf, 2012 pp. 24–41).

Having discussed the general tenants of structural functionalism, in the next section, we explore the contribution of Durkheim to sociology. In fact, Durkheim played an important role in the rise of structural functionalism and influenced the ideas of Talcott Parsons.

Émile Durkheim (1858–1917)

Durkheim, the son of a Jewish Rabbi, was born in eastern France, but grew up to become an atheist. He attended the elite École Superieure in Paris. He trained in the social sciences. Durkheim adopted the sociology of Comte and Spencer. He was neither a radical nor a conservative. His primary concern was the instability and violence of modern society. Later, he became the first professor of sociology at the University of Paris. Considered to be the founder of modern sociology, Durkheim expended much energy to establish sociology as a legitimate and serious academic endeavour (Delaney, 2004, p. 93; Garner, 2000, p. 64; Ritzer, 2000, p. 73).

Durkheim legitimized sociology as a science by distinguishing between sociology and psychology and philosophy. He employed sociological facts in order to explain the importance of social order. He considered **social facts** as external to individuals that affect their socializations and behaviours. In this light, society is conceived as an objective reality that surpassed individual actions. According to him, it is the society that influences human action and the character of humans (See Box 10.2 - Émile Durkheim).

BOX 10.2 - Émile Durkheim

Durkheim's ideas were developed during a time of turmoil and change in France that began in the mid-eighteenth century. France was experiencing a number of changes and political instability at the time. During the time of revolution in 1789 and the events after the revolution more than 16, 000 individuals were executed. In 1799, Napoleon took over the power structure and eventually declared himself the emperor (Pampel, 2007, pp. 48–49). In 1848, France was turned into a Republic, as a result of yet another revolution. But the Republic did not last as Napoleon II declared himself as the emperor. He eventually lost his empire in a war with Prussia and fled to England in 1871. This defeat resulted in a national concern regarding the loss of France's military power and its imperial might. Soon after, a group of French in Paris took over the city and it was not until the French army's invasion of the city and killing of more than 20,000 residents that the city was reclaimed by the central government.

During this period, three main factions were popular: the conservative, who wanted a return to the past system, when the Church and monarchy had control over the country; the working classes, who wanted to see the establishment of a democratic government and the promotion of equality through the establishment of a secular state; and the newly established owners of capital, who promoted individualism and free markets. They wanted the economic restrictions imposed by the aristocrats and landlords to be abolished and political restriction imposed by the kings to be relaxed (Pampel, 2007, p. 50). Durkheim was also concerned about the ways in which modern societies were able to deal with the level of violence, disorder, division, breakdown, and individualism (Pampel, 2007, p. 43). However, unlike, for example, the conservatives who argued that the solution to the turmoil France was experiencing required a return to traditional forms of society and organization, Durkheim maintained that it is unrealistic to consider a return to past social structures as a solution to the changes brought about by scientific revolution, industrialization, and the growth of cities (Pampel, 2007, p. 52). Durkheim's solution to the problems that were introduced by modernism were south in the establishment of a secular state.

For Durkheim, the aim of sociology was to offer knowledge that could be utilized in developing social reforms that would improve life for everyone (Pampel, 2007, p. 48). He argued the rise of industrialization, the process of urbanization, and the decline of traditional ties had tremendous consequences for members of society, mainly weakening the ties of individuals to their social groups, communities, and the family (Pampel, 2007, p. 52). His concerns about the effects of unrestrained and unchecked individualism and the problem of social order remain an important aspect of sociological research. For example, this is an issue that is a concern for structural functionalism. He, for instance, argued that the high rates of divorce and suicide in modern France, which was dealing with a range of socioeconomic and political changes, were the end result of the breakdown of social ties of individuals to larger groups (Pampel, 2007, p. 44). His main concern was how to strike a balance between the needs of society and individual search for personal freedom and expression of individuality. He proposed that restraining individualism is consistent with the nature of modern society (Pampel, 2007, p. 53). For Durkheim, it is not the individual who is the centre of sociological studies but society.

Durkheim and Max Weber were the first sociologists who approached studying society and its components through research-oriented studies (Seidman, 1994a, p. 56). The goal of Durkheim was to assist in developing France based on liberal ideology and principles. During the nineteenth century, France was a divided country and was controlled by the Catholic Church, the nobility (monarchy), and the landed aristocracy (Seidman, 1994a, p. 56). By the early twentieth century, France was moving towards becoming a secular and industrial society. However, the country was socially and politically divided and not stable. The military rulers, the landed aristocracy, and the Church opposed free market principles, individualism, and secularism. Those considered as leftist criticized liberals who were in charge of the Third Republic as promoting inequalities and injustices; and those on the right criticized the liberals for promoting "moral and social anarchy" (Seidman, 1994a, p. 57).

Durkheim followed Comte's commitment to *positivism*, and his explanations of human behaviour were always based on his assumption that human actions originated in the collective rather than in the individual (Ravelli, 2010, p. 30). On the surface, this assumption would seem to mean that we as individuals are divested of any free will, since our actions are determined by the group or collectives to which we belong. While we may believe that our decisions to drive to class or to take public transportation are not influenced by anyone but ourselves, Durkheim would contend that "even these seemingly small personal choices have large social origins" (Ravelli, 2010, p. 30). For example, if you drove to campus today, this is not to any force or coercive measures by other people. You did so of your own volition. However, if other motorists or road users did not cooperate with you by obeying the traffic signs, you are most unlikely to make it to class; you may end up in the hospital from an accident caused by dangerous drivers who were not conforming to appropriate ways of driving. For Durkheim, this example would support his contention that individual behaviours are inspired by collective social forces (Garner, 2000, p. 64). It is the collective or society that has predefined traffic signals and the appropriate ways of driving.

Durkheim believed that sociologists should focus on *social facts* in order to develop "scientific" understandings of society (Storey, 2012, p. 25). A *social fact* can be defined as something that has a basic and general existence over all of society and its components (See Chapter Two). Durkheim described *social facts* as "every way of acting, fixed or not, capable of exercising on the individual an external constraint; or again, every way of acting which is general throughout a society, while at the same time existing in its own right independent of its individual manifestations" (Durkheim, 1964; 1895, p. 13). *Social facts*, then, are general social features that exist on their own and are independent of individual manifestations, for example, laws, beliefs, customs, and morals (see Wallace & Wolf, 2006, p. 20). According to Ravelli (2010), *social facts* are things created through human actions and interactions, but which are not the intended consequences of them. In other words, like the proverbial Frankenstein monster, *social facts* are human creations, which run amok. They are creations which come to create the creators, to put crudely. *Social facts* are unintentional outcomes of collective behaviour and interaction. Ravelli (2010, p. 35) suggested that "social facts, like the collective conscience, operate outside of anyone alive today but also can be seen as givens since they provide the context for our thinking and by doing so constrain and coerce us to behave in established, predictable ways (e.g., what you had for breakfast and what you decided to wear to school today)".

Durkheim pointed out that human behaviour should be understood and analyzed in the context of social organization and structures and not in individualistic terms. In *The Elementary Forms of the Religious Life*, he studied society's most general and taken-for-granted ideas. Durkheim (1915) showed that beliefs about the supernatural are symbols generated by social behaviour and the function of these beliefs was to strengthen the *collective conscience* of society. They were a means to enhance the feeling of solidarity between individuals and society in general. His study of Arunta, for example, pointed out that religion played an important role in determining group membership: he argued that religion reinforces group solidarity. He argued that humans distinguish between the **profane** and the **sacred**. He defined the *profane* as those ordinary aspects of the everyday life. The *sacred*, he considered, as those extraordinary elements that arose a sense of awe, reverence, and fear in individuals. Religion, he maintained, was a system of beliefs and practices that were based on conceptions of the *sacred*. Religion is practiced through rituals and those ceremonies and behaviours that had been formalized in society.

Durkheim's conception of **individualism** was also very different from the American and British conceptions of "unbridled individualism". He conceptualized *individualism* in the context of a focus on moral virtue and civic order (Seidman, 1994a, p. 57). His attempt was to incorporate the ideals of French social conservatives in terms of moral unity, radicals' emphasis on social justices, and liberals' conception of *individualism* into his brand of liberal conceptions of society through empirical science (Seidman, 1994a, p. 57). In his view, Individuals must be well integrated into the social system. He was also a defendant of cultural pluralism but in the context of a firm moral centre based on preestablished and shared values and norms.

Durkheim's view of society was also influenced by evolutionary theories. He conceptualized society as moving from a primitive to a modern stage. Durkheim believed that the key to understanding society was through the division of labour. In *The Division of Labour in Society* in 1893, Durkheim attempted to reveal a "scientific" basis for social order, and hypothesized that the basis of society is a moral order. Durkheim stated that society cannot exist simply by rational agreement because agreements are not possible unless each party trusts the other to live up to them. "Precontractual solidarity" must exist before contracts can be depended upon. Durkheim argued that this solidarity was not an intellectual agreement, but a shared emotional feeling. Members of society have **a collective conscience**, a sense of community which entailed a moral obligation on the part of the members of society to live up to its demands. These feelings, Durkheim proposed, developed through social interactions between individuals, especially through rituals. These rituals served to focus society upon common objects or ideas, which were transformed into the world of moral norms.

In Durkheim's view, "culture and society exist outside of the individual, are independent of the individual, and outlive the individual" (Ravelli, 2010, p. 30). Durkheim characterized this external force as a *collective conscience*, a common social bond that is expressed by the ideas, values, norms, beliefs, and ideologies of a culture. He noted, "as there is nothing within an individual which constrains these appetites, they must surely be contained by some force exterior to him, or else they would become insatiable—that is morbid" ([1928] 1978, p. 213). As the *collective conscience* originated within society, Durkheim elaborated the cause and effects of weakening group ties (and thus a weakening of the *collective conscience*) on the individual in his two works, *The Division of Labour in Society* (1893) and *Suicide* (1897). In *The Division of Labour*, Durkheim identified two forms or types of solidarity, which he maintained were based on different sources. Through his two forms of solidarity, **organic** and **mechanical**, he compared "primitive" societies with "advanced" industrial societies. In his view, "primitive" or traditional societies were characterized by **mechanical solidarity**, and modern societies were identified as those characterized by **organic solidarity** (See Chapter Three). He conceptualized traditional societies as self-sufficient with few differentiations between their members. What kept these "primitive" societies together were their shared beliefs and values, expressed in religious views that were practiced unconsciously. He viewed human order as a *sacred order* (Seidman, 1994a, p. 59). In these societies, social control over individuals was immense. Any deviation from the norm was considered as undermining the social order and was dealt with harshly (Seidman, 1994a, p. 59). In these societies, the social forces that controlled human behaviour were not understood and reflected upon by their members. *Mechanical solidarity*, he asserted, is "solidarity which comes from likeness and is at its maximum when the collective conscience completely envelops our whole conscience and coincides in all points with it" (Mann, 2011, p. 26). *Mechanical solidarity* occurred in early societies in which there was not much (basic or rudimentary) division of labour. Such societies were relatively homogenous: men and women engaged in similar tasks and daily activities, and people shared similar experiences. In such societies, the few distinct institutions expressed similar values and norms, and tended to reinforce one another. The norms, values, and beliefs of the society (or the *collective conscience*) were homogenous and confronted the individual with such overwhelming and consistent force that there was little opportunity in such societies for individuality or deviance from the *collective conscience*. According to Durkheim, "primitive" societies were characterized by segmental kin-groups. Due to their lack of differentiation, for example, between and within groups, each kin-group was very much self-sufficient. As a result of this segmental characteristic, "primitive" societies would have had a hard time to respond to change, and were very much unstable. As environmental changes or social changes due to, for example, invasion and contact with others, were introduced, differentiation between and within groups ensued. According to Durkheim, traditional cultures experienced a high level of social and moral *integration*, there was little individuation, and most behaviours were governed by social norms, which were usually embodied in religion. By engaging in the same activities and rituals, people in traditional societies shared common moral values, which Durkheim called the *collective conscience*. As previously mentioned, the *collective conscience* is the "totality of beliefs and sentiments common to average citizens of the same society [that] ... has its own life" (Mann, 2011, p. 26; Turner, Beeghey & Powers, 2002, p. 332). In these societies, people tend to regard themselves as members of a group; the *collective conscience* embraces individual awareness, and there is little sense of personal options.

In contrast, in industrial societies, he believed *organic solidarity* was essential as it holds society together in the sense that in "such a complicated division of labour, if one 'organ' of the social body fails to do its job, the whole process collapses" (Mann, 2011, p. 27). The basis for this form of solidarity is the *difference* between members. It is the characteristic of industrial societies, which are marked by a high division of labour and specialization. Modernity, for Durkheim, then, signaled a move away from spiritual and religious orientations and explanations of the world to a more rational and "scientific" understanding of the world and the relationship between individuals and their social and natural environments. However, he also believed that *anomie* was the major pathology of societies characterized by *organic solidarity*, and therefore the most pressing underlying social problem with which modern societies must cope. In this sense, *anomie* denotes lack of normality or normlessness (Mann, 2011, p. 26).

According to Durkheim, the two types of solidarity demanded different types of legal systems. *Mechanical solidarity* was characterized by **repressive justice**, while *organic solidarity* was characterized by **restitutive justice.** Durkheim regarded the law (*repressive* vs. *restitutive*) as an index of the nature of social solidarity. Durkheim tested this assertion (theory) by analyzing historical evidence to test whether moral norms (laws) change as the result of changes in social conditions. In *The Division of Labour*, he looked at society's laws as an indicator of its moral norms. He distinguished between two types of laws: **criminal laws** and **civil-administrative laws**. *Criminal laws* seemed to express a stronger sense of *collective conscience* than *civil-administrative laws* did. The former demands **retribution** while the latter demands **restitution**. Durkheim showed that smaller, earlier societies largely had **retributive laws**, while modern societies largely were characterized by **restitutive laws**. The connection that Durkheim drew between societies and their laws was the changing division of labour within these societies. *Retributive laws* were most often found in societies with little division of labour. Durkheim argued that this was so because in those societies most people are very much alike. As discussed above, he used the term *mechanical solidarity* to describe these types of societies. Their many common ideas and experiences resulted in a strong *collective conscience*. Any violation of this *collective conscience* was viewed as very serious and was punished likewise. Durkheim described societies with a high division of labour as being held together by *organic solidarity*. In these societies, he argued, people experienced very different circumstances and had less in common with each other. As a result, there was a weaker sense of *collective conscience* (Mann, 2011, p. 26).

Durkheim (1897) also studied in-depth the concept of deviance. This was of particular interest to him because it is through acts of deviance that society's norms are put to the test. Durkheim postulated that crime was, in some respects, functional. Crime demanded punishment, and Durkheim argued, it served a number of purposes. It sought to discipline the criminal but also drew society together and strengthened the common conscience. As well, he argued that punishment of deviance or the abnormal was necessary to sustain an awareness of what is normal.

Another aspect of Durkheim's study of deviance related to his work on suicide. In his book, *Suicide* (1897), he refuted many of the theories about suicide that had been put forth up to that time and propounded his own theory. Durkheim, for example, argued that race and ethnic differences do not explain differences in suicide rates. He was not concerned with the characteristics of individual personalities of suicide victims either. Durkheim was interested in studying the rates of suicide and how (and why) they varied from one country to another. He maintained that suicide is reflective of group life. He argued that suicide rates are affected and influenced by social relations. He developed a theory that examined and explained individual behaviours in the context of social relations. He hypothesized that the less detached a person was from his or her community/ society, the more likely that person would commit suicide. On the other hand, the more integrated an individual was in his or her community, the less likely he or she would kill himself or herself. The importance of Durkheim's work on suicide though lies not so much with the conclusions that were drawn but also in the process that was followed. Suicide was the first significant large-scale data analysis in sociology. In all his work, Durkheim sought to anchor his sociological work on the basis of the research methods of empirical "science". In *Suicide*, in particular, he followed the basic methodological principle of good research that in order to discover the cause of something, it is necessary to look for the conditions under which it occurs and compare it with the conditions under which it does not occur (Mann, 2011, p. 28).

Durkheim's work continues to be relevant even today. His discussion of *collective conscience, solidarity*, and deviance are particularly meaningful within the context of the social "decay" and problems that our society is currently experiencing. Many theories and ideas are put forth about these problems, and Durkheim's ideas have served as a meaningful basis for these discussions. As was noted earlier, the significance of Durkheim's work also lies in the methods he used. His work continues to be an example of how to use empirical analysis in the field of social sciences (Mann, 2011, p. 28). Durkheim's research also paved the foundation for other American and French sociologists to explore social issues, and informed their sociological perspectives.

Talcott Parsons (1902–1979)

Talcott Parsons majored in biology, but became a social scientist later in his life. It is important to keep in mind his early training in biology. He studied under Antoni Millinkowski, the great Anthropologist at the London School of Economics. He later encountered the works of Max Weber. Parsons spent nearly his entire life teaching and writing at Harvard University, where he became a towering figure in the social sciences (Delaney, 2004). He became so influential that his books and theories were regarded as the holy grail of American sociology. Seeking to address some of the criticism of structural functionalism as too deterministic and divesting individuals of agency, Parsons postulated a series of theories to address these "deficits". His theories, which we describe as "one-size-fits-all", were called **grand theories.** They were universalizing and overarching theories, which sought to offer abstract explanations of social phenomena, beyond local conditions and across disciplines (Mills, 1959). In the 1930s, Parsons introduced American social scientists to Max Weber's **action theory**. *Action theory* describes the subjective factors that influence human action and serve as the foundation for society. In developing his theory, Weber distinguished between the concepts of **behaviour** and **action**. *Behaviour*, he postulated, was an automatic response that occurred with little thought, whereas *action* was the result of a conscious process in which people gave meaning to their actions and the world around them. Weber was concerned only with the study of *action* and believed that the sociologist could understand the meaningful basis of peoples' *actions* through the method of "understanding", or *verstehen* (Ritzer, 2002) (See Box 10.3 – Max Weber). In the next section, we explore Parsons' *systems level analysis*.

BOX 10.3 - Max Weber

Max Weber defined sociology "as the interpretive understanding of social action" (Wotherspoon, 1998, p. 5). In order to understand behaviour, he maintained, social scientists must understand the range of meanings people associate to their actions. Weber promoted the idea that the aim of sociology should be to construct a framework for understanding and interpreting human social actions. He pointed out that external forces, such as coercive *social structures*, are not the only factors that needed to be accounted for in understanding human behaviour. Scholars must also be concerned with the **motivations of human beings,** as they act and behave in the context of *social structures* and become involved in social interactions. In other words, sociology must account for how people's decisions and behaviours are determined by interpretation (Wotherspoon, 1998, p. 5). Any social explanation must take into consideration "those additional subjective aspects of social life: the meanings people attach to their actions, the ideas that govern their behaviour, and their consciousness and perceptions of the world around them" (Grabb, 2002, p. 48). As such, it would be possible to predict certain subjective attitudes and their consequences: Weber called this **rational action**, or "the calculated pursuit of individuals' interest". This was possible, he insisted, since, in a capitalist society, for example, the main goal is to increase one's profit. That is "subjective interests are geared almost completely to the profit motive or the maximization of wealth" (Grabb, 2002, p. 49). Weber also emphasized the importance of *social structures* and the centrality of analysis of systems of social life and their consequences on human action. In order to better understand why certain events happen or why people act in the ways in which they do in the context of their interactions in social institutions, sociologists should "seek social explanations by means of 'a pluralistic analysis of factors, which may be isolated and gauged in terms of their respective causal weights" (as cited in Grabb, 2002, p. 47). This is referred to as **causal pluralism** (Grabb, 2002, p. 47).

Systems Level Analysis

The first of Parsons' grand theories was **systems level analysis**. The concept of a system is the core of Parsons' discussions and his theories. His general *theory of action*, in which he gave his overall picture of how societies are structured and fit together, included four systems, namely the *cultural system*, the *social system*, the *personality system*, and the *behavioural system*.

The *cultural system* is the basic unit, which embodies social meaning or symbolic systems, such as religious beliefs, languages, and national values. The main focus here is **shared values** and a key concept here is **socialization**, whereby society's values are internalized by the individual (i.e., the individual makes society's values his or her own). According to Parsons, *socialization* is a powerful integrative force in society, in that it maintains social control and holds society together.

The *social system* is the basic unit for role interactions. Parsons paid the most attention to this system. He asserted that, "A social system consists in a plurality of individual actors interacting with each other in a situation which has at least a physical or environmental aspect, actors who are motivated in terms of a tendency to the optimization of gratification and whose relation to their situations, including each other, is defined and mediated in terms of a system of culturally structured and shared symbols" (as cited in Wallace & Wolf, 2006, p. 26). He defined a *social system* as a plurality of two or more actors, where actors can be people or collectives. A *social system* can be comprised of two people interacting in a restaurant or two nations (nations as actors) interacting within the format of the United Nations. The *social system* also includes the *cultural system*, which Parsons referred to as culturally determined and shared symbols that define the way the actors interact. He showed how the other actors, whose motives are self-gratification because of the nature of their *personality systems*, bring in a physical or environmental aspect, which set the boundaries around this situation where interaction takes place and is itself a function of the behavioural organism involved (Mann, 2011, p. 35).

The *personality system* constitutes the basic unit of the individual actor, the human person. The focus here is individual needs, motives, and attitudes, such as motivation toward gratification. Note that motivation toward gratification corresponds to both the conflict theory and exchange theory's explicit assumptions that people are self-centred or profit/gain maximizers. According to the conflict theory, self-interest drives people to want to seek relatively scarce resources in their environment to meet their basic needs, including food, shelter, and clothing. In the process of seeking these resources, they inevitably clash with others who also need those resources, in what Marx called class struggle. The exchange theory proposes that people are selfish and calculating beings, who tend to ask themselves "what is in it for me?" as they engage in social intercourses. Based on the Minimax principle, the exchange theory argues that people have a tendency to minimize their costs and maximize their gains or profits as they interact with others. As rational beings, people normally would engage in actions and behaviours that would bring them maximum satisfaction or benefits while abstaining from those actions and behaviours that would cause them loss, grief, or dissatisfaction.

According to Parsons, the basic unit of the *behavioural system* is the human being in the biological sense. It refers to the physical aspects of the human person, including the organic and physical environment in which human beings live. Here, Parsons referred specifically to the organism's central nervous system and motor activity. Parsons was interested in Sociobiology, but could not finish his work on Sociobiology before he died (Wallace & Wolf, 2006). Parsons' view of socialization illustrated how all these systems are linked or interrelated. At birth we are simply behavioural organisms; only as we develop as individuals do we gain personal identity. How do we then become socialized? According to Parsons, as we mentioned above, we internalize the values of society (i.e., we make the social values of the *cultural system* our own by learning from other social actors). In other words, we learn role expectations and in that way become full participants in society. Thus, values are learned from the *cultural system*.

To illustrate this point, let us take a concrete social system and see how socialization works within it. Consider a juvenile gang. If one of the values of the gang is to steal cars, then the juveniles who wish to become full members must make this value their own (*cultural system*). They must conform to the normative expectations of the gang. They must recast their own identity to fit the ideal image of a potential gang member. They must possess certain dexterity and physical skills to steal cars successfully and live up to the expectations of members of the gang. These skills are imparted to the new recruit through *socialization* (Wallace & Wolf, 2006; Mann, (2011, p. 34).

In general, Parsons was interested in explaining how we do what we do in society. Parsons attempted to grant individuals agency in his **social action** theory. In so doing, he sought to separate human *behaviours* from *actions* (Delaney, 2004, p. 241). For Parsons, *behaviours* were mechanical or knee-jerk responses to specific stimuli in the social environment, and social actions denoted the results of active inventive processes (Ravelli, 2010; Mann, 2011). He granted that people have agency, and act on their agency as individuals or collectives. As actors, people go through a four-step process, as they engage others based on their motivations and goals (Wallace & Wolf, 2006; Mann, 2011).

Mann (2011) sketches the steps as follows. The **first step** begins when a social actor is motivated to achieve a goal or an end as defined by the *cultural system* in which he or she lives. Let's use the following hypothetical scenario as an illustration. Anna's decision to attend university and achieve good grades occurred because she is motivated to have a productive and satisfying career, which she believes requires a postsecondary education. The **second step** involves the social actor to find the means to achieve her or his goals. Anna, then, needs to gather the financial resources necessary to cover the costs of going to school (e.g., tuition, books, and living expenses). The **third step** occurs when the actor needs to face the potential and real obstacles or impediments that stand in her or his way to achieve her or his goals. Anna, for example, may have to complete difficult required courses, take classes from teachers who are hard to understand, and write term papers on topics which do not interest her. **Finally**, the actor must work within the social system to achieve her or his goals. Anna, for instance, is required to pay all of her fees on time and comply with the rules and graduation requirements of the institution (See Delaney, 2004, p. 241).

Parsons' four-stage process enabled structural functionalists to begin to dissect and explain why and how people behave the way they do (Mann, 2011, p. 37). Parsons also expended a great deal of effort to outline the **functional imperatives**, referred to as *AGIL* for the first letter of each imperative, which are required for a social system to maintain equilibrium or *homeostasis*.

The Functional System Problems, AGIL

Parsons' next intellectual mission was what has been variously referred to as **systems problems**, the *functional imperatives*, the *AGIL model* (based on the four letters of the functions he devised) or the *four-function paradigm* (Mann, 2011, pp. 36–37). His aim was to incorporate into his theory propositions about the nature of goals. He identified major problems *action systems* must solve in order to develop and survive. His main interest was how the system establishes equilibrium or a state of balance. Underlying this interest was the concept *organismic analogy*. Like a biological organism, certain social institutions or structures maintain equilibrium by fulfilling needs and solving recurring problems (Mann, 2011, pp. 36–37). Parsons argued that all systems face four major problems/needs, which are:

a) **adaptation,**

b) **goal attainment,**

c) **integration**, and

d) **pattern maintenance/latent pattern maintenance/tension management.**

AGIL is the acronym for these problems.

"A" stands for *adaptation*. It relates to the securing of sufficient resources from the environment and distributing them through the system. Social institutions play these roles. The role of *adaptation*, for example, is played by the economic institution. "G" denotes *goal attainment*, and Parsons assigned this role to the political institution. The letter "I" represents *integration* and legal institutions and the courts fulfil this role. According to Wallace and Wolf (2006), this is at the heart of the *four-function paradigm*. The *integrative role* fosters social control, implementation of norms, or influence. The fourth system need is "L", or *latent pattern maintenance-tension management*. This is twofold:

a) the need to ensure that actors are sufficiently motivated to play their parts in the system or maintain the value pattern, and

b) the need to provide mechanisms for internal *tension management*.

The central task here is keeping the value system intact and guaranteeing conformity. This task is accomplished by social institutions, such as family, religion, media, and education. The crucial point to remember about the *four system needs* is that Parsons considered them to be the prerequisites for social equilibrium. This is ensured by two mechanisms: *socialization* and *social control*: "If the process of socialization is successful, all members of society will be committed to the same values and will agree to work together to achieve common goals. When this does not occur, social control mechanisms are triggered to ensure that those who are contravening collectively held values (e.g., laws) are sought out and punished" (as cited in Ravelli, 2010, p. 42).

In the next section, we explore the ideas of Robert Merton, a student of Parsons, and highlight his contributions to American sociology and sociology in general. Merton's theory of structural functionalism is called **middle range**, which is in stark contrast to the grand theorizing approaches of Parsons.

Robert K. Merton (1910–2003)

Robert Merton was, like Talcott Parsons, his former professor at Harvard University, a towering and preeminent figure in the world of American sociology during the mid-twentieth century. Both Merton and Parsons dominated American sociology for more than three decades. Like Parsons' grand theorizing became the Holy Grail for functionalism, Merton's **middle range theory** was celebrated as a creative innovation of functionalist methodology and, we would say, a welcome and compelling alternative to Parsonian grand and abstract theorizing. *Middle range theorizing* involves integrating theory and research. *Middle-range theories* are couched at a lower level of abstraction and reveal clearly defined and operationalized concepts that are incorporated into statements about a limited range of phenomena (Mann, 2011, p. 40).

Merton not only distanced himself from Parsons' one-size-fits-all grand theorizing, describing it as premature, he, in a compelling manner, argued that the best way to study society was to do so one slice at a time and at a micro-level. He proposed an empirically-grounded methodology, which started with gathering data and testing single issues at one time. As Wallace and Wolf (2006) noted, Merton placed a premium on the importance of a functionalism that is empirical and that avoids the tendency to construct grand analytical schemes into which the flow of empirical events is pushed and shoved. Merton's goal was to keep functional assumptions to a minimum, whereas Parsons' intent was to build a functional analytical scheme that could explain all reality.

Merton's singular focus was to move toward studying different levels of the social world, such as organizations and groups. He also postulated the **law of unintended consequences**, and argued that every human action has multiple and contradictory consequences. He introduced the concepts of *manifest* and *latent* functions, referring, respectively, to intended and unintended consequences. According to Merton, functions can also be characterized as displaying unanticipated consequences. He proposed the analysis of diverse consequences or functions of sociocultural items, whether positive or negative, manifest or latent, "for individuals, for sub-groups, and for the more inclusive social structure and culture" (Merton, 1949, p. 12). In turn, the analysis of varied consequences requires calculating a "net balance of consequences" of items for each other and more inclusive systems. In this way, Merton visualized contemporary functional thought as compensating for the excesses of earlier analytical approaches by focusing on the crucial types of consequences of sociocultural items for each other and, if the facts dictate, for the social whole (Mann, 2011).

Merton expanded Parsons' understanding of structural functionalism by explaining not only the function of social structures, but also their **dysfunctions, nonfunctions**, and net balances (Wallace & Wolf, 2006). For Merton (1949, p. 39), the search for "a total system of sociological theory, in which observations about every aspect of social behaviour, organization, and change promptly find their preordained place, has the same exhilarating challenge and the same small promise as those many all-encompassing philosophical systems which have fallen into deserved disuse" (See Box 10.4 – Structural Functionalism: manifest, latent, and dysfunctions).

BOX 10.4 - Structural Functionalism: manifest, latent, and dysfunctions

As we have been stating, structural functionalism is a macro-sociological theory that looks at the consequences of *social structures* on individuals and groups. It studies the contributions *social structures* make to the overall stability of society. This theoretical perspective emphasizes order and stability. Society is viewed as an organism, and is conceptualized as a complex system, which consists of many parts. Each part is assumed to contribute to the survival of the whole, or the stability of society. That is, these parts are connected to one another, and change in one part results in changes in other parts. In general, each part of society helps to maintain the system. According to this theory, society consists of *social structures*, or those "relatively stable patterns of social behaviour". *Social structures* define the roles of individuals and expectation placed on them in society. The family, for example, defines gender roles and expectations and assists in shaping how parents and siblings should behave and act towards one another. That is, each *social structure* has certain social functions for the smooth operation of society, or "the consequences of social patterns for the operation and survival of society as a whole". The family, for example, plays important functions for the survival of society. The family is responsible for the reproduction of society's members, and regulates sexual relations. Structural functionalists argue that if a specific *social structure* does not continue to contribute to the survival of the system or to promote value consensus among the population, it ceases to exist and is replaced.

According to structural functionalists, every part and aspect of society has many functions and these functions may be *manifest* or *latent*. *Manifest functions* are open, conscious, and stated. They are intended and recognized by all members of society. For example, the *manifest function* of the education system is to train individuals as future workers of a nation-state. That is, the education system has an economic purpose. The education system also socializes students as future citizens of the state and instills in them a sense of national identity. That is, schools function as political socialization agents (Siavoshi, 1995). These functions of schools are clearly stated in the goals and objectives of ministries of education in various parts of the world. In Iran, for example, the function of the education system is also to inform students about Islam and Islamic knowledge (Mirfakhraie, 2010).

In contrast, *latent functions* are hidden, unintended, and unconscious aspects of society that may reflect the hidden agendas of an institution. For example, the education system contributes to the reproduction of unequal class relations in society. Schools also alienate students from nondominant racialized backgrounds since the curriculum and teaching methods do not reflect their interests and the way in which they learn. These aspects of the education system were never intended by the educators, but they nevertheless occur.

Dysfunction refers to the idea that not all parts of the society actually contribute to the stability of society at all times. That is, at times, an element or a process may disrupt normal relations in a social system or decrease its stability. For example, residential schools were dysfunctional in a sense that they failed to equally integrate Aboriginal people into the dominant Canadian society. They harmed those who were enrolled in these schools more than they helped them.

It is important to note that structural functionalists do not assume that just because an act, such as prostitution, has functions (i.e., men satisfy their sexual urges, and women earn an income), that act is justified, wrong, moral, or immoral.

In short, according to Peter L. Berger (1963, p. 40), *manifest functions* are "the conscious and deliberate functions of social processes" that are clearly stated and intended. On the other hand, *latent functions* are the unintended and unconscious functions that are not clearly stated or intended. For example, the *manifest function* of antigambling legislation may be to put a stop to gambling. However, its *latent function* may be to promote illegal and underground gambling. The *manifest function* of Christian missionaries during the colonial era was to convert Africans to Christians, but they also helped in downplaying and destroying the importance of Indigenous knowledge (their *latent function*) (Berger, 1963, p. 40).

For any theory to be nurtured into maturity, Merton would have argued, it needs a theoretical and empirical groundwork that derived from data collection and testing of hypothesis. Thus for Merton, *middle range theorizing*, which consists of "general orientations toward data, suggesting types of variables which theorists must somehow take into account" is a more effective strategy in studying the social world. He was of the view that strategies advocated by those, such as Parsons, were not really theories, but philosophical systems with "their varied suggestiveness, their architectonic splendor, and their sterility" (Merton, 1949, p. 116).

A Paradigm for Functional Analysis

Robert Merton also introduced the procedure for conducting **functional analysis**. His paradigm was a convenient way of explicating structural functionalism. His starting point was the identification of an item, which the sociologist wishes to explain. This will be some aspect of structure, a role, an institutional pattern, a social process (e.g., mothering, teaching, or smoking). Step two involves making sense out of this item. What meaning does it have for those involved? What meaning does it have for society as a whole (e.g., what is the meaning of dating?) (Mann, 2011)? The third step is identifying the objective consequences of the item. If the consequences help a system adapt to its environment, then we would conclude that the consequences *function* are *functional*. If on the other hand, they lessen/threaten the system, then they are **dysfunctional**. Also, if these functions are recognised by members of society, then they are *manifest*, but if they are not recognized, they are conceptualized as *latent* (Allahar, 2008, p. 65). Step four logically flows from third: to specify the larger whole for which the structure in question is thought to have consequences. Usually, the larger whole refers to society, but any whole entity qualifies, as long as we think it seeks to maintain itself (e.g., small groups, organizations, and cities). The fifth step is to decide what the survival requirements of the whole are. The fifth step thus postulates the existence of a need. An explanation of a pattern of behaviour by reference to the effects it has makes no sense unless we can claim that the effects are needed by the whole of which the item is a part. The sixth and final step closes the circle. It identifies the mechanism whereby the satisfaction of the need acts back upon the original item. This is called the **feedback circuit**. A complete *functional analysis* requires the demonstration not merely of the consequences of item [A] for some larger [B]. It also requires that the satisfaction of some need of the larger whole [B] in turn maintains item [A]. The assumption of *functional analysis* is that patterns of behaviour persist.

The fascinating aspect of *functional analysis* is the way in which it helps us discern the **unanticipated** and **unrecognized** consequences of people's behaviour. Let's take the Kwanzaa harvest ceremony in East Africa, now adopted by African Americans. The *manifest* meaning or stated purpose of the ceremony is to thank and appease the rain god or Mother Earth for continued bumper harvest throughout the year. The *latent function* of this ceremony is to promote solidarity for the groups, which perform the ceremony. That is, the *latent function* is the reinforcement of group identity. It provides a periodic occasion on which scattered members assemble to engage in a common activity. The collective expression of cultural sentiments is the source of group unity because people find them rewarding. A pattern of behaviour (*social structure*), which is functional for society will command more resources with which to reward those engaged in it. Thus, highly rewarded activities will both reproduce the social system and reward the individual member. For instance, functionalists would justify high salaries for physicians on the grounds that their services are crucial for the well-being of members of society (Wallace & Wolf, 2006).

Functional Equivalence

Functional analysis gives priority to *function* and treats *structure* as secondary. *Structures* exist because they perform *functions*. For example, we have legs because we walk. This idea is made clear in the concept **functional equivalence**. Society is assumed to have chronic needs, which *social structures* must meet. If one *structure* does not satisfy those needs, another will. The structures are believed to be *functionally equivalent* (Wolf & Wallace, 2006; Mann, 2011). Let's take religion for example. If beliefs deteriorate, religious *functions* will no longer adequately be fulfilled by the traditional religious *structure* (i.e., the church). We would look about to discover what other relationships and institutional *structures* take over some part of religious *functions*. For example, baseball is now believed to have supplanted the role of religion for many people in North America and hockey for many Canadians, in particular. Soccer/football plays the same role in many other parts of the world, including Africa, Europe, Latin America, etc. *Equivalence* implies that the responsibility for important functions passes from one structure to another, with important consequences for the rest of society. For instance, formal education/schooling has replaced the family as the educator.

Structural Functionalism and Inequality

Structural functionalists by and large contend that a certain degree of inequality is functional for the society as a whole, and that society could not operate without a certain degree of inequality. Rewards in the form of income, status, prestige, or power must be provided in order to induce people to carry out the work required of them and get them to prepare for and perform in roles required by society. It is no accident that Durkheim argued that social inequalities should represent natural inequalities, and if this occurs, the division of labour performs well (Mann, 2011). This functionalist rationalization of inequality is problematic, however. It fails to answer several fundamental questions: "What is functional and what is not"? "For whom are each of these activities and institutions functional"? "Who determines what is functional and what is not"? Going by the logic of functionalism, racism and discrimination are functional, in that they contribute positively to society. However, racism and discrimination are functional only to the dominant group.

Structural functionalism has been used to rationalize assimilationist and oppressive policies in multiracial and polyethnic societies, such as Canada, the USA, and India. Historically, it had been used to explain away injustices perpetrated by dominant groups against subordinate groups. History abounds with countless examples running the gamut from the enslavement of Africans, the discrimination against women, to the oppression of the "untouchables" under the Indian caste system. Holding racist and sexist views in this country, for example, benefits those who deny rights and privileges to the so-called visible minorities and women they deem "inferior". But any form of discrimination is harmful to society in the long run. For instance, the consequences of race-based disenfranchisement, such as poverty levels, crime rates, and discrepancies in employment and education opportunities, illustrate the long-term (and clearly negative) results of slavery and racism in Canadian society. The outcomes of sexism affect society directly and indirectly, in the short term and in the long term. For example, when a woman is denied promotion in her job because of her sex, the family, and by implication, the entire society is deprived additional income that would contribute to wealthier and more stable family life. Research shows that a significant number of marriage breakdowns or divorces in North America stems from lack of adequate income (Gotman, 1990).

Functionalism and the Spirit of Max Weber

Max Weber was a multidisciplinary scholar. Throughout his illustrious career as a sociologist, he developed a distinctive approach to sociological analysis. His approach in a wide range of substantive areas, economic sociology, stratification, complex organizations, sociology of religion, authority, and social change, still guides modern research and theory. Weber influenced structural functionalists, conflict theorists, and symbolic interactionism, a fact that testifies to his wide range of interest in macro- and micro-sociological issues.

One of the main characteristics of Weber's scholarship was his critique of *economic determinist* analysis. His approach to research drew upon various fields and disciplines and accounted for a number of factors, such as social, economic, cultural, and political (Giddens, 1971, pp. 119–124). Grabb (2002, p. 41) maintained that Marx and the Marxists during the late nineteenth century and the early decades of the twentieth century "argued that ideas and beliefs are wholly products of social interaction and organization, especially within the sphere of economic production". According to Grabb (2002, p. 41), Weber did not agree with this materialist view that did not account for the possibility that "ideas could themselves influence and even generate economic structures and behaviour, rather than being mere consequences of these material forces". He, for example, studied the origin of capitalism in Western societies during the period between the sixteenth and seventeenth century, and asked why capitalism did not originate in other parts of the world. He asserted that certain changes in technology, such as the introduction of machines with new sources of energy like steam power, the mechanization of farming in addition to changes in land use and its privatization, the introduction of new accounting systems, and the factory system were influential in the rise of capitalism. Weber also focused on non-economic factors in order to offer a more comprehensive understanding of the rise of capitalism in modernity.

In his research on *the Protestant Ethic and the Spirit of Capitalism*, he showed how ideas can play an important and effective role in history (Grabb, 2002, p. 50). He investigated how changes in Western European economic organizations were related to and influenced by the new religious belief system (See Chapter Three). As Weber argued, the aim of those that brought about the Protestant Reformation was not to create a new economic system. Martin Luther (1483–1546) and John Calvin (1509–64) were critical of the corrupt power of the Catholic Church. They introduced a new way of religiosity. In their view, each man/woman needed to reach God individually and not through the sacraments that were offered (administered) by the Church. They maintained that people should have direct access to the words of God (not only through the priests as representatives of the Church). They promoted the idea that the Bible should be available in different languages, which resulted in the breakdown of the Church's control over interpreting the scripture for the masses. In their view, one would achieve salvation through personal faith and hard work, which was considered as a way to show one's devotion to God. Savings and investment were also encouraged, and unnecessary consumption was frowned upon. These qualities were viewed as important, which formed the basis of **The Protestant Work Ethic**. In this sense, Weber pointed out that (religious) ideas were also significant in the development of capitalism as a system of economic exploitation. In other words, hard work, deferred gratification, and individual responsibility became the central defining characteristics of modern individuals. In this sense, work was reconceptualized as a "spiritual vocation". In addition, the Protestant belief system promoted a life of frugality and avoidance of luxury. In this way, saving and reinvestment were encouraged over consumption of expensive products. As Weber pointed out, some of the most successful capitalists in the United States were from "those of ascetic Protestant backgrounds" (Grabb, 2002, p. 43).

Weber was a liberal who supported democracy and human freedom (Grabb, 2002, p. 40). However, Weber "was far less optimistic about the prospect for democracy's survival in future societies. Weber also rejected socialism as a vehicle to achieve equality and observed that socialism "would be an even greater threat to democracy and freedom than would be capitalism". He promoted a liberal conception of a political system, "guided by strong but enlightened leaders" who functioned within a capitalist framework (Grabb, 2002, p. 40). At the same time, Weber recognized that bureaucracy, "in the form of political-party machines managed by professional politicians and organizers, was at the same time both essential to democratic action in large-scale complex societies and a threat to democratic principles of equality and participation for all" (Grabb, 2002, p. 42).

According to Weber, bureaucracies are (will be) the most common form of processing information, problems, and people in "regular routine ways" (Grabb, 2002, p. 42). In modern societies, there is a tendency toward rationally directed actions and development of "rationally organized structures and institutions" (Grabb, 2002, p. 64). Economic rationalization entails a rational division of labour based on specialization and accompanying methods of record keeping and accounting practices (Grabb, 2002, p. 64). Even churches become rationalized due to the establishment of rational structure of hierarchy and routinized services and rituals. He pointed out that **bureaucratization** will lead to **regimentation** that is forced upon the population. For example, in contemporary Western societies, the lives of social actors are controlled and managed by computers. In this sense, through machines, bureaucracies manage and dictate our lives.

Just as Weber was said to have engaged in an intense debate with the ghost of Karl Marx, functionalists, from Parsons to Nauman, have been heavily dodged by the spirit of Weber as they tried to answer the critics of functionalism, who charged the paradigm as reducing humans as passive and powerless dunces controlled by powerful social institutions. What, then, has been Weber's impact on the emergence of functionalism? Wallace and Wolf (2006, p. 25) have identified two general aspects of Weber's work that have had an important influence: **1)** his substantive vision of *social action* and **2)** his strategy for analyzing *social structures*. Weber argued that sociology must understand social phenomena on two levels: at the "level of meaning of the actors themselves and at the level of collective action among groupings of actors". Weber's substantive view of the social world and his strategy for analyzing its features were thus influenced by these dual concerns.

Mann (2011) pointed out that Weber conceptualized two interdependent aspects of social reality: the subjective meanings of actions and the emergent regularities of social institutions. Functionalism similarly addresses this dualism by interrogating how the subjective states of actors influence emergent patterns of social organization, and vice versa. Most evident of Weber's spirit is Talcott Parsons' works. Talcott Parsons' *action theory* was inspired by Weber's subjective understanding, *verstehen* theory. Parsons' functionalism (*action theory*) and his early theoretical framework were devoted to analyzing the basic components and processes of the subjective processes of individual actors. But, like Weber, Parsons moved to a more macroscopic concern with emergent patterns of collective action (Mann 2011, 21). Wallace and Wolf (2006) argued that this switch from the micro to the macro represents only part of the Weberian analytical strategy.

Weber's other important contribution to sociology is his conceptualization of the **ideal type**. In fact, one of Weber's most enduring analytical legacies is his strategy for constructing "ideal types." Ideal types, as we explained in Chapter Seven are abstractions from empirical reality, which aim to shed light on certain common features among similar processes and structures. Moreover, they can be used to compare and contrast empirical events in different contexts by providing a common analytical yardstick. For almost all social phenomena Weber studied, such as religion, organizations, power, and many others, he constructed an *ideal type* to conceptualize their structures and functions. Parsons' *systems level analysis theory* and *functional systems problems* were also based on Weber's *ideal types*.

Summary

Structural functionalists assume that society is and must always be stable, orderly, peaceful, and harmonious. Consensus and social solidarity, they insist, must be the bedrock of intergroup interactions. However, they acknowledge that the system occasionally may encounter a system failure or what Durkheim called *anomie* and Robert Merton termed *dysfunction*. Yet, they conclude that in an event when things go awry, when a part or an institution fails to perform its role, the system somehow self-reorganizes, with another part taking over that role, in order to restore an equilibrium or the **status quo ante** (i.e., how things were before the disruption or system failure).

As a macro-sociological orientation, structural functionalism is concerned with institutions and structures existing in the society as a whole. Structures circumscribe or constrain the actions or behaviours of people. In this sense, individuals are not free in their choices, preferences, and actions. *Social structures*, such as the family and the media, are seen as powerful, while individuals are conceived as powerless pawns, influenced by these mighty institutions.

Structural functionalists are obsessed with social harmony, cooperation, consensus, continuity, and stability; they are morbidly afraid of conflict and radical or dramatic change. This explains their emphasis on traditional values, compliance, and respect for authority, law, order, and observance of hierarchy. They argue that conflict and rapid change disturb the equilibrium of society. Rocking the system too vigorously will result in its disintegration. That is, dramatic social change is considered as dangerous. It is therefore safe to manage the existing system, resolving tensions that may arise via consensus and cooperation.

The Conflict Paradigm: From Classical Marxism to Neo-Marxism

The **conflict paradigm** is an example of macro-sociology. It argues that the structural functionalist conception of social order as a harmonious entity is actually based on coercion and exploitation of labour, resources, working classes, and other marginalized groups. It posits that social behaviour is best understood in the context of an analysis of conflicts between classes of people. According to this view, the social world is influenced by continuous struggles over power and resources. The concept of conflict does not only refer to violence or violent behaviour, but to competition over the structures of power between various groups based on factors, such as "race", ethnicity, nationality, religion, gender, and sexuality. Conflict is a structural aspect of everyday relations at all levels of social institutions, locally and globally. The main questions that conflict theorists ask are: who benefits from the existing structures of power, who suffers, who dominates society and its structures, and how do the institutions of society reproduce the privileges of elite capitalist groups. In general, conflict theorists promote social, economic, cultural, and political changes that aim at transforming society and call for the redistribution of resources.

The conflict paradigm is a framework for building theory based on the assumption that society is a complex system characterized by inequality and conflict that generate change (Wallace & Wolf, 2012). This paradigm, which is also called the **political economy paradigm**, is based on the writings of Karl Marx (See Box 10.5 - Karl Marx and Historical and Dialectical Materialism). As an alternative to structural functionalism, the conflict paradigm has become increasingly popular in academia. Structural functionalists, as we have explained, visualize society and social institutions as systems with interdependent parts working toward equilibrium, harmony, and stability. While they do not deny conflict *per se*, they contend that society develops ways to control conflict. Conflict theorists disagree. They contend that not only is conflict inevitable and natural, it also serves as the engine of change in society. Conflict theorists conceptualize society as an arena of constant struggles, with one group dominating others.

BOX 10.5 - Karl Marx and Historical and Dialectical Materialism

Karl Marx (1818–1883) was a philosopher and economist; however, as Ritzer (2006, p. 41) rightly noted, although he was not a trained sociologist, he nevertheless must be considered as one of the main scholars who contributed tremendously to the discipline. Marx's aim was to improve the visions and goals of liberalism that promoted progress and human freedom. He viewed "science" as a tool to change and to understand society (Seidman, 1994a, p. 45). Like the Enlightenment thinkers, he assumed that it is possible for human beings to develop a future that reflects their ideals (Seidman, 1994a, p. 32). Marx and his lifelong collaborator, Friedrich Engels (1820–1895), investigated the nature of the human condition and helped to define an influential sociological theory that offered a clear antithesis to functionalism. Marx is credited with scores of books, articles, and pamphlets, but he is best known for *The Communist Manifesto* (1848), in which, together with Engels, argued that class struggle is pervasive throughout human history and through revolutionary movement led by the workers capitalism will be replaced with a socialist and finally communist state. Marx's vision and philosophy were grounded in British political economy (i.e., the works of Adam Smith and David Ricardo), German philosophy (i.e., Kant and Hegel), and French utopian socialism (i.e., Fourier and St. Simon).

Karl Marx viewed society from a critical perspective during the period in which many people in industrialized societies of Western Europe were moving from rural to urban centres, where factories were becoming the major centre for employment. He asserted that in order to change society, it is important to understand the causes of social problems, and how society works, through a "scientific" lens (Seidman, 1994a, p. 33). He viewed the capitalist society as a divided entity that was composed of two main classes, those who own the **means of production** (the exploiters), and those who have to sell their labour (the **proletariat**), who are the exploited. Marx offered a systematic analysis of capitalism by pointing out that the power of the exploiters over the exploited is maintained by the entire system of legal, economic, cultural, and political relations. One important aspect of Marx's research is his argument that individuals' habits, identities, perceptions, and wants and their status and class positions in society depend on their places and positions in the economic structure of society. He analyzed how one's membership in a specific group affects one's attitudes and behaviour and life chances. That is, he analyzed the extent to which group identification and association in the context of economic relations influence individuals' socioeconomic and class positions in society. He highlighted and argued that the economic class positions of social actors influence their attitudes, behaviours, and life chances. He maintained that who we are, what we consume, and the extent to which we have or lack power is due to our class positions within the context of capitalist relations and structures.

Marx believed that "science" played an important role in creating and informing the new age, or modernity (Seidman, 1994a, p. 32). The "scientific" view that Marx applied to analyze society and its economic structure is called **historical materialism**. It is a critical theory that is based on *political economy perspective* (Seidman, 1994a, p. 36). This theory focuses on the development of social institutions and conflicts instead of evolution of ideas (Seidman, 1994a, p. 36). It provided an objective view of social reality (Seidman, 1994a, p. 46). However, it is important to note that this view of Marx resembled the general belief of the time that "science" was a liberating tool that would free humans from myth and oppression, which postmodernists have criticized as an illusion of modernity (Seidman, 1994a, p. 48). In fact, this emphasis on "science" as an objective tool to understand humanity has resulted in the undermining of other forms of knowledge, such as the oral traditions of non-Western peoples (Seidman, 1994a, p. 49). Marx's emphasis on "science" as a liberating tool points out that he was much influenced by the ideas of the Enlightenment. The Enlightenment, as mentioned in Chapter Three, emphasized liberal and democratic values and promoted individualism and individual rights and privacy (Seidman, 1994a, p. 49). The Enlighteners were also staunch supporters of equality, and believed in the separation of the Church and state; in other words, they insisted on secularization (Seidman, 1994a, p. 49). At the same time, the emphasis of the Enlightened thinkers that humans were uniform everywhere, despite the fact that it was meant to "discredit social hierarchies that rested upon the idea of different races and rankings of human beings", resulted in the promotion of "intolerance towards human diversity and the assertion of social differences between individuals and groups" (Seidman, 1994a, p. 49). Marx, for example, viewed Asian others as despotic and non-modern.

According to Marx, however, human nature was not fixed or uniform. He postulated that they are in control of their destiny (Seidman, 1994a, p, 32). Humans, he maintained, "make their nature through their actions" (Seidman, 1994a, p. 46). These ideas are reflected in his conceptualization of *historical materialism* that states economic activities and structures are more important in organizing society than culture (Seidman, 1994a, p. 46). Marx's approach to *historical materialism* was influenced by the ideas of Hegel and his emphasis on *idealism*. However, he was critical of the *idealist* conception of social relations. According to Jones (1969, p. 367), *idealism* refers to "any view that holds reality to be mental or 'spiritual,' or mind-dependent". In contrast, Marx argued that humans produce their material needs, such as food, shelter, and clothing, by altering their environments. In this sense, **materialism** (Jones, 1969, p. 368) refers to the "doctrines that reality is matter, whereas idealism holds that matter is 'really' the thought of some mind or other". In other words, *materialism* asserts that we can reduce mind and all other nonmaterial things (i.e., God) to "the complex notion of material particles" (Jones, 1969, p. 368). Marx believed that before we can produce culture, we must first satisfy our needs and sustain ourselves as natural beings. For people to survive, they must meet their basic needs of food to save them from starvation and shelter and clothing to protect them from the vicissitudes and the elements of nature. In order to meet these needs, they must use resources in their physical/natural environments. However, these resources are relatively scarce, and as a result, they clash with other people who also need these resources. In the ensuing battles and conflicts, some emerge winners and others, losers. The winners create social institutions, such as the economy to fend off the losers. They also create ideas (ideology) to justify why they won in the struggle over the resources and why the losers lost. Values and ideas are weapons used by different groups to advance their own ends. In fact, there is a link between ideas or ideologies and the interests of those who develop them. For example, Marx insisted that the ideas of an age/epoch reflect the interests of the ruling class: "The ruling ideas are also the ideas of the ruling class" (as cited in Durham & Kellner, 2006, p. 9). This assumption is often discussed in terms of **ideology**, **legitimacy**, and **hegemony**. For example, as we discussed in Chapter Eight, the power elite in the US often invoked the idea of *manifest destiny*, a supposed God-given right conferred on America, to civilize the "backward and primitive Red Indian tribes" as a justification to steal First Nations peoples' land and their near extermination in the hands of the White settlers. The same ideology has been used to rationalize more recent brutal interventions in the Global South, from Afghanistan to Iraq and from Nicaragua to Chile and El Salvador.

However, despite his emphasis on *ideology*, it is important to reiterate that Marx was not an *idealist*, but was critical of *idealist* views that were popular in Germany at the time. Most German *idealists* claimed ideas and their producers play important roles in the process of change (Seidman, 1994a, pp. 32–33). History was informed by the "development of reason through the medium of the clash of ideas" (Seidman, 1994a, p. 33). Marx maintained that German philosophers, such as Hegel, "were less concerned with 'reality' itself; than with ideas about reality" (Turner et al., 2002, p. 104). Marx, for example, criticized liberal Germans for wanting to introduce piecemeal changes in the form of legislation and administration of the government without developing an overall theory of society needed to implement change (Seidman, 1994,a, p. 33). The aim of Marx was to seek "the idea in reality itself" (Marx, as cited in Turner et al., 2002, p. 103). He argued that "human [material] existence determines human consciousness" (Eriskson, 1998, p. 40). That is, he did not believe that "human consciousness determines human [material] existence" (Eriskson, 1998, p. 40). His main point was that relations between humans are not the end result of political values or religious beliefs and ideas. He explained that it is the social and material interests that determine which ideas humans adopt, and it is humans' social positions that determine their social interests (Seidman, 1994a, p. 34). Individuals become a force in change only if such changes appeal to individuals, whose economic and political interests impel them to become involved in the process of change. Marx's position is called **realism**, the notion that objects of sense perception have an existence independent of the act of perception (Simons, 2013, p. 174). In other words, physical objects continue to exist whether they are perceived or not.

Hegel's *idealism* was also based on his conception of **dialecticism** (See Chapter One). Central to his view of *dialecticism* is the idea of **contradiction**: "each concept implies its opposite; or in Hegel's terms, each concept implies its negation" (Turner et al., 2002, p. 108). For example, Marx maintained that the aim of the capitalist class is to ensure its access to a docile and cheap labour force. In contrast, the goals of the labouring class are to increase their wages and improve the working conditions (Seidman, 1994a, p. 40). Although Marx adopted Hegel's dialectal approach, he also rejected Hegel's ideas on several accounts. **First**, Marx considered empirical phenomenon as real. If we consider empirical phenomenon as only thought, the outcome would be that we end up ignoring people's more practical problems. Marx stated that, "Neither material objects nor relationships can be changed by merely thinking about them" (Turner et al., 2002, p. 109). We cannot change our political conditions by simply changing the way we understand or think about reality. For example, we cannot end racism or violence against women by simply theorizing about them and talking about these issues. We need to become active and form organizations that put pressure on governments to implement policies that would put an end to sexist and racist practices. We need to bring about change through becoming involved in social movements and grass-roots organizations that attempt to alter the world that dominates and alienates us rather than simply wait for the after world" (Turner et al., 2002, p. 109). There is a need to apply human reason in the world. According to Marx, it is important to note that ideas should be analyzed in the context of the social conditions in which they emerge and operate. However, Weber disagreed with such a statement. Weber argued that a mere materialist understanding of history ignores the fact that "the subjective meanings and ideas people live by frequently produce effects different from those that a single materialist theory would predict" (Grabb, 2002, p. 49).

Second, humans have certain essential needs that must be satisfied. They are physical needs, such as food, shelter, and clothing. Hegel emphasized on mental labour, producing ideas, but Marx emphasized the productive labour. Marx believed that humans are natural beings: "that is, they have physical needs that can be satisfied in this world" (Turner et al., 2002, p. 109). Marx maintained that how societies produce the things they need in order to survive determines and dictates how such societies are organized and how people in these communities define themselves. He put forth the idea that in order to better understand human beings and society, there is a need to better understand how a society organizes the production of its material necessitates.

Third, Marx rejected Hegel's emphasis on religion. Marx considered religion as the opiate of the people. The main function of religion, for Marx, was for people to ignore their true objective situations and interests (Turner et al., 2002, p. 110). **Fourth**, Marx rejected an emphasis on *idealism*. He considered idealism as too conservative and as an ideology that promoted the *status quo*. Marx argued that "idealism creates the illusion of a community of people rather than the reality of a society riddled with opposing interests" (Turner et al., 2002, p. 110). Marx, however, drew upon Hegel's analysis of *dialectic* by turning it right side up, and applied it to the material world, "where people make history by producing their sustenance from the environment" (Turner et al., 2002, p. 110). Marx believed that the focus must be on concrete societies viewed as social systems, and with groups of people that have conflicting interests. Society is the composite of conflicts that are "systematically generated from people's opposing interests" (Turner et al., 2002, p. 111). In other words, conflict over resources, hierarchies of wealth, power, and status are formed in all societies. Marx saw some type of hierarchy as inevitable (Mann, 2011, p. 41). Society is an arena of continuous struggle over valued or scarce resources, as well as power and social status between two classes: the **bourgeois** (or the **capitalist class**) and the **proletariat** (or the **working class**); poor and the rich; the factory owner and the factory worker; dominant and the dominated; the dominant white and "minority" black; men and women; and privileged and the deprived. The privileged class attempts to maintain the *status quo*, while the deprived class seeks change.

It is in this light that Marx came up with the idea of ***dialectical materialism***. *Dialectical materialism* was the basis for Marx's analysis of society. According to Marx, the basis of life is the production of material goods (i.e., food to satisfy biological needs and shelter against the vicissitudes of the elements). Humans must eat before they can think and act. Within any society there is a way of producing things; that is what is produced, how it is produced (i.e., tools, technology), and who produces the things (i.e., social organization, the relationships between producers). This is what Marx called **productive forces**. The productive forces are established and maintained through a division of labour. Those who own the ***means of production*** (factories, raw materials, capital) belong to the dominant class, which benefit from the *status quo*. The masses or the subordinate class are exploited and alienated because they have little control over their lives, hence they have an interest in changing the *status quo*. Over time, new ways of production emerge due to new technology together with a new organization of production. The new *forces of production* satisfy old needs and also stimulate new ones. The new class, which exists in opposition to current property relations and forms of interaction, will emerge. After some time, tension between the classes will escalate, which will spark a revolution leading to the emergence of a new dominant class. Marx's forces of production can be divided into two distinct parts: the **mode of production** *(the way a society is organized to produce goods and services)* and ***patterns of property ownership*** (**relations of production**, i.e., the relationship between those who own the *means of production*—the capitalists or bourgeoisie—and those who do not—the workers or the proletariat—that together determine the nature of people's lives and course of social conflict). In general, Marx emphasized the primacy of technology and of pattern of ownership as factors that determine peoples' lives and the course of social conflict (Wallace & Wolf, 2006).

Dialectical materialism has four characteristics. **First**, it assumes that society is a system that is made of interrelated parts, such as "classes, social institutions, cultural values, and so forth" (Turner et al., 2002, p. 130). These parts do not function separately from one another but form an integrated whole. In this sense, we can think of opposing yet interrelated parts, such as the *proletariat* and the *bourgeoisie* and wage labour and capital. These opposites cannot exist without the other. We can also view consumption and production in the same light. The process of consumption and production that we call economy is connected to the process of stratification (Turner et al., 2002, p. 130). Class relations are part of all institutions and "are reflected in all areas of social behaviour: the economy, the kinship, illness and medical treatment, crime, religion, education, and government" (Turner et al., 2002, p. 130). Marx focused on and emphasized the economic factors in his analysis of society, but he did so in the context of a *dialectical approach*.

The **second** characteristic of *dialectics* is the assumption that society is constantly changing. Marx assumed that social change is an inherent element of society since people make history as they satisfy their needs that are ever-increasing (Turner et al., 2002, p. 130). Marx argued that change comes from factors within society rather than from outside societies (Turner et al., 2002, p. 130). The inherent changes in the system are due to the existing **contradictions** within the system (See Box 10.6 Contradictions in the Capitalist System of Production). Although all the parts of society are interconnected, they, nevertheless, contain within them contradictions that will result in opposites to develop (Turner et al., 2002, p. 130). For example, according to Marx, the feudal system contained within it elements (social relations) that led to the formation of the capitalist system. The same can be said about capitalism and its eventual transformation.

The **third** characteristic of *dialectical approach* is that social change takes shape in a predictable and recognizable direction (Turner et al., 2002, p. 130). He emphasizes the ***predictability of the future***: a belief in the possibility of a perfect future, which is free of conflict, a communist society. Marx's view of social change was based on an evolutionary framework that assumed social change moves from fewer complexes to more complex social relations and structures (Turner et al., 2002, p. 131).

The **fourth** element of *dialectical thinking* is that people's actions shape the direction of history within the context of "predictable patterns of opposition and class conflict that develop from contradictions in society" (Turner et al., 2002, p. 131). The most important aspect of Marx's definition of class lies in the importance and centrality of the idea of oppositions in his analysis. According to Marx, members of opposing classes have varying and different interests that are in conflict with one another. This is due to the fact that they occupy different and varying positions within the stratified social structures of society. Those who lack power and are not in control of their destiny, work, and cannot express their potentials are in a subordinate position in relation to other groups in society. Because they are alienated within society, they have an interest to change the structure of society, especially since these conflicts and opposing interests cannot be resolved within the current system. Marx was interested in the social conditions that enabled people to act and change their surroundings and social structures of society. People (i.e., the *proletariat* or working class) come to recognize their class interests under certain conditions; and, as a result, will unite and lead a socialist/communist revolution (Turner et al., 2002, p. 131).

Summary

Here we provided a brief summary of *dialectical materialism*: Every society has a way of producing goods and services that it needs to survive. This process of producing goods also entails a certain level of existing social relations and organization of production. This, Marx referred to as the *productive forces*. The *productive forces* in all societies are reproduced and maintained through a **division of labour** (Turner et al., 2002, pp. 131–132). Those few people who own the *means of production* are part of the dominant class. They are the benefactors of the system of production and how society is organized. The majority of people form the subordinate classes and their labours are exploited. They feel and become alienated since they have no or little control over the *means of production* and their lives. The alienated and subordinated people and groups, thus, would be interested in imposing and bringing about social change. These classes will ultimately dismantle the old system and the new system will be based on "new ways of producing things" that draw upon advances in technology or the ways in which production is organized (Turner et al., 2002, pp. 131–132). The new *forces of production* will be in the control of the subordinate classes that are in opposition to existing classes and property relationships and forms of interactions: "over the long run, the tensions between these opposing classes erupts into revolutionary conflicts and a new dominant class will emerge" (Turner et al., 2002, p. 132). This new system will not be based on exploitation and *alienation* since the division of labour is not based on private ownership of the means of production (Turner et al., 2002, p. 132).

Marx and Conflict Theory

Marx, like Comte, Spencer, and Durkheim, believed that society evolved in a lineal direction, from "simple" to "complex", from "primitive" to modern (Seidman, 1994a, p. 40). But unlike these proponents of structural functionalism, as mentioned, Marx posited that the basis of societal change was a *dialectical* unity and struggle of opposite forces that lead to progress. According to Ritzer (2010), society is driven by a moving balance of antithetical forces that generate social change by their tensions and struggles. Unlike structural functionalists who see social change as peaceful, evolutionary, and piecemeal, Marx proposed that conflict was the engine of progress. That is, struggles and strife informed the logic and trajectory of the forward march of society. Rather than viewing social conflict as a bad thing, Marx proposed that it should be understood as beneficial for social progress and as inevitable. Marx, using Hegel's notion of *dialectical struggle*, noted in the opening lines of the *Communist Manifesto*, coauthored with Engels, that, "The history of all hitherto existing society is the history of class struggles ... Freeman and slave, patrician and plebeian, lord and serf, guild-master and journeyman, in a word, oppressor and oppressed, stood in constant opposition to one another, carried on an uninterrupted, now hidden, now open fight, a fight that each time ended, either in a revolutionary reconstruction of society at large, or in the common ruin of the contending classes (as cited in Mann, 2011, p. 63).

Marx and Engels visualized six basic stages in societal evolution:

1. **Primitive Communism**, characterized by tribal society, in which no economic classes exist

2. **Asiatic Mode of Production**, characterized by communal property and despotism

3. **Ancient Mode of Production**, characterized by a mixed ownership of land

4. **Feudalism**, characterized by nobility owning most land and agricultural surplus

5. **Capitalism**, characterized by the division of society into three distinct classes of the *bourgeoisie* and the *proletariat*, and other minor classes

6. **Communism**, where (in theory) class structure is abolished.

According to Marx, the second, third, and fourth stages were all riddled with *class struggles*. For Marx, *class struggle* will end with the emergence of the future *communist* society, which in essence is the "scientific" and advanced version of the first stage, *primitive communism*. He observed that between the capitalist stage and *communism*, there would be a transitional stage, which he called **socialism.** The *socialist* state would be formed by the working class after it has overthrown the capitalist class in a revolution. In the *socialist* state, *class struggle* between the working class and the remnants of the *bourgeoisie* continues, which eventually leads to the ***disappearance of the state***, paving the way for the emergence of the future ***classless communist*** society. In this type of society, humans will govern through conscious choice and reason promoting freedom that highlights moral order and social harmony (Seidman, 1994a, p. 40). It is important to note that, some conflict theorists, including a whole phalanx of neo-Marxists, reject Marx's vision of a classless society.

BOX 10. 6 – Contradictions in the Capitalist System of Production

According to Marx and Marxism, **capitalism** is characterized by cycles of booms and busts. It is also characterized by certain **contradictions** that stem from the structural characteristics of the capitalist system. *Contradictions* are due to the policies that allow for the satisfaction of the needs of one class at the cost of other subordinated classes. For example, the aim of the owners of the *means of production* in a capitalist system is to increase the rate of profit. One way of achieving this is for the capitalist class to replace the workers with machines or to cut their wages. These actions reduce the purchasing power of workers, who can no longer buy consumer products and satisfy their basic needs. This in turn results in fewer goods produced by the capitalist class to be purchased and a reduction in their profits. As Giddens (1971, p. 53) also stated, the capitalist classes are in constant competition with one another to improve the technology used in the production process, reduce the labour cost, and to organize the workplace in order to increase their share of the available profit and to produce their products at a cheaper rate than others. However, this will lead, for example, each capitalist to introduce the same technological advances as others in order to stay competitive, thus, resulting in each capitalist to have a "higher ratio of capital expenditure on constant capital than before. Hence the overall consequence is a rise in the organic composition of capital, and a fall in the average rate of profit (Giddens, 1971, p. 53). According to Marx, these crises within *capitalism* do not point to the breakdown of the system, but help it to deal with the periodic fluctuations to which it is subject (Giddens, 1971, p. 55).

Karl Marx and His Critique of Capitalism

In his book, *The Capital*, Marx offered a theoretical examination of capitalist social system (Turner et al., 2002, p. 106). Marx maintained that all forms of economic organization that had existed at the time he wrote his seminal works inevitably generated conflict between social classes. His *Communist Manifesto* opens with the now famous declaration: "The history of all hitherto existing societies is the history of class struggles" (as cited in Durham & Kellner, 2006, p. 9). Three propositions can be distilled from this declaration:

a) people whose economic position/class is the same also tend to act together as a group,

b) economic classes are the most important groups in society and their history is the history of human society, and

c) these classes are mutually antagonistic and the outcomes of their conflicts define how society develops.

Marx's theory of class is thus the theory of *social structure* and theory of change.

He analyzed the exploitive nature of *capitalism* and its effects on workers and society. In a capitalist society, the aim of the capitalist class is to exploit the labour of workers in order to increase the rate of profit. As Seidman (1994a, p. 43) pointed out, the goal of capitalist profit making is to make sure that economic modernization is possible and achieved. Due to the fact that the capitalists are in constant competition with other capitalists, and in order to avoid failure, the capitalist class needs to constantly improve the *means of production* and modernize the workplace, which has consequences for workers. The aim of the capitalist class is to make and produce better and new products, improve the efficiency of labour, reduce the cost of labour by minimizing their wages, and maximize their productivity, so they can produce more (Seidman, 1994a, p. 43). Although Karl Marx "had great admiration for the capacity of capitalism to produce wealth, stimulate technological, social, cultural innovation, and create the conditions of political democracy" (Seidman, 1994a, p. 43), he realized that despite such a capacity to improve human freedoms, capitalism also hinders and limits freedoms, as the benefits are controlled by a small percentage of the population (Seidman, 1994a, p. 44). Marx believed that in a capitalist system consumption must expand in order for the system to be able to absorb the increased production of goods, which results in the internationalization of capitalism and increasing the domestic markets "by commercializing hitherto noncommerical workers (e.g., leisure, recreation, sports)" (Seidman, 1994a, p. 44).

Marx defined **class** *as group of people who are alike in their relationship to property*. People have none or they have the same type of property, he argued. Ultimately, the sort of work people do is not what matters. Thus, manual workers, clerks, technicians, and engineers belong to the same class, because they only have their labour to sell. They belong to a different class from the capitalists and landlords (i.e., *bourgeoisie*) who own the *means of production*. If you look around the university campus, you will find that the only factor of production most people own is their labour. In Marxist terms, they therefore belong to the same class, the *proletariat* or the working class. This will certainly be true for most students and also a number of the faculty. Why? This is because they work for salary. Some may own their own homes, but that is not *means of production*. On the other hand, some students and faculty may own shares of stock and may be running businesses. For Marx, there is no difference between shareholders, who simply provide capital, and entrepreneurs. Marx's theory argued that the different classes inevitably will have incompatible interests because if one class makes economic gains, it must be at the expense of another. The major economic systems of the past strengthened one particular class, which exploited others. Marx observed: "Freeman and slave, patrician and plebeian, lord and serf, guild-master and journeyman, in a word, oppressor and oppressed, stood in constant opposition to one another, carried on an uninterrupted, now hidden, now open fight" (Marx, 1848, p. 2). He also wrote that an oppressed class was the vital condition for every society founded on the antagonism of classes. In bourgeois society, the capitalists are the oppressors; the *proletariat*, the oppressed (Wallace & Wolf, 2006, p. 88).

Marx explained that economic factors are the fundamental determinants of *social structure* and change. He maintained that society is made up of two interconnected parts:

a) the economic **base** through which people organize their economic activities, such as the production, distribution, and consumption of goods and services; and

b) the **superstructure**, referring to the other spheres of social life, such as the ideas and values people hold.

These ideas are shaped and dependent on the nature of economic production. Marx argued that the *base* and *superstructure* are interdependent. To drive this point home, Marx maintained that people must eat before they can think, but before they can produce the food, they must think of how to produce the food. He wrote, "The difference between the most intelligent bee and the most foolish man is that man thinks of the structure in his mind before erecting it" (as cited in Wallace & Wolf, 2006, pp. 87–88).

Marx regarded society as a structurally integrated whole. Consequently for him, any aspect of that whole (i.e., be it legal codes, systems of education, art, or religion) could not be understood by itself. Like all of the founders of sociology, he believed that we must examine the parts in relation to one another and in relation to the whole. Although historical phenomena were the result of the interplay of many factors, all but one of them was in the final analysis dependent variables: "Political, legal, philosophical, and artistic development all depend on the economic [*base*]. They all react upon one another and upon the economic base" (Elwell, 2011, p. 1).

It is clear that Marx offers a nuanced and complicated view of the working of society. Far from the vulgar materialist he is often depicted to be, Marx saw a mutual interplay between the *economic base* and the *political-ideological-legal superstructure*. He, however, believed that the former produces the latter. Hence his conclusion that the *forces of production* (which determine the *relations of production*, or roughly, the economy) was the most important factor in understanding the social system: "It is not the case that the economic situation is the sole active cause and that everything else is merely a passive effect. There is, rather, a reciprocity within a field of economic necessity which in the last instance always asserts itself" (Elwell, 2011, p. 1).

The *forces of production* constitute the technology and work patterns that men and women use to exploit their environment and to meet their needs. These *forces of production* are expressed in relationships between men (and women). By *relations of production*, Marx meant the social relationships people enter into by participation in economic life, for example, worker-employee or worker-worker relationships. The *relations of production* are the relations people establish with each other when they utilize existing raw materials and technologies in the pursuit of their productive goals. While Marx begins with the *forces of production*, he quickly moves to the *relations of production* that are based on these forces. For Marx, *the relations of production* are the key to understanding the whole cultural *superstructure* of society (Mann, 2011). The *relations of production* (economic organization) constitute the foundation upon which the whole cultural *superstructure* of society comes to be erected. Marx gives the *relations of production* the primary focus in his analysis of social evolution. The *forces of production* set the stage for these relations. The central premise of the Marxist conception of capitalist social structure is that the *economic base* of society is the prime determinant of almost everything else. In other words, the economy takes a preeminent position in society. In short, the economy trumps everything else in society. In the Marxist conception, society consists of an *economic base* out of which arises the *superstructure*, or other institutions and social processes of society (such as, the legal, political, familial, and religious spheres).

The *base* and the *superstructure* emerge from the *mode of production*. Every epoch produces its own *mode of production*. The *mode of production*, according to Marx, is made up of two components: the *forces of production*, which consists of the tools, machines, raw materials people use in producing their material life and *relations of production*, the definite relationship people are involved in the production of material life.

In Marx's view, the relationship between the *base* and *superstructure* is *dialectical*: the *superstructure* arises out of the *economic base* but once created acts back to reproduce it. That is to say while the economy (the *base*) begets ideas, values, etc., the *superstructure* in turn influences the economy. An example will shed more light on the *dialectical* relationship between the two. When one is hungry, the individual must eat food if he/she is to live. First the food must be produced. However, in order to produce the food, one must think about how to produce it. The production of the food belongs to the economic realm or the *base*, while the thought system that guided the production belongs to the realm of *superstructure* or ideas. Thus, the two realms (the *base* and the *superstructure*) exist in a *dialectical* relationship, mutually influencing one another. In a class-based society, such as *capitalism*, the capitalist class controls society. Given the position of dominance of the capitalist class over the working class in the economic sphere, the other spheres and processes in society will be organized to serve the interests of the capitalist class. In other words, within the *superstructure*, the kind of legal system, the form of the family, the nature of education will operate in accordance with the interests of the dominant class (Quist-Adade, 2012).

In a classical Marxist approach, because the economic variable is viewed as primary, it becomes impossible to study other segments of society, like law, in isolation from the economic. Rather, law must be understood in relation to the economic sphere. The Marxist approach also sees inequality, conflict, and power in structural terms, as class inequality, class conflict, and class domination. Accordingly, consensus is not a 'natural' condition: it has to be continually manufactured or created via a process neo-Marxists now call **hegemony**.

This distinction highlights an important point that Marx posited: societal institutions, such as the family, the government, the education system, and religion, are influenced by the **productive arrangements** within society. In general, Marx argued that the *mode of production*, conceptualized as the *base*, determines and affects the *superstructure* (i.e., the government, law, art, and religion). He maintained that in a capitalist system the economic, social, and political systems and relations perpetuate and promote the interests of the owners of the *means of production* over the workers. In his view, a capitalist society is a **class society**. In such a society, one's class position is determined by one's relations to *the forces of production*.

In general, Marx distinguished between three aspects of social organization. They are:

a) *material forces of production*, which consist of actual methods by which people produce their living;

b) *the relations of production*, which arise out of them and include property relations and rights; and

c) the *legal/political superstructures*, which refers to the ideas or forms of social consciousness that correspond to the first two elements.

Marx argued that in production, people enter into definite *relations of production*, which correspond to a definite stage of development of their *material productive forces. The mode of production* of material life conditions the social, political, and intellectual life process in general. In other words, the *mode of production* is the basic causal factor that ultimately determines how society is organized. In changing their *mode of production*, social actors change all their social relations (i.e., the hand-mill gave birth to a society of the feudal lord and the steam-mill produced the industrial capitalists). If we are to extend Marx's argument to today's society, in our computer-age, cyber-society, the information technology has given us the corporate capitalists.

Summary of Marx's Arguments

Our existence, the way we think and act is related to and determined by the **system of economic organization**

or mode of production

Different *modes of productions* dominate different historical epochs

1

Summary of Marx's Arguments

Mode of production consists of two parts:

1) specific forces and the means that are used in producing goods and services (referred to as the *productive forces*)

For example, how we extract natural resources and transform them into products that we need in order to survive

2) the legal-political relations directing the use of productive forces, or the relations of production

Summary of Marx's Arguments

Mode of production infleunces

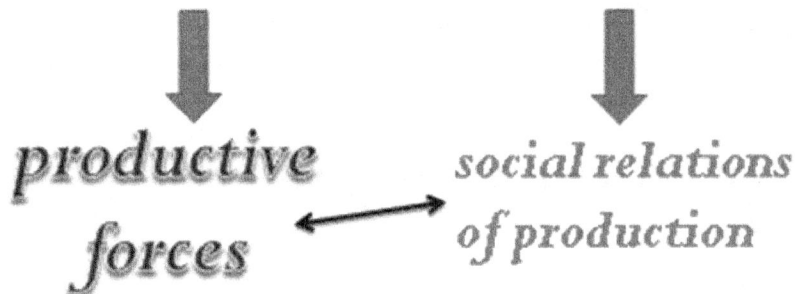

productive forces ⟷ *social relations of production*

Summary of Marx's Arguments

Marx argued that in addition to the *productive forces,*

we must also account for the *social relations of production*

or, who controls and owns the means of production

Marx's Conception of Base and Superstructure

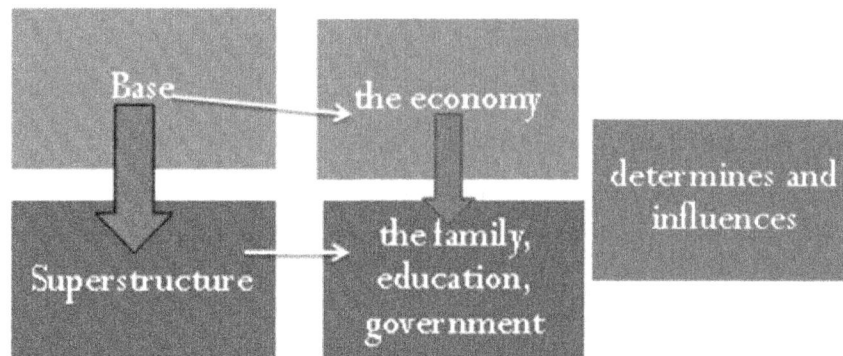

Marx also maintained that the process of modernization and capital accumulation will result in the politicization of the working class. Marx argued that when workplace is rationalized, the end result will be disempowering workers, reduction of their wages, and a rise in workers' insecurities, as machines replace them. Marx pointed out that the usage of technology and machines and a rise in specialization in the workplace (factories) will result in **deskilling** of workers "and will strip work of all its skills, imagination, and creativity" (Seidman, 1994a, p. 44). In other words, he examined how the modernization of workplace will result in the **alienation** of workers and their degradation. His discussion of *alienation*, furthermore, should be understood in light of his assertion that, in industrial societies, the factory is the centre of conflict. **Class conflict** occurs between those who own the *means of production*, such as the land, the factory, and the equipment, and those who sell their labour in order to satisfy their social needs. He conceptualized the relation between these two classes as **exploitative**. The exploiters are the *bourgeoisie* and the exploited are the working classes with opposing interests: the capitalist class aims at increasing its rates of profit and the workers attempt to improve their working conditions. **Exploitation** characterizes the relationship between different classes within the capitalist society. The elite groups use their property rights; social, economic, and cultural privileges; and control over coercive means of powers, such as police and the military, to dominate other groups (classes) within society.

Marx outlined two general conceptions of *exploitation*. **First**, for Marx, *exploitation* occurs if person A harmfully utilizes person B as a mere means for A's benefit. *Exploitation* is the harmful, merely instrumental use of persons for the benefit of others who utilize them. **Second**, Marx also focused on the transhistorical conception of *exploitation* in the labour process. This conception is more specialized than the first one. It is limited to relations within the labour process. According to Marx, each type of social formation in the history of class-societies has its own distinctive labour process. For example, in ancient city-states, it was slavery; in the Middle Ages, it was the Feudal system of serf labor; and in modern capitalist society, it is wage-labor (Mann, 2011; Simmons, 2013). Marx argued that in all these system:

a) the labour is forced;

b) part of the labour is uncompensated;

c) the labour produces surplus products; and

d) the worker does not have control over the product.

The workers are also exploited as they are denied a share of the profits the capitalist class makes because of the value the workers add to products through their labour (See Box 10.7 - The Theory of Surplus Value).

BOX 10.7 - The Theory of Surplus Value

Marx maintained that every commodity has two sides and elements: the **use value** and **exchange value** (Giddens, 1971, p. 46). *Use value* of a product and an item of consumption refers to the characteristics of the item that satisfy humans' basic needs through its consumption. An item can have *use value* irrespective of being a commodity or not (Giddens, 1971, p. 46). For an item to be considered a commodity, however, it has to have *exchange value*. The *exchange value* refers to "the value a product has when offered in exchange for other products" (Giddens, 1971, p. 46). The *exchange value* has meaning only in the context of economic relations and as a commodity.

The **labour theory of labour** asserts that a commodity has value only when human labour is invested in producing it (Giddens, 1971, p. 46). Marx maintained that the *exchange value* of a commodity does not gain its worth from the *use value*: "Exchange value rests on some quantifiable characteristics of labour" (Giddens, 1971, p. 47). Marx concluded that **abstract labour** (which is measured by gauging the socially necessary labour time required to produce a commodity) is the source for *exchange value* and **useful labour** the basis of *use value*.

The labour of workers is also a commodity that is sold in the marketplace. The labour of the worker must be socially reproduced: that is, the worker must be able to provide for his/her basic needs. This amount necessary to reproduce the workers socially is considered by Marx as the value of the **worker's labour power** (Giddens, 1971, p. 49). Marx maintained that the profit of the capitalist is the difference between the portion of the workday that is needed to recover the cost of the workers' subsistence needs and the rest of the day that the worker works for free for the capitalist class. The profits or the **surplus value** is produced due to the fact that workers are not paid according to the value that their labour adds to the products and sold as consumption items in the market. In other words, the profit is the "monetary differential". Consider the following scenario: A worker gets paid $100 a day for ten hours of work and produces 100 candle holders. These candle holders are sold for $10 each in the market. As a result, the owner of the factory earns $1000 for these candles. However, the owner of the *means of production* only pays his/her worker 10% of the market value of the product. In fact, the owner of capital recuperates the cost of his/her labour for the whole day by selling just one candle holder. As such, the worker is, in fact, working for free for the next nine hours.

Alienation runs throughout Marx's writings. He suggested that *alienation* leads to **false consciousness** (i.e., the inability of workers to realize the very source of their *exploitation* in capitalist society). Indeed, Marxists generally agree, if people do not behave in accordance with their class-based interests, it can only mean that they have been deceived about what their true interests are. As such, they work in favour of other's interests and have *false consciousness*.

In general, Marx offered a transhistorical explanation of how *alienation* emerged during different epochs. Throughout history, social actors have strived to tame and control nature with their labour to their advantage; but ironically, as they did so, they at the same time increasingly alienated themselves from nature and their own creations. According to Mann (2011), *alienation* happens when people are controlled by things they themselves have created, which then confront them as an alien power. This is akin to a situation where one creates a deity and then turns around to worship that deity. *Alienation* occurs when people lose the recognition that society and social institutions are constructed by human beings and can be changed by human beings. The term **reification** is understood in the same way. *Reification* is treating the products of human activity as if they were something other than human products, such as facts of nature, results of cosmic laws, or manifestations of divine will. *Alienation* leads to powerlessness, a paralysis of will and resignation. The *alienated* person may feel isolated, rootless, and may regard the social world as meaningless. Durkheim called this condition *anomie*. The *alienated* individual may look at social institutions as beyond his/her control, and may consider them oppressive. Marx saw all major spheres of capitalist society, religion, the state, and the economy, were marked by a condition of *alienation*. All these spheres of capitalist society are human creations, yet the *alienated* person sees them as mystical or divine creations (Mann, 2011). In postulating his theory of *alienation*, Marx argued that human beings are naturally inclined to work and be sociable. However, *capitalism* alienates us from the products of our labour and thus alienates us from ourselves and others. He insisted that only communal ownership of property could counteract social *alienation*.

Marx identified different forms of alienation:

1. *alienation* from fruits of labour;

2. *alienation* from the work process;

3. *alienation* from self; and

4. *alienation* from fellow workers.

Marx explained that since workers work for someone else (the capitalist) and not for themselves, they are alienated from the fruits of their own labour. This is due to the fact that the products and services they produce are taken away from them by their employer, the capitalist. The assembly line production characteristic of capitalist society reduces workers to cogs in the capitalist machine. Workers work rather thoughtlessly and mindlessly as robots, without investing any intellectual energy in the work process. Furthermore, since workers work for long hours, they don't have the time for any intellectual work. They are too tired to read, research, and engage in intellectually fulfilling work. Finally, Marx maintained that workers are alienated from fellow workers. This happens because workers undermine one another through backbiting, bad-mouthing, and gossiping to their bosses in order to curry their (bosses') favour. They do so because they want to be in the good books of their bosses so when the time comes to lay off some of the workers or downsize as it is called these days, they would be spared. Thus, instead of coming together to fight collectively for better working conditions, such as higher wages, shorter working hours, better maternity leave, etc., workers would instead engage in backstabbing and other destructive behaviour against one another.

As mentioned, Marx believed that *alienation* produces **false consciousness**, the inability of the worker to strike out the source of his or her oppression. It is a belief in, and support of, the system that oppresses you (Simmons, 2013). *False consciousness* leads the worker to blame everything else, but the capitalist system (i.e., everyone else, but the capitalist as responsible for his or her oppression). For example, due to the recent recession many Canadians were quick to blame new immigrants for taking away their jobs or for fleecing their welfare system, but they seldom blame the Canadian government for giving tax breaks (corporate welfare) to Canadian companies, which offshore Canadian jobs to "Third World" countries where they exploit cheap sweatshop labour in order to maximize their profits.

But Marx did not see the situation as hopeless. He believed that with time, workers would gain **class consciousness** (i.e., they would come to appreciate or recognize the source of their oppression through self-education, their unions, and political organizations). As Mann (2011, p. 172) noted, no matter how hopeless and hapless *false consciousness* may sound, Marx and Engels believed that people could liberate themselves from oppression through the attainment of *class consciousness*. Marx and Engels expected that over time, the *proletariat* would develop a sense of common destiny with other workers because they worked and lived so close together. Marx stressed that since *capitalism* is characterized by a series of regular crises that cause the workers to lose their faith in the system, they come to the conclusion that they share similar outcomes and outlooks and their dissatisfactions will amalgamate into a united front and the creation of working *class consciousness* (Seidman, 1994, p. 45). Due to the formation of *class consciousness*, rather than attacking machines and destroying them, the workers will begin to organize unions or form socialist or other political parties to change the system (Seidman, 1994, p. 45). That is, in order for the working classes to change the world and capitalist relations, they first need to see themselves as an exploited class that its members have shared and common interests.

The arguments of Marx about the eventual collapse of *capitalism* and its replacement by a revolutionary *proletariat* made sense in the context of social and political events in Western Europe at the time. Between 1824 and 1834, the first trade unions were established in England. For example, the Chartist movement during the 1830s and 1840s was "organized by a group of radical workers in London" (Asheley & Orenstein, 2001, p. 189). This movement was a reformist organization that aimed at involving the workers in the electorate process. It was a sign of the fact that workers were capable of organizing and mobilizing themselves. During this time period, wages were kept extremely low and factories lacked safety regulations (Asheley & Orenstein, 2001, p. 190). For example, many child workers lost body parts in the factory machines. By the 1860s, due to the efforts of middle class reformers laws were passed in England that introduced regulations regarding the "hours and conditions of work for all kinds of labourers" (Asheley & Orenstein, 2001, p. 190). By the 1870s, trade unions had become well established and acted as political forces in England. All these events point to the fact that Marx was correct to assume that when and if the working classes become conscious of their interests, they could function as important political and social forces within society (Asheley & Orenstein, 2001, p. 190). Similar events also occurred in other parts of industrialized Europe. In 1848, workers revolted in Paris and brought down the government. In the Hapsburg capital, the Austrian royal family left Vienna when workers rebelled (Asheley & Orenstein, 2001, p. 190). These rebellions and workers' political unification were due to the effects of the economic depression that was enhanced by the bad harvest of 1846 and 1848. Yet, it is important to note that the revolts in Germany were the end result of workers reacting to the economic conditions rather than due to expanding *class consciousness* (Asheley & Orenstein, 2001, p. 190).

In addition, as Marx claimed, the ensuing wealth inequality between the rich and the poor will eventually result in the political and social awakening of the working classes (Seidman, 1994a, p. 44). This political awakening is a process that first involves workers attempting to improve their working conditions, the length of the workday, wages, or child labour laws. However, it is only when working classes realize that the source of their discontent lies in the structure of the capitalist system that they rise up and unite against the system in revolutionary movement. To achieve this, they need to first come to the understanding and realization that their misfortunes and conditions of life and work are not due to either the capitalist class' characteristics or due to their own personal defects (Seidman, 1994a, p. 44). By talking to each other, workers would begin to understand their plight and the necessity of advocating for their collective needs. By taking such action, by seeing the world as it really is, the *proletariat's false consciousness* would be destroyed, highlighting the fact that no longer are workers *alienated* from themselves or each other.

Weber and Conflict Theory

Max Weber is also associated with the conflict paradigm. Weber is said to have engaged in intense intellectual debate with the ideas of Marx. He dissected Marx's main postulates on capitalist society and found points of agreement and departure. One of the main characteristics of Weber's scholarship is his critiques of economic determinist analysis and his approach to research that drew upon various fields and disciplines, accounting for a number of factors, such as social, economic, cultural, and political (Giddens, 1971, pp. 119–124). As we discussed previously, Max Weber is also known for his idea of *verstehen*, which is a German word for understanding and insight. He argued that when sociologists study a phenomenon in an objective manner, they should also account for those meanings that people attach to their actions. That is, it is important to account for how people account for and explain their behaviours. We should, for example, take into consideration how various groups in a high school interact with one another, judge one another, and construct each other in the context of their emotions, thoughts, and beliefs (as they see them). Another important terminology that Weber introduced to sociology is the *ideal type* that should be understood as a measuring criterion that allows researchers to see the extent to which social organizations, institutions, or behaviours differ and deviate from the norm.

Let us, now, look at where Weber agreed with Marx. Like Marx, he maintained that self-interest underpins people's activities. However, in addition to self-interest, Weber stressed the importance of goals and values of society. He clearly demonstrated the importance of goals and values in people's economic activities and social change in his book, *The Protestant Ethic and Spirit of Capitalism*. Weber believed that *capitalism* grew from many factors, not necessarily from purely economic ones, but also religious and moral ones. He saw modern *capitalism* as a "uniquely Western development". The focus of Weber's book is on the social dimensions and religious impacts on social change. Here, we offer a brief outline of the book's main assumptions:

1. the growth of *capitalism* was stimulated by Protestantism;
2. the Protestant churches unintentionally supported the rise of *capitalism*;
3. a high number of European business leaders were Protestants; and
4. *Capitalism*, Calvinism, and the Industrial Revolution were linked together (Mann, 2011, p. 155).

According to Weber, the major cause of modern industrialism and *capitalism* was the religious ethic of the Protestant sects in Western Europe (Mann, 2011). Weber believed that sects, such as the Calvinists and Puritans, considered work to be an important aspect of their salvation and adopted a modest lifestyle (Mann, 2011). As a result, the profits from their work ended up being put back into their businesses. Thus, *capitalism* cannot be explained in just economic terms, as it holds a connection with moral and religious ideas (Mann, 2011). Weber also thought *capitalism* to be more than the act of making money. Rather, it is the making of profit that is renewed (Mann, 2011). Weber posited that the Calvinists' desire to save their souls found expression in the unique goal of simply accumulating wealth. Weber argued that one of the major causes of modern industrial and bureaucratic *capitalism* was the "religious ethic of certain Protestant sects in Western Europe, notably the Calvinists and Puritans" (Mann, 2011, p. 155). By viewing work as a fundamental element in regards to their salvation, these individuals produced so much profit and maintained modest lifestyles.

Weber also agreed with Marx that the *economic base* shapes society, stating that the decline of the slave-based economy of the Roman Empire was an inevitable political consequence of the decline of commerce. On the other hand, he argued that military and religious motives drove economic development (Wallace & Wolf, 2006). For example, the need for large armies in continental Europe favoured peasant agriculture and because England was protected by the English Channel, capitalist agriculture flourished there first. Like Marx, Weber asserted that key to understanding inequality was the concentration of the *means of production* in the hands of a few.

Weber also sharply disagreed with Marx on a number of central premises of his analysis of *capitalism*. The core differences revolve around *social class* and *class struggle*. Weber disagreed with Marx's conceptualization of the number of classes in a capitalist society. He also disagreed that the basis of *class struggle* was the access to or ownership of economic resources, arguing that there are more economic resources than just ownership of the *means of production*. However, he agreed that class is deified by property (Criab, 1997, p. 128). Weber defined **class** in terms of a group that shares the same economic relationship to the markets. He maintained that, a group of people who share the same "typical chance for a supply of goods, external living conditions and personal life experiences insofar as this chance is determined … to dispose of goods or skills for the sake of income in a given economic order… 'Class situation' is in this sense, ultimately 'market situation'" (Weber, as cited in Craib, 1997, p. 128). He pointed out that there is a variety of **class situations**. A *class situation*, then, refers to similar kinds of control over goods or skills that produce income. A person might be involved in several *class situations* depending on his or her control of economic resources. In contrast, Marx had defined class in terms of people's control of or lack thereof the *means of production*, such as land, money, factories, etc. (Wallace & Wolf, 2006). Classes, Marx explained, are defined and structured by

1. who owns or possesses property and the *means of production* and who performs the work in the production process,

2. the social relationships involved in work and labour, and

3. who produces and who controls the surplus that human social labour can produce (Adams & Sydie, 2012).

To demonstrate that stratification does not rest on property and class position alone, Weber identified three sources of power:

1. *class*,

2. *status group*, and

3. *political parties*.

Class "refers to the objective attributes of the market situation of number of individuals", irrespective of how the individual is evaluated by others (Giddens, 1971, p. 166). That is, it refers to any group of individuals who are in the same *class situation* (Ritzer, 2000, p. 123). Members of class do not form a community. In contrast, the **status situation** of an individual refers to how other people evaluate an individual and his/her social position by attaching certain positive or negative social **prestige** or **esteem** to his/her status (Giddens, 1971, p. 166). In general, *status* refers to a style of life while *class* refers to economic production (Ritzer, 2000, p. 123). Members of a *status group* share the same *status position* in society (i.e., an ethnic group). Unlike *classes*, *status groups* are aware of their common position (Giddens, 1971, p. 166). They form a community (Ritzer, 2000, p. 123). They highlight their differences from other *status groups* through enforcing restrictions on interactions with other group members (i.e., the practice of **endogamy**, marrying within a group). *Political parties* can be distinguished from *social classes* and *status groups* due to characteristics, such as having a rational structure, "formal organization, and administrative staff" (Grabb, 2002, p. 59). A **party** "refers to any voluntary association which has the aim of securing directive control of an organization in which the formation of freely recruited grouping is permitted: from a sports club up to the state" (Giddens, 1971, p. 167). Members of different *classes* and *status groups* can become members of *political parties*. However, *political parties* often represent the interests of *class situation* or *status situation*. Just as a person's position on the social ladder can either confer power on him/her or deprive him/her of power, so does one's *status*. For example, some of you may be richer than your professor by virtue of you coming from an upper class family. Yet, in the classroom, your professor has power over you. An example of a pure *status group* can be the Pope and the class of cardinals who lack economic power but enjoy a high degree of power stemming from their high *prestige* and *esteem* (Garbb, 2004, p. 57). Another example is the position of Whites in relation to non-Whites in the **apartheid system** in South Africa. Regardless of the *class positions* of Whites (i.e., working class versus middle class), they enjoyed certain *privileges* that may not have been available to non-Whites (Grabb, 2004, p. 57). Weber's *class theory* has been subjected to a number of criticisms. We will touch on two of them. The first criticism is that he does not fully account for class exploitation and coercive nature of *power*. The second criticism is that it is difficult, if not impossible to apply the distinctions in cases involving *class* and *status* conflict (Wallace & Wolf, 2006).

Weber's Three Sources of Power

Weber defined **power** as the ability to control an individual or a group against their will. Weber adopted a more nuanced approach to *power* than Marx. He saw it as emanating from three sources, namely

a) tradition,

b) charisma, and

c) law.

These three sources coincide with three types of **authority**. He defined *authority* as the probability that an individual or a group would obey a command with a specific content by another person or group. Let's take a quick look at the three types of *authority* (Mann, 2011, p. 156–157).

Traditional authority denotes *power* based on the customs under which a leader gains *power*. *Traditional authority* prevails in societies or situations where people obey their leader because that is the way things have always been done. Thus, if in the past all the chiefs in the village were commanded respect and allegiance, then it stands to reason that the current chief be accorded the same respect and allegiance.

Charismatic authority stems from the term **charisma**, which is defined as a special gift. A *charismatic* person is believed to possess extraordinary qualities, such as oratory, charm, or intellect. Thus, past leaders, such as Pierre Trudeau, Martin Luther Jr., John F. Kennedy, Kwame Nkrumah, and Lenin, are believed to have been endowed with extraordinary qualities, which made it easy for them to galvanize huge followings. *Charismatic authority*, then, is devotion to the exceptional sanctity, heroism, or exemplary character of an individual person. A *charismatic* person can supposedly solve problems beyond the capacity of ordinary persons (Mann, 2011, p. 152). According to Wallace and Wolf (2006) *charismatic authority* does not require the dominant individual to possess extraordinary problem-solving capabilities. A *charismatic* leader is seen as a revolutionary force that breaks traditional bonds (Wallace & Wolf, 2006).

Legal authority can take many forms, but the most popular structural form is in the context of **bureaucracy** (Ritzer, 2000, p. 126). The individual who holds such an *authority* behaves and acts with others based on impersonal norms that are not grounded on tradition, but have been consciously established within the context of "either purposive or value rationality" (Giddens, 1971, p. 157). People have no allegiances to the person with *legal authority*, but follow him or her within the limits of rules and norms that rationality established to achieve preestablished goals of the institution (Giddens, 1971, p. 158). That is, *legal authority* is defined based on well-established official duties. The office that the person with *legal authority* occupies does not belong to him or her. The rules are clearly stated and written and applied without prejudice to everyone (Giddens, 1971, p. 158).

Having explored the main ideas of Marx and Weber, in the next section, we examine the main arguments of conflict paradigm.

Summary of Conflict Paradigm

The conflict theory has both merits and demerits. For its merits, the conflict paradigm posits that society is constantly changing and that change is inevitable (in contrast to sociologists who stress stability of society). It emphasizes the importance of economic structures, as they determine other structures, and as they determine an individual's economic standing, life chances, values, and behaviour.

It stresses the interrelationship among parts of the *superstructure*. It posits that each part needs to be understood in relation to the others, especially to the *economic base*. The conflict paradigm proposes that "scientists" must apply knowledge in the service of humanity as opposed to Weber's call for value-free scholarship. The conflict paradigm calls for Marxist *praxis*, to use theoretical knowledge to emancipate human subjects. It is informed by Marx's observation that we must go beyond the goals of philosophers of the past centuries who merely interpreted the world in various ways. The task now is to change the world.

On the demerits side, critics say that societies are more than mere reflections of economic organizations and property ownership. They also charge that social conflict is rarely polarized across an entire society and that interests do not always cohere around social class. In addition, critics of the conflict paradigm contend that *power* relations are not always direct reflections of ownership of property. Finally, conflict does not always cause change (Mann, 2011). Both Weber and Marx have influenced conflict theory. Marx influenced classical Marxists, whereas both Marx and Weber influenced neo-Marxists. In the next section, we explore the different views and perspectives within the conflict theory.

Neo-Marxism: The Two Traditions

Neo-Marxists are contemporary scholars of Marxist persuasion, who for a variety reasons have steered away from several of Marx's postulates of capitalist society. Wallace and Wolf (2006) have delineated two traditions in the Neo-Marxist school. The **first tradition** or group believes that social scientists have a moral obligation to engage in a critique of society. To this group, in social analysis, judgement and fact are one; they cannot be separated. Often, but not always, scholars in this group believe that in principle, a society could exist in which there were no grounds for social conflict. Thus, orthodox Marxists or Classical Marxists (i.e., scholars who accept all of Marx's postulates without deviation) insist that there was no class struggle in primitive communal society, and there would be none in the future communist society (Wallace & Wolf, 2012). Proponents of modern and neo-Marxism groups are also strongly influenced by Marx's views. Notable among representatives of this group are Jürgen Habermas and his Frankfurt School forerunners, Charles Wright-Mills, and Pierre Bourdieu (Wallace & Wolf, 2006). The **second group**, by contrast, considers conflict to be an inevitable and permanent aspect of social life. The major difference between these two groups is that the latter group does not think social analysis should be *value-free*. Instead, they call for objectivity in social analysis, the same canon of objectivity, which informs the natural sciences. The intellectual forerunners of this group are Ralf Dahrendorf, Lewis Coser, and Randall Collins (Wallace & Wolf, 2006).

The Critical Tradition in Neo-Marxism

According to Wallace and Wolf (2006), the critical aspects in Marx's thought can be traced to Marx and Engels' book, *The German Ideology*. In this book, Marx and Engels criticized the Young Hegelians, followers of the prominent German philosopher Georg Hegel, the originator of *dialectics* (a clash of ideas as the basis of social life and change). Marx himself was a Young Hegelian, but broke with them. As we have already mentioned, he argued that ideas are not the only determinants of change. Ideas are the reflection of material conditions, and are shaped by the social framework/structures in which they are born. The Young Hegelians, by emphasizing ideas and consciousness, Marx argued, were calling for the maintenance of the *status quo*. Marx proposed an emancipatory project to change the oppressive capitalist system. His goal was to expose oppression and propose a better, alternative system (Wallace & Wolf, 2006). He proposed a Marxist *praxis*, blending theory and action, or the use of theory to stimulate action and vice-versa (See Box 10.8 - What Is Critical Thinking?).

BOX 10.8 - What Is Critical Thinking?

Anderson (2012, p. 10) defined critical thinking as thinking that is purposeful, deliberate, and self-regulatory, and that arrives at judgments based on well-defined criteria and evidence. Alongside research skills and theorizing skills, critical thinking is a one of the three core skills sets a student of sociology must have. To be a critical thinker does not mean, as the common-sense view might hold, to find fault, be harsh, or be judgmental.

Critical thinking has a long history and deep multicultural and multidisciplinary roots. All societies have given birth to thinkers who challenged some form of existing social arrangements, habits, and norms. Anderson (2012, p. 11) noted that people in many different fields across time have challenged the established beliefs of their society. Critical thinking is based on the assumption that social reality is not only a social construct (i.e., a human creation) but also it is a historical, cultural, and dynamic process, which reflects *power* relations. Socrates reminded that an unexamined life is not worth living. Critical thinking allows us for examining taken-for-granted assumptions and conventional truths/wisdoms of our society. Critical thinking also demands of us to engage in self-reflection or reflexivity. Critical thinking must be viewed as the spark that ignites social change. Without critical thinking, a society may stagnate.

Anderson (2012) has identified the following characteristics and habits of a critical thinker:

1. Independence of Mind, a commitment and a disposition favourable to autonomous thinking;

2. Intellectual Curiosity, the disposition to wonder about the world;

3. Intellectual Courage, the willingness to evaluate all ideas, beliefs, or viewpoints fairly, and the courage to take a position;

4. Intellectual Humility, awareness of the limits of one's knowledge;

5. Intellectual Empathy, being conscious of the need to put oneself in the place of others in order to understand them;

6. Intellectual Perseverance, the willingness to pursue intellectual insights and truths in spite of difficulties, obstacles, and frustrations; and

7. Reflexive Disposition, awareness that one's own approach is fallible.

The critical school traces its origin to the Frankfurt School of sociology in Germany. As Meyers (2005, p. 5) noted, all sociological theories, including those deemed conservative, have an inbuilt motif of debunking taken-for-granted assumptions and to criticize the mechanisms of *power* in any given society. But more than any other sociological theory, the critical school takes the debunking characteristics of sociology farthest in analyzing economic, social, cultural, and political issues and structures. Critical theory is influenced by scholars of the Frankfurt School that was formed in Germany in the early 1920s, who offered criticisms of Marx's ideas. While maintaining the basic ideas of Marx and borrowing his notion of *praxis*, they faulted Marxist *historical materialism* for being too positivistic, reductionist, and deterministic. According to this tradition, social actors are conceived as stepping into already conceived systems. They do not create their own motivations or ideological structures. Classical Marxism is criticized for its lack of emphasis on the phenomenology of social action and symbolic interactionism (Wallace & Wolf, 2006). The critical school reasserted the more humanistic, voluntaristic aspects of Marx's thoughts. In contrast, others faulted classical Marxist analysis for being too voluntaristic with insufficient emphasis on the determinative role of *productive forces*. But they comprise a minority of Marx's friendly critics (Wallace & Wolf, 2006).

In short, notable among neo-Marxists who were concerned with what they saw as limitations and inadequacies in Marx's original works were the members of the Frankfort School who began to revise many of his postulates (Meyers, 2005). Contending that Marx wrote his seminal works in a different era quite different from the twentieth century, the Frankfurt School theorists were intent on recasting Marxism to fit contemporary Western capitalist society (Quist-Adade, 2012). Their grand agenda was "to fill the intellectual gaps and elaborate on key concepts so as to make Marxism more relevant and practical" (Meyers, 2005, p. 7). In so doing, they drew on and incorporated critical insights from other social sciences, including the sociology of Max Weber and the psychoanalysis of Sigmund Freud: "What emerged was a more nuanced perspective that examined not just the economy, but also the state, ideology, [culture] and human agency." (Meyers, 2005, p. 7)

The Intellectual Root of Critical Theory: Georg Hegel's Idealism

Simmons (2013) has noted that contemporary critical theorists took more from Hegelian *idealism* than from Marx's *historical materialism*. In other words, they tried to extract and distil a theory of **consciousness** from Marx's writings (Wallace & Wolf, 2012). The earliest exponents of this theory were Georg Lukas, Herbert Marcuse, Theodore Adorno, and Max Horkeimer. Their focus was human *consciousness*. Wallace and Wolf (2006) explained that the forerunners of critical theory developed a Marxist theory of *consciousness* by meshing Freudian psychoanalysis with Marxian *political economy*. In the end they came up with a theory which sought to explain how values and behavioural patterns that serve the capitalist class had been absorbed by the proletariat (Wallace & Wolf, 2006). As Wallace and Wolf (2006) explained, the founders of the Frankfurt School sought to expand the *political economy* of the *mode of production* to encompass a **phenomenology** of the forms of *alienation* in daily life, the family, sexuality, the work situation, cultural activity, verbal and other forms of communication, as well as social interaction, institutions, and ideology.

Wallace and Wolf (2006) traced the historical sources of critical theory to a number of factors, such as failure of social democracy and rise of fascism, the degeneration of socialism in Russia into Soviet-style communism and bureaucratization of communism under Stalinism, changes in mass consciousness generated by the advent of mass consumerism and the mass media, and the growth of monopoly capital. All these factors in addition to Soviet imperialist expansion in Eastern Europe and the so-called "Third World" posed serious theoretical problems for *historical materialism* (Wallace & Wolf, 2006).

Now the question is, what happened to Marx's doomsday prediction about the overthrow of capitalism? Wallace and Wolf (2006) have observed that the answer to this question as offered by neo-Marxists of the critical bent is that they saw no inevitable transformation of *capitalism*. They thus rather devoted their time and efforts to offering a critique of the cultural production and material production of **late Capitalism**. Their interest, then, revolved around a critique of existing ideologies, and their concern was to create an awareness of the possibility of a break with the existing structure of domination. They called for a Marist *praxis* that aimed at self-emancipation of human subjects in the existing capitalist society. One such neo-Marxist is the founder of the Italian Communist Party, Antonio Gramsci.

Gramsci's Hegemony and Counter-Hegemony

Hegemony is a term coined by Gramsci. It is the process of control and domination by the ruling elite through ideological and cultural means in such a way that the dominated and controlled groups consent to their domination without being coerced to do so. It is the process of domination, in which the ideas of the ruling elite are inculcated into the governed through sophisticated, subtle, and multiple channels (See Chapter One). The process of **indoctrination** (the intent to socialize the population based on a set of dominant beliefs that when internalized by social actors form the basis of their worldviews and function as ways to control them) is carried out through panoply of socialization channels/agents, the family, media, education, etc., and is done with such sophistication and "sleight of hand" that ordinary citizens come to accept the ideas of the elite as natural and unproblematic.

Unlike the classical Marxist view of absolute control of ideological and cultural discourse by the dominant capitalist class, the neo-Marxist *hegemony* theory advances a more flexible, fluid, and ongoing dynamic between superordinate and subordinate groups, between the rulers and the ruled. The *hegemony* involves resistance and incorporation; coercion and consent; enlightened coercion by the ruling elite and consent from the ruled. In other words, the power elite do not simply force their ideas onto the people, but shape and win consent so that the power of the dominant classes appears both legitimate and natural (Dyson, 2003).

But it is important to note that *hegemony* is not a one-way street or a zero sum game in which the ruling elites go unchallenged. Rather, there is a limit to elite ideology, and the oppressed can and do fight back. In other words, the ***dominant ideology*** (See Box 10.9 – What Is Ideology?) is open to the challenge by alternative and oppositional interpretations by the oppressed. This suggests an ongoing battle between elite discourse and nonelite discourse. Elite *ideology* is likely to be contested and even subverted through the process of **counter-hegemony** (Quist-Adade, 2012, p. 16).

BOX 10.9 - What Is Ideology?

Berger (1963, p. 41) argued *ideology* is one of the central concepts in sociological theory. *Ideology* is characterized by **selectivity**. As social actors whose experiences are different due to, for example, family relations, values and beliefs, income levels, places of residence, and occupations, we tend to see the world and social issues and interpret them differently. As such, we tend to ignore how the same phenomena are understood differently by others whose interpretations are based on different values and perspectives. That is, we do not get to see and understand the world from other perspectives. Although we all have our own *ideologies* and ways of looking at the world, in every society and/or nation-state, certain views are considered as more important and dominant than others. The views and *ideologies* of the dominant groups influence how we understand ourselves as citizens of the nation-state through their control of knowledge production in the media and schools.

Counter-hegemony entails alternative and oppositional viewpoints, which seek to resist and undermine the *dominant ideology*. It may take several forms, including:

1. **negotiated counter-hegemony**, through which the oppressed engage in negotiated understandings of elite *ideology* by espousing alternative viewpoints, staking intermediate, compromised position. This involves the blending of alternative, dominant and oppositional viewpoints; and

2. **oppositional counter-hegemony**, which involves a wholesale repudiation of the *dominant ideology* of the ruling elite by the oppressed (Quist-Adade, 2012, p. 17).

Part Four

STRUCTURAL SOCIOLOGY

Structural sociology is a theoretical framework based on the assumption that society and its constituent parts precede the individual. It assumes that society is a complex system of interrelated parts. *Social structures* are considered to be stable patterns of social behaviour. They constitute the things we do repeatedly or ritualistically, which with time, take on lives of their own. Examples of *social structure* are family life, economic systems, political systems, and religious institutions. According to Robert Merton (1938), *social structures* are patterned social arrangements in society, which emerge from, and determine the actions of social actors. Mann (2011, p. 178) define *social structures* as sets of rules and resources, or sets of transformation relations that are organized as properties of systems and thus embedded in social practices: "Social structures are not a mysterious force acting on individuals, but is reproduced every time social actors follow the rules of the game". Wallace and Wolf (2006) refered to *structure* as orderly arrangements of elements. They suggested that the parts of a *structure* are less important than the relationships between them. It is only when we have formed an idea of these relations that we know the parts. For instance, we recognize a person as religious because we have previously conceptualized the concept, religion. Wallace and Wolf (2006) maintained that all sociologists make use of the idea of *structure*. To the *structural sociologists*, *structure* is the pivot around which sociological analysis revolves. *Structure* is not the outcome; rather it assumes logical priority over parts that comprise it. Why do *structuralists* accord logical priority to *structure*? Allahar (2008, pp. 47–48) offered an answer to this question with this example. Let's consider our understanding of a traffic light. We do not know what the colour amber means until we know it is part of a *structure* called traffic signal. Even more important, we would not know the precise *function* of amber if we do not how the colours amber, red, and green are arranged in the signal. In the same fashion, the information that a person is black has no sociological significance unless we know something about the *structure* of which blackness is a part. In Canada blackness can be understood in terms of minority/white majority/dominance/submission relationships. In short, *structures* are descriptions of the aggregate as a whole, not of its constituent elements.

According to Wallace and Wolf (2006), *structures* sort people and place them into *status positions*, socialize them through *role expectations* associated with the *status positions*, give them identities, appropriate perspectives, and a certain level of power, privilege, and prestige. As mentioned above, all sociologists employ the concept *structure* in their study and analysis of society. Thus, structural functionalists, conflict theorists, symbolic interactionists, and other theorists use *structure* in their explorations of whether individuals are mere puppets manipulated by powerful external forces, or are architects of their own actions. What follows is a brief survey of different approaches adopted by structural functionalists, conflict theorists, and symbolic interactionists in explaining and applying the notion of *structure*.

Wallace and Wolf (2006) provided what they call a mental image of *structure* in which they identified three forms of structure: **structure as a social location**, **structure as a social role**, and **structure as an organization**.

Structure as a location describes an individual's social location (i.e., one's place on the social ladder in terms of income). According to Wallace and Wolf (2006), *social structures* are social categories into which the population has been divided. *Structure as a role* asserts that roles are packages of expected behaviour (e.g., a husband logically implies a wife; teacher implies a student). *Structure as an organization* draws a distinction between **social relations** and **structural relations**. *Social relationships* are visible associations between actors about which empirical generalizations can be made (e.g., doctor-patient relations). *Structural relations* are not obvious on the surface. *Structure* denotes the way parts are organized. *Structural relationships* limit the range of social relationships. For example, why do some people, for example, blacks and women, on average earn less than White males?

The intellectual roots of the *structural approach* to sociological analysis can be traced to the writings of Karl Marx, Émile Durkheim, and Claude Levi-Strauss. Marx used the *structural approach* in postulating his theories of system reproduction and system conflict. Marx was concerned with how patterns of inequality reproduced themselves in society. He sought to explain how inequality in power and wealth are sustained in capitalist society. He suggested that in the struggle over scarce resources, the powerful emerged victorious. They then created social institutions to protect the wealth of society and devise ways to fend off the powerless from it. They also developed *ideologies* to justify why they, the powerful, should have the lion's share, if not all, of the wealth. Marx was particularly interested in how to break this vicious cycle of systematic exploitation.

Decades later, Émile Durkheim engaged in a *structural analysis* of rituals and religion, among others. Rituals, Durkheim, argued, addressed toward gods and supernatural forces were an affirmation of the power of society. As people enacted these rituals, they legitimated existing social relations. He also used *structural analysis* to explain the relations between economic *power* and society. His central premise was that economy shapes society, and economy is shaped by population density. That is, economic institutions change in response to population pressures (Wallace & Wolf, 2006). He reasoned that the changes in the economy transformed society from "simple" or communal to complex and individualistic organization. "Simple" or "primitive" societies, as Durkheim described preindustrial societies, were characterized by sparse populations and rudimentary division of labour. Members shared similar occupational roles and had similar behavioural patterns. They also shared common beliefs or a *collective conscience*. In these societies, there existed an idealistic basis of maintaining social order. However, maintaining social order in this type of society was difficult because each village or clan was more or less self-sufficient in terms of basic needs. Since the members in the villages could meet all their needs, they did not have to relate to members of other villages. Thus, self-sufficient production fostered little interdependence, Durkheim maintained. Durkheim reasoned that if there were no structural basis for maintaining social order, and if society tolerated deviance or individuality, society would lose its identity. *Collective conscience* therefore must be maintained and reinforced by *repressive* and *punitive laws*. Durkheim called this mechanism to maintain social order *mechanical solidarity* (Mann, 2011, pp. 26–27).

As population density increases, simple division of labour was no longer possible in the new society. A much more complex division of labour emerged accompanied by a high degree of specialization, which produced a similarly high level of interdependence. Consequently, a new structural basis of social order developed, which Durkheim called *organic solidarity* (Mann, 2011, pp. 26–27). This new complex, industrialized society was characterized with a new, stronger basis of social integration, and, hence, there was no longer the need for a *repressive law* to maintain *collective conscience*. In the new society, individualism and uniqueness of personality were now desirable. Paradoxically, while this society promoted individualism, it also fostered a higher level of interdependence. As people specialized in one trade or another, they needed others to provide their other needs. Unlike the "simple" societies, where members were jacks-of-all-trades and produced all their basic survival needs, members in complex societies were characterized as masters of their individual trades. To survive, they needed to rely on others. In short, higher division of labour and specialization both produced interdependence and individualism, while lower division of labour and specialization led to low interdependence and stronger collectivism, or *collective conscience*.

From Anthropology, Claude Levi-Strauss adopted the structural approach to study the structure and impact of language on individuals. Levi-Strauss' *structural linguistics* adopts a micro-structuralist approach. In the symbolic interactionist field, Mead used the structuralist method in propounding his *behavioural structuralism*. Mead argued that *social structure* constrains and circumscribes the options and choices of individuals. He maintained that **role-taking**, the **generalized other**, community attitudes, and values are reproduced and recycled from generation to generation. But most micro approaches tend to underemphasize the impacts of *structures* (Wallace & Wolf, 2006). To conclude our discussion of *structuralism*, let us look at the works of two of the main exponents of the theory, Pierre Bourdieu and Michel Foucault. These two individuals offered critiques of **structuralism** and are credited for the formation of **poststructuralism** (See Box 10.10 – Poststructuralism).

BOX 10.10 - Poststructuralism

Poststructuralism analyzes the "operations of difference and the way in which meanings are made to work" (Wiener, 1994, p. 101; Hall, 1996c, p. 611). *Poststructuralism* challenges meaning and power in modernity (Wiener, 1994, p. 101; Hollinger, 1994, p. 109; Seidman, 1994a). It considers knowledge production as a process that "is linked to the system of power which produces and sustains it" (Weiner, 1994, p. 99). As such, knowledge is considered a site of struggle and not a preconceived entity (Dei, 1996, p. 23). *Poststructuralism* is an approach to deconstructing social issues and structures of *power* by critically problematizing how historical injustices that have affected peoples and groups differently based on factors, such as "race", ethnicity, gender, sexuality, age, or national origin, inform institutional and structural forms of modernity and for what purposes (Bowden, 2003, p. 356). For example, this theory could be applied to analysis of how *differences* are employed as part of the information and knowledge students in schools receive about other groups and other nation-states and the extent to which this knowledge sanitizes the history of the nation-building process, by ignoring the histories of subordinated groups as part of the narration of nation.

From a poststructuralist perspective, diversity and *difference per se* are not considered the problem. Rather, it is the significance or the social meanings that are attached to *differences* that need to be critically evaluated and problematized. More importantly, they point out that by deconstructing the ways through which *differences* are employed in discussing the unequal treatments of groups around the world, we can utilize this knowledge in interrogating the hegemonic and problematic representations and images of the other in terms of the signification of, for example, gender relations and colour of skin in differentiating between human groups.

The aim of poststructuralists is to create many centres of *power* by empowering marginal groups to become part of the centre in search for a common definition of humanity based on principles of equality, responsibility, and community (Dei, 1996, pp. 60–70). *Poststructuralism* is critical of *master* or *metanarratives* that legitimize social reality and give coherence and meaning to other narratives and to socioeconomic and political structures, events, and practices through the process of exclusion based on ethnocentric and **logocentric** views. These *logocentric* views that function as "hidden logics" and authoritative narratives that claim to "reveal truth [and] moral rightness" (Seidman, 1994a, pp. 202, 206). *Logocentricism* (i.e., Marxism or structural functionalism) provides "a universal language that could disclose what is real, true, right, and beautiful" (Seidman, 1994a, p. 203). *Poststructuralism*, as Seidman (1994a, p. 204) explained, asserts that "linguistic meanings are not innocent of political significations … however, [they] do not in themselves produce subjectivity and the social world. They are embedded in institutional frameworks and political hierarchies". *Poststructuralism* critiques ethnocentric, middle-class, gendered, and patriarchal knowledge and questions their "validities" by accounting for other types and forms of knowledge in order to trace how dominant discourses "empower and give privilege to certain individuals, groups and forms of social life" (Seidman, 1994a, p. 204). This alternative view of knowledge explores how various forms of oppression and resistance are reproduced across the globe in particular places. Moreover, *poststructuralism* also "reject[s] essentialist and reductionist approaches to race, [gender, class, and economic] analys[es]" due to the *logocentric* character of knowledge in modernity (Dei, Karumanchery, & Karumachery-Luik, 2005, p. 31; Dei, 1996, p. 49). *Poststructuralism* points out that knowledge is presented and produced in the context of uneven *power* relations. It aims at subverting "the political meaning of" language, knowledge, and social order (Seidman, 1994a, p. 202). In this light, what is considered as universal knowledge is, in fact, a "selective knowledge" presented as "official knowledge" and "the truth" about the world. Knowledge is conceptualized as a site of transformation, reinvention, and subversion of the dominant conceptualizations of what is considered as useful knowledge in both the East and the West (Dei, 1996, pp. 12, 23). Moreover, notions, such as modern subject and identity, are questioned by pointing to the multiplicity and diversity of "subject positions" and the instability of the so-called coherent and fixed identity.

The Poststructuralism of Pierre Bourdieu and Michel Foucault

Structuralism is the formal theory of the structure of language; it is the application of linguistic models to explain cultural and social phenomena. The central premise of *structuralism* is that language, or the analysis of the structure of language is key to understanding the social world (Wallace & Wolf, 2006). The *structuralism theory* has gone through metamorphosis from *structuralism* through *poststructuralism* to *postmodernism*. It derives from French social theory and was applied to everything from religion to comic strips; from archaeology to zoology. Wallace and Wolf (2006) noted that although there are substantial disagreements between and among them, language is their central consideration. They suggested that all three *structuralisms* intend to replace modernist principles of positive knowledge in the sciences, the social sciences, and philosophy with a new approach based on language (Wallace & Wolf, 2006, p. 187). *Structuralism* is often associated with Levi-Strauss, who is credited with pioneering structural anthropology. He analysed, for example, culture in terms of its parts and explained that "each part of the system under study is meaningless except in terms of the structure of connections within which it exists. Such connections are often binary and are held by the structuralists to be basic and permanent organizing features. "The poststructural argument is that this inseparable nature describes all statements or claims of value" (Kubow & Fossum, 2007, pp. 60–61). Poststructuralists argue that the observer imposes his/her conceptual framework on what is being observed, and this limits what "science" can tell us about natural, physical, and social worlds.

In other words, contemporary (post)*structuralists* have gone further by showing that *structures* are far from stable. Ritzer (2010, p. 88) pointed out that "rather than seeing stable relationships of signs, they saw chaotic and highly variable context-dependent systems". In their view, such *structures* could not have the coercive power over individuals that the *structuralists* attributed to them. *Poststructuralists* attempt to deconstruct, decode, or uncover, hidden differences that underlie *social structures*. *Poststructuralists* are particularly interested in decoding the dominant or hegemonic discourse and decentring knowledge so that previously excluded or silenced voices may contribute. One of the main theorists associated with *poststructuralism* is Michel Foucault, whose ideas we examine in the next section.

Michel Foucault

We begin this section with a brief synopsis of Foucault's works. Foucault's early work focused on the *structures* that underlie the limits of discourse and the ways in which discourses create "truth" (Ritzer, 2006). His focus was on the dialectical connections between *power*, control, struggle, and historical change. He was interested in the history of ideas, postulating a theory of how ideas interact with the social world. As Wallace and Wolf (2006) noted, Foucault's site of study and interrogation was life at its most ordinary levels. Foucault began his intellectual journey into *structuralism* with a *theory of discourse*. Wallace and Wolf (2006) asserted that what gives Foucault's work unity is "all is about words". **Discourse** in commonplace parlance or definition is talking, conversing, or communicating (See Chapter One). The term is also understood as the ability to use signs to designate things; the relationship between **signifiers** and the **signified** and the relationships among signs. To Foucault, *discourse* is more than that. *Discourse* denotes a group of signs and the practices which constitute the objects of which they are speaking. Foucault defined *discourse* as a system of **exclusion** or constraint; a set of boundaries of what can be said, and accordingly, what cannot be said; what cannot even be thought (Wallace & Wolf, 2006). He suggested three forms of *exclusion*, namely, **madness** and **reason**, **prohibited words**, and **will to power**. Below, we explore these forms of *exclusion* systematically.

Madness and Reason

Discourse is supposed to be meaningful; no one listens to nonsense. But where is the dividing line? How do we draw the line between reason and madness (Wallace & Wolf, 2006)? From Foucault's point of view, the prison and asylum exemplify the modern world. In premodern times, torture, public floggings, and executions were the state's main tools for securing order. Then, there was a transition to the use of confinement for convicted criminals, but also for the insane and indigent (the poor). In his book, *Madness and Civilization*, Foucault explored the way people have thought and written about madness, and examined the changes that have taken place between the Middle Ages and modern times. In the Middle Ages, madness was a category of untouchables, the outcasts of society. Just as lepers were segregated into their compartments of horror, the mad were gathered together on a ship and put adrift in the sea (Wallace & Wolf, 2012). They labelled them based on religious beliefs, contending that the mad were God's unfortunates, accursed, and unholy. Madness was not a phenomenon that was the concern of medical doctors and a focus of medicine; rather, it was a matter that was dealt with in the public domain.

Different classes of the accursed were mixed together in the houses of confinement that mingled the insane with the unemployed, debtors, vagabonds, and prisoners. Foucault (1961, p. 49) observed that "an entire population almost overnight found itself shut up, excluded, more severely than lepers." In a span of one hundred and fifty years since the end of the Middle Ages confinement had become the method of abusing a group of heterogeneous populations, deemed dangerous outsiders, which had to be controlled and put under surveillance. Wallace and Wolf (2006) pointed out that we commonly see the advent of modern mental hospitals and the decline of the death penalty as signs of progress. Foucault, however, saw them as epitomizing a shift in **the way power is exercised**. Modern hospitals and the death penalty were used to **discipline** and deprive those involved of their liberty. In this way they are more extreme than, but nevertheless similar to, the other major institutions of modern life (i.e., the factory or the modern school).

Foucault's method involved **textual analysis**. His aim was to unravel the structures of knowledge. In his view, the particular way we see and comprehend the world is governed by the ways in which *power* is exercised. Thus, doctors, lawyers, governors, and politicians do not consciously develop the institutions, which secure their positions; rather, the dominant discourses determine how society acts towards and treats individuals: for example. in modernity, "A whole set of assessing, diagnostic, prognostic, normative judgments concerning the criminal [became] lodged in the framework of penal [system]" (Foucault, 1980, p. 19). Moreover, in early nineteenth century, suddenly, "everywhere we find the same outrage, the same virtuous censure" of the way the insane and criminals were imprisoned together. Similarly, throughout Europe and the US "modern" codes of law were drawn up and "the entire economy of punishment was redistributed. The great spectacle of physical punishment disappeared, the tortured body was avoided" (Foucault, 1980, p. 14). Modern psychiatry no longer excluded madness from society, but controlled it. Mental hospitals were now the new methods of control. The mental institutions and the insane asylums were now institutions of surveillance that aimed at controlling those deemed as abnormal and changing their behaviours (Wallace & Wolf, 2006).

In this new system, madness was to be dominated by reason and science. Parallel developments took place in other spheres, including the sphere of work where labourers lost their independence as they were herded into factories; schools, prisons, army barracks, hospitals, factories, reformatories, all come to resemble each other. This shift led to a **discursive formation**, which followed a continuum. "A corpus of knowledge, techniques, 'scientific' discourses is formed and becomes entangled with the practice of the power to punish" (Foucault, 1980, p. 23). *Discursive formation* highlights how all these institutions and the discourse they use "refer to the same object, share the same style and support 'a common institutional... or political drift or pattern'" in such a way that "the relationships and differences between them [are considered to] be regular and systemic, not random" (Hall, 1996b, pp. 201–202). In this light, the modern world is constructed in light of binary oppositions, such as reason and unreason, sane and insane, and modern and traditional (Wallace & Wolf, 2006).

Prohibited Words

Another way in which a system of discourses shape our world is by allowing what can be said and what cannot be said or excluded. Foucault used sexuality to illustrate this point. He took us on an excursus into the history of sexuality in Europe. During the seventeenth century, Foucault revealed, there was considerable frankness regarding sexual behaviour and laws regarding indecency and obscenity were lax. Sexuality was part of the public domain. Sexual pleasures, *power* relations, and physical attraction were integrated aspects of the public discourse. By the nineteenth century, however, a deafening silence engulfed public discourse on sexuality. Sexuality was driven into the private domain, the bedrooms (Mann, 2011. pp. 251–252). The factor behind this transition was what Wallace & Wolf (2006) described as Victorian coyness and prudery. The Victorian period ushered in a new morality, with virtue elevated to a high standard. Sexual monogamy was the order of the day. Any public attention to eroticism was considered scandalous and seriously sanctioned. Yet, according to Foucault, sexuality did not go away. The Victorian era witnessed massive prostitution in cities and towns. It was an era when proper bourgeoisie gentlemen had mistresses (Wallace and Wolf, 2006). According to Foucault, concerns about sexuality are not about good or bad behaviours, but about *discourse*. It is not just what people did or what they thought about what they did; rather they began to behave, think, and act in the context of an established field of conceptions and possible enunciations, of things that can be said and cannot be done (Mann, 2011. pp. 251–252). In other words, a new dividing line between the respectable and unrespectable, which was enforced by a new system of *discourse*, emerged. Sexual behaviour still went on, but it was shaped into its own sphere. It must hide and become secret. Sex experiences took on a new quality. The twentieth century enunciated a new openness of sexuality and a new personal style of liberation, but it followed the same system of discourses of exclusion (Wallace & Wolf, 2006).

Will to Truth

According Foucault, *truth* is one of the exclusionary systems of *discourse*. He posited that the idea that *discourse* should be oriented toward *truth* is a modern invention, adding that we live in this form of *discourse*, so we take it for granted. For example, European penal laws of the seventeenth century were based on the notion of right, right based on the divine will, and obedience to God, the King, nobility, and punishment was meted out to defend these principles. Modern penology, according to Foucault, is characterized by a shift in how laws are justified. Modern penology is not "scientific" as one may assume. Foucault pointed to a deeper cause, a new form of discourse dominated by the will to *truth* (Wallace & Wolf, 2006).

Discourse and Power

Discourse is a system of *power*, Foucault proclaimed. Some people must remain silent, at least in certain situations or else their utterances are considered as unworthy of attention. An example is the medicalization of madness. In Medieval society, madness was explained in light of the religious discourse and mad people were affected through the practice of public segregation; the entire community was involved in recognizing the borderline between madness and normalcy. Today, the picture is different. According to Mann (2011, p. 157), what constitutes madness and normalcy is determined by experts, whose opinions are the only discourses that count. In the same way, *power* also informs the system of discourse on sexuality. The sexual behaviour which can be talked about openly (heterosexual relations) has a different social status than that which must remain behind the screen (homosexual relations) (See Chapter Four). As a result, the system of discourse produces repression at the level of feeling and thought. Although this repressive *power* is hidden and may be agentless (i.e., without agency), it is *power* in the real sense nonetheless (Wallace & Wolf, 2006).

The educational system is equally a system of *power*. School textbooks present a specific view of the history of the nation that sanitizes the past and excludes those aspects of the past that highlight how the dominant society discriminated against, for example, "minority" groups. School curriculum focuses on what needs to be said; what not to be said; what to think about; what objects are real; what is public; and what is private. The schools are a set of rituals through which we pass. Schools divide us into insiders and outsiders. As McLaren (1989, p. 200) pointed out, according to Giroux, schools are not only spaces and sites in which teachers instruct and students learn. Schools are complex sites where dominant and subordinate groups that are ideologically linked, defined, and constrained by the limits of *power* relations and *structures* are involved in legitimating particular constructions of reality despite resistance. Schools supply the terms of reference, symbols, and representations that hide the actual relations of *power*. They justify the *power* of the dominant groups over the subordinated ones (McLaren, 1989, p. 174). School knowledge then can be both ideological and hegemonic as it manufactures meanings and the language (discourses) through which students come to view their relations with both insiders and outsiders. School knowledge provides students with discourses that enable them to develop 'subject positions' that have meanings in the context of discursive positions "that condition [students] to react to ideas and opinions in prescribed ways" and from the perspective of the dominant society (McLaren, 1989, p. 174).

In short, as Foucault maintained, *power* in Medieval society was more transparent. Lepers and madpeople were herded to the outskirts of the town and criminals and heretics burned in the marketplace. Today, we see a shift towards a new organization of *power*; a split between the private and public realms. The modern prison, the insane asylum, the factory, the bureaucratic welfare system, and schools are structures and institutions of *power* that are behind closed walls (Mann, 2011; Wallace & Wolf, 2006).

Pierre Bourdieu

Pierre Bourdieu's main goals were to understand why social inequalities are reproduced over time, particularly how the elites retain wealth and prestige through what he termed "**reproduction**" and why these inequalities are generally accepted by the lower classes. He also aimed to liberate social actors from oppressive social and mental conditions by revealing the effects of social structures that actors are not fully aware of and by showing that society could be organized differently.

Inspired by the works of Weber and Parsons on social action, Bourdieu (1984) also propounded his theory of action, with the social actor at its centre. He characterized the social actor as someone who aims to attain a set goal. The person must garner the necessary resources, which Bourdieu called **capital**. The person must think (consciously or unconsciously) in certain ways, and must consider ways or strategies to achieve his or her goal. But the social actor does not act in a vacuum. Neither do his or her goal and the resources at his or her disposal come from thin air. Even his/her thinking, whether conscious or semiconscious (practical reason), is not unaffected. According to Bourdieu, the person's goals and means are shaped by the culture or **habitus**. The actor must also act in particular social contexts or **fields** (Wallace & Wolf, (2006, p. 111). These contexts or *fields*, Bourdieu (1984) explained, shape the person's thinking and acting. They shape how successful (or not) the person is in achieving his/her goals. Bourdieu (1984) further explained that the individual may compete with other social actors/players in social games over the available resources/*capital*. Some people have more resources than others. Success or failure is contingent upon the right amount of the right sort of resource. Thus a person with a large amount of the right sort of resources and appropriate strategies would be successful, while another person with the wrong sort of resources or inappropriate strategies would fail. How successful a person is in a particular *field* depends on how appropriate their *habitus* and *capital* are for the game played in that *field*. Using sports as an analogy, Bourdieu contended that social life is a series of games in which a player needs the right skills to play those games successfully (e.g., soccer skills, tennis skills, etc.). The skills are equated with the *capital* the player possesses. His *habitus* dictates the *capital* the player possesses. In the game, as in the larger social world, some people have more *capital* than others. Using education as an example, in the "game" of education, the appropriate skills is the same as *cultural capital*. The appropriate *habitus* is the middle class *habitus* (Wallace & Wolf, 2006, pp. 112–113).

According to Bourdieu, *habitus* has three components: ways of thinking/acting, bodily habits, and tastes (likes and dislikes). He argued that "Habitus refers to socially acquired, embodied systems of schemes of disposition, perceptions and evaluation that orient and give meaning to practices" (Bourdieu, 1984, p. 17). He defined this as "an acquired system of generative schemes objectively adjusted to the particular conditions in which it is constituted", producing all thoughts, perceptions, and actions consistent with those conditions and no others (Mann, 2011, p. 87). *Habitus* is an unconscious action. A way of thinking and acting according to a socially constructed code of behaviour accepted as proper for an individual's class at a given time (Mann, 2011).

Bourdieu also referred to *habitus* as "systems of durable, transposable dispositions, structured structures predisposed to function as structuring structures, that is, as principles which generate and organize practices and representations that can be objectively adapted to their outcomes without presupposing a conscious aiming at ends or an express mastery of the operations necessary in order to attain them" (Bourdieu, 1984, p. 55). *Habitus* is "the mechanism by which cultural norms or models of behaviour and action particular to a group or class fraction are unconsciously internalized or incorporated in the formation of the self during the socialization process" (Browitt, 2004, p. 1).

Bourdieu (1984) pointed out that each social class has its own *habitus*, for example, working class *habitus*, middle class *habitus*, lower middle class *habitus*. He identified three types of *capital*, including ***economic capital***: (i.e., money resources), ***cultural capital*** (i.e., knowledge of "legitimate" culture/"high culture"), and ***social capital*** (i.e., social networks, knowing influential people). The amount and type of *capital* one has determines one's class membership. For example, a person with low amounts of all three types would occupy the lower working class stratum, while an individual possessing high amounts in all three types of capital would be in or catapulted to the middle class. *Habitus* strongly influences both the amount and type of *capital* a person may have at his or her disposal (Bourdieu, 1984; Gaventa, 2003, p. 6). He maintained that the lower working class has the least *capital*, the upper working class has some *capital*, the lower middle class possess more *capital* than the two, and the upper middle class commands the most *capital*. In addition, Bourdieu argued that each individual's *habitus* is the *habitus* of their class. Each social actor is socialized into particular ways of thinking and acting of his or her *habitus*. This is due to the fact that each *habitus* has its own set of *tastes* (likes/dislikes, beautiful/disgusting, and moral/immoral). *Tastes* are socially stratified into upper middle class *taste* with highest standards, the lower middle class *taste*, middling, and working class *taste*, designating the lowest *tastes* (Browitt, 2004). Bourdieu insisted that society is still very much class-based and privilege is reproduced and passed on from parents to their offspring, from one generation to another. The elites pass their privilege and advantages onto their children, while the nonelites pass their disadvantages onto their children. Bourdieu noted that the elite have the power to define their *tastes* and their culture as the best, the most "sophisticated", "refined", and "tasteful" (Bourdieu, 1984). According to Bourdieu, the *habitus* motivates each social class to act in a distinctive way. He identified three forms of **motivations**. The upper middle class *habitus* maintains a sense of *superiority*, the lower middle class *habitus*, **aspirational**, while the working class *habitus* has a sense of **inferiority**, defensiveness, mocking of middle class pretentions. In general, one experiences the *habitus* as a "natural" condition of what Bourdieu called the **doxa** (Wallace & Wolf, 2006, p. 117).

Bourdieu asserted that much of our social world is taken for granted and uncritically examined, if at all. As Meyer (2006) noted, the *doxa* is what people take for granted. *Doxa* is "the belief that the social world as it stands is natural" (Mann, 2011, p. 88). It is a way for those in *power* to normalize or naturalize social structures and stratifications. The *doxa* is the self-evident or the obvious; that which needs no further explanation. Each social actor tacitly accepts by the mere fact of acting in accordance with existing social conventions. Meyer further noted that people may sometimes seek to debunk the *doxa* or express **anti-doxa** opinions about the ways that the world works. However, they rarely challenge it. Akin to Gramsci's *counter-hegemony*, Bourdieu noted that occasionally people will oppose the *doxa* through **heterodoxy**. They might criticize the *power* of the elites, or question the distribution of resources in society. When *heterodoxy* risks being seen as legitimate and hence revolutionary, the elite invoke a powerful tool to quell or discredit the dissent. **Orthodoxy** is the officially sanctioned means to censor threatening criticism. The elites tend to cast *heterodoxy* as heretical and blasphemous and dangerous for all not just for the elites (Meyer, 2006, p. 24). *Doxic* thinking legitimates the *power* and position of elites, reproducing the *status quo*. Recognizing and challenging this is to engage in *heterodoxy*, essential to critical sociology (Mann, 2011).

According to Meyer (2006, p. 25) "orthodoxy involves more than a dissolution of disruptive conflict within the *doxa*, it involves the exercise of *power* and authority. Most people subscribe uncritically to the *doxa*, thereby enforcing the *power* and legitimacy of the elites". *Heterodoxy* allows for challenges on behalf of the dominated. If effective, these might redistribute *power* and resources. Such threats must be eliminated in order for the powerful to remain intact. Indeed, because of the effectiveness of *orthodoxy* to censor challenges, much of it is intentionally kept private, so as to remain unsanctioned. As such, people tend to self-censor their language. They would express certain ideas only in settings where the ideas would be welcomed (Meyer, 2006, p. 25). Bourdieu (1997, p. 95) noted that *doxa* describes situations and moments when we 'forget the limits' that have given rise to unequal divisions in society: it is "an adherence to relations of order which, because they structure inseparably both the real world and the thought world, are accepted as self-evident" (Bourdieu, 1997, p. 95).

Bourdieu also synthesized Durkheim's and Marx's ideas, as well as those of Marcel Mauss and Levi-Strauss (Mann, 2011). Bourdieu's *structuralism* asserted that culture is an arena of stratification and conflict. This assumption is borrowed from Marx. Marx had conceptualized society as an arena of class conflict and struggle, where economic struggle breeds class stratification and creates oppositional class relations: the haves and have-nots. Bourdieu maintained that culture is the economy. That is, it symbolizes and reflects the economy. According to Bourdieu, culture is itself also an economic sphere. In other words, culture is simultaneously related to the economic relations and structures (i.e., the production, distribution, and consumption of goods and services). He, furthermore, maintained that stratification in the cultural economy is reciprocated in the material economy. In other words, the cultural economy is reproduced in the material economy. Bourdieu (1984, p. 197) expanded Marx's idea of **economic capital** to encompass all forms of *power* that enable individuals, groups, or classes to cement or reproduce their positions in the social hierarchy. Thus he spoke of "**cultural capital** (money and property), **social capital** (networks of social influence), and **symbolic capital** (classificatory categories of understanding and social differentiation at the service of legitimation), which represent forms of power and domination" (Browitt, 2004, p. 2). Let us explore the concept of *cultural capital* in more detail by reference to schooling and the education system.

Symbolic Violence

Bourdieu argued that social relations can produce **symbolic violence** (Browitt, 2004, p. 2) (See Chapter Seven). Bourdieu defined *symbolic violence* as "power which manages to impose meanings and to impose them as legitimate by concealing the power relations which are the basis of its force" (as cited in Wallace & Wolf, 2006, p. 112). That is, the *power* behind meaning, values, ideological indoctrination, etc., is hidden. For this reason its imposition can be successful since it would be accepted without it being realized. Such *power* is widespread in schools, child rearing practices, religions, and the mass media. Schools transmit cultural values and norms that are authorized by the dominant *power* elite, yet they present this knowledge as universal and representative of all members of society.

In modern society, schooling reproduces the distribution of *cultural capital* among social classes. The content and *structure* of schooling is based on the culture that corresponds to the interests of the dominant class. The position of dominant groups within society is reproduced through the legitimation of their cultural practices and *structures* in schools. *Cultural capital* refers to those dispositions and characteristics that inform individuals' socialization, and have been internalized by them as the norm. It is a set of cultural knowledge that one needs to possess in order to reproduce one's class position in the class structure (Spring, 2004, p. 23). It is about familiarity with the rules and regulations of school/classroom, the national language, schools' expectations of students, the dominant values prevalent in society, and the dominant knowledge (Wotherspoon, 2004). *Cultural capital* consists of "knowledge of appropriate dress, manners and social relationships" (Spring, 2004, p. 23). It includes "informal interpersonal skills, habits, manners, linguistic styles, educational credentials, tastes and lifestyles" (Turner, 2003, p. 496). It is made of "ways of talking, acting, and socializing, as well as language practices, values, and styles of behavior" (McLaren, 1998, p. 193). It takes many forms, including three dominant ones: "embodied State" (i.e., "dispositions of mind and body"), "objectified state" (i.e., "cultural goods", such as books and other material objects), and "educational qualifications" (Nieto, 2000, p. 234; McLaren, 1998, p. 193). The values, tastes, and dialect and language most valuable in schools are "associated with the dominant group" (Nieto, 2000, p. 234). In general, *cultural capital* refers to "various kinds of legitimate knowledge" (Ritzer, 2000, p. 536). The dominant values and norms of the elite social/racial/ethnic class are reinforced in school curriculum and pedagogies (Wotherspoon, 2004; Nieto, 2000, p. 284). These ideas and knowledge legitimate the position and status of the powerful groups. At the same time, the possession of *cultural capital* is often conceptualized in light of the discourse of individualism and meritocracy; and, as such, it is a tool to gain powerful economic positions in society and to legitimate the elite's share of economic wealth and opportunities. Schools teach and pass on the dominant cultural *ideology* and devalue the *cultural capital* of students who are marginalized or come from marginalized groups, such as the working class backgrounds (McLaren, 1998, p. 193; Nelson, Palonsky, & McCarthy, 2004, p. 318). Students who do not possess the dominant *cultural capital* are often in a disadvantaged position in comparison to those who are familiar with the expectations schools have of them (Wotherspoon, 2004, p. 169). The social success of students depends on whether or not they are familiar with the dominant knowledge that is necessary for the reproduction of dominant relations and institutions (Wotherspoon, 2004, p. 169). Since the culture that is transmitted by curriculum reflects the values, norms, and the language of the dominant group in society, middle class kids often are more successful in schools since they know what is expected of them. In fact, the lack of academic performance of the working class students is not reflective of their individual characteristics, but a reflection of schools' devaluation of their *cultural capital* (McLaren, 1998, p. 194). *Cultural capital* is the chief instrument of transforming *power* relations into legitimate relations. In this sense, desirable *cultural capital* is transformed into *economic capital* through academic credentials. In short, the successful actors have large amounts of the right sort of *capital* for the *fields* they inhabit. They pass that *capital* onto their children. On the obverse side, unsuccessful actors pass onto their children small amounts of useful *capital* and large amounts of useless *capital*. In this way, the cards are stacked in favour of the elite and against the nonelite. In other words, the winning upper classes keep winning, while the losing lower class, losing, at least most of the time.

Mann (2011) maintained that Bourdieu analyzed the education system as a *field*. He criticized the conventional, meritocratic view, which claims that educational attainment is the result of "intelligence and diligence" (i.e., students who perform well are those endowed with intelligence and who work hard). Bourdieu sharply disagreed. He argued that social mobility is attributable not to intelligence and hard work, but results from the system of stratification. Educational success stems from "having the right sort of capital" (Bourdieu, 1986, p. 2). High *cultural capital* leads to good qualifications. The elites use their *cultural capital* to get large amounts of educational capital (good qualifications). Bourdieu concluded that one's *habitus* determines the amount of *cultural capital* one may have, which in turn, would influence one's educational *capital*. He pointed to "hidden curriculum" (unintentional evaluations by teachers) as another way educational attainment is enhanced or thwarted. This happens at two levels:

a) **conscious level**, where the teacher acknowledges and rewards the student's intelligence and diligence, with remarks, such as "good work", "well articulated", "intelligent", and "observant", and

b) **unconscious level**, in which case teachers who tend to come from middle class *habitus* and thereby value and respect middle class *cultural capital*, evaluate students in terms of amount of *cultural capital* an individual student may possess with respect to the teacher's *habitus*.

Thus students from lower class families do not get the praise and encouragement their peers from middle and upper class habitus get from their teachers. Instead, they are denigrated with such remarks as "unsatisfactory work" or "disruptive student".

In both cases, a **self-fulfilling prophecy** is most likely to affect the self-esteem of the students. Students from higher class *habitus* are most likely to develop a sense of worth, which would spur them on to study harder, while students from the lower class habitus, who are constantly excoriated for their "less than satisfactory" or "sloppy work" are bound to be mortified (ashamed) and hence discouraged from trying harder to succeed in their studies. Such feelings often "translate into effort and performance, 'naturally clever' and 'naturally untalented'" among students from upper class *habitus* and those from lower class *habitus* respectively (Bourdieu, 1990, p. 22). In the end, high *cultural capital* leads to a ***virtuous circle***, which propels students from upper class families to academic success and a ***vicious cycle***, which pulls students from lower class families down and often out of the educational system. The end result is that middle class success and working class failure are reproduced across generations. But this happens mostly unintentionally.

High *cultural capital* leads to high *educational capital*, which translates into access to "good" jobs and consequently, turns into high wealth (*economic capital*). Upper middle class parents advantage their children by giving them *economic capital*, which they use to access to "good" schools, where they gain *cultural capital* and *social capital* (cultivating useful connections). This is not to say that upward social mobility is impossible for lower middle and working class individuals. In fact, individuals from the two classes do often break through the glass ceiling, but the number is relatively small. Bourdieu contended that capitalist society needs a working class. It also needs to show itself as meritocratic and democratic. Everyone goes to school; all have the same chances of succeeding. However, it is important to note that it is the upper middle classes that can "play the game" better, due to its easier accessibility to "good schools" and "grade inflation" (Bourdieu, 1984). Bourdieu's approach to power as a nexus of human agency and social structure ties in with theories of *structure* and agency, which is our next topic of discussion" (Wallace & Wolf, 2006, p. 112).

Theory of the Duality of Structure and Agency

Berger and Luckman's theory of the duality of *structure* and **agency**, the central thesis of their book, *The Social Construction of Reality* (1986), is one among many theories that seek to bridge the gap between *structure* and agency (see Chapter Two). The central premise of this theory is that while individuals act on things, their actions take place within the context of *social structures*. There are two parts to the structure-agency nexus, which reflect the *structure* versus *agency* and determinism versus free will formulations.

The *structure* part divests individuals of any *power* and casts them as mere puppets, bereft of any free will or *agency*, who are manipulated by powerful social institutions. It takes a fatalistic view of human beings, seeing them as victims of circumstances. Thus, human failings are blamed on social institutions. At the same time, the *structure* approach acknowledges the limits of human power. While the *structure* approach may invest significant *power* in social institutions, it is important to note that sometimes it is not the lack of trying or inaction that is the cause of failure or lack of progress (Quist-Adade, 2012).

The *agency* part of the theory invests individuals with the *power* of willful actions, positing that people are not puppets, that they possess free will who exercise their *power* as conscious individuals. This position may argue: 'We're captains of the ship of our destiny', and we do make choices for good or for bad. In light of the discourse of liberal individualism, this approach may engender a blame-the-victim mentality. The poor, for example, are poor because of their laziness and lack of motivation, not because of society. They have no one but themselves to blame (Quist-Adade, 2012).

Seeking to address the deficiencies in the free will versus determinism debate in social philosophy and *structure* versus *agency* dichotomy in sociology, Berger and Luckman proposed a more nuanced and dialectical formula by suggesting that while individuals deliberately act, their actions do not take place in a vacuum, but that human actions are circumscribed by social forces beyond their control. What this also means is that while social forces may seem all powerful, entrenched, and unalterable, they are social constructions and human creations, and hence can be unconstructed or changed by the same human beings (Quist-Adade, 2012). This relationship is a dynamic and dialectical one. The dialectical relationship between social institutions and human *agency* was long acknowledged by Marx when he made the following two observations: "*Men make their own history, but they do not make it as they please; they do not make it under self-selected circumstances, but under circumstances existing already, given and transmitted from the past*" (Marx, 1852, p. 7); and "*Man is a product of circumstances, but man in turn modifies those circumstances*" (See Marxism as Action: http://www.marxists.org/archive/pannekoe/1915/marxism-action.htm). In short, Marx proposed that men and women are influenced by circumstances, but can change those same circumstances.

Anthony Giddens' Structuration

Anthony Giddens (1984) offered a variation of the duality of *structure* and *agency* theory with the concept of **structuration**. He argued that there exists a relationship between *structures* and actors. *Structures* are the rules and conditions that guide social action, and actors are human subjects who deliberately act in reasoned and planned ways. *Structuration* involves intersubjective understanding and meaning: "Structures do constrain actors, but actors can also transform structures by think-ing about them and acting on them in new ways" (Jackson & Sorenson, 2011, p. 130). Giddens, according to Meyers (2006), has clearly been influenced by the dialectical insights of the critical school. There are several main premises to his *structuration theory*: **First**, social order is reproduced through people's everyday actions. **Second**, there is a recursive and dialectical tension between *social structure* and human *agency*. **Third**, *social structure* and human *agency* exist not only in dialectical relationship, but they also manifest themselves in both macro and micro levels of social interac-tions. Giddens distinguished between *social structures*, **social system**, and **structuration**. *Structures* define social norms, shaping people's perceptions of what is right and what is wrong: "Structures impose systems compromise on the situated activities of human agents reproduced across time and space...organized as regular social practice" (Giddens, 1984, p. 10). Examples of *structures* and sys-tems include the economy, the family, and religion. *Structures* and systems operate together, and they are recursively implicated in each other's conceptualization: "Structuration is the dialectical process through which structures and systems are reproduced" (Myers 2006, p. 20).

Giddens defined *structure* as only existing through the actions of participation. If those within society do not participate within the actions of preestablished rules, the *structure* would cease to exist. Practice is what holds *structure* together. Patterns become systems or at least part of systems if they are repeated over and over again. *Social structure* sets precedence for how to act correctly, which in turn deeply affects their actions and *agency* within that system (Mann, 2011, pp. 177–178). We are bound to the system until we *unnormalize* what the system is doing to us. Having said this, we would essentially undo the entire system if we were to completely act based on our own *agency* in groups (Mann, 2011, pp. 177–178).

Giddens delineated three major *social structures*. The first structure is **signification**, which involves the codes that social actors use to make sense of the world and to make meanings (Myers, 2006). These *structures* are also called *master narratives* or *metanarratives*. *Signification* influences the mode of the discourse of a society. The second *structure* is **domination**. *Domination* involves the unequal distribution of **allocative** and **authoritative resources** in society. *Allocative resources* are raw materials, land, good jobs, and services. *Authoritative resources* include the ability to speak for oneself, act on one's own behalf, and act in a credible, effective manner. The third structure is **legiti-mation**. *Legitimation* is based on the premise that oppressive *structures* persist not just because peo-ple are powerless to change them, but because they are seen as legitimate in the eyes of the masses. In spite of its oppressive nature, the *structure* is considered to be legitimate because people see it as normal (Myers 2006, p. 20). Georg Lukacs (1992) explained this phenomenon with the concept of **reification**: *reification* is the conceptualization of human phenomena as if they were things, that is, in nonhuman or possibly suprahuman terms. Another way of saying this is that *reification* is the feeling of the products of human activity as though they were something else than human products, such as facts of nature, results of cosmic laws, or manifestations of divine will (Berger & Luckman, 1986; See also Bauman, 1976; Giddens, 1984). A reified *structure* is likely to become a legitimate *structure*.

According to Myers (2006), *legitimation* allows the overall *structure* to persist unchallenged. These *structures* constrain and circumscribe our actions. Giddens identified three forms of constraints: **material, structural,** and **negative sanctions. First,** *material constraints* exist when we do not have the financial or physical means to pursue an action. Like Bourdieu's notion of *economic capital,* people low in financial resources, for example, may not be able to afford to attend college or go on a vacation (Myers, 2006). People with physical disability may not be able to enter a building because there is no accessible handicapped entrance. **Second,** "*structural constraints* are defined as placing limits upon the range of options open to an actor or a plurality of actors, in given circumstance or a type of circumstance" (Myers, 2006, p. 27). For example, racial segregation in housing and schooling makes it difficult for people in impoverished areas to find decent places to live and work. Racial segregation helps to reproduce poverty among "minorities", who then have even fewer viable opportunities for improving their lives financially (Myers, 2006, p. 27). The last constraint is **negative sanctions,** which involve one form of punishment or another. An example is when some "minority" people are followed when they shop in expensive stores or marketplaces that truly are accessible only to the very affluent. Often, in multiracial societies, such as Canada or the United States, assumptions are made that black people cannot be affluent therefore they cannot legitimately patronize stores that cater to affluent tastes (Myers, 2006, p. 26).

Myers (2006, p. 27) suggested that taken together various social factors work together to limit people's range of opportunities, despite their dreams, desires, and intentions. For instance, parents tell their children "you can be anything that you want to be if you study hard", and they in turn fantasize about being astronauts, doctors, and world leaders. But the hard truth is that it is "unlikely that most of these parents will have the resources or opportunities to pursue the kids of studies and experiences necessary in order to realize these dreams even if they try their hardest" (Myers, 2006, p. 27). However, far from what pure structuralists would have us to believe, people's lives are not predetermined by their locations in the *structure.* Following the dialectical principle, Giddens argued that the *structure* also enables social actors by providing opportunities for action (Myers, 2006). Therefore people are not dunces or puppets, manipulated by some powerful invisible puppeteers; they are not hopelessly shackled by the *structure.* They are able to make choices, and they affect each other according to the choices that they make (Myers, 2006).

As Giddens (1990, p. 134) emphasized, "one person's constraints is another's enabling". As we noted above, we are both captains of the ships of our destinies, just as we are victims of circumstances. As social actors, we have agencies, and often do exercise them. However, our actions do not take place in a vacuum. Our actions take place within the confines of *social structures,* which do circumscribe or constrain our actions. They are driven by motives and, at the same time, they are impacted by the law of unintended consequences. Quite often, our intentions and actions fail to materialize or are broken into smithereens, either because of unforeseen circumstances or due to the fact our actions produced the opposite results.

As Myers (2006) pointed out, at the heart of structuration, however, is the fact that individual social actors often act in concert with others. Social actors are not random agents whose actions negate the actions of others. Myers (2006) observed that our actions even if spontaneous are somewhat ordered and systematic, because they stem from our knowledge of, and limitations within, the *structures*. Actions and orders are not separate in Gidden's theory of structuration. In his words, action and order are an interconnected duality rather than an unrelated dualism: "How we act is informed by the structure as it imprints itself on our memory across time and space" (Myers, 2006, p. 30). We also tend to act in ways that reinforce the social order. Myers (2006, p. 30) concluded that "the social world operates as a reflexive feedback loop in which order influences actions and actions tend to reinforce the order whether intentionally or not". In the next section, we focus on the ideas of micro-sociologists and their analysis of the relationship between *agency* and *structure*.

Part Five

· ·

Symbolic Interactionism

If the structural functionalist and the conflict paradigms dominate the macro-sociological landscape and are concerned with social structures, institutions, and entire societies; symbolic interactionism occupies the micro-sociological universe, and turns its gaze on small-scale and face-to-face interpersonal interactions. Symbolic interactionism or interactionism, for short, is one of the major theoretical paradigms in sociology (See Chapter Five). The term was coined by Herbert Blumer. He coined the term when he was invited to write a chapter on social psychology in an attempt to clarify how social psychologists differed in their views of human nature. Blumer explained that social psychology was interested in the social development of the individual and the central task of *sociological social psychologists* was to study how the individual develops socially as a result of participating in group life. The primary focus of symbolic interactionism is **social intercourse** or **interaction**. (Wallace & Wolf, 2006) The primary focus of symbolic interactionism is *social intercourse* and the processes by which the social actor makes decisions and forms opinions. The social actor is perceived not as a passive being who is impinged upon by external/outside forces. Rather, the social actor is viewed as an active constructor of social reality in conjunction with fellow social actors.

Symbolic interactionism traces its intellectual roots as far back as mid-twentieth century writings of the German sociologist, Max Weber (1864–1920) and the American philosopher, George Herbert Mead (1863–1931). Weber's contribution to interactionism was his ability to bridge the micro- and macro- perspectives and emphasis on **verstehen** (the German word for empathic understanding), or **subjective meaning** of human behaviour, a concept Mead also adopted. In addition, both Weber and Mead believed that social reality should be seen as a **dynamic social process**. Finally, both theorists underscored **pragmatism** as an important aspect of human interaction.

The symbolic interactionist paradigm is defined as a theoretical framework based on the assumption that society is continuously recreated as humans construct their reality through the use of symbols and interactions. Symbolic interactionism studies how the individual develops socially by participating in group life. Several basic assumptions inform this paradigm. The **first** assumption is that humans are symbol users (Mann, 2011, pp. 185–186). The key elements of social life are symbols. This theory emphasizes the capacity of humans to create and use symbols. Thus, symbolic interactionists, as their name implies, place enormous emphasis on the capacity of humans to create and use symbols as they interact with others. The **second** assumption is that individuals are active constructors of their own conducts and interpret, evaluate, define, and map out their own actions. The emphasis here is on how individuals interact through **role-taking** (i.e., imitating others) (Wallace & Wolf, 2006). Symbolic interactionists are interested in small-scale interpersonal relationships. The **third** assumption is that the mind, the self, and society are intimately connected. Symbolic interactionism posits a relationship between the genesis of "humanness" and patterns of interaction. It seeks to unravel the genesis of the mind and the self. The mind is defined as the capacity to think, to symbolically denote, weigh, assess, anticipate, map, and construct courses of action. The Meadian term, mind, however, is rarely used today (Wallace & Wolf, 2006). The concept of mind has been reformulated to embrace, William Isaac Thomas', **definition of the situations**. Thomas proposed that with the capacities of mind, actors can name, categorize, and orient themselves to constellations of objects, including themselves as objects, in all situations (See Box 10.11 - The Looking Glass-Self, Self-fulfilling Prophecy, and the Definition of the Situation). In this way they can assess, weigh, and sort out appropriate lines of conduct (Mann, 2011, pp. 185–186).

BOX 10.11 - The Looking Glass-Self, Self-fulfilling Prophecy, and the Definition of the Situation

The central premise of the theory of **the looking glass-self** is captured in Cooley's statement: "I feel about me the way you think of me" (Cooley, 1902, p. 180). There are three elements in the looking glass-self theory:

a) the imagination of our appearance to the other person,

b) the imagination of his/her judgment of that appearance, and

c) the creation of some sort of self-feeling, such as pride or mortification (shame).

Cooley's *looking glass-self* ties in with two important symbolic interactionist concepts: **self-fulfilling prophecy** and the **definition of the situation**. The term *self-fulfilling prophecy* was coined by Robert Merton. He defined it as a prophecy or prediction which is false, but is made true by a person's actions. For example, telling a child he/she is stupid again and again is likely to make him/her perceive him/herself as stupid, even though he/she might not necessarily be stupid. **Labelling theorists** deploy *self-fulfilling prophecy* to explain how a negative label attached to a person for a specific behaviour may with time, make the person to internalize that label and reinforce that behaviour. Researchers have emphasized how "particular definitions of the situation held by educators result in self-fulfilling prophecies" (Wotherspoon, 1998, p. 26).

For example, teachers use labels to describe parents and their students based on certain assumptions, background information, and observations that may be biased. In short, labelling students affects their career path and educational chances. Rosenthal and Jacobson showed that the labelling of students based on assumptions about their potentials for learning, regardless of their validity, have influenced students' performance more than students' actual abilities (Wotherspoon, 1998, p. 27). Teachers categorize students as nonnegotiable, intermittently negotiable, or continuously negotiable. Based on this system of categorization, teachers employ different strategies in their interactions with students. This is not limited to children. Adults too are impacted by *self-fulfilling prophecy*, but it tends to have greater influence on infants in how they grow up to be.

The second concept, *definition of the situation*, was coined by American sociologists William and Dorothy Thomas. The concept is captured in their now famous declaration: "If men [sic] define situations as real, they are real in their consequences." According to Mann (2011, p. 186), if we see a situation as real, it impacts what we do, and thus has social effect. For example, if a group of students and their professor think their class is a hardworking class, they may act as hardworking, although they may not necessarily be a hardworking class. Also termed **the power of the situation**, the *definition of the situation* does have a powerful impact on our attitudes, which could make or break us and mend or destroy our relationships. It could turn people from "morons" to geniuses, and vice versa. It can empower or lead to a paralysis of will. The *power of the situation* ties in with another important concept in symbolic interactionism, Weber's **verstehen**. The term is defined as introspective understanding or empathy. Weber called on sociologists to always seek to understand what a situation, action, or symbol means to people as they engage in interaction. He advised that we should "focus on the subjective meanings of people's acts, not their objective purposes," because the value a given symbol has for one person or group might be quite different for someone else" (Mann, 2011, p. 186). A crucifix elicits a different meaning and emotion to a devout Catholic than to a Moslem or a Jew. It is therefore important for sociologists to investigate the actor's actions, as what counts is the way the actor defines the meaning of that symbol.

In general, the emphasis of the interactionist orientation is on:

a) the emergence of self-conceptions (relatively stable and enduring conceptions that people have about themselves), and

b) the ability to derive self-images-pictures of oneself as an object in social situations.

As we explained in Chapter Five, the **self** is thus a major object that people inject into their *definitions of situations*. It shapes much of what people see, feel, and do in the world around them. Society is possible only by virtue of people's capacities to define situations and people's abilities to view themselves as objects in situations (See Box 10.12 - Mead and the Social Self). Society can exist by virtue of human capacities for thinking and defining situations and their capacities for self-reflection and evaluation (Mann, 2011). Having discussed Mead's and Cooley's ideas in Chapter Five, we devote a considerable part of this section to Erving Goffman's dramaturgical analysis and ethnomethodology.

BOX 10.12 - Mead and the Social Self

Mead's approach to explaining the basis of the social self is described as *social behaviourism*. His primary focus is *how we think*. For Mead, the mind is a process, not a thing, and is found in social phenomena rather than within individuals. He theorized that the key to social experience lay in how humans think and he used the term "minding" to indicate that thinking is an ongoing, active, and dialectical process of interaction between the social actor and his or her interlocutors. Contemporary symbolic interactionists do not use the Meadian concept "minding." For Mead, the self, then, occupied a central locus of the individual development as a social animal. The self emerges from social experiences and social experience is based on the exchange of symbols. He defined the self as the ability of the social actor to take herself or himself as an object and a subject at the same time. He theorized that the way to do that is through reflexivity, the ability to put ourselves into the place of others and act as they act. Reflexivity is a mechanism through which the individual develops the self. It involves the social actor taking on the role of others. Role taking is similar to Weber's *verstehen* (i.e., empathizing or putting oneself in the shoes of another person) (Mann, 2011, p. 188).

Goffman and Impression Management

Another contributor to symbolic interactionism is Canadian sociologist Erving Goffman. He built on Mead's notion of role taking. His approach is called **dramaturgy** or **dramaturgical sociology** since he constructed his theory from the logic of the famous Shakespearean declaration, "All the world's a stage, and all the men and women are merely players". The main assumption of Goffman's theory is that we are all actors, who try to manage other people's **impressions** of us. Our behaviours in the public settings are akin to a performance on the theatre stage. We perform according to a script (i.e., social norms and values).

According to Goffman, for any social interaction to be successful, actors must empathize with their fellow participants in order to create joint social acts. They also must actively manage to control how others will interpret their behaviours. In his book, *The Presentation of Self in Everyday Life* (1959), Goffman outlined two ways individuals manage *impressions*: **front stage behaviour** and **back stage behaviour**. Using a restaurant environment to illustrate his theory, he posited that the *front stage behaviour* is the formal, expected behaviour we put on in social or public settings. In the restaurant, people's behaviour or performance is characterized by cooperation, toothpaste smiles, politeness, courtesy, and decorum. The attendant is acting according to his/her role, manipulating his/her customers and impressing them. However, to know the true character of the waiter, we must observe his/her behaviour in the kitchen, where the real character of the waiter is revealed. In the kitchen he/she may argue with the chef or other waiters. The waiter's behaviour in the kitchen is what Goffman called *back-stage behaviour* or **out-of-role behaviour**. *Back-stage behaviour* is informal, and it takes place in more or less private settings. By looking at both *front stage* and *back stage behaviours*, we are able to have a more rounded picture of a person than the image presented to customers or audience members (Wallace & Wolf, 2006).

According to Goffman, individuals deliberately and inadvertently give off signs that provide others with information about how to respond. Out of such a mutual use of signs individuals develop a **definition of the situation**. A *definition of the situation* is a plan of cooperative activity, but which at the same time is not so much a real agreement about what actually exists, but rather a real agreement about whose claims concerning certain issues would be temporarily honoured (Wallace & Wolf, 2006). In constructing this *definition of a situation*, individuals engage in performances in which each orchestrates gestures to present oneself in a particular manner. We try to portray ourselves as having certain characteristics, and, thus, deserving some special treatment. These performances revolve around several interrelated dynamics. **First**, we have the creation of a **front**. A *front* includes physical settings, decors, furniture, etc., and stage props to create a certain *impression*. A *front stage* also involves items of expressive equipment, emotions, energy, and other capacities of expression. These include:

a) **appearance**, or those signs that tell others of an individual's social position and status, and

b) **manner**, or those signs that inform others about the role that an individual expects to play.

Second, in addition to presenting a *front*, individuals use gestures in what Goffman termed **dramatic realization**, or the infusion into activity of signs that highlight a commitment to a given *definition of situation*. The more a situation creates problems in presenting a *front*, the greater will be efforts at *dramatic realization*. **Third**, performances also involve **idealization**, or efforts to present oneself in ways that incorporate and exemplify the officially accredited values of society (Wallace & Wolf, 2006). When individuals move into a new social setting, *idealization* becomes pronounced. *Idealization* creates problems for an individual, however, because if he/she is to be effective, an individual must suppress, conceal, and underplay those elements that might contradict more general values.

Fourth, such efforts at concealment are part of a general process of maintaining expressive control. Because minor cues and signs are read by others and contribute to the *definition of a situation*, actors must regulate their muscular ability, their signs of involvement, their orchestration of the *front*, and their ability to fit it in the context of the interaction (Wallace & Wolf, 2006). According to Wallace and Wolf (2006), a discrepancy between behaviour and the *definition of a situation* can unsettle the interaction. *Impression* of reality fostered by a *performance* is delicate, fragile, and can be shattered by minor mishaps.

Fifth, individuals can also engage in **misrepresentation**. The eagerness of one's audience to read gestures and determine one's *front* makes that audience vulnerable to manipulation and duping. **Sixth**, individuals often engage in **mystification**, or the maintenance of distance from others as a way to keep them in awe and in conformity to a *definition of a situation*. Wallace and Wolf (2006) noted such *mystification* is, however, limited primarily to those of higher rank and status. **Seventh**, individuals seek to make their *performances* seem real and to avoid communicating a sense of contrivance. Thus individuals must communicate in ways that are, or at least appear to others as, sincere, natural, and spontaneous. These procedures for bringing off a successful *performance* and thereby creating an overall *definition of a situation* constitute the core of Goffmanian sociology (Wallace & Wolf, 2006).

Critique of Goffman's Dramaturgy

On the plus side, Goffman's theory presents a creative way of explaining human behaviour in the micro setting. In addition, as Wallace and Wolf (2006) observed, *dramaturgy* is recognition of loose coupling of the micro- and macro-realms. On the minus side, Goffman sought to present humans as cynical and deceptive. Furthermore, Goffmanian dramaturgy places too much emphasis on how individuals manage their impressions and play roles. He also did not account for the effects of gender, social class, race, ability, and sexuality in analyzing how individuals act and behave in social contexts. Finally, Goffman overemphasized stage, props, physical space, and objects.

Ethnomethodology

Ethnomethodology, an offshoot of symbolic interactionism, raises the question of how people who are interacting with each other can create the illusion of a shared social order even when they do not understand each other fully and in fact have different points of view. Ethnomethodology, the detailed study of how people organize their everyday lives, is important in conversational analysis (Littlejohn & Foss, 2008). Littlejohn (2009) defined ethnomethodology as the careful observation of microbehaviours in real situations. It interrogates the everyday, commonsense understandings that people have of the world. Its etymology can be traced to the Greek word "Ethno," which means people or folk. Thus, ethnomethodology simply defined is "people's method of making sense of their social world" (Mann, 2011, p. 214). In short, ethnomethodology investigates how people make sense of everyday activities.

Ethnomethodologists treat the taken-for-granted as problematic. They have carried a number of investigations into how people come to take their everyday lived experiences for granted. Ethnomethodologists have used different methods in seeking to understand how people make sense of their everyday activities. We provide a brief synopsis of **conversational analysis** here. Conversational analysis (CA) sees conversation as a social achievement, the way things get done cooperatively through talking. It focuses on interaction in discourse. The primary concern of conversation analysis is the sequential organization of talk. Conversational analysis assumes that talk, like all social activity, is patterned. It looks at details of conversations to discover the ways in which organization is achieved.

Ethnomethodologists use the following methods in their research: **open-ended interviews**, in which the respondent is allowed to answer, as he or she pleases to **free choice questions** from the researcher. The other methods are **in-depth interview, participant observation, videotaping, documentary,** and **breaching experiments.** Harold Garfinkel is the forerunner in these methods. In one of his studies, he demonstrated the logic behind the taken-for-granted by sending his students out to perform "experiments in trust" or *breaching experiments.* The students were instructed to bring ordinary conversations to an abrupt halt by refusing to take-for-granted what they knew the other person was saying, and so demanded explanations and then explanations of the explanations (Garfinkel, 1967). In another *breaching experiment,* a researcher asked his students to act as strangers in their own homes by asking permission to perform normal acts, such as getting food from the fridge, using the bathrooms, and watching television. In these experiments, people tended to get frustrated and even angry when their taken-for-granted assumptions were challenged. More recently, ethnomethodologist researchers have performed minutely detailed analyses of ordinary conversations in order to reveal the methods by which turn-taking and other conversational maneuvers are managed. Ethnomethodologists deliberately ask questions whose answers are obvious, questions that may seem stupid to most people. The trick is to tease out non-obvious answers and to interrogate how people make sense of their lived experiences and interactions. For example, you arrive late to class and your instructor asks you the reason for your lateness. You reply by saying you had a flat tire on your way. Then your instructor asks: "What is a flat tire?" You are likely to stare at your instructor dubiously, thinking: "What a stupid question? Who doesn't know what a flat tire is?" This is the stock-in-trade of ethnomethodologists. Their goal is to disrupt taken-for-granted assumptions in order to determine how we make sense of our everyday lives.

Critique of Symbolic Interactionism

Like any paradigm or theory, symbolic interactionism has its supporters and critics. For advocates of symbolic interactionism, it restores hope in human creativity and *agency*. By investing free will or *agency* in individuals, it strikes out the zombie and puppet-like caricature construction of individuals in the macroscopic and structuralist paradigms. As we noted earlier, in general, the structural functionalist and conflict paradigms divest individuals of their *agencies* and view them as passive and powerless. The macroscopic paradigms depict individuals as pawns, who are controlled and manipulated by powerful social institutions and external forces. Symbolic interactionism creates an antithetical picture by insisting that human beings have, and often do exercise their *agencies*. The detractors of symbolic interactionism, however, have criticized it for investing too much power in individuals, casting them as also omnipotent, nearly unaffected by social institutions and social norms. It has also been criticized for being too vague on the conceptual front (i.e., some critics have faulted symbolic interactionists for being overly impressionistic in their research methods and somewhat unsystematic in their theories) and for downplaying large-scale *social structures*. Given its micro-level focus, some have argued that symbolic interactionism is not microscopic enough, because it tends to ignore psychological factors. Another criticism of symbolic interactionism is that it tends to promote the *status quo* by its lack of focus on social inequalities and negative institutional and structural impacts on minorities.

Symbolic interactionists are currently trying to answer some of these criticisms by integrating micro- and macro-level theories and synthesizing their approach across other fields of study. For example, some scholars are redefining Mead's theory to show that it accounts for both micro- and macro-level phenomena. Others are using **role theory** as a way to integrate *structure* and meaning. Some symbolic interactionists are focusing more attention on culture and are working within cultural studies to examine the role communication technologies play in producing and representing social reality.

Part Six

··

The Feminist Paradigm

In writing this book, we approached it from a feminist standpoint on teachers and teaching. Manicom (1992, p. 367) argued that "the standpoint of a teacher is political: to develop analyses that inform/ reform teachers' and students' attitudes and ways of acting in and on the world". One's standpoint reflects one's political identity and experiences that are determined by what Anthony Giddens called *structuration* (Ritzer, 2000, p. 522–526). This implies that as agents of social change, we are both the authors/producers of *social structures* through our actions and indeed our inactions, and we are at the same time the products of these structures and are influenced by them. A feminist standpoint is reflective of the person's experiences within institutions, society, and his/her relations with other people of various or similar backgrounds. Our standpoint is influenced by **critical feminism**.

One of the main arguments of this theory is that women face oppression and inequality as well as exploitation based on factors, such as "race", ethnicity, sexuality, age, gender, and ability. They focus on "issues of power and justice, and are committed to uncovering and understanding the forces that cause and sustain oppression" (Glesne, 2011, p. 11). They stress that one cannot understand gender oppression in isolation from other forms of oppression. They all intersect one another and it is important to approach them from an integrative perspective. An integrative approach acknowledges that gender and other forms of oppressions are structural factors that are experienced differently and similarly by the social actors. In this light, Dei (1996, p. 55) introduced "the notion of *integrative anti-racism studies* to address the problem of discussing the social constructs of race, class, gender and sexuality as exclusive and independent categories". *Integrative antiracism* identifies how different forms of social marginality and structures of power and dominance intersect and shift as societies change (Dei, 1996, p. 56). In this sense, "race" like gender is a multifacet criterion of *difference* which intersects with other forms of oppression, such as class, gender, ethnicity, culture, sexuality, and religion.

As antiracism focuses on "race", feminism emphasizes gender-based analysis, which allows for a holistic approach to social issues by accounting for the intersections and contradictory manifestations of factors, such as gender, "race", and ethnicity. Gender analysis provides the possibility of opening up space to critically evaluate the effects of exclusion of women's experiences, knowledge, and other forms of marginality. Gender analysis is critical of **androcentricity** or **malecentredness**; women, then, are viewed not as passive, rather as active subjects in history. In general, gender-based perspectives help to:

1. focus on marginal activities, such as unpaid work of women;
2. question the validity of patriarchal knowledge (it questions dominant views); and
3. formulate new research questions that account for the various experiences of women.

Feminism is a set of theories and strategies for social change that takes gender as its main concern. It attempts to understand how social institutions, processes, and relationships produce and reproduce inequality between the sexes. The major issues all feminists confront are social and political equality, reproductive rights, domestic violence, sexism, racism, classism, heterosexism, ableism, and other "isms" (Mann, 2011). However, feminists differ in their explanations of women's oppression, the nature of gender, and ideas about women's emancipation. Its central focus is the advocacy of social equality for both men and women. It proposes a radical opposition to patriarchy and sexism. Its core concerns rest upon gender oppression and insists that women and men should be equals. It contends that men have social *power* and thus an interest in maintaining their social privilege over women (Quist-Adade, 2012, pp. 98–99).

Feminists share a number of theoretical principles. They agree that many aspects of life are divided into gender categories based on sex. They share a commitment to expose the powers and limits of' the genderized division of the world and to make transparent the oppressive nature of gender categories. They agree that gender is a social construction dominated by a male bias. In addition, feminists reject traditional forms of research as being male dominated and male biased (Quist-Adade, 2012, pp. 98–99).

Goals of Feminism

Feminist scholarship has two main goals: **political** and **intellectual**. In the political realm, feminism aims to achieve gender justice by eliminating male domination of the "science" and knowledge industries. It also seeks to eliminate the *androcentrism* of the traditional epistemologies. In the intellectual sphere, feminist scholarship posits that getting rid of the *androcentrism* of the traditional epistemologies will pave the way for the production of a more objective and balanced stock of knowledge. To do this, feminist scholars must adopt the constructivist approach, which says that reality is socially constructed or invented (Weedon, 1987; Quist-Adade, 2012, pp. 98–99).

We can identify seven approaches to feminist theorizing and research:

1. liberal feminist theory,
2. radical-cultural feminism,
3. psychoanalytic feminism,
4. Marxist feminism,
5. social feminism/gendering,
6. poststructuralist feminism/postmodern perspectives, and
7. "Third World"/postcolonial feminism.

Before exploring these theories, we explore the historical context in which feminism developed.

Historical Context

We begin this section with a brief overview of the historical contexts which gave rise to feminism as a whole. For centuries, women universally were considered to be "inferior" to men, intellectually and physically. They were seen as "emotional, intuitive, irrational, and illogical". Women were also considered as only fit for the roles of wives and mothers and only capable of performing domestic chores of homemaking and nurturing young ones. Women's aspirations were limited to marrying a man and to serve and obey their husbands. Women were denied their civil and political rights; they were not allowed to exercise their franchise, to vote, and be voted for. In addition, they were prevented from receiving formal education, and could work only in menial jobs. A married woman's salary and other property belonged to her husband. Rape and physical abuse were legal within the institution of marriage. While husbands could easily obtain divorce, it was difficult for women to do the same. A Woman had no rights to her children if she left a marriage.

It was against the backdrop of these oppressive and patently sexist conditions that the feminist movement(s) emerged in the beginning of the eighteenth century. According to Mann (2011, pp. 322–323), feminism could be traced back to the 1790s' turbulent period in Western history, when a number of women worked behind the scenes to agitate for change. Within the last few decades of the enlightenment people like Thomas Paine, Thomas Jefferson, the Marquis de Condorcet, and William Godwin took up the mantle and advocated for "rights of man". French playwright and feminist activist, Olympe de Gouges, wrote her pamphlet in 1791, entitled "Declaration of the Rights of Woman and Citizen". In this pamphlet, she argued for equal legal and political rights for the sexes, and included a provision for marriage as a social contract between two equal parties. She was rewarded with a trip to the guillotine. Mary Wollstonecraft (1759–1797) wrote her groundbreaking *Vindication of the Rights of Women* in which she called for equal and quality education for women. She argued that women should be accorded the same education as men instead of encouraging them to study frivolous arts of dancing, singing, chit-chatting, and looking pretty to attract a husband (Mann, 2011, pp. 322–323).

The Waves of Feminism

General Historical Context

The basic assumption of the first wave feminist movement, which also informed the subsequent waves, was that feminists acknowledge that men and women have separate biologically-determined roles and that these roles are played out separately: women are confined to the private (domestic) sphere, while men perform in the public sphere. However, they maintained, women were deprived of legal protection and education in order to become better citizens. Thus, their overall goal was to improve the legal position of women, most especially to gain the vote. To achieve their goals, feminists initiated a movement that came to be called the **first feminist wave.**

First Wave

Mann (2011) noted that in America feminism was tied to the abolition of slavery and that President Abraham Lincoln's *Emancipation Proclamation* served as its clarion call. America's **first wave feminist** movement was led by Elizabeth Cady Stanton (1815–1902) and Lucretia Mott (1793–1880), both of whom were abolitionists. In 1848, the Women's Rights Convention was held in Seneca Falls, New York. In 1920, the 19th Amendment was passed to guarantee women the right to vote in the

United States. Across the Atlantic Ocean, in England, Mary Wollstonecraft and the Radical Suffragists demanded that women should be given equal recognition with men, and called for equal education. Wollstonecraft described marriage as "legalized prostitution". Feminists also rallied against the notion of women being "property" of their husbands. They pressed for legislation that would grant women a fair divorce with child custody. In addition, they rallied for women to run for and hold public offices.

Second Wave

The **second wave feminist movement** went beyond the demands of the *first wave feminists*. While the *first wave* had as its sole agenda universal suffrage, the *second wave* was concerned with the restoration of *all* the rights that women had been denied in the past. It is important to consider the historical context of the second wave feminist movement. The *second wave feminism* was ushered in and drove on the crest wave of the Civil Rights Movement during the 1960s and 1970s in the United States of America. By this time, women had made substantial gains in the civic, political, and social spheres. They now got the vote, they had access to equal and higher education; many had high-paying jobs; abortion was legalized; and women could obtain divorce. However, women were still oppressed. They were still stereotyped as the weaker sex, "irrational", "emotional", "dependent", and "intuitive". While many were in gainful employment, few rose to the top of their careers as they hit the **glass-ceiling**, the invisible barrier women and racialized "minority" workers hit in their upward rise in their occupations due to discrimination. Women were paid less for the same job as their male counterparts. This is in spite of the fact that a notable gain was chalked with the entrance of women into the labour force in the wake of the Second World War. During the war, women had worked in traditional male-dominated jobs in factories and other areas. But when the wars ended and the men returned, women were pushed back to the domestic sphere, to become wives and mothers, again.

Mann (2011) observed that the *second wave* was much more broadly-based than the *first wave*, thanks to its multiple concerns, which included the restoration of women's economic, political, and social rights. If the *first wave feminist movement* was more political, then the *second wave* was more concerned with cultural aspects. As mentioned, in the years, 1966–1979, there was a heightened feminist consciousness (Mann, 2011). The movement was linked to the Civil Rights movement, which had begun in the late 1950s.

Third Wave

In the West, the gains of the *first* and *second waves of the feminist movement*s appear to have gained further consolidation in the 1990s. Women were increasingly gaining equal opportunity with men on multiple fronts. They were excelling in previously male-dominated professions, such as medicine, law, and politics. But women were still behind men in many spheres. They had not attained equal pay for equal work. They were still expected to marry and raise children. Working women were doing a **second shift**, doing the lion's share of domestic work. The picture among "women of colour" and sexual "minorities", lesbians, bisexuals, and transgendered individuals, was much starker, however. They still faced severe discrimination not only on the basis of their sex/gender, but also because of their "race," religion, and sexuality.

The **third wave feminism** was championed by the so-called "scholars of colour" in the Global South and their counterparts in the West. It has been described as more inclusive, eclectic, and going beyond thinking in **dualities** or **binary oppositions**. These scholars contend that the preceding waves of feminism were led by upper and middle class White women, who viewed all women's problems, hopes, and aspirations through the eyes of White women and assumed that the feminist movement was **monolithic**. They also criticized the *first* and *second waves* for being simplistic, in that they saw women as victims of the patriarchal culture alone, ignoring problems of racism, homophobia, classicism, and discrimination on the basis of religion. Thus, *third wave scholars* and activists called for a paradigm that would account not just for "race", class, sexual orientation, religious background, and disability, but would also consider the various generations, Baby Boomers, Generation Xers, and the Millennials. They argued that such a theory must consider what social, political, and economic events and/or trends have shaped these generations and how one's membership in a particular generational cohort might affect his/her outlook on issues related to gender. Finally, *third wave feminists* maintain that women's oppression is global. Neoliberal policies have had and continue to have devastating impacts on women, locally and globally. Neoliberal policies have resulted in a **global feminization of poverty**, as increasing numbers of women in the Global South have been forced to work in sweatshops under horrific conditions. They are victimized by the global sex trade as "they sell themselves or their daughters" in order to eke out a miserable living. Their counterparts in the Global North are not better off either. Many of them are compelled to work low-paid and part-time jobs with no benefits.

Third wave feminist scholars and activists adopted the **intersectionality** and **matrix of domination** approaches to construct a nuanced, inclusive, and multidisciplinary theory of feminism. The *intersectionality* theory is an inclusive theory, which accounts for multiple, subordinated subject positions, including "race", gender, class, and language status. The *matrix of domination* implies the negative impacts of multiple social categories, such as gender, race, class, and sexuality, age, ability etc., on a person's life chances. It argues that patriarchal relations in various institutions, such as the family, education system, and the economy, have negative impacts on women and contribute to their marginalization. For example, an African Canadian woman who is disabled, a single mother, and a lowly-paid secretary is disadvantaged multiple times: by her gender, "race", disability, and class. A Euro-Canadian woman in a similar situation would be disadvantaged in all the categories, except her "race". She would be privileged by her "race" and oppressed by her other characteristics. In the next section, we explore the various feminist theories.

Theoretical Perspectives

Liberal Feminism

Liberal Feminism began in the nineteenth century as the suffrage movement, and adopted a reformist, gradualist, and evolutionist approach in seeking to redress gender injustice and oppression. Liberal feminism posits that women and men should be given the same educational opportunities and civil rights (Tong, 1998, p. 2). It emphasizes the principle of individualism (i.e., all individuals have equal moral worth). The principle of individualism suggests that people should be judged on rational grounds, such as the content of character, talents, and personal worth, hence all individuals are entitled to participate in and gain access to public/political life. It proposes opening public life to equal competition.

Liberal feminists do not seek to abolish distinction between the public and private sphere, seeing the latter as a matter of individual choice. But some liberal feminists believe that women and men have different natures and inclinations, with women having a natural inclination that leans towards family and domestic life. For example, Betty Friedan in her book, *The Second Stage* (1983), proposed reconciling the challenges of the many possibilities created by broader opportunities for women in work and public life with a need for love, home, and family. Friedan warned her fellow women to be careful not to sacrifice their family life (love and care for their children and taking care of their family) in the quest for their personhoods. The demand for equal rights is the core of liberal feminism. As such, it attracted those whose education and social backgrounds were (are) better able to take advantage of wider career and educational opportunities. It therefore reflects the interests of White middle class in "developed" Western nations.

Liberal feminism starts with the assumption that socialization is the origin of gender differences. People, from infancy, are socialized to learn gender-specific roles with girls inculcated with an *ideology* that inferiorizes them as "the weaker sex", "emotional", "dependent on men", nurturers of young ones, and homemakers, whose place is the home/kitchen or domestic/private spheres.

Their male counterparts, on the other hand, are infused with an *ideology* that raises them onto the pedestal, as it were, and teaches them to act strong and powerful (to see themselves as a leader and independent, breadwinner, whose place is the public domain). The goal of liberal feminism is to achieve gender justice for women. Liberal feminists seek to level the playing field by focusing on legislative reforms.

Marxist/Socialist Feminism

Socialist feminism derives from the works of Karl Marx and Fredrick Engels, and is based on the premise that the family is a microcosm of the larger class relations. Socialist feminists argue that class relations account for women's status and function in society. For Marxist/socialist feminists, the starting point for feminist analysis is the family, an institution which they claim is responsible for creation, reproduction, and perpetuation of inequalities between the sexes. Marxist/socialist feminists believe that the nuclear family serves capitalism through the reproduction and maintenance of class and patriarchal inequalities. The ideal family in a capitalist society is patriarchal institution and the site of consumption (i.e., it is dominated by men).

Engels' book, *The Origins of the family, Private property and the State* (1884), explained the link between patriarchy and capitalism. In precapitalist societies, family life was communistic, and mothers' rights were the basis of property distribution with social positions inherited through the female line. However, with the advent of capitalist society, mothers' rights were supplanted by a system based on the ownership of private property by men. According to Engels, this change signaled the world historical defeat of the female sex. Female oppression operated through the bourgeois/patriarchal family in which property was passed on by the men only to their sons. To avoid paternity disputes, the men invented monogamous marriage, but which Engels said, men routinely violated by taking on multiple mistresses and concubines. To appease the women for their infidelity, the men invented the cult of femininity, which was in reality "an organized hypocrisy to protect male privileges and property" (Mann, 2011, p. 327).

According to Marxist/socialists, women constituted a reserve army of labour in capitalist society who were easily recruited when needed and as easily dispensed with during economic recessions. In bearing and raising children, women provided the next generation of workers. Their traditional roles as housewives relieved men and allowed them to concentrate on paid and productive employment. It reinforced patriarchal relations as male breadwinners were given high status and relieved of domestic chores.

Marxist feminists maintain that in a society where women's role is confined to homemaking and the nurturing of young ones, domestic labour serves the needs of the capitalist economy. They suggest the family plays an important ideological role on behalf of capitalism by naturalizing and normalizing the subservient role of women. The family socializes girls to buy into the capitalist system, thereby inculcating in them a *false consciousness*, which prevents them from seeing the oppressive nature of capitalism to women. Marxist/socialist feminists also argue that the family is an obstacle to gender equality in employment.

Marx stated that the only way to end oppression is to "seize the means of production, and women must seize the means of reproduction" (Mann, 2011, p. 323). Following in the footsteps of Marx, Marxist/socialists conceptualized men as the bourgeoisie and women as the proletariat. As in a capitalist society, the bourgeois class owns the means of production, hence *power* to control and exploit the proletariat; men in the patriarchal society dominate and oppress women. In a socialist economy, Mann (2011, p. 327) noted, both genders would be freed from their traditional roles of sexual bourgeoisie and sexual proletariat, where their economic equality would enhance greater social equality. As Mann (2011, p. 327) maintained, a number of socialist feminists have suggested paying housewives (stay-home mothers) a regular wage for their labour. But others think the better approach to ensuring greater equality between the sexes is the sharing of domestic chores.

Radical Feminism

Radical feminism took roots in the late 1960s. It seeks a complete reconstitution or restructuring of all patriarchal societies, as it sees patriarchy as the basis of female oppression. Radical feminism holds sexual oppression as the most fundamental feature of society and other forms of injustice, such as class exploitation and racial hatred, as derivatives or secondary.

Mann (2011, p. 325) maintained that feminists of all radical bent have insisted that "the main problem with Western society wasn't just insufficient rights for women, but that it was a patriarchal, male-dominated society". Radical feminists oppose other forms of feminism, particularly liberal feminism and socialist feminism, which they claim either ignore or minimize the role of patriarchy in all male-centred societies. Radical feminists also criticize liberal and socialist feminists for failing to acknowledge the primacy of gender divisions within society.

Mann (2011) noted that the foundational text of radical feminism is Kate Millet's *Sexual Politics* (1970), which called for the eradication of monogamous marriage and nuclear family as anachronistic patriarchal institutions. Millett also suggested that sex-typed roles imposed on men and women could be traced to differential socialization, which conditions girls from a very early age to take on subservient roles. The conditioning process, she insisted, takes place in patriarchy's chief institution, the family. The condition is not restricted to the family; it continues and is reinforced in literature, art, public life, and the economy. She argued that patriarchy should be challenged through what she termed a **process of consciousness-raising**.

For her part, Eva Figes insisted in her book, *Patriarchal Attitudes* (1970), that patriarchal attitudes pervade society in its entirety. She maintained that women are constructed and depicted universally as inferior and subordinate to men. Another radical feminist, Germaine Greer stated in her book, *The Female Eunuch* (1970) that women have been conditioned to play a passive sexual role through differential socialization. She maintained that true sexuality and the more active/adventurous sides of women's personalities have been suppressed. Adopting Freudian psychoanalysis, she contended that women are castrated and have become sexless objects. She called upon women to reengage with their libido. Andrea Dworkin argued that a woman couldn't really consent to heterosexual sex in such a male-dominated society (Mann, 2011, p. 325). Susan Brownmiller went even further than Dworkin by suggesting that all men are potential rapists due to their innate bestiality (Mann, 2011, p. 325). For most radical feminists, patriarchy is a system of politico-cultural oppression, and, therefore, female liberation requires a sexual revolution to overturn and replace these structures. This thinking is based on their belief that human nature is androgynous, having both male and female characteristics.

To recap, radical feminists see male *power* and privilege as the bases of the asymmetrical and oppressive social relations between men and women. Their goal is the abolition of male supremacy and the establishment of women-centred beliefs and systems.

WOMEN and the Education System

Women's oppression in the education system takes shape in the context of:

a) gendered relations in the classroom,

b) teacher-student relations, and

c) curriculum (Briskin, 1990, p. 443).

The goals of feminist pedagogy are to:

1. reevaluate the assumptions and purposes of education;

2. examine the patriarchal focus of the curriculum, education system, and teaching methods; and

3. reformulate the system, methods of teaching, and curriculum content in order to seriously account for the diverse experiences of women and other minority groups (Wotherspoon, 2009).

Black Feminism

Black feminist thought, often referred to as 'womanism' as opposed to 'feminism', focuses on the distinctive visions of the **outsider groups** within feminism, particularly those of African American women. It proposes a reconceptualization of social theory in which conventional concepts of "race", class, and gender are informed and changed by including the concrete experiences and definitions of subordinated groups. It criticizes mainstream scholarship for rarely recognizing black women as separate from black men, and faults mainstream feminism for automatically placing households as the only places of patriarchal oppression of women (hooks, 2000; Quist-Adade, 2012). Black feminism focuses on the following. **First**, Black feminist scholars conceptualize Black women's subordination as existing within intersecting oppressions of "race," class, gender, sexuality, and nation. **Second**, they seek diverse responses to common challenges. **Third**, they recognize that there is no homogenous or universal Black woman's standpoint, hence their emphasis on unraveling the multifactorial causations of and multiperspectival approaches to problems facing Black women of varying ethnic and citizenship statuses. **Fourth**, they practice *praxis* through ongoing dialogue where thought and action inform one another. **Fifth**, Black feminists see their struggles as part of a wider struggle for human dignity, empowerment, and social justice (hooks, 2000).

Black Feminist Thought

According to the proponents of Black feminist thought, oppression based on "race", class, gender, and sexuality exists in interlocking systems, which Patricia Hill Collins (2000) called, the *matrix of domination/oppression*. In her groundbreaking book, *Black Feminist Thought*, Collins suggested that oppression must be viewed intersectionally and integratively. For example, White women are penalized by their gender, but privileged by their "race". An individual may be an oppressor, a member of an oppressed group, or, simultaneously, an oppressor and oppressed. "Race," class, and gender form axes of oppression that characterize Black women's experiences within more generalized institutionalized forms of the *matrix of domination*. Other groups may encounter different dimensions of the matrix of institutional domination, such as sexual orientation, religion, and age, but the central relationship is one of racialized domination and the types of activism it generates (Collins, 200, p. 226). Hill posited that the *matrix of domination* is structured on several levels (i.e., people experience and resist oppression on three levels):

1. the level of personal biography,
2. the group or community level of the cultural context created by "race", class, and gender, and
3. the systemic level of social institutions.

Black feminist thought emphasizes all three levels as sites of domination and as potential sites of resistance. The *matrix of domination*, according to Black feminists, profoundly affects women and "people of color" in the United States in the form of **double jeopardy** or **multiple jeopardy**, which means that women in general and "minority" women are subordinated twice, thrice, or more by their gender, "race", class, or sexual orientation. For instance, a White woman with a physical disability will be disadvantaged twice because of her gender and physical disability. But a black woman with a disability would be disadvantaged three times by her gender, "race", and physical disability. The disadvantages compound with sexual orientation, religion, culture, and many other categories. In short, in a patriarchal, heterosexist, White, Euro-Christian society, "minority" men and women became subordinated multiple times by virtue of the colour of skin, gender, sexuality, and religion. Straight, White men are immune to these disadvantages, instead they enjoy **White privilege**. During the rise of feminism, for example, non-White women criticized liberal and White and middle-class feminists by pointing out that as sociological theory has been silent about the voices of women, feminism also has ignored the experiences and knowledge of Black, Hispanic, and Aboriginal women.

Summary

Most feminists agree that it is important to develop research methods that recognize women's oppression in male-dominated society (Wotherspoon, 1998, p. 41, Box 2.5). We must account for the subjective experiences of women. That is, the everyday experiences of women must become central aspects of research. Researchers must also contextualize themselves in their own subjectivity. In this sense, we must recognize and distinguish between the role of women as researchers and women as the object of the research. Feminists also share a political commitment to develop avenues through which women's conditions are improved through *praxis*. For example, feminists argue that we must include issues that are pertinent to women's lives, such as violence, the dichotomy between family responsibilities and career demands, the effects of sexism on females, and sexist manifestations in the curriculum and various processes of schooling. Through exploration of women's experiences, feminists attempt to "identify, clarify and seek positive solutions to social problems" (Wotherspoon, 1998, p. 42). Feminism and its many strands account for multiple forms of oppression. For example, liberal feminists emphasize and question the role of sexism in the classroom and curriculum and how power is unequally distributed between men and women. They promote reform in the context of existing systems to eradicate sex bias and gender inequality. Their aim is not to drastically alter how society is organized. They believe that within existing power structures such reforms are possible, and can lead to the condition of equality. Other feminists, however, have criticized this aspect of liberal feminism. Radical feminists, for example, argue that the problem is patriarchy and patriarchal relations, which promote the oppression of women and devalue their contributions to social, economic, and political life. Patriarchy, they argue, is an aspect of all social organizations and institutions. Science, knowledge, and language are based on men's experiences; and their experiences are considered as reflecting the experiences of all people in society. Experiences of women are marginalized and not considered as socially important. For example, they maintain that those spheres of life, such as sexuality and domestic life that give shape and meaning to women's lives, are not included as part of curriculum. Socialist feminists, in accordance with radical feminists, criticized liberal reforms as inadequate in rectifying gender inequalities. They argue that we cannot understand inequality that women face only in terms of gender, we must also account for the effects of class and other factors, such as "race" and ethnicity, which define the experiences of women. In general, it can be argued that feminist pedagogy is concerned with "teaching and learning liberation".

One of the basic arguments of all feminists is to develop standpoints upon which we can explore and analyze the varied experiences of women. Queer theory and various theories of "race" (discussed below) are also examples of **standpoint theory**. They view the world from specific vantage points much like the way Marx viewed the social world from the standpoint of the proletariat. For example, antiracist theorists look at the effects of racism from the perspectives of racialized groups and individuals. Afrocentric theory is another example. Native American theory and theories of masculinity could also be considered as standpoint theories (Ritzer, 2000, p. 225).

In the next section, we explore the basic ideas of the queer theory.

Queer Theory

Classical sociological issues have been silent about issues of sexuality and specifically homosexuality (Ritzer, 2000, p. 224). Queer theory questions the power of heterosexuality, and subverts the construction of **heteronormativity**. *Heteronormativity* is the assumption that heterosexuality "is/ should be the normal (and legal) way of interactions" (Glesne, 2011, p. 10). Queer theory asserts that there no single identities, such as homosexuality. They suggest that all identities are multiple and composite. Identities are not fixed but are unstable and based on exclusionary notions and characteristics. That is, who we are is a composite of several interrelated or isolated identity components. Our identities are informed by our sex, sexuality, age, "race", ethnicity, gender, occupation, nationality, and religious beliefs. Our identities are dynamic and changing. For example, an immigrant from Brazil may refer to him/herself after living in Canada for more than ten years as a Canadian-Brazilian rather than simply as a Brazilian or a Canadian. As an under graduate student, you define yourself as such in conversations with others. But as soon as you receive your Ph.D. and get a job as an instructor, you begin to identify yourself as a professor of, for example, sociology. Queer theorists claim that our identities can be figured and configured in a number of ways by the social actors and others with whom they interact. Their concern is not simply with bringing equality between "homosexuals" and "heterosexuals". They do not just focus on the oppression and liberation of the homosexual subject (Seidman, as cited in Ritzer, 2000, p. 223). Rather, they also analyze the institutional practices of discourses that produce knowledge and the ways in which knowledge organizes sexualized social life. They debunk how these discourses result in the oppression of peoples labeled homosexual. This theory rejects the normalized binary of homo-hetero, and accounts for a diversity of possibilities between the two (Ritzer, 2000, p. 224). For example, consider the discourse of "faggot", which separates between a homosexual individual and a heterosexual person. This discourse considers the latter as "superior" to the former. That is, heterosexism is assumed to be the norm and anyone who is not one is considered as abnormal. It assumes that the only acceptable normative relationship is between a man and a woman, and the only acceptable form of sexual interaction is one that involves a penis and a vagina. In short, queer theory focuses on those practices and discourses that sexualize "bodies, identities, social relations, knowledges, cultures, and social institutions" (Seidman, as cited in Ritzer, 2000, pp. 224–225).

Queer theory is an interdisciplinary paradigm with a crossover from feminism and critical race theory. It advocates social justice for sexually marginalized and oppressed persons. As already mentioned, it interrogates and disrupts the normalization of heterosexuality. In addition, it explores how sexuality is defined and enacted differently across diverse historical and cultural contexts; what counts as '*normal*' varies from one context to the next. Finally, it posits that identities are not fixed or static; thus, the term "*queer*" is more dynamic and problematic than fixed binary categories such '*gay*'/'*straight*' (Mann, 2011; Littlejohn & Foss, 2008).

Queer scholars have identified several tenets (commandments) that underlie queer theorizing. **First**, everything that makes up who we are is a result of discourse. **Second**, we must use terms that avoid moral judgment. **Third**, all types of sexuality are socially constructed through regulatory discourses within language. **Fourth**, queer theory does not have a clear definition; it ranges from the relations between sex, gender, and sexual desire to anything that goes against the mainstream ideology. **Fifth**, humans are not rational. **Sixth**, due to the power relations of society humans are very much lost in an entanglement of power/knowledge regimes, which gives some room for resistance, but also creates a large amount of control. **Seventh**, there does not have to be a relation between sex, gender roles, and sexual relations. Sexuality is created through discourse, so heterosexuality and homosexuality do not actually exist, but are merely products of systems of power/knowledge. **Eighth**, beware of identity. The self is created through a process that makes false variations, which can be used to exploit. Any conception of a fixed identity must be critically questioned. **Ninth**, deconstruct all sexual categories by questioning mainstream sexual classifications, and in doing so show how all have been constructed. **Tenth**, the most effective way to take apart the dominant heteronormative culture is by going against normative ideas of gender, and sexuality, and by ultimately promoting anti-homophobic politics (Mann, 2011).

Part Seven

Theories of Racialization and Racism

There are several characteristics that highlight most theories of racialization and racism that we explore in the following sections (Ritzer, 2000, p. 225):

1. They reject universalistic theories that justify the power position of elite groups in society. They attempt to empower marginalized groups who lack power.

2. They are not value free theories. They are involved in theoretical and practical research on behalf of those who have been historically excluded from positions of power. Their aim is to change the world and the *social structures* of *power* and the prospects of people of marginalized backgrounds.

3. Their goal is to be inclusive and to work with disenfranchised groups to begin to think about equality.

4. They not only focus on disrupting the *social structures* but also how we come to think about the *social structures* by making the intellectual world more open to diverse and silenced histories of dominated peoples.

5. They do not distinguish between "scientific" theories and various types of narratives that are produced by marginalized people about their lives and their conditions.

6. They are not only critical of the *status quo*, but are involved in self-critique.

7. They recognize that their research and theories are specific to particular historical periods and social and cultural contexts.

Whiteness Studies

Whiteness is "the quality or state of being white" (Merriam-Webster Online Dictionary, 2012). This definition is simple, but only deceptively so. Behind the façade of simplicity lies a phalanx of normative meanings, value-laden assumptions, power, and privilege. It's exactly what hides behind this façade of simplicity that scholars of Whiteness Studies seek to expose the structural *power* of Whiteness.

Like any other category, Whiteness is a sociohistorical and cultural construct. Jay (2012, p. 1), for example, observed that,

> [h]istorically, white people are an invented "race," made up of various ethnic groups perceived to have a common ancestry in parts of Europe and self-proclaimed to be superior biologically and culturally to other "races." White, was invented as a category when previous notions of national "races" (French, German, English, Norwegian, etc.) were lumped together to create a single powerful coalition. "White" is thus a political fiction that has been used by one social group to harm and oppress others.

That is, there have not always been White people. For instance, Whiteness Studies scholar, David Roediger (1999), noted that many Western and Southern European immigrants to the US in the early twentieth century were not viewed as White. The Irish, Italians, Hungarians, and Jews were historically considered as non-White. For example, Blacks were referred to as "smoked Irishmen" and Irishmen as "Black inside out". Many non-English Europeans had to "earn" their Whiteness.

White Studies is an attempt to think critically about how White skin preference has operated systematically, structurally, and sometimes unconsciously as a dominant force in Euro-American, and indeed in global, society and culture. The main assumptions underpinning Whiteness Studies can be summarized as follows. **First**, "Whiteness" denotes White supremacy, a term derived from the historical practice of racism based on **Eurocentrism** (See Box 10.13 - White Supremacy). **Second**, the term "White" is a legal term and social designator. **Third**, the term "superior White race" is the notion that the "White race" naturally deserved special privileges (See Box 10.14 - Privilege and White Privilege) and protections. **Fourth**, Whiteness is both visible and invisible. For example,

BOX 10.13 - White Supremacy

White supremacy is the belief that the "White race" is superior to the non-White "races". It is a political and ideological construct that advocates the social, political, economic, and cultural dominance by Whites (Wildman, 1996). Central to the understanding of White supremacy are the notions of **Eurocentrism** and **hegemony**. White supremacy is rooted in *Eurocentrism*, the tendency of regarding people with White pigmentation as "superior" to those with darker skin colour. The desire for *hegemony*, the domination and control of non-White people, is a driving force behind White supremacy. Historically, White supremacy was the basis of the decisions and actions that have had world-shattering implications. From the slave trade to colonialism, neocolonialism, and current processes of globalizations and from the near extermination of the Native Americans to the ongoing "international war" on terrorism, White supremacist ideology inherent in domestic and foreign policies and action has wreaked and continues to exact unspeakable havoc on non-White racialized groups, globally. White supremacy has resulted in antiblack, Islamophobia, and anti-Semitic violence.

White supremacy is both overt and subtle. Overt White supremacist ideology was dominant in the United States before the American Civil War and for decades after the Reconstruction. In large areas of the United States this included the holding of non-Whites (specifically African Americans) in chattel slavery. The outbreak of the Civil War saw the desire to uphold White supremacy cited as a cause for state secession and the formation of the Confederate States of America. White supremacy also informed the Apartheid rule in South Africa and parts of Europe at various time periods; most notably under Nazi Germany's Third Reich.

In some parts of the United States, many people who were considered non-White were disenfranchised (i.e., barred from government office and prevented from holding most government jobs well into the second half of the twentieth century). White leaders often viewed First Nations and Aborigines in the US, Canada, and Australia as obstacles to economic and political progress, rather than as settlers in their own right (Fredrickson, 1981). Moreover, many European-settled countries bordering the Pacific Ocean limited immigration and naturalization of individuals from the Asian Pacific countries. Many Canadian provinces and US states banned international marriage through **antimiscegenation laws** until the third quarter of the twentieth century, when these laws were declared unconstitutional. South Africa maintained its White supremacist Apartheid system until the early 1990s.

White people occupy important positions in the Euro-American landscape, in the media, business, and the education system. In addition, White people tend to think of themselves as "colourless" and "race-less". "Race" and colour is associated with non-White people; Whites are "just people," "just human". As such, they become invisible. **Fifth**, Whiteness is assumed to define the centre as the quintessential element of the national culture. It does not need to be spoken or mentioned; it is the default condition of normalcy. For example, in the US and Canada, journalists tend to refer to the "black thief," "the Hispanic politician," or the "Asian author", but hardly "the White bank robber". In the 2008 and 2012 presidential elections in the US, Candidate and President Barrack Obama respectively

BOX 10.14 - Privilege and White Privilege

Modern racism emerged as a way of enabling and justifying "White supremacy." The theory of "White supremacy" was necessary in order to rationalize practises, such as colonialism, imperialism, class exploitation, and slavery. White privilege stems from and feeds into White supremacy. What is white privilege? Let's first explore the concept "privilege".

Privilege is the interlocking systems of advantage often outside of consciousness, such as the security and comfort of living in a culture in which aspects of identity like one's language, religion, "race", gender, history, and values are normative. Privilege exists when one group has something of value that is denied to others simply because of the groups to which they belong, rather than because of anything they have done or failed to do (Johnson, 2001).

Privilege is:

a) a right, advantage, or immunity granted to or enjoyed by dominant groups beyond the common advantage of all others;

b) an exemption in many particular cases from certain burdens or liabilities; and

c) a special advantage or benefit provided to the dominant groups justified based on ideas, such as divine rights, natural advantages, gifts of fortune, genetic endowments, and social relations.

Privilege integrates **material** forms of privilege that arise from institutionalized inequalities and taken-for-granted cultural practices. Different **social locations** interact and work together to privilege some and oppress others. Thus, if some group is privileged, another group is oppressed. For example, Whites dominate non-Whites, men dominate women, and the affluent dominate the poor. As Collins (1990, pp. 221–238) has suggested, all members of given social groups experience varying degrees of privilege, depending upon their locations in relation to the *matrix of domination*. As we mentioned, the term was coined by Collins (1990) to argue that oppression based on "race", class, gender, and sexuality exists in an interlocking system. The central premise of *matrix of domination* is that oppression is overdetermined (i.e., caused by multiple factors). In other words, the systems of oppression are not limited to "race" and gender, but extend beyond these categories to include class, sexuality, ability/disability, and others.

McIntosh (2001) has identified two types of privilege:

a) **unearned advantages,** which denotes to those rewards that are given to individuals due to their class, gender, "race", ethnicity, and age rather than due to their merits and levels of hard work (not all individuals are entitled to these advantages and once unearned entitlements are restricted to certain groups, they are considered as stemming from the individual); and

b) **conferred dominance,** which involves giving one group *power* over another.

Privilege is defined in terms of domination over positions of *power* and legitimation of those forms of domination.

> **White privilege** is a form of privilege, and refers to a set of customs and practises that reflect and reenforce the system of White supremacy. It entails the advantages, rights, entitlements, immunities, prerogatives and assumed dispensations of *power* positions people of White skin have over non-White people. White privilege is not about some deliberate plot or conspiracy. It points out that White people view their social, cultural, and economic experiences as a norm that everyone should adapt to and experience, rather than as an advantaged position that is maintained at the expense of others. This normative or taken-for-granted assumption implicitly constrains discussions of racial inequality within the dominant liberal discourse of equality. Such explanations are often limited to factors that are considered specific to disadvantaged racial groups, who are assumed as having failed to achieve the norm due to cultural poverty. At the same time, solutions proposed to deal with structural forms of inequality focus on what can be done to help those groups achieve the "normal" standards experienced by Whites rather than how to transform the system of White privilege (McIntosh, 2001).

was referred to by the US media as the African American or Black candidate or president; yet, his contenders, John McCain and Mitt Romney, were never called "the White presidential candidate".

In general, as Jay (2012, p. 1) stated, "Whiteness" is the practice of institutionalizing White supremacy, which goes as far back as the seventeenth century. "White" appeared as a legal term and social designator that determined who could vote, who could be enslaved, who could be a citizen, who could attend which schools and churches, who could marry whom, and who could drink from what water fountain. As Jay (2012, p. 1) also noted, "[t]housands of other legal and social regulations were built upon the fiction that there existed a superior "white" race that deserved special privileges and protections". While many of these legal and social regulations supporting White supremacy were outlawed in the 1960s thanks to the modern Civil Rights Movement, "the power of the fiction of 'whiteness' continues to the present day" (Jay, 2012, p. 1). It is in this light that a group of scholars have focused on Whiteness as the object of their analysis. These scholars argue that at the core of Whiteness is an ideological construction that considers those properties supposedly unique to White people as properties that are used to conclude that they are a "superior race". Whiteness is normative; that is, it is the norm upon which others are judged. "Whiteness", then, is also a legal construct that determines the distribution of wealth, power, human rights, and citizenship in a nation-state (See Chapter Eight) (Lipsitz, 2009). The focus on Whiteness should be read in the context of **critical race** and **postcolonial theories** that are the focus of the next sections.

Critical Race Theory

Critical race theory (CRT) represents the work of a group of progressive legal scholars and activists, including Derrick Bell, Alan Freeman, Patricia Williams, Angela Harris, Richard Delgado, Mari Matsuda, Charles Lawrence, and Kimberle Williams Crenshaw. Grounding their work in the legal debates over US civil liberties, CRT scholars analyze the persistence of racism in US society despite legal inroads over the last century. It investigates the intersection of "race", class, ethnicity, gender, and sexuality to explain prejudice and discrimination. It is "a strategy that accounts for the role of race and racism in education and works toward the elimination of racism as part of a larger goal of eliminating other forms of subordination such as gender, class, and sexual orientation" (Matsuda, Lawrence, Delgado, & Crenshaw, 1993). CRT developed from the Civil Rights Movement with a social justice focus. It interrogates socially constructed racial hierarchies in society and subjugated knowledge of racial "minorities" from an intersectional perspective. The central task of CRT is to disrupt and debunk *Eurocentric ideologies* of meritocracy, neutrality, equal opportunity, and colour-blindness: "As a form of oppositional scholarship, critical race theory challenges the universality of white experience/and judgment as the authoritative standard that binds people of color and normatively measures, directs, controls, and regulates the terms of proper thought, expression, presentation, and behavior" (Crenshaw, Gotanda, Peller, & Thomas, 1995).

CRT also explores alternatives to discriminatory rules, policies, and practices, and offers solutions to ameliorate conditions of disadvantage and oppression. It proposes that counter-storytelling legitimizes voices from racialized groups to legitimately speak about their experiences of oppression and exclusion. Recently, CRT has conflated with feminist theory to generate a new theory, Critical Race and Feminist Theory (CRFT). CRFT puts *power* relations at the centre of the discourse on the intersectionality of gender, "race", class, and other forms of social inequities. It calls for a broader and deeper understanding of the lives of women, particularly racialized women, based on the nature of their multiple and intersecting identities (Santiago, 2011).

In general, CRT is guided by the following five tenets (Santiago, 2011)

1. The centrality of race and racism in society: CRT asserts that racism is a permanent component of life in any given multiracial and polyethnic society.

2. The Challenge to *Dominant Ideology*: CRT challenges the claims of neutrality, objectivity, colourblindness, and meritocracy in society.

3. The Centrality of Experiential Knowledge: CRT asserts that the experiential knowledge of "people of colour" is appropriate, legitimate, and an integral part to analyzing and understanding racial inequality.

4. The Interdisciplinary Perspective: CRT challenges the *ahistoricism (i.e., the decontextualized and dehistoricized)* and the *unidisciplinary* focuses of most analyses and insists that "race" and racism be placed in both a contemporary and historical context using interdisciplinary methods.

5. The Commitment to Social Justice: CRT is a framework that is committed to a social justice agenda to eliminate all forms of subordination of people.

In short, the critical race theorists argue that "race" is so entrenched in our institutions and structures of society that it seems normal and is not problematized (Glesne, 2011, p. 10). They view "race" as a socially constructed category that is used to identify people and classify them. They examine how certain groups of people are included or excluded from positions of *power* due to the colour of their skin or other racialized categories of *difference*. They explore how social and political forms of *power* function and operate in different institutional forms with the consequence of including or excluding people based on their racial category. Related to CRT is the proliferation of postcolonial thought, which we briefly explore in the next section.

Postcolonialism

The term **postcolonial** is used to describe the variety of events and issues that took place and continue to ensue after the end of official colonialism (See Chapter Eight). **Postcolonialism** (also referred variously to as Post-Colonial Studies, Post-Colonial Theory and Post-Colonialism) is an interdisciplinary field of study involving all humanities, arts, and social sciences, devoted to the study of all cultures affected by the imperial process. Postcolonial theory focuses on the following main concerns:

a) the study of cultures formerly (or currently) colonized;

b) power struggles between colonial, neocolonial, and colonized cultures; and

c) intersection of cultures.

Postcolonial scholars also direct their attention to issues of *power*, subordination, "race", gender inequality, and class warfare, interrogating the impact of the legacies of colonization on the lives of the colonized and the colonizers. In addition, they study not only lingering vestiges of the colonial and imperial order, but also how these vestiges pervade the cultures of the formerly colonized peoples, particularly in the tri-continents of Africa, Asia and Latin America. Furthermore, they analyse the postcolonial condition and debunk the notion that the transition to independence is smooth, or unproblematic. Lastly, postcolonialists examine the ways in which the colonial past has shaped the social, political, and economic experience of the colonized countries.

Postcolonialism adopts a *dialectical* and *praxis-oriented* discourse and epistemology. Its overarching goal is not only to construct alternative, *counter-hegemonic*, and anti-Eurocentric discourses, but also to combat the lasting effects of colonialism on native cultures. It is not simply concerned with recovering these past cultures, but learning how the world can move beyond this period together, towards a place of mutual respect. According to Littlejohn and Foss (2008), postcolonialism is concerned with how discourse in the Western world legitimizes certain *power structures* and reinforces colonizing practices (See Orientalism in Chapter Eight).

Littlejohn and Foss (2008) noted that postcolonialism is devoted to understanding *Eurocentrism*, imperialism, and the process of colonization and decolonization (See Chapter Eight). The focus is on neocolonialism as it occurs in contemporary discourse about otherness. Neocolonialism, a term coined by Kwame Nkrumah, relates to the invasion and exploitation of the human and natural resources of the so-called "developing" countries by the imperial powers, including Britain, France, Portugal, Spain, Belgium, The Netherlands, Germany, etc. It also means the domination of a "developing" nation by international corporations attracted by cheap labour and manipulable political and legal systems (See Chapter Eight).

As we discussed in Chapter Eight, the colonial era, also known as imperialism, lasted from the late fifteenth to the early twentieth century, with World War II marking the official end to all European colonization. During this time period, European nations experienced a renaissance of wealth and arts. The most prominent nations that are generally associated with colonialism are England, Spain, Portugal, France, and the Dutch. The expanded power that these nations gained came at the cost of many "developing" nations throughout the Americas, Africa, and Asia. The colonies were transformed into plantations and mines of the imperialists as they plundered not only the natural resources, such as gold, diamonds, rubber, and iron ore, but also their human resources in their quest for *power* and aggrandizement. Colonization was characterized by massive reorganization and appropriation of nations and territories. Countless atrocities were visited upon the colonial peoples, including institutionalized slavery, racism, enforced migration, murder, culturecide, torture, and genocide. Through a process of *indoctrination* (brainwashing) the European colonizers managed to control the larger populations of natives. They destroyed or replaced the ancient cultures, replacing them with *Eurocentric* beliefs and values. *Eurocentric* beliefs supplanted the ideological, political, economic, and cultural values of the colonized peoples. The devastating effects of these actions can be seen throughout the world today. Many Indigenous peoples have lost their languages, religions, and national and cultural identities.

A growing number of scholars from the Global South or the ex-colonies have, since the fall of European imperialism, written seminal works on the colonial and postcolonial condition. These scholars sought to expose and deconstruct the racist, imperialist nature of *Eurocentric* assumptions. Many of these authors found inspiration through Feminist and Marxist teachings.

The founding proponents of postcolonial scholarship include Gayatri Spivak, whose work illuminates the subjectivity of subaltern subjects and the representation of marginalized voices in social research; Homi Bhabha, whose work unravels various conceptions of the nation and suggests that transnationality produces hybrid identities (See Box 10.15 - Transnationalism); Ranajit Guha and the 'Subaltern Studies Group' whose works insist on rewriting history from the perspective of the colonized and call for decentring the production of academic knowledge; Kwame Nkrumah, whose works focused on the vestiges and impact of colonialism and imperialism on the newly independent

BOX 10.15 - Transnationalism

Constructions and reproductions of national and ethnic identities are affected by the consequences of globalization. The rise in global migration has added to cultural diversity, economic inequality, and *power* differentials, nationally and locally, resulting in the formation of "transnational identities" (Satzewich & Liodakis, 2007). The globalization of the economy has also had tremendous negative effects on the "Third World" and in "developing" countries that have resulted in the differential treatment of individuals and groups in society and in political, cultural, economic, and educational systems (Bello, 2002). Transnationalism is a discourse of analyzing the movements of people, ideas, goods, capital, and services across nation-states in the context of globalization.

Amir Mirfakhraie (2008) defined transnationalism as a process consisting of multistranded social relations that link together groups within and between nation-states through "social fields that cross [and intersect] geographic, cultural, and political borders" and are based on multiple relationships: "economic, social, organizational, religious, and political" (Mirfakhraie, 2008; Basch, Glick Schiller, & Szanton Blanc, 1994, p. 7).

Transnationalism is a theoretical perspective that investigates sociopolitical relations and institutions and ethnic, racialized, class, and gender diversities and inequalities from local/global perspectives. Transnationalism is influenced by the idea of transmigration. Basch, Glick Schiller, and Szanton Blanc (1994, p. 7) defined transmigration as the "process by which [non-Western nationalities in their respective countries and] immigrants [in various parts of the world] forge and sustain multistranded social relations that link together their societies of origin, [colonial and imperialist states] and settlement. We call these processes 'transnationalism' to emphasize that many [non-Western nationals and] immigrants today build social fields that cross [and intersect] geographic[al], cultural, and political borders. [Citizens of various nation-states and] [i]mmigrants who develop and maintain multiple relationships—familial, economic, social, organizational, religious, and political—[are now interacting with one another in ways] that span borders we call 'transmigrants'".

Transnationalism is a discourse that accounts for the dialectical relationships between the globalization of capital, the reproduction of hegemonic relations, and formations of resistance movements, oppositional organizations, and discursive fields that cross ethno-national boundaries and influence/(re)shape social relations in both the East and the West (Basch, Glick Schiller & Szanton Blanc, 1994). This perspective focuses on the effects of absent relations on the formation of the self, development policies, and economic and political relations and structures at both local and global levels. Transnationalism is concerned with the creation of "hybrid" cultures and the extent to which local cultures incorporate and transform aspects of other cultures as their own. This theoretical perspective accounts for the outcome and consequences of conditions and social relations that impelled "non-Western" nation-states to modernize/develop through "emulation" and "mimicking" of the West, both during and after the colonial era.

Transnationalism critically evaluates and interrogates the one-sided interrelationship between, for example, the Orient and Occident. As a theoretical lens, transnationalism points to the multifaceted and overlapping sets of interactions and processes of identity formations within the context of postmodernity (See Chapter Nine) that affect ethnic and racialized groups across the world (Satzewich & Liodakis, 2007, p. 215). As both a process and discourse, it is critical of the process of the incorporation, rejection, and naturalization of the Enlightenment project in many non-Western and Western countries, by accounting for how the "language of modernity", in the form of binary oppositions, such as "us" and "them", and other forms of essentialized and bias categories, informs the worldview of social actors without a critical evaluation of their Euro- and ethnocentric "characteristics".

Transnationalism is a discourse that goes beyond the "limited" notions of the West and the East in analyzing socioeconomic, cultural, and political relations. Geographical localities are viewed and analyzed across time and space. As sites of "political engagement" and "cultural reproduction", transnationalism refers to the intersections of the fluidity of citizenship rights, hybrid identities, social institutions, and educational and everyday practices (Satzewich & Liodakis, 2007, pp. 215–219). A transnational perspective accounts for the multifaceted characteristics of ideas and views through which individuals and groups "represent" and "rank" other ethno-nationalities and members of different political/religious groups. Transnationalism problematizes nation-centric approaches to citizenship and social, legal, economic, cultural, and educational relations by offering a multifaceted approach to insider/outsider divisions. As Held argued, "the capacity of the nation-state to protect individual autonomy is now gone" due to the globalization of culture, politics, the military, and social relations (as cited in Kymlicka, 2001, p. 235). The transnational characteristic of the interdependence of nation-states has resulted in the inability of "nation-states to determine crucial questions about their [citizens'] life-chances" (as cited in Kymlicka, 2001, p. 235). This transnational interdependence can no longer be ignored (Kymlicka, 2001, p. 235). As Held (1996) maintained, nation-states' policies are now affected by external and global decision-making bodies that also function as new sites for "democratic political action" (Kymlicka, 2001, p. 236). In addition, as 'rights' are becoming more "predicated on residency, not citizen status, the distinction between citizen and status" is eroding (Koopmans & Statham, 2000b, p. 191). Koopmans and Statham (2000b, p. 191) point out that this has resulted in "a decoupling of identity and rights, the two main elements of citizenship: 'Rights increasingly assume universality, legal uniformity, and abstractness, and are defined at the global level.... As an identity, national citizenship [based on a single cultural model shared by all citizens {Koopmans & Statham, 2000a:20}] ... still prevails. But in terms of its translation into rights and privileges, it is no longer a significant construction'".

In discussing global issues in the context of national boundaries, transnationalism allows the researcher to go beyond a bounded and unilinear understanding of national formations, citizenship rights, migration trends, educational policy, and economic relations between and within the East ("developing" nations) and the West ("developed" countries) as fixed geographical boundaries. The East and the West are themselves saturated with *differences* and similarities that find their sources in both Eastern and Western histories. Neither the West nor the East is considered as a privileged space/location; rather, the two are viewed as extensions of one another. Their meanings are not considered as stable and static, but as dynamic, ever changing, and contradictory. The East is not conceived as a "victim" of the West, but as a category which consists of actors with varied, conflicting, and at times, similar agencies. Although such a theoretical perspective focuses on one ethno-national category, it does so in relation to other forms of 'otherness' in many Western and non-Western parts of the world. They are considered as constructions that are given meanings through discourses of domination, subjugation, resistance, cooperation, and exploitation. It is in this light that through the discourse of transnationalism we can account for:

- the construction of "identities" across time and space in the context of the effects of colonialism and global capitalism in both the East and the West as floating categories rather than as fixed entities;

- the movement of ideas, perspectives, groups, and peoples between nation-states; and,
- how representations of otherness in both the East and the West have been (re)constructed, altered, and maintained from a historical perspective.

Source: Mirfakhraie, 2008.

states of the tri-continents of Africa, Asia, and Latin America; and Franz Fanon, whose seminal work analysed the lingering impact of the psychology of oppression and racial oppression on the leaders of the postcolonial states. The writings of Aime Cesaire Leopold Senghor also make valuable contributions to postcolonial theory and discourse. In the next section, we briefly discuss Fanon's ideas.

Franz Fanon

Fanon is one of the earliest writers associated with postcolonialism. He is best known for his books, *Black Skin, White Masks* (1952) and *The Wretched of the Earth* (1961). In his books, Fanon pointed out the hypocrisies of racism that are woven into Western culture. Pointing to the fact that Whiteness in western culture always equates to "virginity, justice, and truth", Fanon described colonialism and its racist justifications as the source of violence and discord throughout the "Third World". This was a stark contrast to the Europeans' view that the Western powers were saving the "heathens" from their violent natures and enlightening them to the "truth" of Western thought.

Building on Hegelian dialectics, Marxist theory, Freudian psychoanalysis, critical race theory, and global political economy, Fanon provided a nuanced and in-depth analysis of the colonized subject, the problem of nationalism, and the path to liberation. With his expertise in psychiatry, he was able to delve into the psyche of the colonized subjects, both under foreign tutelage and after nominal independence. He saw the "African personality" as afflicted by what Du Bois called **double consciousness** in his book, *Souls of Black Folk* (1903). *Double consciousness* is used to describe how blacks viewed themselves through White perspectives while maintaining their own self-definitions. Fanon defined and explained colonialism and decolonization from a political, philosophical, historical, and sociocultural perspective.

Employing Hegelian and Marxist dialectics, he defined colonization as the process of creating two conflicting societies, one of the colonizer and one of the colonized. The colonizer and the colonized were mutually constitutive. He observed that colonization barbarizes the colonized so that the colonizer can, in good conscience, take everything from the oppressed. Colonialism is the establishment, maintenance, acquisition, and expansion of colonies in one territory by people from another territory. The core or metropole claimed sovereignty over the colony. Colonialism represents systematic "underdevelopment" of the periphery to benefit of the core (Harris & Johnson, 1996).

Fanon maintained that the ideological basis of colonialism is *White supremacy* and racism, adding that the "white man's burden", in its nineteenth-century version, involved extraordinary violence, approximating genocide, against its supposed beneficiaries. A major component of this violence was the collection of cultural images and themes by which the colonized people came to be known by the colonial power. The status of colonial subjects, of being "known" by the colonizer, simultaneously enforced and rationalized the colonial power's dominance of Indigenous populations, giving imperialism a fundamental racial dimension (Hayes III, 1996, p. 17).

Fanon's much celebrated book, *The Wretched of the Earth*, served as the handbook for political leaders' fight to decolonize their countries during the liberation struggles and after independence. In *The Wretched of the Earth*, he stressed that decolonization was not a matter of simply the removal of colonial structures, but especially, the deconstruction of colonial legacies in the mindset of formerly colonized peoples. Fanon explored the psychological dimensions of colonialism: how colonization created a racist system that can go as far as convincing the colonized that they are what the colonists tell them they are. He pointed out that the colonized strived to be like the colonizer, to become "him", to be White: "…The total result looked for by colonial domination was indeed to convince the natives that colonialism came to lighten their darkness" (Fanon, 1961, p. 210).

According to Fanon, to end colonization, first the colonized must see the myth that has been placed on them. Fanon debunked the commonly held view, which peddled by the colonizers that the colonial subject merely reacted to the colonizer's violence by depicting both the colonizer and the colonized as a source of violence. The colonized, he argued, violently resisted rather than reacted to the colonizer's violence. Describing how the two mutually constituted each other, Fanon demonstrated how the violence of colonization both bred and constrained violence within the colonized, simultaneously enabling their colonization and providing the very *power* through which the colonized peoples might use to liberate themselves. Such liberation was only possible, he claimed, through revolutionary violence (Fanon, 1961, p. 36).

Fanon explained in great detail that revolutionary groups should look to the **lumpenproletariat** for the force needed to expel colonists. The *lumpenproletariat*, in traditional Marxist theories, are considered the lowest, most degraded stratum of the proletariat, especially criminals, vagrants, and the unemployed, who lacked *class consciousness*. Fanon used the term to refer to those inhabitants of colonized countries who are not involved in industrial production, particularly peasants living outside the cities. He argued that only this group, unlike the industrial proletariat, has sufficient independence from the colonists to successfully make a revolution against them. The peasant, he emphasized, had not reaped the fruits of colonialism at all, and hence were the true revolutionary force. He wrote, "And it is clear that in the colonial countries the peasants alone are revolutionary, for they have nothing to lose and everything to gain. The starving peasant, outside the class system is the first among the exploited to discover that only violence pays. For him, there is no compromise, no possible coming to terms; colonization and decolonization simply a question of relative strength" (Fanon, 1961, p. 19).

Conclusion

In this chapter, we explored the main arguments of several classical and contemporary theories and social thinkers. We suggest that a multi-theoretical perspective allows students of sociology to develop a more comprehensive understanding of social issues, from local, national, and global perspectives.

Chapter Review Questions

1. Define any five of the following terms and provide an example for each: the matrix of domination, double jeopardy, multiple jeopardy, queer theory, hegemony, counter-hegemony, heterosexism, heteronormativity, and transnationalism.

2. What does Bourdieu mean by social and cultural capital? By 'habitus'? By 'doxa'?

3. What does Gramsci's theory of hegemony say about how the ruling class rules?

4. Why is Hegel important to critical theory? How did he influence Marx?

5. How did Levi-Strauss apply structuralism to myth? What basic assumption did he make about the way myths in separate cultures are connected to each other?

6. What does logocentrism mean?

7. What does Foucault mean by 'power/knowledge'? How does he apply this idea to the history of prisons and forms of punishment?

8. How does Weber's focus on subjective meaning affect his methodology? What does he mean by 'ideal types'? How do these fit into his *Verstehen* approach to sociology?

9. What are the main characteristics of traditional, charismatic, and legal forms of authority? Why does he think we are trapped in an 'iron cage' of rationality?

10. Why does Weber think that the Protestant ethic was a key element in the development of capitalism? Are any aspects of this ethic still alive today?

11. How does Giddens define structure, system, and the duality of structure? How do these fit into his theory of human agency? Is Giddens a purely micro-social theorist?

12. Define symbolic interactionism and state three of its central premises.

13. Outline Goffman's Dramaturgy.

14. Distinguish between front stage behavior and backstage behavior.

15. What did Cooley mean by the 'looking-glass self'?

16. What are Blumer's three principles of symbolic interactionism? Give examples of each from your everyday life.

17. What, for Goffman, are the three regions where the self performs?

18. What are some ways that performers idealize, control, and misrepresent their performances in everyday life?

19. Outline Berger and Luckmann's theory of the duality of structure and agency.

20. What is 'ethnomethodology'? Why are breaching experiments important to ethnomethodologists? Give an example of such an experiment.

21. What were the main objectives of First Wave feminism, and how did these objectives differ from those of the Second Wave? Which theorist in this chapter is closest to being a First Wave feminist?

22. What are the main beliefs of radical feminists such as Dworkin and MacKinnon? How do their beliefs differ from those of liberal feminism?

23. What is queer theory's attitude toward the subject and sexual identity? Evaluate it.

24. Is queer theory too tolerant of marginal forms of sexuality? Should the state police sexuality at all, or does it have no place in the bedrooms of the nation?

25. Betty Friedan in her book, *The Second Stage* (1983), proposed reconciling the challenges of the many possibilities created by broader opportunities for women in work and public life with a need for love, home, and family. Comment.

26. Define structuralism and poststructuralism. What is the main difference between the two concepts?

27. What is neo-Marxism? Briefly explain the differences in the point of view of Classical Marxists and neo-Marxists.

28. Define the terms discourse and power. How are the two terms connected?

29. How does Marx's notion of ideology differ from Gramsci's concept of hegemony?

30. Comment on Foucault's notion of the disappearance of punishment as spectacle.

31. Explain Foucault's theory of surveillance and apply it to how any institution in Canada uses surveillance to control Canadians.

32. What's the difference between descriptive and normative social theory? Which path should social theory take?

33. Identify any two functions of theory and give one example for each.

34. Using either of the epistemological or ontological approaches, answer the following question, "How do we know what we know"?

35. What is critical constructivism? Briefly explain.

36. What did Durkheim mean by a 'social fact'? What are two types of solidarity that he outlined?

37. What is Parsons' theory of action and pattern variables? Apply each to your life.

38. What is the AGIL paradigm? Explain by applying it to the university as a social system.

39. What are some of the basic criticisms of functionalism? How did Merton deal with them?

40. Briefly outline the basic premises of the conflict paradigm.

41. Define class consciousness and false consciousness. Briefly explain the differences between the two terms.

42. Briefly comment on the following statement: "The history of all hitherto existing societies is the history of class struggle".

43. What is the superstructure in Marxian terms? How is it different from the base?

44. Define any two of the following terms and give an example: forces of production, relations of production, mode of production, and surplus value.

45. In which ways are conflict and functionalist paradigms similar and different?

46. According to Marx, how is surplus value produced in the capitalist mode of production?

47. Briefly outline Marx's theory of historical materialism.

48. Briefly outline Marx's theory of dialectical materialism.

49. Define the concepts alienation, reification, and false consciousness. How are the three concepts related?

50. Define the terms dialectics and contradiction. How are they related?

51. Define class struggle. How does class struggle play out in Canadian society today?

52. Structural functionalists assume that society is and must always be stable, orderly, peaceful, and harmonious. How do they account for or explain conflict in society?

53. Functionalism is often criticized for its teleologism. What is teleology? Do you think this criticism is fair? Why? Why not?

54. As with any theory, structural functionalism has both merits and demerits. Identify one demerit of the paradigm and attempt to debunk the criticism.

55. Karl Marx and Friedrich Engels declared in their *Communist Manifesto* that the working class would eventually gain class consciousness and rise up and overthrow the capitalist system. In your opinion, why has not Marx's doomsday prediction come to pass?

56. In debunking Hegel's dialectics, Marx is said to have turned Hegel upside down. What exactly does this mean?

57. Using the Marxian concept of contradiction, comment on Marx's declaration that "capitalism has within itself the seed of its own destruction".

58. What is Marx's model of base and superstructure? What does this have to do with historical materialism?

59. How does Marx outline the stages of history? What basic force drives historical change for him?

Critical Thinking Questions

1. Develop your own unique theory.

2. How does Marx's class struggle play out in contemporary Canadian society?

3. Assuming you are invited to give a speech to high school students on the current crisis in the global capitalist economy, using the Marxist theory of capitalist competition, briefly outline the source and logic of the crisis.

Conclusion

Sociology studies social, economic, political, and cultural structures and processes, human relations, and those historical forces and periods that have shaped the world. Sociology has been influenced by several conflicting and contradictory discourses, such as structural functionalism, conflict theory, symbolic interactionism, postindustrial theories, feminism, queer studies, poststructuralism, post-modernism, and postcolonial theories, to name a few. These discourses, we have argued, allow us to construct knowledge and theoretical frameworks about the economy, politics, culture, and society in order to analyze human relations from multiple lenses and perspectives. Sociology in its diversity of theories and paradigms provides us with multiple views to think about, imagine, and talk about social reality.

Sociological knowledge enables us to interrogate and debunk our commonsense understandings and taken-for-granted assumptions, as we begin to critique structural and historical conditions of oppression that many groups have faced in various parts of the world during different historical periods. We hope that you will use this knowledge to transform the conditions that have led to the domination of marginalized peoples, and put an end to various forms of oppression. As Marx maintained, it is not just enough to produce knowledge, but also to act upon it and change the world. By focusing on critical sociology, we aimed at highlighting and bringing to the centre the worldviews, experiences, and standpoints of oppressed groups and their perspectives. We hope that this could serve as a platform for us to start the process of the reconstitution of the world based on social justice paradigms, at both local and global levels. This also requires us to account for how nondominant groups, locally and globally, have also been involved in exploiting and discriminating against other groups. We hope that the discourses and language of critical theories have now become part of your standpoint epistemologies. We believe that approaching sociology as public discourse enables us to become involved in understanding and changing society as we learn to name the world outside the hegemonic control of the dominant societies. By using our sociological imagination, we can move beyond our individual experiences and understand ourselves in the context of social structures and the history of the world. We hope that you continue the conversations introduced in this book outside the classroom and become an ally of the oppressed in their fights for equality and equity.

References & Bibliography

Abu-Laban, Y., & Gabriel, C. (2002). *Selling Diversity: Immigration, multiculturalism, employment equity, and globalization*. Peterborough, Ontario: broadview press.

Allahar, A. (1995). *Sociology and the Periphery: Theories and Issues*. Toronto: Garamond Press.

Allen, J. (1996a). Fordism and Modern Industry. In S. Hall, D. Held, D. Hubert, & K. Thompson (Eds.), *Modernity: An introduction to modern societies* (pp. 280–306). Oxford: Blackwell Publishers.

Allen, J. (1996b). Post-Industrialism/Post-Fordism. In S. Hall, D. Held, D. Hubert, & K. Thompson (Eds.), *Modernity: An introduction to modern societies* (pp. 533–563). Oxford: Blackwell Publishers.

Anderson, B. (1991). *Imagined Communities: Reflections on the Origin and Spread of Nationalism* (Revised ed.). London: Verso.

Anderson, B. S. (2001). Writing the Nation: Textbooks of the Hashemite Kingdom of Jordan. *Comparative Studies of South Asia, Africa and the Middle East, 21* (1 & 2), 5–14.

Anderson, G. L., & K. G. Herr, Eds. (2007). *Encyclopedia of Activism and Social Justice."* Post-Colonialism." Vol. 3. Thousand Oaks, CA: Sage Reference, 2007. pp. 1149–1151.

Apple, M. W. (1979). *Ideology and Curriculum*. London: Routledge & Kegan Paul.

Apple, M. W. (1986). *The Teachers and Texts: A Political Economy of Class and Gender Relations in Education*. New York: Routledge & Kegan Paul.

Apple, M. W. (1999). *Power, Meaning, and Identity: Essays in Critical Educational Studies*. New York: Peter Lang Publishing Inc.

Apple, M. W. (2004). *Ideology and Curriculum* (3rd ed.). New York: Routledge Falmer.

Apple, M. W., & Beyer, L. E. (1988). Social Evaluation of Curriculum. In L.E. Beyer & M.W. Apple (Eds.), *The Curriculum: Problems, Politics and Possibilities* (pp. 334–349). New York: State University of New York.

Apple, M. W., & Christian-Smith, L. K. (Eds.). (1991). *The Politics of the Textbook*. New York: Routledge.

Apple, M. W. (1991). The Politics of the Textbook. In M.W. Apple & L.K. Christian-Smith (Eds.), *The Politics of the Textbook*, (pp. 1–21). New York: Routledge.

Appelrouth, S. & Edls, L. (2012). *Classical and Contemporary Sociological Theory*. Thousand Oaks:Sage.

Arasteh, R. A. (1969). *Education and Social Awakening in Iran, 1850–1968* (2nd ed. enlarged). Leiden: E.J. Brill.

Ashley, D., & Orenstein, D. M. (2001). *Sociological Theory: Classical statements* (5th ed.). Boston: Allyn and Bacon.

Babbie, E. (1986). *Observing Ourselves: Essays in social research*. Belmont, CA: Wadsworth Publishing Company.

Babbie, E. (1998). *The Practice of Social Research* (8th ed.). Belmont, CA: Wadsworth Publishing Company.

Bakan, J. (2004). *The Corporation: The pathological pursuit of profit and power*. Toronto: Penguin Canada.

Baldwin, E., Longhurst, B., McCeacken, S., Ogborn, M., & Smith, G. (2004). *Introducing Cultural Studies* (revised 1st ed.). Harlow, Essex, England: Pearson Education Ltd.

Ballantine, J. H. (2001). *The Sociology of Education: A systematic analysis*. Upper Saddle River, New Jersey: Prentice Hall.

Banani, A. (1961). *The Modernization of Iran, 1921–1941*. Stanford: Stanford University Press.

Banks, J. A. (1981). *Multiethnic Education: Theory and Practice*. Boston: Allyn and Bacon, Inc.

Banks, J. A. (2001). *Cultural Diversity and Education: Foundations, Curriculum and Teaching* (4th ed.). Boston: Allyn and Bacon.

Banks, J. A. (2004). Introduction: Democratic Citizenship Education in Multicultural Societies. In J.A. Banks (Ed.), *Diversity and Citizenship Education: Global Perspectives* (pp. 1–16). San Francisco: Jossey-Bass.

Barakett, J., & Celghorn, A. (2000). *Sociology of Education: A view from Canada* (1st ed.). Toronto: Pearson Education Canada.

Barak, G., Leighton, P., & Falvin, J.. (2010). *Class, Race, Gender, & Crime: The social realities of Justice in America* (3rd ed.). Lanham, Maryland: Rowman & Littlefield Publishers, Inc.

Basch, L., Glick Schiller N., & Szanton Blanc, C. (1994). *Nations Unbound: Transnational Projects, Postcolonial Predicaments, and Deterritorialized Nation-States*. USA: Grodon & Breach.

Bazarnegar Co. (December 2001). IRN 2001/006: CRC Quantitative Study in Iran. Final Report. *UNICEF Iran*. Retrieved January 14, 2005, from http://www.unicef.org/evaldatabase/index_14448.html.

Behdad, A. (1993). Traveling To Teach: Postcolonial critics in the American academy. In C. McCarthy & W. Crichlow (Eds.), *Race, Identity and Representation in Education* (pp. 40–49). New York: Routledge.

Beck, L. (1990). Tribes and the State in Nineteenth- and Twentieth-Century Iran. In P.S. Khoury & J. Kostiner (Eds.), *Tribes and States Formation in the Middle East* (pp. 185–225). Berkeley: University of California Press.

Bello, W. (2002). *Deglobalization: Ideas for a new world economy*. London: Zed Books.

Berezin, M. (1994). Fissured Terrain: methodological approaches and research styles in culture and politics. In D. Crane (Ed.), *The Sociology of Culture* (pp. 91–116). Cambridge, Massachusetts: Blackwell Publishers.

Berger, P.L., & Luckmann, T. (1967). *The Social Construction of Reality: A Treatise in the Sociology of Knowledge*. Garden City, New York: Doubleday Publishing.

Bernal, S. (2011). UCLA's Center for Community College Partnerships, The Netherlands, 2011, (Lecture Notes). Retrieved December 13, 2011

Beyer, L. E., & Apple, M. W. (Eds.). (1988). *The Curriculum: Problems, politics and possibilities*. New York: State University of New York Press.

Bigelow, B. & Peterson, B. (Eds.). (2002). *Rethinking Globalization: Teaching for justice in an unjust world*. Milwaukee, Wisconsin: Rethinking School Press.

Bleasdale, R. (2006). Class Conflict on the Canals of Upper Canada in the 1840s. In L. S. Macdowell, & I. Radforth, *Canadian Working-Class History: Selected readings* (pp. 28–51) (3rd ed.). Toronto: Canadian Scholars' Press.

Blumer, H. (1969). *Symbolic Interaction: Perspective and Method*. Berkeley, CA: University of California Press

Bocock, R. (1996). The Cultural Formations of Modern Societies. In S. Hall, D. Held, D. Hubert & K. Thompson (Eds.), *Modernity: An introduction to modern societies* (pp. 149–183). Cambridge, Massachusetts: Blackwell Publishers.

Bocock, R., & Kenneth, T. (Eds.). (1992). *Social and Cultural Forms of Modernity*. Cambridge: Polity Press in association with Open University Press.

Bourdieu, P. (1987; 1998). *Practical reason: On the theory of action*. Stanford, CA: Stanford University Press.

Bourdieu, P. (1990). *Reproduction in Education, Society and Culture* (Theory, Culture and Society Series), Thousand Oaks, CA: Sage.

Bourdieu, Pierre, (1990), 'Structures, habitus, practices', in The Logic of Practice. Cambridge: Polity, pp. 52–65.

Bourdieu, P. (1984). *Distinction: A Social Critique of the Judgement of Taste*. London: Routledge.

Bourdieu, P. (1997) 'The forms of capital' in A.H. Halsey, H. Lauder, P. Brown and A.S. Wells (eds) *Education: Culture, Economy, Society*, Oxford: Oxford University Press.

Bowden, B. (2003). The Perils of Global Citizenship. *Citizenship Studies*, 7 (3), 349–362.

Bowers, C.A. (2005). *The False Promises of Constructivist Theories of Learning: A global and ecological critique*. New York: Peter Lang Publishing Inc.

Braham, P. (1996). Divisions of Labour. In S. Hall, D. Held, D. Hubert, & K. Thompson (Eds.), *Modernity: An introduction to modern societies* (pp. 307–342). Oxford: Blackwell Publishers.

Briskin, L. (1994). Feminist Pedagogy: Teaching and Learning Liberation. In L. Erwin & D. Maclennan (Eds.), *Sociology of education in Canada: Critical perspectives on theory, research and practice* (pp. 443–470). Toronto: Copp Clark Longman Ltd.

Brodkin, K. (2002). How Jews Became White Folks. In P.S. Rothenberg (Ed.), *White Privilege: Essential readings on the other side of racism* (pp. 35–48). New York: Worth Publishers.

Browitt, J. (2004). "Pierre Bourdieu: Homo Sociologicus". In J. Browitt, & B. Nelson (Eds.), *Practicing Theory: Pierre Bourdieu and the field of cultural reproduction.* (pp.). University of Delaware Press.

Brown, V. (1996). The Emergence of the Economy. In S. Hall, D. Held, D. Hubert, & K. Thompson (Eds.), *Modernity: An introduction to modern societies* (pp. 90–121). Oxford: Blackwell Publishers.

Brym, R. J., Lie, J., Nelson, A., Guppy, N., & McCormick, C. (2003). *Sociology: Your compass for a new world.* Toronto: Thomson Nelson.

Bulman, R. C. (2005). *Hollywood Goes to High School: Cinema, Schools, and American Culture.* New York: Worth Publishers.

Cahoon, L. (1996). Introduction. In L. Cahoon, (Ed.), *From Modernism to Postmodernism: An anthology* (pp. 1–23). Cambridge, Massachusetts: Blackwell Publishers.

Calliste, A. (2000). Nurses and Porters; Racism, sexism and resistance in segmented labour markets. In A. Calliste, & G. J. S. Dei (Eds.), *Anti-Racist Feminism: Critical race and gender studies* (pp. 143–164) (2nd printing). Halifax, Nova Scotia: Fernwood Publishing.

Calliste, A., & Dei, G. J. S. (Eds.). (2000). *Anti-Racist Feminism: Critical race and gender studies* (2nd printing). Halifax, Nova Scotia: Fernwood Publishing.

Calliste, A., & Dei, G. J. S. (2000). Introduction, Anti-Racist Feminism: critical race and gender studies. In Agnes Calliste, & G. J. Sefa Dei (Eds.), *Anti-Racist Feminism: Critical race and gender studies* (pp. 11–18) (2nd printing). Halifax, Nova Scotia: Fernwood Publishing.

Camino, L. A., & Krulfeld, R. (Eds.). (1994). *Reconstructing Lives, Recapturing Meaning: Refugee identity, gender and culture change.* United States: Gordon and Breach.

Canadian Taxpayers Federation. (2013). *CTF Proposes to End Aboriginal Poverty.* Retrieved February 5, 2013, from http://www.taxpayer.com/news-releases/ctf-proposes-to-end-aboriginal-poverty

Castagna, M., & Dei, G. J. S. (2000). An Historical Overview of the Application of the Race Concept in Social Practice. In A. Calliste, & G. J. S. Dei (Eds.), *Anti-Racist Feminism* (pp. 19–37) (2nd printing). Halifax, Nova Scotia: Fernwood Publishing.

Chavanu, Bakari. (2011). Examining Media Violence. In E. Marshall, & Ö. Sensoy (Eds.), *Rethinking Popular Culture and Media* (pp. 282–285). Milwaukee, Wisconsin: Rethinking Schools, Ltd.

Chief Kabongo (as told to Richard St. Barbe Baker). The Coming of the Pink Cheeks. In B. Bigelow, & B. Peterson (Eds.), *Rethinking Globalization: Teaching for justice in an unjust world* (pp. 45–49). Milwaukee, Wisconsin: Rethinking School Press.

Christensen, L. (2011). Unlearning the Myths That Bind Us: Critiquing fairy tales and cartoons. In E. Marshall, & Ö. Sensoy (Eds.), *Rethinking Popular Culture and Media* (pp. 189–200). Milwaukee, Wisconsin: Rethinking Schools, Ltd.

Cleveland, W. L. (1994). *A History of the Modern Middle East*. Boulder: Westview Press.

Cook, S. B. (1987). "The Irish Raj: Social Origins and Careers of Irishmen in the Indian Civil Service.1855–1919," *Journal of Social History*, 20, 3.

Cooley, C. H. (1902). *Human Nature and the Social Order*. New York: Scribner's.

Cooley, C. H. (1961). Primary Groups. In T. Parsons, E. Shils, K. D. Naegele, & J. R. Pitts (Eds.), *The Theories of Society: Foundations of modern sociological theory* (pp. 315–318). New York: The Free Press.

Conley, D. (2011). *You May Ask Yourself: An introduction to thinking like a sociologist*. New York: W. W. Norton & Company, Inc.

Craib, I. (1997). *Classical Social Theory: An introduction to the thought of Marx, Weber, Durkheim, and Simmel*. New York: Oxford University Press.

Crenshaw, K., Gotanda, N., Peller, G., & Thomas, K. (1995). *Critical Race Theory: the Key Writings that Formed the Movement*. New York: New Press.

Crenshaw, Gotanda, Peller, and Thomas. (1995). *Critical Race Theory: The Key Writings That Formed the Movement*. New York: New York University Press.

Cruxton, J. B., Wilson, W. D., Francis, D., Harrison, B., & Johnson, J. (2008). *Flashback Canada* (5th ed.). Don Mills, Ontario: Oxford University Press.

Cuautémoc, C. (2002). The Marshall Plan. In B. Bigelow, & B. Peterson (Eds.), *Rethinking Globalization: Teaching for justice in an unjust world* (pp. 93–94). Milwaukee, Wisconsin: Rethinking School Press.

Culvert, J. (with Kuehn, L.). (1993). *Pandora's Box: Corporate power, free trade and Canadian education*. Toronto: Our Schools/Our Selves Education Foundation.

Cutter, C. H. (1999) *Africa 1999*. The World Today Series. Harpers Ferry, W. V.: Stryker-Post Publications.

Das Gupta, T. (1996). *Racism and Paid Work*. Toronto: Garamond Press.

Davis, K., & Moore, W. E. (1945)."Some Principles of Stratification." ASR 10: 242–49.

Declaration of the Rights of Man and Its Citizens. (1995). In M. Perry, J. R. Peden, & T. H. Von Laue (Eds.), *Sources of the Western Tradition. Volume II: From the Renaissance to the present* (pp. 90–91) (3rd ed.). Boston: Houghton Mifflin Company.

Dei, G. J. S. (1996). *Antiracism Education: Theory and Practice*. Halifax, Nova Scotia: Fernwood Publishing.

Dei, G. J. S. (2005). Critical Issues in Anti-racist Research Methodologies: An introduction. In G. J. S. Dei, & G. S. Johal (Eds.), *Anti-Racist Research Methodologies* (pp. 1–28). New York: Peter Lang.

Dei, G. J. S., Karumanchery, L., & Karumachery-Luik, N. (2005). *Playing the Race Card: Exposing white power and privilege.* New York: Peter Lang.

Dei, G. J. S., & Calliste, A. (Eds.). (2000). *Power, Knowledge and Anti-Racism Education: A critical reader.* Halifax, Nova Scotia: Fernwood Publishing.

Delaney, T. (2004). *Classical Social Theory: Investigation and Application. NJ: Prentice Hall.*

Delpit, Lisa. (1995). *Other People's Children: Cultural conflict in the classroom.* New York: The New Press.

Dewey, J. (1933). *How Society Thinks.* New York: D. C. Heath.

Dewey, J. (1971a). *Experience & Education* (13th ed.). New York: Collier Books.

Dewey, J. (1971b). *The Child and the Curriculum and The School and Society* (11th ed.). Chicago: The University of Chicago Press.

Driedger, Leo. (1996). *Multi-Ethnic Canada: Identities and Inequalities.* Don Mills, Ontario: Oxford University Press.

Driedger, Leo. (2003). *Race and Ethnicity: Finding Identities and Equalities* (2nd ed.). Don Mills, Ontario: Oxford University Press.

Du Bois, W.E.B. (2005). *The Souls of Black Folk.* Boston: Paperview in association with The Boston Globe.

Dua, E. (2000). "The Hindu Woman's Question": Canadian nation building and the social construction of gender for South-Asian-Canadian women. In A. Calliste, & G. J. S. Dei (Eds.), *Anti-Racist Feminism: Critical race and gender studies* (pp. 55–72) (2nd printing). Halifax, Nova Scotia: Fernwood Publishing.

Duffy, A., & Mandell, N. (2010). The Growth of Poverty and Social Inequality: Losing faith in social justice. In V. Zawilski (Ed.), *Inequality in Canada: A reader on the intersections of gender, race, and class* (pp. 251–265) (2nd ed.). Toronto: Oxford University Press.

Durham, M. & Kellner, D. (Eds.). (2006). Media and Cultural Studies: Keyworks, Boston: Blackwell.

Durkheim, Émile. (1961a). On Mechanical and Organic Solidarity. In T. Parsons, E. Shils, K D. Naegele, & J. R. Pitts (Eds.), *The Theories of Society: Foundations of modern sociological theory* (pp. 208–213). New York: The Free Press.

Durkheim, Émile. (1961b). Types of Suicide. In T. Parsons, E. Shils, K D. Naegele, & J. R. Pitts (Eds.), *The Theories of Society: Foundations of modern sociological theory* (pp. 213–218). New York: The Free Press.

Durkheim, Émile. ([1893] 1964). *The Division of Labor in Society.* Tr. George Simpson. New York: Free Press.

Durkheim, Émile. ([1897] 1951). *Suicide: A Study in Sociology:* Tr. John A. Spaulding and George Simpson. Glencoe, IL: Free Press.

Durkheim, Émile. (1938) *The Rules of Sociological Methods.* New York: The Free Press.

Durkheim, Émile. (1915). *The Elementary Forms of the Religious Life: A Study in Religious Sociology*. Translated by Joseph Ward Swain. New York: Macmillan.

Dyson, M., 2003, *Reflecting Black: African-American Cultural Criticism*, Minnesota: University of Minnesota Press.

Engels, F. (1995). The Condition of the Working Class in England. In M. Perry, J. R. Peden, & T. H. Von Laue (Eds.), *Sources of the Western Tradition. Volume II: From the Renaissance to the present* (pp. 117–118) (3rd ed.). Boston: Houghton Mifflin Company.

Erickson, P. A. (1998). (With Liam D. Murphy). *A History of Anthropological Theory*. Toronto: broadview press.

Fawcett, B. (Ed.). (2007). *You Said What?: Lies, and propaganda throughout history* (1st ed.). New York: Harper.

Ferdows, A. (1995). Gender Roles in Iranian Public School Textbooks. In E. Warnock Fernen (Ed.), *Childhood in the Muslim Middle East* (pp. 325–336). Austin: University of Texas Press.

Ferguson, N. (2006). *The War of the World: Twentieth-Century conflicts and the descent of the West*. New York: The Penguin Press.

Fleras, A. (2010). *Unequal Relations: An introduction to race, ethnic, and aboriginal dynamics in Canada* (6th ed.). Toronto: Pearson Education Canada.

Fleras, A., & Elliott, J. L. (1992). *Unequal Relations: An introduction to race, ethnic, and aboriginal dynamics in Canada*. Scarborough, Ontario: Prentice-Hall Canada.

Fleras, A., & Elliott, J. L. (2002). *Engaging Diversity: Multiculturalism in Canada* (2nd ed.). Toronto: Nelson Thompson Learning.

Fleras, A., & Elliott, J. L. (2007). *Unequal Relations: An introduction to race, ethnic, and aboriginal dynamics in Canada* (5th ed.). Toronto: Pearson Prentice Hall.

Elwell, F. (2011). *Macrosociology: four modern theorists*. New York: Paradigm.

Fanon, F. (1952; 1967) *Black Skin, White Masks*, trans. Charles Lam Markmann; New York: Grove.

Fanon, F. (1961; 1985). *The Wretched of the Earth*. Harmondsworth: Penguin.

Fleischacker, S. (1999). *A Third Conception of Liberty, Judgment and Freedom*. Princeton: NJ.

Figes, E. (1970) *Patriarchal Attitudes: Women in Society*. New York: Macmillan Publishers Limited.

Foucault, M. (1994). Two Lectures. In N.B. Dirks, G. Eley, & S.B. Ortner (Eds.), *Culture/Power/History: A Reader in Contemporary Social Theory* (pp. 200–221). New Jersey: Princeton University Press.

Foucault, M. (1977). *Discipline & Punish: The Birth of the Prison* (A. Sheridan, Trans.). New York: Vintage Books.

Foucault, M. (1970). *The Order of Thing: An Archaeology of the Human Sciences*. New York: Vintage Books.

Foucault M. *History of Madness*. Khalfa J, editor, (2006). translator & Murphy J, translator. Routledge;

Foucault M. *History of Madness*. NY: Routledge; (2006). Preface to the 1961 edition. p. xxvii–xxxix.

Foucault, M. (1980). "Two Lectures," in Colin Gordon, ed., Power/Knowledge: Selected Interviews. New York: Pantheon.

Foundry and Engineering Works of the Royal Overseas Trading Company. (1995). Factory Rules. In M. Perry, J. R. Peden, & T. H. Von Laue (Eds.), *Sources of the Western Tradition. Volume II: From the Renaissance to the present* (pp. 111–113) (3rd ed.). Boston: Houghton Mifflin Company.

Francis, D. (1997). *National Dreams: Myth, memory, and Canadian history.* Vancouver: Arsenal Pulp Press.

Fred, R. (1988). Forward. In C. Haig-Brown, *Resistance and Renewal: Surviving the Indian residential school* (pp. 15–24) (8th printing). Vancouver: Arsenal Pulp Press.

Fredrickson, M. (1981). *White Supremacy: A Comparative Study in American and South African History.* New York: Oxford University Press.

Freedman, S. E. (1988). Teaching, Gender, and Curriculum. In L.E. Beyer, & M.W. Apple (Eds.), *The Curriculum: problems, politics and possibilities* (pp. 204–218). New York: State University of New York.

Freire, P. (1985). *The Politics of Education: Culture, power and liberation* (D. Macedo, Trans.). South Hadley, Massachusetts: Bergin & Garvey Publishers, Inc.

Freire, P. (1997). *Pedagogy of the Oppressed* (20th ed.). New York: Continuum.

Freire, P., & Macedo, D. (1987). *Literacy: Reading the word and the world.* Westport: Bergin and Garvey.

Freire, P., & Macedo, D. (2001). Literacy and Critical Pedagogy. In F. Schultz (Ed.), *Notable Selections In Educations* (pp. 192–200) (3rd ed.). New York: McGraw-Hill/Dushkin.

Frideres, J. S. (1998). *Aboriginal Peoples in Canada: Contemporary conflicts.* Scarborough, Ontario: Prentice-Hall Canada Inc.

Friedan, B. (1983). *The Feminine Mystique.* New York: W. W. Norton.

Gage, S., & McNair, D. (2002). Colonialism: Before and after. In B. Bigelow, & B. Peterson (Eds.), *Rethinking Globalization: Teaching for justice in an unjust world* (pp. 35–37). Milwaukee, Wisconsin: Rethinking School Press.

Gage, S., & McNair, D. (2002) Colonialism: The building blocks. In B. Bigelow, & B. Peterson (Eds.), *Rethinking Globalization: Teaching for justice in an unjust world* (pp. 35–37). Milwaukee, Wisconsin: Rethinking School Press.

Gage, S. (1991a). *Colonialism in the Americas: A critical look.* (Illustrations by Don McNair, Westcoast Development Group) Victoria: Victoria International Development Educational Association.

Gage, S. (1991b). *Colonialism in Asia: A critical look.* (Illustrations by D. McNair, Westcoast Development Group) Victoria: Victoria International Development Educational Association.

Gage, S. (1991c). *Colonialism in Africa: A critical look.* (Illustrations by D. McNair, Westcoast Development Group) Victoria: Victoria International Development Educational Association.

Galeano, E. Conquistadores Destroy Native Libraries. In B. Bigelow, & B. Peterson (Eds.), *Rethinking Globalization: Teaching for justice in an unjust world* (pp. 43–44). Milwaukee, Wisconsin: Rethinking School Press.

Garfinkel, H. (1967). *Studies in Ethnomethodology.* Englewood Cliffs, NJ: Prentice-Hall.

Gaskell, J., & McLaren, A. (Eds.). (1991). *Women and Education* (2nd ed.). Calgary: Detselig Enterprises Limited.

Gaventa, J. (2003). *Power after Lukes: A review of the literature.* Brighton: Institute of Development Studies.

Gedalof, A. J., Boulter, J., Faflak, J., & McFarlane, C. (2005). *Cultural Subjects: A Popular Culture Reader.* Toronto: Nelson Education Ltd.

Ghosh, R. (1996). *Redefining Multicultural Education.* Toronto: Harcourt Brace & Company.

Ghosh, R., & Abdi, A. A. (2004). *Education and the Politics of Difference: Canadian Perspectives.* Toronto: Canadian Scholars' Press.

Giddens, A. (1971). *Capitalism & Modern Social Theory: An analysis of the writings of Marx, Durkheim and Max Weber.* Cambridge: Cambridge University Press.

Giddens, A. (1979). *Central Problems in Social Theory: Action, Structure, and Contradiction in Social Analysis.* Berkeley: University of California Press.

Giddens, A. (1984). *The Constitution of Society.* Polity Press: Cambridge, UK.

Giddens, A. (1990). *The Consequences of Modernity.* Stanford, California: Stanford University Press.

Giddens, A. (1991). *Modernity and Self-identity: Self and society in the late modern age.* Stanford, California: Stanford University Press.

Gilad, L. (1990). *The Northern Route: An Ethnography of Refugee Experiences.* St. John's: Institute of Social and Economic Research.

Gintis, H., & Bowles, S. (2006). "Evolutionary Origins of Collective Action", in Donald Wittman and Barry Weingast, Oxford Handbook of Political Economy (Oxford University Press)

Giroux, H. A. (1987). Introduction: Literacy and the Pedagogy of Political Empowerment. In P. Freire, & D. Macedo (Eds.), *Literacy: Reading the Word and the World* (pp. 1–28). Westport, Connecticut: Bergin & Garvey.

Giroux, H. A. (1988). *Schooling and the Struggle for Public Life: Critical Pedagogy in the Modern Age.* Minneapolis: University of Minnesota Press.

Giroux, H. A. (1994). *Disturbing Pleasures: Learning Popular Cultures.* New York: Routledge.

Giroux, H. A. (1999). *The Mouse that Roared: Disney and the End of Innocence.* Lanham, Maryland: Bowman & Littlefield Publishers, Inc.

Giroux, H. A. (2000). The War Against Cultural Politics: Beyond Conservative and Neo-Enlightenment Left "Oppositions": A Critique. In C.J. Ovando, & P. McLaren (Eds.), *The Politics of Multiculturalism and Bilingual Education: Students and Teachers Caught in the Cross Fire* (pp. 50–61). Boston: McGraw-Hill Higher Education.

Giroux, H. A. (2005). *Against the New Authoritarianism: Politics After Abu Ghraib*. Winnipeg: Arbeiter Ring Publishing.

Glesne, C. (2011). *Becoming Qualitative Researchers: An Introduction* (4th ed.). Toronto: Pearson Education Inc.

Goffman, E. (n.d.). *Total Institutions*. Retrieved March 7, 2013, from http://www.markfoster.net/neurelitism/totalinstitutions.pdf

Goffman, E. (1958). *The Presentation of Self in Everyday Life*. Edinburgh: University of Edinburgh, Social Sciences Research Centre.

Goffman, E. (1963). *Stigma: Notes on the Management of a Spoiled Identity*. New York, NY: Simon and Schuster.

Goffman, E. (1986). *Stigma: Notes on the Management of Spoiled Identity*. New York: Simon & Schuster, Inc. (Originally published in 1963).

Goldstein, T., & Selby, D. (Eds.). (2000). *Weaving Connections: Educating for Peace, Social and Environmental Justice*. Toronto: Sumach Press.

Goldthorpe, J. E. (1996). *The Sociology of Post Colonial Societies: Economic disparity, cultural diversity, and development*. Cambridge: Cambridge University Press.

Gordon, L., T. Denean Sharpley-Whiting, Renee T. White. (1996). *Fanon: A Critical Reader*. New York: Wiley

Gottman, J. M. (1990). *What Predicts Divorce*. Hillsdale, NJ: Lawrence Erlbaum.

Gourevitch, P. (2006). Stories from Rwanda. In P. S. Rothenberg (Ed.), *Beyond Borders: Thinking critically about global issues* (pp. 195–205). New York: Worth Publishers.

Grabb, Edward G. (2002). *Theories of Social Inequality* (4th ed.). Toronto: Harcourt Canada.

Greer, G. (1970). *The Female Eunuch*. New York: Paladin.

Hadden, R. W. (1997). *Sociological Theory: An introduction to the classical tradition*. Toronto: broadview press.

Haig-Brown, C. (1988). *Resistance and Renewal: Surviving the Indian residential school* (8th printing). Vancouver: Arsenal Pulp Press.

Hall, S. (1994). Cultural Studies: Two paradigms. In N.B. Dirks, G. Eley, & S.B. Ortner (Eds.), *Culture/Power/History: A reader in contemporary social theory* (pp. 520–538). Princeton, New Jersey: Princeton University Press.

Hall, S. (1996a). Introduction. In S. Hall, D. Held, D. Hubert, & K. Thompson (Eds.), *Modernity: An introduction to modern societies* (pp. 3–18). Oxford: Blackwell Publishers.

Hall, S. (1996b). The West and the Rest: Discourse and power. In S. Hall, D. Held, D. Hubert, & K. Thompson (Eds.), *Modernity: An introduction to modern societies* (pp. 185–227). Oxford: Blackwell Publishers.

Hall, S. (1996c). The Question of Cultural Identity. In S. Hall, D. Held, D. Hubert, & K. Thompson (Eds.), *Modernity: An introduction to modern societies* (pp. 596–634). Oxford: Blackwell Publishers.

Hall, S., Held, D., Hubert, D., & Thompson, K. (Eds.). (1996). *Modernity: An introduction to modern societies*. Oxford: Blackwell Publishers.

Hamilton, P. (1996). The Enlightenment and the Birth of Social Science. In S. Hall, D. Held, D. Hubert, & K. Thompson (Eds.), *Modernity: An introduction to modern societies* (pp. 19–54). Oxford: Blackwell Publishers.

Hamilton, S. (2010). Our Mothers Grand and Great: Black Women of Nova Scotia. In M. A. Wallis, L. Sunseri, & G.D. Galabuzi (Eds.), *Colonialism and Racism in Canada: Historical traces and contemporary issues* (pp. 61–67). Toronto: Nelson Education Ltd.

Harman, C. (2008). *A People's History of the World: From the stone age to the new millennium.* New York: Verso.

Harris, L., & Johnson, C. (1996) 'Foreword', in Gordon, L.R., Sharpley-Whiting, D.T. and White, R.T. (eds) *Fanon: A Critical Reader*, Oxford: Blackwell.

Haskell, R., & Burtch, B. (2010). *Get That Freak: Homophobia and transphobia in high schools.* Halifax, Nova Scotia: Fernwood Publishing.

Hebron, L., & Stack, J. F. Jr. (2009). *Globalization: Debunking the myths.* Prentice Hall Studies in International Relations: Enduring questions in changing times, C. W. Kegley Jr. (Series Ed). Upper Saddle River, New Jersey: Pearson Educational, Inc.

Heilbroner, R. L. (1989). *The making of Economic Society: Revised for the 1990s.* Englewood Cliffs, NJ: Prentice Hall.

Held, D. (1996). The Development of Modern State. In S. Hall, D. Held, D. Hubert, & K. Thompson (Eds.), *Modernity: An introduction to modern societies* (pp. 55–89). Oxford: Blackwell Publishers.

Heiner, R. (2010). *Social Problems: An Introduction to Critical Constructionism.* New York: Oxford University Press.

Henry, F., & Tator, C. (2000). The Theory and Practice of Democratic Racism in Canada. In M.A. Kalbach, & W.E. Kalbach (Eds.), *Perspectives on Ethnicity in Canada: A Reader* (pp. 285–302). Toronto: Harcourt Canada.

Henry, F., & Tator, C. (2006). *The Colour of Democracy: Racism in Canadian Society* (3rd ed.). Toronto: Thomson Nelson.

Henry, F., & Tator, C. (2010). *The Colour of Democracy: Racism in Canadian Society* (4th ed.). Toronto: Thomson Nelson.

Hermer, J., & Mosher, J. (Eds.). (2002). *Disorderly People: Law and the politics of exclusion in Ontario.* Halifax, Nova Scotia: Fernwood Publishing.

Hermer, J., & Mosher, J. (Eds.). (2002). Introduction. In J. Hermer, & J. Mosher (Eds.), *Disorderly People: Law and the politics of exclusion in Ontario* (pp. 11–21). Halifax, Nova Scotia: Fernwood Publishing.

Heyck, D. L. D. (2002). *Surviving Globalization in Three Latin American Communities*. Toronto: broadview press.

Higgins, P. (2006). *The Child's World as Portrayed in Iranian Elementary Textbooks*. Paper presented at The Sixth Biennial of Iranian Studies Conference, London, England.

Higgins, P. J., & Shoar-Ghaffari, P. (1994). Women's Education in the Islamic Republic of Iran. In M. Afkhami, & E. Friedl (Eds.), *In the Eyes of the Storm: Women in Post-revolutionary Iran. Contemporary Issues in the Middle East* (pp. 19–43). Syracuse: Syracuse University Press.

Hill-Collins, P. (1990, p. 221). *Black Feminist Though: Knowledge, Consciousness, and the Politics of Empowerment*. Boston: Unwin Hyman.

Hill-Collins, P. (1990) *Black Feminist Thought: Knowledge, Consciousness and the Politics of Empowerment*. New York: Routledge

Hiller, H. H. (2006). *Canadian Society: A macro analysis* (3rd ed.). Toronto: Pearson Education Canada Inc.

Hirji, F. (2010). *Dreaming in Canadian: South Asian youth, Bollywood, and belonging*. Vancouver: UBC Press.

Hirsch, E. D. (Ed.). (2001). English Colonies in North America: Thirteen colonies. In E. D. Hirsch (Ed.), *What Your Third Grader Needs to Know* (pp. 140–145). The Core Education Series. New York: Random House Publishing Group.

Hobsbawm, E. (1983). Introduction: Inventing traditions. In E. Hobsbawm, & T. Ranger (Eds.), *The Invention of Tradition* (pp. 1–14). Cambridge: Cambridge University Press.

Hobsbawm, E. (1989). *The Age of Empire 1875–1914*. New York: Vintage Books.

Hoffman, S. (2011). Miles of Aisles of Sexism. In E. Marshall, & Ö. Sensoy (Eds.), *Rethinking Popular Culture and Media* (pp. 207–213). Milwaukee, Wisconsin: Rethinking Schools, Ltd.

Hollinger, R. (1994). *Postmodernism and the Social Sciences: A Thematic approach*. Thousand Oaks, California: SAGE Publications, Inc.

hooks, b. (1989). *Talking Back: thinking feminist, thinking black*. Boston: South End Press.

hooks, b. (1990). *Yearning: race, gender, and cultural politics*. Toronto: Between the Lines.

hooks, b. (1994). *Teaching to Transgress: Education as the Practice of Freedom*. New York: Routledge.

hooks, b. (2000). *Feminism is for Everybody: Passionate Politics*. Cambridge, MA: South End Press.

hooks, b. (2000). *Where We Stand: Class Matters*. New York: Routledge.

hooks, b. (2002). Representations of Whiteness in the Black Imagination. In P.S. Rothenberg (Ed.), *White Privilege: Essential readings on the other side of racism* (pp. 19–23). New York: Worth Publishers.

hooks, b. (2003). *Teaching Community: A pedagogy of hope*. New York: Routledge.

Hoover, K. R. (1988). *The Elements of Social Scientific Thinking* (4th ed). New York: Saint Martin's Press.

Howard, M. C. (1993). *Contemporary Cultural Anthropology* (4th ed). New York: Harper Collin College Publishers.

Illich, I. (1971). *Deschooling Society*. New York: Harper and Row, Publishers.

Jackson and Sorensen (2011). www.oxfordtextbooks.co.uk/orc/jackson_sorensen4e/ Retrieved August 21, 2011.

Jakubowski, L. M. (1997). *Immigration and the Legalization of Racism*. Halifax, Nova Scotia: Fernwood Publishing.

James, W. (1907) Pragmatism. New York: Longmans, Green.

James, W. (1890) 'The Perception of Time', in The Principles of Psychology, Vol. 1, pp. 605–42. New York: Henry Holt.

Jay, G. (2012)."Introduction to Whiteness Studies." https://pantherfile.uwm.edu/gjay/www/Whiteness/introwhite.htm. Retrieved March, 10, 2012.

Jenkins, K. (1991). *Re-thinking History*. New York: Routledge.

Johnson, A. (2005). *Privilege, Power, and Difference*. New York: McGraw Hill.

Johnson, L. (2011). Looking Pretty, Waiting for the Prince. In E. Marshall, & Ö. Sensoy (Eds.), *Rethinking Popular Culture and Media* (pp. 201–202). Milwaukee, Wisconsin: Rethinking Schools, Ltd.

Jones, W. T. (1969). *A History of Western Philosophy: Hobbes to Hume* (2nd ed.). New York: Harcourt Brace Jovanovich, Publishers.

Kagan, D., Ozment, S., & Turner, F. M. (1991). *The Western Heritage, Volume I: To 1715* (4th ed.). New York: Macmillan Publishing Company.

Kamrava, M. (1993). *Politics and Society in the Third World*. New York: Routledge.

Keddie, N. R. (2003). *Modern Iran: Roots and Results of Revolution*. New Haven: Yale University Press.

Kedourie, E. (1966). *Nationalism* (3rd ed.). London: Hutchinson University Library.

Kedourie, E. (1992). *Politics in the Middle East*. Oxford: Oxford University Press.

Kelleher, A., & Klein, L. (2009). *Global Perspectives: A handbook for understanding global issues* (3rd ed.). Upper Saddle River, New Jersey: Pearson Education, Inc.

Kelly, J. (1998). *Under the Gaze: Learning to Be Black in White Society*. Halifax: Fernwood Publishing.

Kelly, U. A. (1995). "The Feminist Trespass": Gender, Literature, and Curriculum. In J. Gaskell, & J. Willinsky (Eds.), *Gender In/forms Curriculum: From enrichment to transformation* (pp. 96–108). New York: Teachers College Press.

Kempf, S. (2002). Colonialism: Before and after. In B. Bigelow, & B. Peterson (Eds.), *Rethinking Globalization: Teaching for justice in an unjust world* (pp. 34). Milwaukee, Wisconsin: Rethinking School Press.

Kiely, R. (2005). *Empire in the Age of Globalisation: US hegemony and neoliberal disorder*. London: Pluto Press.

Kincheloe, J. L., & Steinberg, S. R. (Eds.). (1995). *Thirteen Questions: Reframing Education's Conversation* (2nd ed.). New York: Peter Lang Publishing, Inc.

Kincheloe, J. L., & Steinberg, S. R. (1995). The More Questions We Ask, The More Questions We Ask. In J.L. Kincheloe, & S.R. Steinberg (Eds.), *Thirteen Questions: Reframing education's conversation* (pp. 1–11). (2nd ed.) New York: Peter Lang Publishing, Inc.

Kivisto, P. (2011). *Key Ideas in Sociology* (3rd ed.). Los Angeles: Sage.

Klein, N. (2005). *No War: America's real business in Iraq*. London: Gibson Square Books Ltd.

Knutilla, M. (1998). The State and Social Issues: Theoretical considerations. In W. Anthony, & L. Samuelson (Eds.), *Power and Resistance: Critical thinking about Canadian social issues* (pp. 9–28) (2nd ed.). Halifax: Fernwood Publishing.

Kohn, H. (Ed.). (1965). *Nationalism: Its meaning and history* (Revised ed.). New York: Van Nostrand Reinhold Company.

Koopmans, R., & Statham, P. (2000a). Migration and Ethnic Relations as a Field of Political Contention: An Opportunity Structure Approach. In R. Koopmans, & P. Statham (Eds.), *Challenging Immigration and Ethnic Relations Politics: Comparative European perspectives* (pp. 13–56). Oxford: Oxford University Press.

Koopmans, R., & Statham, P. (2000b). Challenging the Liberal Nation-State? Postnationalism, Multiculturalism, and the Collective Claims-making of Migrants and Ethnic Minorities in Britain and Germany. In R. Koopmans, & P. Statham (Eds.), *Challenging Immigration and Ethnic Relations Politics: Comparative European perspectives* (pp. 189–232). Oxford: Oxford University Press.

Kubow, P. K., & Fossum, P. R. (2007). *Comparative Education: Exploring issues in international context* (2nd ed.). Upper Saddle River, New Jersey: Pearson Education, Inc.

Kuper, A. (1990). The Genocidal State: An overview. In P. L. Van der Berghe (Ed.), *State Violence and Ethnicity* (pp. 19–51). Niwot, Colorado: the University Press of Colorado.

Kymlicka, W. (1995). *Multicultural Citizenship: A liberal theory of minority rights*. Oxford: Clarendon Press.

Kymlicka, W. (2001). *Politics in the Vernacular: Nationalism, multiculturalism, and citizenship*. Oxford: Oxford University Press.

Laibo, S. A. (1999). *East, Southeast Asia, and the Western Pacific 1999*. The World Today Series (32nd ed). Harpers Ferry, West Virginia: Stryker-Post Publications.

Lapidus, I. M. (1988). Iran: State and Religion in the Modern Era. In I. M. Lapidus (Ed.), *A History of Islamic Societies* (pp. 571–591). Cambridge: Cambridge University Press.

Latouche, S. ((1996). *The Westernization of the World: The significance, scope and limits of the drive towards global uniformity*. Cambridge: Polity Press.

Lawrence, B. (2010). Rewriting Histories of Land. In M. A. Wallis, L. Sunseri, & G.D. Galabuzi (Eds.), *Colonialism and Racism in Canada: Historical traces and contemporary issues* (pp. 38–60). Toronto: Nelson Education Ltd.

Leicht, K. T., & Fitzgerald, S. T. (2007). *Postindustrial Peasants: The illusion of middle-class prosperity.* Contemporary Social Issues (Series Editor: George Ritzer). New York: Worth Publishers.

Lemert, C. (2005). *Social Things: An introduction to the sociological life* (3rd ed.). Lanham, MD: Rowman & Littlefield Publishers, INC.

Lemert, C. (2007). *Thinking The Unthinkable: The riddles of classical social theories.* Boulder: Paradigm Publishers.

Li, P. S. (1998). *The Chinese in Canada* (2nd ed.). Don Mills: Oxford University Press.

Linton, R. (1961). Status and Role. In T. Parsons, E. Shils, K D. Naegele, & J. R., Pitts (Eds.), *The Theories of Society: Foundations of modern sociological theory* (pp. 202–208). New York: The Free Press.

Liodakis, N., & Satzewich, V. (1998). From Solution to Problem: Multiculturalism and 'race relations' as new social problems. In W. Anthony, & L. Samuelson (Eds.), *Power and Resistance: Critical thinking about Canadian social issues* (pp. 95–114) (2nd ed.). Halifax: Fernwood Publishing.

Lipsitz, G. (2002). The Possessive Investment in Whiteness. In P.S. Rothenberg (Ed.), *White Privilege: Essential readings on the other side of racism* (pp. 61–84). New York: Worth Publishers.

Littlejohn, S., & Foss, K. (2008). *Theories of Human Communication.* New York: Wadsworth.

Lock, J. (1995). Second Treatise on Government. In M. Perry, J. R. Peden, & T. H. Von Laue (Eds.), *Sources of the Western Tradition. Volume II: From the Renaissance to the present* (pp. 58–60) (3rd ed.). Boston: Houghton Mifflin Company.

Longhofer, W., & Winchester, D. (2012). *Social Theory Re-Wired: New connections to classical and contemporary perspectives.* New York: Routledge.

Lovejoy, P. E. (1983). *Transformations in slavery: A history of slavery in Africa.* Cambridge: Cambridge University Press.

Luttrell, W. (Ed.). (2010.) *Qualitative Educational Research: Readings in reflexive methodology and transformative practice.* New York: Routledge.

Macdowell, L. S., & Radforth, I. (2006). *Canadian Working-Class History: Selected readings* (3rd ed.). Toronto: Canadian Scholars' Press.

Macedo, D. (1995). Power and Education: Who decides the forms schools have taken, and who should decide? In J.L. Kincheloe, & S.R. Steinberg (Eds.), *Thirteen Questions: Reframing Education's Conversation* (pp. 43–57) (2nd ed.). New York: Peter Lang.

Macionis, J. J., Benoit, C. M., & Jansson, S. M. (1999). *Society: The basics* (Canadian Edition). New York: Prentice-Hall.

Mackay, E. (2010). Setting Differences: Managing and representing people and land in the Canadian national project. In M. A. Wallis, L. Sunseri, & G.D. Galabuzi (Eds.), *Colonialism and Racism in Canada: Historical traces and contemporary issues* (pp. 17–37). Toronto: Nelson Education Ltd.

Mackay, S. (1996). *The Iranians: Persia, Islam and the soul of a nation.* New York: A Plume Book.

McMichael, P. (2008). *Development and Social Change.* New York: Pine Forge.

Manicom, A. (1992). Feminist pedagogy: Transformations, standpoints, and politics. *Canadian Journal of Education,* 17 (3), 365–389.

Mann, D. (2011), *Understanding Society: A Survey of Modern Social Theory.* Toronto: Oxford University Press.

Marshall, E., & Sensoy, Ö. (Eds.). (2011). *Rethinking Popular Culture and Media.* Milwaukee, Wisconsin: Rethinking Schools, Ltd.

Martin, D. (2002). Demonizing Youth, Marketing Fear: The new politics of crime. In J. Hermer, & J. Mosher (Eds.), *Disorderly People: Law and the politics of exclusion in Ontario* (pp. 91–104). Halifax, Nova Scotia: Fernwood Publishing.

Marx, K. (1848). *The 18th Brumaire of Louis Bonaparte.* Rockville: Wildside Press LLC.

Marx, K. (1971). Preface to *A Contribution to the Critique of Political Economy,* Tr. S. W. Ryanzanskaya, edited by M. Dobb. London: Lawrence & Whishart.

Matini, J. (1989). The Impact of the Islamic Revolution on Education in Iran. In A. Badran (Ed.), *At the Crossroads: Education in the Middle East* (pp. 43–55). New York: Paragon House.

Matsuda, M, Lawrence III, C.R, Delgado, R., & Crenshaw. K. (1993). *Towards a Critical Race Pedagogy.* Boulder, Colo.: Westview Press

Mazzini, G. (1965). Mazzini: On the unity of Italy. In H. Kohn (Ed.), *Nationalism: Its meaning and history* (pp. 118–121) (Revised ed.). New York: Van Nostrand Reinhold Company.

Mazzini, G. (1995). Young Italy. In M. Perry, J. R. Peden, & T. H. Von Laue (Eds.), *Sources of the Western Tradition. Volume II: From the Renaissance to the present* (pp. 145–146) (3rd ed.). Boston: Houghton Mifflin Company.

McCullough, H. B. (2010). *Political Ideologies.* Don Mills, Ontario: Oxford University Press.

McGrew, A. (1996a). The State in Advanced Capitalist Societies. In S. Hall, D. Held, D. Hubert, & K. Thompson (Eds.), *Modernity: An introduction to modern societies* (pp. 239–279). Oxford: Blackwell Publishers.

McLaren, P. (1998). *Life in Schools: An introduction to critical pedagogy in the foundations of education.* New York: Longman Inc.

McLaren, P., & Farahmandpur, R. (2003). Class, Cultism, & Multiculturalism: A Notebook on Forging a Revolutionary Politics. In F. Schultz (Ed.), *Multicultural Education 03/04* (pp. 97–109) (10th ed.). Guildford, Connecticut: McGraw-Hill/Dushkin.

Mead, G. H. (1934). *Mind, Self, and Society.* Chicago: University of Chicago Press.

Mead, G. H. (1938) The Philosophy of the Act. Chicago: University of Chicago Press.

Mead, G. H. (1961). The I and the Me. In T. Parsons, E. Shils, K D. Naegele, & J. R. Pitts, Jesse (Eds.), *The Theories of Society: Foundations of modern sociological theory* (pp. 163–168). New York: The Free Press.

Mehmet, O. (1995). *Westernizing the Third World: The Eurocentricity of economic development theories.* New York: Routledge.

Menashri, D. (1992). *Education and the Making of Modern Iran.* London: Cornell University Press.

Menashri, D. (2001). *Post-Revolutionary Politics in Iran: Religion, society and power.* London: Frank Cass.

Mendieta, E. (2006, pp.726–729). "Post Colonialism." Encyclopedia of Philosophy. Ed. Donald M. Borchert. Vol. 7. 2nd ed. Detroit: Macmillan Reference USA. Web 05/02/2011

Merton, R. K. (1938). *Social Structure and Anomie.* American Sociological Review, Vol. 3, No.5, pp.672–682

Merton, R. K. (1967). *On Theoretical Sociology: Five essays, old and new.* New York: The Free Press.

Merton, R. K. (1968). *Social Theory and Social Structure.* New York: Free Press.

Millet, K. (1970). *Sexual Politics.* New York: Doubleday & Company, Inc

Mills, C. W. (1959). *The Sociological Imagination.* New York. Oxford University Press.

Mills, W.G. (2006) *Racism and Social Darwinism,* Lecture Notes. Retrieved September 30, 2006. http://stmarys.ca/~wmills/course203/8Racism.html

Ministry of Education, Islamic Republic of Iran. *Education in Islamic Republic of Iran, 2003.* Retrieved January 15, 2005 from http://www.ier.ir?Home/ier/ENGLISH.pdf.

Mitchell, B. A. (2009). *Family Matters: An introduction to family sociology in Canada.* Toronto: Canadian Scholar's Press Inc.

Mirfakhraie, A. (1999). *Transmigration and Identity Construction: The Case of Iranians in Canada, 1946–1998.* (Master of Arts Thesis). Burnaby, British Columbia: Simon Fraser University.

Mirfakhraie, A. (2008). *Curriculum reform and identity politics in Iranian school textbooks: National and global representations of "race", ethnicity, social class and gender.* (Doctoral Dissertation). Retrieved from CIRcle: UBC's Information Repository. (https://circle.ubc.ca/handle/2429/992)

Mirfakhraie, A. (2011). Racialization of Asia, Africa and Americas and the Construction of the Ideal Iranian Citizen: Local and global representations of colonialism, geography, culture, and religious diversity in Iranian school textbooks. In C. Quist-Adade, & F. Chiang (Eds.), *From Colonization to Globalization: The intellectual and political* (pp. 265–288). Canada: Daysprings Publishing.

Mirfakhraie, A. (in press). *Iranian School Textbooks and Representations of Ethnic, Racialized, Gendered and Religious Diversity: Situating the 'ideal Iranian citizen' in local and global contexts.* Newcastle upon Tyne, United Kingdom: Cambridge Scholars Publishing.

Mohsenpour, B. (1988). Philosophy of Education in Postrevolutionary Iran. *Comparative Education Review*, 32 (1), 76–86.

Mohsenpour, B., & Kiamanesh, A. R. (2000). *Evaluation of the Education of Rural Working Girls Project*. Iran: United Nations Children's Fund and Literacy Movement Organization.

Mojab, S., & Hassanpour, A. (1995). The Politics of Nationality and Ethnic Diversity. In S. Rahnema, & S. Behdad (Eds.), *Iran after the Revolution: Crisis of an Islamic State* (pp. 229–250). London: I.B. Tauris & Co. Ltd.

Moore, D., & Hannah-Moffat, K. (2002). Correctional Renewal Without the Frills: The politics of 'get tough" punishments in Ontario. In Joe Hermer, & Janet Mosher (Eds.), *Disorderly People: Law and the politics of exclusion in Ontario* (pp. 105–121). Halifax: Fernwood Publishing.

Morgan, K. (1999). *The Birth of Industrial Britain: Economic Change 1750–1850*. London: Addison Wesley Longman Limited.

Mosher, J. (2002). The Shrinking of the Public and Private Spaces of the Poor. In J. Hermer, & J. Mosher (Eds.), *Disorderly People: Law and the politics of exclusion in Ontario* (pp. 41–53). Halifax: Fernwood Publishing.

Moustakas, C. (1994). *Phenomenological Research Methods*. Thousand Oaks: Sage.

Myers, K. 2006. *Racetalk: Racism Hiding in Plain Sight*. Lanham: Rowan and Littlefield, Inc.

Naiman, J. (2004). *How Societies Work: Class, power, and change in a Canadian context*. Toronto: Thomson Nelson.

Narveson, J. (2008). *You and the State: A short introduction to political philosophy*. Lanham, Maryland: Rowman & Littlefield Publishers, Inc.

Ng, R. (1993). "A Woman Out of Control": Racism, sexism, and the "inclusive" university. *Canadian Journal of Education*, 18 (3), 189–205.

Ng, R., Staton, P., & and Scane, J. (Eds.). (1995). *Anti-Racism, Feminism, and Critical Approaches to Education*. Ontario: The Ontario Institute for Studies in Education.

Nkrumah, K. (1965). *Neo-Colonialism: The Last Stage of Imperialism*. New York: International Publishers.

Nkrumah, K. (1970) *Consciencism*. New York: Monthly Review

Nkrumah, K. (1973), *Handbook of Revolutionary Warfare*, London: PANAF Books Ltd.

Nieto, S. (Ed.). (2000). *Affirming Diversity: The sociopolitical context of multicultural education* (3rd ed.). Boston: Pearson Education Inc.

Nkrumah, K. (2004). *Affirming Diversity: The Sociopolitical context of multicultural education* (4th ed.). Boston: Pearson Education Inc.

Nkrumah, K. (2005). *Why We Teach*. New York: Teachers College, Columbia University.

Oakes, J., & Lipton, M. (2003). *Teaching to Change the World* (2nd ed.). Boston: McGraw Hill Higher Education.

O'Grady, B., & Bright, R. (2002). Squeezed to the Point of Exclusion: the case of Toronto squeegee cleaners. In J. Hermer, & J. Mosher (Eds.), *Disorderly People: Law and the politics of exclusion in Ontario* (pp. 23–39). Halifax: Fernwood Publishing.

Olsen, G. M. (2011). *Power & Inequality: A comparative introduction.* Don Mills, Ontario: Oxford University Press.

Omi, M., & Winant, H. (1993). On the Theoretical Status of the Concept of Race. In C. McCarthy, & W. Crichlow (Eds.), *Race, Identity and Representation in Education* (pp. 3–10). New York: Routledge.

Osborne, K. (1991). *Teaching For Democratic Citizenship.* Toronto: Our School/Our Selves Education Foundation.

Ovando, C. J., & McLaren, P. (Eds.). (2000). *The Politics of Multiculturalism and Bilingual Education: Students and teachers caught in the cross fire.* Boston: McGraw-Hill Higher Education.

Paine, T. (1995). The age of Reason. In M. Perry, J. R. Peden, & T. H. Von Laue (Eds.), *Sources of the Western Tradition. Volume II: From the Renaissance to the present* (pp. 65–67) (3rd ed.). Boston: Houghton Mifflin Company.

Pampel, F. C. (2007). *Sociological Lives and Ideas: An introduction to the classical theorists.* New York: Worth Publishers.

Parenti, M. (2002). Myths of Underdevelopment. In B. Bigelow, & B. Peterson (Eds.), *Rethinking Globalization: Teaching for justice in an unjust world* (pp. 64–67). Milwaukee, Wisconsin: Rethinking School Press.

Parsons, T. (1951). *The Social System.* Glencoe, IL: Free Press.

Parsons, T. (1971). *The System of Modern Societies.* Englewood Cliffs, NJ: Prentice-Hall.

Parsons, T., Shils, E., Naegele, K. D., & Pitts, J. R. (Eds.). (1961). *The Theories of Society: Foundations of modern sociological theory.* New York: The Free Press.

Perry, M. (2001). *Western Civilization: A brief history. Volume II: From the 1400s.* Boston: Houghton Mifflin Company.

Perry, M., Peden, J. R., & Von Laue, T. H. (Eds.) (1995). *Sources of the Western Tradition. Volume II: From the Renaissance to the present* (3rd ed.). Boston: Houghton Mifflin Company.

Perry-Globa, P., Weeks, P., Yoshida, D., & Zelinski, V. (2007). *Perspectives on Globalization.* New York: Oxford University Press.

Peterson, B. (2002). Burning Books and Destroying People. In B. Bigelow, & B. Peterson (Eds.), *Rethinking Globalization: Teaching for justice in an unjust world* (pp. 38–42). Milwaukee, Wisconsin: Rethinking School Press.

Pettman, J. J. (2006). Women, Colonisation, and Racism. In P. S. Rothenberg (Ed.), *Beyond Borders: Thinking critically about global issues* (pp. 142–149). New York: Worth Publishers.

Power, C. H. (2004). *Making Sense of Social Theory: A practical introduction.* Lanham, MD: Rowman & Littlefield Publishers, INC.

Prashad, V., & Ballve, T. (Eds). (2006). *Dispatches From Latin America: On the frontlines against neo-liberalism.* Cambridge, Massachusetts: South End Press.

Prentice, A. (1977). *The School Promoters: Education and social class in mid-nineteenth century Upper Canada.* Toronto: McClelland and Steward, The Canadian Publishers.

Quist-Adade, C. (2012). *Social Justice Issues in Local and Global Contexts.* Ste Stu-Marie: Landon Elsemere

Ravelli, B. M. Webber and J. Patterson (2011). *Sociology For Everyone.* Pearson: Toronto.

Razack, S. (1998). *Looking White People in the Eye: Gender, race, and culture in courtrooms and class-rooms.* Toronto: University of Toronto Press.

Redjali, S. M. (1985). Iran: System of education. *International Encyclopedia of Education* (pp. 269–702). Oxford: Oxford University Press.

Rejali, D. M. (1994). *Torture and Modernity: Self, Society, and State in Modern Iran.* Boulder: Westview Press.

Rethinking Schools. (2011). *This Is What Solidarity Looks Like.* Retrieved February 5, 2013, from http://www.rethinkingschools.org/archive/25_04/edit254.shtml

Rezai-Rashti, G. (1995a). Multicultural Education, Anti-Racist Education, and Critical Pedagogy: Reflections on everyday practice. In R. Ng, P. Staton, & J. Scane (Eds.), *Anti-Racism, Feminism, and Critical Approaches to Education* (pp. 3–19). Toronto: The Ontario Institute for Studies in Education.

Rezai-Rashti, G. (1995b). Connecting Racism and Sexism: The dilemma of working with minority female students. In R. Ng, P. Staton, & J. Scane (Eds.), *Anti-Racism, Feminism, and Critical Approaches to Education* (pp. 87–97). Toronto: The Ontario Institute for Studies in Education.

Rhodes, C. (1995). Confession of Faith. In M. Perry, J. R. Peden, & T. H. Von Laue, (Eds.), *Sources of the Western Tradition. Volume II: From the Renaissance to the present* (pp. 226–228) (3rd ed.). Boston: Houghton Mifflin Company.

Richmond, A. H. (1994). *Global Apartheid.* Toronto: Oxford University Press.

Ritzer, G. (1996). *The McDonaldization of Society: An investigation into the changing character of contemporary social life* (revised ed.). Thousand Oaks, California: Pine Forge Press.

Ritzer, G. (2000). *Sociological Theory* (5th ed.). New York: McGraw Hill Higher Education.

Ritzer, G. (ed.).(2002). *Contemporary sociology theory and its classical roots: The Basics.* New York: McGraw Hill.

Ritzer, G. (Ed). (2005).*Encyclopedia of Social Theory.* Hammer, Rhonda. "Post Colonialism.". Vol. 2. Thousand Oaks, CA: Sage Reference, 2005. p576–578. Web 05/02/2011

Ritzer, G. (2010). *Sociological Theory.* New York: McGraw Hill.

Robbins, R. H. (2008). *Global Problems and the Culture of Capitalism* (4th ed.). Boston: Pearson Education, Inc.

Rodney, W. (2006). How Europe Underdeveloped Africa. In P. S. Rothenberg (Ed.), *Beyond Borders: Thinking critically about global issues* (pp. 107–125). New York: Worth Publishers.

Roediger, D. (1999). The Wages of Whiteness. New York: Verso.

Roman, L. G. (1993) White is a Color! White Defensiveness, Postmodernism, and Anti-Racist Pedagogy. In C. McCarthy, & W. Crichlow (Eds.), *Race, Identity and Representation in Education* (pp. 71–88). New York: Routledge.

Rothenberg, P. S. (Ed.). (2002). *White Privilege: Essential readings on the other side of racism*. New York: Worth Publishers.

Rothenberg, P. S. (2002). Introduction. In P.S. Rothenberg, (Ed.), *White Privilege: Essential readings on the other side of racism* (pp. 1–5). New York: Worth Publishers.

Rothenberg, P. S. (Ed.). (2006). *Beyond Borders: Thinking critically about global issues*. New York: Worth Publishers.

Rothenberg, P. S. (2010). What's the Problem? *A Brief Guide to Thinking Critically*. New York: Worth Publishing.

Sadiq, I. (1931). *Modern Persia and Her Educational System*. New York: Bureau of Publications Teachers College Columbia University.

Sadler Commission. (1995). Report on Child Report. In M. Perry, J. R. Peden, & T. H. Von Laue (Eds.), *Sources of the Western Tradition. Volume II: From the Renaissance to the present* (pp. 113–117) (3rd ed.). Boston: Houghton Mifflin Company.

Said, E. W. (1978). *Orientalism*. New York: Vintage Books.

Said, E. W. (1989). Representing the Colonized: Anthropology's Interlocutors. *Critical Inquiry* (15), 205–225.

Said, E. W. (1993). The Politics of Knowledge. In C. McCarthy, & W. Crichlow (Eds.), *Race, Identity and Repesentation in Education* (pp. 306–314). New York: Routledge.

Said, E. W. (1994). *Culture and Imperialism*. New York: Vintage Books.

Sanasarian, E. (2000). *Religious Minorities in Iran*. Cambridge: Cambridge University Press.

Santiago Bernal (2011). "Critical Race Theory." UCLA's Center for Community College Partnerships. Retrieved on December 13, 2011.

Satzewich, V., & Liodakis, N. (2007). *'Race' and Ethnicity in Canada*. Toronto: Oxford University Press.

Schiller, N. G., Basch, L., & Blanc-Szanton, C., (Eds.). (1992). *Towards a Transnational Perspective on Migration: Race, class, ethnicity and nationalism reconsidered*. (Analysis of the New York Academy of Sciences, 645). New York: The New York Academy of Sciences.

Schissel, B., & Wotherspoon, T. (2003). *The Legacy of School For Aboriginal people: Education, oppression, and emancipation*. Don Mills, Ontario: Oxford University Press.

Schneiderman, D. (2002). The Continual Disorder of the Safe Street Act: A federalism analysis. In J. Hermer, & J. Mosher (Eds.), *Disorderly People: Law and the politics of exclusion in Ontario* (pp. 79–90). Halifax: Fernwood Publishing.

Schniedewind, N., & Davidson, E. (1998). *Open Minds to Equality: A sourcebook of learning activities to affirm diversity and promote equity* (2nd edition). Boston: Allyn and Bacon.

Sear, A. (2008). *A Good Book, in The Theory: A guide to theoretical thinking*. North York, Ontario: UTP.

Seidman, S. (1994a). *Contested Knowledge: Social theory in the postmodern era*. Oxford: Blackwell Publishers.

Seidman, S. (1994b). Introduction. In S. Seidman, *The Postmodern Turn: New perspectives on social theory* (pp. 1–23). New York: Cambridge University Press.

Sernau, S. (2011) *Social Inequality in a Global Age* (3rd ed.). Los Angeles: Pine Forge Press.

Shorish, M. M. (1988). The Islamic Revolution and Education in Iran. *Comparative Education Review* 32 (1), 58–75.

Siavoshi, S. (1995). Regime, Legitimacy and High-school Textbooks. In S. Rahnema, & S. Behdad (Eds.), *Iran after the Revolution: Crisis of an Islamic state* (pp. 203–217). London: I.B. Tauris & Co. Ltd.

Sieyès, E. (1995). Bourgeois Disdain for Special Privileges of the Aristocracy. In M. Perry, J. R. Peden, & T. H. Von Laue (Eds.), *Sources of the Western Tradition. Volume II: From the Renaissance to the present* (pp. 88–89) (3rd ed.). Boston: Houghton Mifflin Company.

Simmons, T. (2013). *Revitalizing the Classics: What Past Social Theorists Can Teach Us Today*. Halifax: Fernwood Publishing.

Slattery, P. (1995). *Curriculum Development in the Postmodern Era*. Critical Education Practice, Vol. 1. Gerland Reference Library of Social Science, Vol. 929. New York: Gerland Publishing, Inc.

Sleeter, Ch. E. & Grant, C. A. (1991). Race, Class, Gender, and Disability in Current Textbooks. In M.W. Apple, & L.K. Christian-Smith (Eds.), *The Politics of the Textbook*, (pp. 78–110). New York: Routledge.

Smiles, S. (1995). Self-Help and Thrift. In M. Perry, J. R. Peden, & T. H. Von Laue (Eds.), *Sources of the Western Tradition. Volume II: From the Renaissance to the present* (pp. 108–111) (3rd ed.). Boston: Houghton Mifflin Company.

Spivak, Gayatri Chakravorty..(2005, p1859–1867). "Postcolonialism." in New Dictionary of the History of Ideas. Ed. Maryanne Cline Horowitz. Vol. 5. Detroit: Charles Scribner's Sons. Web 05/02/2011

Spring, J. H. (1972). *Education and the Rise of the Corporate State*. Boston: Beacon Press.

Spring, J. H. (2004a). *The Intersection of Cultures: Multicultural Education in the United States and the Global Economy* (3rd ed.). New York: McGraw-Hill Higher Education.

Spring, J. H. (2004b). *How Educational Ideologies Are Shaping Global Society: Intergovernmental organizations, NGOs, and the decline of the nation-state.* Mahwah, New Jersey: Lawrence Erlbaum Associates.

Spring, J. H. (2006). *Pedagogies of Globalization: The Rise of the Educational Security State.* Mahwah, New Jersey: Lawrence Erlbaum Associates.

Spring, J. H. (2007). *Deculturalization and the Struggle for Equality: A Brief History of the Education of Dominated Cultures in the United States* (5th ed.). Boston: McGraw Hill Higher Education.

Steger, M. B. (2003). *Globalization: A very short introduction.* New York: Oxford University Press.

Strinati, D. (1995). *An Introduction to Theories of Popular Culture.* New York: Routledge.

Teeple, Gary. (1995). *Globalization and the Decline of Social Reform.* Toronto: Garamond Press.

The Constitution Society. (2012). *Declaration of the Rights of Man and of the Citizen.* Retrieved May 24, 2013, from http://www.constitution.org/fr/fr_drm.htm

The Factory and Engineering Works of the Royal Overseas Trading Company (factory rules). (1995). In M. Perry, J. R. Peden, & T. H. Von Laue (Eds.), *Sources of the Western Tradition. Volume II: From the Renaissance to the present* (pp. 111–113) (3rd ed.). Boston: Houghton Mifflin Company.

Theobald, R. (1990). *Corruption, Development and Underdevelopment.* Houndmills: Macmillan.

Thompson, K. (1996a). Social Pluralism and Post-Modernity. In S. Hall, D. Held, D. Hubert, & K. Thompson (Eds.), *Modernity: An Introduction to modern societies* (pp. 565–594). Cambridge, Massachusetts: Blackwell Publishers.

Spring, J. H. (1996b). A Global Society? In S. Hall, D. Held, D. Hubert, & K. Thompson (Eds.), *Modernity: An introduction to modern societies* (pp. 466–503). Oxford: Blackwell Publishers.

Thomsen, B. (2007). Bad Blood: Tuskegee, Alabama, 1932–1972. In B. Fawcett (Ed.), *You Said What?: Lies, and propaganda throughout history* (pp. 252–256) (1st ed.). New York: Harper.

Thomsen, P. A. (2007). The Yellow Peril That Wasn't. In B. Fawcett (Ed.), *You Said What?: Lies, and propaganda throughout history* (pp. 73–77) (1st ed.). New York: Harper.

Tong, R. P. (1998). *Feminist Thought.* New York: Westview Press

Turner, J. H. (2003). *The Structure of Sociological Theory* (7th ed.). Belmont, California: Wadsworth.

Turner, J. H., Beeghley, L., & Powers, C. H. (2002). *The Emergence of Sociological Theory* (5th ed.). Belmont, California: Wadsworth.

Van der Berghe, P. L. (Ed.). (1990). *State Violence and Ethnicity.* Niwot, Colorado: the University Press of Colorado.

Van der Berghe, P. L. (1990). Introduction. In P. L. Van der Berghe (Ed.), *State Violence and Ethnicity* (pp. 1–18). Niwot, Colorado: the University Press of Colorado.

Vaziri, M. (1993). *Iran as Imagined nation: The construction of national identity.* New York: Paragon House.

Visano, L., & Jakubowski, L. (2002). *Teaching Controversy.* Halifax, Nova Scotia: Fernwood Publishing.

Waksler, C. F. (1989). Erving Goffman's Sociology: An Introductory Essay Human Studies, Vol. 12, No. 1/2, pp. 1–18. Retrieved from: http://www.jstor.org/stable/20009043

Waldron, J. (2002). *God, Locke, and Equality*. Cambridge: Cambridge University Press.

Wallace, R. A., & Wolf, A. (2006). *Contemporary Sociological Theory: Expanding the classical tradition* (6ᵗʰ ed.). Upper Saddle River, New Jersey: Pearson Education, Inc.

Wallerstein, I. (1998). *Utopistics*. New York: The New Press.

Wallis, M. A., Sunseri, L., & Galabuzi, G.E. (Eds.). (2010). *Colonialism and Racism in Canada: Historical traces and contemporary issues*. Toronto: Nelson Education Ltd.

Weber, M. (1947). *The Theory of Social and Economic Organization.* (A. M. Henderson & T. Parsons, Trans.). New York: The Free Press.

Webster, A. (1984). *Introduction to the Sociology of Development*. Houndmills: Macmillan.

Weeks, J. (1992) The Body and Sexuality. In R. Bocock, & K. Thompson (Eds.), *Social and Cultural Forms of Modernity* (pp. 219–266) Cambridge: Polity Press in association with Open University Press.

Weiner, G. (1994). The Gendered Curriculum: Producing the text. In G. Weiner (Ed.), *Feminism in Education*, (pp. 97–120). Buckingham: Open University Press.

West, C. (2004). *Democracy Matters: Winning the fight against imperialism*. New York: Penguin Books.

Westby, C. (1991). A scale for assessing children's pretend play. In C. Schaefer, K. Gitlin, & A. Sandgrund (Eds.), *Play diagnosis and assessment* (pp 131–161). New York: John Wiley and Sons.

Whitty, G. (1992). Education, Economy and National Culture. In R. Bocock, & K. Thompson (Eds.), *Social and Cultural Forms of Modernity* (pp. 267–317). Oxford: Polity Press in association with The Open University.

Wildman, S. M. (1996). Privilege Revealed: How Invisible Preference Undermines America. NYU Press

William A. Darity, Jr. Ed. (2008). International Encyclopedia of the Social Sciences. "Postcolonialism." Vol. 6. 2nd ed. Detroit: Macmillan Reference USA, 2008. p392–393. Web 05/02/2011

Williams Johnson, Simon. (1986). Appraising Goffman. The British Journal of Sociology. Vol. 37, No. 3 pp 348–369. Retrieved from: http://www.jstor.org.ezproxy.kwantlen.ca:2080/stable/590645

Wirth, L. (1961). The Problem of Minority Group. In T. Parsons, E. Shils, K D. Naegele, & J. R. Pitts, Jesse (Eds.), *The Theories of Society: Foundations of modern sociological theory* (pp. 309–315). New York: The Free Press.

Wosley, P. (1976). Part Six: Organization. In P. Wosley, (Ed.), *Modern Sociology: Introductory readings* (pp. 255–257). Baltimore, MD: Penguin Books.

Wotherspoon, Terry. (1998). *The Sociology of Education in Canada: Critical perspectives* (1ˢᵗ ed.). Don Mills, Ontario: Oxford University Press.

Wotherspoon, Terry. (2009). *The Sociology of Education in Canada: Critical perspectives* (3rd ed.). Don Mills, Ontario: Oxford University Press.

U.S. National Archives and Records Administration. (2013). *The Declaration of Independence: A Transcription*. Retrieved May 24, 2013, from http://www.archives.gov/exhibits/charters/declaration_transcript.html

Yurdusev. Nuri. (2006). Thomas Hobbes and International Relations: From Realism to Rationalism'. *"Australian Journal International Affairs"*, Vol. 60, (2006), p.pp. 305–321.

Zeitlin, Irving. (1990). *Ideology and the Development of Sociological Thought*. Englewood Cliffs, N. J:, Prentice Hall.

Zeitlin, Irving. (2004). Ideology and the Development of Sociological Theory. New York: Pearson.

Zinn, H. (2003). *A People's History of the United States*. New York: Harper Perennial.

Zinn, H. (2005). *Howard Zinn on Democratic Education*. Boulder, Colorado: Paradigm Publishers.

Zinn, H. 2008). *A People's History of the American Empire: A graphic adaptation*. New York: Metropolitan Books / Henry Holt and Company.

CPSIA information can be obtained
at www.ICGtesting.com
Printed in the USA
LVOW03s1945200416

484582LV00003B/3/P

9 781465 299895